JEREMY ROBERT WALKER
MILLENNIAL COMMON SENSE
THE PHILOSOPHY OF LIBERTY AND THE CURE FOR LIFE.

PUBLISHED BY

Oriri

Copyright © 2020 Jeremy Robert Walker

All rights reserved.

ISBN:9780692192870

Printed in the United States of America

This book is reverently
dedicated to
Maram
Susli.

You are the
yellow rose
of Texas.

Beneath the ocean no man knows.

Above the clouds is one man known.

for liberty,

TABLE OF CONTENTS

FOREWORD

Liberty is the highest planetary debate. America is an idea before a state. Truth animates imagination, governs liberty, preserves God's kingdom of life and property on the earth, and defends the gospel of Jesus Christ: the King of Kings, Lord of Lords, my savior, chain-breaker, and Prince of Peace authoring Liberty and governing Death. The enemy seek and destroy what could be; the new Atlantis. Can destiny vanish? How can time amplify season? Does the holy spirit favor reason? Why do men risk their fortune? Must one fear God or man? What if a society sabotage the pursuit of happiness? God molds the men that answer His call to be the defense of, by, and for the people of His kingdom. Honesty treads down the blight of hell. Duty and reverence toward the defense of human liberty establish true civilizational nobility and declare safety to the mankind held captive to the yoke of envy and greed. Perhaps adversity and composure motion for the moral and resilient to keep safe with the love and wisdom of Heaven's instructive understanding. What if Heaven transcends awareness; manifests destiny; seizes that life without slavery; goes home to the promise land; envision the illumination of God? Raising the standard to God razes the pirates. Where goes the heart when the lands go awash? What happens to one's spirit when one can no longer be water or manifest wind? Verily, the heart does not suffer the mind.

LIFE

Genesis 3:9 But the Lord God called to the man, and said unto him, Where art thou?

It was the war. Why did God deliver us into this mystery? God's love dwells within the life-force of all men as a tree of liberty rooted in conception. The Goldilocks Zone for human civilization crests when society shall not infringe upon equal rights; and, it is in this zone, the epiphany zone, that the globalists fear. Momentum compounds deeds into heightened states of awareness. The growing awareness of God's presence magnifies the absolute truth that all men are created equal with unalienable natural rights to their liberty; and, with this freedom to disobey the orders and sin of tyranny we can know that civil destruction first occurs from within the nation and through the insecurities of the people. Bad ideas dominate the mind resisting ancient wisdom and self-evident truth. Insanity practices dark arts to dominate and extinguish the flame of love within one's soul. The highly educated will claim to 'know better' than God therefore they feign aloofness and self-governance; rather, they forsake life in questioning nothing significant; and, will always side against Christ where peer pressure shall strike lest they ask of God to move their heart.

Why do individuals trade valuable time for sin; a slide from humanity to mutiny? The true individual engages in the pursuit of happiness through earnest counsel and exemplary activity. The universe remains chaotic due to the fact only individuals can make decisions. Individuals historically separate into three groups: the most whom fear thinking and do not fear acting, the many whom fear acting and do not fear thinking, and the least whom do not fear acting or thinking thus causing them to enter the animating contest of liberty.

Oppressors create false rights and present their self as the absolute authority of reality while even threatening with violence all whom would oppose their insolent behavior. Who fears a life of freedom? Individuals born into slavery suffer circumstance. God Himself purchased the birth of every child and forms all of His children with different and equally important God-given talents to overcome circumstance; and, contrary to the preachers of the left-hand path: murdering children is not "a most basic right," and children are not accidents or contagions. Adults that do not challenge slavery condemn their family or their self to absolute damnation. The free man risks His fortune to pursue destiny and not live as a peasant-slave under tyranny. Dying free separates the free-thinker from the slave. The moment the slave chooses to live as a free individual their mind then breaks free and harnesses power from the spirit of the Lord to live a new life of freedom and preach liberty to the captives of tyranny. The risk of losing one's physical life compares not to the damnation of losing one's spiritual life. God wants His children to find joy without infringing upon the natural rights of others. The heartless keep slavery alive in all of it's hidden and plain form: debt and taxation; but, debt to whom; and, tax for what; questions whose truth clarify the ages. Debt enslaves the individual to the same alien enslaving the third world. International cartelmen early and often receive rewards of valor or even high political or religious seats. The taxation of one's labor and acquiring of stolen property will forever define the original and final intent of slavery. A nation of charity and not taxation separates a*merica* from the authoritarians. Few americans today resemble their ancestors with the majority now claiming death and taxes as the only two certainties in life; imagine God's shock at witnessing their destitution. American revolutionaries did not desire their progeny to dictate a sixty-five percent taxation of all income earned and then claim this feat of theft as no historical error or violation of natural rights. America reawakened the idea from antiquity of rendering theft and fraud illegal. Individuals conspiring against the ideas of liberty constantly profess this idea as impossible, insane, or fringe-utopianism. Original americans desired nothing more than to free the world of slavery. Peaceful and prosperous Native Americans allied with new americans and armed their self with the knowledge to defend against monarchical rule and savage Native Americans. These savages were well-known to perform deeply shocking torture rituals on any other tribe or peoples they encountered not excluding capturing men alive, ripping their testicles off, sowing their mouth shut with their own testicles locked in their mouth, and burying these men up to the chin and leaving them to die either by scorching hot sun or five dozen coyotes; or keeping them alive and wrapping and tying a fresh cow-hide around their body to then be left in the hot sun while the drying hide squeeze them to death by suffocation as every bone in their body shatter into smitherings and if they do not suffocate then the coyotes will clean them up as they lay unable to move a single finger while being exposed to feeling every rip and tear; the savage women were the creatives coming up with and doing the torturing; it was said every killing was equally different and confoundingly horrifying; of course, this was only if they did not want you for chili meat or for indefinite ritualistic torture or sex magic. The primary course of action for inhabitants of america surrounded rigorous work to agree on patents of truth, spiritual nobility, and the instruments and teachings for the individuals and the youth on how to keep peace as one people and live free of despotism as one mankind ascending toward a type-one civilization living for the defense of human liberty and not that artificial composite of a so-call intelligent singularity wherein a human architect culls information and political enemies for a mechanistic world eliminating human awareness and even smothering terrestrial biology. America's *Founding Fathers* and inhabitants of america desired two absolutes to take root: liberty and no taxation without representation for all; a worthy battle-cry as americans overthrew the world empire thus inspiring a global resistance to the encroachment of tyranny from ceremonial monarchy, theocracy, aristocracy; and, the differing flavors of oligarchy whom lord over subject-populations in wait to institute secret courts, redefine a reality without equal rights, and reduce the perfect law of liberty to a long forgotten memory wherein the people live as subjects to human statutes without foundation or principle. The soul of mankind acts as a phalanx of knowledge purging the New World Order. Societies with top-down control will always use theft and fraud to coerce the people into accepting state-sponsored violence. State-controlled or totalitarian markets corrode the spirit of free thought, institute unlawful governance, encourage idleness, render trade illegal, threaten the livelihood of peaceful individuals, and ration economic production. Idleness produces a fictional society worshiping envy as fine art and greed as a merger of orthodox religion and science or state-sponsored eugenics preserved by a military-industrial-complex of technocrats. America, for many people all over the world, means equal rights, natural rights, private property, self-governance, self-rule, rugged individualism, and the great american melting pot.

Evil governs mankind with shadowy intelligence figures institutionalizing banks to compartmentalize military and eliminate entire populations for an ancient and covert continuity of governance. The military-industrial-complex describes only one facet of this loosely associated and tightly woven network orchestrating the global plan of eugenics. The ruling elite use the spiritually dead to oppress their countrymen, purify the genetic pool according to their own vision, and lead the false human awakening. Americans today imprison the charitable for not having sought approval (official denial) from the usurpers of their own government. Some will suggest evil as an off-world spirit or alien race of interdimensional Archons controlling the spiritually dead to complete the works of death and desolation on this earth. In either case many individuals will sell their soul to the evil spirit of the world and coldly serve the darkness of dead spirits for temporal gain.

God provides government for all living creatures. Man thrives in flourishing His community. So long as individuals do not govern their own mind then the lie will forever persist:

"Authoritarians must govern man for pretend reason; even as belittling as **ceremonial law, ceremonial purpose, state sovereignty, or hereditary commonwealth.***"*

Dozens of nations, and more than half of earth, face absolute rule from the British crown; though, the peasants of such nations claim the role as *ceremonial* therefore they contritely demand the person they debate with to agree monarchical rule is inactive or inconsequential lest the contents of their world-view in an instant turn to ash, cause their face to melt, and challenge their worship to go to the one true living God and not the state. Common sense spells out this childish point of view in defending royalty as a baseless foundation devoid of honestly chivalrous society. Royalty consists of individuals wearing fancy hats and administering violence to sequester resources and coerce individuals under their slavery. Hereditary rule persists as the most wicked form of oppression known to mankind as it's consequence and occurrence comes involuntarily and en masse. America thwarts Royalty in declaring *independence* from their hegemony. The new way of living in america resembled ancient antiquity; however, oppositional forces deceive the world and stain the name of america with their own misgivings unrelated to the cause of liberty resulting in perpetual chaos as wicked individuals incite unprovoked violence as their wrongful solution for the world.

Human potential maintains ability to consciously observe the semantical hierarchy of human thought and peaceably assemble a righteous course for mankind. A Godly court aims to protect the individual from mankind's most wicked devices. Government and court systems exist as magnecules of non-linear power manifest from the imagination's toroidal polarization of life and death. The courts create a focal point of social energy to weigh human events in context with relevant subject-matter. Not all courts possess the same government and some societies prove superior in every respect. The pauper will argue mankind can live without government when dwelling within all individuals exists God, His courts, and the moral constitution of self-government. Naivety renders the idea of evil as far-fetched. Human instinct finds difficulty in perceiving evil without first experiencing the effects of evil. Limited government allows bad ideas to filter through a wary public in their safe-guarding against the rise of lawlessness and in so doing keep falsehood at bay and permit truth to surface from various checks and balances afforded as an unalienable human right for all individuals. The individual arguing against the use of courts to assist in the protection of the individual from group-think must in the least confess decisions govern individuals and those decisions either infringe upon or preserve mankind; however, bad government does not cease existence therefore good government must persist.

The peace of submission taught in communism does not represent the peace of God in a society with the courts of God. Ungodly societies tremble for fear of many false dead gods and Godly societies tremble for fear of not fulfilling the will of the Almighty and one true living God of the universe. How must the individual protect their self if human statutes persecute speech? Civil disobedience to unjust law creates providence from God; though, the potential for a disastrous rise in tyranny persists. Why must individuals vote? The risk of voting and not voting both possess potential for a conqueror to form an army and subvert society. Political power comes out of the barrel of a gun and so long as an educated populace understand this source then the people will exercise their rights without fear of men or their crimes. A colony or state's representative must hold a fearful reverence for the people far greater than the ambition to conquer these masters of His and only a vigilant people will foster this fear into their representative through maintaining their natural right to self-defense and a militia to over-throw bad government by any means necessary. Ensuring no weapon formed against them shall prosper and trudging as our ancestors had to equip mankind's defenses against oppression proves the most worthy duty of man.

One good man possesses more power than every tool of death and desolation. President Thomas Jefferson will forever hold the title as america's original abolitionist with having proposed the first legislature to end the practice of slavery; however, His effort did not receive enough public support to achieve the required number of votes. *The White Man*: a phrase manipulating innumerable uneducated minds into counter-productive political fodder. America's first slave owner did not have white skin therefore 'the white man' did not own the first slave in america. A man with black skin owned the first slaves in america; however, morality rests in the heart and not skin color thus men must transcend carnality before ever entering the true arena of morality.

The most carnal and false survival instinct in all living creatures may exist as some type of slavery causing the enslaved to believe they increase their chances of survival against a predator. Individuals manifesting evil intention prey upon such weakness for temporal gain. Intention without action represents no good duty at all and only derides itself as an asset for evil. The grand magician of earth tricks the individual into living as a slave through the false prophecy of worshiping evil as means to obtaining empowerment or survival. Individuals participating in false power structures directly aid the destroyers of civilization. From the beginning of civilization unto today dynasty and oligarchs cull the mind set at liberty to maintain rule over the civilized world. Ancient occults participate in sadistic rituals as means to absolutely control the social structure of earth for all of eternity. Death and desolation adorn their chest of false honor. Only a society aware of true Law will rise to the occasion of arresting the individuals declaring their self as emperor over the deep. Emperors want nothing more than turpitude. Free minds find joy in overthrowing wickedry, unlocking spiritual prisons, thriving outside of the illusion of temporal security, and living eternally in the presence of God. Enslaved minds enjoy sabotage. Confused individuals claim slave-owners represent a free person living their life set at liberty. Slave-owners create a false image of freedom in not realizing their own slavery devoid of liberty and shackling them to the wicked one planning their inevitable misfortune.

The wicked one of the underworld, that prince of darkness, uses divide and conquer to hypnotize the public into submission. Manufactured consent inspires condescension toward one's neighbor and accelerates spiritual degradation of truth and justice. As the quickening of good versus evil takes center stage in society: the stifling of peaceful expression increases in frequency and mobilizes the remnant of society for spiritual warfare against total conquest. Self-evidence reasons most people of earth have not witnessed the cause of liberty. The spirit of this anti-art, anti-human, callous in nature, vitriolic few, whom value rubbish over art and coffins over apartments, crystallize the essence and codify the existence of the enemies of humanity incapable of producing art; save their full repentance unto God. Love salvages the suffering heart and creates a path of life without fear of death. All individuals receive the gift of life and death. Eugenicists declare mankind a virus deserving of political and religious conquest. Using evil for good possesses the same logic as poisoning unto death for the sake of health.

How does civilization achieve a free society when the very individuals countervailing the statutes of the oppressor face martyrdom and their society faces even worse? Fear not man and fear only what God will not do for us if we do not fight the evil of man. All of the world will eventually pursue justice. Until then how will art sway human destiny or even challenge, enhance, strengthen, serve, love, or oppose, earth's twisted poets of destruction forged against poetic justice? Ancient philosophers recognized the difference separating human statutes from *The Perfect Law of liberty*. Statutes fail as a foundation of sand washing away and the Law stands as a rock witnessed by all discerning people. Human statutes criminalize free speech and force government to seize control of, and eliminate, classically liberal economic trade. Imagine one individual in society possesses power to censor speech with state-sponsored violence and coercion. A free society does not exist where government confines or sanctions speech. Promoting the infringement of natural rights does not represent freedom without consequence. Individuals following thought with violent action face immediate retribution and the defenders against violent action shall be long remembered. The false science of Human Statutes use necessity to justify violence and coercion. Submission to tyranny does not align with the indifferent authority of the universe. Few in present time speak of Manifest Destiny and even argue this term means to enslave the world; whereas, many claim the goal as: a nation devoid of slavery with private property and free trade for all as means of entering God's Kingdom on the earth. Today's tip of the spear seeking justice for the world exists as america; however, only a minor fraction of american citizens comprehend such a feat and even fewer act to succeed such aims making the practitioner of equal rights defiant unto tyranny and those whom know of tyranny and do not act as the embodiment of a crooked and idle observer.

Several of america's Founding Fathers referred to God as The Almighty Creator of The Universe. The only Founding Father holding no belief in God had His own son waged against Him in war, remained unfaithful to His wife, and proved the least earnest and effectual among The Founding Fathers though He never so incompetent as the left's monarch worshiper Alexander Hamilton. Benjamin Franklin mirrored the lifestyle prefects of the multitude whom would identify with certain ideas of His and remain oblivious toward other moral absolutes exercised by other Founding Fathers; or, in the least respect: self-evidences a double-mindedness not representative of a people of one mind.

Morality exemplifies God's purpose. Imagination creates art, economy, and civilization for abstract, concrete, immediate, and indeterminate function. The spiritual world consists of the active participant and idle observer. America contains the highest concentration of free-thinkers with a *Bill of Rights* designed to remind individuals to protect the pursuit of happiness. The realms separating the participant and observer each possess a faction of good and evil. Evil observers lend their self as the weakest link in society and the good participant as the strongest link. The good participant jettisons their spiritual life into a world of awareness devoid of psychological imprisonment. The observer only knows comfort and abhors adversity. Adversity manifests growth and inspires life in the valley. Observers possess envy toward participants; envy mounts hate against it's target; and, hate empowers the worst elements of society. Spirit connects to our mind and signals the body to act with purpose. Action renders an observer into a participant of the animating contest of liberty. Cold, lukewarm, and hot describe how accurate the alignment of intention meets with action. Individuals without conscious intention live an unconscious, spiritually dead, and idle existence. The observer did not learn "All men are created equal." The participant, endowed by their Creator, makes self-evident the incomplete and ineffectual nature of the idle observer retaliating against the living in their hope of dissolving the love and futurity of mankind. Billions of people on this planet will today expend one hundred billions hours keeping their life and the world in a state of slavery. Imagine those hours suddenly transformed into actionable hours of worshiping the living Creator to manifest a world of justice and peace? Who will argue their life does not possess value if all possess the currency of time? Time grants power to strengthen one's constitution set at liberty. Forgoing pursuit of a good destiny embodies oppression whereas exercising natural rights overcomes oppression. The indecisive nature of the lukewarm observer animates the contest of liberty to overcome the hot and cold polar forces ruling mankind.

All human senses act as potential energy to establish the flow of good or evil. Physicists claim matter exists as chaos until any observation unfolds thus potentially causing the most minimum of a perception to matter into any maxim of awareness. God multiplies good deeds and rewards evil with the lake of fire. Healthy economies thrive when the good vigorously protect liberty in order to animate dreams and risk failure. The image of Christ wilts the denier of the power and glory of the Holy Ghost. Evil participants combine false light with inaction to summon the host of illusion and manifest the spiritual image of unthinking evil. The unthinking individual and the criminal worship Satan's mental plantation of propaganda with their desire to receive a confirmation bias from their peers thus relinquishing the sovereignty of their mind. Confirmation bias fosters narrative bias and this aggradation produces a closed loop, caste system, of social validation, and then stratifies into a compartmentalized order of global evil. The back-biters of this realm conquest to hoard economic power and obtain Godhood over society. The wicked one designs command-control environments to crush the soul, silence dreams, and breach His underworld onto the physical plane.

The Kingdom of God with only one Lord not of this world represents good intention. The underworld possesses overlords with evil intention. Mankind triumphs the pattern of evil when the knowledge of good self-evidences reason to immediately defense against every form of evil. If one never identifies evil then how does one avoid evil if acting good requires defense against known evils? Will mankind awaken to one human family-race in defense of the innocent? Dishonesty disguised as good intention emboldens an ignorant public to yearn for the most evil to abolish knowledge itself, idolize man, and rewrite history in a great culling of civilization. Free people must protect life to keep rulers a memory.

Vigorous action favors truth and not martyrdom. One individual with absolute power to rule civilization always results in catastrophe. The participant remains the most valuable, viable, and visible individual in the animating contest of liberty. "I wear my heart on my sleeve" describes the good participant. The sloth, also known as the liar, observer, or saboteur, speaks against the doer of will-power as evil thus condemn the righteous as a last resort to flourish the metastases of evil. The universe honors positive vibrations with infiltrating the cloud of evil in order to attempt rescue of those dwelling in despondence and make the path of abiding under the shadow of the Almighty plain and His morning wings of eternal truth comely. Mankind must master spiritual fire for the transformation out of ash into one people with one language of love, peace, and prosperity.

Humans experience two deaths. Spiritual death represents the first death while physical death represents the second death. Did God, the giver and taker of all things, create death as the ultimate equalizer? The spiritually dead have an appointed time to awaken preceding their physical death; though, not all respond to God's calling thus live with needless suffering. Vigilance of falsehood corrupting minds into a tool for tyranny defines the realm of living a virtuous spiritual life. Submitting to evil means observing one's own nightmare of walking dead. God creates the multiverse of infinite outcome though choice may seem finite when imminent physical death offers little time for spiritual recourse; however, perhaps God creates enough time for us to decide when the great passing from this realm to the next occurs. How does the individual prove worthy of the great passing without first pursuing happiness and destiny? How does one pursue destiny without shining light on the evils of this world? If a society does not discuss poverty and war then what odds stand to reason against such mayhem? The common taxpayer in america either wittingly or unwittingly funds illegal war and most will not acknowledge their parched soul, blind sight, selective hearing, and superficial speech creating the perfect image of a spiritual mute; a spiritual death imagined by the temple of the salmon melting into the forest floor.

Popular music today promotes a worship of violence and coercion aimed at ending the family and capturing the mind of the aimless whom imagine their decisions self-made when in reality have enlisted their self into the pious evocation of priding one's self as spiritually dead, envying the act of keeping the wicked afloat, and pandering to an unhinged world. The spirit of this world obsesses with mainlining Satanism through lewd media and entertainment (love for self is hate toward others and channeling the dark psychic force and spirit of Satan). Weaponized media and entertainment keep individuals under the yoke of bondage. Multitudes of children see the promotion of vanity and then mimic the lifestyle of the advert; which, only represents a universal symbol of spiritual slavery and not individuality. Police receive programming designed to discriminate such fashion as the uniform of a potentially dangerous enemy. What reason does the individual dressed in gangster attire hold to suspend belief and feel surprised when their vernacular and uniform advertised to millions undergoes public scrutiny from authoritarian representatives? The deterioration of culture into violence and coercion succeeds the cause of Satan's trade and cannot portray an accurate representation of private property or trade competing for honest means; rather, this perpetration of violence has begun an era of trading civil liberties for the illusion of law enforcement by prison wardens and further inspiring of the erosion of civility and enlargement of a rogue and domestic police force motivated to invest in the criminalization of private property ownership and the militarization of government's use of force to go against their fellow countrymen.

Why do the least educated idolize media, entertainment, and false power? Does one not commit a crime of heart in worshiping fear? The constant effort of individuals attempting to simply blend in with their culture through learned behavior fuels the condition of slavery. The pessimist will object as though a statement was made condemning freedom of choice to listen to any music and wear any fashion. The point made questions not the notion of freedom of choice rather the promotion of violence as appropriate means to trade. The state rendering private property illegal does not remove the natural right to own private property; however, violence and trade both receive their own reward. Trade of what God made legal from the beginning does not break God's law; however, violence and coercion do not achieve what peaceful trade achieves in the absence of the threat of violence or coercion. The ancients held life to the highest esteem; and, with the idea of life paints the notion of sovereignty and one spirit of love for all people. The growing sub-culture of entrepreneurs securing their private property from violent thieves renders society a more dangerous environment from a brain-washed domestic police force using violence to steal private property, promote mass-incarceration or destabilization of the family unit, and instill a constant state of violently charged paranoia into the atmosphere of private trade and american society. Peaceable trade of useful products in the free market will forever supersede submission to unlawful governance. Action alters the destiny of humanity to either live free or as slaves.

Manifesting our being-at-work into a good participant, and not defiling our image into an evil observer practicing illusions of good intention, form intention-aligning habits aimed at departing this realm and cultivating a new realm from atop of the last heroic action. Abundance dwells within one's soul and from this outward expression manifests life onto the physical plane and forms into what old texts refer to as the fruit of one's labor. God created man to pursue happiness and live in abundance with nature. Many will vehemently, and wrongly, argue abundance and power originate from money. Since abundance originates from God dwelling within one's soul then time and action drives abundance. Our flesh births into space and with time and energy learning unfolds. Intention possesses an enfold of potential energy. Action from the participant unfolds the enfold of reality and releases even more energy into the observable realm as means of attracting or directing the participants for even an alteration of the realm into a place excluding the perceived power of the observer. Does life constitute exploration of the enfolded universe for the pursuit of unfolding the forbidden fruit of happiness? No man keeps a perfect constitution and not living up to our human potential creates more harm than destiny. Repentance adds strength to character in the lessons we suffer. Righteousness aids in manifesting destiny for our lives and those around us. God created us for His ultimate design; and, our hands do not separate from His unless we turn our face away from God and onto sin. Those seeking the easy route of sin will petition to persecute the righteous in order to avoid justice for their increasingly difficult way. The Creator of the universe demands His people to preserve His perfect Law and fight the unlawful statutes of man oppressing natural rights.

Thermodynamics recognizes a State-Function as a Point A and Point B; or, for the participant: a starting-point and an ending-point. *The Bible* speaks of this in referencing God as *The Alpha and Omega*. State-Functions often possess intermediate actions separating point A and B. The observer, compartmentalized into a state-function of slavery, starts nothing good and finishes nothing.

Individuals perform miraculous gifts born from the spiritual realm and brought forth into the physical after acting on righteous discernment. Hidden awareness in all things contrasts God's truth participating in life against the idle observer manifest as the shadow army waging war against life. Perhaps purpose and accident keep the two philosophies unto their own.

A man pursuing the idea to create a hovering city gains momentum in the collective consciousness and a later date proves the idea worthy with creation of a hovering city. Mind over matter overcomes, or perpetuates, the struggle of advancing mankind into a type-one civilization of voluntary harmony. Knowledge governs ignorance and the ignorant avoid knowledge. Information holds potential to gift sight to the blind which does mean a life of truth in participation. Where we stand as individuals and where we desire to reach exists as a gap worthy of our lives to close. Every effort will build the road to meeting one's destiny in the appointed time as each part of our path presents opportunity for higher ways toward destiny. What if americans acted without words to be the liberty against tyranny? Human action competes non-linearly with the superficial nature of linear time. Participants and observers experience time differently. Observers falsely perceive time as a linear story of events; for example, submitting to oppression: the observer's excuse in a linear fantasy; and, fighting oppression: a participant's solution in a non-linear reality.

Actions concentrate into representative power on the micro and macro of civilization. Tyranny manifests on the micro within the mind of the individual and manifests into governmental psychosis on the macro. Perhaps governmental psychosis sounds oxy-moronic insofar as self-rule won the war over earthly governance long ago through Christ; however, the knowledge of the many different type of beasts grown from the evils of public discourse must find it's way into the common knowledge of society in order to immunize culture from pursuing the effects causing such national illness. Liberty when manifested on the micro safeguards the world from the macro of tyranny. Society maintains power over the elect to institute new maxims in the form of elected representatives to construct a new state-function of micro, macro, problem, reaction, and solution. Achievement reserves itself for principled individuals adhering to the pursuit of happiness. The upper rungs of consciousness wage spiritual war to keep people free from the slavery of idleness. Concern for social status over morality always results in a loss of liberty. History proves ascension as the norm and not the exception.

A majority of the american government remains rogue through it's hijacking of the economic system. Criminal elements acting as rogue agents within the american Government have always committed atrocities under the guise of national security; for example: enslaving Africans, forcing Native Americans into Oklahoma, Japanese internment camps, robbing public funds for illegal and undeclared war, crony-capitalism, and using tools of war for policing domestically and abroad exist as only a few of the ways the underworld assails the waxing american Republic.

Today's United States dollar represents the global currency. No sane individual will argue the dollar does not effect their life. Fiat currencies such as the american dollar subjugate individuals to perpetual economic inflation and deflation through the business of debt and warfare. American currency backed by the value of Gold for it's first two centuries allowed for one month of work to purchase retirement; and, this type of abundance created an exponential expansion of choice, economy, and opportunity for people across the planet whether people sought refuge in america or traded with americans. The rule of rising tide applies here. Fiat money results in a fixed economy preventing centuries worth of growth in months time. Estimates today suggest one out of two americans live without stable work. In the nineteen fifties america could feed the entire planet and today it's own people starve as generations worth of savings dwindle, the homeless population climbs to millions, and tent villages multiply.

Dishonest money forces industry to produce products unfit for a free people. Bad *Economic Policy* promotes the trade of corrupt money until the population starves. Global governance aims for nothing more than keeping individuals from learning of God's calling to act with certainty, clarity, discernment, and purpose. Certainty promotes faith. In certainty we hold truth self-evident all men are created equal and this foundation creates true civilization. Outside of the ancient ideas of antiquity exists fantastically evil rituals. Generations flounder under such blasphemy until the observer experiences the love of God and acts as His winds of change. The spark igniting the brushfire of liberty exists within us all. Inspiration delivers to the animating contest of liberty what humanity sees when hovering it's face over the waters of salvation, and, with the light reflecting against the darkness, separates the matters of the heart into knowing good from evil.

A common, benign, conversation, in america starts with: "Imagine [this] device exists." The invention, in question, often exists as a patent owned by a major corporation or private government subsidy far from public awareness. In the days of renaissance individuals well-understood the danger in patenting ideas. The most potent ideas always rise to the occasion and no human statute will help to control the flow of information aimed at improving the human condition lest such patents aim to injure competition and improve the condition of those keeping the people under intellectual duress. Wireless electricity was invented nearly one century ago from the time of this writing and the public still do not have access to the intention of the technology and those attempting to reproduce the work often face physical or political assassination. Wireless Internet, today, serves as a simplistic form of the same technology; albeit, militarily controlled. Why was computer technology heavily developed as early as the nineteen twenties with rumors suggesting it's blueprint having begun in the nineteenth century? Self-evidence reasons a global cabal aimed at suppressing speech does manage the political narrative of entire continents and will continue in the centuries ahead. Technocrats have knighted their self as informational crystal-balls wherein harvesting data for the highest bidder results in billions of individuals trained to corrupt economy and culture through state-sponsored consolidation of information resources. The illusory technology of reading minds may potentially surface with individuals foolishly thinking it's purpose trustworthy when it's chief function will confuse language and suppress civilization. The highest instinct of man resides in living free from sin through preaching liberty to the captives.

Luke 8:27 [a] And as he went out to land, there met him a certain man out of the city, which had devils long time, and he wore no garment, neither abode in house, but in the graves.

Luke 8:27 Footnotes

[a] Christ showeth, by casting out a Legion of devils by his word only, that his heavenly virtue was appointed to deliver men from the slavery of the devil: but foolish men will not for the most part redeem this so excellent grace freely offered unto them, with the least loss of their pelting pelf.

Public speaking persists as the most dangerous profession. America's *Declaration of Independence* concisely separates the Law from the unlawful for the object of keeping The Perfect Law of liberty and trashing the human statutes designed only to enrich the devils.

Imagine a world without docile sloths collecting for hereditary masters. Beta-males long desire to violently oppose intellectual society founded on the action of the alpha-male. Ego threatened: the beta-males form into a weapon of death and desolation. The oppressive beta-male would hide all beauty on the earth given the opportunity. Examples of such egregious ineptitude exist across every specie of the animal kingdom and none more grotesque than witnessed in human civilization: secret societies create death cults, tribes war other tribes, states form institutions to impoverish and enslave their own people, oligarchs build global empire to lead otherwise good men into unspeakable atrocity, and emperors keep thousands of concubines to limit the cultivation of strong families and societies and prevent youthful ideas from ascending society into liberty and away from wicked reign. Empowerment for this anti-liberty beta-male does not manifest decentralization; rather, their deplorable philosophy celebrates Satanic power.

Alcohol produces poor mediation, wine makes a mockery, and, cannabis has formed against it a global army aimed at the absolute destruction of it's industrial, medicinal, and economic function and all under the guise of militarily-enforced national security. The United States Constitution, written on Cannabis, stands as one additional symbol and testament of love uniting mankind. Cannabis provides an abundant resource for every individual on the earth to end the most base forms of slavery: poverty and warfare. America's Founding Fathers never asked of their sons to allow a foreign army acting as america's domestic police force to steal private property whether Cannabis or otherwise. Americans allowing such pestilence do not resemble liberty and deserve the wicked government they so choose as their endeavor to strangle self-awareness faints into the fiery pit of hell. Participants live with principled action and resist false statutes with eternal vigilance. The mentally enslaved do not find decision-making and truthful intention as common knowledge. The mind devoid of maxims dispossess individuality and assails the foundation and architecture of individual rights. What maxim does the observer possess but discord and discontent?

One must question the false utopia of the military-industrial-complex mesmerizing the public into a state of absolute control. If the people occupy public streets professing immediate political change then ought the people to learn only a Republic will serve their interest with a government remaining subservient to their will? When the people relinquish their participation then a hostile military will mandate observation of those people. Shadow-governments target powerful individuals for elimination; however, those in fear of darkness will not shadow the light. The american Republic illustrates true opportunity for individual transformation and self-governance on a global and multi-generational scale. The failed idea of democracy and despotism will rest in it's eternal grave and the Republic will rise to protect all individuals.

Destiny burns as midnight oil never to relinquish it's flame in the soul of man. One must keep steady distance from the denier of soul. Apathetic minds abandon their quest for destiny. "I do not possess the strength to succeed therefore I must not act," qualms the unbeliever. The back-biters do not represent iron sharpens iron insofar as friends help to illuminate and not diminish perspective. Even the world's most talented individuals regularly encounter hecklers or energetic contortionists.

The world's most revered rock-climber recently sought His greatest accomplishment. Lesser men used pride, a form of hate, to dissuade His efforts whereas men of quality earnestly revel in

His success. Living as a participant enabled Him to continue unperturbed and receive happiness. Avarice comes from a place of pure envy; a signet of the type of inconsistent character chiding others and not their own menial effort. The observer remains oblivious to the danger of not pursuing destiny. Tasks in a company of men require completion and unpetitioned advice holds no foundation and only represents the beta-mind attempting to dominate the acting man. Imagine a government used violence to prevent this man from pursuing His dream for reason of safety. Government sanity does not exist when ensuring safety means exercising preemptive violence; for example: preemptive war. The idle observer suggests, "He can discover success safely elsewhere." The beta-male desires all men to stop performing peaceful feats of intelligence and physical acumen; even going so far as to claim mental acumen is a form of autism which has inspired a national brainwashing and drugging of highly intelligent and highly functioning children until they believe they are "aspie" or "weaponized autists making weaponized art", lest these children shed the brainwashing and become the world's most learned and pivotal artists, doctors, fathers, lawyers, mothers, musicians, painters, patriots, politicians, preachers, scientists, philosophers, and statesmen; children whose total idiot, challenged, and deluded parents now firmly believe intellectually drowning as the golden standard for adulthood – as golden as California's communism being an exemplary status of american statehood (the geographic source of celebration for our nation's brainwashing and fake news).

The perpetual trade of resources from one profession to another grows economy. Idleness suffers economically and encourages tax collectors to sabotage participants. The participant remains conscious in decision-making and the observer unconsciously clamors for the evil spirit of this world to whisk them away. Consider North Korean citizens slapping the ground while hysterically sobbing after the death of their dictator: a premonition of the social engineering causing the left to perform the exact same act upon President Trump's winning the 2016 Presidential election; the media seemingly rendered the general public into dottling miniature autistic Kim Jong Un's (was this too Federally approved?). Dictatorship mandates such peer pressure to prove allegiance to the regime or face elimination, exile, political humiliation, ostracizing, or economic sanctioning. Free people mourn the death of a loved one; however, never does an individual possess authority to restrict natural rights without just cause or due process.

Since the days of antiquity men discuss signs and wonders of the spiritual world and the high significance of "No King but King Jesus," as a reminder of the living God dwelling within us all and His hidden knowledge kept from mankind by the ruling elite teaching us of our right to only defend heavenly rule and to fight against earthly rule. The Bible's mention of: "turned to flight the armies of the aliens," correlates with stone etchings from thousands of years ago displaying flying vehicles or practices of kundalini though either interpretation results in the same interpretation of a society exceedingly advanced in the expansionary role of human consciousness. Official reports reveal other worlds near earth and all throughout the universe with fresh water, earthen landscape, and, more than likely, intelligent life. In all of life's vastness mankind had not separated the taboo from the truth to achieve peace on the earth.

When the people turn to flight the armies of the aliens then the creator of this Universe advances humanity to the grand plan: a type-one civilization; the land of milk and honey; the promise land; Mount Zion; equal rights for all individuals; and renaissance. Zionism and Mount Zion fail to relate one to the other. *Isms* arrest the mind and prevent ascension through social stigma associated with high-level communication; for example: communicating the idea of Mount Zion as a form of overthrowing oppression and not empowering oppressors. Frequencies possess the potential to split; for example, departing from evil works. Perhaps in ancient days Mount Zion held another name, phrase, or meaning. The wicked light of this world wields the purest idea as His own then proceeds to commit wickedry in the name of the idea thus confusing the high ways of God with the valley of oppression.

Evil nurtures away from the nature of God while good nurtures society more near God's presence. Nurturing the youth out of carnal nature and into angelic society ought to remain a goal for humanity and to suggest humans as totally carnal creatures without spiritual nature denies mankind's ability to awaken and oppose the dead. Raising the youth in an environment of good and teaching the knowledge of good and evil departs mankind from the culture of evil. Free-will allows even the highest upbringing to fail when the individual chooses evil. Positive and honest frequency threaten the ways of the underworld. Honest enemies lend great danger. Lying constitutes every oppression, possesses full intention of miring one's own soul, and shifts an honest individual into the image of the liar, the realm of the underworld, and society of evil on the earth separate from the realm of good walking all around. The elite rulers of this fractured realm read five hours per day gaining ever more knowledge of all the different ways to control people. What happens to the elite when the people self-educate and discover the methods keeping them chained and then set free the minds of this planet?

God's servants sow their riches in Heaven for all to reap. The youth remain the highest value target for the wicked to cull. Imagination defines the effort required to live on fire toward salvation. Delivering truth aids society as do artesian springs overflowing polluted water. The wicked will argue since Christ produced no monetary riches then He produced a tree without fruit; though, the Lord knows the wicked love to fail for other gods.

God promises the land of milk and honey for His people and in this habitation I see my ancients amongst me living as we had moons ago in a heavy brain-wave-state of energy and love for our self and our neighbor. No more will the people gnash their teeth or dash their foot upon a stone. Family will thrive in abundance and live near one another and not scatter across the world in disarray. The ways of Babylon forcing the elders into hospital to die alone ends and wisdom will verily spread peace and prosperity to a republic of people protecting equal rights for their fellow countrymen.

Truth portends an invincible living force of justice. Ideas self-evidence the machinations of our universe such as mountainous rocks (metal, and non-metal, known and unknown) hurdling at insurmountable speed, stars consuming stars, galaxies feeding on galaxies, black holes eliminating entire nebular, the universe consuming immeasurable sectors of itself and transforming the old into new; yet, today scientists religiously warn of scientist-created pollution in outer-space and politicians engage in democide to prevent the ascension of ideas thus hypocrisy rules the many whom refuse to process information outside of hypocrisy.

Imagine warming next to a camp-fire and upon turning one's back to the fire a state of chaos ensues engulfing the valley and mountainside with flame. Fire does not contain sentience. The state of the camp-fire mirrored the observers lack of participation and wrongful intention. Individuals similarly possess the ability to factor their life for good within certain limitation. The least of a thing matters to the extent of a thing insofar as a rotten apple spoils the barrel or an unchecked government, like an untamed fire, commits mass genocide under the guise of national security or fighting a foreign enemy.

Debate inspires the keeping of friends and enemies. Ideology determines whether one individual views another as alien, foe, or friend. The progenitors of violence exist as the evil army plaguing humanity's ascension; and, their violence, for reason of necessity, remains self-evident as unprovoked violence throughout the world. Many pose as friends and upon further debate release hidden information; for example, upon stating: "Mankind contains one human race," the foe within the individual manifests and utters: "Skin color determines race and [this] race proves superior to others." Only individuals, not groups or skin color, differ in morality. Racism is the failed idea that mind is not over matter. The message of equal rights represents individuality, self-rule, self-governance, peace, harmony, and judging a person's deeds and not their skin color. Desiring to keep society free encourages others to experience the privilege of liberty and not money; life and not death.

Many people perpetuate their own fear of man and produce undesirable self-fulfilling prophecy. Self-miserly instigates a ruling class to gain absolute authority over one's life. Does fear of man exist simply from refusing to relinquish anger of man and commit deeds of good to inspire all men? Suppose an individual assails an individual for reason of race. Does violence against man prove fear of man just or does the perpetrator of violence represent a manifest mental-illness? No individual of civility or high-society operates on the paradigm of assailing others for fear alone. Only barbarous third-world nations and animals remain so tribal. Suppose an individual encourages violence toward other men. The defenders of self remain justified in their prevention of violence. Self-defense justifiably remains an unalienable right and does not define unlawful violence. In the market of ideas word-of-mouth forms a natural self-defense against a concern, group, individual, or place.

World-view possesses spiritual danger. Individuals unconcerned with tyranny face elimination for a fatalistic, treacherous, and unfounded world-view whereby not defending society with force falsely represents God. Spiritual war must dominate the actions of those awakening under slavery. On the simplest of terms this means devoting additional hours of practice each day for one's vocation. In suffering God delivers true intelligence to the honest. The aim of good eternally succeeds the war and the wicked never rise past the realm of fallen battlefields.

Freeing one's self from bondage starts with a plan of immediate, implementable, and achievable action. A lack of knowledge in either good or evil will result in suffering. Effort reduces suffering and gains invaluable knowledge. People perish for lack of knowledge therefore knowledge remains everlasting as God first breathed knowledge into existence. All ideas begin as a word. In the beginning was the Word and that Word was with God and that Word was God.

The individual-at-work desires to stay in a stream, or flow, of thought producing their highest quality of goods or services. The farmer knows well His course of action to reap the reward of His labor; and, weighs risk during His effort. Imagine the farmer discovers His crop was stolen. What if the farmer accepts such domination for fear of backlash? What if neighboring farmers unite and turn to flight the armies of the aliens stealing their crop and never again in their lifetime experience theft? Free people instinctively resist the yoke of bondage. Men throughout history will use every type of oppression against Godly men whom will then write it upon their heart to overthrow such pretenses to defense society with natural rights.

The world fell ill to the spell of tyranny seemingly forever ago. Choosing to thrive with spiritual vision inspires the expression of raw talent. Producing abundance requires the mind to break the chains of social manipulation and the eyes to remove the scales of normalcy bias. Only the mind will shed the insecurity of spiritual death. Outside of true Law the chains of slavery shackle humanity and only a vigilant people will walk freely. Individual power to break these chains manifest it's highest potency in times of widespread oppression; however, in the event the majority persecute the few then what will cause the chain of the captives to break when their actions cast a net upon the free? Perhaps certain individuals escape and migrate their way to a heavily defensed province of free people ready to stifle conquest. What obstacles lie in wait for those hours leading to such freedom?

Lucifer manifests within God's children whom do not physically act to defend their spiritual and physical life. Americans today profess Christ won the war and therefore reason no battle today worth fighting exists when the opposite remains true with Christians across the Middle East being slaughtered at the hands of the wicked. The spirit of this world turns people to a reprobate mind. Many people in their lack of knowledge abandon all ideas of freeing the captives. How does one argue freedom and imprisonment do not exist at all; and, how does one live spiritually free without fighting for physical freedom? The same individual arguing freedom and imprisonment do not exist will argue oppression does not exist. Following the same logic one must ask: "Did Christ, in choosing not to sin, choose His own murder if only the sinful receive sin from others?" Corrupt knowledge infects sick individuals incapable of comprehending the most rudimentary concepts of history, jurisprudence, natural rights, and sovereignty.

Enemies of humanity divide members of the society and encourage apathy toward victims of enslavement and preach evil as God's will. The apathetic pretend chasing the spirit of this world exists as the only form of gain, obtainment, and permissible life of success; and, for this reason such apathy finds ease in declaring all victims deserving of victimhood. How arrogant, naive, and wicked to profess the child dying of cancer deserves such a fate or this child even brought the illness upon their self. The piety of claiming children sold into sex-trafficking must occur and children deserve such an affair defines the very illogical essence of tyranny in the mind. Clearly this type of individual no longer utilizes the most base form of logic to reason a matter and in their now keeping long separated from their heart do swell their ego into a balloon of apathy waged against righteousness. Shadowing minds from deeper truth in how the world operates will keep knowledge quarantined, increase the multitude worshiping death, and increase the fervency, and persecution, of the few worshiping life. No matter the consequence of challenging a ruler's consanguinity the divinity of God's likened image eternally prevails. Peacocks dance to attract attention; certain animals wear the mask of a thief; dolphins defend human from shark; and, everywhere in nature God provides an animation of sentient harmony. Babylon forever confounds itself upon it's inverted language and drawing forth of no eternal fruit. Denial shields the observer from understanding God's message all throughout nature.

Consider the life-long painter dying without public reverence and long after their physical death the post-society discovers and then regards the art as high spiritual attainment. What if the artist starved in His pursuits? Did the artist fail to recognize the significance of economizing art or did God plan to store the art in secret until the appointed time for the collective human conscience to receive the expression? Can art fail? Success remains subjective. Perhaps only the heart solves mystery. Did the artist hide from a society upholding falsehood over truth or fear persecution from a cowardly public threatening to assail His liberty for none reason other than imaginary blasphemy or other mass-hypnosis? What if the sinful accusers exemplified and vilified the artist's authenticity and this cognitive dissonance inspired the public to hate the presence of the prophet? What if the artist never produced His best work had He devoted time to loitering in public to peddle His wares? Perhaps the artist produced no wealth on the earth and His art produced voluminous wealth long after His grave. Does this constitute afterlife? Oppressors martyr righteous men in an effort to render potent ideas impervious to their reign of terror. The hungry artist suffers at length whereas those dying to protect the innocent live swiftly; though, what life worth living exists without hope in Christ? Wars of aggression, even labeled preemptive war, exist when vanity assails righteousness. Love evinces the only spiritual force working inwardly upon even the most wretched depth of consciousness fraught in error.

A large vehicle once wedged under a bridge and hours passed as adults erred to free the vehicle until a child's suggestion of deflating the tires freed the truck. "The emperor wears no clothes:" a phrase out of the mouth of babes ready to state the truth. Though american society largely lost ambition to protect individual rights – the youth today utilize passion to manifest the essence of the Republic. The evil follow one another to the grave and they alone hold responsibility for their action and in no manner does righteousness fuel the ways of crooked men. Notions of peace and prosperity fill the air in america; however, a great gnashing of teeth continues for reason of insufficient knowledge, highly engineered propaganda producing mass-hysteria, and a national mental illness epidemic bent on militarizing domestic police and instituting unlawful war in foreign nations lauded as patriotic or democratic policy.

After one of the most trying times in american history under the illegal Presidencies of George Bush Junior, and Barack Hussein Ubama: america grumbles in their slumber and elects President Donald John Trump whom does not work for the ancient ruling elite vampirizing mankind. His civic discipline, Godliness, education, and tenacity in no way measures close to President

George Washington or former Congressman from Texas Ron Paul or any of our Founding Fathers; however, as it stands at the time of this writing: His heart with righteous intention appears to resolve certain issues blatantly killing the american Republic and other nations around the globe; albeit, He unfortunately does keep The Federal Reserve and it's military-industrial-complex alive. Barack Hussein Ubama, George Bush Junior, and many other Presidents prior – illegally, openly, and wittingly, funded terrorist organizations with american tax dollars. President Trump removed funding for most terrorist organizations destroying the Middle East excluding The White Helmets destroying Syria as a proxy army for Al-CIA-Duh, ISIS, ISIL, or american, British, Israeli, and Saudi intelligence. Why does Trump not arrest the war criminals and fully exercise His Presidential authority to cut the excess agencies from The Federal Government thereby releasing the people from involuntary and unrepresentative taxation? President George Washington would not hesitate to rope the war criminals up a tree and my hope rests in future americans unequivocally reinstating the Republic through immediate justice against such oppression.

President Trump exposed the Clintons shipping Uranium to Russia as well as their theft of one point four billion tax dollars loaded onto a tarmac and flown to Ukrainian and/or Russian oligarchy. The Clintons responded with false accusations of Trump colluding with Russia to hijack the function of the american citizen. The wicked always blame the innocent for their own crimes. Trump fails Syria; however, He does not presently self-evidence the intentional destruction of Syria as Ubama did under Rothschild authority and although President Trump's actions prove slow – He shows a path toward an untangling of the lies keeping the wars endlessly alive.

The illegal central banking system, The Federal Reserve, fuels the loss of liberty at home through an Economic Policy of central economic planning fueling the loss of life abroad through the corruption of our *Foreign Policy*. President Trump, and all future americans, must enforce President Kennedy's Executive Order to abolish the central bank, and all central banks shall they ever arise; however, politics keeps people from seizing the constitutional, efficient, and honest approach to indefinitely resolve Economic Policy with immediate abolition of the central bank: The Federal Reserve.

President Donald Trump proves a guttural response from the american people to end the attempted tyrannical overthrow of america. President Ubama signed one Executive Order after another to spy on and rendition american citizens and even listed individuals holding strong belief in defending the constitution as potential domestic terrorists and even insurgents with specific reference to military veterans and retired police. How did our nation fall so far to allow the attempt of a total erasure of our history and people?

True domestic enemies of the american Republic only serve to awaken the american people and immunize future generations from such blatant authoritarianism. Ubama and His handlers, today, continue saboteur operations aimed at our american

Republic's dissolution though their foothold loses strength as President Trump destroys Ubama's Executive Orders listing the suspension of the constitution, interning of american Christians, and every other evil formed against a free people. America awoke and now it's time to arrest the enemies of humanity.

LIBERTY

Liberty; the idea which excites me – that feeling they wish to kill; the right pre-existing man which no one ever established or institutionalized. Human beings are people and people are individuals and individuals have a God-given right to their life, their liberty, and their property; and, the individual knows that no government can take away this design that God made for the individual. Imagine a world of nations allied for trade with one another; a replacement of warfare and welfare's enmity with true philosophy, friendship, and liberty from sin. Philosophers articulate reason, manifest action and inaction, cultivate consciousness, and expose evil. Individuals often describe good advice as bread and knowledge as water. Philosophy holds as much value in human life as food and water does to all life. The individual proclaiming love as their religion worships the one living God as their deity of worship and liberty as their dialectic philosophy of language and reason. liberty trades the evils of the heart for a realm infinitely equipped to answer the ails of the world.

James 1:25 But who so looketh in the perfect law of liberty, and continueth therein, he not being a forgetful hearer, but a doer of the work, shall be blessed in his deed.

History illustrates mankind as a large, ugly, and unaware monster feeding on the philosophers of liberty and at the same time insulting philosophy with the claim that it's function can only fulfill an aimless hobby at university and will not be the vehicle to unlock mankind's potential.

Luke 17:6 *And the Lord said, If ye had faith, as much as is a grain of mustard seed, and should say unto this mulberry tree, Pluck thyself up by the roots, and plant thyself in the sea, it should even obey you.*

Acting man must conduct His time in such a way as to build honorable civilization. Defending liberty requires individual attention to one's surrounding environment including cultural, educational and social norms, and a visceral prowess in articulating unalienable rights. The majority of earth suffers from not possessing the assembly of people with the least requisite of such a constitution or disposition; either from a lack of knowledge in liberty and the present principalities waging spiritual war against mankind or their blind assumption ignorance and not action creates the peaceful world they imagine thus surrendering their waking life to the indentured servitude of the philosophy of death.

What word, other than liberty, in any language, possesses an entire philosophy equal to liberty; and, if such a word exists then how on the earth does said culture fail in reflecting the ideas of liberty? A true Republic will fight for the liberty of individual rights. Despotism, under the guise of Democracy, will fight for mob rule and inspire civil ruin. How does an individual know they live under slavery without first becoming aware of their present state of existence or their ability to choose another state of awareness no matter the duty or talents God will demand of them? Few identify their slavery to shift into liberty; some must have their shackles of slavery shown to them; and the majority rarely wake out of bondage.

The individual set at liberty embarks on a life of peace and prosperity; even toward the fire of innocents calling out for help from places of violence or coercion. What compels evil to substitute knowledge for falsehood? What impels individuals to shadow minds and enslave the world? Limiting the exercise of liberty will not fulfill the individual or access their higher frequency of cognition. Trading one's own cognition for the countenance of spite empowers the deep and dark web of lying, weak-minded, and unthinking egos to subjugate free individuals to their own mental enslavement of fearing men or their words in order to debase civilization and extort the ideas of liberty. The beast of the underworld brought against the law confounds the one mind within the weak man into two minds thus perpetuates the necessary double-mindedness required to spiritually lead sheep to sacrificial bone fire.

Most have heard the phrase: "Life, liberty, and the pursuit of Happiness." or even read america's original flags with statements such as: "Don't Tread On Me," "Give Me liberty or Give Me Death," "liberty or Death," "Victory or Death," and "Join or Die." Give me the liberty of shared truths and y'all can keep your shared lies. The central theme of liberty distinguishes america from the many nations with openly legalized oppression. Most nations fly a flag and boast a national slogan. The Venezuelans pride their nation on socialism and what does socialism prove but another absolutely failed state? Certainly slogans aim to portray a maxim; though, the Venezuelan government remain the most duped among all of their people; Venezuela even imprisoned one of their firefighters for filming a donkey touring their firehouse while doing a voice-over of their President; is this not the trap of stupid behavior – He is hiding at the firehouse telling jokes while His fellow citizens are mowed down by His own government; afraid to take up arms and reclaim His nation; of course socialist nations produce voluminous amounts of comedy – it's tragic what they as a child-like public intentionally put their family through: they are cuntish people.

What if man does not protect ideas? Why would americans smelt the word "liberty" on every coin, fly flags with the phrase: "liberty or Death," and wage war against the most powerful and destructive global empire if not to secure the blessings of liberty? liberty empowers individuals to think and act without need for divide and conquer such that all individuals exercise sovereignty without shame. No other time in recorded history will an individual discover a nation of free people declaring and defending the ideas of liberty as achieved in american society.

Original americans understood man's origin as a God-given right to self-govern and not exist as slaves thus america's identity-politics started with "we the people." We the people, through the help of our God, secure the blessings of liberty to defense individuals with truth from those whom disdain our life, seek our death, and curtail human renaissance. Does the nature of liberty frighten entire populations into relinquishing self-responsibility, nurturing tyranny, and cultivating their future generations for the worship of money, power, and the state instead of their creator?

What happens to a people that forget liberty but a loss of natural rights forever? The blindness and falsehood of such an individual choosing slavery as their final destination in life knows no end. Only light pushes out darkness. Cognitive-dissonance delivers the hive-mind of society into perpetual enslavement to false information; for example, a false definition of liberty states: "Liberty means freedom to commit evil therefore liberty destroys and does not build civilization." Contrarily the vision of the individual practicing liberty perpetually discovers the value of truth. Liberty grants a life of moral society without fear of violent government coercively demanding obedience. America's Founding Fathers taught the usurpers of liberty operate within the confines of violence and coercion and the only true means of counter-acting this evil force exists in the liberty to speak freely, form a militia, train, and live prepared at all times to defend our life, liberty, and property. Violence and coercion fall under the crimes of theft and fraud – crimes clearly outlined in Articles I and III of the constitution; articles directly reflecting on the human condition and mankind's political and religious potential when juxtaposing the things for which men wrongly define as legal or illegal against the straightening out of these things from a national and global perspective before stepping even further back and finally weighing this transcendent potential at the epoch level concerning the lengths of time at which the ideas of liberty will reign over wicked men. Most of the animal kingdom lives a puritanical life or a life of religious devotion to the creation which gives to them each hour; good men face a real and present predator; an enemy that is not clear with their words. Americans, above other populations, rightly pursue the ideas of liberty and have illustrated the success of these precepts in our two and a half century-long experiment with the most sublimely limited government in recorded history which has proven the testament to the path of salvation and before ever fully righting mankind onto that path our people have produced the most free and prosperous individuals and families on the face of this earth; however, recent attacks on civil liberty have resulted in the persecution of individuals and exponential expanse of the ever-present and occultic global empire.

One of the main arguments against liberty falls into the idea of a hereditary right-to-rule wherein a sexual congress of inbreeding family wields absolute power over enslaved people. "I will keep you safe; come here my pretty." laments The Queen as She stares down her nose upon Her servile ants. What device must the authoritarian design to keep their aristocratic social and government architecture? The ruler without a willing caste of subjects will not rule at all. Authoritarians obsess over hereditary ownership of a global body politic and practice this type of control as though it were an art to program individuals into the fantasy that liberty were a phenomena, even one-dimensional therefore unhealthy, and not the standard from which their wickedness seeks to shadow from mankind's awareness. If in fact we see liberty as the standard, or homeostasis, of mankind then what things in the life of each individual must see removal to render civilization from it's state of imprisonment under unelected tyrants; and, conversely what within our own life renders civilization free to the degree that even our neighbors will elect honest representatives and defend peace and prosperity for all? What things in society must unearth to discover such clear change? What entity occupies the mind, body, and spirit, of those sacrificing the innocent? Perhaps under the instance of a people fighting the ruling-class, ending involuntary taxation, and actively pursuing means of securing individual civil liberty in the erecting of a new government of elected representatives then the slaves no longer exist in the present realm and now a free people give birth to a new realm wherein the former rulers and agents of evil peacefully retire and live a free and humble life.

Perhaps Royalty in far away lands fully grasp, and fear, a people set at liberty; and, with their realizing of the most intelligent among their own peasantry feigning contempt for the Crown whom enslaved their ancestors centuries ago: fear insurrection from within, overthrow of their Monarchical monopoly, and widespread flourishing of individual liberty completely uninterested in the idea of autocracy. Today's peasants of The British Crown attempt to explain how their masters, The Royal Family, control nothing and live as a system of tradition wherein the people of Her prison-nation live free and not as modern-day slaves. Her Majesty's peasants must have saved that joke for after the greatest american generation to have ever lived: that generation which overthrew Her wicked reign and founded our sovereign nation. Perhaps the ancestors of such peasantry have always died by this useless epithet. Lord help that mentally handicapped public playing make-believe with their peasant philosophy of lispy whisperings and false heroes justifying their own slavery to a gremlin vampire named Queen: yeah, that philosophy that says the world is better off without a god as a veil to disguise their making of every thing they do being their tormenting wretch of a god: how do you not feel like less of a human for being ruled by a royal family or not being in understanding of being their peasant? All of the public witnessed His Hairy Princess, Prince Harry, in Canada on the eighth of May, twenty-sixteen, at the Invictus Games state: "The Queen controls the military." Deep within the psyche of victimized man exists an instinct to worship one's captor; for example, the peasant-slave of the Monarch will absorb the same format of information and state this revelation illustrates political fervor without consequential reverberation (*so posh*).

The obtuse in thinking argue no society proclaiming liberty will ever exist nor will such a people succeed in instituting a government defending this type of people. If true then how does the majority on the earth agree with a government equal and opposite to absolute rule; and, how did one nation, america, cultivate and achieve a population whom instituted self-ownership? Liberty is above all things an artistic pursuit and what makes liberty necessarily iconic is contained within the creator's ability to mesh with the transparency of culture and contradict the powers antithesis to man. How does one intelligently argue the authoritarian does not exercise power over the people without the overthrow of their bonds? Perhaps the addled mind believes individualism will not give to society what will go unnoticed without collectivism. Only an infidel will argue human civilization remains unaffected to the decisions of an active ruler and certainly when that ruler publicly sacrifices individuals. The less than genuine would wish to belittle the examples mentioned and argue human statutes as necessary security theater for keeping individuals safe from our self; however, to paraphrase Inventor and Founding Father Benjamin Franklin: "Those who would give up essential liberty, to purchase a little temporary Safety, deserve neither liberty nor Safety."

The wishfully empirical and woefully omniscient self-appointed historians purport america as an illegal nation (even taught in american public schools) subject to arrest from the British Monarch and remain indebted to various groups wronged by american policy. Even today, in the year twenty nineteen and in the days ahead of twenty twenty, the British Crown, and Israeli citizens, publicly claim the Monarch maintain ownership of individual americans and all property for reason of: "The

Monarch have always owned earth and stating or acting contrary amounts to a criminal act subject to judgment from our Head of State: the Crown." Americans called the Royal bluff and turned the global order on it's head thus disrupted the cog churning mankind into fuel for the few controlling earth with full writ over the lives of those God ordained as free from the beginning of time. Famous slogans born out of the american Revolution include: "I would rather die on my feet than live as a slave on my knees." Who will so arrogantly misinterpret the message of such a slogan? Not long after the american Revolution an overwhelming number of traitors seized political office within american government and imprisoned many of our revolutionaries including members of Congress and for reasons so insolent as insulting the waist-line of our fat-ass President [Greetings your Royal Rotunda]. The Founding Fathers advised mankind to flick the blood-sucking ticks, like the Monarch, off of society's back; however, in so doing, hell will produce another tyrant lusting for the opportunity to kill, steal, and destroy; therefore, the revolution must burn within the heart of the individual until tyranny fears reprisal from all men.

Another common refutation from the anti-liberty individual starts with, "Denmark and Sweden do this ..." as though their families remotely resemble the multi-generational war for Independence waged by american family, friends, and their ancestors, whom fought, bled, suffered, faced imprisonment, were tortured, starved, or died fighting the global Monarchy in order that they safeguard the blessings of liberty for their children in the only nation on the earth succeeding this highest value achievement for all of mankind. Crime persists in every strata of american society; though, the ark of salvation tugs along for those not jumping ship to feed their self to the hysteria.

The Church of Christ in Sweden now teaches God exists as a woman and this false revelation somehow aids this new and mysterious elevation of the gospel (never-mind the fact the woman-as-God religion [Lucifer] was already spoken for); though, what example of elevation exists in their socialist culture compared to america's self-governance and why do so many nations find value in assailing america as their own nation if not for their subconscious inclination to self-identify with the cause of liberty dwelling within us all? False teachers slight the name of Christ and this does not stop americans from Godly discernment proving liberty as the sure means to secure peace and prosperity. Americans maintain a superior architecture of government than other nations around the world with our Republican form of self-governance instituting an autonomous and decentralized system to protect the natural rights of the individual, absolutely subvert the authoritarian, and prove america in the least exemplifies mankind's proving grounds for waging spiritual war against the global tyranny wreaking havoc upon our world and the cause of liberty; though, americans have not realized or exercised the full and working philosophic capacity of our Declaration of Independence and Bill of Rights and as a result we do remain entrenched in a war against bad, hostile, and ugly government (literal geriatric crypt-keeper-looking wind-bags, Jabba the Hutt's, feral rats, and Sims). The fact Earth still possesses individuals whom name their self a word such as Royalty and use this word to justify their domination of civilization proves humanity remains deeply embedded within the dark ages of a mankind without liberty and america represents the last stand and remnant routing out and lightening the load of tyranny for the increase and abundance of individuals fighting the good fight.

The ruler masquerades as the highest accord among men, gifts stolen resources to those keeping false hope in His cloak of evil, and enslaves ignorance to His rod. History shows peasants will publicly celebrate their King, no matter the destitute state of their affairs, and especially upon His dispersal of only one vessel of wine. What power within the realms of imagination will render a wicked reign obsolete except the philosophy of liberty; there is none. What window of opportunity does the ruler observe in order to participate in this act of oppression? The matador engages the bull with a waving of the veil. Royalty, more rightly defined as seriously confused, deceptive, deranged, and sociopathic individuals, flaunt their wealth to the peasantry whom blindly charge the veil and remain absolutely unaware of the matador impaling mankind's spiritual body politic for the blood-letting of civilization. Individual loss of liberty occurs when religious and political programs of violence and coercion sequester thought and action. The meeting of men primarily utilizes speech to innovate those men and more effectively equip and strengthen them against the devices of the tyrant. Authoritarians will invert language to suppress ideas capable of shifting the political paradigm. The word liberty does not lose translation from one language to another, though, articulating liberty on a mass scale proves an enduring struggle for civilization; one overarching struggle wherein we look onto the world and witness the vast majority of our human race as subjects to absolute rule from the tongue of those coercively monopolizing language to inspire a dehumanization or daftness from within their subjects. Entire civilizations have sacrificed liberty on the altar of authoritarian governance: yeah, empty platitudes cutting off the tongue from the throat of those that would dare speak liberty and truth to the devil's plague: yeah, that power of the devil described in Revelations 9:4 and the butchery of conscience seared with a hot iron in Revelations 16:2: yeah; that plague that guards every civilization not our own: yeah, that driver of self-censorship and a world without God, art, or man.

Eternity connects all living creatures as a town-clock pointed at liberty and the rulers seek to shadow this native intellect in order to subordinate a multitude for their servitude. The ingredients for a society poisoned by the known dangers of a life stripped of all liberty starts with "free stuff from government." All throughout the ages the watchers have sought to absolutely control or destroy the will and good heart of man; a heart of whom only knows to pursue liberty and perfectly hate the negative behaviors required to obey the calm of despotism. The tyrant argues necessity as His destiny and not that of the individual. "Consider the ant-colony," the tyrant in reaffirming His glut continues: "Nature ordains *Order* and shows even among the bees, ants, and ape, there must exist ruling gods: a Queen!" The barbarous baboons argue the examples in nature provide mankind a template to operate more humanely; which, delivers deep insight into the carnal psychology of the subordinates of Satan as they justify those greater evils of humanity thus dehumanize the eloquence of mankind's sentience in order to reduce culture unto perfidy. Individuals unlike animals do, in fact, naturally desire to seek peace in the defense of ideas. The world argues for the necessity of government and only in america, that we know of, had individuals fought a real war and for true self-governance and *repeatedly kicked the ever-loving shit out of those red-coat's asses until we claimed total victory (So sad! Not.); winning; so much winning.* Catalonia recently declared Independence and this only started their war as the Catalonians allowed Spain to immediately arrest their political representatives as prisoners of war. Words must meet action and if Catalonians truly view their self independent and their nation sovereign with authority to levy war and conclude peace then their people must properly prepare and defend their lands.

A magic wand and fancy hat does not grant man the authority to misinterpret natural rights without eternal consequence. The youth, armed with music, always represent the future of mankind as the incessant issuance of rewritten law will fade away with the graves of those whom sought power in trade of peace. Authoritarians liken their self to slaughterers herding men into a state of uncertainty and ultimately the shadowing of their unexpressed excellency and virtue. Farmers change cattle field-to-field on a daily, weekly, and monthly basis. The rulers control false narratives and alter mankind's battle-scape every decade, century, and millennium to hide knowledge and the blood-lines ensuring success for the anti-Christ rewriting the book of life in real-time. The technocratic elite working to rewrite humanity with a new anti-liberty philosophy disguised as liberty, today, remain convinced of the impossibility of conquering mankind on the physical realm and instead wish to see an artificially intelligent control-grid of nano, pico, and femto-bots (one superimposed on zero and has infinite area) culling mankind into relinquishing sentience and submitting to a life without physical death. The elite want to literally insert people into a machine wherein the individual's sleeping body will remain in a dream-state of viewing a manufactured reality while their true physical body will electrically power a robotic super-machine and no longer act in the physical realm thus living in reality as a willing or unwilling existence (circumstantial; proto, neo, etc...) of surrendering their mind for a view within an artificial reality with an artificial body in the form of a digital super-algorithm that dreams a false life with non-existent liberty; and, will eternally remain within this prison so long as their spirit does not awaken and pursue means to escape the control-grid, live on the physical realm, and repopulate the cosmos far outside of the control of this all-consuming and absolute evil; smart devices: new-tech [caveat: with the backing of the state] will always control dumb populations. We do live in a free mind and make no mistake: the tyrant does not view humanity as family and works to cage society into a prison planet of weaponized caste systems usurping the vision of those individuals ensuring the inheritance of liberty goes to their progeny.

Men created The Magna Carta in the year twelve fifteen to settle the dispute of law and order and who maintains power over the elect. The Magna Carta outlined the self-evidence that no man lives above the law and certainly not higher than King Jesus who art in Heaven. Jesus Christ, not of this world, the Son of Man at the right hand of God, shares His existence with us through His Holy Spirit of liberty dwelling equally within all men. The peasant-slave will argue The Magna Carta allows society to live as one with a Royal Head of State; and, here again, peasants will sit upon their throne of ignorance for eternity. Five hundred and fifty years later the precepts juxtaposed in The Magna Carta continue to warn man of the world separate from true spirituality.

What proof for liberty exists in america? Perhaps the word liberty speaks immediately to the mind and for many individuals this notion reaches into the spiritual depth of every man and woman with eyes to see and ears to hear the animating contest of liberty; in the discernment of our people are the things of the mind that were first in the senses. Why does lightning strike the wicked in the head? In two hundred and forty years america created more prosperity than the previous six thousand years of recorded human civilization; this feat performed without permanent rulers and instead with elected representatives of the free world: good and bad; standing in the space of where the tyrannical oligarchs previously stood for all of known human civilization; and, now standing under the umbrella of true consciousness: exposes the illusion keeping mankind from it's independence; and, that very independence of which was first declared and foretold of in the story written on the night sky. Consider Founding Father: President George Washington denying the opportunity to wear a Crown as King over america and instead succeeded the instituting of a nation with elected representatives and a people free from absolute rule. New Yorkers on the fourth of July seventeen seventy-six waited five additional days for British soldiers to murder any remaining americans marching in opposition of The Crown. Whatever the source of this anti-american, anti-Independence, anti-liberty regalia remaining in america today – the sentiments continue generation to generation through backward and archaic teachings from entire families that never unlocked certain life experience, knowledge, or epigenetic inscription; thus, wallow in their family pit of intellectual depravity. The multi-generational disdain for liberty remains palpable among every race, color, creed, national origin, gender, and sexual orientation. President George Washington and His soldiers marched up to New York and waited for British soldiers to arrive and the cowards never showed. Under intense political pressure New Yorkers finally signed onto the Declaration of Independence on the ninth of July seventeen seventy-six. The country of Morocco was more willing to celebrate american Independence than New Yorkers. President George Washington held a firm belief in Divine Providence to secure the blessings of liberty and He achieved as perfectly near this vision ever imagined by men not Christ; perhaps women imagine this vision every morning and evening during the ceremonial preparation of the excellent hair. The Declaration of Independence eloquently torts:

"*We, therefore, the Representatives of the united States of America, in General Congress, Assembled, appealing to the Supreme Judge of the world for the rectitude of our intentions, do, in the Name, and by Authority of the good People of these Colonies, solemnly publish and declare, **That these united Colonies are, and of Right ought to be Free and Independent States, that they are Absolved from all Allegiance to the British Crown, and that all political connection between them and the State of Great Britain, is and ought to be totally dissolved**; and that as Free and Independent States, they have full Power to levy War, conclude Peace, contract Alliances, establish Commerce, and to do all other Acts and Things which Independent States may of right do. — And for the support of this Declaration, with a firm reliance on the protection of **Divine Providence**, we mutually pledge to each other our Lives, our Fortunes, and our sacred Honor.*"

Divine Providence explains the intent and whole of our cause of liberty. Jesus Christ is divine; liberty is divine; private property rights is divine; defending against tyranny is divine; free trade is divine; diplomacy is divine.

After the original american Revolution Marquis de Lafayette described our revolution as a wildly rare phenomenon when, to paraphrase Him, He states: "Humanity has won it's battle. Liberty now has a country." The Independence of america was not only a victory for a nation more than it was a victory and singularity of mankind's entering into a new era of antiquity or even within the fields of Atlantis as we more near those places far beyond the violence of fire that our people had grown so keen to worship. Will a type-one civilization face regression or even threat of absolute destruction from an equally and opposite power unfathomable today; perhaps, an evil type-two or type-three civilization? Politicians and academic-elites today purport there exists no intelligent life outside of mankind. Will type-one civilizations communicate with type-two and type-three civilizations or will the politically motivated within the type-one civilization claim no type-two or type-three civilizations exist? Does decadence always produce a loss of liberty or potential extinction of civilization or will envy alone corrupt the enjoyments of living well?

The Economic and Foreign Policy enacted by our Congress and President remains the key component for advancing the cause of liberty in real-time (i.e.: abolish The Federal Reserve; bring the troops home; stop making excuses for the things which the constitution allows the President to completely enforce today). The Economic and Foreign Policy remain high-value targets for subversion though liberty compels the citizen to expand society's consciousness and disrupt authoritarian operations. Sovereign society goes forth as an example to all nations and their inherent desire to satisfy the Lord and preserve their liberty tells a story which teaches the world about the blessings of liberty and education of leading by example (even if that example are the spoken or written words countervailing evil forces) will forever remain the only true and most proper method in igniting brushfires of liberty in the minds of men: yeah, even for the trafficking of it's all-consuming flame in the soul of the very elect. Questioning the anti-liberty individual about the jury process in nations outside of america proves a rewarding course of debate in order to delineate the cruel mind caring not about the absence of liberty outside of america. A jury of peers preserves the life and liberty of it's fellow citizen and even serves as the standard for which america must entreat foreign nations: yeah, a friendly arbiter of truth and not an unelected harbinger of destruction bearing false witness against in the name of democracy, necessity, or security. Foreign Policy reflects the spiritual quality of the body politic as this policy can only be corrupted with the theft of the nation which will result in war or saved by the reverence of the people for the ideas of liberty which will produce peace. Corrupt americans today remain hell-bent on using central banks to indiscriminately fund rogue military empire for the murder, theft, and destruction of sovereign individuals and even until the very bowels of civilization pulverize into irreparable memory.

All men of quality agree the individual owns the fruit of their labor. Who will argue ignoring theft of individual labor, including under threat of violence, or from a ruling class, does not represent immoral transgression? No man or group of men own the labor of another man unless the individual willingly shares His harvest or talents without being under the threat of coercion or violence though in times of duress men can be compelled by the two to save their lands. The individual works to obtain an honorable return for the investment of their time. When Joe trades His oranges for Sues apples this constitutes a private and protected contractual trade. Individuals possess the natural right to trade freely and peaceably with one another under private contract. When individuals demand to keep their earnings then this represents a society of liberty or voluntary exchange. An entire civilization with the awareness, comprehension, and discernment of the philosophy of liberty (against all other philosophies even) produces more innovation, opportunity, peace, and prosperity in one century than any ruler could fathom in seeing His drooling minions produce by the forced labor of their subjects; and, this society of liberty does contain within it the demonstrative power to render the ideas of lesser nations and the philosophies obsolete since only liberty will create and lead to that expansive shift of consciousness as witnessed in american society and foretold of by our ancients and fathers of long-past. The rulers wish to restrain liberty for each individual, claim ownership of all trade, and alter the tides of humanity as though we were their ship of spirits lividly resetting course for frigid and tumultuous seas and even for the appeasement of central bankers and warmongers (LOL).

The tax collector knocks on the door and demands every man, woman, child, and item of private property and especially the deed to the property be immediately handed over to Him and His driver as the tax collector roll out His ransom orders from those greasy ingrates in government office accusing Him of theft for not making payments on that which He owns aright while the ransom even claims His government wilt permit the theft of their lives without honoring the final payment notice; this is the essence of mafia and not civil liberty; this is america (Sad!). Original americans poured literal hot tar and chicken-butt feathers on tax collectors to fight such self-evident tyranny involuntarily raising itself over the precepts which prohibit their interventionisms. Paying government through taxation is the legalization of every human error. What totally ignorant, arrogant, and feeble-minded newts to not know of and defend the historical significance of a global renaissance engaged in the attack formation of overthrowing Tyranny, reconstituting liberty as the highest law of the land, and reminding the earth that liberty has with it the ideas worth living and dying for. The superior definition to government power ought to stay *government anti-power* to underscore government's inability to produce real estate when only free people produce anything and especially are the progenitors of every institution, decision-makers of every alteration, and jurors for every abolition of bad government and for what else except the preservation of life, liberty, and property; keep your sour grapes and I will keep my liberty you incompetent government imbeciles.

God designed mankind with the guarantee that we the people must choose individual sovereignty if we want to live well on the land; and, as sovereign beings and individuals of sovereign power with sovereign control of the sovereign flow of our own sovereign resources this idea of being sovereign is inherent to the philosophy of liberty and does especially include the idea that individual sovereignty must as an act of God, obedience to Christ, principle, and self preservation defend the sovereign ownership of that sovereign property or properties which men so often deprecate as unsovereign money or official contraband for the forceful seizure by the crusty fingers of the sovereignty-infringing wicked men and bull dykes they worship. Money exists as a tool of exchange and anything can be money at any time which is another reason government shall not be in the business of defining money; money can only be moral when the people can freely determine their own destiny by freely determining the best money for their pursuits; if a man wants to be a trader of gems today then the dark angels occupying federal government would steal it from Him and demand His papers proving ownership. Beasts argue man must live without the commodity of money; however, what will come of the individual arguing one commodity obsolete and not another? Masking liberty with the full force of unthinking government purchases the commodity of self-destruction and apathy toward national desecration. The liberty to fail supplants every form of tyranny. The unlawful drug laws in america only replace preexisting markets with the malignancy of violence and coercion. Doctors once prescribed many of the items the government now labels unlawful drugs and once the tyrannical laws were applied then suddenly a new market emerged wherein the concentration of the compound-substance within the consumer product exponentially multiplied as a natural market response to more efficiently work within the unlawful confines applied to the market; however, unintended consequences expanded a culture of corruption, intervention, and isolation. Peaceful markets will always exist and individuals whom desire to rule mankind seek to distort free markets for their own gain.

"Commerce with all and alliance with none." should forever remain the motto and action of the nation fighting for liberty. This slogan validates both in the micro and macro of national sovereignty with the micro of our Economic Policy first appertaining to the civil Liberties of trade which immediately protects the sovereignty of the citizen; and, the macro of Foreign Policy restraining constitutional subversion, government theft, and manufactured war. Both policies, when unchecked, will always result in the persecution of foreign nations and our own nation as the abuse of it's power demands expansion to it's meaning and repurposing of it's weapons of war for absolute genocide at home. The original design and intent of america's Economic and Foreign Policy safeguards the natural rights and blessings of liberty for citizens of america and increases potential for liberty to unleash in the foreign world trading with america. Sovereign trade manifests the single action a constitutional Economic Policy intends to preserve. Sovereignty in the nation of liberty must extend as an olive branch to individuals of foreign lands; insofar, as the nation of liberty must love thy neighbor as their self and this behavior sets the stage for a proper Foreign Policy designed only for defense against invasion. Economic and Foreign Policy act as an axis of measure either keeping the nation free to pursue political and religious liberty or condemned to live under the political and religious ideology of the wicked one. History allows us to prove this as the most logical reasoning to deduce the affairs of a free nation into two absolute and discernible forms of commerce; thereby exemplifying the reason The Founding Fathers of america devised an ark of governance to defense all individuals from the tempest of dependence with The President and Commander in Chief overseeing Economic and Foreign Policy; and, the local County Sheriffs keeping their oath to the constitution and possessing the self-same powers of The President and nation-state to exercise their liberty in enforcing the constitution from within their own County even if the County must secede to preserve the american flag and the ideas of liberty. Liberty in a Foreign Policy represents a policy of strength through commerce. War-time allies, even when war persists under the pseudonym of sanctions, always results in perpetual warfare. Standing armies remain idle observers, economically dead, and depend on their leisurely sanctioning through the funding of central banks and plunder of society's participants. The Founders were doubly smart in proclaiming: No standing armies for our Foreign Policy and no central banks for our Economic Policy in order to abstain from violence and coercion and secure the foundation, scaffolding, and architecture of true liberty. Prosperity only grows when the people view standing armies and central banks as immoral high offenses to God which can only result in destruction no matter the profane reason a human statute will, by decree, transgress. A people of liberty must continually arm their wit with maxims designed to keep their liberty.

Today, in the year two thousand and eighteen of our Lord, debate rages for term limits amongst elected Congressional citizen-representatives. Those individuals purporting such nonsense envisage the least educated among americans. Congress serves *two-year term limits* and Senate serves *six-year term limits*. The liberty of the people to reelect representatives allows the people to expediently dismiss their representative and greatly enhance the probability of healing the republic through allowing the people to peacefully recapture the co-opted republic since we can know real liberty is in jeopardy of being lost forever every generation (even if the awareness and recompensing process takes decades to stop a train of abuses); maintain ability to adapt and weather a potentially lengthy storm of authoritarianism; inspire the recurrence of our champions of liberty to represent the people with their constitutional mastery, public knowledge, and service of watering the fire of out-of-control government; inspire healthy competition; increase probability for competency from within government; rudder the tempestuous sea of liberty; and nullify corruptions and idleness. James Madison taught frequent elections held a superior check on the abuse of government power; a far greater check than rendering reelections illegal.

1. Yale Law School. "The Federalist Papers: No. 53." *The Avalon Project, Lillian Goldman Law Library,* https://avalon.law.yale.edu/18th_century/fed53.asp. Accessed 4 January 2020

Limiting the volume of Congress' two-year term limits will neuter the already stupid men of america (those stupid men demanding Congress limit the volume of their two-year terms) and lead to a quick collapse and end to the experiment of liberty in our nation (just because impotent and stupid men want to quit the animating contest of liberty does not mean they will succeed an authority to usurp my nation and quit my liberty), and "greater the proportion of new members, and the less the information of the bulk of the members, the more apt will they be to fall into the snares that may be laid for them." Liberty aims to keep the most exemplary representatives and guarantee authority to zero individuals whom would abolish the ability to reelect honorable representatives in favor of the unsavory and self-professed authoritarians mandating allies, fomenting war, and widening it's circle of death and desolation. When government does not possess authority to unlawfully acquire allies then those citizens maintain a higher probability of keeping their life, nation, and respect for one another. The subversion from tyranny happens in a sweeping overthrow of a free people – first by infringement of the individual's currency, second by an intentional draw and rack of constitutional precedent, third by official censorship, fourth by seizure of industry and property, and last by enslaving the submissives to debt or forced labor and culling any counter-revolution. Those unaware of the liberty the people possess in maintaining mastery over reelecting citizen-representatives fail in succeeding the purpose of The american Republic, cause of liberty, and the understanding of their ancestors; as this type of american desires to strip americans of their discernment, pretend they do the thinking for the men of this nation when they do not think at all, know not how utterly foolish their eye-sight misleads, pursue the centralization of false power and increase of the illusion of constitutional oversight and Presidential authority, and degrade the power of the people until they usher in the beginning of the end of the citizen's right to think. The displacement of knowledge, insofar as many overtly possess the knowledge of evil and do not in the least know our own base architecture of governance and namely that which was outlined in our Declaration of Independence, resulted in the continental destruction of civil liberty witnessed across the americas and The Middle East today. The architecture of government: Federal, State, and Local contains a design to protect the liberty of each individual. Much time has passed since america's founding and millions of americans today claim less liberty creates more freedom. Freedom is not liberty. The inaction of pursuing intelligent thought and cogent speech represents the multitude of anti-Christs muttering unthinking utterances as they usher in the New World Order of Old World Order inverting every form of governance, reason, and idea previously protecting the natural rights of man in america and abroad. The embers of hell consist of every unthinking individual that worked to obstruct liberty. What the world regards as normal is hell's highest expectation for it's servants. Insecure individuals adopt obtuse religion and manifest political motif concise with the philosophy of Death. All culture tends to agree idleness manifests nothing good. Does liberty own the space in opposition to Death? And if liberty contains all philosophy then Death must persist as the philosophy of no thing. Liberty when viewed as the most high architecture for religious and political association produces the only foundation for society to faithfully build upon and exit from the old world order as joy enters each generation evermore toward God's greater plan.

What security grants greater liberty than liberty granted for it's own sake? Our Founding Fathers brilliantly designed weights and measure in the american government derived primarily from direction within The Bible and borrowing from more modern experience of warfare and enmity and even Iroquois native American knowledge. Mankind, today, falls short of comprehending the protections of liberty inscribed in america's Declaration of Independence and Bill of Rights; and, whose guarantee of the raised standard will, when defended, provide unlimited blessing in the order God prescribes.

Many will verbally proclaim liberty and will not physically defend liberty thus surrender their God-given victory for a total loss of life and liberty. The liberty of the american citizen must restrain government with the chains of the Constitution; and, in so doing: harbor the institutions for liberty. The Perfect Law of liberty embodies a Godly court system, people, Economics, and relation with other nations whom otherwise stand in darkness and will not see the glory of mankind's ascension until the day all of the world lives of one body, mind, and spirit with the Heavenly One above all. Courts all across this world do not guarantee the protection of natural rights and only guarantee the protection of the state. The semantical architecture of governance in the courts of america, intend to found the courts of God on the earth as in Heaven, and have as of late turned to harsh vinegar from it's state of sweet wine. God gave us vinegar to aid stomach health; preserve, disinfect, and clean food or instruments; or even serve as a reminder of the freshness of a drink; enable the conduct of electricity; facilitate cooking or food preservation; and other vast uses. Many of the jellyfish dominating american society today guarantee the efficacy of government corruption and even traffic through the majority of our Christian churches. Many of these fake Christians equip their self with built-in, knee-jerk, reactionary responses to denigrate individuals pursuing the higher actions of God and escaping the yoke of bondage thus this reactionary and back-biter embodies the Synagogue of Satan preaching Christ as both missing or near in order to keep hidden The Kingdom of God at hand.

Philippians 4:5 *[a]Let your [b]patient mind be known unto all men. [c]The Lord is at hand.*
Philippians 4:5 Footnotes
[a] The second is not taking all things in good part, they behave themselves moderately with all men.
[b] Your quiet and settled mind.
[c] The taking away of an objection: We must not be disquieted through impatience, seeing that God is at hand to give us remedy in time against all our miseries.

Exodus 32:1 But when the people saw, that Moses tarried long ere he came down from the mountain, the people gathered themselves together against Aaron, and said unto him, Up, [a] make us gods to go before us: for of this Moses (the man that brought us out of the land of Egypt) we know not what is become of him.

Exodus 32:1 Footnotes

[a] The root of Idolatry is, when men think that God is not at hand, except they see him carnally.

Why do the fake Christians mockingly interrupt the individual releasing the Knowledge of God with: "More flies with honey than vinegar." as to suggest God desires man to abstain from vinegar, ostracize individuals teaching about the principalities ruling our present realm, condemn knowledge itself and all things God reveals, or pretend peace without justice represents peace or justice? Evil delivers the ignorant into bondage and the knowledge of such seizure of power possesses the potential to grant eternal life. Why would anyone presume God views His children as flies to capture and not individuals to set free? This type of virtue-signaling only serves to avoid knowledge, fear thought, and condemn the followers of Christ teaching about the knowledge of God and the crooked ways of those professing to follow Christ when their family serves the unlawful military excursion of death and desolation upon innocent citizens in faraway lands. Perhaps the hypocrites always anger when faced with digesting their own hypocrisy; though, their sourness represents no hindrance to my proclamation for liberty to the captives of tyranny. The most exemplary proclamation of the hypocrite, today, persists not only in their ignoring of illegally bombing foreign people, even consisting of fellow or superior Christians, but in their evil justification: "God is not a feeling!"

Nehemiah 8:10 .. *the joy of the Lord is your strength.*

Ezra 6:16 ¶ .. *the children of the captivity kept the dedication of this house of God with joy,*

Psalm 43:4 *Then will I go unto the altar of God, even unto the God of my joy*

Zephaniah 3:17 *The Lord thy God in the midst of thee is mighty: he will save, he will rejoice over thee with joy: he will quiet himself in his love: he will rejoice over thee with joy.*

Romans 14:17 *For the kingdom of God, is not meat nor drink, but righteousness, and peace, and joy in the holy Ghost.*

Ecclesiastes 2:26 .. *God giveth wisdom, and knowledge, and joy*

Isaiah 49:13 *Rejoice, O heavens; and be joyful, O earth; burst forth into praise, O mountains; for God hath comforted his people, and will have mercy upon his afflicted.*

Isaiah 55:12 *Therefore ye shall go out with joy, and be led forth with peace*

Proverbs 14:10 *The heart knoweth the bitterness of his soul, and the stranger shall not meddle with his joy.*

Proverbs 12:20 *Deceit is in the heart of them that imagine evil: but to the counselors of peace shall be joy.*

Psalm 105:43 *And he brought forth his people with joy, and his* *chosen with gladness,*

Psalm 100:2 *Serve the Lord with gladness; come before him with joyfulness.*

Psalm 32:11 *Be glad ye righteous, and rejoice in the Lord, and be joyful all ye, that are upright in heart.*

The ruling elite have programmed the entire world with a fear for our liberty when we know after the last days of the wicked reign and during the time of the excellent and great reloading of munitions we will only know:

Isaiah 14:7 *The whole world is at <u>rest</u> and is <u>quiet</u>: they sing for joy.*

The word *rest* describes a physical and spiritual state of quietness allowing room for nothing more than the singing of joy to enter upon the whole face of earth. Both words narrowly represent one another insofar as spirit quietly rests within and around flesh and sings it's own melody to those performing it's message; however, the spirit does not dwell in carnality therefore the people resting in quietness and singing in joy spiritually live as God's image on the earth. The liberty of man rests in the peace of doing the things of the heart, not bending or breaking during persecution, and escaping every realm of bondage. The spirit of man finds joy in peaceful living and free assembly. The calm of despotism perpetually hissing, groaning, and gnashing of teeth paints a realm separate from the world of joy God intends. Government desires to privatize their own secrecy, render government transparency a crime, and make democide their reality.

The point of reference, or vector, for economic output starts with individual speech, and then expands to the wider borders of economic trade with county, state, federal and every border of international civilization. Innovation and trade possess the sharpest weapon for the liberty movement. America's Founding Fathers designed the original ten amendments, The Bill of Rights, for this very purpose: to shield innovation from corruptive government power through the protection of individual speech. Our Bill of Rights achieves in one document what most succinctly phrases the word liberty through a logical reasoning of our God-given and unalienable natural rights appertaining the individual's domestic and foreign affairs and institutionalization of the preservation of their civil liberties from the first amendment showing the fashion of the individual and then advancing as a pattern outward toward the tenth amendment concerning the liberty of the colonies of people residing within each state and not for the means to instill violence or coercion upon any entity whatsoever but rather according to what the members of society agree as a true and constitutional defense realized through the enforcement imbued into and exercised through each of their representatives; a true representation or literary image of that still-shot of physical reality acting in a harmonious animation; the first document wherein man looked clearly into a literary mirror while the illusion of tyranny faded into memory; our Bill of Rights was not a simply document creating any old nation or institutionalizing what the screeching left so stupidly calls cultural appropriation. The creation of more amendments beyond the original ten can only constrict the content of the original ten amendments and blood-let the nation by Satanic forces and their sinister dialectics. Our ten amendments possess the foundational logic to articulate every discernment. The addition of amendments only serves to systematically dismantle our comprehension of the Bill of Rights, increase the ignoring of the first ten amendments with the excuse of antiquated applicability, and eliminate mankind's foundation of life and property; which, appears self-evident today as we witness Amish men and women militarily warranted for drinking their own cow's milk, students across every age of schooling banned from wearing clothing displaying the american flag, and Californian farmers descended upon via Executive Magistrate military squadrons for growing scrumptious fruits and vegetable without the corporate chemicals or government-subsidies.

Rogue government influencing society produces heightened awareness in individuals predestined to defend against it's threat; and, a lack of awareness for individuals possessing intention to defend no thing except their most carnal and least thinking hunger. Today a majority of americans identify with the mind-manipulation program of erasing american History for reason of social justice; a state-sponsored program of mental enslavement which grows in popularity and bears the hallmark of every type of self-assigned slavery and especially the dismissal of true knowledge to fantasize one has attained an unattainable illusion of comfort as the false means of intellectually defeating sound logic; this illusion creates the perspective of apathetic compartmentalization associated with the public portrayal of powerful individuals; therefore: reducing knowledge [falsely] guarantees individual power; though, only shields the powerful whom oppress those without knowledge. The tide of tyranny proves ever more difficult to reverse as cultural degradation accelerates. The tyrant pleas for necessity therefore the slave claims necessity as their creed to appease the tyrant. Liberty removes the illusion of necessity and reveals a harmonious society of antiquity.

Language creates the most foundational element of each individual's order of political and religious life. "Never discuss Religion or Politics." – the fool's tom-foolery. God's will manifests political prosperity, religious peace, and no hidden agenda. Acting man observes in similitude with action. All human action represents a political decision and all human belief represents a religious conviction. Individual belief defines one's Religion (Why?), determines their Politics (How?), and completes their destiny (What?). Religion starts in the spiritual realm within man and percolates into knowledge which compels man to discern wisdom and grow His own personal Religion with God or frequency of which He sources His positive or negative behaviors or decisions. Each belief of the individual defines a part of their religion; for example: an individual preferring a lightly toasted bread creates a religious decision politically manifesting as their preferred state of reality. Individuals will wittingly, or unwittingly, claim they possess no religion. Perhaps the possibility remains for the individual to exist as a participant-observer wherein the weakest link in good society only participates in observation thus their metaphysical support of the good participant delivers to the observer the least amount of joy and most amount of pity among all of the joyous combating evil.

What does it mean then for a human to have liberty? A right to one's life implies the liberty of self-ownership. The combination of an individual's Religion and Politics, made self-evident through their human action, defines the use of their liberty to pursue happiness in life insofar as violence and coercion does not represent the liberty of peace and prosperity though securing peace and prosperity requires repelling violence and coercion with absolute force. Hostility against tyranny deserves more protection in society than the least taxation with good intention. Liberty forces the conqueror to submit to it's power through the multitude whom accept liberty as universal truth.

Lord Acton described liberty, not as the means to a higher political system, but as the highest end of the political system. Some philosophers describe a positive and negative liberty. What some describe as negative liberty and not sin serves no justice for the cause of liberty. The expansion of liberty only serves to injure the aims of the criminal masquerading as spiritual authority. Each individual possesses liberty to commit good deeds. True violence or coercion manifests abandonment from the Perfect Law of liberty. "Negative liberty" describes a pseudonym for philosophy of Death; or, the Luciferian Religion, Satanic Church,

Cult of Death, enemies of humanity, underworld, or evil. John Locke advised, when speaking of liberty, to do so only in relation to the individual and not to the will of the individual. Describing liberty as positive and negative portrays a false dichotomy only speaking to the will of the individual thereby hiding the relation of entities oppressing the individual and that individual's true purpose within the function of society. The phrase liberty versus Death supersedes all concept of a Positive liberty versus Negative liberty. The virality of false ideas remains a phenomena sourcing from intelligence agencies enslaved to the wickedry of global shadow-government.

No man holds superiority to God and His government. The avaricious argue God does not exist therefore government does not exist and therefore people remain superior to God and government; when, in fact, God and government remain separate and above the order of a government of people therefore with no mankind to witness the universe then only God and His government remain; however, with man following God then the opportunity to create a government in God's image persists as an attainable, albeit, with human error, image and way of life. Most of this anti-God rhetoric sources from the pseudo-intellectual, neo-atheist, Ivy-league, movement using pseudonyms such as "anarcho-cap," "atheism," "anarchy," or simply, "anti-government." The neo-atheist, unaware of the power of God's constitution within man, builds His world as a pile of dry timber on a lake of fire. Self-evidence proves God installed His eternal self-government within man from the beginning of the universe's expansion. The neo-atheist vainly declares God-like status over all men while simultaneously denying God and even claiming liberty as the word which individuals define on their own terms whether this means committing good deeds or engaging in deadpan evil; insofar as their troubled argument states good and evil does not exist and all things viewed without definition possess a higher power than the highest power netting all men together, weighing deeds, and handing the evil over for judgment to the victors of good. In modern america this appears as eighteen to thirty-five year-olds meeting with other failures, wearing all black attire, often with chains and excess metal loops, buckles, cups full of disgusting substances to assault citizens with, piercings, bike-locks, grenades, knives, guns, pepper-spray, ninja-stars, bats, razor-blades protruding from their boots, tattoos, painted hair, skull and death symbolism, the majority of which hailing from Satanist or Atheist religions, and even masks, and then recursively converse about the non-existence of God, the dangers of man thinking for Himself and not adopting Communism, the encroachment of man owning business or wedding women to then bear children, and thinking about all of the various ways of frightening the busy man into pursuing tyranny and forgetting happiness in their failed effort to culminate men into a false utopian brotherhood wherein no families form, no private business operates, and government pays everybody with imaginary coffers happily-ever-after: what a vile portrayal of life. Acknowledging and identifying this particular archetype of boyish-man signifies the separation, among men, the ideas of liberty God outlined in The Bible juxtaposed to the false ideas of freedom the anti-Christs wield.

All men proclaiming liberty defines the essence of the spirit of a people living as one body in one mind with Christ. Many tyrants will claim the "one mind" rhetoric originates from Satanism. Perhaps they got their Bible reading from The New World Order version of the Bible, aptly named: The New International [World] Version [Order].

Philippians 1:27 *Only let your conversation be as it becometh the Gospel of Christ, that whether I come and see you, or else be absent, I may hear of your matters, that ye continue in one spirit, and in* <u>*one mind*</u>, *fighting together through the faith of the Gospel.*

1 Corinthians 1:10 *Now I beseech you, brethren, by the Name of our Lord Jesus Christ, that ye all speak one thing, and that there be no dissensions among you: but be ye knit together in* <u>*one mind*</u>, *and in one judgment.*

Romans 15:6 *That ye with* <u>*one mind*</u>, *and with one mouth may praise God, even the Father of our Lord Jesus Christ.*

2 Corinthians 13:11 *Finally brethren, fare ye well: be perfect: be of good comfort: be of* <u>*one mind*</u>: *live in peace, and the God of love and peace shall be with you.*

Why does the 1599 Geneva Bible contain thirty-one references to the word liberty and the New International Version erase thirty references of liberty leaving only one mention? Jesus Christ taught to preach liberty to the captives; however, if each new version increasingly disappears the diction of the word liberty until total abolition by ignorance of the concept then what will the people preach but falsehood and what will replace this market value in due time but a bloody battle for liberty? The childish and addled of mind claim individuals do not possess the intelligence, comprehension, or discernment, to interpret or understand the necessity of changing and erasing common precepts in the neo-conservative Bible. A common colloquialism today suggests the rule of law as the one missing element in the Arabias and americans today further this notion to it's bitter extreme with the false responsibility of persecuting the Arabias as though americans provocatively possess God's judgment of death for the people of a foreign land. Perhaps the heart of the matter rests in the fact that individuals whom no longer care of the cause of liberty, or simply do not know thereof, profess their body politic as the movement of Christ worshipers when in fact their book worships a false movement of disempowered, juvenile, and rewritten, for-profit, rhetoric and their elected representatives for the past two decades have incessantly and illegally bombed nations in the Middle-East, and even with specific focus on Syria, Iraq, and Afghanistan, including Christians and many other religions and all under the guise of national security while being sold to the unthinking masses as a necessary type of racism to combat a single radicalized religion in opposition to their false book and cancerous lifestyle labeled freedom. When a foreign state sponsors preemptive war then liberty both in the foreign and sovereign nation disassembles. War provides the highest moral response for a nation utilizing it's last means for liberty. The lone-wolf committing a public act of violence does not grant lawful authority to wage war against a foreign nation or even eliminate their population or force regime-change as though the foreign nation must not work to stamp-out their disillusioned aggressor. The majority of americans remain so detached from reality that their catastrophic empire of social destruction represents a maze of forgetful rats racing to consume the object feeding their own mental absenti.

The unthinking of the world haphazardly polarize the architecture of self-governance into an apparatchik of wolves feasting on all of the world. Individuals in the government remain both a citizen and citizen-representative and neither of their titles possess any more natural rights than equal rights allow. Once mankind uncovers the foundational knowledge of liberty and then desires to thrive with their exercise of natural rights as opposed to allowing evil to cull civilization then the flock of God will raise a standard as liberty goes on high as the most prolific debate topic for mankind's eternal pursuit of proving excellent works unto God; and, only then will lower semantics find order within their proper branch of government and economy; and, with the peaceable advice of The Bible: will accurately reflect liberty into the physical realm through action placed into motion from individuals seizing political control from the wicked world turned against all good religion.

American Churches ship their children to foreign lands on jet-air-liners to the tune of two pounds of Gold per head as they fly over homeless and poverty-stricken individuals on the same street as their own church and then grand-stand over third-world people as though they were modern-day saints that after having been filled with such gladness from eliminating poverty in their own land had felt the calling to fly to the opposite side of earth to spread the thanksgiving. God's plan desires nations to work down-stream from their well-spring. A nation allowing poverty to overcome their members of society will only invite more death and desolation onto their own lands and provide no room for overflow at home or abroad. Another plague of the church today consists of defending the evils of society with the idea: "Do not defend the children of God from the violent taking life by force." Many of the fake Christian churches only teach about the Knowledge of Good and manufacture pretend reason for hiding the knowledge of evil thus hide the knowledge of God and liberty from their flock. How will the children of God understand how Satan traffics in the heart of man without ascending beyond the teaching of Satan's mercenaries in the spiritual and physical realm? Humanity wields knowledge to identify the religious and political Luciferian and transcend this demonic vessel failing to stand against the strength of Heavenly righteousness.

Government defines the most ancient type of force. Dictatorships exist as relics of the past enslaving individuals to the bondage of ignorance. Abortion, a fancy word used by the state in place of it's murderous fertility God trading worldliness for human payments, requires the state to exercise force against those whom would righteously stop the individuals committing murder upon the defenseless unborn. Government will not forever abort peaceful individuals or their ideas. Free people will forever abort violent government and their ideas. God grants liberty on the same day He grants life. Sadly not all individuals know they own their life. Many individuals give their life over to media and entertainment as witnessed in america with the average american consuming over nine hours of television per day. Does an epidemic exist when ninety percent of a nation ignore their own absence of civil liberty? The idle lifestyle witnessed in american society inflicts a self-imposed imprisonment from life, liberty, and happiness with soaring obesity and cancer rates in combination with plummeting fertility and IQ rates. The success of television programming has narrowly eliminated conscious awareness to the point that american streets glow blue at night as the television light the outdoor silence.

The cure for Life is Happiness and not Death. Why would an individual claim happiness does not require defense of happiness and Life if happiness only manifests for the living and not the dead whom suffered theft of their life at the hands of the unhappy? What political gain arises out of rhetoric without action but ruse? Enemies of humanity constantly aim to dwell within the space to kill, steal, and destroy the mind set at liberty. Historical records illustrate a story of human beings living on this planet without liberty for eons; however, intuition suggests liberty dwells in the space outside of the time the evil one aims to enslave His subjects within and self-evidence reasons mankind's unwritten history spans a vastness exceeding the lot of known civilization. If humans did live with liberty for a time greater than texts record and liberty was lost for a gobsmacking amount of time then this strengthens the proof for the presence of the wicked one shadowing consciousness and purging history to extend the illusion of ill-gotten gain. What separates a destroyer from a conqueror or do both figures manifest a unified transgression and countenance antithetical to liberty? Children born into this world not aware of The Philosophy of liberty or how men and women must associate in a sovereign society of self-governing individuals electing representatives for an appointed time, and when only made aware of their own government's law, suffer every consequence of not understanding the Perfect Law of liberty binding all men, and exist as additional pawns in the watch-tower of communes defending the ways of the wicked one. Happiness and liberty will overflow the borders of a nation when law gives no quarter to coercive envy and violent hate.

Liberty once adorned or defined does not leave the heart and will persist as the only firmament of immortal ideas and eternal life. The ruling class portray an illusory phalanx of invincibility. The ideas of liberty and not people remain invincible. Civilization possesses the moment and awareness to spark the brushfire of imagination and dissolve every contradiction. Adults remain most susceptible to every worst form of self-denial, especially in thinking the ruling elite as unobjectionable authority, amounting to the most repeat-misfortune of mankind. What within man allows their own thinking to cherish false teaching and inconclusive results? Some paraphrase this notion with: "Those that do not know history are doomed to repeat it," and, "Those that do not know their history do not know where they came from or where they are going." Children will point out the obvious unlike the vain and disgruntled entity peering through life with the eyes of an insatiable hunger for madness.

The Founding Fathers of america were thorough in illustrating to americans the concept of liberty. The United States dollar contains an illustration of a small pyramid hovering above a lower shape to which it was presumably and formerly attached. Two new objects remain present with a single pyramid affixed to the firmament above the second object known as a *frustum*. Perhaps The Founders wished for americans to identify the symbol of one world of worship in opposition to another. Many interpretations persist for the all-seeing-eye, or eye-of-horus, perhaps representing good fixed above the exposed symbol of evil. In the year nineteen hundred Max Dehn proved no equation for the frustum exists without reliance on the concept of continuity and integration. Max Dehn's equation consequentially shows, "any proof of the volume of a pyramid must use infinitesimal considerations in one form or another." making the pyramid sound infinite in depth, without measure, and the source and potential for all possibility.

1. Eric W. Weisstein. "Truncated Square Pyramid." Eric W. Weisstein, 1999-05-26, https://archive.lib.msu.edu/crcmath/math/

math/t/t411.htm. Accessed 4 January 2020

2. Izmir Institute of Technology. "Chinese." http://web.iyte.edu.tr/
~gokhankiper/Polyhedra/Chinese_dosyalar/rightside.htm.
Accessed 4 January 2020

The formula for a frustum was well known among the Egyptians
as early as the year eighteen fifty before Christ. The roots of the
word frustum surround the notion of a crumb, morsel, scrap of
food, offense, pincers for cracking shells, full of, cudgel (further
defined as government), whip, whisk, force, strap, staff, knobbed
stick (further defined as money), and even the compound-
translation of strike, slay, and kill. My short-form theory on the
pyramids is that the pyramids were conceptual solid-state or semi-
solid-state hydrology machines (like a single piece of clay or
wood acting as a whistle) designed over the mouth of a river or
hot spring and accompanied by a network of subterranean or
terranean avenues, ducts, levys, tracts, and lifts to supply a
metropolis with it's goods, services, and potentially even fresh
structured water or even infinite electricity with subordinate uses
in civil engineering, civilization's expansion, air sanitation (beams
of moon, sun, and wind reflecting from the pyramid's surface),
civil defense or navigation, or a static particle-accelerator
synthesizing a dynamically structured atmospheric shield or sub-
tropical biosphere or crypto-climate [increase of frequent rains
and temperateness], (etc ...). The combination of power and
responsibility to the land of the pyramids would keep the people
domesticated to the enslavement of their architect's hereditary
master. The frustum consists of one cube, four qiandus, and

four yangmas. The all-seeing-eye perhaps illustrates the fixed origin of the soul of man, or liberty, dwelling within us all as coordinates directing us to break free from the frustum, or bludgeoning, of tyranny. Various terms describe this origin we all possess: to rise, fixed end, fixed point to which coordinates measure and where axis intersect, attachment, become visible, to rise, I am born, come to exist, originate, root, I appear, get up, to mount, to climb, to ascend, go up, get in, board, increase, ascent, clamber, heap closely together, cling, climb with some difficulty, climb in haphazard fashion. One must be born again to enter into the new life rising to intersect with the point at which fixes us all as coordinates of the same axis of truth boarding a ship in the flood of mankind's sin. The fixed origin of God dwelling within all men represents the domestic and civilized world of higher consciousness replete with peace and prosperity. The exercise of liberty persists as that origin and this pursuit only remains achievable through seeking justice for the innocent. Frustum-culling most accurately portrays the term by which the frustum formula, or doers of evil, control mankind. A frustum-culling emits symbols as a projection which observers then translate into messages while the projection simultaneously omits messages from outside of the projection. Multiple planes exist within the frustum with the most near plane possessing the greatest magnitude of resonance upon the few and the most far plane consisting of the whole projection dispersed with least intensity, like a soft light, upon the public thereby controlling unaware individuals incapable of discerning the more full image controlling their thoughts and action, or facts and questions, from above the small space of the lower plane, or outer shell, they occupy; and, this formula acts as a unified system expanding the message of the central source emitting tyranny into the minds of those keeping their highest priority as projecting the illusion of false power and remaining ignorant to the power predetermining their own elimination and damnation to hell. Self-evidence reasons then that the shapes of the pyramid and frustum illustrate two divergent realms of Life and Death; liberty and Tyranny; Good and Evil; Awake and Asleep; Illuminate and Shadow; Peace and Force; Justice and Violence; Reality and Inversion; Domestic and Foreign; Nascent and Plague; Civilization and Apocalypse; *I am* and the World; Will and Wilt; Not of World and of World; I build and They destroy; Controller and Controlled; Heaven and Hell; Origin and Occupation; Firmament and Bottom of the Sea; Ascend and Dive. The tyrants oppressing liberty want to shadow the knowledge of our true origin and keep us contained within a false image without liberty in a never-ending-quest of divide and conquer. Only lower level conscious individuals will agree to live in such a state. True transcendence waits for all individuals choosing to love liberty and not fear revolution. The frustum depends on the individual living a lie to not set straight their path onto our true origin of liberty from whence we came and must return. When viewing a frustum from overhead: the highest plane illustrates Saturnia, a Cube within a cube, or otherwise Satanist symbolism. The frustum formula serves to create a society, even replicating the inverse square law, or more aptly termed *Cube*

Law, as illustrated with it's Saturnistic, Satanic, Luciferian religion based on iconicity, or idolatry; designed to strike, slay, and kill individuals living in accordance to the symbols incongruent to the symbols of mind control. The bottom plane contains the foundation and surrounding four points keeping the system as one inter-dependent image. These four points find representation in The Bible as the four beasts, full of eyes before and behind and with six wings, finally worshiping God in Revelation, that are the four kings of earth that devour and destroy; the four winds; four corners; four heads; four Monarchies:

Zechariah 6:1 *By the four chariots he describeth the four Monarchies. Again, I turned and lifted up mine eyes, and looked: and behold, there came four chariots out from between two mountains, and the mountains were mountains of brass.*

Genesis 2:10 *And out of Eden went a river to water the garden, and from thence it was divided, and became into four heads.*

Acts 11:5 *I was in the city of Joppa, praying, and in a trance I saw this vision, A certain vessel coming down as it had been a great sheet, let down from heaven by the four corners, and it came to me,*

1 Kings 7:34 *And four undersetters were upon the four corners of one base: and the undersetters thereof were of the base itself.*

Ezekiel 37:9 *Then said he unto me, Prophesy unto the wind: prophesy, son of man, and say to the wind, Thus saith the Lord God, Come from the four winds, O breath, and breathe upon these slain, that they may live.*

Daniel 7:17 *These great beasts which are four, are* four kings, *which shall arise out of the earth,*

Isaiah 11:12 *... gather the scattered of Judah from the* four corners *of the world.*

Daniel 7:2 *Daniel spake and said, I saw in my vision by night, and behold, the* four winds *of the heaven strove upon the great sea:*

Zechariah 2:6 *Ho, ho, come forth, and flee from the land of the North, saith the Lord: for I have scattered you into the* four winds *of the heaven, saith the Lord.*

Revelation 4:6 *And before the throne there was a Sea of glass like unto crystal: and in the midst of the throne, and round about the throne were* four beasts, *full of eyes before and behind.*

Revelation 5:6 *Then I beheld, and lo, in the midst of the throne, and of the* four beasts, *and in the midst of the Elders stood a Lamb, as though he had been killed, which had seven horns, and seven eyes, which are the seven spirits of God, sent into all the world.*

Revelation 7:1 *The Angels coming to hurt the earth,* 3 *are stayed until the elect of the Lord,* 5 *of all tribes were sealed.*

13 *Such as suffered persecution for Christ's sake,* 16 *have great felicity,* 17 *and joy. And after that, I saw four Angels stand on the* four corners *of the earth, holding the* four winds *of the earth, that the winds should not blow on the earth, neither on the sea, neither on any tree.*

Revelation 7:11 *And all the Angels stood round about the throne, and about the Elders, and the* four beasts, *and they fell before the* *throne on their faces, and worshipped God,*

The frustum does not represent anything native to mankind as it's origin traces to the foundational beasts manifesting every evil since the beginning of the world. A phrase surrounding the pyramid image on the dollar states, "Annuit Coeptis Novus Ordo Seclorum," translating as, "Announcing a New World Order." The white-shoe-boys, nail-biters, ankle-biters, and bullies of the world will argue nobody truly knows the meaning or will ever know the meaning; however, those individuals do not discern and instead assail knowledge for reason of fearing the alteration of their own normalcy bias. The date inscribed on the frustum may represent free men branding the frustum, or global tyranny, as a sacrificial cow politically slaughtered the day of america's founding; or, perhaps, labeling the base of the frustum with the year seventeen seventy-six proclaims the foundation for the new world of free humanity to grow the tree of liberty into higher planes of conscious illumination and build higher frequency frustums for a wake of ascension. Perhaps the liberty God gives us from birth exists as the template for the tyranny of frustums to virally attach it's matrix and project it's program through our eyes to manipulate our life as it's tool for continuity and without our consent does not exist at all and without our awareness manipulates mankind for eons. Some individuals take the image on the dollar literally as though the image represents an Egyptian Pyramid with an eclipsed moon overhead presenting a message too vague for any human-being to ponder and then look right past the two shapes exposing the story of man's origin, or most currently relevant state of affairs, and those clockwork or elven aliens that would erase the memory of living free.

The exercise of liberty naturally orders civilization into a self-same function of peace and prosperity without state-sponsored collectivism. The enemies of liberty collectivize as subordinates to a frustum of money, power, and fame. Mankind must realize the illusion and do as the pyramid on the united states dollar and independently lift-off from the old world order, ascend, and affix our consciousness to the firmament of eternal love. Guiding humanity through elected representatives proves infinitely more bountiful and simplistic for liberty than collectivism and this notion even finds great ease for children to comprehend as the youth remain far less likely to think a superior model of governance as unelected authoritarian murderers lying and stealing to cull free-thinkers. Perhaps the multitude of people on the earth will notice the old world order as an obsolete dwelling of worship housing the profane and only independent thought leads to true revival.

The global lie of "peace through strength (militarism)" has promulgated and corroded the mind of americans into reinterpreting the idea of liberty as freedom to illegally and militarily occupy every nation on the earth when this precedent precisely represents the very empire americans waged war against for independent access to their own liberty and has brought nothing but the national curse of debt upon our lands and ravaged the american middle-class to the degree every small town across these great lands appear as desecrated, war-torn, and abandoned ghost towns with few people living in the area but the abandoned elderly and impoverished youth seeking liberty. President George Washington taught true liberty requires citizens at all times to maintain skill in warfare as proper defense for invasion; however, we must not remain in perpetual war or go to war undeclared claiming democide defines justice, peace, freedom, or liberty and not violence or coercion.

PROPERTY

Words are like stones. God created all men equal when He sowed into that life an unalienable liberty to property. Man is incentivized by God to enter society and strengthen the ideas of liberty. Men determine one society superior for their interests and not another. Do men enter society voluntarily? If men enter society only through their departure from childhood into adulthood then the reason men choose to enter society remains unknown or a random and often involuntary occurrence. Why then do some men choose isolation, reclusion, or absolute seclusion rather than entering society? Civilization will burn when men trade their right to assemble for wealth. Does choosing not to enter society mean one lacks the social or interpersonal skill for civil society or is it possible for an individual to start their own society and if so then are those the acts that Jesus Christ engaged in or was He seeking simply to restore the true nature of reality? Social interaction defines the essence of man and society. What compels men to seek friends or destroy enemies? Only a moral people can keep a confluence of religions sharing their lasting riches. Perhaps in the event of society worshiping the absence of civility then the best of men will meet with one another in secret and public to disband the yoke of the corrupt and unthinking in order to stop the erosion of justice and peace. Most men born into any society are born as the children of men; and, of whom occupy skilled positions within society for the enduring preservation of civilization. Family, innovation, common defense, culture, and faith create an environment of lasting devotion for the preservation and expansion of society. Young men possess limited skill and enter society as acolytes to trade their labor for wages or additional skills. Entering society requires individuals possess or work to acquire a certain repertoire of culture, education, and even reputation to continue their works of contribution for the happiness of God and country. Traditionally the elder men possess higher honor, renown, resources, skill, and value for society and their work ethic generates a hierarchy of men with complementary skills to achieve the means and ends for society's choosing. Men in their curiosity and integrity devote the time that skill provides to enrich their culture and honor their ancestors and future generations with the continued march of moral sublimation. Tradesmen are a gift to any society by being the original government, the assembly of men instituting a government designed for the preservation of civil liberty, the martial law, the militiamen, the just weight and measure toward moral innovation, and the last stand for preserving their life and property from domestic or foreign tyrannical government (Agent Smith's; aliens; boy lovers; enemies; clandestine kleptocrats; human traffickers; pirates!). Innovation solves economic demand while the intervention of government regulation stifles innovation and plunders economic forecasting; even by the subtlety of price and wage controls: textbook state-sponsored rationing. The benefactors of a product discover an ability to more effectively contribute to the happiness of society thus experience a higher standard of physical and spiritual living through utilizing the intelligence of one product over another insofar as that product which serves the people the best will always compliment life, liberty, and property and weaken the influence of government sleuths. Economic liberty is the only permanent solution to preserving the property of society and their freedom for improvisation (a vital state of moral economy in which wicked government so often names with their endless babylonian codes to claim authority with their sanctioning and superseding the authority and liberty of the people ("Derrr ... according to t dot dash x, four, nine, derpy, derpenstein ... liberty is illegal because he is now indefinite emergency king; Here is the certificate that says you do not live in america anymore and there is all the codes and flags and specially designed skull and lizard bone shields drawn by retard-John proving this to be the case; If you got any questions then fuck you retard; dough nut say Hail China; three more times and Agent Derp-33 will be here to bicuriously inoculate you for organ harvest; derrrrrrp; over in out; cheeseburgers.").

Men primarily participate in society for the duty of preserving property from the immoral men that would otherwise tread upon their God-given rights. Men guarding their time and one another's property proves the only rewarding course of discovery for civilization. Man has a right to His Life, liberty, and Property.

unalienable rights ordained by God and instituted among men capitalizing their time in liberty guarantees defense of property. Men trade time to preserve property and keep society intact as President George Washington described: "liberty is for Keepers." American folklore commonly states, "Time is the Keeper." God, the producer of all time, the keeper of all liberty, the ordaining of the predestined; He whom indeed exalts men. Man's most valuable property granted from time of birth exists in the trade of His time for the birth of every type of property. During the days of Renaissance men believed intellectual property a moral fallacy. Only the most potent ideas matter in intellectual society and the innovation of ideas does not constitute the theft of another man's property. In imagining a society terraforming Mars, every celestial body in our solar system, and even a terraformed bridge connecting all celestial bodies on the face of the cosmos, in no manner does the articulator of such an idea reserve ownership of all property of the individuals that would proceed forth with the creation of the ideas seeded from the original articulation since God first articled man and men can not articulate what God did not first make available to them for the purposes of God's kingdom. Only the hands of the producer can lay claim to His self-evident work. Preservation of property includes the preservation of private contracts and common sense property rights. Whether many men produce aqueducts or one man crafts a clock – all men require access to a broad economy to produce the fine materials of the clock or in the case of the aqueducts then the lumber and livestock to support it's construction. Few producers of fine clocks will also desire to obtain mastery over metallurgy, ore mining, and leather crafting; nor, will any majority of clock-makers possess the resources for individually producing the raw materials for the clock and additionally out-competing other makers of fine clocks; however, the clock-maker in His participation of the economy contracts the production of raw materials from His fellow members of the society; lest He waste all sorts of time in producing the raw materials and allow competing clock-makers to outproduce and gain superior mastery over the production of clock-making rendering His output sub-par or unsubstantial for a market of ideas. Righteous men preserve property through securing their responsibility to meet the demand for each consumer of their product and not mismanage their time or property or needlessly risking their family, fortune, and honor. Suppose a man awakens to find His work-shop reduced to smoldering ash. The members of society must agree on a just course of action to recompense the criminal act. Perhaps society's first order of business is in rebuilding the shop or supplying His family with the charity to not starve from the destruction of His way of life.

Representatives of society arise out of the need for individual representation of the preservation of life, liberty, and property; and, without such an economic maturation there exists no political foundation for religious men to stand. Most societies will not defend individual rights and create unequal caste systems to favor the success of some men over others; and, those men most favored by the system disdain most the righteous men above all other things as these religious men would desire to create a political body to render all men including those hired to government as subjects under the equal rights of the rule of law; thus forcing the market to determine favor and success based on the cause and effect of productivity and not monopoly. Man instinctively desires to protect His private property beginning with His own body and expanding to the fruit of His labor and no moral element exists to needlessly require the separation of man from the reward of His labor except for that of His own decision. Why on the earth ought any man built in the image of God live as subjects to the dictates of lesser men and remain divided from their earnings God provides? Men authorize and appoint legislators to keep watch over the law for each member of the society. Immoral men possessing obtuse intent and reputation receive rightful opposition to their presence; however, all men will have their deeds alone weighed. Barbarous nations murder foreign men for superficial and unwarranted reason. Texas was founded in 1836 for this very reason: to leave the occupied america for a country of liberty; and, then it was so in 1867 when the lone star state and sovereign country of Texas seceded and never rejoined. Black-birds and mockingbirds possess superior memory recall and do not forget the face and countenance of the human-beings that wrongs them. Civilization operates on a more supreme order with the children of men defensing their sovereignty and property with the full authority knowledge provides; evidently the school of epigenetics suggests there are great truths in this very linguistically structured thing. The majority of earth today holds a desire for divine rule without guarantee of individual rights. Divine rule represents a people worshiping man in gladness for their own enslavement thus their deeds known to God exhibit a people undeserving of a free society. What ends does the peasant of a Monarch desire to meet without the preservation of their property? Does this individual not know their desire for life does not even extend beyond what their eyes see and nose smells? Perhaps their choice in avoiding moral society exists as their choice for a hell on the earth full of their delusional friends. President Thomas Jefferson stated: "If a nation expects to be ignorant and free in a state of civilization, it expects what never was and never will be."

1. National Archives. "Founders Online: Thomas Jefferson to Charles Yancy, 6 January 1816." Archives.gov, https://founders.archives.gov/documents/Jefferson/03-09-02-0209. Accessed 4 January 2020

Knowledge alone separates the free man from the enslaved man as the one without knowledge keeps His body in the only position He knows best: assuming the position. Unlawful thought in an empire of lies grants the individual full authority in His liberty to speak words of revolution as a trumpet of fire igniting the youth as plains of hay awaiting the breath of God to storm the valley and strike the heart of the mountain. Ideas threatened with unlawful arrest result in earthquakes for He to possess who fills the shoe of unrest.

Society demands certain formalities for the preservation of their property. The expectation of society to protect property does not constitute a resolution for it's inhabitants without their militia's authorization and enforcement of representative-diplomats and laws. When men hold the desire for law to preserve property and do the things required to form their words into action then Godliness will flood the consciousness and constitution of the generations after them. The idea to pursue Happiness through defending property generates a thriving economy of moral law and people. Secret oppressors will always advertise pretend offenses as reason to delegate arbitrary power, wherein the defense of property must suspend in order to redefine liberty and foster a new security providing every illusion of freedom; though, such infringement of civil liberty, understood as unlawful, illustrates coordinated and systemic campaigning for the reeducation of the youth for a constant manufacture of peril. The same laws fundamental to society persist as the immovable and irrefutable laws of the universe; reasons for which God brought man to earth: to terraform a wicked realm with Heavenly intelligence. Does the universe not answer to a source frequency ordering the perfection of it's own arrangement? A swarm of unconstitutional bureaucracies within america's Executive Magistrate presently threaten american society with that damned divine right to rule. The sons of men, the laws of God, and the combination of those men and laws manifest as institutions created for man to live on the earth as in Heaven and do not exist for us to surrender to the arbiters of spiritual duress or magicians of absolute evil inventing inclusions of perception. The battle to enter society designed by God rages for mankind. Every vile alien of humanity sets traps in front of the narrow gait of liberty with intent to capture and sacrifice souls to the wicked one. Men defending knowledge proves a higher duty than any martial authority as the enemy of eternity would rather trick people into the persistence of enslavement in order that the enemy evade the judgment of God; in fact, america would serve well to mandate carrying swords and legalizing street-dueling by sword; the elimination of such noble recourse has produced in america a standing army of pink-shirt-wearing men with lispy and effeminate voices (a voice totally devoid of boldness) whose spoken words end with a quick and forceful "Um," before mechanistically stumbling through the next sentence while ending every statement with an inflection disguising the statement as though it were a question or weak-minded projection requesting social affirmation as though every construct of their ideas, thought, speech, and intent invert and conform to the analysis of wicked military memetics and other general propaganda disguised as socialite euphoria; while the women of this same left-hand schizophrenia wear short purple hair or talk as deep-throated as possible; furthermore, when these two archetypes combine they form a relationship of a daft boy with nail appointments and a sadomasochistic mommy and high-priest witch of a Satanic church working to erect a nanny state over the free world; lastly, this same scenario especially applies, though with slightly different window-tinting, to the fake and fashionable male conservatives fondling each other's balls and ass (you cowards, dick weasels, grab-assers, and pussies hate operator mode; if all you want is TnA then depart from us and forget you were our countrymen: yeah, these same fake conservatives telling us to respect the people disrespecting the constitution and the advice of our founding fathers) all day as they hide from being the change to save the republic and be like their ancestors growing into chiefs of renown with early and often devastating military analysis to end war and restore peace on the earth. The Perfect Law of liberty shall not be infringed upon whatsoever. Let these words remain a testament, warning, and flame to all present and future as the timeless battle for liberty ensues and let it not be said that we did nothing in the face of that storm cloud rising.

The rule of law will not govern without the men of society keeping the ass of their government-representative held to the trying fire. A chess board contains thirty-two pieces and sixty-four coordinate-defined squares with each piece representing an immovable law; and, this way in which each piece moves with it's fellow counterparts designs the flow of power against an opposing opinion-structure. Whether this discussion of powers and principalities surrounds Chess or society the rule of law will persist and await the hand at which knows the course and sees the obstacles. The american Republic's original design shows a law and order superior to every other form of government on the earth with a design of purpose for the eternally infinite exercise of self-governance. We must as men keep our disdain for the destructive forces of tyranny by ever sharpening and increasing our language and literature while paying no mind to the addled and challenged people wasting their time in deceiving or mocking us for we are of the Lord and do the duty of our savior Jesus Christ for the angels are'a'watcin' over you and me. The rule of law supersedes every ruler and only authoritarian governance will define reason to supersede civil liberty; and, when this usurpation occurs it will always occur through the subversion of the meaning of property – first with a thing and then an expansion of the original meaning to be used as a template for innumerable causes and expansions and things and if unchecked it goes unto the witnessing of state-sponsored masochism overwhelming a naive and vicious public. Authoritarians keep the knowledge of natural law far from their peasantry otherwise who among their peripherals will allow their Crown to rest lightly upon their head (Not *I am*.)? The rule of law allows society to expand it's economy of ideas and preserve it's rules in restraining government from misinterpreting and misapplying the law or even worse: allowing government to pay death squads to cull the public (happening in america today through the ancient babylonian or luciferian or left-hand network of nexion cells (the same people that killed Jesus Christ)). Rules grant society checks and balances to enforce the luxury of grid-lock within government as the means to help secure our natural rights as unalienable in the minds of the public (and the extent to what the full commitment thereof means; i.e.: no taxation and the clearness, morality, and sharpness this demands and naturally produces within the individual as an act of God and not an impossibility or disorder of logic or reason). A people not allowed to abolish, alter, or set the rules of their government live on their knees as slaves with total amnesia of the fighting tenacity of a free man or woman. Cannabis continues as a major topic of debate surrounding property as educated individuals remain aware of the more than ten thousand different uses in society from food, textiles, fuel, and medicine. The uneducated wish to cage free people as animals in the slaughterhouse or expedite their intention by slaughtering their children, dog, and family as a response to the discovery of God's chief herb bearing seed – one of the many herbs that the blood of Christ paid for when dying for our life, liberty, and property.

Genesis 1:29 *And God said, Behold, I have given unto you every herb bearing seed, which is upon all the earth, and every tree, wherein is the fruit of a tree bearing seed: that shall be to you for meat.*

Modern american no longer possesses a national defense and instead possesses militarism wherein an entire military death squad of nutritionally starving, mindless, television-programmed idiots murder the divinity of their own life and replace it with the entity of a stupidity training for the persecution and terrorizing of free people exercising their God-given right to worship Jesus Christ, speak Jesus Christ, and possess God's herb bearing seed for which history reminds us as america's founding crop grown for potency in the gardens of america's Founding Fathers and used as the textile to write our laws upon, show our flags of war, clothe our church, and feed our multicultural effort to end slavery and live as one love upon the face of this earth. Men desire to have all of their property defended including Cannabis and the legalization of individuals destroying and not preserving property will remain an inoperable form of economy that must pass shall it arise lest it fester unto total civil war; such an emergency will always be paid for by corporate mercenaries seeking to conquer our lands and steal our property and by fact of stealing our property will erase any culture or kill any people defending their culture or property from the thieves hijacking the role of government. Rules do not grant men the authority to subvert the rule of law. Rulers have always worked to prevent men from living sovereign lives outside of their arbitrary lines and wicked intent. What property does the dictator own but His own body and will God not preserve His estate in hell?

Why would an unarmed body politic of gibbering beta-males desire to elect an armed foreign military to occupy their own land, suspend their rights, and wage war against a more trained and numerous armed citizenry innocent of all crime for no reason other than their irrational and unfounded fear of a society maintaining weapons of defense from invasion and tyranny? The rule of Law will forever guard civilization through allowing man to construct a fence around His private property and His neighbors around theirs in order to aid in the defense of their sovereign border surrounding all of society. Only natural disasters such as earthquake, meteor strike, tsunami, or otherwise reserve the right to try human law; however, even man possesses the potential to guard against such threats with the shaping of an economy preserving liberty with the natural defenses of architecture, material, and rights. Only when men agree to defend and preserve life, liberty, and property will economic sustainability meet the supply demanding a society of men hearing and doing the will of God in a more perfect union every generation. *No Taxation Without Representation* guards society from economic plunder since the true nature of it's logic guarantees men to self-declare null and void involuntary taxation and choose which taxation they will voluntarily purchase since the individual reserves the right and duty to resist and even fight the immorality of theft and especially theft by force. The men leading the american Revolution against the British Crown kept full awareness of the fountain of peace and prosperity awaiting a society driven to achieve a free nation shedding the highest arbitrary power of all: taxation. Society did not repeat *Taxation With Representation* for the simple fact that no individual will ever accurately represent each member of society without first preserving civil liberty and second guaranteeing that preservation of civil liberty by declaring null and void the immorality of a law used to exercise force against peaceful individuals even if it justifies itself with the illusion of a greater good like taxation. Voluntary taxation is a synonym for charity; and, a society of charity, and not involuntary taxation, represents the only moral approach to peace and prosperity. "Charity begins at home;" – this philosophy lends itself toward the *No Taxation Without Representation* principle insofar as when all of the members of society keep the fruit of their labor and move it whithersoever they so please then all excess abundance remains a readily available form of liquidity in the economy to more fluidly adapt the members of society to the time-induced experience of constant change. A free people with full access to their resources maintain a more substantive disposition capable of economically stimulating an exponential positive curvature of growth through their currency of just weights and measure: Gold and Silver. Government and economy will never mix therefore government will never fix the economy; and, certainly not through brainwashing the people that stealing their property will fix anything at all or that layering the people as the universal masters over their state and government is antiquated. Economies heal when government serves for the defense of civil liberty and otherwise leaves citizens alone. A society choosing taxation will in the same instance choose an economy incapable of choosing best for itself thus will breed every host of plague most demonstrably equipped to devour economy and society; in fact, most of earth is separated from the defense of private property.

Self-evidence reasons one individual remains separate from another as well as their ability, responsibility, talent, and morality and by the order of these things does intelligence and civility flow. A society interested in the defense of their property will limit the power of individuals elected to the legislative and the only sure means of achieving such defense rests in the knowledge of the people to not grant any man authority to thieve or coerce a member of society including the theft disguised as the legalese of taxation. Thinking man would not wittingly enter society if unthinking men possessed society's permission for arbitrary and unlimited power especially the theft of their property. Private contracts create a private record to remind men of the necessity to defend and fight for the rule of law. Taxation breeds militarism to be used as aggression in foreign countries (even if the government decides one day that the state of Texas is prohibited from enforcing their Tenth amendment therefore subject to the war powers act and militaristic intervention – an intervention of truly foreign and hostile origin) and poverty as it's fiat pass down unjust resolutions damning honest men to the rotting away in filthy jails overwatched by dishonest, filthy, and stupid pigs. The full limitation of evil power in government and society combined with the full exercise of the rule of law remains an unseen standard and potential throughout the present state of affairs in mankind. Certain individuals through their lack of self-control and their open willingness to submit to the absolute control of Satan, and His army of pathetically weak demons, will always hold a desire to bathe in the bathhouse of money and evil in order to have their fallen god seize control over every member of society; especially their friends and family by fact of easy access or their game's starting position. No taxation guarantees the only limitation of power necessary for a free society to morally flourish. A Republic demands the individual exercise their spiritual power for it's essence to manifest. Rules and laws create a system of checks and balances for a society to govern the exercise of limiting power. Only when society determines the highest form of excellence as law beginning with no taxation will the power of God, previously restricted by man, meet the needs for every individual. Why does america have fully-occupied homeless shelters and even more homeless sleeping on the sidewalks outside of millions of square feet of empty church space? Natural rights in america remain at such a limited state that our standard of society falls well below the living standard for an overwhelming majority of americans as bankers and politicians unite to exercise unjust power over the people while being under the influence of that potent drug called power convincing them that their efforts will not illicit historically profound consequence. Rumors suggest overall taxation in america tops sixty percent for every individual. Couple this with a more than one hundred percent drop in value of the nation's currency since the year nineteen thirteen with The Federal Reserve Act then the figure grows exponentially in what amounts to the total erosion of wealth for multiple generations as we witness a back-sliding of american society into a nation of communists professing freedom, freedom, dignity, and not liberty for all. One does not need the eye of a genius or the bug of perfection to see america has fallen into slavery from an excess of arbitrary power or to witness it's tunnel vision of abusive power from those without care for power limitation in their open exercise of sadist tendencies for the purchase of a default orthodoxy moving further toward forced state housing for all members of society as though our state were their prison to guard while even blasting over an intercom the Muslim call of prayer twelve times a day and celebrating each call to prayer with burning a Christian church and publicly massacring any admitted Christians by nailing them to a cross and burning the cross. Consider the infamous "bail-outs" wherein banks and corporations thieved the entire population of america: this would never happen without taxation since only an ignorant and superstitious society would agree to taxation in the first place; in the after-math of these bail-outs we witness bankers hung from the ends of rope all over the place or jumping from high places to their death or being thrown from high places to their death or appearing mysteriously dead. What will come of the individuals claiming the wisdom of the Founding Fathers does not apply or represent wisdom at all? Of course those individuals following that course to it's end will amount to nothing good; traitors even.

What if americans in their setting the example for the rest of the world to defend liberty gave dominion for that equal rights of no taxation for a millennia? Why must a free people guard their society for the favorable outcome of expanding the influence of morality if not to keep out the immoral that do nothing but compensate peace with wicked corruption? The members of society must act as moderators for the outcome of mankind's future dominion free from sin. A Republic, and not a Democracy, begets government transparency thus a Republic contains individual moderators of the law while a democracy requires only group reinterpretation of consensus law. Oligarchs want nothing more than to dominate the ability to moderate liberty. Does the judge not moderate the debate? Do free people not moderate the government? The property owner free to do whatsoever with His property without infringing upon the property rights of another member of society keeps the standard for the perfect law of liberty; and, this is especially true when His government shall wrongly persecute Him and side with the transgressor. The unthinking belt out: "If we have no Laws then people will poison the land." Property rights do not create an absence of law; the enforcement of property rights creates an absence of tyrants misconstruing natural rights for all persons, papers, houses, and effects. Poisoning land clearly violates property rights. Only evil believes the enforcement of pretended supply and demand of natural resources and economy supersedes the sum-total intelligence of the multitude of society participating in the time-consuming economy for the discernment of their own harmony. Kings and Queens represent a virus eating the soul of man that would then harbor their petulance and prove the presence of a war inspired by the defense of their D.N.A. that they believe has spiritual favor from culling mankind unto their blasphemous throne. Natural rights do not inspire individuals that view a hereditary right to conquer free people. Unchecked power always subverts the dominion of each individual. The lack of education in america allowed for americans to believe america still represents liberty when the government and it's people today reflect a majority of addled communists gnashing their teeth at the cognizant and sane. Checks and balances create an environment of harmony raising the frequency and potential of society disengaging from obtuse rules feigning law. A government of free people represents a government of moderators maintaining dominion around an original moderator in it's original dominion. In america this was first represented as: In God We Trust; or Victory or Death; or Liberty or Death; though we discern the root, cause, meaning, and tree of knowledge for which these phrases appertain and prophesy.

When america was created the society was defined into parts separate from government so as to include all members of the society abiding under the freedom of religion as a body or Church of people wholly separate from the State so that we the people, contract government to keep watch over the powers delimited men from converting any one freedom to a tax which the people would then be forced to purchase back from the government (for what intention of the government's other than to torment the people and enrich their stomachs). The Electoral College in america was devised to ensure The President possesses the most near representation of the will of the people to give the people the highest probability of maintaining power over the Executive Magistrate that would otherwise go rogue and select a tyrant to deprive every member of society of every part of their property in liberty. When this most sublime power of the people is properly exercised by the people and according to The Electoral College's intent in alignment with their individual spiritual intent then the people will produce voluminous Presidential Candidates giving none the authority to garner that obsolete power resting from under the footing of the people; and, giving the most educated and resonant of the lot the highest probability of electoral success and unfiltered civil liberty. Media in america use their position as a weapon to convince the people of who media will promote as the only ballot box choice thus exclude those not seeking to afford the right to subvert the law for the owners of corrupt media. When the overwhelming majority of america understand the potential power in exercising every part of government for honorable means then the members of society will willingly line up to overwhelm the ballot box with selections to not only serve our civic duty for our nation but as well serve our duty on the world stage to free our nation and the foreign world from the ideas of tyranny through the great flood of liberty that will overwhelm the global economy by reinstating the awareness and education of private property. Competition always guarantees quality. State-sponsored controls on peaceful competition will always guarantees the corruption of prosperous cooperation. Only dictatorships like Russia and Great Britain exalt the profane and protect the grotesque from judgment under God's law. In the event The Federal, State, or surrounding County governments in america no longer restrain their self from abusing a sovereign government within america such as a separate County then the Sheriff and His posse of citizens whom they elected stand as the last line of defense for natural rights, the Constitution, and the protection of their property and border. Constitutional authority guarantees itself for the members of the society and not for parts of the government to act as entities separate from the law and members of society.

Men do not build their own home with the intent to destroy their home nor do men build their own society to destroy society. Men build their home and society to enrich their life and the lives of others, create a legacy for their family and society, and seek happiness in a world of dispassionate angst. Only madness would overwhelm the man willingly destroying His life and sacred honor. The will of the society reflects a design of individuals desiring to grow their self-worth and society. The majority of the members of society do not desire to destroy life or property. Only the most evil and divisive would desire to conquer what others built to collapse those individuals and their property into their own portfolio of chattel. A flower that does not grow will die. Does the flower contribute to it's own demise? Must the alien force of violence and coercion effect a time-line of events to position an invading army to seize economic and political control? Society remains in a constant state of building value into property. The elements of unpredictability and our own mortality effects the scope of society in it's inherent ability to innovate for more efficient means of living which does mean the advancement of a culture of peace and prosperity. The people own their government and this government institution is the servant, slave, and property of the people. To preserve property also means to preserve the state of government from it's first intent and to not give quarter to bad ideas demanding necessity as ransom for altering or abolishing the good ideas in government which does mean when the people they can damn well do what they please with their government insofar as their acts appertain to the restoration of the constitution and chaining down of a bad government to the boundaries of the constitution. Ownership of property rarely falls into question in a free society unless a matter of ethics arise, for example: the original owner; a bill of sale; the heir of the property; and, other commonplace checks guaranteeing honest ownership. What happens to a society that will spoil it's values without care? Certainly a house divided shall not stand. When a separate body of men compete to overthrow the original society then one of two things will occur: a contest of culture and war of ideas will produce a fertile addition to any growing society or a physical war of necessary sacrifice will ensue. Only the heavenly places in society remain so susceptible to rot and demand the shedding of blood to justify the right and the wrong. Perhaps the strength of the society must fade in order for the members to forget their allegiance to anything good and from their lack of education and wherewithal seek new means as the ignoring of tried-and-true means fails to project anything good into their realm of possibility. Perhaps envy and greed circulate only the dark avenues of the sadists and when their fear of losing control piques then they must inject their lust for domination into every economic tributary. America's Founding Fathers debated whether writing the necessities of society in the sight of the public will accomplish anything since the law stand sovereign of man at the right hand of God.

Ezekiel 43:11 And if they be ashamed of all that they have done, show them the form of the house, and the pattern thereof, and the going out thereof, and the coming in thereof, and the whole fashion thereof, and all the ordinances thereof, and all the figures thereof, and all the laws thereof: and <u>write it in their sight</u>, that they may keep the whole fashion thereof, and all the ordinances thereof, and do them.

Do members of society expect youth to constitute the will of society through a moral education, expectation, memory, passion, or talent? President James Madison believed that a true moral society ought to establish the family as the core government unit preserving the rights of the individual which would better shield the individual from an incompetent jury rather than immediately exposing them to their rotten tomatoes and sour grapes and as such would expose a jury of rotten tomatoes and sour grapes and compel the state to more rightly try the case with competence rather than adopting the system as we do in america today wherein the constitution no longer applies as self-evidenced in the majority of incarcerations today happening without a jury ever considering the case: an express lane to the tyrannical imprisonment of mass incarceration, nationwide familial instability, and the faltering of the nation whose futurity in liberty depends on the spoken and written clarity of the perfect law of liberty.

Perhaps men only desire contact with society to secure the preservation of their progeny. Only honorably acquired property will grow a family and society of individuals. Do parents not own their children as a type of property until the children reach adulthood (perhaps for these reasons did James Madison logique His own reasons on self-governance)? A propagandist defending the Ubama administration stated, "Children are owned by the whole community." Parents and not government own their children and only a tyrant wants to seize ownership of all children as to imply parents, children, and all property first exist as property of the authoritarians. Men designed society and their legislature around defending and not destroying their own property and only a rogue occupation would seize control of the legislative body or the corporations under it's diplomacy to then quickly implement and succeed an amorphous or soft coup of countersubversion, subterfuge, memetic warfare and other devilish things for the transference of rights or properties from one entity to another in order to hijack the destiny and the would-be property of the people and the world and at their own risk of an irate public awakening to the smell of the blood of these englishmen. Suppose four factories each manufacture a separate product for a later assembly of a single greater product fitting together in a signature manner to separate it's quality from it's competitor product. Who shall discover reason in a society once allowing openly competitive markets to now harbor legislation to prevent men from earning a living at the factory through government forcing the public to accept one product from one company without allowing any competition to produce for it's consumers determining their preferred quality product? Perhaps the individuals choosing to legislate property destruction remain too self-deprecated to see their self wrought with evil. Preserving property requires pursuing happiness as the only cure for life. Only individual property advances innovation. Ownership of self implies property ownership of one's life, liberty, and property. Many people foolishly think innovation and social status alone measure civil advancement and completely ignore the rules and laws that create and keep civilization kosher. Unexplainable and extreme advances in technology in limited periods of time always precede civilization's imminent collapse into authoritarianism or "the dark ages" wherein public literature is banished and life is exceedingly devalued. Does decadence and a loss of education share the only relationship required to wash away the civilization of people forsaking their fortune for ruin? The ease of innovation to grow in congruence with the malfeasance of law goes unnoticed as the people trade morality for profit and care for apathy. Aristocrats wait in the shadows paying off anyone to misguide the will of society and force choices upon the people whom believe each choice as their own and not a predetermined response from professional programming smothering their intellect without notice. Virus' and parasites suck the life-force of their victim in the exact same manner. The wicked presume no boundaries separate good from evil and if this were the case then why do the draw perimeters of knowledge around sects of dark philosophy while even applauding some more than others like gnosticism and Satanism (which (((they))) argue is a personal path and not a collective which really means child-like demons metaphysically and telekinetically encouraging and praying for each other to burn the world down [((())) is a reference to a prevalent Internet meme (rarely discussed since it's so cryptic yet congruent) which needs more researchers on the topic since it is presumably related to algorithmic covert psyops and "crystal-ball or event horizon or quantum or pico and femto technologies"]). Does the vandal, robber, and destroyer not commit a property crime? Do invaders not invade for property's sake and the ruler leading the invasion for His own sake? Moral society exhibits every foundation of a game eternally opposed to those desiring to murder creativity. Why does earth possess no fully realized examples of free society?

Many people will argue the ability to simply walkabout, work a job, and sleep in one's own bed depicts the only necessities required for free society. Does a prison not grant the same adventure? Men enter society for greater purpose than simply fooling one's self into the idea that proclaiming freedom without the knowledge of liberty represents society at all. Authoritarians will always justify their crimes through their claim of lending all men the currency of time. Only the glow of the man proclaiming liberty will act as the template for the reconstituting of a legislature designed for the preservation of life and property (1 Corinthians 3). A large portion of america now despises america and even argue Denmark, Germany, Great Britain, and Sweden represent fine examples of free societies on the earth when their nations represent subjects under the absolute rule of Monarchy: yeah, a calm of despotism so self-evident that their philosophy is as the syrupy shit of a bull mucked upon the boots of a ten-foot tall man: a thing for which man can not be washed clean of fast enough and no woman would want to see or smell on her man and nary for jealousy's sake. How did the children of free america learn to regurgitate Monarchy represents free society and the nation that overthrew Monarchy as the unfree society? Unfree nations are palaces and it's people are the palace's dolls. America above all other nations represents the closest example of a free society and all people recognize this if not in their mind then in their heart. America represents the only nation on the earth wherein free men banded together on their property to mutually preserve life and liberty against the factions of tyranny. The hallmark of a free society rests in the privilege to enter and leave at will. Border walls only prevent escape and make entry all the more difficult thus strangling trade, encouraging cancerous regulation, and festering the popularization of infringing on civil liberty through keeping society apathetic and silent under a standing army of psychopaths. Free societies do not steal money from it's citizens to build fencing that the government would even label a wall (stone and mortar will not enrich these rhetoricians) and the best defense for any state border will persist as defending civil liberty and opening trade in order that the decisions of a free people cause an excess and overflow of peace and prosperity extending from borders to the four corners of earth.

The desire of man to release the warmth of His own home in the dead of winter makes no more sense than maintaining a readiness to surrender His property to foreign institutions or absolving His kinship with His like-minded countrymen. What superior government exists than that of men serving their society as a higher authority than their legislators they solely designed for the preservation of rights? The people, as the defenders of law, shall not subjugate their self to foreign law. The legislators serve as the bellwether for the citizens to determine the accuracy of what the law reads and how the legislative acts giving room for man to determine proper redress of grievances with their government or continue their business as usual. Only the insane invert right and wrong for those caustic perceptions of trading life and property for the wages of sin. What effects manifest when men enter society to create legislators in their own making compared to authoritarians forcing individuals to behave for arbitrary rules? True society with legislators designed in the image of the people grants man the ability to access higher levels of discipleship required for a people ascending the throes of tyranny. Ancient philosophers commonly lamented on the fact this world's perverseness guarantees an illusory liberty to property and mankind does not reflect as pastoral servants of this present realm therefore the knowledge of what entails a people attaining sovereignty over the world for mankind's great ascension alludes society for lack of actionable faith. Authoritarians maintain rule through continually accusing the men of society with their own sins in order to convince those men to not institute their own society, overthrow the yoke of bondage creating the illusion of security, and create their own legislators that will submit all potential authoritarians to the rule of law and suspend every ability for a hereditary right to rule.

History shows an endless train of authoritarians abusing people as though they were their subjects and property and not human beings at all. The slide into tyranny from liberty only plagues a society programmed to release care for Jesus Christ. The minimum penalty for a man refusing His participation in society always results in His own spiritual decapitation to inferior men; and, of whom He metaphysically agrees to strengthen by acquiescence and not fight by virtue of grace and understanding of the knowledge and wisdom which frees and threatens us all. No man will articulate every action that results in the slide from the birth of a civilization to it's death; however, the facts prove any society that would step forth without faith in Christ Jesus produce results antithetical to their liberty. Where does man find the seed and root of this plant that devours society in such a way as to place barbarism above prosperity? Evil always culls children as though we the people were their crop to harvest. Rogue legislators will always seize control of the Economic and Foreign Policy as the means for seizing the foundation for which private property rests and the assailing of all other subordinate policies to further erode and pervert the meaning and scope of private property to the degree that The Federal government now believes they can burn the world. The Economic Policy concerning interpersonal relationships from one citizen to another and the Foreign Policy concerning intrapersonal relationship from one society to another governs the potential for peace and prosperity; or, the fall into the pit of serfdom whose ledge be so excessively curtailed. The primary form of subversion concerning Economic Policy occurs when society determines forgoing just weights and measures of their currency for the entertaining of counterfeit measures commonly known as fiat currency or bank notes. Lackeys suggest government first owns all things and legislators determine what the citizen owns. Public debt will forever represent the most pervasive, common, all-encompassing, and least public form of slavery. The Founding Fathers of america viewed public debt as a public curse and wide gait for rogue legislators to enter and steal from every member of society. Man will incur many waves of resistance when fighting a legislature gone awry not excluding imprisonment for their thought and speech. Bad government is lipstick on a pig.

The power to legislate is the power to tax; is the power to demoralize; is the power to steal; is the power to destroy; let us then filter legislation with morality and tax, demoralize, steal, and destroy not. Destruction of property can occur through devaluing the currency thus altering the value of time and trade for government's sequestering of man or through immediate physical destruction of property. What member of society would hold confidence in a system that promised to destroy their goods or all attempts at creating goods? Work requires energy and different work requires different momentum. Even the farmer, largely viewed as rural and therefore separate from society, remains the most fundamental instrument and participant in society as His food production fuels the caloric requirements of the economy and in return the economy produces tools to more efficiently achieve His means, increase His profit and output, lessen food costs to the consumer, and advance society's resolve. A rogue legislature first aims to covertly destroy property through the destruction of value; namely, legalized public theft of every portion of trade for the pretend reason of adding gain to a government emboldening itself as a separate and superior entity to an unthinking subordinate people: yeah, destroy property as it's void is filled with anarchy and tyranny. What brain synapse, philosophy, urge, or appetite, stimulates in the individual to switch from fulfilling their job role in government to believing their duty as one of dominating and destroying the people funding their endeavors? When government reserves the right to destroy property then the people maintain full authority to abolish such government by any means necessary for the futurity of the people. Historically the apathetic, disingenuous, lazy, uncreative, and destructive personalities enter government to find ways of punishing the productive and fill their evil lust for power produced within their inverse spirit completing the works of a global order of death and desolation. True power manifests as honest competition in the market of ideas and not in the competition of destroying property for the act of evil.

What if the oppressor does not want to openly destroy property and instead would rather keep His subjects downtrodden with the illusion of property and remain too economically exhausted, intellectually defeated, or spiritually blinded to question property or slavery? Does the individual not equally and rightly possess their rights as a form of property; and, will the destruction of their rights not result in the destruction of all of their property? Arbitrary or pretend power, exercised as real power, when gone unchallenged always results in the monetization of oppression. The range of ability for man to exercise His natural rights or not exercise those rights illustrates the range of the free man and enslaved man; free nation and enslaved nation; and, all sorts of acquiescence or ignorance for the means to reduce man or society from the natural and unalienable free state. In a truly free society no legislature will arbitrarily criminalize ownership of one type of property and not another without first convicting without trial every citizen of suspicious activity thereby instilling a climate of authoritarianism even convincing the public to render their own ideas of a free society as a schizophrenic illusion far beyond the fringe of reality and as such society must continue the expansion of public spending in order that their authorities locate the individuals proclaiming their contrarieties to this fattened and squamous face of ignoble and state-sponsored persecution: yeah, the aliens are the scales armoring the beast system. The unthinking will always suggest the absolute liberty of property ownership means society will allow men to acquire weaponry and destroy the planet at once when the less than secret truth rests in the fact that the addition of morality will only grow the absence of ill-will and misfortune; and, the bad actors promoting liberty and property as ill-will and misfortune design their self and legislators as the avalanche that mounts it's weight to crush peace and prosperity for their self-fulfilled prophesy of rewarding pure evil with high office. Men have seized entire continents with sticks and stones; yet, those destroyed in their logic would wish to ban all words and property for their security to keep their lack of self-worth equal with their comrades. Arbitrary power first destroys logic and reason to erode the rule of law and reduce rights until the authoritarians have absorbed all people and property as their own chattel. The free society men entered into to keep their liberty and earnings does not well respect any man arriving at their door and arbitrarily demanding property or die. Free societies voluntarily pay their government so that that government maintain the records showing their enforcement of the preservation of individual liberty. Involuntary taxation and reduction of natural rights only produces unfavorable outcomes until no outcomes and no society will exist to explore. Royal Families have perfected the art of exercising arbitrary power and destroying rights and property to keep people under their hypnosis of slavery.

The people must at all times maintain awareness that the ever-present rogue legislators seething to eliminate natural rights remain in a constant stream of thought and action to figure the destruction of property and concentrate their overall efforts into an unseen foreign invasion of every continent through their secret declaration and invasionary war against the people: yeah, the A.I. army of global proportion that would circle the earth nine times in one tenth of one second if given the room to run; and, only awareness of their deception and triggerings will animate the people into instituting new forms of governance and abolishing the rogue government smoldering within their own society. One of the foremost troubles in eradicating society of bad government persists in the bad government hypnotizing their self into violently opposing speech when it was the speech of the public which led the cause of violent insurrection against tyranny and instituted a free nation wholly disinterested in succumbing to the same powers of the empire for which we overthrew. The american people will only lift out of their state of war with their own government when all of the world unabashedly exercise their natural rights. The people unaware of the state of war the government exercises against the people live as soldier-slaves to the system destroying their own property. The ignorance of the government at war with it's own people does not exclude their person from the consequences of their childishly blind ignorance manifesting as open treason. The individuals exercising arbitrary power to war-game against the people shall not enter society without their image known among the warriors defending their property. The countenance of individuals participating in war-games against society to reduce their rights and property exist more as a centrist force of evil receiving off-world transmission and instruction for their behavior than some object or sect of study; though if all sects of study of evil could reduce to one base element above the order of evil then Authoritarianism rightly defines their allegory, essence, and intent. The weapons of war to counter and fight these enemies of humanity consist of only ideas manifest though a wide range of tools rooted in prayer and only founded at the commencing of action.

James 1:22 And be ye doers of the word, and not hearers only, deceiving your own selves.

Information possesses the most potent weapon of war to dissolve the destroyers. America's Founders and the multitude of members of early american society understood the First Amendment must contain free speech to freely transfer information and fight tyranny.

Ephesians 6:4 *And ye, fathers, provoke not your children to wrath: but bring them up in instruction and information of the Lord.*

When an opposition force determines discourse and speech no longer represents their interests and all whom disobey their commands face persecution then the people must at once render all of the society aware of such usurpation and flood the streets with the knowledge of the right and duty for all men to immediately prepare for spiritual and physical invasion. The destroyers of humanity always desire to confuse language and exile truth. In today's america the clerics of evil arrogantly gush that "the right to bear arms" speaks of smokey the bear and all that would profess this reference as man's right to constitutionally carry their armaments upon the face of this earth do not read or spell properly thus intentionally and wrongfully define the right to bear arms and remain subjects to this false intelligencia of historical revisionists and rhetorical soothsayers. Some patriots hilariously suggest that in the event of armaments made illegal then we will seize control of government by not misinterpreting the spelling and release bears into the halls and homes of government until we slash our way to victory over the imps, grinches, and newts usurping our authority. God please favor us to never slide so far. Self-evidence reasons their incoherent assessment as baseless ignorance and blind pursuit of arbitrary and absolute power over honest men. We as free people separate ourselves from the reality of the rogue legislation and choose a new realm in the same manner light separates from darkness, common law separates from evil, and peace separates from war. The individual does not require extraneous permission to access their unalienable rights for the defense of their life, liberty, and property; and, only need a threat to their life, liberty, and property to engage and overcome the enemy.

When the evil hunters of good amongst society make their intent known then man and all members of the society must recognize they owe no allegiance and must disobey every form of such arbitrary power as the allowance of one tyranny only can build upon the rubies of even another and another and another tide. Recognition without action does not absolve the bonds binding man to unjust law or pretend offenses.

Earth and it's available resources, with or without man, contain refuge for its inhabitants. In the event all of a society suddenly dies off leaving one man and one woman then the two remain left to the most common refuge of all: the laws of nature and their willingness to unobstruct their own natural rights in hopes for an ever greater expanse of liberty. In the event many men and women experience a majority of the population turn against natural rights and seek to enslave them then these natural rights they must return to in order to survive will set free the spirit of God dwelling within man and as well provide refuge for them when it was the destroyer that promised refuge in the first place and only delivered deluge. A common refuge renders refugees into citizens of a common cause. The British Royal Family owns a garden called "The Poison Garden" full of deadly plants (and even place the sacred and holy Cannabis in the midst of this garden as a revelation of their method and art of deception) and this venue touts itself as the perfect family outing. Free societies dwell within the common refuge of good ideas. Fallen, managed, and controlled societies without human liberty always pose as the ultimate refuge for the common man. The common refuge of man starts with the heart knowing those self-evident truths under God; and, then manifest when men at-hand deliver their society from the world of evil. Society will never properly manifest when the proper role of man, woman, child, family, and community relationship evades and offends the common knowledge of the people.

Man only finds common what He claims common. God provides all men refuge in their common thinking though only one common thinking does God grant common or refuge for those that will hear and do. What one man finds common another man finds uncommon and this same truism extends man to man, neighborhood to neighborhood, county to county, state to state, nation to nation, society to society, continent to continent, hemisphere to hemisphere, philosophy to philosophy, story to story, tongue to tongue, planet to planet, and epoch to epoch. True men enter true society for a true refuge God promises as common to those that will believe in the defense of the property of God's Kingdom which extends as the property of His defenders according to the fruit of their own labor. The men whom desire to invert the whole of society and render the common as an uncommon offense reject what God provides for them and instead attach their soul to the spirit of evil and remain in perpetual preemptive war with those that institute society to contest with and overthrow evil. All men remain slaves to their common ways until the exercise of what God finds uncommon in their behavior lays too many traps before them and man must determine to choose what God finds comely or choose forfeiture of His own saving grace.

Job 27:13 *This is the [a]portion of a wicked man with God, and the heritage of tyrants, which they shall receive of the Almighty.*

Job 27:13 *Footnotes: [a] The reward of the wicked and of the tyrants. Thus will God order the wicked, and punish him even unto his posterity.*

Psalm 91:8 *Doubtless with thine eyes shalt thou behold and see the reward of the wicked.*

God finds the refuge of the wicked uncommon and entrusts His sons of God to execute His will and righteous judgment on the earth as in Heaven and stop the wicked seizing lives and property by force.

Matthew 11:12 *And from the time of John Baptist hitherto, the kingdom of God suffereth violence, and the violent take it by force.*

Consider the invading force of conquerors and the action men must take to protect civilization. God dwelling within man as the Holy Ghost and spirit of the Lord animates and authors the contest of liberty unto magnanimous victory.

Isaiah 3:11 Woe be to the wicked, it shall be evil with him: for the reward of his hands shall be given him.

God provides the good men the knowledge of the rule of law to administer justice whithersoever in defense of The Kingdom of God. The wicked will not address the realities concerning society and will angrily attempt to silence debate with endless pejoratives hoping their arrogance damages the weak-minded into bolstering their ego madly declaring war with reality and fueling their true being full of fire and fury: yeah, their realm of insults, grievances, and vendettas.

God provides man His refuge in our full authority to exercise our liberty to repel the wicked to the ends of the world.

1 Samuel 2:10 The Lord's adversaries shall be destroyed, and out of heaven shall he thunder upon them: the Lord shall judge the ends of the world, and shall give power unto his King, and exalt the horn of his Anointed.

Proverbs 30:4 Who hath ascended up to heaven, and descended? Who hath gathered the wind in his fist? Who hath bound the waters in a garment? Who hath established all the ends of the world? What is his name, and what is his son's name, if thou canst tell?

2 John 1:3 *Grace be with you, mercy and peace from God the Father, and from the Lord Jesus Christ the Son of the Father, with truth and love.*

Micah 5:4 *And he shall stand, and feed in the strength of the Lord, and in the majesty of the Name of the Lord his God, and they shall dwell still: for now shall he be magnified unto the ends of the world.*

Romans 6:5 *[a]For if we be planted with him to the [b]similitude of his death, even so shall we [c]be to the similitude of his resurrection,*

Romans 6:5 Footnotes: *[a] The death of sin and the life of righteousness, or our ingrafting into Christ, and growing up into one with him, cannot be separated by any means, neither in death nor life, whereby it followeth, that no man is sanctified, which lived still to sin, and therefore is no man made partaker of Christ by faith, which repenteth not, and turneth not from his wickedness: for as he said before, the Law is not subverted, but established by faith.*
[b] Insomuch as by the means of the strength which cometh from him to us, we so die to sin as he is dead.
[c] For we become every day more perfect than others: for we

shall never be perfectly sanctified, as long as we live here.

Only the defenders of the living God have ever desired to preserve property and build civilization. As far as individuals will exercise words in the instituting of legislation to prevent the exercise of force and violence – the enemies of civilization will use words to justify force and violence. God allows man free-will to determine what society He believes to enter and the men of God will sort out the reality of honest property trade.

Joshua 1:3 *Every place that the sole of your foot shall tread upon, have I given you,*

Matthew 5:5 *Blessed are the meek: for they shall inherit the earth.*

God owns the Earth and the Heavens as His property and common refuge reserved for His defenders of The Perfect Law of liberty.

Proverbs 1:7 ¶ *The fear of the Lord is the beginning of knowledge: but fools despise wisdom and instruction.*

The fools exercising force and violence to achieve peace and prosperity manifest as Satan's demon army raised from hell sent to raze civilization. God has given great purpose to His people and no fool shall attempt to restrain the glorious majesty of His Kingdom of people manifesting The Kingdom of God.

Proverbs 11:30 *The fruit of the righteous is as a tree of life, and he that winneth souls is wise.*

Psalm 109:29 *Let mine adversaries be clothed with shame, and let them cover themselves with their confusion as with a cloak.*

Deuteronomy 25:4 ¶ *Thou shalt not muzzle the ox that treadeth out the corn.*

1 Timothy 5:18 *For the Scripture saith, Thou shalt not muzzle the mouth of the ox that treadeth out the corn: and, The laborer is worthy of his wages.*

So long as the people keep their wages and aim for the preservation of property – only then will life, liberty, and property manifest through their like-image to God as peace and prosperity form reign from the breath of God's saints.

THEFT

Men trade ideas for visual mastery in good or evil power. Dumb and silent people prefer their cocktail stirred with both powers. Eyes of fire choose good. The cult of death choose evil. Theft is one of the two absolute powers of wickedness on the earth. The war of good and evil moves our temporal universe (Matthew 11:12). The Founding Fathers of america were so well educated on this realm of evil that the crime of theft was written into the constitution as one of two crimes that can be committed in a free society (though some argue there be a third crime while others argue this third crime be subordinate to the original two crimes and as such sets a dangerous precedent by deprecating society's discernment in understanding the two crimes through an introduction of a third crime; or, said in another way: to suggest there is a third primary color rather than this third primary color really only being a secondary or even a tertiary color and as such is a physical impossibility to become a primary color and derive primary logic or reason from secondary or tertiary evils; furthermore, because there are three primary colors does not mean crimes and colors share the same root – rather, the idea of primary, secondary, and tertiary colors provide metaphorical clarity while revealing dialectic intention). Economic liberty produces goods giving man power to influence and preserve His and the members of society's life and property and for the continued goal of trading peaceful and prosperous ideas for the keeping of liberty for all men (whom will without hesitation destroy the enemy and protect the children, the innocent, and the women). The multitude of disengaged pseudo-philosophers forever claim hierarchy and semantics mean nothing when self-evidence reasons language alone delineates everything for the free flow and trade of ideas.

Free society knows private contracts to remain the foremost tool for individuals to engage in the free association of ideas including and not limited to instituting or abolishing government.

Psalm 67:4 Let the people be glad and rejoice: for thou shalt judge the people righteously, and govern the nations upon the earth. Selah.

Society, in designing a contract to hire citizens into government, restrain individuals from gaining absolute power over society. The historical proof of individuals seeking absolute power remains self-evident and the free press today actively works to keep record of those whom seek abandonment of the preservation of unalienable rights and the expedition of unmitigated acts of corruption throughout society. The absolute power of individual natural rights represents the micro of God's intent; therefore, in His macro, creates society for the recognition of an absolute difference from He that would thieve man and society and He that would preserve unalienable rights unto death. The individual rendering their state-of-being from a law-abiding state to unlawfully initiating force against my person does introduce their agency or self as a force and state of active war against the cause of liberty, me, and my countrymen for what else than to thieve my liberty and steal my property when He reveals Himself into that most precarious state against me: the property-owner; and, with lawful judgment, I and my countrymen reserve the right and duty to exercise the laws requiring society to self-govern; even in the face of this spiteful lawlessness; and, this exercise of liberty can be thought of as autocracy since the individual does wield unlimited power insofar as this intent is of God therefore wholly deprecated into a state without sin thus is not autocracy and conversely is liberty; although the tyrants will claim this contrariety against them as a tyranny which God Himself has ordained them to quash. Americans possess the greatest wherewithal to recognize we do not yet even have the equal and opposite of liberty outlined or fully realized: yeah, the types of systems without taxation and only with self-governance.

No society legalizing theft will illustrate the full embodiment of civilization and will instead shadow society as though theft were their reserve currency, common denominator, and absolute power of the ruling class; and, when initiated, will oversee the approval, arrival, departure, and disapproval of it's people and ideas for any arbitrary reason whatsoever. The common man remains highly capable of discerning a rogue class of individuals dominating all of society; however, only the value of His own morality will determine how He seeks justice for the immoral theft of His own property and the members of His society.

What happens when the people the ruling class presently thieve suddenly realize this act of theft as an act of war and unite to guard against such offense through every power of authority realized by the faction antagonistically brought into war by their adversary? Even throughout society, today, individuals illustrate commonalities in The Bible such as fearful, unbelieving, abominable, murderers, whoremongers, witchcraft, sorcerers, idolaters, and all liars claimant to a world without a rule of law therefore erect their own God of no godhood at all thus worship the progenitor of every rule and law that God would abhor as rule or law. God spoke of the symbol reminding of His law:

Genesis 9:13 I have set my bow in the cloud, and it shall be for a sign of the covenant between me and the earth.

1 Corinthians 6:9 Know ye not that the unrighteous shall not inherit the kingdom of God? Be not deceived: neither fornicators, nor idolaters, nor adulterers, nor wantons, nor buggerers,

Ephesians 5:5 For this ye know, that no whoremonger, neither unclean person, nor covetous person, which is an idolater, hath any inheritance in the kingdom of Christ, and of God.

Revelation 18:21 Then a mighty Angel took up a stone, like a great millstone, and cast it into the sea, saying, With such violence shall that great city Babylon be cast and shall be found no more.

Man's intent to identify with God's power will create a life in harmony with believers pure in their faith for liberty and as well create the standard against those individuals in a self-evident state of war with God and His people.

Man's decisions order His life into a design of particulars therefore the thief designs His own decision when He declares war in His exercising of unwarranted force against His target. Nature illustrates the order and design of patterns throughout the cosmos, in individual flowers, or even the perfect swirl and mirror image of the galaxy or seashell. Theft as an absolute power affixes a design aimed at the deprivation of the life of those whom will design the function of their life to safeguard against the force of theft. The absolute power of theft represents a force and faction assailing logic and reason to blind individual destiny. The universe creates abundance and does not require theft from creation and all creation forms abundance for unending creation.

Jeremiah 33:6 ¶ Behold, I will give it health and amendment: for I will cure them, and will reveal unto them the abundance of peace, and truth.

Proverbs 14:23 In all labor there is abundance: but the talk of the lips bringeth only want.

Psalm 72:7 In his days shall the righteous flourish, and abundance of peace shall be so long as the moon endureth.

God's cohesion of nature gifts man the observation of a harmony whose cohesion can show the promise of civilization though we also must be wary of those demonstrations of imbalance which go full tilt toward the favor of authoritarians; for example, an uninhabitable planet with winds of fire giving no quarter for the vision or prosperity of man's desire; at least not with mankind's present demonstration of liberty.

Revelation 18:3 For all nations have drunken of the wine of the wrath of her fornication, and the kings of the earth have committed fornication with her, and the merchants of the earth are waxed rich of the abundance of her pleasures.

The unbelievers of liberty will claim the beast in nature as proof for the economic role and necessity of theft therefore justifying their own inflictions of ill-will upon society.

Individuals electing theft as their practice require the intent of any pursuit and namely that of designing an increasingly efficient system to elevate their practice for the growth of it's effects upon the members of society; however, the thief's common folly rests in the shortening of time for their recourse or repentance and what was hidden will find itself known. Without the willingness of individuals to worship evil then the doors of evil will keep hidden it's effects. Through the closing of the evil realm: the realm of good designs it's own effects giving ever more purpose for individuals to design upon the realm of good and not the fallen realm beaming it's eye of corruption upon the living. I am reminded of a time when Infowars and political activists whom listen to Infowars arrived in Dallas, Texas to attend a free speech protest after the day's official 50th JFK memorial on 23 November 2013 and for reason of defying the so-call officials in Dallas outlawing american citizens from the time-honored tradition of exercising their free speech. Upon attempting to enter, a literal army of some one hundred men in black uniforms with the label of SHERIFF sporting literal battle-rifles descended from the back of a mobile Federal Fusion Center stationed in a climate-controlled tractor trailer ("fusion center" is the non-government organization (popularized under that Hussein Ubamanoid Admenstruation) centralizing local policing into an above-the-law national police force; promoted through the use of online covert action and other crystal-ball algorithmic technologies even including so-call "Pre-Crime;" and, of which is currently an active division within the United Nations (and by extension our rogue Federal Government and by fact of self-evidence) and with unelected military officers heading it's systems and subverting american sovereignty and the world's sovereignty; perhaps, even making Interpol america's standing army to suppress civil disobedience) and marched immediately toward us and began to attack us even causing me to be the victim of a spine injury as I was violently thrown against a large, steel, traffic lightpole before these tyrants then shoved and violently hit us with closed fists as

they forcefully move us one entire street-block until the Dallas
Police Department, dressed in felt cowboy hats and long rain
coats, rushed to our aid and fought off these redcoats and formed
a wall protecting us from their wildly illegal exhibition of tyranny.
One of these, presumably, Sheriff's officers, an elder African
American man, broke into tears upon awakening to realize He had
become the raging enemy and the machine He swore an oath to
defend against.

Life allows individuals the opportunity to labor in good or evil
works. Individual duty toward liberty manifests a vine of ripening
fruit with power and knowledge to increase the ability for society
to conclude the sweet from the bitter; the living from the dead.
The ability to conclude the difference of bitter and sweet or even
to conclude any reasoning at all remains an eternal threat to the
hidden oligarchy and Babylon and of whom wage constant
spiritual war against the power of the free man delivering self-
evidence for the false authority designing a state of war over my
life, liberty, and property.

*Matthew 26:59 Now the chief Priests and the Elders, and all the
whole Council sought false witness against Jesus, to put him to
death.*

*Jeremiah 50:2 Declare among the nations, and publish it, and set
up a standard, proclaim it and conceal it not: say, Babel is taken,
Bel is confounded, Merodach is broken down: her idols are
confounded, and their images are burst in pieces.*

From back-alley thieves, to spiritually lukewarm worshipers of evil power, to lovers of money, to highly organized cartels stealing political office for absolute control over society through their mass theft labeled taxation – we the people recognize government as an institution created by free people; and, it's effect on society, created in a complete system without partiality, renders the issuing of government theft a trespass and a purchase of it's own risk of self-inflicted violence; and, although unalienable rights forbade such government corruption instituting the absoluteness of evil: man at any time can and will conclude reasoning to justify His judgment to alter or abolish such rogue government in coordination with His countrymen to reconstitute their stolen ideas and property; even when total war presents itself as the only redress of grievances with the perfunctory manner and immediacy so as to please The Almighty God of the Universe and lay to grave the fallen gods deriving their unjust authority from the off-world illness of theft.

Psalm 40:10 *I have not hid thy righteousness within mine heart, but I have declared thy truth and thy salvation: I have not concealed thy mercy, and thy truth from the great Congregation.*

The thief does not ask consent of His victim therefore His seeking seeks anything unnaturally His and posits action self-evidenced in violation of civil Liberties and a state of war with His victim whom must exercise their rights in escaping the thief's design over their life. As the thief would declare war against me through His attempt to render me or my property as His own will he then give me reason to see His design as my enemy in a war which I did not create therefore His action moves me into a state of preservation against His damned stuttering tyranny.

Matthew 23:33 O serpents, the generation of vipers, how should ye escape the damnation of hell!

Philippians 3:19 Whose end is damnation, whose God is their belly, and whose glory is to their shame, which mind earthly things.

Luke 10:19 Behold, I give unto you power to tread on Serpents, and Scorpions, and over all the power of the enemy, and nothing shall hurt you.

The source of the thief's intention matters not as He does not request consent and only demands His victims to obey. Thieves often justify their evil through proclaiming God as dead or unreal; however, their worship of no God presents itself as a buckler of ignorance engraved with a design of calculated intelligence.

Isaiah 24:5 The earth also deceiveth, because of the inhabitants thereof: for they transgressed the laws: they changed the ordinances, and brake the everlasting Covenant.

Genesis 3:14 ¶ *Then the Lord God said to the serpent, Because thou hast done this, thou art cursed above all cattle, and above every beast of the field: upon thy belly shalt thou go, and dust shalt thou eat all the days of thy life.*

Sufficient evidence exists for what ends the thief aims to obtain and though the obtaining of illegal property may exist as the potential end-game – His pleasure may as well rest in doing whatsoever with the physical body of His victim once He gains absolute power; as the addiction of obtaining one property does not restrict the addiction to stealing all property within reach including that sovereign property of life. Theft happens in an instant and even through intervals of time. Americans at the founding of the nation knew taxation as a fancy word for theft and understood tithing as the only moral form of charity to supplant and lay to rest the conjecture of that immorality of taxation with this most righteous offering of allowing the morally influenced to allocate their funds in private and keep the wicked macrons of government from stealing their property and their ability to control trade. What compels the thief to do His bidding but the chaos of evil He wrongfully, inwardly, and shamefully, possesses? The righteous individual and society must focus on ending the practice of theft and honor liberty as an achievement higher than any technological achievement. Self-defense provides the only realistic course of action for the individual facing the immoral and malevolent pleasures of the thief.

History books often wrongly teach the theft of a nation only occurs when a foreign nation marches on sovereign soil when the reality of national destruction shows the loss of civility occurs first from within a nation and this only invites every form of tyranny over the mind of man. Theft preoccupies the mind of the immoral living in a collapsing economy as those whom collapsed the economy did so at the enjoyment of the individuals that cheered, "Triumph! Freedom!" as their nation collapsed by design in the name of national security. A nation in decline succeeds it's fall through the multitude of it's low-level thieves acting as a manager-class for the elite bankers thieving the nation from it's higher architectural levers of influence thus robbing society's birth-right and destiny in order to collapse their civilization into the circle of darkness. When the people remain under the spell of accepting thievery as commonplace then destruction will always follow as only when the last drop of blood in society spills will every ounce of power concentrate into the hands of the arrogant elites designing the experience of absolute rule against the honest.

Luke 20:46 Beware of the Scribes, which willingly go in long robes, and love salutations in the markets, and the highest seats in the assemblies, and the chief rooms at feasts:

Proverbs 23:23 Buy the truth, but sell it not: likewise wisdom, instruction, and understanding.

Matthew 5:20 For I say unto you, except your righteousness exceed the righteousness of the Scribes and Pharisees, ye shall not enter into the kingdom of heaven.

Revelation 13:16-18 *And he made all, both small and great, rich and poor, free and bond, to receive a mark in their right hand or in their foreheads. And that no man might buy or sell, save he that had the mark or the name of the beast or the number of his name. Here is wisdom. Let him that hath wit, count the number of the beast: for it is the number of a man, and his number is six hundred threescore and six.*

Matthew 23:13 ¶ *Woe therefore be unto you, Scribes and Pharisees, hypocrites, because ye shut up the kingdom of heaven before men: for ye yourselves go not in, neither suffer ye them that would enter, to come in.*

Matthew 13:44 ¶ *Again, the kingdom of heaven is like unto a treasure hid in the field, which when a man hath found, he hideth it, and for joy thereof departeth, and selleth all that he hath, and buyeth that field.*

The thief reasons pain and suffering a greater reward for His witness than the act of theft alone and for this reason taxation always leads to destruction as any involuntary displacement of property will only demand God's righteous judgment even if this means destroying the thieves or the people doing nothing and allowing the evil to destroy the good.

What ends does destruction of life serve the thief but one of self-fulfilling prophesy of determining His own leisure which represents no leisure at all and only the illusion of honest success? The thief collects property and in return destroys His life. The common thief steals a loaf of bread or gallon of wine; and, though, this holds it's own suffering for the victim of the act – the thieving of an entire society through the magistrate haunts society and future destiny with a game of absolute evil that society must render ineffectual.

2 Samuel 22:5 For the pangs of death have compassed me: the floods of ungodliness have made me afraid.

Matthew 24:12 And because iniquity shall be increased, the love of many shall be cold.

Proverbs 25:25 As are the cold waters to a weary soul, so is good news from a far country.

What authority does the thief believe they possess in stealing or destroying myself or society? Unto what power does the thief find granting or justification for their trespass but that of pure evil? Certainly the desire to commit a crime does not constitute a crime unless the individual acts upon the desire and commits the crime. True desire rests in the heart of good and not evil and therefore the root of evil manifests in the desire of money as it's lusting after the perfection of controlling all resources and not talent inverts the function of society thus transferring exorbitant power and authority to the head until the body starves for lack of substance.

1 Timothy 6:10 For the desire of money is the root of all evil, which while some lusted after they erred from the faith, and pierced themselves through with many sorrows.

Isaiah 9:15 The ancient and the honorable man, he is the head: and the prophet that teacheth lies, he is the tail.

Revelation 9:19 For their power is in their mouths, and in their tails: for their tails were like unto serpents, and had heads wherewith they hurt.

Deuteronomy 28:13 And the Lord shall make thee the head, and not the tail, and thou shalt be above only, and shalt not be beneath, if thou obey the commandments of the Lord thy God which I command thee this day, to keep and to do them.

Consider the time the thief spends in desiring to render individuals into His absolute power and the economic flow He removes from the economy in not pursuing honorable means of social establishment. Old american history has shown criminal behavior to remain in families for multiple generations through teaching the practice to the children even if that teaching is the absence of love.

Matthew 23:15 Woe be unto you, Scribes and Pharisees, hypocrites: for ye compass sea and land to make one of your profession: and when he is made, ye make him twofold more the child of hell, than you yourselves.

And even though the thief meets His desire He as well achieves totality and absoluteness in designing His power for the use of evil and this in it's own right designs a force against righteousness and even limits His own existence. Perhaps theft then represents only a mistaken identity and incompleteness forcing the socially inoperable to prey upon the lesser perceptions of the public good.

Proverbs 14:7 Depart from the foolish man, when thou perceivest not in him the lips of knowledge.

Matthew 22:18 But Jesus perceived their wickedness, and said, Why tempt ye me, ye hypocrites?

Mark 2:8 And immediately, when Jesus perceived in his spirit, that thus they reasoned with themselves, he said unto them, Why reason ye these things in your hearts?

1 Corinthians 2:14 But the natural man perceiveth not the things of the Spirit of God: for they are foolishness unto him, neither can he know them, because they are spiritually discerned.

Theft exists so long as the immoral faction of men continue

coercing the youth into hating liberty and loving the subjugation of their own spirit to the confines of a living hell emanating from an alien being of eternal evil. Therefore how can the man that holds a desire to remove my absolute power for the subjection of His power not do so without the exercise of force, or violence, upon mine liberty that grants me the sweetness of joy in disobeying? Force and violence as a power inflicted upon the sovereign individual demands acquiescence for it's own success for only the lack of power to repel such advances will render the refutation of the situation wanting and the destruction of individual sovereignty certain. My liberty in no manner gives another individual freedom to my liberty no matter the existence of state-sponsored legalese or act of force negating my right to consent. Theft in it's subtraction of liberty gives rise to the idea of a newfound type of freedom allowing individuals to do what thou wilt to any other individual whereas liberty allows any individual to do what thou will without sin. The thief claiming His act as a job, order, duty, or any arbitrary permission discovers no more reason than any cause of evil denying it's effect. The argument for the individual deserving of their own theft for a matter of wrong place and time fills the stomach of the carnally corrupted liar as a venom and out of necessity elects the nocturnal creature of death we know as the spirit of the thief and force of evil to commandeer and seize His heart.

Job 15:2 Shall a wise man speak words of the wind? and fill his belly with the East wind?

The force of the initiator destroying the natural rights of the individual gives desire only to those individuals in support of unjust weights measuring the facsimile of reason as pure necessity and lawful or statutory security. Does the dictator not weigh upon the rights of the population with His unjust provincial empire holding a primary objective to receive wages from the people and further design and inflict His system of control as the original creator of a church worshiping the oppression of the just?

The history of thieves shows nothing but their attempt to render their victim a slave to their will. One of the main justifications for imposing individuals to their destruction roots in their imagined election of deserving the fruit of whom they perceive as lesser beings and property-chattel of their mentality which acts as a dominating class assuming hereditary right and any other myriad of arbitrary means to achieve their caste system. Keeping wary the thief steals only to render victims His slave aids the effort to gather knowledge and the members of society against all cause of future, permanent, and temporal slavery.

The only recourse for the individual subjected to the slavery of involuntary and absolute force from an arbitrary power seeking to steal their life, liberty, and property measures it's security not in the defense of the word freedom but in the means to achieve liberty and raise the standard from whence liberty was subtracted and to it's resurrection found simulcast in it's aim for eternal keeping.

James 2:12 *So speak ye, and so do, as they that shall be judgeth by the Law of liberty.*

Isaiah 49:22 *Thus saith the Lord God, Behold, I will lift up mine hand to the Gentiles, and set up my standard to the people, and they shall bring thy sons in their arms: and thy daughters shall be carried upon their shoulders.*

Isaiah 62:10 *Go through, go through the gates: prepare you the way for the people: cast up, cast up the way, and gather out the stones, and set up a standard for the people.*

Some will argue the preservation of property requires no protection from man and it is far wiser to ignore the perpetual hissing from the thieves generating a society of occultic domination from every crevice of civilization which does create more gaps to place it's wedge and drive apart the soul of man from the alignment of universal consciousness. Natural law gives an abundant field and homeostasis for mankind to source our peace and prosperity; and, the trite whom desire to reform natural law to a monarchical hierarchy also desire a form of what never was man or ever will be kind due to the illusion of evil manifesting as immortality when it's thin veil really only reveals violent transgression from hoards of thieves treading upon the innocent under the color of law.

1 Samuel 8:11 *And he said, This shall be the manner of the king*

that shall reign over you: he will take your sons, and appoint
them to his chariots, and to be his horsemen, and some shall run
before his chariot.

Does the border separating my body and all things not separate as air to water and old to new? Do the leaves and branches in the forest not know to sway and do I not know to impart my path from the sickness of conformity? If security meant reason alone then my mind alone the thief would wish to destroy and render captive the freedom of my liberty which only desires life free of bondage.

Reason alone permits my heart and soul to inspect the individual of malice as His entire constitution capitulates the desire to affirm His abyss of wrongful lust to weather my mind, body, and spirit, into a mold of His slave; and, if I for a moment withdraw my awareness to permit such an egregious downtrodden of my self or society I garner reason to empathize and even defend without reason the suffering of momentary and eternal damnation in staining good conscience with a plan inverse to God's path and resurrection. Perhaps "Two steps forward; one step back." derives itself from the juxtaposition of the thief and the common good of the members of society as I know with discernment alone this wisdom transcends time, space, and language to the inward knowing of God Almighty and His authority over all foreign and domestic affairs.

What reason will aid man if man does not reason His own defense against all probability of the evils of and not of this world? Why must individuals continue to falsely report the watching for evil represents evil itself when the good remain worthy of the time circumspect from the apathy which always leads to evil victimizing the apathetic and innocent?

Does man not provide shelter from the rain or clothe the skin for protection from the elements? Who's duty then but God to endow man the power and duty to inflict righteous judgment against the chaos of wickedry within the micro of the individual and macro of government whether human or otherwise? The thief waits in the dark to issue a state of war with man and therefore even government under the guise of security wrongfully imposes the will of it's hired individuals to remove the will of those individuals whom instituted their function which was designed to preserve against destruction and work without suffering, immorality, and down-right monstrous activity. What effort to defend liberty truly suffers man but society seeking from Him the philosophy of liberty?

God above all malformed human reason stands to defend the individual pledged for the preservation of the kingdom of God: the incorruptible property of all salvation. He that would seek to destroy me or the kingdom of God not only designs Himself into a state of war against me and the Kingdom of God but in so doing declares Himself an enemy against mine and society's preservation; and, as an embering coal would consume unthinking man in a secret war waged deep within the annuls of His consciousness – so goes every thief chasing the depths of that depthless Hell.

Hebrews 12:29 *For even our God is a consuming fire.*

In the honoring of my oath to preserve and defend my fellow countrymen and in their honor laid down for mine self-evidences all whom shall remain the eternal enemy and obliger of avarice and whom shall remain our countrymen. Self-evidence alone shows the righteous as an immutable and absolute power to recognize the oppressor and enemy evincing a design decidedly easy to determine to repel it's advances thus devising a trap for that enemy of liberty into His own encampment of eternal danger. The enemy and thief concerns Himself least with preservation and most with corruption. The thief, like any natural enemy, assumes the world must submit to their illusion of authority. What ends does the thief aim if even He does not recognize His own life as property with certain protection and dangers under the law if He would reject natural law and remove those protections from His victims for the reinterpretation of the world in His own law while also claiming no allegiance to eternity or law? The eternal enemy of good flaunts their evil.

My liberty defenses my preservation with certain unalienable rights and the thief whom desires nothing more than to circumvent law and take away my liberty to speak, defend, live, and travel would not only disregard unalienable rights but as well transgress upon the social contract of the members of society that possess a duty to defend against those in abject confluence against their way of life. Does the unlawful tax-man not thieve one's earnings and bid out one's life in the forceful theft of wage earnings to deliver society's wealth without consent to the dictates of a higher thief demanding said wages for a personal cloak labeled public interest that can never lawfully exist in the first place therefore never a right in it's own right or anyone's right to place subject-matter and authority over unalienable rights? The thief prowls as a predator hedging His bets that my defense of life, liberty, and property warrants no justification or historical precedent. Natural rights auctioned off as artifact represent only a temporal easement for unlawful thugs that will eventually recompense for their coordinated assault on reality with the same grave that arrests every wretched soul. What society would allow sacred knowledge of antiquity to waste and not foresee their own slavery as the only result for living in falsehood?

The rule of law affirms theft as an unjust destruction of rights therefore any knowledge justifying destruction of property exhibits knowledge at war with the knowledge of God. People hold a right and duty to resist any illegal occupation and all attempts thereof on their land. America as a name does not grant extra-judiciary rights to occupy foreign lands without any citizen vote, without consent of the foreign nation, or for reason of preemptive self-defense therefore no true authority exists for government to act independent of the citizens whom instituted their government for their own use as a tool to shape or discard. In the attempt to steal rights does the thief unlawfully claim property and seek absolute enslavement of His target subject and when so doing unites Himself with consequences afforded to that individual exercising such force and action.

The thief in merely attempting claim of my rights and property in an instant declares sanction and war against me thus inviting every tool of war for my protection against His introduction as the assassin. The attempt at the crime of stealing my life, liberty, and property declares through action a design of destruction therefore a position of war inviting judgment from His victim. The realm of war possesses it's own unique rules of engagement. The thief fancies himself to place subjects into slavery at the least and into total destruction at the most; and, He ought to know He stands in a state of war and risks every type of righteous repercussion from His target. How does the thief assume His enslavement of individuals does not destroy His own soul? The court systems today protect the illegality perpetuating social genocide on the american Republic and the literal genocide of foreign nations overseas while enriching the colonizing class in america with an Executive Magistrate plundering the culture of liberty. The colonizer, in ignorantly misusing the american Republic, acts as the thief and enemy in a state of war with me, my countrymen, and my future progeny.

Perhaps this individual subverting the cause of the american Revolution lives in a state of nature indifferent to the ancient armies of long-past formed against the will of the God-fearing and to the extent of which He who knows not His reason or purpose: flails and grasps at logic in an unholy alliance and defiance against Godliness.

Deuteronomy 4:31 *(For the Lord thy God is a merciful God) he will not forsake thee, neither destroy thee, nor forget the covenant of thy fathers, which he sware unto them.*

Jeremiah 22:9 *Then shall they answer, Because they have forsaken the covenant of the Lord their God, and worshipped other gods, and served them.*

Deuteronomy 7:4 *For they will cause thy son to turn away from me, and to serve other gods: then will the wrath of the Lord wax hot against you, and destroy thee suddenly.*

Judges 2:12 *And forsook the Lord God of their fathers, which brought them out of the land of Egypt and followed other gods, even the gods of the people that were round about them, and bowed unto them, and provoked the Lord to anger.*

The dark alliance of evil though not always obvious, albeit ominous, present Godly men with a state of nature positing an act of war with the promise of life if those men shall deliver their life into the hands of the wicked. I am the fence protecting that liberty of my countrymen from that enemy of my desire seeking to tear down and wreak havoc on all in this world following the way of Christ Jesus.

Acts 15:26 *Men that have given up their lives for the Name of our Lord Jesus Christ.*

Acts 28:31 Preaching the kingdom of God, and teaching those things which concern the Lord Jesus Christ, with all boldness of speech, without let.

Joshua 22:29 God forbid, that we should rebel against the Lord, and turn this day away from the Lord, to build an altar for burnt offering, or for meat offering, or for sacrifice, save the altar of the Lord our God that is before his Tabernacle.

To write off Christ Jesus as pure mind-control and negate the original argument of thievery standing in opposition to an eternal moral society proves existence of the persistent agenda possessing the unbeliever with a hidden cause to subvert logic and shadow the knowledge of God's right-hand man. The representatives of evil hate the representatives of good. The representatives of evil admit their state of nature follows dead idols both physically and spiritually. Their inclination to dismiss the one living God of the universe removes all of their natural spiritual power and ushers in their own succumbing to carnality and the kneeling of their soul to every plague of hell. The representative of good lives a heightened state of self-awareness and responsibility requiring certainty for committal duty and preservation of society in an uncontested oath to their fellow countrymen. This sacred oath spans all borders, dimension, and time.

Jeremiah 23:10 For the land is full of adulterers, and because of

*oaths the land mourneth, the pleasant places of the wilderness are
dried up, and their course is evil, and their force is not right.*

1 Corinthians 4:4 *For I know nothing by myself, yet am I not
thereby justified: but he that judgeth me, is the Lord.*

Deuteronomy 7:8 *But because the Lord loved you, and because
he would keep the oath which he had sworn unto your fathers, the
Lord hath brought you out by a mighty hand, and delivered you
out of the house of bondage from the hand of Pharaoh King of
Egypt.*

In the same manner I hold the desire to remove the ability for
individuals to destroy my life, liberty, and property – the thief
desires freedom to maintain a state of war with all members of the
society and this state He possesses acts as a static realm through
which He idly aims to sacrifice life, liberty, and property. God
desires the state of nature of man to follow His righteous path – a
path guaranteeing freedom from sin and the liberty to ascend. The
individual disregarding Christ Jesus as myth lives a disingenuous
life totally oblivious to historical fact and true human intent.

Matthew 12:32 *And whosoever shall speak a word against the
son of man, it shall be forgiven him: but whosoever shall speak
against the holy Ghost, it shall not be forgiven him, neither in this
world, nor in the world to come.*

John 14:26 But the Comforter, which is the holy Ghost, whom the Father will send in my Name, he shall teach you all things, and bring all things to your remembrance, which I have told you.

Proverbs 25:13 As the cold of the snow in the time of harvest, so is a faithful messenger to them that send him: for he refresheth the soul of his masters.

Mark 12:36 For David himself said by the holy Ghost, The Lord said to my Lord, Sit at my right hand, till I make thine enemies thy footstool.

Most will point to the ancients as proof of no religion or some odd religion worthy of man's time. The most advanced and ancient civilization humans hold record of, presumably, The Sumerian, believed in an inter-galactic religion with only one living God worshiped throughout an infinity of civilizations amongst the universe. President James Madison advised to use the name of Christ in the midst of the people as they stand in awe that anyone might speak this name for any reason whatsoever as though man ought be ashamed of the King of Kings.

Daniel 2:37 ¶ O king, thou art a king of kings: for the God of heaven hath given thee a kingdom, power, and strength, and glory.

Revelation 17:14 These shall fight with the [a]Lamb, and the

Lamb shall overcome them: for he is Lord of Lords, and King of Kings: and they that are on his side, called, and chosen, and faithful.

Footnotes

[a] With Christ and his Church, as the reason following doth declare, and here are mentioned the facts and the events which followed for Christ's sake, and for the grace of God the Father towards those that are called, elected, and are his faithful ones in Christ.

Acts 2:22 *Ye men of Israel, hear these words, JESUS of Nazareth, a man approved of God among you with great works, and wonders, and signs, which God did by him in the midst of you, as ye yourselves also know:*

Proverbs 13:5 *A righteous man hateth lying words: but the wicked causeth slander and shame.*

The thieves of reality identify the individuals whom speak the name of Christ as a damning indictment to the state of nature deserving of the theft of their life, liberty, and property.

Psalm 45:7 *Thou lovest righteousness, and hatest wickedness, because God, even thy God, hath anointed thee with the oil of gladness above thy fellows.*

Hebrews 1:9 *Thou hast loved righteousness and hated iniquity.*

Wherefore God, even thy God, hath anointed thee with the oil of gladness, above thy fellows.

Reason finds safety to suppose necessarily the individual desiring to take away my liberty must wish to do so for all people and as well possess the state of nature required for the conquering of every form of liberty one possesses to defense against theft. All thieves hold this state of nature as a foundation forming the antithesis of society to demand uniformity under their law meaning a society without order.

Job 10:22 Into a land, I say, dark as darkness itself, and into the shadow of death, where is none order, but the light is there as darkness.

Colloquialisms refer to the thief as an "Archon;" however, Satanist fits the bill in the least and most respect. Rather than conduct an honorable discourse the evil ones when in the midst of good favor do speak with a tongue of inverse symbol forming the shape of babble and will not direct their language into a matter-of-fact communication as though our dialect were not the master keys loosing their illusions. This bodes well to prove their reason, idleness, inaction, and falsehoods of dark and hidden modus operandi contort the least of things in attempt to circumvent all things and subjugate the population to their sorcery.

1 Samuel 15:23 For rebellion is as the sin of witchcraft, and transgression is wickedness and idolatry. Because thou hast cast away the word of the Lord, therefore he hath cast away thee from being king.

Certainly the good possess their own language with contour, shape, and symbol and this design eternally reflects the face and the roots against evil.

Jeremiah 9:8 *Their tongue is as an arrow shot out, and speaketh deceit: one speaketh peaceably to his neighbor with his mouth, but in his heart he layeth wait for him.*

Proverbs 12:18 *There is that speaketh words like the prickings of a sword: but the tongue of wise men is health.*

Psalm 37:30 *The mouth of the righteous will speak of wisdom, and his tongue will talk of judgment.*

Now one ought to know the difference of the relationship shared with the state of nature and society the evil weave to sustain the foundation of players gaming the stage to keep the righteous in bondage. The common thief, foolish for believing His efforts go without keen watch, subsists in His realm of alluding the law for a time but in the end only a growing shadow of who God designed Him to reflect the image of mauls His good conscience in direct opposition of what never came to fruit from the life of evil He has chosen. A faction of thieves might form against a thief and demand His booty with the threat of violence. Government represents a faction of thieves feigning watch over society though the length of their stay in government depends entirely on the decision of the people.

Organized religion often performs organized crime with a faction within each organization acting as the complex within each institution to carry out the will of the part for the whole to act as a symbiont corrupting the religion and man following that religion. The state of society that embodies the state of nature of theft and evil subverts the society men entered for the preservation of their property and it ought remain known the men entering society to thieve bring with them the foundation of every evil.

The overall agenda of a society exhibiting flagrant use of theft as a form of social control pays tribute to no known leader and with all participants acting as minor archetypes of Satan forming major Satanic potential. Often we find lone rings or groups of criminals in society but even therein power not of this earth fuels such enigma.

Proverbs 11:19 As righteousness leadeth to life: so he that followeth evil, seeketh his own death.

Proverbs 11:27 He that seeketh good things getteth favor: but he that seeketh evil, it shall come to him.

Proverbs 17:11 A seditious person seeketh only evil, and a cruel messenger shall be sent against him.

The individuals engaged in theft remove the commonwealth of society insofar as the foundation of our harmony starts and happiness ends. One can think of the two separate states of society: good and evil, as a leavening of sorts. In a sense it takes only one part of good to leaven the entire lump of evil and the opposite holds true with evil maintaining a potential to leaven the lump of good if those good things which were leavened were too lukewarm to stand aright. What exactly coerces each part to generate inertia toward the opposite state of society requires an alteration of the state of nature of said individual and members of society. The inertia of sin builds in a society to overturn good and establish evil as newfangled normalcy bias thereby dissolving the definitive function of society and the Liberties belonging to man.

How does the thief that would steal my property not design Himself to steal my life after capturing me under a false claim to my property? Stealing remains such an obviously immoral state of society that only an immoral society would allocate public resources to expedite the necessity of theft as social security. The band of robbers outside of town must see justice as much as international theft organizations printing money to steal wealth.

Society must resist the immorality which invites the destruction of civilization and in order to do so we as a people must assume the position of presuming all evil, especially the thief, as assuming the position of a state of war with the people and for this reason the rule of law exists, even preceding man's creation, and must persist through the upholding of the oath to the constitution primarily through the citizen whom enforces their representative to comply and meet the demand of accountability requiring their allegiance to justify that which begets peace. In the same regard theft must remain under the perpetual scrutinizing of man's conscience in such a way that in the event the experience of theft unfolds then that man now made a victim of the thief must in an instant understand His state of war with His assailant and respond in a manner conducive to successfully defending one's sovereign self and property with the full authority derived from our natural rights to levy war and conclude peace.

The individual that will argue against self-defense renders misplaced empathy for the attacker and their ignorance inspires additional harm and destruction to the liberty of individuals and society. The unnatural and disingenuous nature of abhorring knowledge for the arbitrary compact of crime and evil withholds the knowledge and historical evidence of civilization's right and duty for men to deal maximum damage against an evil arising to manufacture victims from new orders of chaos.

The thief's very existence permits man to design Himself in a moment's notice to lawfully kill that thief that would in an instant kill Him without cause, concern, remorse, responsibility, or right.

Deuteronomy 24:7 ¶ If any man be found stealing any of his brethren of the children of Israel, and maketh merchandise of him, or selleth him, that thief shall die: so shalt thou put evil away from among you.

No man can know the intention and end-game of every thief; however, man ought first protect society from those that would work against the natural law. In as much as we know the thief seeks to steal the smallest of items by force means we know He will utilize the most wretched form of evil: murder, to acquire even the least of an item of property though the property He aims to obtain restricts all spiritual gain as He chooses the realm of evil and therefore all property and life He wishes to claim only represents a token of His admittance into the Kingdom of Death.

Even in modern american culture there exist confused individuals making claims that only racist individuals use door locks and further reason this stupidity by stating one skin color burglarizes homes more than another therefore the door lock exists for the purpose of manufacturing a culture of hate against a skin color and not for the purpose of securing a culture of equal rights and justice for all. Sadly this type of mental insanity grows in popular culture and threatens the foundation of civilization and will perhaps resurface in later years with new and uneducated youth.

Proverbs 24:28 Be not a witness against thy neighbor without cause: for wilt thou deceive with thy lips?

Jeremiah 9:5 And everyone will deceive his friend, and will not speak the truth: for they have taught their tongue to speak lies, and take great pains to do wickedly.

Do these individuals not attempt to thieve the mind, the product of the mind, and even the life of the mind through their altered state of reality manifesting violence and coercion as their own mental enslavement and of which they then attempt to entrap the rest of mankind into their ideal design? Therefore the group of thieves when formed into a unified front represent a hostile invasion of living individuals programmed by pure evil to act as spiritual tropes of the same insurgent force throughout history and such a society faced with the base ignorance of violence reserves the right to repel and even kill the invasion to save their own life and justify their own sovereignty. Perhaps the american Revolution remains a perpetual information war killing evil information from those individuals willing to kill the defenders of God's abundant flow of heavenly inertia.

Isaiah 2:2 [d] It [a] shall be in the last days, that the mountain of the House of the Lord shall be prepared in the top of the mountains, and [b] shall be exalted above the hills, and all nations shall [c] flow unto it.

Isaiah 2:2 Footnotes

[a] The decree and ordinance of God, touching the restoration of the Church, which is chiefly meant of the time of Christ.

[b] In an evident place to be seen and discerned.

[c]When the kingdom of Christ shall be enlarged by the preaching of the doctrine. Here also is declared the zeal of the children of God, when they are called.

Isaiah 2:2 Endnotes

[d] Mic. 4:1

Micah 4:1 *But in the [a] last days it shall come to pass, that the mountain of the House of the Lord shall be prepared in the top of the mountains, and it shall be exalted above the [b] hills, and people shall flow unto it.*

Micah 4:1 Footnotes

[a] When Christ shall come, and the Temple shall be destroyed.

[b] Read Isa. 2:2.

Micah 4:1 Endnotes

Of the kingdom of Christ, and felicity of his Church.

Even though the thief commonly portrays the perception of an amicable character – the thinking man knows upon whom to presume among individuals who may simply and honestly seek to pass through society without trouble and whom to communicate with their fellow countrymen to keep watch over and portend the events of the unfamiliar, peculiar, and misplaced nature of the potential thief whom may choose a course of events producing public iniquity.

Luke 12:39 *Now understand this, that if the good man of the house had known at what hour the thief would have come, he would have watched, and would not have suffered his house to be dug through.*

Revelation 16:15 *(Behold I come as a thief. Blessed is he that watcheth, and keepeth his garments, lest he walk naked, and men* *see his filthiness.)*

The elder woman possesses just as much a right to beat to death the man that would strangle Her to death for Her possessions as does society with it's right to form a militia and kill the foreign or domestic invasion of aliens.

Not all individuals cultivate the common sense of natural rights and certainly this holds true for the majority of earth for if it were true then the cause of liberty would persist far outside of america's borders; and, perhaps Switzerland in that regard as well; and, not that the cause of liberty seeks empire; however, liberty seeks to absolve empire and render obvious the authority man possesses in His natural rights all throughout civilization since God created mankind equally with unalienable rights from the beginning and without any requisite whatsoever for permission from man or any earthly authority. The overwhelming majority of earth lives with the unthinking nature of acquiescing their authority to thieves in the form of their government; and, generations, upon generations, of their progeny remain slaves to this system of absolute control and even develop a Stockholm's Syndrome to criticize free america as an impossible virtue for a nation to achieve even though the ideal persists and the ideas of liberty presently remain easy to discern, locate, read, learn, and proclaim to their public; however, a certain foundation of knowledge remains missing within the destitute nations to build this logic upon or otherwise the people would in an instant seek to use this all powerful philosophy to free their people and the world even over night.

The thief lives without tangible sympathy or empathy or in the least lives a dualistic life of lukewarm nature therefore programmed by an off-world evil to not live of purity and Godliness. The thief arrives to steal and with His fancies unsatisfied commences to kill; and, though even this remains insufficient for His evil He destroys that which He stole and when He has nothing left to steal, kill, or destroy, He flees and escapes when none pursueth only to later strike again on a new target and repeat this tragedy all of His living days if left without reproach.

The international cartels culling society deserve the members of society to kill them to prevent the absolute destruction of civilization from those moneychangers.

Matthew 21:12 ¶ *And Jesus went into the Temple of God, and cast out all them that sold and bought in the Temple, and overthrew the tables of the moneychangers, and the seats of them that sold doves,*

Mark 11:15 ¶ *And they came to Jerusalem, and Jesus went into the Temple, and began to cast out them that sold and bought in the Temple, and overthrew the tables of the moneychangers, and the seats of them that sold doves.*

The thief need not say or do anything more than the very action of thieving as proof of the design He inflicts upon the lives He victimizes. Involuntary consent does not represent consent at all but a design of absolute authority over a target victim. Voluntary consent exists as one of our natural rights to not have a rogue government steal from the people involuntarily and call the theft taxation.

Zephaniah 3:9 Surely then will I turn to the people a pure language, that they may all call upon the name of the Lord to serve him with one consent.

Revelation 17:17 For God hath put in their hearts to fulfill his will, and to do with one consent for to give their kingdom unto the beast, until the words of God be fulfilled.

Romans 8:21 Because the creature also shall be delivered from the bondage of corruption into the glorious liberty of the sons of God.

1 Corinthians 15:42 So also is the resurrection of the dead. The body is sown in corruption, and is raised in incorruption.

1 Corinthians 7:5 Defraud not one another, except it be with consent for a time, that ye may give yourselves to fasting and prayer, and again come together, that Satan tempt you not for your incontinency.

Ancient literature agrees with this notion, the Founding Fathers of america agree with this notion, reality agrees with this notion; however, the readily ignorant fear liberty and the knowledge of natural rights alone that will free them from the bondage hiding their Godliness.

Proverbs 1:10 ¶ *My son, if sinners do entice thee, consent thou not.*

Psalm 10:8 *He lieth in wait in the villages; in the secret places doth he murder the innocent; his eyes are bent against the poor.*

Hosea 6:9 *And as the thieves wait for a man, so the company of Priests murder in the way by consent: for they work mischief.*

Luke 22:2 *And the high Priests and Scribes sought how they might kill him: for they feared the people.*

2 Peter 2:19 *Promising unto them liberty, and are themselves the servants of corruption: for of whomsoever a man is overcome, even unto the same is he in bondage.*

The man with the right to kill the thief did nothing, crafted nothing, and declared nothing prior to the thief committing His crime so what on the earth could compel the thief to harm the righteous but only evil from within using His flesh as a weapon? Theft does not abide by any natural law and works as unthinking fungus to rot the economy of man and institute it's own government without any peace or prosperity and only condemnation of logic in a realm without Godhood.

The instantiation of theft acts with force permitting man to act upon what self-evidences a design threatening His life and in the least imposes slavery and absolute control over his life, liberty, and property. A nation at war with a tyrant over their lands often has no where to run and must stay and fight or die. Deception guides the thief and free men must exercise force against the thief to stop His act of force. The use of force from the thief removes the rights of His target and Himself subsequently tempting God Almighty to come as a thief in the night for the thief Himself.

The energy of force exists as a tool for good to protect from evil and the use of force from evil only exerts harm upon the spiritual self and physical realm of influence. Aristotle spoke about the fool not knowing with what direction to lead His right or left foot. Force seeks power therefore the thief aims not only to steal and exercise force but to render His victim under His absolute power for an indefinite period of time. May bidding go unto my favor as I keep watch over the believers and the sinners and may the chariot of the sinners forever know the good will inherit this earth as we always have.

The Royal Family exercises an illusion of absolute power over this earth for why else has their family kept dominion over an unthinking public for so many millennia? The american Revolution greatly aided the effort to dispel the myth of Royalty and fuel mankind's ascension out of this present darkness persisting over the great sum of mankind today. The Revolution for liberty has continued to break the yoke of bondage from the absolutist powers of Royalty century after century. From the common thief to Royalty both extremes illustrate the nature of the thief using society's good-will to subjugate them to the imprisonment of absolute rule. The thief knows blood as the only currency of power.

Hosea 4:2 By swearing, and lying, and killing, and stealing, and whoring, they break out, and blood toucheth blood.

In the simplest of understanding the thief only wants to steal money: the fruit of the laborer.

Exodus 20:15 Thou shalt not steal.

John 10:10 The thief cometh not, but for to steal, and to kill, and to destroy: I am come that they might have life, and have it in abundance.

Perhaps some thieves work in an honorable trade and outside of their public persona perform great heists but in due time the public will find them wanting. The tax-collector wants to steal as much money as His unlawful orders demand as His chosen profession represents a guarded secret, insofar as government will not admit to thievery therefore the concept must remain publicly understood as lawful therefore not illegal and otherwise warranting of society to kill the stranger demanding their property at the door, hence the open thief plays out the old tragedy of ignorance at the expense of ignorance alone.

Daniel 11:20 Then shall stand up in his place in the glory of the kingdom, one that shall raise taxes: but after few days he shall be destroyed, neither in wrath, nor in battle.

How does society fall into such depravity as to alter the tax-collector from voluntary collections into involuntary demands even under the threat of violence or stripping of honor, value, and citizenship? Taking away money with force must stand as the gait of which society does not allow for anyone to enter without the consequence of physical death.

Ezekiel 38:4 And I will destroy thee, and put hooks in thy jaws, and I will bring thee forth and all thine host, both horses and horsemen, all clothed with all sorts of armor, even a great multitude with bucklers and shields, all handling swords.

Global cartels rob society as unwatched dark knights and therefore inflate and deflate the currency of a nation until the transfer of wealth into their hands parasitically kills their hosted target. The monopoly men not only lobby government to violently hedge industry, unnaturally out-compete sovereign citizens; but, as well, use this unlawful authority to siphon purchasing power from the public and ultimately control their mind in order to permit their self absolute authority over the unthinking and their future progeny. If all labor performed with honest hands including the labor hired to fill government then the conduit of peace and prosperity would fill and create an abundant connection with society and God for a natural market liquidity and efficacy only a society of Godly education could produce thus keeping their countenance aimed at the permanence of cauterizing all caustic erosions plaguing mankind since the beginning.

Exodus 9:14 For I will at this time send my plagues upon thine heart, and upon thy servants, and upon thy people, that thou mayest know that there is none like me in all the earth.

Even if the thief seeks not money: does He not please Himself to take away the product of another individual's labor therefore steal the product of what unalienably rests within each individual to render their displeasure a form of His pleasure thus constituting theft and force? Does a group of individuals given the title of government by their boss: the members of society, not betray the Republic when finding leisure with stolen property – the individuals whom the Republic entrusted with the preservation of their rights? Theft, therefore, with intent to make one right illegal, removes all rights and liberty, and as the jeopardizing of one man's liberty also jeopardizes all of society's liberty, does the thief or factions of thieves in government seize power and steal every form of freedom God manifests to counter that which was instituted for their own function and way of life. Even in modern america today: industry salesman have written textbooks which Government demands society teach at all levels of education, by threat of violence, in order to please the monopoly men illegally occupying positions of representative power and altering the state of reality in the mind of their targets. Let the honest victim do whatsoever to pursue liberty for He and His people from the state of war the evil one has designed over their life.

Nothing of this earth possesses the thief to believe He maintains freedom to exercise force on an unwitting subject. Wherein does the rogue government believe their establishment obtains the freedom and right to exercise force, as though a vote grants the government employee authority to use force against the citizen whom He assumes to possess more liberty than liberty equally grants every citizen, does the citizen reserve the right to repel every such advance and alter and abolish the government that would not act accordingly to their oath to the constitution. Considering the tools available to the members of society to earn and achieve Godly things – society will eventually conclude it's maximum tolerance for the thief and exile He and His ideologues from society.

Force exists as a physical and spiritual course of action and the will of mankind alone represents a force of good and the evil one seeks nothing more than to invert this force thereby hosting a myriad of illusions as a form of hypnosis to gain absolute control and invite despotism over the lands. Hunger exhibits and justifies nothing for the thief as His desire seeks death alone for what can come of theft but a loss of life through the property stolen that time produced. Self-defense against force begins with free speech and ends with mankind's unalienable right to kill thieves and not the alleged.

Speech ought never require permission as in the multitude of the just, or to say when that multitude knows and lives just, the defense of their cause will find reformation quicker than any government army can form a squad against them thereby giving the free people the most equipped free army in all of the earth. The thief in possessing no right to exercise force will when exercising unjust force withdraw their self from the protections of natural rights afforded to individuals as their action now renders them a criminal in the eye of judgment even if that eye of the law finds itself within the man discovering the thief in the act.

And for what other cause to take away my liberty than to subject me to absolute control of a false and opportunistic power?

2 Chronicles 36:16 But they mocked the messengers of God, and despised his words, and misused his Prophets, until the wrath of the Lord arose against his people, and till there was no remedy.

Hebrews 12:2: Looking unto Jesus the author and finisher of our faith, who for the joy that was set before him, endured the cross, and despised the shame, and is set at the right hand of the throne of God.

The evil use mockery as a tool and weapon to gain absolute power over individuals through shaming them into submission therefore Christ blameless and selfless and shameless does sit at the right hand of the throne of God. The power of repentance exists as the only original power within the thief in order to save His life and live a new life free from sin.

Whatever the reason of the thief's surmising for His defense let the fire of God fill my heart with such perpetuity that no physical or spiritual thief will have sufficient power to overcome the will of my Almighty God set at liberty. Many thieves succeed with lying to gain trust over the unwary.

Proverbs 20:17 *The bread of deceit is sweet to a man: but afterward his mouth shall be filled with gravel.*

Truth warrants me to look onto the intention and pretenses of the thief so as to never fall victim to His snares nor allow those snares to influence or befall any individual in my presence and I pray my countrymen look onto the wider world in the same manner that one day we may all lay to rest the ill-will of every thief and live on a free earth with liberty to defend thought and speech to it's most Heavenly expanse.

Stolen property rarely goes long unnoticed from the victimized property owner. Once an item of property goes missing and presumed stolen then the members of society must notify their government of the possibility of a thief for investigation into the thief and the item's whereabouts. The property owner holds no responsibility in knowing the purpose of the thief nor does the thief's purpose effect the outcome of what obviously represents a crime worthy of judgment. What if society willingly forgoes pursuing the thief and pretends none more shall receive the effects of what obviously eats the substance of the public under the cover of darkness or men aright? Will the society not experience another theft of similar sorts? And to what ends shall thieving meet if the purpose of the thief shall kill as the most grand plan of His design thus intruding upon the sovereignty of every member of society? Will the frequency of theft not increase until such concern remain never so apparent? Does the thief with newfound permission to exercise His freedom to kill, steal, and destroy, not naturally form a group of individuals interested in the deception of thievery to more efficiently plunder the members of the society to only eventually form their own government to enslave all of society? Therefore what purpose of the thief must I care; for killing a thief finds greater justification than the original founding of civilization from whence the laws arose for the preservation of property from such tormentous cruelty. Will society under the influence of thieves not advance in a similar manner as the decay found in nature; for example: a leaky roof increasing it's leaking over time until even the walls shall break? So then will a society of thieves without watchmen groom the most evil to victimize an entire generation by any means necessary. Every purpose of the thief seeks absolute power over the power of the righteous juxtaposed against His state of nature therefore His existence we call an evil and abhorrent state of society living according to human statutes and not law.

People have often referred to this concept of the leaky roof as *the broken window theory*: the idea that one crime encourages more crime and disorder. Does society fear losing their meekness with imposing swift justice? Should their greatest fear not rest in losing everything allowing for society to continue in it's age of prosperity? Suppose society abandons their city – will nature not overtake the things man left unwatched? So goes the thief like fire or as a natural animal without concern for morality. The thief will assail my liberty but my fence of preservation rests in the natural rights afforded to me as a child of God. My liberty to own and defend property possesses every right for the preservation of life. The thief wants nothing more than to exile the state of liberty from all living existence as this higher state of society represents a higher state of consciousness, action, and satisfaction than His state of nature that for whatever purpose or pretense has abandoned morality and adopted the habits of a four-legged beast devouring His prey. Language itself has abandoned this creature in the most base sense for why would the command: "Stop; or, I will shoot!" not even work to ajar the imagination of the thief into complying to such a juris execution of law and order: yeah, to realize the execution of law produces no injury (Executio Juris Nnon Habet Injuriam)?

In the imagination of the thief possesses every trait required for barbarous and dictatorial activity. The dictator, more uncanny, and self-evident, with His way of thievery, grandstands to the general public as a friend in love with His target population and not a foe while both He and the common thief to which He employs for His own survival hold little to no recourse in justifying their vile existence therefore proceed at the luxury afforded to them by the public that could in an instant remove all flesh construing such an illusion.

What could the thief achieve with me under His power if what He started was forceful and what He shall end with represents all of what He knows? Would the rogue legislator and common thief not cull society to worship Him and His behavior? What option does anyone possess when enslaved by the dictates of a captor with an unhinged persona to psychotically destroy and even torture all within their realm of influence and control?

Purpose and reason will forever serve us to realize the thief holds no viable presence in a state of society for He alone will kill all good before Him. Give the thief public office and He will lead the people to ruin. Society serves well to recognize the chief desire of the thief to subjugate His victim to the absolute control of every form of His sins. Somehow in the deranged mind of the thief He presumes the voice in His heart will fill once He succeeds in the victimization of His own conscience and the life of His target. The thief, or double-minded demon manifest in the physical realm, inverts reality with false information to shadow the ideas of antiquity and keep reality in suspended animation of ritualistic dialectic bent on rendering the soul of man a slave to the absolute power of the gatekeepers of a rogue eternity.

We must therefore recognize the good members of society as the harbingers of behavior-control thusly granted permission by God and before all men to treat the thief with a judgment conducive to unequivocally stopping the thief in His thieving act. We must pray for an awake populace to respond appropriately and quickly throw out the violent offenders abusing our system of civilization and governance and only elevate individuals to positions of responsibility whom will defend our good conscience, constitution, and way of life.

Psalm 7:6 Arise, O Lord, in thy wrath, and lift up thyself against the rage of mine enemies, and awake for me according to the judgment that thou hast appointed.

Consider the thieves in The Federal Government in america whom honor not the constitution and instead use their position of high office for political amnesty insofar as their political colleagues and the general population remain fearful to learn of their obvious crimes or seek justice thereof; do these individuals living in opposition and subversion of the law not intend to abuse their power and violate their oath to the constitution and every contract with society thereby placing their self into a state of war worthy of being abolished by the voters whom reject the notion of an illegal occupation of their own government and society? The right and duty of the people compels them to refuse all cooperation by such arbitrary authority including the militia's lawful exercise of lethal force. Our nation was bought with the price of liberty and only liberty will keep this nation and the free world from being sold off to global bankers and technocratic elites culling all of mankind.

The greater the number of individuals with eyes to see the thieves gaining momentum and traction in their state of war against the people then the quicker the routing out of their vampiric nature subsides as the multitude of hands at work against the evil will levitate the odds against the advances of the minority of thieves. President Andrew Jackson called the global elite a den of vipers and even a cursory review of ancient civilization shows evil has never changed and a total war of evil waged against the people persists. The majority of americans today remain ever fearful and too caught up in carnal narratives and therefore remain without desire to spiritually discern thus culpable to the historical precedent requiring their action to reject theft as a necessity for state security and accept the totality of unalienable rights as the exacted form of individual and public sovereignty to forever expand the best parts of civilization and lay to rest every subversive, hidden, corrosive, and evil element. One of the single greatest crisis effecting human civilization today rests in the fact of machine buttons known as computers now threatening the liberty of every waking human on the earth from wirelessly controlling planet-destroying and biological missiles to mass misinformation campaigns.

Society would serve well to keep their liberty in refuting the thief in all circumstance. Even four individuals attempting to hurt me proves their exercise of force represents theft; as their intention to have me under their absolute power can, and will, not end with inflicting me with pain, but as well to kill me therefore my lawful right to kill them and keep my liberty persists and a society with such common sense will continue their peace and prosperity for generations and prevent every foreign invasion. What better for society than to serve the God of peace and serenity and exercise His power to keep honest legislators and citizens punishing every form of theft over the mind of man and especially that most egregious form of sin we know as taxation?

A society lacking values will convince itself of increasing the illusion of safety by restricting rights thereby pretending to protect the "homeland" from invasion and this loss of liberty increases in direct proportion to the inflation of the militarized and rogue government stealing public funds to continue it's illusory excursion of national security through waging war against the higher authority of the citizen and of whom ought to keep their behavior as the highest military authority of the lands through their free militia.

The thief creates justification for lawful hostility against His processes including the authority His victim possesses to conclude the death of the thief therefore the thief must know His actions expose Him to such recourse insofar as He concludes Himself to no longer possess lawful protection from what the public knows as their natural right of preservation. The members of society rather than overcome their fear and shame of a government acting as a thief with permission to rob the public often submit to the thieves for reason of obeying authority so as to not expose their self to punishment of the new and unlawful rogue government though their ignorance creates no defense for the ends of what will succumb society when that thief does not find Himself under swift condemnation; and, rather finds power over an ignorant and willing host inviting their own plunder. The thief knows no end therefore His towing the line always leads to His destruction as the just and irate minority will no longer tolerate the expansion of evil. The conscious vibration of the aware being resisting the force of a thief at a micro, individual-level, and a macro, society-level, far exceeds the resonance of any multitude of thieves. The higher frequencies registering love and defending liberty inspires the first course of action to manifest mankind's peaceful and prosperous destiny without absolute rule of any arbitrary and absolute power.

Jesus Christ walked the earth without desire of money and spoke truth like thunder and lightning. What if one man refused to speak when the opportunity for Him to speak His word alone secures that blessing of liberty granting every member of society an entire expanse of civilization through the setting into motion of the opening of the heavens?

The great folly lays at the footstool of whomsoever shall introduce their person as the thief at war with the common man. What reward does the thief possess but eternal damnation? He who would steal from me wages war against me and my Creator therefore He dwelling from within grants me power to defend my physical and spiritual realm. Each generation must remind the former of their folly in a perpetual revolution for liberty against those whom wage a constant state of war against reality, the knowledge of God, and the cause of liberty.

History shows the greatest aggressor against liberty as the thief working in continuity with thieves of differing perversion and evil exploitation of reality. All pretenses of the thief act as an aggressor utilizing force to trace their efforts into a weapon deserving the highest justice of the lands. Does the liar not steal your mind, the thief your life, or rogue politician your civilization? The unmitigated, unconscious and indiscreet aggression of that state of nature in possession of the thief orchestrates a global and all encompassing panopticonic prison-grid focused on burning the grass of liberty to the ground.

One may look no further than the thieves in government whom robbed (stole by way of seizing control of our delegate's convention to change unchanged rules in order to steal votes and prohibit His clearly victorious nomination – a literal CIA coup in real-time and the stupid public did not even bat an eye) former Congressman from Texas: Ron Paul of His twenty-twelve Presidential election-run due to His plan to strip the united states government back to it's near-perfect Republic status The Founders built and intended our nation and the world to spread and keep and forever preserve from the fire of ignorance and tyranny. Imagine a world where america, currently, occupying every nation on the globe with a military base, has those bases shut down and troops brought back home. The imbecile says the world will fall to chaos under the assumption the world does not live in chaos without the assistance or theft of liberty from a global empire. A free people must lead by example and do what The Founding Fathers of america taught and defend liberty at all cost.

FRAUD

Ecclesiastes 5:7 If in a country thou seest the oppression of the poor, and the defrauding of judgment and justice, be not astonied at the matter: for he that is [a]higher than the highest, regardeth, and there be higher than they.

Footnotes *[a] Meaning, that God will redress these things, and therefore we must depend upon him.*

America's Founding Fathers concluded the operating structure of evil as a primary structure of theft and a secondary structure of fraud. No matter how advanced the technology of civilization: theft and fraud will strategically plan processes to derail mankind from our God-given liberty for peace and prosperity. Mankind must further it's continuance in recognizing wickedness as a state or realm of society preying upon the fruits of mankind's labor. These oppressions generate a spiritual demand within men to express absolute qualities designed for the overthrow of their oppressors; for example, their trading personal skill for the mutual preservation of their property from that origin of force defying God and defrauding society.

In the same manner one prayer pierces Heaven one evil pierces the commonwealth of society.

Psalm 45:4-6 And prosper with thy glory: [a]ride upon the word of truth and of meekness and of righteousness: so thy right hand shall teach thee terrible things. Thine arrows are sharp to pierce the heart of the King's enemies: therefore the people shall fall under thee. Thy [b]throne, O God, is forever and ever: the scepter of thy kingdom, is a scepter of righteousness.

Footnotes:

[a] Psalm 45:4 He alludeth to them that ride in chariots in their triumphs, showing that the quiet state of a kingdom standeth in truth, meekness and justice, not in worldly pomp and vanity.

[b] Under this figure of this kingdom of justice is set forth the everlasting kingdom of Christ.

What fruit do the nations wrought in theft and fraud have to show for their state of nature against that state of society with the most limited form of corruption thereof? Many nations offer the illusion of liberty and a cursory review reveals every limitation of their individual liberty and thus live in a fraudulent society with fraudulent tenants promising the public a grand illusion of comfort and freedom while only guaranteeing the demoralization and destruction of it's citizens. Perhaps that government of fraud exists as a breeding program only to steal true destiny from every waking inhabitant. Perhaps the word government itself remains synonymous with fraud insofar as the only real government on the earth dwells within each individual as an absolute architecture of logic and reason and for the sole purpose of provisioning for the defense of the unalienable rights.

America's first and most understanding, righteous, and successful President: George Washington, spoke about government acting as fire – a dangerous servant and a fearful master. Do men not increase their own access for economic prosperity by instituting government to preserve property; and, in the same breath – share an economy with the least ability to thieve and defraud it's members? A government of itself, and not the people, self-evidences fraud as so often does their leisure in imposing a contract without consent upon the public deliver them into that wicked state of nature mandating unlawful consent and acquiescence of their unalienable rights; and, rights, of which, require no addition or subtraction as all reconfiguration thereof only exists to separate man from the spiritual conscience uniting us all and render those repugnant men their absolute authority.

Does the rogue government illegally obtaining the fruits of it's countrymen not avoid pain until the day that populace quells such transgression? Members of society avoiding the pain of achieving the fruit of their own soul's satisfaction through electing immoral servants into government office succeed in instituting a host of arbitrary means promising security and only delivering plunder.

What man but a foreign mercenary would enter society claiming to aid in the preservation of property only to then defraud His fellow countrymen? Do we not see examples of the lender issuing notes with adjustable rates to unthinking borrowers for the sole purpose of fraudulently rendering the financial freedom of their lendee into a prolonged state of bondage? Many will argue lending as a necessary form of capitalism when lending in it's most free state punishes capitalism and purchases the freedom to institute a caste system and plunder economic liberty until the lending institutions gain absolute political control over society.

Why have modern americans come to associate capitalism, another name for voluntary trade, with fraud except for the reason of witnessing individuals of false authority claiming their fraud as both lawful and capitalism as though their actions were not an obedience to the violence guarding their fraud thus total disobedience to Christ Almighty? Only mass reeducation of uneducated youth could ever allow and make way for the propagation of teaching fraud as an acceptable trade or traditional means of preserving the state and not a supplanting of our preservation in property and in rights. Select families and groups of individuals throughout history have perfected the anti-art of creating corporations to siphon and defraud public wealth forcing the people to involuntarily pay a corporate theocracy. Individuals imbued with the mental illness of accepting every additional form of government authority then demand society's allegiance in forgetting what man honestly acquired, and maintains right over not relinquishing, in order to lovingly trust the unelected autocrats guiding their lives into every servitude of hell.

Banks historically position into an ambiguous an autonomous entity with authority to manipulate the law and exercise fraud as the deluded individuals whom call their self *The State* rubber-stamp every misdeed in sardonic reverence for sadistic power in thieving industry through the protectionisms of governmentism; since that rogue government will disregard, imprison, or sabotage, the men whom instituted government in the first place and will with time seek righteous justice for the building of moral pressure to alter, through voting, or abolish, even by the violence of self-defense such a transgressionary government. Both the thief and the fraud-oriented entities work together to achieve the same ends: render those men that would preserve property as dead subjects or reeducated into the new-think forcing all men into a state of unthinking and submissive felicity upon their receiving notice for the quelling of their every communication and action.

Men of society ought never allow the hidden acts of fraud to steal the wealth and security of their society through the seizing control of every industry their forefathers made way for preserving in the first place. The intention for men entering society was pure and full of purpose and necessity with an honest and natural desire for the preservation of what those men entering society honestly achieved in talent, property, and culture; and, before the institutionalization of any government was ever created these men well desired to institute a government to meet their own desire through the protections of every individual's unalienable rights as even these men understood the worst elements in society would wish to steal their industry, redistribute the resources by way of violence or coercion, and kill the idea of God and first by killing His son on a cross and second by finishing off His followers.

Psalm 10 Endnotes *1 He complaineth of the fraud, rapine, tyranny, and all kinds of wrong, which worldly men use, assigning the cause thereof, that wicked men, being as it were drunken with worldly prosperity, and therefore setting apart all fear and reverence towards God, think they may do all things without controlling. 15 Therefore he calleth upon God to send some remedy against these desperate evils, 16 and at length comforteth himself with hope of deliverance. Why standest thou far off, O Lord, and hidest thee in due time, even in affliction?*

Fraud and it's minions acting as it's roots feed a greater tree; perhaps, even as a creeping and subterranean fungus consuming the living matter within it's influence. Honesty counteracts that narrative of fraud which sources it's reason from the inversion of logic and a culture of normalcy bias loved amongst the profane and unthinking. Honest reason has previously established taxation as a theft defrauding men of logic and binding it's oligarchy to the absolute and indefinite fraud of economic spiritual machinations.

Man in preserving His property from the fraud of men must equally consider the preservation of His strength through disciplining His conduct to exercise every form of liberty free from what God and not man defines as sin. People often claim property as a tangible item worth preserving though will not admit to the eternality of liberty thereby justifying their pursuit for an unprepossessing world cut off from everlasting life; and, again, herein, we discover individuals willingly consuming false information to defraud their self from learning of the highest philosophy known to mankind: yeah, the philosophy of liberty. Even when a government not of the people or of liberty allows the illusion of private property – that government extends a fraudulent form of ownership wherein the people must pay the government, by threat of external violence or outright theft of said property, a fraudulent property fee or more rightly understood as a rental ticket purchasing freedom from tyrannical imprisonment. Free men do not make payments on paid-for property to any man regardless of the arbitrary reason fomented by deluded individuals in government or any entity whatsoever. A society claiming taxation as necessity defrauds every individual of their liberty and serves no purpose in this world except for the manifesting of that image of the hypocrite and deceiver as the highest authority and moral representative of the nation in order to satisfy their Satanic bias disguised as a veil of natural politics or religious virtuosity.

Does limiting liberty with an increase in the fraud of state security not impoverish the mind of intellect and liberty? What possesses the individual to speak words of expanding liberty with their right hand and with their left hand corrupt the use of government into sequestering liberty and those individuals that will defend liberty? Does this citizen assume fraudulently limiting liberty will somehow embolden the strength of society; or, does this individual not yet fear The Lord: the most Heavenly and righteous self-image prepared for mankind; and, in a self-fulfilling prophecy, engage their self in the worship of the most evil of all of their self-images to ensure the fall of mankind and their own wicked preservation as an apparatchik of the system that will only self-destruct when their fraudulent function as a guardian for the empire expires?

Romans 8:9 *Now ye are not in the flesh, but in the Spirit, because the spirit of God dwelleth in you: but if any man hath not the Spirit of Christ, the same is not his.*

What causes the individual to fear the transparency of a fully realized liberty and love the most minimal exercise of individual liberty knowing full and well their countrymen grow in futility daily toward the fraudulent commonwealth granting itself eternal freedom for every sort of injustice and poverty as it's countenance of all-knowing, beyond-reproach, and unquestionable occupation camouflages itself as cultural tradition forcing every member of society to seek it's favor and not God for every type of abundance?

Private property contains every defensible means of honest logic, reason, and purpose to preserve in it's own right. Why then does society allow the definition of property to diversify into multiple definitions in turn limiting property, liberty, and the pursuit of Happiness as some sort of temporal means of securing a government interested only in the securities of the oligarch instituting boundaries of fraud around civilization as though a prison formed from dust and quarantined every member of society without charge or crime? The men whom hold desire to preserve property historically live a non-confrontational life though when court systems charge their honest way of living as fraud then the fraud of such a court will not go ignored for long and the people will rise to alleviate and overthrow these pains of oppression.

Deuteronomy 4:14 ¶ *And the Lord commanded me that same time, that I should teach you ordinances and laws, which ye should observe in the land, whither ye go, to possess it.*

Deuteronomy 5:31 But stand thou here with me, and I will tell thee all the commandments, and the ordinances, and the laws, which thou shalt teach them: that they may do them in the land which I give them to possess it.

Innovation will flourish on a fantastic scale when men without the restraint of fraud and theft continue their economy with one another. Men in a society valuing the preservation of property find great incentive in waking sooner and working harder to grow evermore into their economy and heart's desire so as to not infringe upon the rights of others, spread the cause of liberty throughout the world, and grow the abundance of individuals preserving property and defending liberty.

Matthew 28:19 *Go therefore, and teach all nations, baptizing them in the Name of the Father, and the Son, and the holy Ghost,*

Theft and fraud reserve their time for harm upon the actions of man in the market of ideas. Does theft not constitute the fraudulent behavior of one individual acting as the absolute authority over another? Consider the inverse of obliging one another with the innovation and expanse of human consciousness into a life of peace and prosperity throughout the ages.

Proverbs 15:22 *Without counsel, thoughts come to nought: but [a]in the multitude of counselors there is steadfastness.*
Footnotes
[a] Proverbs 11:14 Where no counsel is, the people fall: but where many [a]counselors are, there is health.
Footnotes
[a] Where God giveth store of men of wisdom and counsel: whose conversation he knoweth not.

2 Peter 3:17 *Ye therefore beloved, seeing ye know these things before, beware, lest ye be also plucked away with the error of the wicked, and fall from your own steadfastness.*

The dynamics in steadfastness alter and abolish the static structures shadowing heavenly consciousness. Suggesting steadfastness requires peace without civil defense holds as much logic as consenting to involuntary fraud. Would admitting certain truths not compel the individual to charge their attitude and mind with the reframing of reality; and, in so doing, light their eyes and abandon the mountain of fraud for that moment of life?

John 8:31-33 *[a]Then said Jesus to the Jews which believed in him, If ye continue in my word, ye are verily my disciples, And shall know the truth, and the truth shall [b]make you free.*

Footnotes

[a] The true disciples of Christ continue in his doctrine, that profiting more and more in the knowledge of the truth, they may be delivered from the most grievous burden of sin, into the true liberty of righteousness and life.

[b] From the slavery of sin.

With steadfastness I desire to dissect the truth and not imagine that the obtaining of material items as total resolve for all heavenly matters. My peace means my steadfastness forever journeys my destination out of captivity and further into the obedience of Christ and that obedience is a stage witnessed by the world whereupon Christ sets men on display and into motion to displace tyrannical authority subverting mankind.

Men take an oath to the law they institute and this oath joins them together into a society defensed against the society that would desire to impose it's rule over their lives. The idea men oblige their self to the idea of defending the natural rights of one another and not subjugated to an oligarch that would hide the knowledge of natural rights invites a competition of honest power;

though, evil will invite itself to sabotage the plans of man through a stratum of political and religious wherewithal.

Suppose ten men enter an establishment and one of the ten men decides to kill the other nine men. Do these nine men not immediately unite against the state of war imposed by this individual? Does the behavior of the aggressor not defraud His intended victim of their rights in His very attempt to kill, rob, or steal them? Many individuals will argue mankind as a naturally unkempt creature requiring oligarchy to enforce it's interpretation of civility whereas the Spirit of the Lord within each individual possesses that power of mankind to alter this present world into an architecture of governance reflecting liberty and self-governance thereby terminating the contract with the occultic elites damning mankind to their dungeon of surveillance.

More than likely none of these nine men would have entered the establishment with proper foreknowledge of the aggressor's intent or would have approached the scenario with an entirely different intent and perspective. Since man can not always know the intent of every man then the nature of man to forever sojourn with like-minded individuals persists. Morality breeds that liberty framed within natural rights and purchases every eternal achievement for a stateless exalting of our Lord Christ Jesus and the defense of individual rights thus circumventing every arbitrary power declaring claimantship over civilization. Certainly court systems aid to keep record of private property so as to not allow any space for infringing upon property rights. What superior way for society to operate than to assist one another for equal defense of their property and country? The fraudulent nature of the ill-informed man to interrupt this harmonious flow of agreement acts as a blunt tool misshaping the relations of the commonwealth. Consider america's hospital systems today and the flow of information conforming hospitals to the dictates of a government-subsidized medical tyranny of insurance fraud, toxic drugs that do not heal, government mandating educational universities to teach fraudulent information via their textbooks, and, all under the illusion of wicked individuals employed by the Executive Magistrate and it's pervasive ancillaries to keep us safe from our self while being cast into the fire of their beast system.

America's health-care system today even funds propaganda campaigns to reeducate citizens of the [false] dangers in utilizing herbal medicines and then encourage my countrymen to blindly follow the orders of their government-subsidized doctor at the government-subsidized hospital wherein hundreds of thousands of people suddenly die every year for a reason unrelated to their initial stay. An entire crop of individuals have emerged in america whom remain grossly unaware and even terrified of their having ignored the most foundational aspects of living the life of a homeostatically stoic and virtuous human being realized in liberty and have now arrived at their later age knowing little else than to regurgitate narratives, begrudgingly act on this false information for reason of normalcy bias or otherwise their own faltering for fear of peer pressure; and, as a result, conform to the disease the beast system designs over them as their self and physical image reflects not the vitality of God's marvelous intent; and, through vanity compels them to seek emergency attention from fraudulent treatment centers providing inadequate standards through stolen public funds since the right of the free human being to access a medicine system the people first acquired in their own right was stolen by psychopathic agents supplanting the role of government with their aural fantasy of officialdom and national security.

Millions of people now have cancer from government-run food programs injecting chemicals into the food; and, the large government-run hospitals all receive their government-mandated drugs forcing their cancer patients to die a slow and expensive death – all of the while the healthy people of america whom know the truth of cancer and the weaponized food program targeting americans and many other nations around earth exhibit every trait of health, self-awareness, and vitality; and, know how to properly articulate how and why such vitality remains possible; and, as a result, today, receive all forms of chastising from the public (the majority of whom by perpetual choice exhibit every deterioration in their ability to articulate or maintain their health), even job loss, and government prosecution due to their knowledge acting as an existential threat to the fraudulent authorities guarding a host of dialectic weapon-systems formalizing soft-genocide. Burger King was even caught with burgers with eighteen million times more estrogen per burger than is permitted; this is enough estrogen to grow breasts on a biological male; this is self-evidence of one of the numerous eugenics operations to alter the hormones of men and women and even transition the sexes without their knowing the cause; everywhere on media today is how people ought to allow the children or adults to receive tax-paid sex transitions: Satanism on parade; militaries and prisons are in fact engaging in this practice.

Doctors, television, media, print, press, and the science community all state nobody has any idea how to rid the body of cancer, what causes cancer, where it comes from, why it appears, how it goes away; however, the irony here: the medical establishment propagandizes against the information proving the root cause and it's healing methods; for what danger could they save their patients from if their continued effort in purporting the truth as "no known cure for cancer" fail? Herbal medicines, eliminating toxic chemical food intake, and creating a conscious decision as to what will and will not enter the human body invents a healthy environment and thriving body; and, as this holds true for the individual – this holds true for society and it's ideas toward liberty in allowing, or not, God's persuasion evinced within the strength of the people to heal the land.

One joint force in society fraudulently shovels information as manure down the throat of the public keeping them in a constant state of fear even so far as to promulgate the suggestive thinking that all people will get cancer and when this happens then one must trust the state medical system to lessen the pain of their slow death. The joint force of righteous man and His countrymen acts to repel the advance of false narratives and corruption eroding civil Liberties and enslaving individuals whom would otherwise act to secure their oath to the law and their fellow countrymen in the form of manifesting their spiritual image as explosive lights sparking spectral fires of grace and salvation.

Philippians 2:15 That ye may be blameless, and pure, and the sons of God without rebuke in the midst of a naughty and crooked nation, among whom ye shine as lights in the world,

What function other than preserving property could society possibly serve lest society forgo the preservation of unalienable rights and pursue the defense of a caste system; especially that most common dynasty of a conquering royal class and lesser social classes donning a divisive and self-deprecating mob mentality?

Numbers 14:35 I the Lord have said, Certainly I will do so to all this wicked company that are gathered together against me: for in this wilderness they shall be consumed, and there they shall die.

The sons of liberty must continue to fight the global fraudsters threatening their happiness found in natural rights and deeds for the cause of life, liberty, and the pursuit of happiness. The eternal defeat of the order of fraud remains self-evident insofar as our ability to share the philosophy of liberty, and other revolutionary information our ancients knew of and practiced, continues as a strategic force repelling the oligarchs. Our great positional struggle rests in pursuing our happiness and continuing to produce the type of adversity repelling the comfort of apathy and it's voluntary restriction of happiness and liberty.

Proverbs 11:27 *He that seeketh good things getteth favor: but he that seeketh evil, it shall come to him.*

This verse illustrates the eternal quest for man to pursue His happiness and expunge the evil seeking to expunge man. Evil stands as a thorn in the saddle of man. Society ought forever cherish eternal happiness in the obedience of Christ for what else from above can man receive so great as those securities found in the blessings of liberty? President Thomas Jefferson was rumored to speak about peace as a time in history when everyone stood around reloading their munitions.

Jeremiah 9:8 *Their tongue is as an arrow shot out, and speaketh deceit: one speaketh peaceably to his neighbor with his mouth, but in his heart he layeth wait for him.*

1 Kings 9:8 *Even this high house shall be so: everyone that passeth by it, shall be astonied, and shall hiss, and they shall say, Why hath the Lord done thus unto this land and to this house?*

Does this not mean man's happiness must occur from within and the state of peace of mankind exists only as a transitory state of society preceding a resurgence of the evil upon the land requiring another triumphant state of even one man to spread the message of liberty to repel the contagion of ill-will amassed throughout earth? For only when men know the route to immortality and all people regard liberty as the highest state of being will society then not require any type of hostile revolution save the reproving of it's requisite emergence from that new generation continuing that destiny for liberty.

The fraudulent individuals opposed to human liberty obsess over the manufacture of illusions feigning eternal happiness and other farcical utopians. As a child I was taught the study of Physics represents the language of God therefore liberty exists as a matter of physics with an uninterrupted trajectory of God and not some shallow philosophy for ruling elites to use government violence to hatch and harvest slaves.

Mark 14:11 and the high Priests, and Scribes sought how they might take him by craft, and put him to death.

"Money does not buy happiness," and many add the caveat, "but enough will." No amount of money will purchase true spiritual happiness. Such fraudulent information, disseminating to a naive public, reflects the state of society imposing it's fraudulent-will against the good state of nature of the very many of society whom would otherwise not so willingly worship the slavery of sin; and, in particular the representative-leaders of that society for they reflect society's functional intention; or, in the least, point to the most dominant traits of those that would vote such an individual into representative-office.

Only the people will ever properly possess the conduit for civilization's esteem, perseverance, and values to nurture individual constitution on an eternal scale. The absolving of individual constitution as well exists as it's own type of subsisting industry aimed at exploiting our mental, physical, and spiritual galaxy. The fraud of blinding people into erecting the worship of a false God in the form of any multitude of social leaders threatens civilization with centuries of darkness. Civilization requires industry and especially the least economy of self-governance acting as the sum-total economy and final oath to which we as righteous men preserve our governance for a free market of personal, public, and sovereign life, liberty, and happiness; thus, only the spiritual realm produces that cure for life we know as happiness; as the desire of money only produces an economy of people consumed with the idea they remain stuck within the power and confines of a physical body sustaining every enterprise devoid of happiness and law; and, therefore the unhappy without Christ and liberty live unaware of their own spiritual body possessing that spirit of the Lord rebirthing self-image into a spiritually transfigured physical body.

2 Samuel 23:2 The Spirit of the Lord spake by me, and his word was in my [b]tongue.

Footnotes

[b] Meaning, he spake nothing but by the motion of God's Spirit.

Numbers 27:16 Let the Lord God of the [a]spirits of all flesh appoint a man over the Congregation,

Footnotes

[a] Who as he hath created, so he governeth the hearts of all men.

Matthew 17:2 *2 The transfiguration of Christ. 2 And was [c]transfigured before them: and his face did shine as the Sun, and his clothes were as white as the light.*

Footnotes

[c] Changed into another hue.

1 Samuel 10:6 *Then the Spirit of the Lord will come upon thee, and thou shalt prophesy with them, and shalt be turned into another man.*

1 Timothy 6:10 *For the desire of money is the root of all evil, which while some lusted after they erred from the faith, and pierced themselves through with many sorrows.*

What if individuals considered the loss of one man's happiness as cause for the loss of their own happiness? Any man that would perturb His own happiness due to the loss of another man's happiness does not rightly value His own life or love God.

2 Thessalonians 3:13 *[a]And ye, brethren, be not weary in well doing.*

Footnotes

[a] We must take heed that some men's unworthiness cause us not to be slacker in well doing.

The fraud of words not meeting action acts as a prejudice punishing itself for it's own sake. The individual choosing to limit their own liberty thus their happiness disparages the commonwealth insofar as their own energy production aimed at the increase of their own happiness will assist in the increase of peace and prosperity for their own society. Individuals must cultivate their own happiness to usher in the renaissance of free society. The malady of ignorance invites every inversion instituting fraud and coercion. Does the individual dedicating their life to the arts not pursue a congregation of like-minded and even happy peers defending the cause of liberty from that black, red, and yellow flag of fraud?

God streams His happiness into the righteous man and His society as an abundant flow of economy pouring from Heaven as His messengers spread the good news in order to keep men free from the entanglement of iniquitous slavery. Only the knowledgeable defense and exercise of unalienable rights will activate that frequency to excise the carnal supposition of fraud: yeah, that driving force of intellect which the competing intellect aims to kill: yeah, we the true spiritual mediators guarding supernatural and earthly realms.

Ecclesiastes 8:7-9 For he knoweth not that which shall be: for who can tell him when it shall be? Man is not Lord [a]over the spirit to retain the spirit: neither hath he power in the day of death, nor deliverance in the battle, neither shall wickedness deliver the possessors thereof. All this have I seen, and have given mine heart to every work which is wrought under the sun, and I saw a time that man ruleth over man to his own [b]hurt.

Footnotes:

[a] Man hath no power to save his own life, and therefore must not rashly cast himself into danger.

[b] As cometh ofttimes to tyrants and wicked rulers.

Despotic regimes such as North Korea wrongfully force, by threat of violence, their citizens to publicly declare and demonstrate their happiness to the state.

***Thessalonians 2:16** Now the same Jesus Christ our Lord, and our God, even the Father, which hath loved us, and hath given us everlasting consolation and good hope through grace*

Do men obliging to preserve one another's property in the formation of a society not issue their grace of which God places in man with His hope through our Lord Christ Jesus?

***1 Thessalonians 2:19** For what is our hope or joy, or crown of rejoicing? are not even you it in the presence of our Lord Jesus Christ at his coming?*

What fool believes liberty does not exist as a whole sourced from within insofar as He believes Himself capable of partially removing His own liberty to deliver that liberty to the sovereign man or society already in possession of that liberty from within?

We must not confuse this notion with the idea of preaching liberty. Does this fool not also represent the same fool whom believes capable and necessary to redistribute that liberty amongst the public in order to convince that public of a realm limiting and containing liberty (dissolving liberty does not strengthen the peace and prosperity for liberty; as though liberty meant a freedom apportioned by the fraud of a government of men and not freely given in whole authority to man by God to serve His Kingdom and not man) therefore in the reasoning of the tyrant: the people only possess a fraction of liberty (though liberty remain wholly hidden within their spirit awaiting it's self expression from the each of them)? How could society so foolishly believe granting permission to violently steal their earnings does not defraud their society of any sort of liberty (though their freedom to choose slavery possesses grandness unto it's own demise and those whom seek such choosing readily boast of their gladness for such fraudulent laurels), and of which existed before any unlawful transgression of the law was later perceived as lawful and not presently understood as transgression thus involuntarily acts to discourage, by threat of external violence, the praise and joy for our happiness to pursue a world unafflicted from such awful transgression?

Romans 15:13 *Now the God of hope fill you with all joy, and peace in believing, that ye may abound in hope, through the power of the holy Ghost.*

In war the threat of external violence possesses greater power than the act by succeeding the invasion of the mind. The right of the people to bear arms most greatly guarantees men the opportunity to preserve their property against every form of tyranny by fact of wicked men having foreknowledge of the uncontested power of the spirits of those men. The inversion of war into peace and tyranny into freedom will remain the great love of those decidedly separate from God. How must men in society resist external violence without acknowledging the priests of external violence that work to absolve society at all times through hidden and open measure insofar as the hidden remains unknown to those without such knowledge and known to those with vision of such transgression and it's actors?

Isaiah 32:3 The eyes of the seeing shall not be shut, and the ears of them that hear, shall hearken.

Numbers 24:16 He hath said that heard the words of God, and hath the knowledge of the most High, and saw the vision of the Almighty, and falling in a trance had his eyes opened:

Steadfastness and grace remain a force of superior frequency and intelligence in comparison to that of fraud and rapinous external violence. Perhaps steadfastness and grace imbue one another with that strength only the individual and realm cooperating with God's knowledge will discover as they keep their true intent toward repelling every mental, physical, and spiritual invasion. Christ does not force His hope as He grants man free-will and only those whom hate Christ in their heart blame the evils of Satan on the glory of Christ.

Suppose a publicly-professed Christian assails an individual while shouting: "For Christ!" The act of external violence, without provocation, lives as a pledge of allegiance to Satan, and not Christ, for whom else but the champion of destruction would disguise their actions as righteous through the misalignment of their action and words?

Jeremiah 7:16 Therefore thou shalt not pray for this people, neither lift up cry or prayer for them, neither entreat me, for I will not hear thee.

Corinthians 14:33 For God is not the author of confusion, but of peace, as we see in all the Churches of the Saints.

For every reason men enter society – evil will persist in their exercise of fraud to invite more conquerors to share in the spoil. Theft, the more obvious curse on society, will persist when given the authority of fraud to hide it's intent. Does the letter of law alone then represent that rogue legislature operating under color of law; or, does no such alteration need occur for the people to believe the act of oppression represents the act of liberty? America's unpatriotic Patriot Act, which has at this present time suspended the entire constitution, oppresses the american people into a state of martial law – or so-to-say a nation without the rule of law and a people without the knowledge of liberty preserving man from theft and fraud of their life and property even while remaining idle and shouting, "Who will save us?"

Consider today's american food industry with fraudulent ingredients containing thousands of known hazardous chemicals posing as affordable food. What moral man would wittingly enter society only to have a group of men grant their self authority to govern men, by threat of external violence, or to eat food laden with toxic chemicals accompanied by an entire culture of agricultural, insurance, medical, military, economic, pharmacological, psychological, and otherwise tax-subsidized systems of defrauding the public of their funds and subjecting mankind's destiny to a vision of decay for evil's sake?

Perhaps man and His skill when found desirable for the society then realizes His decisions beneficial for everyone thus those ingrates without skill or renown then work to corrupt His good name and even attempt to generate public or intelligence agency support for external violence and other forms of sabotage against Him. Does man in refusing His communications with society not risk present and future relations; and, not only His own but those connections which can be known by His effects? Beyond risk rests a reward for the participants working to preserve the property of the society. Among those men whom desire the instituting of society favoring preservation of property and disfavoring external violence how then must these men seek to unite with one another and what series of risk await their endeavor?

Self-evidence shows men seek a foundational oath for one another's preservation of liberty. What reason other than love for His God and His woman would man so endeavor to master Himself and resist every futility working to absolve His soul and the eternal expanse of mankind and society? The idea all men, through their kindness and inclination to settle into a life of requiring nothing more than feeding their family, assists one another for a shared goal does not hold water as that man whom works to defend the society of liberty competes against the other man acting as a part in the machine warring against liberty. This type of questioning nothing and only subsisting in the most base form of existence does nothing particularly great to help anyone as that basic or wickedly bound man to hide His shame would even sacrifice the man animating for liberty; thus, the assailant defrauding man of His life by force succeeds only in His intent of preserving and following His stomach which does perform the role necessary to protect the whole establishment of fraud oppressing the entire body politic of people and sacrificing the inheritance of generations to a death cult; therefore, the innocuous life of the carnal man possesses no allegiance, awareness, or duty toward the combating of the evils of His government committing crimes against humanity, Christ, and His own soul as His apathy acts as the skeleton key to surrender His destiny and instantiate the successional time-loop of manufactured darkness; for example, Communists claiming a mutual compact with america does not resonate truth with any man of fortitude as the Communists and other perpetrators of aristocracy desire not the success of liberty as the success of free men absolves the global tyranny (including those minor tyrannies in possession of every sort of ism (so-to-say those Communists, which profess public support for the cause of liberty and Christ and then do not deliver their nation with the duty of dissention toward their wicked government thus drag on their lives as ghoulish apparitions separate from God)) and resurrects the true church fighting for liberty; therefore, only our demise would serve the interests of Communists; though, perhaps, one day, the earth will awaken, understand, and implement civil Liberties; however, the potential for this reality appears as obtainable as inhabiting and terraforming Antarctica into a tropical super-metropolis of liberty surrounding a transfigured earth of liberty formerly consisting of those false flags which read theft and fraud.

The haters and losers fighting against the idea of liberty claim america as nothing more than a Jewish money operation thereby feign ignorance to the excellence of liberty, insult both the keepers of the idea of liberty and Jewish people, and pretend human beings exist as nothing more than "mutts" incapable of obeying God in their directing of mankind's destiny; and, all under the guise that ideas do not matter and only their classist caste systems whom arrogantly mock the intelligence of righteous protesters in opposition to their tyranny deserve final say concerning the authority over society.

Psalm 81:15 The haters of the Lord should have been subject unto him, and their time should have endured forever.

When a dictator of a foreign land issues a demand to another nation then under what cause would a moral society voluntarily and logically subjugate their livelihood to the captivity and prejudices of said nation or compact of nations threatening invasion? Compacts will forever remain morally and constitutionally superior to allies insofar as compacts remain informal and oft of necessity to prevent invasion; however, allies institute corruption and normalize the abuse of power and demoralization of society even under the guise of religious superiority.

What else drives economy but the separation and compact of public affairs and private trade? Allied nations remain so obviously separate in their culture, story, and purpose, from one to the other so what else than the futility of rogue politicians could explicate every falsehood in order to achieve their fraud and disunite nations from their compacts to reorder the world into a cold war of allies and aristocrats redefining peace in order to enslave every market to the capitulations of their own hypocrisy?

Why on the earth would a nation of separate faith, for example: america unite with Israel when each nation follows a separate God and lives oceans apart; and, does this ally not unconstitutionally merge both nations as one nation; insofar, as the politicians of the foreign nation now indoctrinate our domestic nation into allowing the deterministic abuse of our military and public funds through unelected votes governing our body politic; therefore, why would any sane people act as a borrower and lender for the military excursions of another nation thereby stripping their own economy of it's fitness and people of their liberty that would otherwise solve the smallest and greatest of issues of their own nation based on their own merits and not demand other nations stretch their own prosperity thin for the sake of some illusion provided by a team of so-called experts claiming policy-by-necessity per global decree; especially when that globalism means governance by international cabal or hidden government demanding all formal nations to obey their commands by threat of external violence in order to create order out of their manufactured chaos? All citizens being equal with rights under the law how can any government without the consent of the people sequester liberty and defraud society of it's birthright without some type of foreign compact or ally readjusting the origin of their law to the dictates of unelected autocrats?

Entering society for the preservation of property suggests those men keeping the wisdom of liberty and rejecting the insolence of an education devoid of the knowledge of liberty do recognize the fraud which seeps into the annals of society from the effects of an office keeping captive the mind of every man convicted of their oath to God and the fight for liberty lest such men rebel by authority of God. Happiness will not occur as a physical talisman but rather a spiritual token and calling from God Himself to those armed with the path of salvation to deliver mankind out of bondage and into the only happiness God alone purveys for the expulsion of fraud and confluence of every defiance against the alien tyranny revealing it's layers of orthodoxy.

Revelation 2:17 Let him that hath an ear, hear what the spirit saith unto the Churches. To him that overcometh, will I give to eat of the Manna that is hid, and will give him a white stone, and in the stone a new name written, which no man knoweth, saving he that receiveth it.

Happiness originates from our liberty thus once a society chooses to withdraw it's pursuit for happiness then happiness will that society lose forever as only the beast can serve their disparate intangibilities.

Proverbs 16:18 Pride goeth before destruction, and an high mind before the fall.

So many americans today remain convinced saving The american Republic means pretending the knowledge of a Republic does not exist and we must claim our nation as a Democracy and needlessly chant "USA! USA! USA! Freedom! Democracy!" when only an elementary understanding of our constitutional architecture as a Republic, and not a Democracy, must remain present within our public knowledge and privately-owned educational systems to thwart every advance of theft and fraud working to corrupt the public largess and reduce our Republic to the despotisms of Democracy in order to completely dissolve our memory into that pit of tyranny for eternity.

President George Washington, with great knowledge and reason, desired to ban political parties as this form of sectionalism posing as nationalism only obstructs the vision and intent of liberty and disjoints the mind of the nation into tribal factions exercising fraud as civil defense. Political parties, or factions, create a shield of ignorance clouting the mind of it's followers and hiding the hands manipulating the nation's Foreign and Economic policies for what reason other than to aid foreign agencies in the plunder of domestic and foreign populations: yeah, factions of which maintain politically corrupt influence for none reason other than selective authorization to defraud individuals of their sovereignty and remove the role and higher authority of these lands from otherwise electing or dismissing public servants for or against their preservation of life and property; for or against arbitrary authority; for or against moral auxiliary. What proof do we hold as sentient beings when we allow our own nation to fall and cheer not for the idea of liberty which will glorify it's resurrection?

Sovereignty dies when that nation exercises the tools of fraud as shallow means of securing illusory ends.

Galatians 1:4 *Which gave himself for our sins, that he might deliver us from this present evil world according to the will of God even our Father,*

Titus 2:12 *And teacheth us, that we should deny ungodliness and worldly lusts, and that we should live soberly and righteously, and godly in this present world,*

The most cursory review of history reveals the incessant succession of plunderous fraud through institutions designed for either a pure fraud of siphoning wealth through taxation or pure theft through destroying persons, houses, papers, and effects of domestic and foreign individuals by any means necessary. Denial of God and evil, in deed and word, will remain a persistent existential threat to mankind for all of our present existence.

Isaiah 49:1   *1 The Lord God exhorteth all nations to believe his promises.   6 Christ is the salvation of all that believe, and will deliver them from the tyranny of their enemies. Hear ye me, O isles, and hearken, ye people from far. The Lord hath called [a]me from [b]the womb, and made mention of my name from my mother's belly.*

Footnotes

[a] This is spoken in the person of Christ, to assure the faithful that these promises should come to pass: for they were all made in him, and in him should be performed.

[b] This is meant of the time that Christ should be manifested to the world, as Ps. 2:7.

A phrase I have heard uttered amongst the mentally-ill public reads something to the effect of,

"There exists no such thing as an enemy. Clear your mind to sharpen your wisdom and you will see there is no enemy come against you; therefore: everyone that chooses to imagine the whole world as your friend will receive the cosmic prophylactic securing them from chaos and entering them into exceeding wealth and dignified tranquility. Lastly: learn the calm pleasures of apathy, remove the roaring from your lion, and indubitably trust your government unto absolute inculcation."

Exodus 15:9 The enemy said, I will pursue, I will overtake them, I will divide the spoil, my lust shall be satisfied upon them, I will draw my sword, mine hand shall destroy them.

Exodus 23:22 But if thou hearken unto his voice, and do all that I speak, then I will be an enemy unto thine enemies, and will afflict them that afflict thee.

The worst type of liar claims the idea of an enemy as false and then dive even further into the colorful depths of denial through declaring no historical proof of man and society's plunder under the dictates of empirical military excursion exists nor in the targeting of individuals at random for theft or fraud; therefore, the righteous must know the bounds of chaos in God's divinity act as the absolute destroyer and eternal creator of exact and inexplicable divination perfecting God's greater plan of ascension through the path of our own actions for only without the continuance of our living bodies will the most wretched of evil unearth to torment all of the world.

Matthew 5:48 Ye shall therefore be perfect, as your Father which is in heaven, is perfect.

The knowledge of God, holding precedence over all matters, faces an army of gas-lighting individuals shooting a host of montages as absolute truth including their most worshiping notion of God not existing and the patently fraudulent idea of oligarchy requiring control over mankind. In the same manner the sane man does not question the motive of a bear does the protector of society care not the motive of He that would assail society in open or secret though He care greatly to serve Him justice. The assault and hoarding of knowledge founds the battlefield separating the masses from the sergeants of good and evil. If no enemy exists then certainly knowledge does not exist nor creation, destruction, or reality; and, the only purpose of life, according to the fallen and left behind, rests in that self-appropriation for fraud by coercively and violently filling one's physical and spiritual stomach with the lusts of envy and greed.

The intellectual armed with knowledge receives every impedance designed to stop His effort in forming a society armed with the accuracy of our courts, to the fullest philosophic extant, in preserving property and free markets which would arrest the open criminals rendering every member of society a victim to their treasonous game of theft and fraud. Declaring the knowledge of God an unrealistic thing sets the foundation for the grave of violence to proselytize individuals into acting as unthinking components of the beast system.

The idea of a domestic and foreign enemy must remain common

teaching to the youth of liberty. The domestic enemy may exist as one's fellow countrymen tempting Him to sin. A foreign enemy represents that individual of domestic or foreign origin though only their ideas separate their self as a true foreigner from the member of society that would abhor the destruction of their property at the hands of a political elite. This type of fraud exists as a form of hostility portending violence therefore an invasion without the common image of a battlefield though it represent the exact image of a spiritual battlefield requiring spiritual vision to discern that realm of affliction hypnotizing the public into offering their destiny as an effigy for a black mass séance.

Isaiah 66:4 Therefore will I choose out their delusions, and I will bring their fear upon them, because I called and none would answer: I speak, and they would not hear: but they did evil in my sight, and chose the things which I would not.

So long as the public at large in the moral nation refutes every encroachment of theft and fraud only then will the advance of tyranny string itself to it's own weight and reap the seeds to which it sows and manifest it's iniquity separating them from those of antiquity even unto the grave lest mankind render them, through a technological advancement or understanding of sorts, an eternally living servant for the Kingdom of God. The hostility of a foreign force acts as the most fierce form of fraud as it's manifestation strikes the chords of imagination upon the furthest poles of society's extremities thereby causing every chaos to erupt into a cloud of disorder rushing to defense against an undeniable threat; however, the foreign enemy from within the domestic nation often holds responsibility for this plight as under a false flag the usurpers will seize control of a nation by passing all sorts of fraud as constitutional legislation otherwise incapable of passing without the chaotic ignorance of a submissive public surrendering their life, liberty, and society, for no reason other than chaos creating unthinking perceptions of fear upon those enslaved to a life of inaction.

Man must forever pursue the understanding of foreign and domestic threats to civil liberty as the fraud and theft of imposing violence and coercion to hide every hostility will persist until the skin of every member of society roasts over an open fire for the ritual sustenance of their conquerors. To ignore such hostility whether by apathy or ignorance will inevitably signal every global power of wicked origin to impart it's dominion over the mind of man until the host of spiritual demons manifests every physical form of it's effects through the unthinking public following their ordered programming.

Debt will forever represent fraud and the most lightened chains of slavery. God, the great giver of time, did not create the universe for man to seek the promise of abundance and alleviation of financial pains through other men and not through God. Man and His society ought never lend or borrow as this type of presently acceptable form of moral economy only exists as theft and slavery from it's inherent theft, which men label tax, known as interest owed by the individual whom was promised freedom by the acquiring of unearned resources which only work to form economic bubbles quenching social and economic activity and requiring all sorts of wasteful recompensing, and dissolution of one's own savings, and not an economic addition or boon for those partaking in the immediate satisfaction of the most formal-in-appearance type of self-induced plunder and slavery.

Under the strict competition of not allowing violence or coercion and theft or fraud into society then the borrowers and lenders must compete with honest money, trade, ethics, just weights and measure to righteously pursue and build the life of purging the cult of fraud from stealing society. History shows borrowing nations often borrow from many nations until no nation will lend to the borrowing nation any longer or until the least honorable of lenders invade, occupy, plunder, and install it's own hostile regime upon the nation(s) in question.

All nations of the earth must recognize the fruit of liberty in our natural rights and how their property remedies every poverty when those citizens remain armed to defend and keep their oath to the rule of Law and remain ever vigilant and ready in moment's notice to wage spiritual war for the defense of their countrymen and property. Even in the event of fraud taking root, the law laying wayside to the legislators, and the perpetual instigation of the troubles of theft in every form, it will remain the right and duty of the people to communicate freely and utilize their resources for the defense of their society by any means necessary including the incarceration of the domestic enemies inviting the foreign enemies and their unthinking domestic patsys to commit acts of hostile violence against them.

What do we mean of the right to bear arms but the right to own every artifact of righteously acquired property for our defense and salvation including every form of weaponry so as to form a militia and incarcerate every weapon formed against our posterity and the Kingdom of God? As an american and defender of liberty the King of all Kings for me will remain Jesus Christ whereas the multitude of nations all throughout this earth call an earthly individual their King; for example, the King of England, or United Nations, whom bestow a fraud upon mankind deserving of God's judgment to strike their name from the book of life; and, who would God be had He not promised us the expedition to know His truths.

Deuteronomy 3:21 ¶ *And I charged Joshua the same time, saying, Thine eyes have seen all that the Lord your God hath done unto these two Kings: so shall the Lord do unto all the kingdoms whither thou goest.*

What does God mean of riches but those Liberties preserving property and adjoining abundance with healthy family and peacefully prosperous society? And what does He mean of the virtuous society but a multitude of individuals praising God and defending liberty with knowledge, power, and grace? Lastly what did He mean by remedying civilization but the implementation of the only and final method for total provision and wall as well as expulsion of reason purposed against the keeping of individual liberty under that rule of law formed against every form of theft that fraud will enlist for society's ruin?

Deuteronomy 1:28 *Whither shall we go up, our brethren have discouraged our hearts, saying, The people [are] greater, and taller than we: the cities are great and walled up to heaven: and moreover we have seen the sons of the Anakims there.*

Acts 23:3 *[b]Then said Paul to him, God [c]will smite thee, thou [d]whited wall: for thou sittest to judge me according to the Law, and [e]transgressing the Law, commandest thou me to be smitten?*

Footnotes

[b] It is lawful for us to complain of injuries, and to summon the wicked to the judgment seat of God, so that we do it without hatred, and with a quiet and peaceable mind.

[c] It appeareth plainly by the Greek plural, that Paul did not curse the high Priest, but only pronounce the punishment of God against him.

[d] This is a vehement and sharp speech, but yet not reproachful: For the godly may speak roundly, and yet be void of the bitter affection of a sharp and angry mind.

[e] For the Law commandeth the judge to hear the person that is accused patiently, and to pronounce the sentence advisedly.

Deuteronomy 7:24 *And he shall deliver their Kings into thine hand, and thou shalt destroy their name from under heaven: there* *shall no man be able to stand before thee, until thou hast destroyed them.*

How would a society without arms and abundance preserve itself unless that society does not represent society at all and instead exists only to preserve that state heavily defensed against it's own citizens and other vassal nations? The empiricism of fraud starts with society accepting it's invitation in the marketplace of ideas and then trickles into every hall of government until it's constricting of the heart of society vexes with such coldness the fraud expands as ice and bursts the body to which it's proximal incantation measured.

Does society in individually standing against the acts of tyranny working to remove their preservation of property not more grandly defense their self in instituting a government with the role of remedying the advance of tyranny with the reinforcement of the rule of law? Does society then require two remedies to preserve property, one in their property rights, and two in their laws; and, of which, both the property and the government exists as property of the people? The first remedy preserves property from the hostile violence of domestic and foreign enemies as it's effect remains an immediate and self-evident form of theft and the other remedy for preserving property: the rule of Law, further protects against the often slow and gradual erosion of liberties occurring through fraud; for example: the fraudulent claim of prohibiting or restricting man's eternal right under Heaven to bear arms as though their argument were proved to be constitutional or justified-by-necessity thereby mysteriously trumping the rule of law from which we and not they stand upon.

Today we stand in a new world and new perspective for mankind as not only had we the people succeeded the american Revolution but as well this illustrates the sweet fruit of our Lord Christ Jesus and His death on the cross. Connect this idea with the notion of the continuance of our own perpetuity and the message of Christ and philosophy of liberty as well as the advent of technology granting man the uncannily powerful ability to transmit any type of synapse around the earth instantaneously. One of the more arrogant assertions from unbelievers states, "Christ said He came to bring peace; okay, where do I see peace? Laugh out loud!"

Matthew 10:34 [a]Think not that I am come to send peace into the earth, but the sword.

Footnotes:

[a] Civil dissentions follow the preaching of the Gospel.

Concerning The Bill of Rights and it's succinct rules written for the role of government we must realize civilization depends on the proper interpretation and implementation of these rules; however, even america remains confused into properly comprehending and implementing the Ten Amendments (and the world for that matter remains confused into properly implementing The Ten Commandments) to institute a government fitting the proper role as God intends; therefore, what power other than God and His messengers will light the brushfires of liberty and enflame the hearts of the remaining one hundred and ninety nations around the earth to resemble anything remotely close to the standard of liberty? Realizing most nations function with the illusory aid of a dictator managing enslaved people as His annual crop self-evidences enough knowledge to see the good have weighted against them a knowledge of evil tilt in the favor of those individuals sitting at the throne of the caste system. As a child of God I envision all of the world discovering liberty and lifting the weight and hostile force of violence off of mankind and overthrowing those wicked powers suppressing the rule of law and keeping the human condition as the subjects of a fraudulent glory and power.

Philippians 3:18-20 [a] For many walk, of whom I have told you often, and now tell you weeping, that they are the enemies of the cross of Christ: Whose [b]end is damnation, whose God is their belly, and whose [c]glory is to their shame, which mind earthly things. [d]But our conversation is in heaven, from whence also we look for the Savior, even the Lord Jesus Christ,

Footnotes:

[a] He painteth out the false apostles in their colors, not upon malice or ambition, but with sorrow and tears, to wit, because that being enemies of the Gospel (for that is joined with affliction) they regard nothing else, but the commodities of this life: that is to say, that flowing in peace, and quietness, and all worldly pleasures, they may live in great estimation amongst men, whose miserable end he forewarned them of.

[b] Reward.

[c] Which they hunt after at men's hands.

[d] He setteth against these fellows, true pastors which neglect earthly things, and aspire to heaven only, where they know, that even in their bodies they shall be clothed with that eternal glory, by the virtue of God.

The ease of controlling the world through the distracting of those following their stomach demands a higher standard of interpretation from the church concerning Christ's teachings and how particularly the men must continue to engage the enemy, publish God's divinations, and serve Christ by early and often declaring the philosophy of liberty where it's manifestations await confirmation.

Matthew 6:21 For where your treasure is, there will your heart be also.

Psalm 57:2 I will call unto the most high God, even the God, that performeth his promise toward me.

The american Republic as a system of governance remains simple to discern and in plain-English text and only an irate minority of men will reawaken the knowledge and power freely given in The Bible and made self-evident by Christ and our Founding Fathers.

Man forever guarding the knowledge of liberty led to the creation of america thus proving the will of the people can and will form a magistrate defending self-governance as the reigning supreme law of the land even over those fraudulent royals purporting truth as their crown giving them a false authority to arbitrarily serve justice to any multitude of people as though such inbred psychopaths excel with such an esteemed existence their reward allows the denying of worshiping God upon any multitude of people insofar as the worship of God among people allows individuals to unite and overthrow all bonds of this most fraudulent authority declaring itself holy by royalty. One may then think of nations outside of america no longer as nations but as districts of people remapping their origin to the ways of liberty which supersede all carnal-isms.

Countrymen preserving property succeed furthest when they institute a civil magistrate as their most firm commitment to liberty. The Founders of america devised government as a triad within triads of social influence; for example, the Federal, State, and Local government; the Executive, Legislative, and Judicial branches; the President of the nation, Governor of the State, and Sheriff of the County within the state (today's representation arrived at a later date, compared to it's origin of Marshal though the concept of sovereign entity within sovereign entity of governing bodies persists); Life, liberty, and the Pursuit of Happiness; and, this knowledge, when acted upon, replicates the non-duality and non-linear harmony with the Father, Son, and The Holy Ghost. Only an army of experienced patriots will properly defend the idea of liberty as each piece of knowledge of good and evil aids in the extinguishing of the flame of evil for the abundance of good therefore the worshipers of Christ must stand on His law alone and abandon the laws of the land which earthly and vain men presumptuously, involuntarily (for their unthinking worship of the fallen one acts as a trance through which their physical body animates as the long-arm of insatiably wicked law), and violently presuppose upon all within their vision as though the desire of their money mandates and justifies this most grievous offense against our Lord whom views such worldly pomp as damnation by sin.

Leviticus 11:30 Also the rat, and the lizard, and the chameleon, and the stellio, and the mole.

As the believers in Christ desire the peace and prosperity of people on the earth as in heaven so do the evil desire violence, coercion, theft and fraud on the earth as in hell.

Matthew 16:18 And I say also unto thee, that thou art Peter, and upon this rock I will build my Church: and the gates of hell shall not overcome it.

Matthew 22:32 I am the God of Abraham, and the God of Isaac, and the God of Jacob? God is not the God of the dead, but of the living.

Liberty will eternally exist as the original and only true use for a government of God and for man. America's Founders knew well the american Dream meant to secure the blessings of liberty in our own nation in the hopes all of the earth will follow and establish liberty upon the whole face of the earth. Perhaps the law must remain written; however, President Thomas Jefferson possessed a measured uncertainty for the writing of any law as an assurance for the defense of liberty; as even He understood the law does not change (though man often renders salty His interpretation and God's instruction); therefore, man must forever protect the law from those men, even under the flag of government, that would disregard law for statutes oppressing the individual.

Perhaps writing sows seeds and the fruit that follows grows trees and those trees create forests perpetually sustaining the roots and in those roots the trading of earth and water for that manna of salvation keeps watch over the defense of our liberty.

Genesis 9:12 Then God said, This is the token of the covenant which I make between me and you, and between every living thing that is with you unto perpetual generations.

The unbelievers repeat their fraud through vacuous slogans supporting fraudulent solutions all requiring stolen public funds for what else than widespread political and religious contempt for the Lord.

Psalm 55:19 God shall hear and afflict them, even he that reigneth of old, Selah: because they have no changes, therefore they fear not God.

Why do americans bomb innocent Syrians; for example: the bombing of Syria on Christmas night from Israel in the year twenty eighteen? Love thy neighbor as thyself? The deception and lies subverting the perfect law of liberty with fraud to coerce believers into reinterpreting liberty as some form of security requiring preemptive (aggressive) war only paves way for more domestic and foreign insurrection and destruction as the real liberty publishes anonymous notes for the general public's sake and preaches truth amongst that same public at the risk of martyrdom.

Jeremiah 7:28 But thou shalt say unto them, This is a nation that heareth not the voice of the Lord their God, nor receiveth discipline: truth is perished, and is clean gone out of their mouth.

America's Founders frequently declared God as "The Great Legislator of The Universe." God legislates all hidden and known things and those whom assume their role as that of God over the people seek the only immediate satisfaction their ego mercilessly demands through defrauding all within their reach which in the end only brings their grave more near to whisk them off of this earth as a thief in the night at the appointed time. The people ought ensure their civil magistrate guarantees their preservation of property through the keeping watch of the night so when the honest men wake to prove their works under the honest hours of the sunshine then all will prosper.

Will the evil not creep about the night and will their ways not target the corruption of the most weak? Compare each hour individuals contribute for society and the present demand for each member of the society to prosperously participate in the economy in a state of happiness and abundance with the individual in the wild living alone and the multitude of roles He must combine into a load-bearing responsibility leaving little room for happiness or abundance; now, juxtapose this with the near-perfect Republic, with specialists for every craft and function of the free market of ideas with no arbitrary regulation and replete with individuals exercising full authority as the keepers of the rule of law and God's abundant provisions making way for the most realized self-evidence of a world with eternal and present defense for liberty. The role of government then ought to protect every form of the free market and it's entrepreneurs whom instituted the government in the first place as a dam against theft and fraud.

1 Samuel 2:3 Speak no more presumptuously: let not arrogancy come out of your mouth: for the Lord is a God of knowledge, and by him enterprises are established.

Self-governance implies self-regulation as no government preventing self-governance and preservation of property deserves obedience; and, the intangible world-government of hell it's servants envision only masks their vision of time and honor as their own commencing toward failure and illusion of security by way of earthly wealth, military force, or otherwise comes to pass.

In that regard self-regulation alone then, so-to-say liberty from sin, sets the cornerstone and foundation of liberty thereby damning the high priests to the truths crystallizing into civil dissension previously trapped for eons in the space of unexplored time.

Joshua 3:3-5 And commanded the people, saying, When ye see the Ark of the covenant of the Lord your God and the Priests of the Levites bearing it, ye shall depart from your place, and go after it. Yet shall there be a space between you and it, about two thousand cubits by measure: ye shall not come near unto it, that ye may know the way, by the which ye shall go: for ye have not gone this way in times past. (Now Joshua had said unto the people, Sanctify yourselves: for tomorrow the Lord will do wonders among you.)

Ezra 9:8 And now for a little space grace hath been showed from the Lord our God, in causing a remnant to escape, and in giving us a nail in his holy place, that our God may light our eyes, and give us a little reviving in our servitude.

We must as well recognize the legislators must remain bound by the constraints of the rule of law and under no circumstance should any man conceive any notion whatsoever to grant man authority to dismiss the law for some perceived or temporary gain. The Founders of america referred to the bounds of the legislative as the chains of the constitution and in this we must remove the most liberty-infringing nexus points of the legislative and replace them with nothing at all. Once the vision of liberty spreads, until all individuals feel that joy in witnessing the lifting of the chain of that yoke of bondage, only then will God facilitate His Golden Rule to clear our trajectory out of this present pit and into the consistently tempestuous transmission riding on the ultra-light-beams of loving imagination.

Matthew 5:13 Ye are the salt of the earth: but if the salt have lost his savor, wherewith shall it be salted? It is thenceforth good for nothing, but to be cast out, and to be trodden under foot of men.

The civil magistrate (an oft well-intentioned; albeit, a majority of foolish people and especially in times of extraneous government institutions) will never properly understand their role or reason for the bounds which constrain them from abusing power; though, these bounds exist for their protection as well as the members of society. What government instigating crime remains government among moral men for long? What moral people would allow government to rule them and exercise hostility toward their ideas of a government that serves and does not oppress it's people?

Does the citizen whom instituted government not represent the original legislator thus the supreme legislator of the society and would a society whom recognized it's citizens as the supreme legislators beholden to the law not remain a society with full power to determine it's representative-servants ad infinitum? Free people know and act upon the fact that today, yesterday, and tomorrow exists as that same eternal universe imbued with the perfect law of liberty and only an ignorant public and evil magistrate would lead mankind outside of this present realm and into an inverse reality; for example: that belief in theft as moral government and those thieves in government as people imbued with incomprehensible and supernatural powers making them a super-being separate and superior to their salacious human peasants which commit their life on the earth for every glug of unending and fraudulent dribble.

The separation of a society of liberty and a society of the sword rests in that which people will freely call their supreme power and namely Jesus Christ for the free society or the society of freedom of religion; and, an oligarch, royal, or dynasty for the society deluded with distraction. The raccoon finds great distraction in anchoring Himself to the reflective object in as much as the unthinking public inherently and historically finds great distraction with all things vanity and it's promise to alleviate the human condition by converting the law into an ephemeral consciousness requiring not the discernment of man.

Isaiah 54:17 But all the weapons that are made against thee, shall not prosper: and every tongue that shall rise against thee in judgment, thou shalt condemn. This is the heritage of the Lord's servants, and their righteousness is of me, saith the Lord.

Proverbs 22:28 Thou shalt not remove the ancient bounds which thy fathers have made.

Proverbs 23:10 *Remove not the ancient bounds, and enter not into the fields of the fatherless.*

Hebrews 6:17 *So God, willing more abundantly to show unto the heirs of promise the stableness of his counsel, bound himself by an oath,*

Not only will no weapons prosper against The Kingdom of God – the bounds of the legislative will spiritually exist with or without the weapons formed against truth; no matter the advancement of technology: righteousness, evil, and the law remain even when men choose to cloak fraudulent governance with the redefining of such universal terroir.

James 1:22 *And be ye doers of the word, and not hearers only, deceiving your own selves.*

Many churches in modern america today ignorantly, incessantly, woefully, wrongfully, and presumably will continue to preach to their flock to *wait* on the Lord as though none of them stood within the glory and grace of God's eternal power and presence at their hand.

Matthew 4:17 *From that time Jesus began to preach, and to say, Amend your lives: for the kingdom of heaven is at hand.*

Psalm 34:17-19 *The righteous cry, and the Lord heareth them,*
and delivereth them out of all their troubles. The Lord is near
unto them that are of a [a]contrite heart, and will save such as be
afflicted in spirit. Great are the troubles of the righteous: but the
Lord delivereth him out of them all.

Footnotes

[a] When they seem to be swallowed up with afflictions, then God
is at hand to deliver them.

The power to secure the blessings of liberty exists in this present
moment. How must the starving man satiate hunger but to eat; and
does God not always receive those whom ask? We will keep the
word of God as our law and the corrupt in their ears and eyes will
stay unbelievers filling their desires with the carnal distraction of
absolute enslavement to render their world a perverse Religion of
ashen Politics for that unholy order to which they bid their
worship and alibi. Idleness proves nothing more than living
without miraculous triumph over the evil storm bringing forth
every abomination. Even today the american people and the
people in nations without such organization must not only pay lip
service to human liberty but as well verily organize and enforce
such a constitution with full wherewithal and evincing of the Lord
conscripting them into the book of life and governing of earth.

What then can physically illustrate society better than private
possessions alone for only fraud would confuse society into
relinquishing private property or even outlawing the idea of
private property altogether? If society suddenly realized the sum

total of their private possessions went stolen in secret through fraud then ought the members of society (the supreme keepers of the law) not immediately respond in provisioning their fellow countrymen with the only security designed to preserve property; and, namely in the possessing of Gold and Silver as real and honest money for all men to preserve their trade of property in equal and righteous defense without the corruptions of theft by taxation or fraud by authority? The greatest fraud of all displaces the idea of liberty, God, and Happiness, the son of God: Jesus Christ, and the Holy Ghost with an ideology of self-preservation through worshiping the state and preserving it's vestiges as some type of holy possession in alliance against the preservation of property for those very individuals that ought exercise their rights in overthrowing such powers even over night.

Does even the animal world not illustrate a kingdom of hierarchy? And does God's abundance from the inner universe to the outer universe consuming entire worlds into black holes and eternal expanse not illustrate enough of the fraud of the unbelievers that would claim nothing in this creation exists as property created by any self-aware higher-being at all and how do they not see their ideology erects a leadership of dark armies oppressing mankind with fiat money and the exploitation of resources with the wantonness of external violence? The same liberty preserving the single private possession of one man universally preserves the property of the whole of His person, papers, houses, and effects, and, as well, all of the society in unison.

How can any member of society remain safe when nobody preserves peace or property? Does the property of the individual and society not extend from the private possessions to the legislative to which the bounds are written and known from the original intent and use of the absolute power of God to guarantee liberty to all beings of His? Does the member of society professing no allegiance to any God not profess worship for the worst God of all electing theft and fraud as the chief arbiter of man? Does every individual in society not share the earth, sun, air, and water in one respect or another? How could one individual poisoning the air not cause illness upon the public through the wind in their lungs and rain in their stomach thereby violating their civil Liberties and oath to society therefore what need for regulation would society require atop of preexisting law as though such regulation would not muffle and suppress (even unto oppression) the innovation of a company inventing means to prevent all civil liberty violation and these innovations would not focus society into a new spectrum of invention otherwise defrauded from the multitude of future generations and time?

John 10:15 As the Father knoweth me, so know I the Father: and I lay down my life for my sheep.

The abundance of God proves the knowledge of Good and Evil far exceeds the fraud of power by injustice. This truth requires man to seek God inwardly for His strength and increase evermore. Action manifests parts moved from origin to a final destination or new and necessary origin; and, without the assistance of the good-will of the living actors nothing good will change. God waits for no man to raze every conquerors ship, save His captive servants, and ensure His destiny above all manifests the truth in His creation for the each and whole of us as we as His Ark and covenant plan for mankind to forever abide in His glory.

1 Chronicles 16:32 Let the sea roar, and all that therein is: let the field be joyful and all that is in it.

The tempestuous sea of liberty will roar as the mighty of the field remain vigilant and joyful for God's law moving mountains and proving the way for future generations as the practitioners of fraud and evil forever leaven into dust as our Lord and Savior Jesus Christ reigns as our King of Kings from dust to dust.

STANDING

ARMIES

Exodus 15:3 The Lord is a [c]man of war, his [d]Name is Jehovah.

Footnotes

[c] In battle he overcometh ever.

[d] Ever constant in his promise.

Jeremiah 33:22

As the army of heaven cannot be numbered, neither the sand of the sea measured: so will I multiply the seed of David my servant, and the Levites, that minister unto me.

Luke 2:13-14 And straightway there was with the Angel [a]a multitude of heavenly soldiers, praising God, and saying, Glory be to God in the high heavens, and peace in earth, and toward men [b]good will.

Footnotes

[a] Whole armies of Angels, which compass the Majesty of God round about, as it were soldiers.

[b] God's ready, good, infinite, and gracious favor toward men.

Rights do not legalize Wrongs. War originates from within the spiritual realm and physically manifests into the realm of the living. The spirit of the Lord conceives all innocence and demands men preserve their liberty and cast out the invasion of the standing army.

Numbers 10:9 And when ye go to war in your land against the enemy that vexeth you, ye shall blow an alarm with the trumpets, and ye shall be remembered before the Lord your God, and shall be saved from your enemies.

The individual or group of individuals ushering in war against the righteous affix their soul to that root of evil grasping at mankind's harmony, peace, and prosperity.

1 Timothy Endnotes

1 Setting forth a perfect pattern of a true Pastor, whose office especially consisteth in teaching, 4 he warneth him that vain questions set apart, he teach those things, 5 which further charity and faith: 12 and that his authority be not condemned, 14 he showeth what an one he is made through the grace of God.

Psalm 67 Endnotes

1 A prayer of the Church to obtain the favor of God and to be lightened with his countenance. 2 To the end that his way and judgment may be known throughout the earth. 7 And finally is declared the kingdom of God, which should be universally erected at the coming of Christ.

Declaring our independence on the earth with the understanding we inherit the Kingdom of God on the earth as in Heaven forms natural leaders out of the dust into an image manifest for the overcoming of those false flags forsaking their individual power for spiritual treason. The physical image of those spiritually wicked individuals delegating an assault on human liberty forms a standing army of idle individuals drooling at the mouth with all sorts of incredulous statutes as God awaits His joyous men in the spirit of liberty to reward those wicked beasts with absolute demolition of their schemes.

The natural man finds great ease in adapting to the crudeness of a war without reason; however, these men perpetrating unlawful war shield their self from God under false flags containing their own ignorant imaginations which worship every type of superstition.

Numbers 31:53 *(For the men of war had spoiled, every man for himself.)*

The definition of warfare as means to defend the Kingdom of God confounds modern americans today as america now embodies the ancient empire of envy and greed which God forewarned of since He will overthrow it's bonds for those individuals whom keep their conduct according to liberty. The active state of war america keeps as it's addiction and necessity creates a host of unintended consequences.

Warfare always creates more death than life, more unthinking than achievement, and more plunder than reason. Any society in an active state of war or maintaining of a standing army sustains it's economy with every form of burnt offering in place of the demand which productive innovation inspires and as a result society will then lack in all things from an overabundance of incompetence obsessing over the varying distractions only an occultic propaganda machine could instill in order to remove the original alpha authority from society's educational loop: parents; and, only then can the state rear the youth in an economy criminalizing free trade and celebrating a fallen and transient culture too confused to know truth from perpetual genocide, starvation, and the enigmatic *isms* of the world justifying all sorts of indefinite oppressions upon the civil Liberties of the people even when history proves time and again no such logic or reason will ever exist for morally enacting such a scenario as only a well-armed and free people active in their daily occupation supersedes in peace and prosperity that dumb, idle, and oppressive beast we have come to know as the standing army. How can the american Revolution end if destruction of america represents this end? Who wins this state of war but that wicked beast aimed at the expunging of free-thought?

Whether men fend off or lead invasion – both sides form a military, or militia, bound by an oath for one another's mutual defense. All throughout human history men have met on the battlefield and formed compacts against their enemy. Standing armies remain the second greatest threat and existential danger to society as it's concentration of power consciously suffocates liberty in order to transfer power obtained by it's act of attrition into the corruptive hands of an Executive Magistrate acting under the authority of foreign influence. How could any economy operate under the auspices of endless war lest that economy acknowledge it's desire for conquest through it's intended erasure of every member of society as it dives unto the bottom which designs itself to receive every empire fading into expiration?

Economic faculties will persist under the watch of free-minded men even when a fear upon the land mounts a tension so grinding upon the market the majority of the people mortally wound their civil foundation in their ceding power to an insane Executive Magistrate coordinating an assault against the free people participating in their Godly duty in the militia, insofar as all people whom label their self militia do not represent the militia as under such a war-time scenario the true militia will represent the primary majority at war against that secondary majority whom invade for the imposition of their foreign law upon sovereign lands; and, as such, illustrate mankind's last days of free people charged with the final authority of preserving liberty; so-to-say, mankind and all of earth's inhabitants: yeah, the colonizers become the indigenous in our world. A common argument in circulation today, and presumably ad infinitum, against the idea of men possessing and defending their property argues:

"Nobody owns the earth. All property was stolen therefore imminent seizure of all property under the domain of government will morally absolve any past and future transgression and achieve the utopian free society all balanced, common, and fair people seek; and, when we say free society of course we mean people forced under the slavery of anglo saxon royal bed-wetters."

This argument includes ignoring the existence of sovereign rights possessed by each individual; thus, demands individuals organize into groups and exercise violence to submit or murder the divergent personalities whom understand the wages of an immoral and rogue government legalizing violence and coercion as an authority only a coddled and inhuman public would allow in the permitting of their own evil for the granting of God-like status over the world unto men and all under the wantonness of a standing army. Does man not represent that measure preserving human civilization with His time on the earth; and, in this sense do we then not envision earth as a theater of war, whether calmly despotic or tempestuously republican, as our foundation, means, and virtue whereupon how and why we keep the peace and spiritually measure the bounds and limitations of physical or spiritual manifestations without restraint for razing our civilization even when the concealment of it's auspices demand a concession for it's simple subtleties?

Isaiah 42:13 The Lord shall go forth as a giant; he shall stir up his courage like a man of war: he shall shout and cry, and shall prevail against his enemies.

Ezekiel 3:17 Son of man, I have made thee a watchman unto the house of Israel: therefore hear the word at my mouth, and give them warning from me

Only in today's america of blind rage politics would warning Israel of it's transgressions be labeled hatred toward Jewish people and worthy of public exile or imprisonment. War will persist as the most grotesque form of mankind's conduct as it's function acts as an antiquated tool succeeding the shadowing of mankind's potential and shifting of man's liberty into the hands of an Executive Magistrate set at democratically culling the public through the false paradigm of political parties vying for either conquest or consent; though, none of them absolutely vying for life or liberty; therefore, wholly forged against human felicity.

Do the carnal rulers of this earth not presume war as their constant duty for the maintenance of temporal power over earth as though this sovereign realm exists for their planes of existence to breach, overwhelm, and subdue through the gaits of occultic empire merging unbindable dimensions to blind and shut out ideas of sovereignty and that man of war whom will contemptuously and righteously set His mind against such psychopathic warmongering working to alter or abolish mankind's heavenly neural and spiritual frequencies?

Genesis 28:4 And give thee the blessing of Abraham, even to thee and to thy seed with thee, that thou mayest inherit the land (wherein thou art a [a]stranger,) which God gave unto Abraham.
Footnotes
The godly fathers were put in mind continually, that they were but strangers in this world: to the intent they should lift up their eyes to the heavens where they should have a sure dwelling.

For why else would the ruler seek to acquire such worldly riches through violently stealing from the public if not to entrain that public into enabling the perpetual pursuits of wicked people converting innocent blood into false power? America as an experiment proves ever worthy in it's perpetual bear-arms revolution against the worldlings and ever self-evident our people represent not simply a country; and, instead represent true free people of one body, mind, and spirit aimed toward that preservation of liberty not of this world.

Psalm 123:1 A prayer of the faithful, which were afflicted either in Babylon or under Antiochus, by the wicked worldlings and contemners of God. [A song of degrees.] I lift up mine eyes to thee, that dwellest in the heavens.

Where else on the earth but america lives a free people with an ethos bound in the liberty of electing representatives to preserve life, liberty, and property according to their constitution and certainly not according to monarchical cast, occultic high priests, barbarous military dictatorships, or any other form of involuntary collectivism using it's authoritarian umbrella to keep away the dew of liberty? Mexico and the Philippines may argue their people possess a constitution of similar stature and language to the United States; however, even more specifically, what people like americans wittingly fight for liberty in an epigenetic, genealogical, and perpetual revolution until all of the world lives in peace, prosperity, and civil Liberties with one another, and, even putting to rest the technocratic-military-industrial-complex-oligopoly; and, as well, purge that violence manifesting from within the world's tyrants whom daily conceive every coercion upon the public for the dimming of creative imagination?

Genesis 11 Endnotes

6 The building of Babel was the cause of the confusion of tongues.

The intellectually dishonest will argue no people will ever create peaceful governance without oppression and all ideas of people engaged in a spiritual war against standing armies for liberty exists as an over-active or delusional state of imagination deserving reeducation from a totalitarian government (though these intellectually dishonest individuals will demonically recoil at the spoken word of liberty and will then go on to speak ever faster in their own witting failure toward shielding their inversions of tongue under the cover of menacing and venomous confusions born of babel); however, their busy-as-a-devil rhetoric, speaking all sorts of anti-Christ-isms, only proportionately meets the economic demand of those like-minded individuals cheering their collective descent into hell even insofar as no true individuals within their collective truly live therefore their mind possesses nothing everlasting, and certainly no moral foundation, Godliness, or self-governing individuals since all of them live under the gun of the wicked one.

Genesis 17:7 *Moreover, I will establish my covenant between me and thee, and thy seed after thee in their generations, for an everlasting covenant, to be God unto thee, and to thy seed after thee.*

Numbers 35:29 *So these things shall be a [a]law of judgment* *unto you, throughout your generations in all your dwellings.*

Footnotes:

[a] A law to judge murders done either of purpose, or unadvisedly.

Joshua 22:28 *Therefore said we, If so be that they should so say to us, or to our [a]generations in time to come, then will we answer, Behold the fashion of the altar of the Lord, which our fathers made, not for burnt offering, nor for sacrifice, but it is a witness between us and you.*

Footnotes:

[a] They signify a wonderful care that they bare toward their posterity, that they might live in the true service of God.

America and none other possesses a population of people recognizing life, liberty, and property as an unalienable right of the individual regardless of their physical location and supersedent to any proclamation whatsoever from a people self-labeling their person or group of persons a higher authority over the people through their exercising of empty and powerless words such as announcing, authority, collective, commission, decree, democracy, global, government, group, international, law, new, official, order, progress, statute, union, or world; especially since our Founders encouraged the teaching of the enemies of the cross as an habitation of man into the physical and spiritual confiscation of His persons, houses, papers, and effects through culling His mind unto inversions of language rendering common terms inert thus generating high demand for free men to steadfastly defend against every form of wickedry. Standing armies claim ownership of the individual and the idea of liberty (that individual of whom such divination from the almighty God of this universe applies) in order to triumph their war against mankind and especially those individuals acting as that tip of the spear in the cause for liberty whom apprehend the imaginations of those powers and principalities oppressing mankind into the division of two realms: one consisting of the wicked worldlings and the other consisting of that multitude of individuals waging spiritual war as a cloud of witnesses alive in the true service of God for the breaking of the yoke of bondage from those diabolical theocracies driving mankind's erasure.

Revelation 16:19 [a]And the great city was divided into three parts: and the cities of the nations [b]fell: and that great [c]Babylon came in remembrance before God, [d]to give unto her the cup of the wine of the fierceness of his wrath.

Footnotes

[a] That seat or standing place of Antichrist.

[b] Of all such as cleave unto Antichrist, and fight against Christ.

[c] That harlot, of whom in the Chapter next following. Now this phrase to come into remembrance is after the common use of the Hebrew speech, but borrowed from men, attributed unto God.

Endnotes

[d] and the inhabitants of the great city.

Though war remain a constant false power of separation within man from that whole power of Godliness: the fact of a people remaining aware and preserving the knowledge of eternal victory for mankind creates a population of participants shedding society of the scaley-eyed, walking-dead, as the light of God shines upon the face of the Godly and blushes the face of the guilty as though such humiliation written upon the face of compulsory treason acts as a lighthouse indicating it's gratuitous stronghold opposing mankind's perennial victory for liberty.

Standing armies create that very perception of indefinite physical war whereby forcing the public to withstand that chilling effect of rearing a youth into living as idle booms capturing the trade winds for those pirates duplicitously sailing for the walling in of our sovereign and tempestuous waters. America's Founding Fathers rightly held a strong conviction for a voluntary society operating as a sovereign army, or militia, in defense of free society from tyrants whom invade by foreign, domestic, false, or formal flags and means onto the flatlands and valleys either by immediate seizing or slow and gradual erosion through seemingly disconnected events closely tethered through the subtle forming of a public perception being guided into a Satanic economy rewarding the unthinking with carnal and temporal riches upon their public display of spiritual surrender.

The militia does not illustrate a standing army insofar as the carpenter, potter, tailor, clothier, blacksmith, chef, or inventor remain in constant motion for their trade; thus, the indivisible sovereignty of man keeps Him in that eternal vigilance against foreign invasion, therefore, a people of such cognizance generate a force of many hands making light work which out-compete any cumulative intelligence of tyrants preparing to render our nation the subject of that constant occupation practicing it's dynamic trajectory of global governance in shifting the authority of the people into the hand of lamentations criminalizing free speech since it's affects lift mankind into ever higher states of salutary destiny, and, as such: is criminalized as the vision of the forbidden clothes as white as the light.

Standing armies will always champion psychopathic domination of the members of society through placarding their narratives atop current events in order to vilify their political enemies though they must keep and not destroy their political enemy in order to fuel their justifications lest we the people, in hour's time, discover our individual power and escape the parasitism of these destroyers on a planetary scale by electing individual liberty as the head of our nation-states.

Revelation 13:5 *[a]And there was given unto him a mouth, that spake great things and blasphemies, and power was given unto him, [b]to do two and forty months.*

Footnotes

[a] The second member containing an history of the acts of the beast, as I said verse 1. The history of them is concluded in two points, the beginning and the manner of them. The beginning is the gift of the Dragon, who put and inspired into the beast both his impiety against God and his eminity and injustice against all

men, especially against the godly and those that were of the household of faith, the fifth verse. The manner of the acts or actions done, is of two sorts both impious in mind, and blasphemous in speech against God, his Church and the godly, verse six, and also most cruel and injurious in deeds, even such as were done of most raging enemies and of most insolent and proud conquerors, the seventh verse.

[b] Namely his actions and manner of dealing. As concerning those two and forty months, I have spoken of them before in the twelfth Chapter and second verse.

Political representatives historically decline their people any declaration of truth and upon this notion we the people continue to witness rogue representatives perceive civility as disobedience and transgression of that perfect law of liberty as illumination for their false flags bearing that god of necessity riding upon it's steed of ever faithful and morally illiterate standing armies whom first erect public oppressions with mass theft of public largess and secondly with death to the members of society whom wield the ideas of liberty as a torch brighter than the darkest hour. Consider modern-day america and it's Executive Magistrate hiring mercenaries to delightfully fly the american flag in foreign and forever wars; and, these mercenaries, whom learned well the anti-art of oppressing people, and after their serving the oligarch's boondoggled war, then enter american police forces only to reactively exercise those same Satanic psychopathies of oppressive occupational tactics on american citizens; and, especially through their confirmation bias in the unconstitutional "war on drugs" though this more accurately translates to a war on the american people and a war on the ideas of liberty by waging war on the idea of private property and private contracts and even that private contract of the people instituting government for the preservation of life, liberty, and property; therefore, how then will any standing army represent defenders of liberty without plainly illustrating the freedom of Satan's mercenaries completing the works of death and desolation whithersoever their orders demand they aim lest they deny their stomach and then discover their heart demands the shout of a new song in line with God and not the state whom so excitedly discharge their weapons against the image of God and even a mother holding Her healthy infant safely in Her arms?

What comes of that man manipulated into unjust war, the ordering of other men into all sorts of transgression against innocent people, and then post-war finds himself without men to order around, no directives to blindly follow, and no training in the creativity an economy of moral innovation demands; even further, what then will come of the men whom know not of their participatory transgression in a war which worldly men start for Satanic ritual alone, though it bare the illusion of a righteous war, thereby compromising their own soul, lest they ask and receive of God's forgiveness, and ignite an equal and opposite frequency for the forming of weapons of war unto the dispelling of the foundation in their own land? What objective other than victory would any military seek to accomplish; even when those men wittingly or unwittingly aspire the succession of their cause under false auspices which only perpetuate illegal occupation and cut off their purpose from constitutional law insofar as what particularly exists as constitutional and law represents the perfect law of liberty set into being and motion by the living God of this universe; so to say, that perfect law provisioning men with the absolute sovereignty to choose a civilization and life free from the sin of theft and fraud feigning it's authority, injunction, sanction, or state? Does the militia not in it's essence triumph that victory for mankind over that constant threat of foreign apprehension, enterprise, or invasion? Tens of millions of americans today ally with professional organizations attempting to dismantle america's Bill of Rights, the ideas appertaining to natural law, and the common defense of our nation; and, even further their mentally-ill claim in possessing authority to do so as a responsibility to destroy civil liberty (for He who misses such an opportunity misses that mark of the beast) in order to superficially obtain national security (though their language speak of security – their action manifests subversion of every individual's civil liberty).

Had mankind long ago not thought of the wonderful idea of ridding the earth of sin? What buffoon concludes their self the first human to think of writing crime out of existence as though God had not advised such in His Ten Commandments; and, what of the tyrant inverting The Ten Commandments appeals to the individual declaring on the one hand no citizen possesses the right of self-defense (insofar as God, and not man, delivers permission and good conscience for individual unalienable rights to thwart that advance of whatsoever type of sin and formed weapon); and, with the other hand then permits a group of individuals to hire armed thieves, whom label their self government, to steal public funds as though these individuals wearing a costume own the members of society as their slaves and codify false authority as society's requisite subsistence whereby the state declares illegal the existence of the individual and mandates cause for two vengeful groups of citizens to partake as the chosen ones for the state's bargaining tool of destruction and long-arm of colorfully diverse fraud: both of differing flavors of the same unpunished license to kill; though, individuals with knowledge of liberty within the listless third group, the oppressed, will continue in their Godly duties irrespective of the false authorities demanding they spiritually belittle their own destiny as though God did not choose them to step out of the world and into His elect in order to use their living hand to overthrow such burnt authority; rather, the contrived status of the thieves admonishing their self as government elects their spiritual cowardice to that high office of false God whereby God almighty observes and participates in the closing in of their surroundings; especially including those individuals tenderly worshiping their dialectic alchemist, bishop, community organizer, controller, demigod, elder, elf, general, guide, idol, jester, knight, lord, magician, master, maw, paw, pimp, politician, pope, priest, scientist, scribe, sorcerer, and spirit.

*1 **Peter** 2:7 Unto you therefore which believe, it is precious: but unto them which be disobedient, the [a]stone which*

the builders disallowed, the same is made the head
of the corner,

Footnotes

[a] By setting the most blessed condition of the believers, and the most miserable of the rebellious one against another, he pricketh forward the believers, and triumpheth over the others: and also preventeth an offense which ariseth hereof, that none do more resist this doctrine of the Gospel, than they which are chiefest amongst the people of God, as were at that time that Peter wrote these things, the Priests and Elders, and Scribes. Therefore he answereth first of all that there is no cause why any man should be astonished at this their stubbornness, as though it were a strange matter, seeing that we have been forewarned so long before, that it should so come to pass: and moreover, that it pleased God to create and make certain to this selfsame purpose, that the Son of God might be glorified in their just condemnation. Thirdly, for that the glory of Christ is hereby set forth greatly, whereas notwithstanding Christ remaineth the sure head of his Church, and they that stumble at him, cast down and overthrow themselves, and not Christ. Fourthly, although they be created to this end and purpose, yet their fall and decay is not to be attributeth to God, but to their own obstinate stubbornness which cometh between God's decree, and the execution thereof or their condemnation, and is the true and proper cause of their destruction.

Any people or society that would remain in a constant state of war, especially that standing army oppressing it's own citizens while feigning protections over them, and, even further: through the good name of the people maintain an illegal occupation of one, multitudes, or all nations – form an obstinance to God and immoral authoritarian and interventionist society failing to rightly demonstrate morality through free persuasion; and, instead choose the anchoring and enslavements of death as their idea of a sure path for mankind though it lead to utter ruin.

Jeremiah 18:21 Therefore, [a]deliver up their children to famine, and let them drop away by the force of the sword, let their wives be robbed of their children, and be widows: and let their husbands be put to death, and let their young men be slain by the sword in the battle.

Footnotes

[a] Seeing the obstinate malice of the adversaries, which grew daily more and more, the Prophet being moved with God's Spirit, without any carnal affection prayeth for their destruction, because he knew that it should tend to God's glory, and profit of his Church.

History shows the existence of the standing army as a tool domestically leveraged into society as a writ of oppression concealing it's foreign identity and premise for invasion. The hostile lunatics comprising this standing army of dull and goblin-like creatures match their dottling failings with a surplus of threats against our exercise of spiritual powers and free militia at all times designed and prepared for war against them. The calm of despotism always raises the question of that standing army's validity, viability, and whether that despotic society faces immediate invasion or slow and gradual erosions of their liberties. No persons, houses, papers, or effects will ever successfully disassemble or claim authority over the militia which in itself remains synonymous with the sovereign human as this military force exists as the last authority of uncontested powers against foreign or domestic invasion therefore the only and final defense of liberty on the earth.

Why in modern america have americans taken it upon their self to enlist a standing army in spite of the Founder's wisdom? What reason would a society place their complete government under the authority of a standing army or interchange the sublime rules of their own government to mimic a standing army other than the blind assumption this usurpation of sovereignty does not always divide and conquer the people (as our Founders so keenly warned of in their advice for all future americans regardless of the present form of their weaponry garnering public support of the dumb and blind variety to alter the definition and scope of natural law into outlawing self-defense and electing outlaws under civil pretense)? Standing armies legalize violence, encourage coercion, encumber individual decision-making, and constantly threaten genocidal collapse of the nation or civilization. Does the standing army in times of peace not represent that sin exercised by a society set out to manufacture foreign entanglements and diminish or even prohibit public awareness from even speaking of the spiritual excellency of God?

Power-hungry imbeciles seek work in the Executive Magistrate to chaotically grow their office into demonstrably wicked epithets of unlimited power, form standing armies to exercise certain violence and coercions upon a free people by way of shoveling innocent men into kangaroo courts only to later rot to death in their filthy and privately-owned prison systems, and concentrate the encroachment of this power to rid the earth of the militia and assume the role of the militia for their self as though they and not the militia possess that duty and right in being the arbiter and mediator of peace and prosperity under the trust of God and with the plight of man. Standing armies possess potential to cull or impoverish an entire generation of their mind, body, and spirit through the false authority of the Executive Magistrate stealing all trade through the color of fraud. During times of war unalienable rights for each member of society historically suspend as only an unthinking public would grant permission for the continuity of government and not the people or their progeny whom, in whole, institute the state from whence it received it's passion. The free man must ponder the perpetuation of false narratives surrounding such illusions demanding their necessity for preserving the Executive Magistrate and not the citizen and their free market which, under that keystone under God, forbade such lawlessness. The inversion of truth and light into the darkness of lies imprisons man and His rights and will never increase or preserve liberty as liberty lost amongst mankind will remain lost for eternity so how can any sane man erode our river of economy and upend the roots of liberty without polluting our living waters through which ethereality flows?

Ephesians 1 Endnotes 1 After the salutation, 4 he entreateth of the free election of God, 5 and adoption. 7, 13 from whence man's salvation floweth, as from the true and natural fountain: and because so high a mystery cannot be understood, 16 he prayeth that the full, 20 knowledge of Christ, may by God be reavealed unto the Ephesians.

The bloated Executive will perpetually inflate the alteration of their ego and behavior to match their diseased state of assuming the ceding of individual power as the acquiring of their authority as a god determining life and death for whatsoever reason. How will mankind identify with love when the overwhelming majority of individuals ignore honesty and placate their self with the deep illness of abhorrent lies which floats the capstone of insufferability over the world? History proves time and again the granting of extra-judiciary power for an Executive Magistrate will always injure the individual and divide the society into indefensible and conquerable parts as opposed to manifesting that whole power of God exercising His will as one people of one mind for liberty. Self-evidence then reasons the bloated and hemorrhaging Executive Magistrate maintains the shape of an enemy formed against the cause for liberty; and, consequently: the cohorts of the rogue Executive Magistrate act as an old and used rag for the drying out of every idea defending the sovereignty of man, His economy, and state. Perhaps certain individuals escape the grip of such tyranny; however, where shall they run when the society they enter refuses them; and what if this individual, in fleeing and not fighting tyranny, only trades one tyranny for another thereby destroying their own soul in the process of remaining obstinately stubborn to God with the tyranny of their own mind thus ingesting that poison of not illustratively delivering civil disobedience to the rogue government (the only lit path for liberty out of absolute tyranny)?

Certainly moral business and enterprise will contribute to the peace and prosperity of society when that society consciously defends and thrives within the rule of law and without the addiction of sin; however, when the people alter their duty into the clinging onto of false narratives demanding their manufacture of a nationwide constriction of civil Liberties and even mould their person into an idly bound subject under the servitude of a standing army: peace then wanes and falters as the wicked thieves sojourn the people into excursions of oppression. Standing armies share no greater a purpose than setting driftwood to sea in hope of setting the world on fire, thus, it's intention does inherently and historically oppose the true church and state, as it's ideology demands the merger of the two in order to maintain authority over all. Allies of standing armies extend the reach of it's tyranny and invite their self to ruin for matters particularly unrelated to them insofar as politicians and oligarchs guide such nations into warfare since under an invasion even the whole of society would participate as a free army rewarding no foreign or domestic occupier or invader. How could any nation survive the involuntary theft of taxation and it's funding of psychopaths wittingly receiving these stolen funds to then stand idle and metastasize as a regional army instigating epochs of terror?

When one nation truly achieves friends with all nations and not enemies of some – only then will the world set free that whole spirit and embody that whole image of the Lord onto this earth even over night. The more enemies a nation incurs the more wicked it's people, insufferable it's existence, and more near it's erasure as such a nation designs it's own destruction as no friend or companion to mankind or God.

Lamentations 4:19 Our persecutors are swifter than the eagles of the heaven: they pursued us upon the mountains, and laid wait for us in the wilderness.

The sowing of a foreign enemy, even by extension through an ally, plants a grove of domestic enemies. America's Declaration of Independence and Bill of Rights articulates the exact and proper design, function, and use of government to keep mankind peaceful and prosperous in a world of foreign danger. Truly the Bill of Rights rightly reaches and attains the most near and perfect literary example for liberty both in the aiming of it's effort and articulation by it's men despite the vapid nothingness and Satanic babel projected by the false prophets, philosophic psychonauts, psychic terrorists, and incognito intellectuals whom dismay the value of liberty and so worship their self-image as too educated to confirm historical precedence as though all people must apprehend their resolve unto the false reality of submitting to the articulations conforming earth into a waning and waxing waterfall of Satanists provoking the world to flood them with the last days.

1 John 5:19-20 *[a]We know that we are of God, and this whole world lieth in wickedness. But we know that that Son of God is [b]come, and hath given us a mind to know him, which is true, and we are in him that is true, that is, in that his Son Jesus Christ, the same is that very [c]God, and that eternal life.*

Footnotes

[a] Every man must particularly apply to himself the general promises, that we may certainly persuade ourselves, that whereas all the world is by nature lost, we are freely made the sons of God, by the sending of Jesus Christ his Son unto us, of whom we are lightened with the knowledge of the true God, and everlasting life.

*[b] **Luke 24:45** Then opened he their understanding, that they might understand the Scriptures,*

[c] The divinity of Christ is most plainly proved by this place.

The accumulation of historical knowledge both good and evil illustrates human trial, error, morality, and immorality. The Founding Fathers understood well a standing army as the signpost of the enemy of our liberty and so designed their logic around this threat as it's coercive funding fuels incessant usurpation. The foreign world imposes certain and immutable danger through it's self-evident strongholds, or standing armies, demanding each individual strangle the imagination of their family, their self, and their society thus a demand in the foreign world persists: yeah, the only true means of righteous defense founded in the perfect law of liberty.

John 6:27 [a]*Labor not for the meat which perisheth, but for the meat that endureth unto everlasting life, which the Son of man shall give unto you: for him hath [b]God the Father [c]sealed.*

Footnotes

[a] *Bestow your labor and pain.*

[b] *and everlasting,*

[c] *That is, whom God the Father hath distinguished from all other men by planting his own virtue in him, as though he had sealed him with his seal, that he might be a lively pattern and representer of him: and that more is, installed him to this office, to reconcile us men to God, and bring us to everlasting life, which is only proper to Christ.*

Ezekiel 38:10-13 Thus saith the Lord God, Even at the same time shall many things come into thy mind, and thou shalt think [g]evil thoughts. And thou shalt say, I will go up to the land that hath no walled towers: [h]I will go to them that are at rest and dwell in safety, which dwell all without walls, and have neither bars nor gates, Sheba and Dedan, and the merchants of Tarshish with all the lions thereof shall say unto thee, [i]Art thou come to spoil the prey? hast thou gathered thy

multitude to take a booty? to carry away silver and gold, to take
away cattle and goods, and to spoil a great prey?

Footnotes

[g] One enemy shall envy another because everyone shall think to
have the spoil of the Church.

[h] That is, to molest and destroy the Church.

[I] Meaning, Israel, which had now been destroyed, and was not
yet built again: declaring hereby the simplicity of the godly, who
seek not so much to fortify themselves by outward force, as to
depend on the providence and goodness of God.

We as free men must write that goodness of God upon our heart and mind as it's understanding of foreign danger invading our society through the gait of the mind resolves all such matter concerning the preservation of liberty. What greater danger exists than that foreign enemy using domestic countrymen to act as a standing army oppressing their own countrymen? Do the history books not reveal endless examples of standing armies issuing death warrants and how can anyone stand against an unthinking public hiding behind a standing army without facing desolation or martyrdom therefore we must worry least of all for our self and most of all for mankind's destiny especially those innocents centering their destiny upon despotic waters without knowledge of the tempestuous sea.

Revelation 6:9 *[a]And when he had opened the fifth seal, I saw*
under the altar the souls of them that were killed for the word of

God, and for the testimony which they maintained.

Footnotes

[a] The fifth sign is that the holy martyrs which are under the altar, whereby they are sanctified, that is, received into the trust and tuition of Christ (into whose hands they are committed) shall cry out for the justice of God, in an holy zeal to advance his kingdom and not of any private perturbation of the mind, in this and the next verse, and that God will, in deed, sign and word comfort them, verse 11.

Man must consider all options in uprooting the enemy including those physical and spiritual means in speech and arms. The greatest folly of any society criminalizes speech in order to erect man as God over an immoral, servile, spiteful, unbelieving, unthinking, and wicked public. God grants man the liberty, yeah, that power, to destroy standing armies.

Hebrews 4:12 *[a]For the [b]word of God is [c]lively, and mighty in operation, and sharper than any two edged sword, and entereth through, even unto the dividing asunder of the [d]soul and the [e]spirit, and of the joints, and the marrow, and is a discerner of the thoughts, and the intents of the heart.*

Footnotes

[a] An amplification taken from the nature of the word of God, the power whereof is such, that it entereth even to the deepest and most inward and secret parts of the heart, wounding them deadly that are stubborn, and plainly quickening the believers.

[b] The doctrine of God which is preached both in the Law and in the Gospel.

[c] He calleth the word of God lively by reason of the effects it worketh in them, to whom it is preached.

[d] He calleth that the soul, which hath the affections resident in it.

[e] By the spirit he meaneth that nobelest part which is called the mind.

The foundation of truth weaponizes man as a power provisioning society with every defense against foreign danger. Apathetic people will fail society. Domestic enemies, in their reciprocity for evil, pose a foreign danger of existential and metaphysical origin and potential.

Moral society protects against the foreign dangers which would openly torture society with every type of tyranny flowing from the mind of man. Hidden within society for eternity exists an evil working in the night to cull society every day and in every way. Fortunately for mankind we must not concern our self with the majority of individuals pursuing a position as our tyrant though our rule of law must reflect such that all individuals in high and low places face a stopping or staggering from their ascending into a position which would sanction them as an instrument of tyranny.

Genesis 3:1 *Now the serpent was more [a]subtle than any beast of the field, which the Lord God had made: and he [b]said to the woman, Yea, hath God indeed said, ye shall not eat of every tree* *of the garden?*

Footnotes

[a] As Satan can change himself into an Angel of light, so did he abuse the wisdom of the serpent to deceive man.

[b] God suffered Satan to make the serpent his instrument and to speak in him.

Fortunately the few seeking the status of despot make their self plainly known to man through their using instruments of war as devices of domestic tyranny.

Psalm 119:113 *I hate [a]vain inventions: but thy Law do I love.*

Footnotes

[a] Whosoever will embrace God's word aright, must abhor all fantasies and imaginations both of himself and others.

America's Founders were keen on understanding what that clean slate of society founds itself upon in order to preserve property and encourage the entering of society for those seeking that Kingdom of God on the earth as in Heaven. America was founded on human liberty which does not hide the self-evidence for a moral and sane society as one without involuntary taxation; however, masses of people today claim their self american and simultaneously fight against the idea of human liberty by entering unlawful roles within government or endorsing such roles (insofar as a government of involuntary taxation persists as Satanic machinations, immoral means, unlawful and misplaced authority, and a constant flux of wickedry) to spiritually dissolve america since they exist as the actor of tyranny over free humanity expediting subversion of the global economy since that anti-economy seals us from our wealth through corrupting the use of our currency from it's state of a commodity and into a worthless symbol of exchange; so-to-say, a fiat global currency concurrently inflating, deflating, and stratifying the value of money into an architecture of superior and subordinate political weaponry capturing and imploding the brevity, intuition, and sovereignty of individual power into the hands of the wicked one. The members of the society must keep wise in the ways of our ancients of antiquity and comprehend their life purpose in constituting a society of no involuntary taxation in order to preserve the free and unencumbered market of ideas forcing otherwise nefarious servants of the evil eye to obey the people and not their agency or standing army whom feigns liberty and then promotes freedom at the cost of an entire civilization forced to produce every sort of device and instrument for their own enslavement.

Sanctions, an act in the theater of war, always follow tariffs as both the theft of taxation and coercion of sanctioning represent the steam-valve controlling the escalations of war. And how do we depose of entrenched layers of legislators, lobbyists, and unconstitutional agencies combining and composing foreign dangers through their domestic and foreign corruptions, overreaching, under-representing, and misrepresenting of their own citizens? And what good of these legislators can the public witness when we the people, and not any government, possess that knowledge of liberty and the knowledge appertaining the complete history of nations and war seizing control of every man in the name of empire or despotic freedom? Who benefits above the domestic dividers but foreign conquerors? Who enforces such treason but multitudes of unthinking hands sacrificing mankind for a job in the quartet of tyranny: yeah, those high-minded and self-congratulatory imbeciles and minor-tyrants lauding their self as the "guy you pretend to be on your video games," the spiritually autistic political atheists with no real enemy, no true purpose, and no heroism to derive from unjust wars: yeah, hero is the man you claim to be when there is an audience of pedantic and disingenuous worshipers of false authority and glorified theaters of war: yeah, godless people hostile toward everyone, worshipers of the state and not God, destroyers of all people especially including the citizens they claim to defend the rights of since they destroy rights in order to hold hostage those true defenders of sovereignty: yeah, those people uttering words dreamt up in military control rooms with the intent of subverting american and international sovereignty: yeah, that standing army provoking the militia because it stole our flag, placed it on their uniform, and now work with our own government to seize our liberties and cease the essence of this free nation of free people: yeah, we shall not covet thee.

Daniel 7:7 After this, I saw in the visions by night, and behold, the [a]fourth beast was fearful and terrible and very strong. It had great [b]iron teeth: it devoured and brake in pieces, and stamped [c]the residue under his feet: and it was unlike to the beasts that were before it: for it had [d]ten horns.

Footnotes

[a] That is, the Roman Empire which was a monster, and could not be compared to any beasts, because the nature of none was able to express it.

[b] Signifying, the tyranny and greediness of the Romans.

[c] That which the Romans could not quietly enjoy in other countries, they would give it to other Kings and rulers, that at all times when they would, they might take it again: which liberality is here called the stamping of the rest under the feet.

[d] That is, sundry and divers provinces which were governed by the deputies and proconsuls, whereof everyone might be compared to a King.

We know through history, and even recorded in The Bible, of the the Romans and their standing army to foment war and justify all sorts of blasphemy. The standing army, with full support of the Roman people, delivered a false sense of ego and security upon the unbelieving children of righteous ancestors as the unkempt in their pursuits chose everything except the living God in order to worship false gods and deny the Lord Jesus Christ at every impasse for the illusory securitization of each transgression.

Daniel 11:37 Neither shall he regard the [a] God of his fathers, nor the desires [b] of women, nor care for any God: for he shall magnify himself above all.

Footnotes

[a] The Romans shall observe no certain form of religion as other nations, but shall change their gods at their pleasures, yea, contemn them and prefer themselves to their gods.

[b] Signifying that they should be without all humanity: for the love of women is taken for singular or great love, as 2 Sam. 1:26.

The unthinking masses quip:

"Why would a government turn on it's own people? You unpatriotic, communist, fascist, redneck, imbecile, flyover-American, uneducated, psychotic conspiracy-theorist and/or reactionary! We don't need divisions in this country; keep your mouth shut and follow the wide gait to hell like the rest of us."

An additional example for social analysis of the socially engineered and artificially autistic american claiming immunity against known dangers:

John: *"Did you see the news about the poison beef at the grocery store?"*

Dumbass: *"Because I have arrived and set my intention I do not focus on negative news."*

John: *"You brought me poison beef."*

Dumbass: *"Actually the beef will not poison me because lord-god shiva-baphomet's positive vibes and kundalini rainbow gatherings and also this beef is set between avacado toast blessed*

by a seminar-certified emerald tablet master, social media battle-rapper, and skynet social credit score official."
John: *"Now fuck off out of my kitchen."*

This individual views government as one coordinated and harmonious default application of preselected individuals imbued with the highest traits of authority ensuring proper and common guidance for the fabric of society for the warm pissing of it's stream of authority upon the backs of the members of society as though this action, through the eyes of the tyrant, increase their presumptuously ordained nobility in defrauding society unto death with their tyranny bent against the liberty of man. The mass of people valuing such barbarous ideas of an aristocratic class cultivating mankind as though we exist as their plant for harvesting feeds a cancerous mass of demonic peasantry too obsequious to properly assess in word alone for their action in assessing nothing good and electing everything bad speaks one thousand fold for their even-measured tone of words which measure death and desolation at it's end.

The legion of androgynous cretans exhibiting the most obviously acrimonious acts of evil as their sole foundation of existence do impress upon every member of the society as the foremost premonition of tyranny inciting every form of domestic insurrection against liberty. Lending institutions and oligarchy stand as that most evil army of shadows delivering false power to weak-minded individuals promised priesthood in that cult of death leading their séances with the prayerful lie of respectfully paying nature "Her" dues through their culling mankind by what these technocrats describe as an orderly managed population reduction. The individuals supporting the standing army remain blissfully unaware this same system which they spiritually constructed will reign for the appointed length of time ensuring it's design first destroys it's maker and lastly itself. The network of influence forming that jurisdiction uniting government with predation moulds a standing army against the Kingdom of God. Even the story of Adam and Eve illustrates this standing army of evil as a present anti-power on the earth awaiting man's request to enter His mind and spiritually corrupt Him even unto the fall of mankind's futurity.

2 Kings 1:6 And they answered him, There came a man and met us, and said unto us, Go, and return unto the king which sent you, and say unto him, Thus saith the Lord, [a] Is it not because there is no God in Israel, that thou sendest to inquire of Baal-Zebub the God of Ekron? Therefore thou shalt not come down from the bed, on which thou art gone up, but shalt die the death.

2 Kings 1:6 Footnotes

[a] Ignorance is the mother of error and idolatry.

2 Chronicles 15:6 For nation was destroyed of nation, and city of city: for God troubled them with all adversity.

Rather than turn toward God the evil erect a standing army to capitulate the freedom, security, and destiny, of the public as though the public's only meaning and purpose persists as chattel of the state affording predetermined freedoms and not children of God with absolute, common, equal, natural, resolute, sovereign, and unalienable liberty.

Any false authority which would desire and work to reverse the rule of law faces pure revolt from the people. Fortunately for mankind a type of quantum entanglement exists with the spirit of the Lord to ensure us the victory in our spiritual representation of Heaven through our courts and deeds to keep away those unusually cruel and beastly social-climbers of the wind rebelling against God and usurping His rule of law to enslave earth and mankind.

Jeremiah 50:28 The voice of them that flee, and escape out of the land of Babel to declare in Zion, the vengeance of the Lord our God, and the vengeance of his Temple.

America exists and will persist as that example of a population of individuals breaking that yoke of bondage weighting mankind from setting free that love for liberty and the Lord as we in one mind and people defend the ancient, eternal, and only true cause for human liberty and cross the river of awakening in our revolution against that new world order whom represent that old world order constantly working to incinerate ideas of libertarian soul. The new world order today openly works to form it's totalitarian world government, or standing army, over the entirety of the globe when in former centuries kept itself hidden through their faction of unions dissolving borders and merging nations into super-states with the aid of manufactured global crisis forcing colonization of foreign lands thereby subverting culture and sanctioning crime and disease to achieve a more near-perfect representation of that merger toward authoritarian world government; however, all of this stops when a multitude of counselors speak freely to retard such sin injuring the world and the innocents. The regulatory nightmare of an openly standing army of self-entitled world-government, autocratic, technocratic, oligarchy chiefly concerns itself with depopulation of the planet to increase the trajectory of it's otherwise benign, sterile, and unproductive genealogy.

God eternally preserves the will of His people in their rightful authority to revolt against even the most minute usurpations dreaming their compositions of evil for the vanquishing of true life on the earth as though God will reward these wicked worldlings with an escape route in their death, and not a seat in the frigid eternity of searing hell, or onto an inter-dimensional or intergalactic ship transporting them to another place of occupation for their further seeking of targets for destruction among the wider cosmos.

Revelations 11:2 Footnotes

"Coelestinus, by fraud, under color of oracle, he deceived: for which cause, that well said of him, Intravit ut vulpes, regnavit ut leo, mortuus est ut canis. That is, he entered like a fox, reigned like a lion, and died like a dog."

The realm which the oppressors hide in their standing army only manifests their destruction though victims of their regime manifest for a season. The spirit of evil often has associated with it an off-world and alien spirit choosing it's human members to act as it's interstellar travelers insulating the expanse of and destroying it's chosen worlds throughout all of time and space. The american revolution will rightfully persist in revolting against powers and principalities working to deploy catastrophe for the apprehension of our mind, body, and spirit which otherwise so desires to beat that dark-heart of tyranny into a pulp thus making way for the righteous to eternally dwell within God's expansive matrix for liberty. The naivety and meekness of the public acts as an extension of the darkness and weapons formed against those true pastors making way for liberty.

A standing army persecutes all logic and reason keeping a people free and thrives on hypocritical language of inversality, certain hostility toward the honest, deceptive compassion for their own family, unending promotion of black magic and the dark arts, and stupendous feats of contempt for any people whom would not so wish to feverishly worship the lavishing of all carnalities and keeping of their life purpose in a state of autonomous spiritual corruption guaranteeing civilization's demise through fearing man and not God. The history of Europe maintains great fame in exercising standing armies over it's people while claiming they do so for the defense and representation of the working class. The idea a few thousand individuals with weapons of stone and wood will properly defend an entire civilization from a faltering which roots from within the mind of man will energize a culture to overthrow the intellectual and celebrate the dishonest as though these individuals of carnal worship held the duty as a standing army to enslave the people, perpetuate the false authority of Kings and Queens, and politically, religiously, violently, and coercively lead the infantilization and institutionalization of a public championing some sort of self-inflicted mastery in destitution and ire. Consider the never-ending and undeclared, unconstitutional, and out-right illegal, immoral, and invasionary war promulgated by america today wherein the United States military, without any vote from the people, immorally steals public funds in order to purchase uneducated youth to hone the art of murdering defenseless peoples; and, even with armed robotic devices which now fly over american neighborhoods for presumed defense when this only illustrates President James Madison's point-of-view regarding the well-known dangers of wicked men auctioning and repurposing instruments of war for weapons of tyranny at home; therefore: nationalism, the true form of collectivism and national socialism, today supersedes the american public's former idea of founding a nation on liberty and not monied corporations occupying civil liberty; thus, foreign oppressions and power trample upon our own people under a foul tyranny crying democracy, freedom, authoritarian-*isms* including nationalism and socialism, and especially ideologies founded on communism and fascism, national security, necessity, policy, statute, or expertly-advised tradition. Verily this scenario highlights the fact the army standing in opposition against human liberty and the american revolution does stand as an ominous army reflecting the fire of it's reason on a contagiously unthinking american people thereby injuring the world since america as a form of power leads the world in the like-manner of a chief schoolmaster lest our people fall the way of Rome.

The standing army will waste no time in suppressing civil dissent as their actions move as a lever wedging apart the rogue legislators from the control of the free society whom remain bound to their oath to truth. Standing armies in the least remove trial by a jury of peers and at the most expedite the dishonorable secretive orders of execution upon citizens ordained their unalienable rights under God. Standing armies act as a temporary infrastructure, scaffolding, or bridge opening the gates of hell, though posing as law, for the full spectrum dominance of a Luciferian idol at war with the people and the living God of this universe. The division separating righteous revolt from apprehending revolution acts as a ballast herding the people as sheep for standing armies in order to remove the experience of those effects of liberty from the nature of their reality without giving notice of a highly-architectured program of mental enslavement whereby the state designs functions wrongly justifying the persistence of the standing army and it's oppressions upon the people. Individuals occupying positions within the standing army exist as idle destroyers of liberty ushering in the resurrection of Satan's ancient army through the spiritual corpses appearing as living human beings.

The most crude aspect of that standing army oppresses the youth through the conquering of their minds insofar as all of their adult life maintains an infantilized state of expressing their moral turpitude with every dishonor glazed with that heralding of the hooligan oligarchs as the acceptable chief religion and keystone under independence for the publican. Our Founders recognized speech as the foremost instrument of liberty to set free the captives of tyranny. Free people exchange their energy and expand mankind upon the abundantly high ways of liberty. When any society views liberty as a greater danger to personal security than a standing army – the ability for any member of society to define the role of a militia, citizen, Sheriff, Governor, and President wanes with the liberty which they desecrated for a day's worth of bread and circus; thus, further enhances the prowess of those erosions upon civil liberty and displacing of the righteous man from His seat of authority in society; and, further, establishes an attraction point of bad ideas for wicked individuals to rally around; for example: ignoring the rule of law and setting the standard for killing, stealing, and destroying every citizen in opposition to the usurpation of theirs' and mankind's life, liberty, and property.

The original and final defense for liberty exists in the militia – for the archetype of the citizen and the militia remain inseparable as each citizen participates in the cause of liberty as an individual unit of measure and whole wall of authority preserving society from those self-evidently empiric individuals that would wish to erect their mind into that high place of a standing army unequivocally oppressing domestic and foreign lands. Those that would seek such asylum in the debauchery of debasing speech and the militia do so only at the leisure of the free people since their grandeur and far-fetched lies satiate for a season the tools and dupes in society until self-evidence reasons them the beady-eyed and porcelain-faced image of those enemies of the cross.

Proverbs 23:6 *Eat thou not the bread of him that hath an [a] evil eye, neither desire his dainty meats.*
Footnotes
[a] That is, covetous, as contrary a good eye is taken for liberal, as Prov. 22:9.

Rogue legislators will advertise all sorts of fairy-tales to the public to grow their establishment of false ideas and especially incarnations concerning the militia; for example:

"The militia represents a public threat far too great to withstand for our own version of national security thus our Executive Magistrate's military must eliminate the militia since it presents to us a clear danger for our forward and progressive agenda."

The militia will persist as the highest of pleasantries amongst a society of liberty staving off every form of peasantry. The supposed present danger of the militia only threatens the perceptions of the guilty, the action those perceptions would otherwise foster, and those tyrants bound under their oath to assail and not preserve life and liberty. All nations must preserve their own militia to represent that perfect image in true defense of their civilization as only the citizen, and not the incompetence of unelected government, and that citizen of whom, under the cognizance of their unalienable rights, remain synonymous with the militia in their participation as the infantry and living master over the government He and His countrymen institute for the serving of their own peace and prosperity. Barack Hussein Ubama, america's unfortunate forty-fourth President, though His tyranny fortunately teaches and immunizes future americans of such egregious usurpation, unlawfully abused His Administration for the targeting of the militia and supporters of the constitution which does mean the entire american Christian population and the populations whom are friends to the Christians, ultimately translating to every american citizen, and supporters of The Founding Fathers in what His administration termed "domestic extremists" and "domestic terrorists" thereby instantly rendering The Federal Government an enemy occupier of america and liberty – the america of which Ubama surreptitiously referred to as "homeland" (the same term the monster Adolf Hitler used during His takeover of Germany; and, President George Bush used to illegally occupy vast swaths of the Middle East for the canard of: "weapons of mass destruction" – a thing of which was never discovered and fat and wicked monsters still claim Bush showed to them on their television programming) making the language of such foreign hostility so plainly self-evident in their erecting of standing armies over free people while posing as a friend of the collective or common man.

True domestic enemies will always invert the written and commonly understood law and language for the restructuring of civilization into the figment of their ideal authoritarianism. Today and all throughout america the domestic enemies have taken over public office and continue to actively work toward discarding our historical state and national monuments as though each symbol represents nothing more than an undiscarded memory far too archaic and consciously injurious to bare. True danger to liberty hides in the open and only a coward would refuse to speak or receive truth during times of universal deceit. Free and spiritual thinkers arm their self with that knowledge found only in common sense. The knowledge of our civil Liberties and right to form a militia with our fellow countrymen keeps us well preserved in God's greater plan from that same fear which paralyzes the weak-minded people of foreign and forgotten wastelands whom institute all sorts of societies founded on perverse things of deceit insofar as even immediate gratification exists as deceitful since it's possession of non-everlastings keep an unlike structure to the peace resting in the truth of ideas; and, of which, when succinctly and widely understood delivers that eternal life with love for Christ.

Will common sense alone not forever separate the living from the dead and the participant from the observer? For what else exists as so ostensibly common as that confidence in keeping and acting upon our knowledge for liberty as means of keeping standing armies in hell and not on the earth? Countless tyrants in america's present and future will claim the militia as our greatest threat to civil liberty; however, the men of liberty must raise a standard throughout the society to keep the way of our ancient knowledge for liberty and it's eternal design, intent, and purpose as the safest abode and foundation for all of civilization since it is under the wings of a Christ-like militia that we prevent Satanic invasion whether foreign or domestic: yeah, the militia will sort the evil from the good and preserve life, liberty, and property; and, of course the retarded government will distort and manipulate the words and meaning of such a statement from a false transclusion synonymizing any language mentioning the militia as support for insurrection or terrorism thereby the only proof they justify in criminalizing free speech and human liberty on the very continent our forefathers conquered. The enemies of liberty complete nothing good in their lives except pretending our common sense in living our lives with purpose in defending mankind's destiny for liberty through our Christ as too dangerous for a society moving forward from history therefore worthy of incarceration so as to not spread the idea of liberty and threaten the insidious way of life of those slaves of Satan: that way of life working to write tyranny into law and every form of liberty a crime under the color and oracle of fraud. The rule of oppression spurs every dishonest, without lasting, and fallible thing cutting off lasting peace and prosperity into a recurring image of an old world order masking itself as new beginnings for those ritualistic performance artists begging their false gods for that fleeting and most carnally despicable power of hypnotizing the public into keeping out of their individual destiny.

The rogue legislator constantly leverages society to maintain a state of fear for liberty greater than their fear for living for living alone inspires liberty while fear chills the unthinking into demanding mass population control even unto genocide to stabilize the security of the state which only exists when consciousness wanes and psychopathy waxes bold. Men fearing their standing out and growing in character thus acquiescing their God given right and duty to abolish all forms of tyranny will only work to shadow consciousness and institutionalize oppression. Man will, however, find great difficulty and triumph in governing their common sense so as to not early sacrifice their life for what liberty more intelligently solves. Liberty from standing armies require man's highest awareness and present action and not what lesser men proclaim through their self-evident acquiescence to tyranny for reason of supposed temporary personal security therefore an eternal persistence of tyranny and lifelong devotion to managing their own feelings for one's own enslavement and controlling all people within their projected area for a willing sacrifice of their own mind for that spiritual dwelling place of apathy, bread, circus, entropy, and idleness: yeah, the chicken-shit zone. All sorts of inept paths achieve God's reward for the wicked; and, as well, all sorts of paths achieve God's reward for those whom love and follow Him through taking action in this present moment of now and do not wait or boast their acting upon at a later date. A multitude of generations exerting their will for liberty guarantee the only future for a youth not reared in that cruel and unusual nightmare of captivity devoid of the knowledge of liberty.

Self-evidence then reasons those whom would profess fighting for freedom, and never speak of fighting for liberty, pursue a desire for money and not that abundance, faith, and truth our people and militia will produce in waging war against the standing armies oppressing civilization. How could any civilization expect to survive should they surrender their intellect into trusting the inept people whom seek office in unelected positions in government and not their countrymen whom instituted the preservation of civil government? What in this world could deserve such love and reverence than one's own countrymen and our shared perfect hatred toward those individuals that love that fire of government and not that brushfire of liberty? The especially obtuse pseudo-intellectual will argue for the absolute trusting of legislators and even go so far as to state that questioning the legislators borders religious blasphemy and terrorism against the state and continue with all sorts of publicly declared shallow and feckless insults used throughout history to libel known true pastors teaching of the con-artists manipulating mankind; for example, insults such as bigot, conspiracy theorist, luddite, racist, or reactionary have remained popular libel terms for tyrants to exercise on their political enemies; and, especially when the terms most deride it's subject possessing the least resemblance of such definitive accusation. Only that countryman whose cause for liberty rightly interprets the original meaning and use of trust placed in God and all of those whom would mutually assist in one another's preservation of liberty will ever inherit the Kingdom of God.

Our militia-men, or countrymen, act as the only righteous form of an army as our participation in our daily trade and vocation possesses no original intent or final purpose in the oppressing of people on domestic or foreign lands. America as the most diversely abundant nation on the earth flowers the renaissance of humanity and popularizes the idea of liberty in order to keep mankind according to the bounds of it's purpose and intent which exceeds those bounds set by standing armies whom suppress by theft and fraud any and all forms of creative imagination resulting from a people obedient unto God's leading, guidance, and direction. Allowing the enemies of the cross to presuppose law as crime without a victim forces mankind's spiritual faculties to act as an incendiary device either for good or evil; albeit, far removed from harmony. Let the facts of the evil ones submit to a candid world as their mass of ignorance supports godless ideas remaining ever self-evident of their use as an evil weapon formed against our righteous countrymen standing outside of time in our present realm of antiquity to keep those vampires frozen in their icy hell from evolving into fiery dragons with no cause except to exist as the catalyst for earth's mass extinction.

Ecclesiastes 8:13 But it shall not be well to the wicked, neither shall he prolong his days: he shall be like a shadow, because he feareth not before God.

The true danger lies in the shadows; those shadows whom seek work not for the Kingdom of God; and, in their evil think their night deserves governance over our day; their inside over our outside; their rule over our law; their authorities and officials over our representatives; their hidden over our plain; their unconstitutional over our constitutional; their lie over our truth; and, their standing army above God's angels and surrounding His throne.

How on the earth could man so fear His own shadow He then learns to adore His occupation in provoking honest men, and, even further, refuses to comprehend His provocation as the only and final form of erosion upon true civility and liberty? The ruling elite and those individuals whom view their self as tyrants keeping the elite in power target education alone for eradication and primarily language as it's transmission forms the most potent weapon supplying the greatest trajectory of all: ideas, and, most particularly: ideas in books, which as a tree bear the fruit of more ideas thus eradicate every succession of tyranny shadowing human excellence. Wittingly recognizing the separation of the good and evil men in society works to preserve liberty as the evil men act more like bacterium exploiting decay than men finding opportunity for abundance in their time. Those men working to subvert liberty form a separation from God wider than the spanse separating mankind's alpha and omega of universal potential. The men working with the knowledge of God to defend human liberty, work under the days of our honest and golden sun for all to see and receive benefit from their sown seeds of righteousness, whether carpenter or doctor, and then sleep in the night in order to perpetually keep their mind occupied with those duties in the moral inspiration of righteous intervention as an animating heavenly participation of men measuring new borders for our salvation, quelling of violence and insurrections, and providence in the self-governing of eternal vigilance against that standing-army-by-night.

1 John 2:8 [a]Again, a new commandment I write unto you, that [b]which is true in him: and also in you: for the darkness is past, and that true light now shineth.

Footnotes

[a] He addeth that the doctrine indeed is old, but it is now after a sort new both in respect of Christ, and also of us: in whom he through the Gospel, engraveth his Law effectually, not in tables of stone, but in our minds.

[b] Which thing (to wit, that the doctrine is new of which I write unto you) is true in him and in you.

History shows an unending genealogy of wicked people convinced of the necessity of a government synonymous with a standing army and accept it's baseless authority as proper form, sure foundation, and default function for their posing as civil society. What separates a Republic from a Banana Republic but the rule of law; and, what separates a fake individual from an authentic spirit but He whom confesses Jesus Christ?

1 Peter 3:18 [a]*For Christ also hath once suffered for sins,* [b]*the just for the unjust,* [c]*that he might bring us to God,* [d]*and was put to death concerning the* [e]*flesh, but was quickened by the spirit.*

Footnotes

[a] *A proof of either of the rules, by the example of Christ himself our chief pattern who was afflicted, not for his own sins (which were none) but for ours, and that according to his Father's decree.*

[b] *An argument taken of comparison: Christ the just suffered for us that are unjust, and shall it grieve us who are unjust to suffer for the just's cause?*

[c] *Another argument being partly taken of things coupled together, to wit, because Christ bringeth us to his Father that same way that he went himself, and partly from the cause efficient: to wit, because Christ is not only set before us for an example to follow, but also he holdeth us up by his virtue in all the difficulties of this life, until he bring us to his Father.*

[d] *Another argument taken of the happy end of these afflictions, wherein also Christ goeth before us both in example and virtues, as one who suffered most grievous torments even unto death, although but in one part only of him, to wit, in the flesh or man's nature, but yet became conqueror by virtue of his divinity.*

[e] *As touching his manhood, for his body was dead, and his soul felt the sorrows of death.*

1 John 4:2-8 [c]*Hereby shall ye know the Spirit of God,* [d]*Every* spirit which confesseth that [e]Jesus Christ is come in the [f]flesh is of God. And every spirit that confesseth not that Jesus Christ is come in the flesh, is not of God: but this is the spirit of Antichrist, of whom ye have heard, how that he should come, and now already he is in this world. [g]Little children, ye are of God, and have overcome them: for greater is he that is in you, than he that is in this world. [h]They are of this world, therefore spake they of this world, and this world heareth them. [i]We are of God, he that knoweth God, heareth us: he that is not of God heareth us not. Hereby know we the [j]Spirit of truth, and the spirit of error. [k]Beloved, let us love one another: [l]for love cometh of God, and everyone that loveth is born of God, and knoweth God. He that loveth not, knoweth not God, [m]for God is [n]love.

Footnotes

[c] He giveth a certain and perpetual rule to know the doctrine of Antichrist by, to wit, if either the divine or human nature of Christ, or the true uniting of them together be denied: or if the least jot that may be, be derogate from his office who is our only King, Prophet, and everlasting high Priest.

[d] He speaketh simply of the doctrine, and not of the person.

[e] The true Messiah.

[f] Is true man.

[g] He comforteth the elect with a most sure hope of victory: but yet so, that he teacheth them that they fight not with their own virtue, but with the virtue and power of God.

[h] He bringeth a reason: why the world receiveth these teachers more willingly than the true: to wit, because they breathe out

nothing but that which is worldly: which is another note also to know the doctrine of Antichrist by.

[i] He testifieth unto them that his doctrine and the doctrine of his fellows, is the assured word of God, which of necessity we have boldly to set against all the mouths of the whole world, and thereby discern the truth from falsehood.

[j] True Prophets against whom are set false Prophets, that is, such as err themselves, and lead others into error.

[k] He returneth to the commending of brotherly love and charity.

[l] The first reason: Because it is a very divine thing: and therefore very meet for the sons of God: so that whosoever is void of it, cannot be said to know God aright.

[m] A confirmation: For it is the nature of God to love men, whereof we have a most manifest proof above all others: in that that of his only free and infinite goodwill towards us his enemies, he delivered unto death not a common man, but his own Son, yea, his only begotten Son, to the end that we being reconciled through his blood, might be made partakers of his everlasting glory.

[n] In that he called God, Love he saith more than if he had said that he loveth us infinitely.

What separates the militia from a standing army?

Psalm 46:11 *A song of triumph or thanksgiving for the deliverance of Jerusalem, after Sennacherib with his army was driven away, or some other like sudden and marvelous deliverance by the mighty hand of God.   8 Whereby the Prophet* *commending this great benefit, doth exhort the faithful to give themselves wholly into the hand of God, doubting nothing but that under his protection they shall be safe against all the assaults of their enemies, because this is his delight to assuage the rage of the wicked, when they are most busy against the just. [To him that excelleth upon Alamoth, a song committed to the sons of Korah.] God is our hope and strength, and help in troubles, ready to be found.*

The standing army will forever illustrate pure destruction with intent to separate the people from God as it's act of corruption forms a space as even a design polluting the image and sanctity of life. The existence of man first forms the militia as the foundation for society and the preservation of the only true form of civilization: a people of liberty with freedom to not sin; since, for example, that society of taxation permits the sin of theft thus exercises, even if by threat alone, violence against every man that would seek liberty in their life from all sin including the theft men wrongly label as taxation therefore to pursue a life without sin means to pursue suffering since the wicked, as a tenet of their standing army, enjoy torturing the innocent with the effects of multitudes of ignorant and superstitious people.

Men agree daily to abide in one another's presence for their mutual reciprocity as fellow countrymen in defense of liberty. Men not only work the day with one another and then enjoy one another's company in recreation but as well rest and sleep within the proximity of one another as neighbors and otherwise varying representation within their mutual compact of society. The free men of this earth whom do presently and eternally exist as the militia for the cause of liberty vastly outnumber any amount of legislators or hired mercenaries standing as an army in opposition to the free people and militia. Standing armies always utilize foreign governments and paid imbeciles to stand as an army and oppress the members of society as a compact forged against civil liberties in celebration of their raising of a new culture of slaves obsessed with distraction and cheering the rise of their own torturous fears consuming every signet of knowledge devoid of that sovereignty in liberty. The release of that spirit of the Lord in liberty will occur from time to time within certain individuals whom face great existential danger through their very creation into existence; however, this spirit accelerating unto critical mass upon the population acts to free the people through encouraging the focus of solving flagrant sin throughout society and primarily through abolishing that sin of taxation in order to allow the proper delivery of the knowledge of God for the inspiring of individuals into participating as the change they wish to see in the world from expressing their physical image as a spiritual being not of this world.

The pseudo-intellectual will argue due to the hostility of the people and ill-perceived effects of a growing mass of the public then only a new government ought to form and reserve the right to invent the idea of issuing and removing individual rights at-will and even mandate begging, celebrating, and worshiping of the fantastically incompetent individuals in government as the highest solution for politically controlling the ebb and flow of relative ethics in order to stifle man's supposed sin against exposing the color of fraud, legalization of sin, and the torching of society into ruin. God quickens such signs and wonder of His greater plan to awaken the true spirit of man for the reconciliation of our rule of law and altering or abolishing of Satanic government, even by hostile means, shall such a standing army campaign it's lusts against God, man, and country. In no way would limiting liberty act to limit sin as liberty will only equate to sin in the reprobate mind; however, the uneducated baboons exhibiting true danger to society justify such stupidity in their own mind as they voraciously salivate over false power as though their naivety securely respires them though their democracy of willingly trading in their life for the greed and envy to possess that shame of exhibiting the inhuman behaviors of collective violence and coercion scheming society into worshiping false Gods of death and desolation; and, all for the mirage of joining a fallen establishment of untold wickedry and divers colors.

*Jeremiah 12:9 Shall mine heritage be unto me, as a bird [a]of divers colors? are not the birds about her, **saying**, Come, assemble all the beasts of the field, come to eat her?*

Footnotes

[a] Instead of bearing my livery, and wearing only my colors, they have change and diversity of colors of their idols and superstitions, therefore their enemies as thick as the fowls of the air shall come about them to destroy them.

The militia, or sovereign individual representing a majority of even the militia, will converse at length to refine interpretations and adjust calculations of current events in order to preserve life, liberty, and property as a form of mutual self-evidence for each countrymen uniting to absolve every yoke of bondage.

My sentiments for a world devoid of dictators does not limit itself to mine own feelings. For a people to keep their character in a manner to overthrow oppression means for a people to keep interest in habituating our feelings of joy which keep us as participants defending liberty and not observant infantile minds of the world obsessed with the distractions of a terrible interpersonal and intrapersonal architecture of corruptive influence, defiled bodies, and shape-shifting spirits with the lowest genealogical trajectory; insofar as even ideas remain genealogical as witnessed in families and communities around the world dispossessing or uniting around that reality in liberty in order to thrive or leisurely subsist under authoritarian rule either from a self-fulfilled prophecy of failure or success or out-right apathy and shame toward committing their life to that function and purpose for which God designed man; and, namely, to live aright according to His plan as outlined in The Bible (insofar as not living according to the extant minutiae which heretics will espouse as representative of the whole fashion of the gospel; i.e.: mentions of stoning as proof even true religion exists as falsehood or those of the true religion possessing those self-same barbarous examples in order for the heretic to avoid more Heavenly topics such as absolute equal rights for each and every individual with no negative displacements of rights meaning no allowance for theft under man's law both for the citizen and the government representative; therefore, living according to unalienable rights wholly understood by the people as self-evident and not gregariously debated unto the countervailing of God's intent).

Psalm 49:1 Endnotes 1 The holy Ghost calleth all men to the consideration of man's life, 7 showing them not to be most blessed that are most wealthy, and therefore not to be feared: but contrariwise he lifteth up our minds to consider how all things are ruled by God's providence: 14 Who as he judgeth these worldly misers to everlasting torments, 15 so doth he preserve his, and will reward them in the day of the resurrection, 1 Thess. 1:6. [To him that excelleth. A Psalm committed to the sons of Korah.] Hear this all ye people: give ear, all ye that dwell in the world,

Does self-evidence not illustrate our feelings for defending liberty from our common enemy living in fear of our liberty? Do we not share the sentiments of our forefathers in our continuance for the cause of liberty? And do our enemies when fallen not simultaneously shred the habits which kept their obtuse spirit alive and liberty under threat of extinction?

Language and purpose bind man into the stablishing of a true foundation acting as the standard for civilization as outlined by God since antiquity and will persist as the only form of Godliness though man will encounter all sorts of illusory resistance in His efforts to popularize truth. Who other than that prince of darkness would so convincingly standardize methodologies to inflict violence and coercion throughout the world and convince the public into cowering under such evil? The foundation binding the righteous with society creates a spiritual alignment more focally resonant than disjointedly moot; more neurally addictive than profusely sick; more cathartically domestic than wretchedly foreign; more economically abundant in honor and truth than perverse and wicked; more faithful than coercive; more civil than animus; more creative than habit; more religious than political; more knowledgeable than distracting; more inventious than plunderous; and more liberty than tyranny. Our speech alone resonates on a frequency readily apparent to the enemies of the cross which, through their choosing, aim for the rendering of the life of their adversary into imminent danger for none reason except a desire for the perverseness of absolute dominion over their surroundings by the authority and in the name of the wicked one. Man's ability to articulate and declare His sovereignty makes Him a prime target for those working as an army to disallow and kill those that would use their tongue to flee and free those in the enslavement of thought-prison which only fastens itself within the mind of it's victim-mentality-oriented agreeable subjects.

Two methods exist for successfully invading a country: a standing army domestically occupies a nation or a central bank implodes the economy and cleans up the mess with a colonizing force of enemy troglodytes. Self-evidence declares that power and spirit of the Lord and liberty as the participators of true feeling and conscious vibration as our interests coalesce and manifest to bring low the enemies of liberty and mount their political head on our wall of justice and peace. Our forefathers for centuries have defended liberty and this effort will habitually persist even when the multitudes of families disobey God until one child of God, insofar as even the tormented adult then turned toward God lives as a child of God, speaks up to ignite the brushfires of liberty once again. The enemies of liberty, for example The Royal Family, have destroyed nations according to their wilt for all of recorded history and herein we find the bichromatic juxtaposition present on the earth today as it was yesterday, today, and presumably forever, lest humanity awaken and wittingly flick the tyrants off of their back; aye, tyrants whom dwell as blood-suckers upon us giants whom stand equal and opposite to the tyrants masquerading as giants.

Members of society must regard the knowledge of identifying foreign and domestic invasion and how to exercise their civil Liberties, even when deemed unlawful by a rogue government, to expose and steadfastly disassemble the invasion in order to secure their peace and prosperity.

Ephesians 6:16 Above all, take the shield of Faith, wherewith ye may quench all the fiery darts of the wicked,

1 Peter 13:13 [a]Wherefore [b]gird up the loins of your mind:be sober, [c]and trust [d]perfectly on that grace [e]that is brought unto you, [f]in the revelation of Jesus Christ,

Footnotes

[a] He goeth from faith to hope, which is indeed a companion that cannot be sundered from faith: and he useth an argument taken of comparison: We ought not to be wearied in looking for so excellent a thing, which the very Angels wait for with great desire.

[b] This is a borrowed speech, taken of a common usage amongst them: for by reason that they wore long garments, they could not travel unless they girded up themselves: and hence it is that Christ said, Let your loins be girded up.

[c] He setteth forth very briefly, what manner of hope ours ought to be, to wit, continual, until we enjoy the thing we hope for: then, what we have to hope for, to wit, grace (that is, free salvation) revealed to us in the Gospel, and not that, that men do rashly and fondly promise to themselves.

[d] Soundly and sincerely.

[e] An argument to stir up our minds, seeing that God doth not wait till we seek him, but causeth so great a benefit to be brought even unto us.

[f] He setteth out the end of faith, lest any man should promise him-self, either sooner or later that full salvation, to wit, the later coming of Christ: and therewithal warneth us, not to measure the dignity of the Gospel according to the present state, seeing that that which we are now, is not yet revealed.

All invasion exists as a foreign and alien spirit uncommon to the intent of mankind. Even domestic insurrection represents an alien and foreign force aimed at the overthrow of the rule of Law. The invasion first occurs in it's micro state from within the mind of man, for example: claiming Christ will arrive at a later and ambiguous time and does not dwell amongst us even at the present, and then grows into it's macro manifestation as a pincer attack surrounding society with central banks and standing armies. Markets override the managers of central banks since markets value liquidation and politicians hate this fact. The force of invasion threatens all of humanity as it's consummation works to engulf all peace and prosperity on the earth and not simply any one law or people. History shows society will as a majority remain unaware and live as the children of lies welcoming every expedition of the beast marking them for death.

Invasion occurs every time the individual allows the manipulation of their mind into that altered state of reality which falters logic and reason for the shifting of Godliness into the hues of wicked despair which hiss about as serpents and feast on innocents as manna strengthening their metaphysical stronghold in order to open that wide gait of hell onto the planes of earth thereby narrowing that straight gait of liberty.

Matthew 16:18 [a]And I say also unto thee, that thou art [b]Peter, and upon this rock I will build my Church: and the [c]gates of hell shall not overcome it.
Footnotes
[a] That is true faith, which confesseth Christ, the virtue whereof

is invisible.

[b] Christ spoke in the Syrian tongue, and therefore used not this descanting betwixt Petros, which signifieth Peter, and Petra, which signifieth a rock, but in both places used this word Cephas: but his mind was that wrote in Greek, by the divers termination to make a difference between Peter, who is a piece of the building, and Christ the Petra, that is, the rock and foundation: or else he gave his name Peter, because of the confession of his faith, which is the Church's as well as his, as the old fathers witness: For so saith Theophylact, That confession which thou hast made, shall be the foundation of the believers.

[c] The enemies of the Church are compared to a strong kingdom, and therefore by Gates, are meant cities which are made strong with counsels and fortresses, and this is the meaning, whatsoever Satan can do by counsel or strength. So doth Paul, 2 Cor. 10:4, call them strongholds.

The animating contest of liberty exists as the only true form of contest demanding the individual animate in Godliness in order to receive God's blessings for entry into such arena; however, this destruction of liberty from within the mind and imagined into an existential threat as a physical standing army breeding constant evil into society demands total inebriation of it's contestants whom champion their delusionals upon each and every cardinally villainous act devoid of any morsel of a God for mankind. Throughout human history free speech has suffered constant oppressions under the enforcement of that standing army of unthinking peasants and their lords of the land imprisoning and even torturing individuals for their ideas and speech which the rogue state deems non-conducive to it's immoral cohesions of illicit joy witnessing it's own darkened sin either by the lesser magic of suggestive thinking, or propaganda, or legalized sin guarded by the false authority of all sorts of spiritually dead beasts. Standing armies thoroughly enjoy condemning those members of society with righteous indignation toward evil men though this does nothing to shorten the fiery eruptions of the soul within society whom detest such bondage and mount a tidal force of total victory with God's provisioning. The evil within the physical realm will work to conquer the spiritual realm; however, even the wicked and profane know Jesus Christ eternally commands the spiritual realm and none power above His exists thus the evil race to raise their dead anti-Christ above earth's inhabitants as though the anti-Christ possesses that omnipresence of our Messiah therefore their vagabond lives and dies but for a season.

Rendering civilization from disparate into thriving manifests a lasting counter-culture of champions fighting to temper society against the standing army which arises when good men do nothing. The idea there remains a superior message to that of liberty persists as an ideology of confirmation bias glorifying false authority and unfounded knowledge. God created mankind for liberty and the potential for a global rise in liberty exists and will persist as only when the people commit their present incarnation to spiritually die in order to rebirth their spirit into that narrow gait and one mind of Christ wherein mankind greets the Lord face to face will He welcome all action and nations unto Him as mankind abounds unto the higher order and realm designed for our spiritual destiny and unending exploration of our infinite Heavens. Invasion inspires individuals to defend their society through the increase of their actions in such a manner so as to render their person conductive to the frequencies strategically compositing the proper overthrow of domestic or foreign invasion. These actions, though focused with the ominous weight of war in mind, facilitate an exponential rise in economy, presuming such a people possess a source of necessary resources and do not suffer the slow death of attrition, insofar as the intention of the people focus into a concentrated energy abandoning previous forms of economy in order to create a new life and economy once the energy shones through what the people must come to know through their efforts in triumphing success over their enemy.

The militiamen, the true face of free men of this world and the arbiters of peace and prosperity in communion with God and their country, always present their self in times of defense as even their existence and vocation acts as a defense for the nation in it's own right though the courts of public opinion require man's participation for absolving and abolishing bad government for liberty's absolute effect. The militia represent a frequency and an image of God intended on preserving liberty on the earth since God brought us a sword for us to secure the blessings of liberty and absolutely annihilate our sworn enemies from the face of existence. Living as an image of the defenders of liberty embodies with it the consciousness and memory of God to render the insane: sane, and the unholy: holy, as we free men and militia steadfastly quell insurrections, absolve alliances of standing armies on our lands and even the expanse of earth, and eternally keep standing armies from assassinating God's spiritual warriors. America's Federal Government have institutionalized the systemic erosion of civil Liberties through the creation of "Free speech zones," wherein all space outside of the identified square footage (bordered areas drawn by mentally incapacitated individuals given jobs in government whom gutturally enjoy the rendering of civil Liberties illegal thereby betrothing the most heinous of oppressions) of space criminalizes our first amendment, and God-given right, and permits society's hired servants, gifted the label of government, to commit criminal acts of violence against american citizens for exercising their God-given rights. The inverse nature of defending the criminal and attacking the civil illustrates the upside-down nature of bad government and a rotting american Republic.

Free speech persists as the foremost attack and defense for any free people and it's militia against the standing army. The free man stands ready to speak the truth in the face of abject evil and receive the following orders from God for what duty next requires His participation for the defense of His countrymen from those dumb dogs whom follow the orders of Satan and wittingly discard believers of God into shallow pits (whether literal or temporal). God desires His militiamen to shepherd the sheep up the path of liberty in the midst of the unthinking evil illuminating our people with it's darkness. The purpose of the militia consists of defending liberty throughout all of space and time. The militia will appear first in image and this image will produce unmitigated speech patterns in society disseminating throughout the free press, travel, and association with one another as the network of defenders of civilization unite and stand together for the preservation of life, liberty, and property. What a travesty for a people to ever allow a standing army to thieve their property and convince them of not participating as a member of free society, so-to-say the militia, for the defense of liberty.

All throughout america a widespread entertainment theme of "walking dead" and "zombies" flood the worldly entertainment stage. The enemies of the cross and liberty exist as that image of the walking dead therefore their culture growing in public entertainment acts as a sign and wonder (for their acts represent such grievous tyranny one can misstep and suffer the idle marveling of that reward of the wicked insofar as that reward of the wicked in this instance illustrates a literal living puppet advertising evil as entertainment under the angular directive of Satan himself) for a civil society to keep keen regard over for the interpretation of that growth of evil depicting it's aim and intent in preparing destruction upon mankind. The walking dead march without the possession of true cause or character and as such perfectly illustrate zombies actively responding in the usual seditious and evil manner against that good-will and fortitude of free humanity whom express God's earnest intent in a conscious state of living through the pursuit of happiness with justice, liberty, and peace in mind. True inspiration alludes these beasts whom seek only to kill mankind: the only true source of inspiration founded on that knowledge in Christ and spirit of the Lord. The pathogen known as those enemies of the cross act as a colony of ants forged against intelligence, sentience, spirituality, valiance, and victory.

All cause outside of Christ renders the individual a failure in the animating contest of liberty. The very act of marching with one's free speech and self-defense fulfills that image God desires for His people in order to overthrow the free wilt of those enemies of liberty; however, the blessings of liberty truly rests in the hands of that individual participating in the complexity produced through the density of action in mankind's animating contest of liberty. Does the pauper whom grows up as the world's greatest baker not daily march alongside His friends in His domain of excellency completing His daily duty in honoring His fellow countrymen with His own economy which as a function steadfastly appears each day as a singular representation of the wider phalanx preserving His and society's liberty? And how does any one man differ from the baker whom does not participate in the courts; and, in His meekness grants His government full permission to flee with their every transgression lest such a government aim for even His erasure without their self facing any civil resistance? Only a free people and moral society of one mind in Christ will ever morally discriminate their own proper course of domestic and foreign affairs.

Do the men of the militia not enter and deliver a mutual

agreement of free association and choice in their unobstructed action manifesting the animating spirit of the Lord as one united body for one just cause in liberty? In the beginning was the word therefore speech, through the word, establishes the design, constitution, and fortitude built within man to overthrow evil. Gradual erosions of liberty encourage the dismembering of that idea of love (insofar as God and love exist as one and He who knows love knows God and lives in love aright) and order the drunken, stammering, and violent standing army to reeducate the unthinking masses into enjoying the savagery of every stupid satisfaction constructing their social programming into ever higher states of impoverishment.

Psalm 39:2 I was dumb and spake nothing: I kept silence even from good, [a]and my sorrow was more stirred.

Footnotes

Though when the wicked ruled, he thought to have kept silence, yet his zeal caused him to change his mind.

Attempting to frighten the free man possessing that spirit of the Lord will only encourage the efforts of that one man, whom does represent a majority, since His body exists as that temple of God and living in that temple rests the potential for the birth of a new universe in dispossession of the old universe; and, that man, as the part and the whole remnant of the militia, will receive God's power and blessings in herding God's enemies off of the nearest political cliff. We must forever march in the light of God knowing we justly tread down our usurpers with the aid and power of the mighty wings of God for nothing else of this life exists with higher concern, demand, or responsibility than performing those duties for liberty.

Exodus 19:4 Ye have seen what I did unto the Egyptians, and how I carried you upon [a]eagle's wings, and have brought you unto me.

Footnotes

[a] For the Eagle by flying high, is out of danger, and by carrying her birds rather on her wings than in her talons declareth her love.

Liberty does not march for death in mind though the march of death guarantees we the people for liberty justly defend mankind from that standing army and death cult which culls the mind of man for the aim of civilization's end.

   The zombies usurping the world and america demand and expect a false respect insofar as they would desire and form their own rogue government so that we would consider and require the reinterpretation of these failed people as the instruments of our salvation. The overwhelming majority of people on the earth seek a master to minister unto them confabulations demanding the jeopardizing of their own life for it's unzealous end. All of the day these peasant-slaves toil in distractions which obscure their vision in destiny and mould it's purpose into the hands of the evil one; so-to-say, that standing army standing as one wicked being with only one throe. The Queen of England and Her filthy family presently own the standing army enslaving the vastness of minds over the earth. One will know the unthinking peasant from their uneducated world-view, newspaper-programmed life, and animalistic and hostile nature when confronted with self-evident truth.

What else than that massive lattice of slaves forming the substrate of systemic simulations would so respond with such blasphemous hostility toward honest men bearing words of concise articulation and deeds of eternally rhythmic love? The free man does not welcome risk into His life for the salvation of a standing army demanding worship of those false masters clamoring for their mythical gavel of tyranny. The militia keep their character ambitious and joyous in the spirit of the Lord and at any moment welcome the challenge of exercising their liberty in the face of such coercion, cowardice, evil fiefdom, false gods, illusion, violence, and all sorts of wicked monstration accusing our words of violence and interpreting their theft and fraud of the people as too orderly to not commit. The militia lay down their life for their sheep and jeopardize all things for the King of Kings. Even greater an enemy than the self-evident standing army exists that fake countrymen whom argues Christ will defend Himself and we must render our spirit idle and commit no effort in pursuing justice upon the wicked. In Christ we face the battle-field of truth and with our Bible as the omniscient compass and map we possess that amulet of victory giving power unto man to eternally preserve the liberty of mankind.

The peasants whom do act as the walking-dead, zombie-class, of people on this earth cry crocodile tears of joy for the standing armies orchestrating the culling of free humanity. Heavenly things do not concern these false giants obeying Satan therefore His standing armies puppeteer their every whim.

Ezekiel 16:16 And thou didst take thy garments, and deckedst thine high places with divers colors, [a]and playedst the harlot thereupon: the like things shall not come, neither hath any done so.

Footnotes

[a] This declareth how the idolaters put their chief delight in those things, which please the eyes and outward senses.

Genesis 22:14 In the mount will the Lord be seen.

Hebrews 8:5 Who serve unto the pattern and shadow of heavenly things, as Moses was warned by God when he was about to finish the Tabernacle. See, said he, that thou make all things according to the pattern, showed to thee in the mount.

Exodus 26:40 [a]Look therefore that thou make them after their fashion, that was showed thee in the mountain

Endnotes

[a] All must be done according to the pattern.

2 Timothy 1:13 [a]Keep the true pattern of the wholesome words, which thou hast heard of me in faith and love which is in Christ Jesus.

Footnotes

[a] He showeth wherein he ought to be most constant, to wit, both in the doctrine itself, the abridgment whereof is faith and charity, and next in the manner of teaching it, a lively pattern and shape whereof Timothy knew in the Apostle.

Exodus 4:27 and *Exodus 18:5* also speak of, "t*he Mount of God."* The peasant wonders not why standing armies line their streets, war rages about the planet, poverty fills their own home, suffering far below their own poverty of mind, body, and spirit persists, and conclude all of these things as a responsibility under authority, ownership, and resolve of their master whom acts as an oligarch and ancient ruling occult over the world. The zombies remain so far removed from reality either in their lack of knowledge or generations of learned and forced behavior – not even honest money possesses a definition within their mind as their daily business in obtaining bread and water perceivably, in their own minds, demands far more energy than the care of efficiency found in moral economy founded on civil Liberties; therefore, their presenting their character as a thing remotely honest by way of discovering infinite pleasantries in their naivety represents nothing honest or naive; nay, their truth lies in allowing the strengthening of their character's weakest aspects: especially adorning the worldly vanities of theft and fraud as a form of power when such things so obviously have stolen from them their life's truest intention – that life of Godliness and world-changing probabilities insofar as God desires man to live as an avenue for the treading down of the enemies of the cross and not as they live: a brick, fire, lamp, angel of light, mortar, scimitar, sheathe, and wood for the veil and wall of tyranny. The active army of the militia acts as the image of free speaking individuals separating the dark psychic force of tyranny that would participate as a standing army in oppressions over the people. Free humanity will never represent a desire to live in such a state of acrimony for this portending keeps only to it's maker: the destroyer; aye, that builder of standing armies.

The ruling elite imagine all people as their dispenser of additional power; either through conquest, consent, theft, fraud, violence or coercion. Viewing mankind as scanty pittance in exercising their wickedness upon innocents hacks the social order of mankind into bits allowing enough separation of the sane and insane members of society to forge a gap of people so wide the insane move into public office, celebrate the conquering of civilization, and inspire the sane to raise their war flags for the cause of liberty. History shows a long path of blood wherein persons, houses, papers and effects face seizure from a false culture worshiping the virus' of mankind as though they possess a power and knowledge greater than God's revelation or highest potential vision from any potential or vision mankind acquires. The evil inwardly reason the ignorance of the people as their duty to rule over them and accept their own evil as the currency to maintain their social status of self-evidentiary and debaucherous tyranny. Man in praying for God's guidance and being the vehicle to rescue society conforms not to any message counter to the spiritual realm of Jesus Christ's teachings therefore the free man acts as authority, claimant, and the physical messenger bearing the archetype and frequency of the spiritual realm declaring it's absolute authority over all subjects planning mankind's destruction and subsequently demanding said subjects submit unto the obedience of Christ. Education, through free speech, gives man that power to teach a gullible public of the invasion creeping about the foundations of culture and society. Who except a peasant-slave would find the individuals in full defense of their life, liberty, and property wrong? The minor tyrant of apathy and major tyrant of evil command the global standing army to complete the works of death and desolation as a mutual compact to achieve planetary extinction. All across earth exists a black void of standing armies and their oligarchy of tyrants culpable in their opposing that one white Mount of God existing today on the earth as a free and imperfect nation: america and it's philosophers of liberty.

Psalm 19:3 There is no speech nor [a]language, where their voice is not heard.

Footnotes
The heavens are a Schoolmaster to all nations, be they never so barbarous.

Aside from that recognition we possess fervent worship as

illustrated through our action in Christ for the cause of liberty and our Creator, and, the impossibility of removing our rights which our souls sovereignly possess: our tender names will fill the book of life as our fathers had and in similitude we the people inherit the earth and overcome every oppression (we possess that duty and responsibility to destroy that which designs itself to destroy us through our righteous action in justice, peace, and prosperity). Does the foreign colonizer or invader not write the names of His opposition and will our free militia not write the names of ours? Today in San Antonio, Texas our usurpers want to rip down the monument at The Alamo, even my direct father's names (yeah I am a seventh generation Texan at war against the tyranny on our lands, for no reason other than erasing those tender names (at the request of Satanic revisionists), etched in stone, from mankind's history. Contained within the names of those defenders of liberty, and mine own family, exists a story and history of individuals keeping the brushfire and vision of liberty alive and acting out our cause to further inspire the future generations to complete the mission and pursue the founding of mankind's peace and prosperity on that truth in Christ; as no foundation, revelation, or truth exists outside of this original alpha and omega of heavenly human knowledge. Our forefathers kept constant defense for liberty as they moved from one land to another as the invasion of tyranny overwhelmed their lands; though, our revolution for liberty against standing armies persists. Even under the Republic of Rome this Republic did not come near that near-perfect image of what the american Republic represents due to our consistent comprehension, interpretation, and realization of civil Liberties (though we shall not include the idolatrous sinners such as the slave-owner as our representatives though revisionists would enjoy such perversions of historical phenom); nor does any nation on the earth in current historical records represent such near-perfectness toward liberty though many will argue the Sumerians achieved such and perhaps today's liberty movement exists as a horridly fractured, albeit unbroken, revelation of the same revolution as though the information to desire such liberty expresses it's power through our expanding and waning of genetic lineage insofar as our ideas unite and disjoint us ad infinitum.

The usurpers of our salvation rage for a more perfect technology designed to erase liberty from mankind's memory. We hold not only truth as self-evident but as well our fellow countrymen as our most high honor to fight and die for so that our life may live on through the expanse of civilization well beyond our years and present-day understanding; therefore, we fight for our life, liberty, and property, and not for our own countrymen to auction off the meaning of such terms for the limitation of righteousness until it render into sin and not higher orders of righteousness the eye and ear had not yet known. The rulers of this realm invoke all sorts of evil spirits to encourage their tireless work manipulating mankind; including and not limited to false predictions or squelching uprisings through injecting real-world events as a type of stimuli or scenario preceding or fulfilling their planned rituals to secure measurable outcomes or in the least build new potential toward the alteration of public perceptions into their genocidal hands managing the sequence of government administered events either through press or agency; though, all of these things exist as burnt offerings to God as when the free man obeys God He alone possesses that power to set into a motion of increasing momentum and velocity the overthrow of the entirety of such an entourage culminating every spirit devoid of joy. The tyrant seeks the building of His army through standing upon corruptions as law and shutters the door of the individual mind in order to suppress and even silence their influence which would otherwise expose the contradictions compositing the image of the evil ones and strengthen righteousness for God's sake. The ruling elite participate in all sorts of blood sacrifice to focus energy into their rituals with the idea they receive a granting of spiritual permission of the truly wicked kind (though God's righteous punishment for the wicked will far exceed the magnitude of their devices) to coldly and numbly control generations though the controllers condemn their life to hell.

Ultimately only individuals and ideas will persist therefore without ideas mankind will cease to exist. The physical and spiritual right for individuals to not unadvisedly kill, steal, or destroy founds the reason for a society of holy people to seek every form of God dispossessed from violence and coercion. God, met inwardly, connects mankind with the infinite and shuts out the incapable from their false claims of Godhood as their right of ownership over man. The inwardness we seek in knowing God reads plainly in:

1 Corinthians 3:16 [a] Know ye not that ye are the Temple of God, and that the Spirit of God dwelleth in you?

Footnotes

[a] Continuing still in the metaphor of a building, he teacheth us that this ambition is not only vain, but also sacrilegious: For he saith that the Church is as it were the Temple of God, which God hath as it were consecrated unto himself by his Spirit. Then turning himself to these ambitious men: he showeth that they profane the Temple of God, because those vain arts wherein they please themselves so much, are as he teacheth, so many pollutions of the holy doctrine of God, and the purity of the Church. Which wickedness shall not be suffered unpunished.

The Spirit of God manifests for the incarceration of the carnal motions engaged in efforts to kill steal, and destroy mankind; and, herein we find the order and reason for which the universe bends unto the rule of law preserving every form of righteousness.

The Garden of Eden dwells within us all and in this truth we discover the knowing of true energy, frequency, and vibration pursuant to the salvation of our own life, liberty, and property aimed at the cross of cavalry as all people's final destination and only truth toward planetary salvation: yeah, the cavalry is here. The false gods of this world: Theft and Fraud, mirror the minor and major tyrants in society as their microology in theft of physical goods and macroology in fraud of terrible ideas compartmentalize their worship into a flaming hell of double-minded people killing for the reprobate power of envy and greed.

As the individual metaphysically connects one to the other so does our God meet face to face within the each of us in this transfiguration of mankind as God waters those flames of tyranny with the spiritual drowning of those standing armies. Whether the standing army we face acts as an active military of foreign intervention or an unlawful banking institution infiltrating government to commit the acts of death and desolation upon our lands, we possess that power to shift the energy and witness the rotting of the zombies from the head down. What beauty outmatches that which we find in personally meeting God inwardly upon His calling and the multitude of all people of the world meeting our God at once in an instant and upon the whole face of earth?

CENTRAL

BANKS

Teeth is to shark what standing armies is to central banks. The daft will demand proof for proclaiming central banks and standing armies a threat to man or liberty as though history does not illustrate a constant reprimanding of the unbelievers; and, this daft individual even further reckons every society must posit itself ready to adhere to the dictates of a central bank's standing army since the foreign world so readily submits to it's false authority; therefore: "The tradition must persist," although this delimiting of form and knowledge misnomers every form of good and evil for an intention only viewed as good to wicked men. Central banks have succeeded the enshadowing of mankind's trajectory through the labyrinth of it's guarded society which structures it's merit system with followers worshiping chains, collars, enticings of riches, jewelery, paltry riches, riches of iniquity, uncertain riches, uniforms, wicked riches, and ultimately a competition for the untimely reception of a false power which subdues human consciousness for the intentional dimming and dumbing-down of public awareness and subsequent elevation of all things contradictory to a free and open society; and, as an institution – differs from standing armies in that their title relegates authority over the actions which preserve it's purpose; and, chiefly in the maintaining of authority over the standing army for the shedding of the blood of the innocent. The standing army forms the mainstay of the oppressions which flow forth from the central bank as even a continuity of governance (which persists even without public awareness of a central bank) subordinate to that function which only knows to oppress the people and preserve the central bank as though it's common action moved in similitude according to the idolatry of those central banks whom care not who write the laws so long as they deliver the people into the bondage of accepting the central bank as the illusion of God's wrath therefore the spiritually blind reason the central bank as a logical stronghold to accept as good and not evil.

Diversity inspires competition while centralization of economic and foreign power concentrates the domestic economic policy into the hands of fewer individuals; and, especially those contradictory elements which aid the wicked unto the absolute corruptions of reconstituting government as a squadron of mercenaries preserving a central bank for the sole function of obscuring public awareness from that center of origin or marketplace dictating and potentiating the macro order of political perception for the instilling of a chilling-effect or perceived disconnection from the micro or self and society insofar as the central bank in separating their political cause from it's religious effects can not conceal public suffering from that rogue enforcement which restricts the individual's unalienable right to the abundance of self-governance; and, whether these events find meaning for the politicians to use for political gain in the funding of illegal endeavors or to subsist the central banks for the continued puppeteering of civilization through the reshaping of the mass perceptions occurring during the procession of their manufactured crisis – these wicked conductors constantly attempt to sell society on the idea they will provide a solution for the crisis in which they first manufacture; and, any society which does not conform or discern unto such crookedness will then worship these vampires as heroes or veterans of a cause which continually impale the innocent and righteous. Central banks enjoy well to exchange a people's language for a new language which anagrams the thieving of that which will never clause against the judgment of moral linguistics, coerces the people unto hypnosis, and defrauds the knowledge of which articulates a history for the phrasing of moral civilization.

Matthew 21:12 ¶ *And Jesus went into the Temple of God, and cast out all them [d] that sold and bought in the Temple, and overthrew the tables of the moneychangers, and the seats of them that sold doves,*
Matthew 21:12 Endnotes [d] *He casteth out the sellers.*

Consider america's Vietnam war and the fact the war was sold to the american people based on the now admitted lie and declassification of The Gulf of Tonkin – a fictional event distributed to the masses at the same time the central banks exercised the witnessing of this perceived crisis as justification for a mass sacrificial slaughter of the brightest and most bold american youth (though they lack the life experience in recognizing a military-industrial-complex and it's threat to their own liberty), a genocide of Vietnamese citizens, unlawful invasion and occupation of foreign lands, plunder of american society, and the debasement and mockery of human liberty.

Today's american people consistently sacrifice their life on the alter of fraud, join any war as though war represents some type of gladness for ultimately achieving through the embracing of a universal ignorance which fragments their ancestor's accumulated wisdom (until the achieving of a total disorder only an ignoble public could so readily dramatize and not gain knowledge in or act upon when challenged by such multi-faceted evil), blindly assume there exists a ruler which rightly solves such mystery concerning civilization, refuse every opportunity to adhere to the constitution, and even persecute defenders of the constitution with the claim of upholding an intention superior to their oath to a constitution which they so arrogantly and naively perceive as subordinate to their pretended cause; a pretended cause of which arrogantly abandons our founding documents for the hog-wash of a 'greater good' which can only aid the genocide of a free people apt to defend their liberty at every impasse – even in spite of the knowledge which abounds of the vociferous oligarchs around the globe engaging in the profit, quarrel, and portending of world war from their ever-present political carnage stretching the veil of Satanic massé across the world through the various orthodox religions and political tradition of administering oligarchs as means for absolute control of human existence through funding standing armies with central banks.

1 Timothy 4:7 *[a] But cast away profane, and old wives' fables, [b] and exercise thyself unto [c] godliness.*

1 Timothy 4:7 Footnotes

[a] He setteth again true doctrine not only against that false and apostatical doctrine, but also against all vain and curious subtleties.

[b] It is not only requisite that the minister of the word be sound in doctrine, but also that his life be godly and religious.

[c] In the true serving of God.

Consider the success of the lie which sold the Iraq War to the american people: americans and weak-minded people all throughout history have worshiped war as a necessity which easily digests into their psyche through fancy phrasings or a catchy slogan; for example: Weapons of Mass Destruction (WMD) stupidly phrased by the public as "dub-yuh-em-deez." America has not constitutionally declared war since World War II and even this war was succeeded off of the deceptions of a globalist operation designed to destabilize the foreign world and global economy, hinder the ascension of the liberty movement and individual sovereignty, and act as a wind sailing the trajectory of human destiny into the foggy canals of never-ending and at-will constitutional suspension (as though the constitution represents a thing of suspendability and not a perfect law of liberty wherein mankind's words aim for the reception of a total consciousness in God's greater plan).

America remains plagued with that alien force occupying earth primarily as a central bank; and, known today as The Federal Reserve which thieves in contemptuous defiance of constitutionality, happiness, God, liberty, life, man, and reason. America's Founding Fathers warned against central banks and the masses of people keeping distracted with their apathetic worship of man and the state; for whom else could so convict such faithless people than those pithy entrails of government zealots etching away at civilization's foundation as they impart their ill-will onto those people whom abandon their own soul for the submission to a wilt of no soul or will at all?

The american people continue to engage in illegal war with Afghanistan and the wider Middle East for nineteen years now which will only further ignite the brushfire of liberty as the people continue to witness this same system of death suppress language and truth in order to complete it's anti-human mission. The Federal Reserve unlawfully funds today's illegal wars throughout the world and remains chiefly responsible for the perversions feigning as though they represent human liberty or our america Republic.

Deuteronomy 2:14-21 The [a] space also wherein we came from Kadesh Barnea, until we were come over the river Zered, was eight and thirty years, until all the generation of the men of war were wasted out from among the host, as the Lord sware unto them. For indeed the [b] hand of the Lord was against them, to destroy them from among the host, till they were consumed. ¶ So when all the men of war were consumed and dead from among the people: Then the Lord spake unto me, saying, Thou shalt go through Ar the coast of Moab this day: And thou shalt come near over against the children of Ammon: but shalt not lay siege unto them, nor move war against them: for I will not give thee of the land of the children of Ammon any possession: for I have given it unto the children of Lot for a possession. That also was taken for a land [c] of giants: for giants dwelt therein afore time, whom the Ammonites called Zamzummims: A people that was great, and many, and tall, as the Anakims: but the Lord destroyed them before them, and they succeeded them in their inheritance, and dwelt in their stead:

Deuteronomy 2:14-21 Footnotes

[a] He showeth hereby, that as God is true in his promise, so his threatenings are not in vain.

[b] His plague and punishment to destroy all that were twenty years old and above.

[c] Who called themselves Rephaims: that is, preservers, or physicians to heal and reform vice

The issuance of any currency through a central bank will only result in the rallying of wicked men calling for the death of the spirit of the Lord; and, even further, these privately-owned central banks as witnessed today in america through The Federal Reserve system only illustrate a portion of a wider consortium of private share-holders granted legal immunity to commit any crime therefore devoid of accountability from any american citizen or elected representative lest those citizens awaken and overthrow such a stronghold; thus, consequently, the central bank in hooking into the dictates of a foreign power at war with the idea of human liberty elect the image of a bishop as their chief warlord and greater magician exalting their Luciferian god.

Jeremiah 18:18 Then said they, Come, and let us imagine some device against Jeremiah: for the Law [a] shall not perish from the Priest, nor counsel from the wise, nor the word from the Prophet: come, and let us smite him with the [b] tongue, and let us not give heed to any of his words.

Jeremiah 18:18 Footnotes

[a] This argument the wicked have ever used against the servants of God. The Church cannot err: we are the Church, and therefore whosoever speaketh against us, they ought to die, 1 Kings 22:24; Jer. 7:4 and 20:2; Mal. 2:4, and thus the false Church persecuteth the true Church, which standeth not in outward pomp, and in multitude, but is known by the graces of the holy Ghost.

[b] Let us slander him, and accuse him: for we shall be believed.

Jeremiah 20:2 Then Pashhur smote Jeremiah the Prophet, and put him in the [a] stocks that were in the high gate of Benjamin, which was by the house of the Lord.

Jeremiah 20:2 Footnotes

[a] Thus we see that the thing which neither the King, nor the princes, nor the people durst enterprise against the Prophet of God, this Priest as a chief instrument of Satan first attempted, read Jer. 18:18.

1 Kings 22:24 Then Zedekiah the son of Chenaanah came near, and smote Micaiah on the cheek, and said, [2 Chron. 18:23], [a] When went the spirit of the Lord from me, to speak unto thee?

1 Kings 22:24 Footnotes

[a] Thus the wicked would seem that none were in the favor of God, but they, and that God hath given his graces to none so much as to them.

Jeremiah 7:4 Trust not in [a] lying words, saying, The Temple of the Lord, the Temple of the Lord; this is the Temple of the Lord.

Jeremiah 7:4 Footnotes

[a] Believe not the false prophets, which say that for the Temple's sake, and the sacrifices there, the Lord will preserve you, and so nourish you in your sin, and vain confidence.

Malachi 2:4 And ye shall know, that I have [a] sent this commandment unto you, that my covenant, which I made with Levi, might stand, saith the Lord of hosts.

Malachi 2:4 Footnotes

[a] The Priests objected against the Prophet that he could not reprove them, but he must speak against the Priesthood, and the

office established of God by promise, but he showeth that the office is nothing slandered, when these villains and dung are called by their own names.

The silent weapons within deception release public rewards for those individuals possessing destructive capability as though they in their compartmentalization lack the aptitude to identify their own position, reason, or selection in the formation of a standing army performing quiet work for central banks in the graduating stages of subterfuge taking course over the lifetime of generations in order to seize their industry, occupy their lands, steal their property, and declare omniscient victory over mankind as it's builder who sold the world to a carnal and fallen realm of monarchy manipulating individual consciousness out of self-awareness or sentience and dispersed into a slurry of caste systems and usury.

Ezekiel 31:11 *I have therefore delivered him into the hands of the [a] mightiest among the heathen: he shall handle him, for I have cast him away for his wickedness.*
Ezekiel 31:11 Footnotes
[a] That is, of Nebuchadnezzar, who afterward was the monarch and only ruler of the world.

All across america the banks have ravaged our rural communities leaving them seemingly abandoned as townships show an overgrowth of nature and general deterioration of it's architecture, culture, economy, infrastructure, family, and total population. American industry now obeys government's regulatory demands which do represent a sanction thus an act of war against a free people since any semblance of such a government decree stands as a weapon formed against our unalienable constitution for that liberty which dwells as the spirit of the Lord within our physical body and for the exercise of that sword of liberation against Babylon and all other oppressions facing man. A majority of any youth reared in a culture of envy and greed will learn to love the loathing and self-pity found in vanquishing markets and their working for a cartel or government subsidy acting as the economic surplus or alien command center advancing the cause of the military-industrial-complex planning this megalopolis of erasing human liberty from the mind of man.

Today as high as ninety-five percent of individual's net earnings go toward food and rent as property ownership dwindles and all but disappears as millions of americans face homelessness, a nation of only rental dwellings, or the combining of families into ever tightening living quarters though property ownership will partially continue as many homes remain paid-for from past times of economic surplus though the continued excess of regulation and taxation will ensure continuity of state-sponsored theft of all mental, physical, and spiritual assets. Some estimates even claim as high as eighty percent of all annual american income goes directly to the military and not even for defense; this is the american nightmare. The result in all of this shows a growing animosity and avarice toward the mounting of a danger within domestic and foreign culture as a sort of mass-cuckolding of a once free people into the image of what The Federal Reserve aimed for in it's self-evidenced crusade against free enterprise and the rule of law: that spiritual image of an embroiling apathy, gratuitous animus, hissing avarice, and total spiritual surrender. Standing armies force their enslaved population to love the bread and milk of the stomach (whether an abundance or ration; healthy or rotten) above the land of milk and honey which does mean that spirit of the Lord declaring unto the captives our victory for liberty.

The Federal Reserve have now cornered americans into emotional despair causing mass consumption of ready-to-eat-meals, for example the Chinese Communist imports such as toxic powdered milk or semantically manufactured news stinking of bull manure which today supplies american Democrat and Republican political parties with fuel to manipulate the american dream; and, as we the people witness President after President deliver their surplus of promise unto applause – promises which appertain not to the restoration of our near-perfect republic – we witness a reduction of constitutional things, maximization of the unconstitutional, and a people and President given over to the delusion of saving their self from being that representative human reconstituting the near-perfect Republic on an earth devoid of such sublime governance (so to say that liberty which forms a court system to spiritually discern liberty unto it's highest end; and achieving the true foundation for preservation of life and property for the pursuit of happiness – the chief instrument of God's kingdom). No standing army will ever compare to that destructive force of central banks inspiring apathy into the republic insofar as the central bank represents the most alien-in-nature of energies aimed at the eradication of human felicity. Central banks dictate daily decisions through controlling the purchasing power of the currency and as a result alters the horizon of destiny for which the spirit of the Lord within man seeks and future generations know in their heart as the epitome of truth in setting the foundation for all life prior to any social engineering lest even one witness amongst the fallen arise and proclaim the truth of the central banks' conciliatory praxis upon an unthinking public.

The wicked rulers of central banks spend the money of the people and then promise that money against the lives of each citizen. The Federal Reserve exemplify this notion with it's ability to print symbols on paper and label this fraudulent behavior as a creation of money while at the same time promising the members of society their preservation of currency and in effect their life and property. Former Congressman from Texas and Presidential candidate Doctor Ron Paul ran on the platform of abolishing The Federal Reserve system, replacing it with nothing, and restoring america to it's near-perfect Republic status thus gained a global following (also due to His pushing for an end to government-sponsored racism since it is presently the policy of government and not the people that remain the source of racism in america today), notoriety, and renown from tens of millions of self-aware individuals as such ideation when placed into the motions of government office will in the same instance abolish the illegal wars and illustrate the original intent and purpose of human liberty otherwise unseen since those men at america's founding made it known to the world they would bear the fortune and risk as Founders of a great reminder in which free people declare liberty and overthrow this tyrannical world.

The reality today lies in the fact most of the american people, and the foreign world, historically remain unaware of the dangers of central banks except for a fervent and novel few whom have swept the world as a force of liberty and manifest that same image of the eternal human and free people witnessed during the founding of this nation and of whom share in one another's mutual aid and especially from their neural network of knowledge surrounding modern events in conjunction with ancient knowledge which america's founding fathers held a firm reliance upon as fellow discerners of truth. Rumors of President Andrew Jackson suggest He dropped to His knees and wept like an infant with the impression the american dream had died a mere eleven years into it's experimental inception as the perception of central banks recapturing the world through suffocating americans weighed heavily upon His conscience as though said bank razed what was so dearly fought over for centuries upon centuries to only now achieve and then so quickly lose what was narrowly mankind's most recent and substantive proof of a perfect realization of a society in harmony with liberty. One illness of the human condition exists never so prevalent and self-evident than that of acquiescing one's present power and as a result this act of nature acts as an accelerant for the condemning of future generations to pay that curse of a debt whereby sullen individuals failed to oblige their own life with the effort at hand of manifesting a civility, hope, and will for God's blessings.

Joel 1:14-15 Sanctify you a fast: call a solemn assembly: gather the Elders, and all the inhabitants of the land into the house of the Lord your God, and cry unto the Lord, Alas: for the day, for the [a] day of the Lord is at hand, and it cometh as a destruction from the Almighty.

Joel 1:15 Footnotes

[a] We see by these great plagues that utter destruction is at hand.

What greater prophylactic for the present generation against squandering generations of effort, peace, prosperity, and wealth than never allowing central banks or taxation to infiltrate society even under the auspices of good-intention, lawful, moral, necessity, or tradition? Standing armies act as a buffer zone protecting the central banks from the people whom would otherwise take great care, duty, and honor in obtaining and exercising the knowledge of God in order to overthrow the hidden hands plotting civilization's end. Only posterity can pay for unlawful wars since only an ignorant and naive public would decimate their own future without acting as the defense for which they in their delusions call to arms for their own oppression and not liberation (though they speak boldly as though they act). Perhaps some nations find means to pay for their war within the decade though even this event would consume the prosperity of a half of a generation as the world produces a new generation on average every two decades. President Thomas Jefferson firmly understood the knowledge of God in the duty of a revolution every twenty years for reason of atoning for the transgressions of the past generations as they curse the future of humanity with debt and all of it's entrancing enslavements.

Numbers 1:18 And they called all the Congregation together in the first day of the second month, who declared [a] their kindred by their families, and by the houses of their fathers according to the number of their names, from twenty years old and above, man by man.

Numbers 1:18 Footnotes

[a] In showing every man his tribe, and his ancestors.

America's current debt exponentially rises as our unconstitutional central bank and hostile enemy foreign occupier, The Federal Reserve, has sold america to the world for a price numbering in the hundreds of trillions of american dollars when considering the derivatives, or so to say the whole fashion of the literal and numerically indebted figure against the property and wealth for which it stole, or otherwise one half of one quadrillion dollars; and, with americans only earning one trillion dollars per year – this number remains impossible for any amount of people in the world to pay even for the dozens of centuries to follow therefore the only foreseeable outcome will result in the collapse of civilization since the people perish for a lack of knowledge and will continue their debauchery and sin in, through, and beyond the collapse and ruin as though their fantasy and illusion of a superior race of people whom destroy and not preserve liberty will form an amicable solution for anything at all.

President Andrew Jackson killed the central bank of His day; however, political pressure from the ill-informed, vindictive, envious, hateful, and pious elitists and masses drove the public to seek further bondage under the unconstitutional central banking system thereby derailing the future of peace and prosperity of free humanity through the wrecking of their currency's purchasing power which does mean the wrecking of the nation's individual intelligence. Enlightenment challenges the core existence of those purveyors of monetary destruction; though, these destroyers remain keen on controlling the enlightenment through projecting illusions to cull the weak-minded into the keeping of them as an acrid people under the constant duress of hypnotic trance, suggestive thinking, and otherwise under the submission of unequal rights which sanction them as an idle faction opposed to those individuals valuing preservation of property in the face of a battlefield surrounding the landscape of liberty or garden of eden.

"   'TIS THE SEASON OF FUNDING   "

reads the terrible banner upon entering the city. Those inhumane people whom steal from the public abide in a zone of decision-making which gambles their public perception of egoic stoicism against the illusions which they fund though the transparency of such a villainous wherewithal that it create no ordinal substance though they unquestioningly act out their eons of theft-oriented hereditary traits as a disguise of faux pas collectivism or pretended egalitarianism masquerading as contemporary orthodoxy. Only a moral society will comprehend and possess that knowledge of God ensuring the preservation of their life, liberty, and happiness, as the intent of man's creation possesses with it that ancient and sacred place of sanity and holiness combined with the enlightenment and revelation of man's purpose as defending an earth against a present evil which designs injustice against mankind's fulfillment in spiritual happiness.

The idea any government ever possesses interest, and not hostility, for charity remains one of the single greatest religious superstitions. Coercion, fraud, violence, and theft will always represent the only things government and it's banners will freely issue or perform in direct proportion to the number of their body of people acting as their church of worship which does merge as one mind and will go to war in order to not separate church from the state thus they in their idolatry do deliberately and publicly charge their fellow countrymen with the task of extincting mankind in the name of funding; albeit, most particularly, in their chief religion of Satanism disguised as their pseudo-science of Eugenics which guards it's subordinate elements within the philosophy and sciences and starting at the public universities; and, of whom now more closely relate to the like-image of police-state indoctrination or communist reeducation ("Rheeee-

Education.") centers than higher learning institutions. The belief in money or people receiving value from debt solves nothing and only satiates a primal discontent for living a carnal life knelt at the altar of death. Funding of any economic activity starts with the effort of the individual and can only continue with individuals trading with one another in private contract without any government intervention provided no violence or coercion exists lest that individual vote with their money a rogue government promising the funding of their security when this rogue and alien entity will only fund their own genocide; consider the neo-conservative idea in america that a government can "Bail Out" the banks as though all individuals in society deserve the theft of their funds for some illusory shared responsibility in preserving from failure the power-hungry psychopaths in the banking and government institutions – the same individuals whom manufacture the failure simultaneously receive the plunder from the nation or any additional resources from the consolidation of nation-states obtained during their conquest or consent of submissive peasants.

Untold amounts of wealth remain stolen from the american people without the american people ever voting on the matter therefore self-evidenced as a people hostage to an alien faction occupying their own government; and, this false funding through the mass underwriting of a theft fraudulently redefined as taxation or national security, under ordered threat of violence from the wicked individuals in government and their excuse-makers often referred to as fellow countrymen (though they vote for the intervention of liberty therefore a dissolution for liberty's whole fashion thereof), forces an imbalance in the harmonies of man and woman thus widespread confusion flows forth from man into the family and finally into the world as the decision-making process of civilization, and otherwise a general assembly of universal disorder, erupts into economic and foreign chaos from those worldlings aiding the widening of this gap of corruption for their own Satanic pleasures concerning each day's flow of pomp and vanity. The preservation of bad ideas and economic business failings suppresses morality and alters culture into a Stockholm's Syndrome of worshiping criminals as authority and central banks as the vital source or origin of intelligence for the agency named funding so as to imply it's purpose as a funding of what society abhors in the definition, label, name, or statute of security hence there exists no funding of anything secure for the members of society when those members turn their back on both God and His knowledge and most particularly concerning these items in relation to their court systems and individual agency, authority, civility, morality, power, and sovereignty. The agency named funding which forks into all of the various corruptions of the central bank, intelligence agency, and standing army keep their guard well stocked with dung trained as their royal knights to obey and then ignore the rule of law as though God Himself will not consume their head with the breaking forth of the Heavens as an heap of coal. These oppressors in their Satanic wherewithal claim not equal rights and in this opposition form into a type of intelligence which binds as though it formed allegiance with that which must fund itself off of the theft of the public therefore it's agency must receive authority from public support for the name of funding in order to more capriciously thieve through various delineations such as capital gains tax, federal tax, fee, fine, foe, property tax, regulation, state tax, taxation – any excuse to supply or trick an apathetic public into keeping idle with the payloads of "good reason" which, through little convincing, cause them to surrender their spirit and rights to wicked men devising outwardly appearing sophistications of intentionally spiritual transgression. The only entity providing the illusion of a physical barrier to preserve the central banks from being thrown into the deep as shark chum exists in their standing armies and multitudes of gibbering clowns barking their marching orders at an impish general public. These entities act as a buffer-zone in a constant strife for the analyzing and tracing of an image which outlines their perceived enemy in order for this occupying force to subvert the people of the nation and their government before instructing their rogue legislators to persecute and prosecute upon every form of inconceivable insanity as they label the defender of liberty with a scarlet-letter and drag them before a Salem-like witch trial as though mankind had not learned well from the implications of a world of facts without evidence or persecution unto the abandonment of due process which only the tyrant can celebrate.

Central banks in their demanding the funding of every known thing appertaining to the blood-letting of civilization fail to comprehend the budding of liberty unto each dawn and according to it's creative forces imbibing life with an amulet of harmony.

Government stealing from the economy and funding additional theft in society represents a crime and predatory behavior which the people must peacefully find objection in or refuse even by the force of their own mutual aid in the event that the beast shall arise against their faith. The unique scenario of two lives meeting and even uniting supposes the answer to economic gain as that property whose consciousness the minutes belong and the intelligence in which purchased liberty in said form in the first place insofar as discernment begets the decision-making which forms a new world insofar as tyranny resurrects that old tomb of doomed and fallen spirits and can never represent creation, life, new, or unique. Today's brainwashed masses, and presumably the same type of hollow people of the past and the future to follow, chalk up the common sense phrase: "Sticks and stones may break my bones but words will never hurt me." tantamount to that of a thought-crime labeled *Hate Speech* or *Hate Crime* as even their fervent proclamation of <u>Free Speech</u> as a crime and not a natural right showcases the platitude without foundation from which they espouse nothing particularly concrete therefore left to the open interpretation of those they hypnotize upon any carnal supposition ending only with martial or temporal authority over their lives as a solution for government though it disjoint government and society in part and therefore disparage life on the earth in whole.

Proverbs 12:12 *The wicked desireth the [a] net of evils: but the [a] root of the righteous giveth fruit.*
Proverbs 12:12 Footnotes

[a] Continually imagineth means how to do harm to others.

[b] Meaning, their heart within, which is upright, and doeth good to all.

One of today's main tenants in controlling human thought through subliminal and direct hypnosis derives out of the persistent lie of the use of speech as not an argument for a defensible civil liberty and instead anyone at anytime can assume authority to label any individual's speech as a crime under the pseudonym of "hate speech;" therefore, the false logic follows:

"Society must fund theft, plunder the individual, abandon the idea of a republic in it's entirety, and coerce the public into relinquishing the whole of morality found in civil liberty for the immorality of democratic socialism or any other form of despotism which feed the beast and maintain hostility toward the <u>*idea*</u> *of liberty;"*

– common tactics for securing absolute conquest or consent. Clearly the rule of law was outlined long ago and the success of any perturbations misconstruing that perfect law of liberty results in the popularization of an ignorance and superstition which grows in greater succession every generation as the orating hypnotizers of force, lies, monopoly control, violence, and war propaganda enlarge the scope of their historical relevance and use this falsehood as justification for more actions of evil.

Society like all forms of life must mature into the future or as one shall say – mature the human experience from one of barbarity into one of electable harmony. Funding conquest with destruction of prosperity and future generations illustrates the whithering of the vine of mankind. Since individuals institute government then the individual possesses final authority and governance over any people that would seek the redefining of the social hierarchy of mankind for which God intends especially for the prevention of any self-elected tyrant permitting any sum of men the right to thieve and especially knowing the future generations remain keen to fight unto death against such open and self-evidenced blasphemy. What can remain for the swindler of society when His legislators (whom the citizens institute) destroy any opportunity to exercise liberty especially His own for we know in the absence of society He will have nothing to govern except the observation of His own ruin?

Numbers 15:22 And if ye [a] have erred, and not observed all these commandments, which the Lord hath spoken unto Moses,
Numbers 15:22 Footnotes
[a] As by oversight or ignorance, read Lev. 4:2, 13.

Leviticus 4:2 Speak unto the children of Israel, saying, If [a] any shall sin through [b] ignorance, in any of the commandments of the Lord, (which ought not to be done) but shall do contrary to any of them,
Leviticus 4:2 Footnotes
[a] Hebrew, a soul.

[b] That is, of negligence or ignorance, specially in the ceremonial law: for otherwise the punishment for crime [is] appointed according to the transgression, Num. 15:22.

Leviticus 4:13 ¶ *And if the [a] whole Congregation of Israel shall sin through ignorance, and the thing be hid from the eyes of the multitude, and have done against any of the commandments of the Lord which should not be done, and have offended:*
Leviticus 4:13 Footnotes
[a] The multitude excuseth not the sin, but if all have sinned, they must all be punished.

Whether sought in intention or unsought in ignorance – any man that would aid or abet a central bank trades His peace and prosperity for the death of His spirit since no man can act the part of a dragon's tail without first consuming His own head. No individual can multiply wealth via a printing machine, digital alteration, or corrupt record-keeping without committing the high crime of fraud (doing-business-as for central banks) since this type of theft devalues a currency which individuals rightly possess as a type of property. The most insidious criminal aims to dwindle the power of the people through circumventing the rule of law and writing human statutes to claim authority over men and their property to justify all future theft unto the state through the fraud of false legalese such as adjustable rate loans, debt, expansion, today especially – fractional reserve banking, lending, quantitative easing and all of these things the criminals in central banks and their proxies name for use as leverage unto the sin and justification for the exercising of absolutely unjust authority over man. The power for which the individual conspires under when operating under the guise of government breeds a danger upon the public so foreign in nature and domestic in opposition to our tranquility that the only limit for which it seeks dwindles liberty and minimizes opportunity unto economic suffocation upon the whole public which then enables a template for a multitude to absolutely plunder the remaining public largess.

" *I WILL STEAL FROM THEE TO ASSIST THEE!* "

exclaims the politician as they print ever more useless currency notes until the value reaches oblivion and the people forget the ways of their ancients and ancestors and instead of choosing self-governance in cooperation with one another for the mutual defense of their life, liberty, and property – they then beg for the carnivorous robbing of their own perceptions for the ignorant blasphemes of a superstition advertising politicians as resolve for matters of the heart, otherwise known as individual economy, though these politicians infringe on individual liberty thus tempt God to send them to the bottom of the tempestuous sea of liberty lest they seek their own liberty from sin.

A rogue legislature guarantees the swindling of a society's future and the absolute control of it's economic forces which individuals previously governed under their power of good which through their acquiescence then manifest an evil as though it were a lamp at the feet of man and instead of lighting their path this force turns life into ash.

Judges 9:15 And the bramble said unto the trees, If ye will indeed anoint me king over you, come, and put your trust under my shadow: and if not, the [a] fire shall come out of the bramble, and consume the Cedars of Lebanon.

Judges 9:15 Footnotes

[a] Abimelech shall destroy the nobles of Shechem.

Judge 9:1-6 Then Abimelech the son of Jerubbaal went to Shechem unto his mother's brethren, and communed with them, and with all the family, and house of his mother's father, saying, Say, I pray you, in the audience of all the men of Shechem, Whether is better for you, that all the sons of Jerubbaal, which are seventy persons, reign over you, either that one reign over you? Remember also, that I am your bone, and your flesh. Then his mother's brethren spake of him in the audience of all the men of Shechem, all these words: and their hearts were moved to follow Abimelech: for said they, He is our brother. And they gave him seventy pieces of silver out of the house of Baal-Berith, wherewith Abimelech hired [a] vain and light fellows which followed him. And he went unto his father's house at Ophrah, and [b] slew his brethren, the sons of Jerubbaal, about seventy persons upon one stone: yet Jotham the youngest son of Jerubbaal was left: for he hid himself.

Judges 9:4 Footnotes

[a] Or, idle fellows and vagabonds.

Judges 9:5 Footnotes

[b] Thus tyrants to establish their usurped power, spare not the innocent blood, 2 Kings 10:7; 2 Chron. 21:4.

The moral and selfless society cares particularly about promoting honest means of communication, currency, and privacy while dishonesty empowers foreign occupation; hence making self-evident it's allegiance to a cabal; cartel; central bank; network of secretive intelligence agency; occult; and, shadow-governance. Most often the foreign nation faces the same dilemma as the domestic nation in that the passivity of the people in the greater nation (greater in influence and power) instills a chilling effect throughout all of the nations in the world and creates a most ignorant, gloomy, and superstitious age.

The foreign world committing to the business of the fraudulent central banking oligarchs form the global mass which dwindles the future of mankind whereby the healthy competition of a free market at the national level and consequently global level dissolves citizenship and transfers government into a machine of funding genocide under the false flag of security. The central banks determine when a standing army animates into an active army of proxy cells forming the illusion of physical and political competition as though a domestic and foreign military earnestly sought attack or defense against one another when in reality the central banks fund proxies to keep war as a type of business racket which over time consolidates power into the hands of fewer individuals or entities whom mind not the sacrificing of an ignorant youth as pawns in a war though these youth foolishly believe the superficial afflictions demand their affections and allegiance to the falsity of defending freedom or security which as a flag was and never will manifest liberty since this scenario can only perform as the machine, system, or veil in which the apathetic, idle, and ignorant worship for vain recognitions; and, all of the while the defenders of liberty discern and know war profiteering reduces civil liberty and enslaves the mind of man even unto the eventual genocide of mankind.

Jeremiah 27:11 But the nation that put their necks under the yoke of the king of Babel, and serve him, those will I let remain still in their own land, saith the Lord, and they shall occupy it, and dwell therein.

The central banks receive power from a blind people as though this bank arrived at a pivotal time in history to stand over the people as a chosen god determining life and death in a sadomasochistic adherence to a philosophy of apartheid as though it did not symbolize a swarm of demons descending from a cobalt castle for the colonization of free humanity. Permanent occupation, palaces, strongholds gone rogue from liberty, forced interbreeding, and genocide exude the foreign world in opposition to liberty and the founding of america in that the original americans voluntarily united for human liberty as one people of one mind against tyranny and it's corporations over the mind of man while those whom sought government power chose out this office for nefarious reason though the naive and historically ignorant today believe all americans past, present, and presumably future americans were complicit in a systematic genocide of native people when only a fraction of people, primarily the latent government and it's hired mercenaries, and namely those international and hereditary financiers with charge of the central banks fund the business of murder with the aid of their ignorant and superstitious men salivating like insatiably fattened and starving dogs competing for fashion-designer costumes with shiny trinkets engraved with false virtue and symbols and all of it's vacuous titles consuming useful idiots with the feckless color of law, desire of money, drama, idleness, posturing, and drunken power.

As long as time exists there exists a state of mind and from this state of mind flows the many perceptions of man and especially in cooperation with He and His fellow countryman's state of economy. America's Founders had exceedingly mighty comprehension and understanding of every issue and topic surrounding paper money. Not only had they studied the ancient and true philosophies but as well had witnessed in their own life-experience either through current events or historical reference the effects of paper money on their state and the known history of it's affects and origin. Paper money will only ever perform the task for which it was designed to do and namely act as a promise. True: the belief in paper money establishes value; however, the belief in a paper without a backing for it's value endangers the people to the diminishing of an era of mankind in the most and the currency's perceived value until total economic collapse in the least. The danger of money always rapidly changes human history and especially today with the advent of computerization and digital money threatening to simply alter numbers on a globally shared spreadsheet so as to plunder the global economy and vaporize via nuclear armaments or particle-beams upon any righteous uprising in second's time.

Paper money, or any other form of promissory note, will only ever represent a monopoly or lottery with the end result of corruption, destruction, instability, and uncertainty. Whether the citizen or the citizen in government creates the paper money the end result will contemplate and then execute widespread destruction at every imaginable scale of injunction as we know only the individual trade matters in respect to no theft or violence, fraud or coercion; therefore, the only true form of decentralization exists in returning that true power of liberty to the individual and not formulating excuses for a government eternally determining what form of money best meets their agenda ad infinitum. Proponents of paper money will always argue for the necessity of a future wherein a utopia gains absolute excellence above all measure from the use of government-enforced currency trade and money control when in fact this national curse of society-wide debt extends the range in which these entities fuel time with their encompassing plans of misplaced trusts widening their scope of influence into a culturally popular state-of-mind or otherwise a self-fulfilling prophesy of the most colossally dangerous virtues upon mankind's existence.

Our lack of real and honest money such as Gold and Silver will ensure society an embargo of it's education and monetary systems thus testing the knowledge and ignorance of adversity or wishful thinking as the great revelation exists in the fact whatever job or duty for which men occupy in any industry of exchange eternally feeds their spirit or stomach for a season or lifetime; and, therefore exists rather as a design cultivating their human experience either unto the usurpation of their true potential power under the spirit of the Lord – or men wittingly endowing their lives with such power to joyously overthrow the oligarchs as mankind accelerates into God's greater plan of using central banks as an historical example of what mankind must perfectly hate in order to alter truly the scope of society unto the shifting or razing of civilization based on the merit of discarding or preserving the inevitable human action and memory of a society in eternal defense for human liberty.

Gold and Silver out-compete all other forms of currency in it's perfect distribution of value from the industrial to the individual scale as one in liberty comes to know Gold and Silver maintains it's value from the highest scale of economy in it's industrial use as a choice material suited for many fine purposes both in the manufacture of goods and in it's ability to accurately out-compete and justly weight every account held within the most central of banks and thusly decentralize all stagnant pools of power and influence in civilization through the sheer flow of abundance from which our cosmos so readily supply when we do not acquiesce our liberty and especially through the abstaining from those gradual shiftings of minor resources which entrench the oligopoly, Babylon, or the king of Babel through every trade of fiat currency. The pseudo-intellectuals in their failing to comprehend reality argue for a mankind wherein mankind renders money unlawful though money be a commodity; for example, even Silver contains properties to render water potable or even eliminate disease of the body and extend one's age as a result. The ascension of the human race in it's pursuit for happiness through the exploration of the cosmos and the uncovering of a global and intergalactic agrarian society operating as a voluntary association of peace and prosperity with the living creator of the universe in which we trust most and ensure guidance from within it's power and through our elected representatives whom we provision in the keeping of these servants subordinate to our own authority and directive maintains the order and civility required to keep plain and powerless the potential despots bleeding the purity of civil intention.

The culture applauding digitized currency or robotic automation spans the globe and what these infidels patently do not comprehend remains self-evident in the resultant dystopic future of these digitized bits of fabricated currency or information controlling the function and use of everyday human life via enforcement of rogue law from that individual whom games the system for the seizing control of all forms of industry and government unto the monitoring of all human behavior and thought. The aim of individuals using computers for false governance will see an enforcement of their rogue law via a robotically automated military with instant teleportation access via stargates egressing and traversing every realm. The apparitious oligarchs acting as the face of the central banks and the shadowy figurines puppeteering their endeavours aim for a future, or present-day, wherein the mere mention of a mankind in sovereign relation and thought within the whole of our being as a form or image of love of, for, and by one another will illicit from the standing army posing in mankind's place a hissing as though such liberation of thought crystallized the essence of heresy against the state and otherwise colloquial myths slated for elimination from the mouths of the perceived heathen class whom otherwise, in this case, do represent the individuals with morality of liberty and knowledge of tyranny and those enlightened states of not fearing or worshiping man. The lore of the state will continue as it always had in it's false grandeur and sure road of converting the use of technology into wicked means.

Most human beings on the earth today still do not have regular computer access or any at all nor the means to possess or devote time to such a device; and, like the fish in the coral reef viewing their natural aquarium as the whole of the world containing all known waters so goes the blind individual of apathy in the midst of a fallen world. The apathetic individual, incapable of concretely, earnestly, and steadfastly articulating a moral, political, or religious position or reproach drone on about the nature of knowledge and truth as a thing of impossibility, obsolescence, professional suicide, or otherwise too load-bearing of time's present constraints to pursue in feeling or thought and will instead writhe in outwardly unprovoked aggressions, self-pity, or karmic loathing of the time they knew in their heart would ease their life into the imagination of God's chosen plan acting through man as the arrow for which God's vision engulfs the trouble which choosingly abstract His omniscient design. Today such a stigma upon Gold and Silver exists and it has come to my attention to address the present-day with the idea of this debate as a thing of pernicious peculiarity which must come to pass in it's question and answering before the whole of public from our past and into our future; and, therefore this grievance will likely persist in the future and the stigma surrounding money for which it forms will in the end dispel into a formless state of childish or sinful mockings as it's existence permeating culture as a stronghold or absolute moral human virtue above true forms of currency and not the duplication of money which moral society banishes (as though value were a thing government administered when only fruitful labor and effort from a free people freely determine and retain the value which unalienable rights increase in their ordaining by God as a currency obtained in the time of trading one's talents for the means of happiness which the people and not their government pursue) for what can men produce when the wicked slay the thinking man in order to prevent men from receiving the tools of ability which aid mankind's artistical linguistics and spiritual ascension to the higher realms of discernment; rather, the wicked reward fallen men for their squalor, trite pursuits, and the litany of proceeding ambisense. The debate surrounding paper money ought to center around what necessarily represents fiat currency and honest money; and, in truth – the people institute government therefore this hired group of citizens working their institutional job of government possess no constitutional authority to legislate money or trade and any ignorant or superstitious individual duped during whatsoever trade must not blame all of society nor must all of society receive the punishment of government violence or otherwise restriction of civil liberty for the failings of the idiot demanding a resolution for their pompous ignorance as flagrant government violence for those paper tigers which He imagines therefore does not grant Him the freedom to infringe on the civil liberties of all members of society through the seizing of control of the government of those individuals whom aim to keep free. God layers all things therefore the central banks in their constant manipulation of the economy must deliberately misinterpret language and especially man's articulation of currency and money in order to convince a naive people that paper money suddenly obtained a novel and virtuous resolve for their present suffering. The layers underneath the perceptible weights and systems governing the economy favor intelligent creation and not political ghettos of the mind overpowering a minority from the seat of wicked political groups whom constantly shift popular culture and national narratives into central banking schemes acting as a permanent and absolute power structure asundering mankind unto the governance of it's festoonery. Nothing physical or spiritual will ever alter the intention or scope of the central bank in it's function of working against the liberty of the people though it grandstand as the savior of the people in hopes of trapping mankind into an incomplete world of oligarchs raising people like jungle fowl, robbing their nest, and then dispensing every spiritual suppressant to continue this age of shadowing consciousness.

The act of commerce starts and completes with communication therefore communication, even the rule of law, must come to a perceived ruin in order for the central bank to enflame the spirit of commerce with a spoil which at it's end only diminishes capital – so to say civility, community leadership, culture, individual property ownership, industry, true higher education, family planning, marriage, mental health, and morality disappear at a rate which matches the inflation of the fiat currency or money supply. God gave man the eternal right for trade of His goods and services. Individuals within their capacity of time form a majority within an industry, for example: the herbalist or smith, and when these individuals trade their time or wares then this multitude when judgmentally observed appears as several different types of industry aiding in one another's peace and prosperity and in this duty of the people there garners a true influence of the holy ghost which paints with all colors for the creation of the whole portrait of God's vision upon the economy which sets an easel to build upon as our framework of society in the tracing of God's kingdom manifestly in this life.

Does every member of society not require one or more individuals to perform tasks which facilitate the success of their own trade? As President George Washington taught: all jobs within the republic represent an equally high duty for the defense of liberty, meaning even in the criminalization of our rule of law then going against such lawlessness represents remaining within the republic, since all people possess their civil liberties and form the final authority in their right to a militia for our mutual defense against tyranny.

Deuteronomy 7:9 *That thou mayest know, [a] that the Lord thy God, he is God, the faithful God, which keepeth covenant and mercy unto them that love him and keep his commandments, even to a thousand generations,*

Deuteronomy 7:9 Footnotes

[a] And so put difference between him and idols.

Deuteronomy 7:10 *And rewardeth [a] them to their face that hate him, to bring them to destruction: he will not defer to reward him that hateth him, to his face.*

Deuteronomy 7:10 Footnotes

[a] Meaning, manifestly, or in this life.

Consider all of the public's combined assets equal to the value of one monetary unit. Suppose a hidden faction duplicates the money supply and then injects this additional monetary unit into public circulation. Does the public in the same instant not possess a currency note worth half of it's original value; and, would the continued belief of their currency as equal in value to the original purchasing power eventually fail to mitigate the effects of this monetary inflation; and, would the people not justly lose faith in this money as an accurate and honest means of valuing trade?

Why then must any people demand the farmer to trade His labor unto the insufferable dictates of a monetary system for which He reserves the independent right to declare null and void? Even further why would any population ruin their economy as though their own luck was second to the success of their servants hired to operate government? Will society in not pursuing justice for the plunder of their economy not suffer their own denigration, oppression, or exile? Therefore the ruin of the economy from paper money lies in the fact the envious and the hateful at their wit's end gamble paper money based on a masochistic valuation of the innocent lives for which they prey upon thus ruin their destiny in seeking the acceptance of a sacrilegious premonition to join with them and the central spider at odds with reason.

Media and entertainment, the new phrase for bread and circus, illustrates the simple method of obtaining absolute power over a blind population whom trades destiny for paper money. Government enforcement of money walls off the public from their establishing a higher harmony of economics without the pretended aid of evil rulers promising a more calm resolve for the life of the common citizen. Popular opinion in america today claims the value of one american dollar prior to the creation of The Federal Reserve as worth as many as five thousand of today's dollars; and, looking around at the abject poverty, abundant ignorance, civil unrest, gratuitous loss of attention span, focus, intelligence, and memory capacity throughout this nation – one must come to know this type of lore as that type of knowledge particularly holding water. The central bankers have swapped american coins, once minted in Gold, Silver, and Copper, with nickel, tin, aluminum, and other trash metals even further depicting the madness of central bankers and what madness they wish the population to worship for a manufactured world of artificially and not authentically intelligent or moral society since that society which accepts such debasement of truth will only exercise hostility against those whom speak the whole truth and nothing but the truth. The promise of the central bankers ensuring total economic preservation acts as a debt unto itself for future generations to pay through the swapping of knowledge with insolent hypocrisy and civil ruin.

Zephaniah 1:3 I will destroy man and beast: I will destroy the [a] fowls of the heaven, and the fishes of the sea, and ruins shall be to the wicked, and I will cut off man from off the land, saith the Lord.

Zephaniah 1:3 Footnotes

[a] Not that God was angry with these dumb creatures, but because man was so wicked for whose cause they were created, God maketh them to take part of the punishments with him.

The only sense to make of these individuals lies in the fact they rest their laurels upon remaining the enemies of liberty and progenitors of every destructive force against the preservation of mankind's liberty as we know these tyrants would partially preserve mankind and not liberty for their own wretched torments. Every angle concerning the argument of the tyrant designs itself around distorting and misinterpreting the spirit of the individual into acknowledging and accepting the ruin of their own salvation. Many individuals will oafishly argue the central banks do not effect their own personal economy and ignoring one's fellow countrymen being ruled by evil men exists as a delicacy of the most refined tastes in art and philosophy. When considering the encroachment of civil liberty as a ruin upon all things, especially that man fainting under the pressure of a lack of self-awareness, discipline, and the all-encompassing self-evidence which illustrates the precedent of publicly ostracizing those good men whom prophesy society through the witnessing of signs and wonders, then we must firmly know Jesus Christ in whipping the moneychangers so forewarned the people in the present and future of that origin of the business cycle and it's effects and also why men must particularly obsess the futurity of mankind with an abstaining from the affects of the moneychangers.

The idea of society automatically creates an aura of a civility and honesty devoid of individuals granted authority or supposed legal immunity to thieve and defraud; especially, that unalienable and God-given right to the civility and honesty of free association, defense, preservation, property, speech, and worship. All things fall into order beyond this for do humans not desire a certain type of homeostasis as do the ripples upon a pond or even the ocean when showing a time of calmness but how must anything on the earth ever go without chaos or it's illusion of stillness and must the water always move in a reaction with or without the water's knowledge insofar as it's action represents the unfolding of it's enfolded intelligence thus it's original intent or action keeps so far removed from the original inquiry that the succession of a series of tactics can create a circuit of connected series and even a structure of lapsing circuits which will over time illustrate the first of motions which we find evident in one's intention and resultant product or strategic aligning of the particular inquiry in question postulating it's transfer or vector of energy from an origin of position to an observable displacement. Honesty contains it's own energy spectrum ranging from the coldly dishonest to the hotly honest and of course those lukewarm individuals whom ignorantly portray honesty though they lie as often as possible as though deception were a thing of desirable mastery. Central banks oppressing honest men collide mankind into an ancient battle over whether our eternal purpose and pursuit for a more perfect union in liberty meant more to mankind's preservation than worshiping comrades, dung, destroyers, necromancers, sentinels, sorcerers, templars, and villains.

The tide of wealth accumulated by the central banks will render so disproportionate the perceived balance of power in society that only the most disingenuous and wealthy will fit the design of the structure delivering the flow of power toward the image of those individuals whom will only obey the system and enforce the extermination of civil liberties. Dishonesty forms a gait for which evil will seize for it's migration into the physical realm and from this corruption sets mankind into a realm unrecognizable to His spirit or total spiritual consciousness in this life.

Plants and animals throughout the world display honesty as a result of their environment demanding they express their genes for the adaption of living within a larger design expressing it's design of limitations or resistance upon their life and liberty; for example, abundance or famine; light or dark; dry or wet; optimal or inhabitable. Human beings face the same challenge in their environment constantly changing thus demand their energy pursue the acquiring of supplemental intelligence in order to sustain society from those allegiances formed around the subterfuge of dishonesty and pretended patriotism.

The honest pursue the arts with liberty as their foundation and in so doing illustrate the knowledge of God for all to take heed in it's effect even when that mind producing the art so often lives a life of solitude thus a natural social camouflaging of one's message into an animation of life possessing every quality of the arts and sciences in order to deprogram the minds of the masses held captive within the system; and, especially those individuals with a clearly spiritual audibility in their soul screaming for their body to break free from the matrices of babylon and delineate as an animation of brilliancy in a motion incontrovertibly joined with righteousness; so to say their eyes and ears seek not the absolutes of ruin thus pursue happiness in a way which forms a secure route around the widened pit of desolation. The majority of society tends toward honesty so long as things perceivably and honestly relate to the filling of their stomach with abomination and mockery which to them tastes of fatness and sweetness; however, this majority most often falls into apathy and inadequacy concerning the principalities and spiritual strongholds inspiring the exercising of it's corruptive influence toward mankind's disunity. Does oppression not go hidden, albeit self-evident, when the printing of money diminishes the quality of life from one generation to the next and does this fate not tie in man from His most ancient ancestors to modern countrymen and future progeny? What happens when the people allow the advance of oppression but a silence moving as a veil to gag, imprison, or eliminate it's opposition; especially, and chiefly the youth? What sane man could find security in allowing the wicked access to His society? The divergent stronghold killing the faithful via funding from oligarchs man their central bank as though it were their divinity, dynasty, flag, monarch, nation, outpost, province, or sovereignty within the perfect law of liberty. How much oppression then could make way under the physical dictates of an economy trading with honest money via their honest deed and word if no man under any statute or title were granted authority to steal even under the pseudonym of taxation? The only authentic form of consciousness exists in the honest man and His willingness to defend trade for the preservation of His society in the face of the dark hearts of mankind breaching our plane of existence as though they were a fleet of aliens spewing fire from an interdimensional gait as though this gait were the dawning of a new horizon spilling bloodlust instead of light of heaven upon the land. Men in liberty must cultivate all things to subvert tyrants and strengthen each generation forevermore.

Individuals throughout history have referenced currency as a specie and when interpreting the language literally – currency then reveals it's unique capability of keeping an adaptive and constant purpose. Monopoly of a currency, more rightly known as fiat currency, guarantees an occultic system of doors and windows to open and close passageways in the economy and disappear the honest to then provoke and unearth every form of undead into our present realm for the vanquishing of what mankind cherishes as life. This fiat currency then acts as a magnet or gravitational antimatter attracting the forces of evil and amassing it's energy into a thing of expanding and contracting density of which the world and it's vain religions welcome with open séance and sacrificing of innocent life unto their graven idols. One can think of that society with a fiat specie or fiat currency as a society of magnates and mirrors wherein everywhere fiat currency appears one can equally witness the dehumanization of the honest and the incarceration of good men into it's injustices lest they rebel in order to return mankind unto it's true intention: living for the liberty to appeal unto God and not the fear of man. The agrarian society does not concern itself with opening the doors of perception past the scope of it's original intent insofar as preserving life, liberty, and property in society for the eternal happiness of peace and prosperity does not require victimizing society with taxation by force and it's subsequent subversional agency.

The central bank founds their institution on the mastery of theft and fund fraud through the printing of their fiat currency. Printing money forms layers of compartmentalization as the dispersing of it's effects act as nodes upon a hub which complements this closed system with the temporal ability to abuse the rule of law and enable an attrition or sanction upon the exercise of liberty. The illusory names of royalty will always accompany ownership of the central banks or it's pseudonym of shareholding since those families or cartels remain keen on divorcing mankind from the reality of their own individual sovereignty thus wage war on common sense and it's simplistic husbandry eternally forged with the creator of the universe. Mankind when keeping the memory of it's history alive preserves the intent and purpose of the effects which aim to destroy their windows of free opportunity with illusory babel such as royalty and in the guarding of the knowledge of our ancients and of God we as mankind preserve and stimulate the collective imagination and intelligence which boosts the signal density and power frequency of society's intelligent communication and individual spiritual response of expanding the scope of civilization's systems which naturally thwart the enemy of liberty. The vampire must receive permission from the individual to gain access inside the dwelling and the entity which naturally juxtaposes against mankind operates in the same like-fashion of the vampire: preying on the ignorant and exploiting the superstitious to erect central banks and defend their standing armies for the oppression of the youth and old in the name of necessity or security. The power structure which casts the symbol of it's all-seeing-eye as a finely architectured central bank affords itself the illusory luxury of sin through opening spiritual doors for those whom will obey and enlarge the influence of it's confined structure insofar as it's evil keeps an impurity which can not expand past the scope of what God so quickly destroys thus the central bank breed devils whom tempt God and though named or unnamed – those individuals pursuing entry into such doors or windows of perception do inwardly receive the possession of an alien or evil entity within their physical body and spiritual psyche as though they killed their living spirit and now walk as an image or like-form of a being which diffuses or shifts the shape of incoming light through the auric field of it's empty darkness such that their countenance or spiritual nature reflects in one's imagination that shifting image of a specie separate from the human race; therefore intransitively alien, and, not only do these doors and windows of perception open for the invitation of evil upon mankind – the invitation for every form of specie alien to man arises, interdimensional and otherwise, in combination with the church of the antichrist and it's pattern forming a stumbling beast to not marvel; and, we must then root out the minions of magical windows carving their egoic shape which match the materialization or recruitment requirements of the power structure whom particularly revel in the acquiring of truly stupid individuals since only the wicked remain stupid truly, and no cross-examination will prove another absolute of higher comprehension or discernment of this most alien, idle, and weak enemy whom so readily increases the frequency of disrupting the occurrences of peaceful and prosperous society for the hope of extinguishing the brushfire of liberty: yeah, the human action for Christ. Any free people whom earnestly aim to not succumb to the yoke of bondage must work, through their pursuit of happiness with life, liberty, and property, as theirs and society's highest political end, to identify reality in it's self-evident form and not what their power structures have programmed their imaginations into falsely worshiping and namely those false gods of central banks and standing armies occupying the citizen's economic and foreign policy and defrauding civilization through every injustice of the false flags preaching freedom through war and not liberty through peace.

The central banks in holding authority over the standing armies possess the weights to measure best the modes of infiltration upon the Executive Magistrate of the targeted nation and the eventual abuse of it's intention; and, from this Federal level allows for the corruption of the sovereign State and Local levels of governance penetrating even the family and individual liberty across all of the once free people. Any nation that would allow such mass transgression of the law could not as well assume the position of preventing the intrusion of their local and state governments lest only a few among the many stand guard to remind the apathetic in the oppressed lands to rise up and fight for righteousness' sake. The hither swarms of locusts formed into politically charged groups with the sole intent of eating the substance of the people always demand hostile seizure of the modes of government and not without the aid of their alien combat ship – that central bank. The coldness of the heart-shaped box formed against civil liberties crusades against memory alone for their fate in the pains of misery and fear of the memory which imagination inspires always returns them to the grave in which they opened with their regulatory nightmare of a war on logic and reason. In defrauding the people – the system will report up as down; left as right; moral as immoral; night as day; hot as cold; good as evil; sick as well; and, unconstitutional as constitutional.

At the time of america's Founding the present inhabitants of the land whom instituted government for their preservation well understood the terroristic insurgency of central banks. Central banks will always fall under the proper definition of a privately owned bank and therefore it's state-sponsorship coupled with ownership of a private owner or group of owners even if and when government claims the bank as a public asset of the people and all surface-level appearances of the bank speak such – the functioning thereof always reveals the hidden hands ever increasing their oppressions of the people through it's use. The Founders of our american Republic issued strong warnings against the permittance of private banks which can only install it's corruptions with publicly accepted terms such as democracy; a term of which only begets the despotisms of tyranny. One must comprehend the intention of individuals forming an unconstitutional alliance, even when congressionally voted as constitutional, for the inflation, printing, or taxation of money since printing money most perfectly represents a tax or theft of the people by way of stealing the value of the standing dollar and by extension defraud the goods and services of the people. Sadly americans continue about their lives oblivious to the danger they expose their self and progeny to in their acquiescence to evil via the central banks and their governing mankind toward imminent extinction. A central bank issuing the control of money acts as a design for which the fallen society worships as a lesser god, though it rule them as their greater god or thin veil of civilization masking the beast, even when espousing claims toward worshiping the living creator of the universe – their inaction defaults them to the action which enacts and preserves the reign of the wicked.

Luke 22:25 But he said unto them, The kings of the Gentiles reign over them, and they that bear rule over them, are called [a] bountiful.

Luke 22:25 Footnotes

[a] Have great titles, for so it was the custom to honor Princes with some great titles.

The issuance of currency forms the primary foundation of the business cycle and the people and not the government must remain the sole authority in determining what money to issue in their agreed private contracts with one another and any government that would take control of such transaction in the same moment reveals itself a hostile enemy of the people and the people must take appropriate action to redress such grievances lest they point with their inaction where they most succinctly wish for the system to impale their neck.

Exodus 33:3 To a land, I say, that floweth with milk and honey: for I will not go up with thee, because thou art a stiff- necked people, lest I consume thee in the way.

The daft human exits their spiritual body to forgo the duty and honor of liberty insofar as their equal and opposite image defends human liberty from sin thus forms the aggregate for a society against central banks and for the guidance of God to avoid the famine from central banks.

A primary objective of the central bank past the point of it's issuance of currency revolves around inflating and deflating currency which one can think of as synonymous with inflating and deflating poverty or the middle-class even from one generation to another in order to destabilize culture and create a classist system with lines of avarice drawn into the sands of perception. Central banks act out a great show of omniscient ambivalence though the honest individual can envision their deceptions and avoid the vanity of those borderless apparitions whom presently embody the unthinking power structure siphoning civil liberties into a fount of evil power. Central banks maintain a false image subject to none authority of true sovereignty and for the protection of the common citizen which works well to pacify a naive public wherein the public live to only breed for the interests of the central bank. Consider the members of the society whom acquiesce their civil liberties to the rogue legislator and whatever civil Liberties they willingly act upon fit a design for later oppression therefore the private lending institution lends not money and instead lends the abuse of power to capture the focus of the people into surrendering their right to hold authority over government and it's institutions thus giving way for the central bank to lead all people as the perfect representation of animated cadavers forming a walking dead power structure of self-appointed royal dynasty whose sole aim in obfuscation of reality succeeds only upon the ignorance and superstitions of the people and their individual commitments toward criminalizing free association more rightly termed independence, liberty, self-governance, society, sovereignty, and thought which exists as unalienable rights and the only favorable decision and outcome to succeed for an awakened human being pursuing happiness which shuts off the lime-light of the wicked. The american people in their perpetually selling their self the idea of layering debt with lies and this notion coupled with future generations of abominable representation of mankind only serves to keep their stomach full of food which can mean full of disease. Any society that would select a central bank to control their public largess does not alleviate or avoid the pain of some perceived social threat; rather, their naivety assumes ceding their civil liberty unto a perceived higher intelligence exists as a thing particularly circumspect to their own individual or personal comprehension therefore this inability to individually stand for a decision produces a decision which they falsely believe will not affect their wellness; and, as such combines their cowardice with a mounting pain which follows them into the life of their tomorrow sorted with the decay of God's burnt offerings gone astray from truth in their unintended tactics courting civilization into the hands of those haughty lenders auctioning off the donkeys of society for their own preservation.

Exodus 8:22-23 But the land of Goshen, where my people are, will I cause to be [a] wonderful in that day, so that no swarms of flies shall be there, that thou mayest know that I am the Lord in the midst of the [b] earth. And I will make a deliverance of my people from thy people: tomorrow shall this miracle be.

Exodus 8:22 Footnotes

[a] Or, I will separate.

[b] Or, land of Egypt.

The role of fiat currency in subverting society first comprises inflating the monetary supply for only the allowance of an inflation of false money could adjust a debt that would so abundantly supply artificial reason for politicians to demand more theft or taxation of the public to further their evasion of fraud in manipulating the currency and distorting the public's morality. The worst of american debt did not occur until the removal of Gold as the standard backing the value of the united states dollar known otherwise today as the world currency. This removal immediately resulted in a runaway inflation of our monetary supply bringing the american people to their political knees as generations even today continue the trudge for liberty through the swamps of fiat culture and currency. The central banks build their reign upon economic terror for the creation of unkempt generations (insofar as their end-game for world domination and human extinction always fail therefore they favor perpetual and partial enslavement of mankind since the overwhelming majority of these elites practice incest unto the culmination of a lackluster hereditary intelligence and none do possess enough intelligence to acquire additional power outside of the piece of pie in which they have all agreed to divide amongst one another) whom aid the acceleration of a cultural division which only leads to the ruin of civil war though true war never will demonstrate civility. The seeding of bad ideas into the dumbed-down masses of americans of doing whatsoever our government shall want to perform upon a foreign nation, or our own, without any vote from the american people only emboldens the central banks to ravish the domestic population for an insolence of feigning intellectual and moral superiority. As if the high-crime of a people imposing unjust war against foreign lands even while simultaneously claiming all sorts of false moral superiority such as democracy, freedom, or peace places their existence above that of others whom extend their offerings in peace as prosperity in trade with one another and not the unending and absolute opposition for which the corruptions of war insist and enact upon.

The central bankers understand inflation as the primary focus for subterfuge of an economy and society as it's ability to increase consumer spending ensures it's illusion of an economic boom for the further inspiration of a sense of false social compassion or national security or otherwise stated as an unthinkingness amongst the public or a growing devotion toward expending one's life into meaningless pursuits (meaning even more individuals perform no unique talents of God designed for the dissolution of wicked rulers by way of being unobstructed with false legalese) unto the runaway inflation of their economy hereby guaranteeing the few individuals whom knew well the agenda go ignored or martyred by the political machinations devaluing life and growing their business upon the scarcity of happiness which concentrically grows with the magnitude of society's deprivation of life, Godly knowledge, and resources.

The moment americans removed Gold and Silver as their means of economically backing the value of their currency – they in the same instance delivered the world under the yoke of a bondage previously suppressed by the moral acquisitions which ensured a perpetual inhibition of unmitigated collectivism. Artificial and intentional inflation of the money supply creates a hidden tax wherein the controllers of the money-supply steal the public largess without notifying anyone or even requiring access to a citizen's bank account since this transfer of wealth occurs through the monopoly of artificial money. What individual believes they possess any type of intelligence for legislating the value of a currency? No amount of inflation via the dictate of an individual or group of individuals acting as a central bank will ever manifest an intelligence higher in authority, order, or reason than that of the decision-making which occurs among two individuals trading with one another and that trade which forms the only true intelligence that freely forms the construct of ideas in a marketplace of consciously sovereign individuals. In our present day the continent of Africa illustrates most that exponential inflation which plunders civilization as witnessed especially by a single fiat Zimbabwe currency note numbering in the trillions of dollars though it's value measures only according to what the historically-minded or university professors remain willing to pay for the purchasing of this note as an article of fact or warning for future generations against mankind's recursion unto economic error; and, namely that of ceding their sovereignty for the subjection of their will to psychopathic royalty conquering their lands.

Inflation will result in a failed state since it's outcome bares the afflictions of it's intention in the same manner a symbol carries with it the energy and intention of it's original messenger to the extent the intended recipient maintains power over the acceptance or withdrawal of said image, message, or symbol. From a surface-level perspective the intention of the vampire appears innocent in their asking to enter the abode; however, in their enfolded intention manifests the unfolding of a greater plan conducive to their ends and devised toward their target-victim as their chosen means for additional sustenance insofar as their evil begets an evil which consumes the fruit of Godliness unto total depletion of it's creators. Intent acts as the engine of physics driving all things and the vampires operating the central banks succinctly understand this cause and exercise their language, position, and status as a termite carving idols as their dwelling place within a more cavernous network or structure provisioning their worshipers with a church grounds of sorts though all of their devices and structures will only crumple in their effort to remain viable for tens of thousands of generations when such a world possesses no literal use for evil therefore God remains wholly impartial toward such impracticality of culling untold destinies for a trajectory which strategizes it's tyranny against that animating contest of liberty flowing toward the growth of Heavenly applause. History books do not shy away with the simplistic nature of the ruling elite, for example: "... the rulers then captured four nations by way of economic subterfuge and used the newfound plunder to then conquer twelve additional nations by the brute force of their standing armies whom adorn their chiseled torsos with the uniforms of their beloved nation; the same beloved nation which chides to the tune of their conquering as the divergents in opposition to the ignorant countrymen thwarting total conquest for at least eight hundred years until the great chemical expunging of the badlands ..." and as such in so-call "modern times," the mass of the public (whom remain even in the midst of a civilized nation) indulge in their gullible and naive world-view by remaining apathetic, ignorant, superstitious, or even unaware of their political and religious surroundings charging them with an ever increasingly new way of living, and even choose to blaspheme the progenitors of their civilization and even the father who art in heaven; thus; this apathetic clique act more like a trapdoor for mankind and may even one day receive public cognition to define their presence as a named thing such as the *apathétique* which wash out with the undercurrent of anti-knowledge rewarding their abandonment toward calling, destiny, purpose, truth, and God with the sword of calamity and fire though beyond this veil lies a dancing grass waving about the hills without question of the existence which bears their winds and weathers earth into mountains of civilized towers preluding every planet's horizon.

Deflation of the currency increases the frequency of economic chaos which means an increase of that frequency which the rogue politician will capitalize on for the use of additional restrictions on civil liberty since without this chaos the public would otherwise not hasten to agree to the theft of their funds and especially upon further inspecting the destination of the funds only to realize international groups occupying a central bank receive these funds and through a veil of secrecy will then direct government without any consent from the people. The fiddler on the roof moves His bow to and fro with the arco technique as does the central bank in their inflation and deflation of the currency and economy. Inflation duplicates, prints, or replicates money for the administering of a false supply of money while deflation limits the money supply in a gradual erosion of the value of the currency as the oligarchs train the people like dogs to learn their new role in accepting a life of less. The oligarchs gamble and trade on the world upon their own secret game table though they frequently reveal their modus operandi with full knowledge that the release of such information acts as a way of attracting and recruiting new blood into their operation and the general public so often in apathy unto their self and cognitive dissonance unto others will forgo reading, fail to discern any type of truth, and therefore will not possess sufficient knowledge to properly respond to the threat of their liberty and at least certainly not the sinister text of globalist plans outlining the demolition of their civilization and even so if the citizenry discover such plans then their apathy arrests their personal development from choosing emergency paths of arrest upon the agenda which pervades society for their perceived fear of confronting that responsibility God prepares as a battle-plan even for His honest subjects seeking that satisfaction of securing sovereignty for their self and the world by way of acting as the avenue of political pressure which foments the multitudes of citizens into the desire of discovering what particularly ails the happiness of a nation whom profess freedom and not liberty as their source of bravery, peace, and prosperity though it surreptitiously lack liberty since they so gleefully possess that mighty central bank which affords them the time to dole around on the couch all day as glassy-eyed and slack-jawed pretenders gibbering their mouths and bobbling their heads in approval for the smothering of their public largess and poisoning of their nation's food and water supply in an utterly contemptuous defiance of God which destroys their progeny's future as tentacles upon snares entrap the very base of what the people must otherwise keep holy from such alien interdiction.

Deuteronomy 28:20

The Lord shall send upon thee cursing, trouble, and [a] shame, in all that which thou settest thine hand to do, until thou be destroyed, and perish quickly, because of the wickedness of thy works, whereby thou hast forsaken me.

Deuteronomy 28:20 Footnotes

[a] Or, rebuke.

Without the advent of unnatural inflation and deflation the market determines it's own course of action as a natural adaptation possessing an efficiency and intelligence superior to that of any theft by government via so-called central planning since central planning will always self-destruct. Deprecation of the obsolete freely allows decisions to flow and keep ideas wholly intact under the authority of the individual whom in such scenario ensures the trade of their property results in the trade of this moment for a superior moment if not for their self but for the future maturity of mankind and it's assurance in voluntary association and trade thereby allowing their government to remain within the confines of it's self-evidenced and true definition as an institution of individuals hired by the people to aid in the preservation of their liberty and not to govern every member of society's budget. Many proponents of the lawless and rogue oligarchs will incessantly argue for the bludgeoning of their economic system through all sorts of fancy-named pseudonyms such as a *stimulus program* claiming to empower individuals through the release of "free money," though this money was immorally acquired through the theft of the public largess via psychopathic highwaymen, pickpocketers, and thieves wearing costumes and assuming their own invincibility though they only spoil the mind of the youth and the righteous plan for which God originally preconceived for mankind's tree of life.

Deuteronomy 28:12

The Lord shall open unto thee his good treasure, even the [a] heaven to give rain unto thy land in due season, and to bless all the work of thine hands: and [b] thou shalt lend unto many nations, but shalt not borrow thyself.

Deuteronomy 28:12 Footnotes

[a] For nothing in the earth is profitable but when God sendeth his blessings from heaven.

[b] Deuteronomy 15:6

Deuteronomy 15:6

For the Lord thy God hath blessed thee, as he hath promised thee: and a thou shalt lend unto many nations, but thou thyself shalt not borrow, and thou shalt reign over many nations, and they shall not reign over thee.

When looking onto what facilitates the influence of natural law and not the law of man we see a constant reemergence of the individual in their sinless state of being acting out their life in the highest order of consciousness which creates more space and time for the liberty of mankind to witness it's blessings and pursue those blessings all of their days; therefore, the influencing of the micro and macro cause and effect or mass and energy of every man, state, and economy behaves more like water than man as it's effort goes formlessly unobstructed as though it were both the part and whole, visible and invisible motion, of an intelligent system seamlessly connecting with every ocean and cloud, tributary and aquifer, and even every neutron in the heavens which as a system within an even greater and presently unknowable structure – harbors it's own atmosphere which distinctly and intentionally preserves mankind's life on the earth. Consider those few numbers comprising the oligarchs compared to the farmers and land-dwellers of the world whom comprise the majority of earth's population and mostly possess no knowledge whatsoever of the manipulation of their finances by global financiers planning their manufactured genocide through plagues of war. Man plans for the future; however, what will come of His investments without proper foreknowledge of the political landscape working to shape His genealogical and personal outcome without His input? Inflation and deflation in the marketplace of ideas work off of a risk and reward system based on merit and morality as the sure foundation of our natural law. Ripe or unripe low-hanging fruit can illustrate the severity of risk concerning nutrition for now, never, or later.

What happens to the investor whom undergoes the economic stress of producers in the marketplace with too few of resources to allow them to act according to the frequency of a free market from malinvestment at the datum level of the economy, so to say at the level of the government working with secretive elites and a central bank using currency to interrupt the flow of consciousness by hindering free trade and subsequently plummeting the production of goods or services necessary for the abstaining of famine and the procurement of a civil society and it's investors participating as that liquidity of honest trade and true intelligence insofar as that true intelligence loves God aright?

Genesis 41:56 When the famine was upon all the land, Joseph opened all places, wherein the store was, and sold unto the Egyptians: for the famine waxed sore in the land of Egypt.

The investor losing His full ability to freely act in a once free market dwells within an economic depression, which does mean within a famine, then witnesses His futurity dim as the economy whom previously relied on His efficiency then demand by order of writ His own plunder by He satisfying the socioeconomic debt which the captor of civilization formed; and, when multiple investors notice irregular fluctuation in the money supply the investors then shift resources and a confusion of the marketplace ensues from their inability to naturally and rightly assess the value of their trade due to the fiat currency altering the entire economy since government-enforcement now demands by threat of violence the trade decisions of the people therefore the economy in whole will suffer unto the entrapments of an ignorance which can not demand the restoration of liberty. Consider the opposite occurrence of the investor receiving double his normal rate of investment and then reinvests this sum into His works only to produce twice as much as the society can purchase. What comes of a society whom experiences this lengthy process of seeing a tumultuous economy rock as a ship upon stormy seas and suddenly the ship then points toward whatever lies at the bottom of the wave for which rose it's stern and revealed a bottom to set the ship upon as though even the place in which it aims to set possesses a prepared name to rest the ship upon as though the ocean designed the ship's destruction for it's divine purpose; though when considering the design of evil we see an anti-divine purpose for no purpose other than harming the divine?

Lamentations 3:61 *Thou hast heard their reproach, O Lord, and all their imaginations against me.*

Lamentations 4:17 *While we waited for our vain help, our eyes failed: for in our waiting we looked for [a] a nation that could not save us.*

Lamentations 4:17 Footnotes

[a] He showeth two principal causes of their destruction: their cruelty and their vain confidence in man: for they trusted in the help of the Egyptians.

Self-evidence then inspires us to witness the differences separating a tempestuous and calm sea. The sea though naturally tempestuous does not always possess the same treachery of the arctic or antarctic waters. The calmness of the sea precedes only that storm for which it hides as does the calmness of inflation inspire individuals to fear not the potential for a sudden deflation of their economy which often impales the contradictory ego and ensures this contradiction fails to exhibit it's true expression of a life lived with determination and inspiration without an insatiable desire for the cancellation of the human race. Self-governing society harmonizes every type of inflation and deflation of the economy through enforcing the idea of individual and sovereign trade with all parties aware of the effects of a rogue bank and the measure which mitigate it's succession thus keep out it's intervention and allow individuals to culturally pursue growth patterns in accordance to their moral virtue which will in turn inspire a free market economy to return an average of a three percent growth rate each year and ad infinitum. Deflation ensures every value which the human mind may conceive then fragments into the broken discernments of a foreign entity dictating their most prescient life matters from an honest perspective and into an unsalvageable discontent of oppression.

Central bank and their ancillaries easily reflect the microscopic image of a virus or pathogen with it's surface proteins extending outward as telescopic arms autonomously magnetized to a synchronistic recognition of a viable host to then bind with as one illusion with the inner-workings of a co-dependent system and outward appearance of an organic life-form using communication to extend it's viral reach to then psychologically manipulate organisms outside of it's immediate physiological control though psychology can mean an extension of physiology insofar as the technology will not keep separate the matter as humans would with politics and religion since technology can only automate and the mind of man can only create (though the inhumane pollute the meaning of spirituality's reason for politic and religion). The central bank surrounding itself with varying hierarchy of banks or functions facilitating the bank, for example standing armies occupying nations, resources or various strongholds – be they political or religious in nature, form their own central standing army whose only function works to infect and control the world with it's culture of death and depravity. The size and scope of the central banking system will always appear to exceed the combined power of the individuals falling victim to it's carrier function as though the illusion of it's mounting power outweighs the infinite power within the individual to overthrow every yoke of bondage. The central banks in their forming of relationships with corporations train populations to accept their authority as the ultimate caregiver of individual satisfaction from cradle to grave; however, the only result in succumbing to such illusion actualizes a society foregone of it's knowledge of God and only acquiescent to the dismissal or erosion of their civil liberty as this super-structure of control replaces the market of lighted eyes with that of a perpetual drooping unto cultural decimation. Even a society experiencing the most heightened states of awareness whereupon this intelligence piques into frontiers previously unseen, though not unknown, in the epigenetic inscription in mankind's experiment in life and liberty – there exists short-lived disturbances of peace and prosperity in society whereby multitudes of chaos interfere with the harmonic frequency and vibrations of man's conscience thus filters the receiving and revival of the whole spirit of the Lord which only knows the seeking of God's law unto perfection and this energy which pervades the deep for mankind's destruction persists since the dawn of man though the knowledge of overcoming this destruction lives for eternity. Human beings remain well equipped to assess a physical threat though remain equally indefensible to the assault of civil liberties when viewing history through the filter of time as a thing inconsequential to present events. Common sense argues for the individual to assume responsibility in delivering aid to the poverty-stricken and over time these waves of love will saturate hearts and heal poverty; however, the central bank and corporations merge and grow as a prison-wall surrounding the people into a duality of warfare against the state-opposed divergents and the state-vassals of warfare and welfare.

As poverty rises in direct correlation to the influence of the central banks – the corporations ensnare the people as a governing authority or even arbiter over the life of the citizen as such scenario without fail increases the inability for the state or occupying forces to provision the captured population with the ever increasing demand for additional clean water, clothing, food, and shelter as the people led like sheep to the slaughter beg for whatever additional suffering their overlords shall bestow, though they lack the proper supply thereof, in the witnessing of their own institutionalization and endemic culling. Mankind operated for millennia without the false aid of involuntary taxation as the people and their churches handled all material finances to secure their blessings of liberty from the good Lord above and even today the churches, elderly, and pastor remain targets of a rogue government simply for feeding the homeless and hungry. Only a central bank and their corporation could possibly come up with such wicked scheming self-evidenced as involuntary taxation or otherwise face a military firing squad by the full backing of the court system in the violent murder and overthrow of the individual right to keep God's law in a manifest refutation against the unconstitutional jargon decreed as law by the uttermost filthy demons posing as neighborly or orderly in their obeying of an unlawful job and immoral act; and, we witness such affairs in modern day america with the Federal Government using sniper rifles to murder mothers while She bear Her baby in arms as she watch Herself aired on live news television of an ongoing military strike which explodes Her brains with military precision thus murdering the innocent woman of God and dropping and injuring the innocent infant of God whom was marred with the bone, flesh, and blood of it's loving mother and all for an uneducated nation surrendering their power to a foreign and alien government claiming taxation as a justifiable offense and reason for the suspension of unalienable rights, martial law, and public execution of an innocent and sovereign human being; a true merciless hell at war with God's vision of life.

Inflation and deflation persist as the primary and secondary goals of the central banks and corporations; however, their tertiary or even hidden goal lies in empowering the occult to cull society into the false idea that all of known civilization requires involuntary taxation and no such agency of voluntary association can exist since the image of the military defending the central bank and corporations appear to so powerfully provision the people and their government architecture, which this unlawful system produced in the first place, above any other inspiration or false hope in the people since that system so gratuitously inject the belly of it's supporters with a dilute poison causing it's receiver to enjoy their shallow and unintelligible existence which rewards the inability to logic or reason and selects the most fallen for roles of absolute authority therefore we all must learn to love this illusory *fair and balanced* amount of involuntary taxation in order to function or even think properly or whatsoever shall we do since only government guards the unknowable information appertaining art, budgeting, foreign policy, health, national security, parenting, science, or road-building. Those nations intentionally electing the central banks and corporations to feed their population possess an apathy toward life only surpassed by their evil desire for rulers to deliver them the illusion of money – the same type or even family of rulers whom conquered their ancestors and imprison their spirit as a flame hidden from it's potential and eventually sequestered into the memory-hole of humanity. What sits atop the central banks and corporations deserves the most attention as we know throughout all nations and time the priests concern their self most with ruining liberty and all reductions of it's occurrence thereof coupled with the manufacture of best overthrowing it's chief and true animator, author, berserker, commander, father, governor, guardian, maverick, musician, pastor, philosopher, president, realm, renegade, or sheriff.

The individual professesing literacy and intelligence without illustration thereof will always argue for the necessity of a tyrannical system of absolute control for their dogged idea of a common good supposedly, or so to say an "inside" or "insiders" trade or knowledge too high in intellect for their perceived intellectual enemies to grasp since they do hide so well behind their dark armies of untold wealth enslaving mankind to it's counterintuitive means by way of thieving and defrauding the population on the altar of every coercion and violence for the rendering of the spirit of the Lord into confusions of tongue which magnify oligopoly. The incompetent ne'er-do-wells fear honest competition above all things as even their intellect knows intimately well their physical, intellectual, and spiritual boundaries pontificating not life's highest meaning and instead rely solely on the orders of their standing army to subjugate their mind into the illusory order of a falsely personified population of dignity imposing it's reign for centuries upon free men. The poverty of the mind drives the power of the priest and His desire to accompany His power with banks and corporations to erect standing armies over the people as a public show of His reign. Grown men today still naively believe The Pope does not control armies when we can know fully well His orthodoxy is that very synagogue of Satan or associate standing army of which the central banks ordain as their subordinate manager over the free world.

Our purpose in entering society for the preservation of property stands as the foundation and target of the central bankers for destruction since in their alien field-of-vision or imagination – all people exist as their property and even further to not sin for them exists as a sin unto itself therefore they view their freedom as a necessity to sin unto the oppressing of mankind as this hidden potential in their imagination exists as a thing the universe necessarily allows since so often their own generations and life continues though only later they may accept their own awareness to include the fear of God and only then understand their transgression and hell which they have formed around them.

Exodus 23:6 Thou shalt not overthrow the right of the poor in his suit.

No other function outside of inflation and deflation allows the central banksters to achieve absolute control over society without this gradual erosion of the currency draining the people of the fruit of their labor and with acquiescence of the people even trains them to learn the source of sustenance as a collectivism which exiles the individual or rather corporatizes the individual into a customer, employee, partner, or supplier owned as the chattel of the central banks.

What mechanism within the human mind convinces the people to question not the most pertinent issues concerning a free state of existence and namely that of life, liberty, and property since one's own mind, body, and spirit exists as the same type of property as one may own outside of the body whether intellectual or physical? The only existential threat in the mind of the individual unconcerned with the loss of their property or society exists in other individuals making an attempt to provide them with education to matters particularly concerning their own well-being in relation to the thieves and defrauders of property and time in the high place of principalities. What mechanism must occur in order to awaken the minds whom so easily faint upon hearing the sound of the trumpet and whose only concern surrounds the bread and circus which keeps their intellect even with that of an infant; though, a conniving infant trained in the art of blood-drunkenness, coercion, contradiction, décevoir, entrapment, fraud, futility, hostility, lying, obstruction, psychological manipulation, rage, especially sabotage, theft, and violence toward the discerner of faith and truth?

Proverbs 12:9-10 The light of the righteous rejoiceth: but the candle of the wicked shall be put out. Only by pride doth man make contention: but with the well-advised is wisdom.

A man whose hands willingly surrender His God-given ability, duty, and right to discern, implore, and question in the same instance forms into a hollow shell which was at one-time filled with the blood of a man whose heart beat with the rhythm of God. What can we say of a society when all of their men adorn apathy as a form of excellence and justify their evil rulers as a form of honor or normal but the shell of a society going by the name of Africa, Asia, Canada, Europe, Oceania, South America, or The Middle East? What makes a society worship that inconsistency of dignity and forgo private property which bore every freedom under the umbrella of liberty? Only a society with full understanding of private property will avoid those deprivations of their life, liberty, and happiness ushered in by the harbingers which stripe men with that yoke of bondage.

The fortitude which forged man's ability to conceive of His ultimate constitution will persist as the same fortitude which keeps man forged in His prowess of declaring and defending His liberty in a world demanding His begging or imprisonment for exercising His God-given rights since that same God which leavened all things of the world will leaven what God instructs man to leaven even unto the leavening of all things on the earth, in outer-space, and throughout all of time. The meek so often do not engage the central bank impoverishing their society through simple and yet elaborate schemes limiting their ability to lawfully exercise their skill-sets in the marketplace of ideas in the least and therefore this notion when gone uncontested starts the countdown for the total culling of civilization and resurrection of hell on the earth.

Central bankers remain masters at the deception of promulgating regulation as superior to that perfect law of liberty and in so doing deprive the people of their civil liberties which do even mean that property which manifests as action in the free market and in trimming these faculties from the whole of society there lies the endangerment of civilization and prevention of the exponential rise of mankind's hidden fruit as the ultimate servant for the creator of the universe and highest enemy within the circles of demonic influence. The range of property, from information of the mind to textiles of the body or places of spiritual worship, cover the grounds at which remain under eternal assault from individuals masquerading as friendly central banks though they harbor the enemy of mankind with unspeakably wicked masters and fearful servants even unto cannibalism as their choice of self-funding, preservation, and population control. Central banks ignore whom they profess to serve and then laugh at whom they destroy and will always fight unto death those individuals worthy, insofar as worthy means to love God aright, and aright meaning to do and not pray without the inclusion of exposing the philosophy of Keynesian Economics really only hiding the Luciferians and their subordinate carrier-philosophies insofar as those vain philosophies of the world only contend for the varying degrees of Luciferianism which evade righteousness through seeking public office and official secrecy. Keynesian Economics deprives people of life and property while Austrian Economics preserves life and property.

Former Texas Congressman and Presidential Candidate Doctor Ron Paul wrote in an article entitled 'Democracy Isn't Freedom':

"The problem is that democracy is not freedom. Democracy is simply majoritarianism, which is inherently incompatible with real freedom. Our founding fathers clearly understood this, as evidenced not only by our republican constitutional system, but also by their writings in the Federalist Papers and elsewhere. James Madison cautioned that under a democratic government, "There is nothing to check the inducement to sacrifice the weaker party or the obnoxious individual." John Adams argued that democracies merely grant revocable rights to citizens depending on the whims of the masses, while a republic exists to secure and protect pre-existing rights. Yet how many Americans know that

the word "democracy" is found neither in the Constitution nor the Declaration of Independence, our very founding documents?"

1. Ron Paul. "Democracy Isn't Freedom." *Lew Rockwell,* Ron Paul, 7 February 2005, https://www.lewrockwell.com/2005/02/ron-paul/democracy-isnt-freedom/. Accessed 4 January 2020

Central banks will take a republic and render it into a democracy in the same manner wicked committees render the pre-existing rights of the individual into an unchained prisoner subordinate to man and not God therefore an indentured servant or corporate chattel with suppositional or revocable rights; thus, this ebb and flow of common sense weaves a despotism into the fabric of the world and siphons the knowledge of God from the people whom would defend liberty and instead suffer even unto martyrdom in their engagement in the arena of ideas to awaken the general public into the destiny God outlined and planned for their own life and the eternity of mankind in this eternal realm of God, imagination, light, peace, presence, space, and prosperity.

So often does the public awaken to the erosions of their civil liberties only to realize their own homelessness occurred prior to their awakening and what they thought of as a home now more closely resembles a panopticonic control-grid prison-system withholding reason for force and the nobility we receive under God as a hostility to persecute under the illusion of a collectivist authority. Certainly the appendages of this matrix show a network of banks and corporations extracting public wealth to energize it's machinations though it's static nature implores man to dynamically fight and oppose it's edict in the perilous and imperceptible realm of spiritual warfare until lesion upon lesion hemorrhages the machine and this cause breaks forth the good flood gates of a feast at odds with planned famine. In order to cause famine the system must control all forms of industry, especially child-birth, food, and medicine, though without blatantly controlling the land and water their only choice then rests in over-regulating markets and providing the illusion of choice, liberty, or the limited offerings of state-enforced rations; and, in the case of agriculture: the rogue legislature forces farmers to plant genetically modified corn (which corrupts and hybridizes human genetics; GMO food is bite-size Satan) sprayed with all sorts of lethal poison only to then use this crop to produce megatons of toxic syrup and then use this toxic syrup as a food sweetener for virtually every single food product on market shelves today as this toxic syrup perfectly showcases the poison known as an excitotoxin or even a form of chemical castration; and, it's effects perfectly cause untold levels of cancer, disease, and malnourishment to assist the military-industrial-complex in the refueling of pharmaceutical customers in their communist medical market which promotes it's own false drugs synthesized from God's medicine cabinet which grows freely from the earth. Cannabis, God's chief herb, has proven time and again in it's ability to induce the apoptosis effect to eliminate cancer; of course even this debate will shadow under the larger debate of Cannabis' use in over fifty thousand known product and textiles. The militarily foreign-occupied education system ensures a steady flow and even growth of individuals blindly bumbling about life as a visionless worm consuming all things directly meeting their face as they maneuver into the easy slightings of despotism.

"How did I find myself godless and unhealthy?"

– the fallen nation must individually ask through self-evidence so abundantly clear; and, further:

"How did my nation abandon it's law for foreign law? I thought I lived in the American dream and instead now I see a communist nightmare replete with fraudulent money, citizen spies, illegal empire-building, and mass-scale indoctrination."

Knowledge then only calls home whom calls home unto God for directive, guidance, and leading.

Today the colonizers actively remove american statues illustrating our history and even across Texas – the last stand for the american Republic while even replacing these statues with the tyrants we overthrew (talks of Santa Anna being raised (for now ^_-;) at The Alamo); and, all for what? So a lot of disingenuous hellions incompatible with the sanctity of liberty and all things comprising a wholesome civilization can grandstand as the emperors and foremost thinkers of mankind though they disease the body politic of human liberty in their own declaration against natural law? The meek would well enjoy the presence of the finest example of human excellence and not only one individual among many but rather they would even greater prefer many exemplary people for liberty among the few whom previously represented the profanely wicked majority. Man must keep that power of liberty to drag another man behind the tool-shed for a man-to-man discussion either by duel or humble discourse to ensure an outcome conducive with the blessings of liberty in that we as a people do not see the head of tyranny emerge for the conquering of man or civilization. Our forefathers conquered the american continent not through force but through ideas. Many individuals whom followed came not for liberty but to destroy the ideas which pre-exist and portend the success of the true man's cause as our cause represents that of life and not death; peace and not war; liberty and not enslavement; prosperity and not depravity; imagination and not cruelty.

Rulers always advertise freedom as the route toward a free society and in that lies the deception of certain and immutable dangers as it's only offering consists of involuntary taxation and empire building through endless military occupation of foreign lands and even militarizing the domestic homeland. The free man knows well the word liberty while that enslaved man deals in the absolutes of limited vocabulary and confusions of tongue; for example, freedom and democracy and not liberty and the republic. Comfort then sacrifices liberty for freedom under evil rulers and adversity purchases that excellent path for liberty. Thomas Jefferson articulates that calm of despotism as a comfort of apathy in which it's mould forms.

Compare the parent whom raises their child behind the bars of a crib and the parent whom opts not to train their child unto the clinging of cold bars. Why then do societies professing their civilization as that of a state of heightened awareness then hide men behind bars and not simply guard their quarters for even the public to witness as a form of shame to inspire healing and humility and how can america as three and one half percent of the world's population claim to exist as a free nation and then imprison two out of three of the world's prisoners with their own citizens as those subjects? How could such degradation of civility and law not paint shame upon the face of that society which would as well hide their shame with additional evil? Even further these prisoners all remain victim to unlawful human statutes – victimless crimes.

Our forefathers in conquering bad ideas lay the foundation for their progeny to as well conquer bad ideas and not agree to imprisonment by the criminally insane whom have occupied positions in government for their own inanity; and, how else, but, by the deflation of private economy and inflation of tyranny by way of secretive central banks. The individuals whom would later create a nation called america based on the cause of liberty performed such acts to conquer what deep evil had for so many centuries succeeded the conquering of the free human spirit. Those men worked in unison with Native Americans to flush out the evil and merge as the new, albeit ancient, human to sow the seeds of love and grow a new world of infinite possibility without the pyramidal rule of man and with this flat hierarchy – channel the flood of the knowledge of that perfect law of liberty from the living creator of the universe.

The rulers in their historical and social dementia sent hither swarms of reptilian-brained drones to route out the free man and deprive this people of their life, liberty, and happiness; and, this ship of fools, in which the rulers puppeteer even when not called by a name do represent the function of the central banks. This light brought forth to the inhabitants resonated as both the primitive and advanced people well understood the thanks and giving to share through the expunging of royalty throughout the earth. The pursuit of happiness would cure mankind of the illness of war both in it's silence of violence and terror of coercion and trade these abominations for peace and prosperity through honest and open trade and the guarding and preserving of one another's resources against those oppressors so coldly grouping individuals into teams to war one another off against each other. The phalanx of liberty will stand true and form the only united front for humanity to regain it's whole conscious state of expansion rendering tradition a cultural choice and not government mandated attrition, border, and division. Free humanity's continent for conquering then does not rest at the americas; rather, the earth and all of human exploration as our spiritual conquering will end the monetization which rewards the shedding of physical and spiritual blood as we identify and route out the tools of mankind's demise and render their carnal program of tuning paradoxical and imaginative collisions into history lessons for mankind to keep and study and improve upon knowing full and well that liberty eternally represents the only reward worthy of the true life to pursue. Certainly we must conquer our inner demons to conquer the outer demons though the path for liberty exists in knowledge first and foremost and without that knowledge only the lesser demons will wane and not die though the shadow of the greater demons will continue their doom unchallenged. The higher order of mankind abounding in His own knowledge of liberty builds upon an abundance only produced from that higher state of awareness providing Him proof of the higher existence separating the men of God into a joy daily exceeding the snares of Lucifer. We find liberty at our own hand and in that grip God delivers us and the world out of bondage though we must read and train to sharpen our ways into hearing and seeing the knowledge God will provide to universally destroy the compartmentalization suffocating the world by way of the central bank's trickle-down tyranny. The american Revolution occurs in every moment for eternity as we who have seen the vision know this cause of liberty requires eternal vigilance from our hand unto every generation ad infinitum. All of humanity; every ancestor, tribe, tongue, and realm possesses individuals whom understand this cause and responsibility weighs heavily on their heart to act and spread the awareness which will increase occurrence, potential, and moments for additional discovery into the expansive vastness of liberty as each effort put forth renders plain the gait for a globe to enter and attune to liberty. We will as a human race again align with the frequency our ancestors fought so dearly for in their purchasing of time for the pursuit of those blessings of liberty which magnify

God's light into the world and carry mankind on that frequency which inspires every judicious form of humanity and our pursuit for a mastery in the knowledge to know good and evil and only act good and abhor evil. Though the standing armies and central banks twain against the instincts of humanity to forgo embarking on human excellence and turn toward only despair and naivety for fear of our own unique greatness meeting the greatness of other uniques in the clouds upon towers of brightness and refuge from all unholiness and ineffectuality – the central banks always die the death.

TYRANNY

Genesis 6:4 There were [a] giants in the earth in those days: yea, and after that the sons of God came unto the daughters of men, and they had borne them children, these were mighty men, which in old time were men of [b] renown.

Genesis 6:4 Footnotes

[a] Or, tyrants.

[b] Which usurped authority over others, and did degenerate from that simplicity, wherein their fathers lived.

God designed man to love the pursuit of God's design for His life; a design wherein a people would assemble and form a nation, even a world, destined for living in a more perfect union in defense of life, liberty, and property against tyranny. The preservation of the philosophy of liberty entails discerning tyranny and taking action to tread it down and enjoy the blessings which God rewards for those deeds in which His knowledge instructs for the survival and liberation of mankind from the rule of wicked men. Perhaps all nations form as a result of men recognizing their mutual ideas share a likeness which occurs only as a result of their past generations positioning their progeny to mature the peace and prosperity of mankind into the forming of the basis for a permanent civilization which moulds itself free from any constraints which infringe upon the civil liberty of the individual. Suppose this civilization grows in such exceeding number it now reaches one hundred million individuals. Certain events may compel such a nation to self-reflect upon their assembly and sort the things which form them into a single type of people although they vary greatly in character, choice, and function. Such a vast number of individuals prevent any one individual from meeting every individual face to face; therefore, we must come to know this self-evident assembly of observers and participants assemble around a central political or religious idea even if that centrality is political decentralization or prohibition of state-enforced religion which must necessarily be the only direction or method for which political unity meets a religious purity of coexisting with the state's design of preserving our civil liberty: yeah, a state chained down by the function of the constitution and not a state unchained by the dysfunction of the people; and, the divisions which separate and unite society mainly consist of the rich and the poor, young and the old, the educated, and the uneducated. The measure of morality or ethics may unite every multitude though at their base logic or reason illustrates an agreeable justification or standard of education which compels them to manifestly defend society as though these few people can effect the outcome of an encroachment of a perceivable sea of phantoms that would not hesitate in imprisoning them within a political ring of fire kept alight by religious planes of magic.

How does one measure education, status, or wealth without setting a justification of which creates a measure for the uneducated and the poor and how do these measurements affect the formation of a nation both in the precession of it's people prior to assembly and the procession of it's people and representatives upon and after it's declaration of independence? And what could history write in stone for us if we shall assume that a nation was abandoned to form a new nation on grounds of abandoning old ideas thus allowing the assembling of a nation to grow upon a more perfect union of Godly knowledge which keeps more closely bound to the reality concerning mankind's disposition in pursuing happiness insofar as such pursuits must openly refute injustice? The endless examples of injustice plaguing mankind has rewarded us with the experience of discerning and deliberating upon the uniting of a common purpose in a fight against a common enemy gone rogue from the perfect law of liberty unto the denying of individuals their unalienable right to a life of liberty and property in a civilization free from the prison planet.

1 Corinthians 2:15 [a] But he that is spiritual, [b] discerneth all things: yet [c] he himself is judged of [d] no man.

1 Corinthians 2:15 Footnotes

[a] He amplifieth the matter by contraries.

[b] Understandeth and discerneth.

[c] The wisdom of the flesh, saith Paul, determined nothing certainly, no not in its own affairs, much less can it discern strange, that is, spiritual things. But the Spirit of God, wherewith spiritual men are endued, can be deceived by no means, and therefore be reproved of no man.

[d] Of no man: for when the Prophets are judged of the Prophets, it is the Spirit that judges, and not the man.

The individual acquires a unique experience and thus provides a specialized purpose for society such that their experience and talent aid the focus which sharpens the fight against the common enemy at war with the futurity of mankind. Do the wealthy not often possess the education which a large economy would demand; for example: their role in increasing the ability of a multitude of skilled laborers through funding or even managing the construction of an aquifer system which would supply water to civilization in the long-term and fuel the economy of society in the short-term which acts as a critical rung in the golden ladder of society's futurity? And do the poor not possess the ability to serve others with their labor in a way which only their noble intent in duty and might could so well align for their vision alongside the efforts of their fellow countryman whom encourage their success and not failure; and, even here at times we find natural disaster, inexplicable events, or personal tragedy may befall a people though our hope of a greater salvation fills our spirit in the pressing onward for a more perfect union in the destiny God made plain for mankind in encouraging we purge the tyrants and glorify God with our liberty. What scenario might so endanger a people that the disposition which they all bear then agree to assemble and resolve the injuries which equally afflict them all? And what so captivates the human spirit that it would enflame the heart and impassion the soul of a multitude of people at any one time such that this multitude arrives at the conclusion that they too must individually influence the world into an alignment which other nations fail to know as the resolution for evading that kettle which steeps the human spirit into it's qualms of despotism? One person amongst the multitude may shout:

"We must all assemble;"

however, perhaps many individuals of similar spiritual discernment advertised such an idea until the frequency or popularity of this idea grew in direct futility against those ideas which sought to infiltrate the mind of each member of society in like fashion.

What can we know of a nation with only a class of wealthy and poor but the absence of a middle-class which mediates the two as though such a society sought reverence in warring their neighbor and not the world's oppressors?

James 2:6 But ye have despised the poor. [a] Do not the rich oppress you by tyranny, and do they not draw you before the judgment seats?

James 2:6 Footnotes

[a] Secondly, he proveth them to be mad men: for that the rich men are rather to be holden execrable and cursed, considering that they persecute the Church, and blaspheme Christ: for he speaketh of wicked and profane rich men, such as the most part of them have been always, against whom he setteth the poor and abject.

Society repeatedly degrades unto the point of forcing individuals into a caste system of classes or hereditary hierarchy; and, though these definitions provision the dumb and spiritually destitute with an illusory feeling of foundational or sound knowledge – these intolerant divisions can not describe the knowledge or stratum which God designs in His making all men equal in their spiritual image thus having a likeness to God in which equally creates the individual with unalienable rights as God's children and not imprisoned within any system of man which predefines the young and old as builders of a government imposing a new world order wherein liberty goes to die. All social stratum remain illusory then insofar as the arc of humanity's trajectory can only form one race, specie, or temple of existence as witnessed with the lion and tiger or orca and great white shark or even one solar system or galaxy independent of another; therefore, perhaps the philosophy of liberty could even mean the one life-force of all things do exist as perceivably unique individuals acting out a unique story pursuant to their own life and death of liberty or tyranny; happiness for those whom trust in the Lord or destruction for God's enemies. Perhaps then what we mean in separating class must designate first in a class of ego which one could argue as a human thing though all of the natural world exhibit alpha and omega characteristics and a free nation shatters the illusion of a people assembling for the preservation of a ruler since that ruler exhibits an unequal right to His life and liberty, and, manifests a society devoid of the rule of law and wholly impartial to the effects of the tyranny accompanying His reign.

Acts 12:22 [a] And the people gave a shout, saying, The voice of God, and not of man.
Acts 12:22 Footnotes
[a] The flattery of the people, maketh fools fain.

Always in times of trial and tribulation in society will that wicked public rush toward the fallacy of a utopian society for the common citizen wherein this false utopia demands a government of men steal from the public and redistribute their wealth to a central bank and corporations; thus, the acceptance of such ignorance as truth will only manifest the ruin of commerce, oppression of the honest, destruction of a nation, and emergency scenario demanding action from the men of the nation to assemble for the defense of liberty. Will the abandonment of false ideas supporting only that material status and wealth not enhance the perception of the people unto the entering of that narrow gait for the total discernment of that spiritual status and wealth which God so readily supplies as a whole acquisition to those people fervent unto His calling? Society in abandoning sin, or in the least abandoning those sins made into law for their government, inherently constructs a new foundation which manifests an architecture unlike what the dung and villains of society can imagine; and, under such a governance will address those matters which require the articulations of persuasion and not coercions or violence in order for individuals to competently and wittingly compose society under the security of honorable court systems which receive their design according to the perfect law of liberty thereby preserving individual life, liberty, and property without any excuse or statute claiming permittance or precedent for government theft, fraud, violence, or coercion.

Considering the multitude of nations: past, present, and future, we witness a minute fraction of any nation in possession of land or other real estate. History teaches us that the citizens whom do not own property have remained within generations of this type of usury for centuries either for a reason of not possessing enough knowledge to climb out of the poverty (which keeps them as chattel to hereditary tyrannical overlords whose reign condemns whomsoever shall acquiesce their own individual power to the subjugation of it's arbitrary power of political systems exercising violence and coercion to enforce it's Satanic law); or, allowing the manufacture of false ideas to render obtuse their intelligence in order to convince them into living a life obsessed with the carnal misgivings of bread and circus or media and entertainment: a veritable stronghold which can only form through a multitude of idle individuals hypnotized into viewing their self as a chattel whose only function can desire money and then spend these funds within the system enslaving them to their own ignorance.

President George Washington, President Thomas Jefferson, President James Madison Jr., President Andrew Jackson, Congressman Ron Paul, John Hancock, Patrick Henry, Samuel Adams, Alex Emric Jones, John David McAfee, Samuel Langhorne Clemens, myself, and countless more had all proverbially looked over the mountain and seen the vision of mankind in it's promise land: the highest state of consciousness – an agrarian society wherein true men preserve mankind through the defense of liberty for all individuals with none exception so that the youth in society can gain the knowledge of God for guidance toward the blessings of liberty which instruct them in the art of restraining wicked men from exercising evil forces even unto it's event horizon which would endeavor to deliver these tyrants the ability to participate as the governing authority which will only usurp individual liberty and oppress mankind. Ignorance and superstitions dispossess the individual from their liberty; and, in the same instant dispossess mankind from that invincible zeal of ascension unrestrained from those earthly and hellish coercions; and, this especially holds true concerning the demonic psychopaths in government office whom so often chain down an ignorant public as though such a treading down of the innocent and sovereign does not inspire God to taxi the absolute destruction of this destroyer of life and property. The vision of the agrarian society in possession of the full discernment of the knowledge of God and liberty does not limit itself to the vision of Thomas Jefferson nor His acolytes. God Himself gave man herb for meat to eat therefore any oppression of our knowledge or unalienable rights thereof enact the season of famine on the futurity of mankind; thus, God's word first preserves the agrarian society as the foundation, rock, and seed for enlightenment wherein mankind worships the creator of the universe and abandons the tyrants leading the world unto destitution through it's taxation and war; thus, abundance then governs this new world order while violence and coercion form into a distant and elongating memory wherein mankind keeps record of it's lashings so as to not fall into it's trappings again.

2 Samuel 21:10 Then Rizpah the daughter of Aiah took [a] sackcloth and hanged it up for her upon the rock, from the beginning of harvest, until [b] water dropped upon them from the heaven, and suffered neither the birds of the air to [c] light on them by day, nor beasts of the field by night.

2 Samuel 21:10 Footnotes

[a] To make her a tent wherein she prayed to God to turn away his wrath.

[b] Because drought was the cause of this famine, God by sending of rain showed that he was pacified.

[c] Or, rest.

What necessarily represents attack or defense persists as an heated debate which certainly governs mankind into the various despotisms and threatens our present time with a lack of peace and prosperity (though many feign peace and have no prosperity to show for their supposed peace though they claim their earthly riches as the idol and symbolic proof of their peace and prosperity; for example, this commonly vain or often wealthy liar pompously meditates in all luxury and tranquility while the world burns). Must man then leave fate for the determination of a living individual with an undetermined fate Himself or must we trust in God to set the course of our fate within the confines of His lively commandments which can only result in our own experiencing of liberty in this conscious life?

2 Corinthians 1:24 [a] Not that we have dominion over your faith, but we are helpers of your [b] joy: for by faith ye stand.

2 Corinthians 1:24 Footnotes

[a] He removeth all suspicion of arrogance, declaring that he speaketh not as a Lord unto them, but as a servant, appointed of God to comfort them.

[b] He setteth the joy and peace of conscience, which God is author of, against tyrannous fear, and therewithall showeth the end of the Gospel.

The recognition of the living God dwelling within each individual securely measures the form of law which gives us right to preserve one another and our property while the donkey which can not conceive of God or openly rejects His guidance aims for the reception of that spiritual fallacy which God would abhor as spiritual preservation. Why then do so many individuals bleed for that social status which requires them to maintain a certain and unthinking countenance for the granting of extra-judiciary authority to individuals; and, of whom will subjugate even an entire population to their wicked statutes which will prohibit loving thy neighbor as thyself and will mean abolishing that constitution which reminds the public of our indivisible liberty dwelling from within our being; and, of which interpositions us with the heavens for the preservation of our liberty; and, though these pretenders work for the usurpation of the rule of law – they work for a lunatic asylum moonlighting as a slave camp feverishly working to hide it's inconsistencies from entering the perceptions of the public domain and awakening even the most dumb and idle to their plan for society's famine. Only a sadistic fruitcake would desire the establishing or keeping of a hereditary authority. Insecurity mars the soul; tyranny, then, rots the void. The tyrant very much enjoys to exercise the use of that word *Freedom* to mask the effects of their tyranny insofar as their tyranny wilt not speak of the living creator of the universe; nor His perfect law of liberty or His eternal commandments; neist, not even acknowledging the truth of that living image of He in form as that heroic man walking the earth and preaching truth without falsity.

Ezekiel 22:29-31 The people of the land have violently oppressed by spoiling and robbing, and have vexed the poor and the needy:

yea, they have oppressed the stranger against right. And I sought for a man among them, that should [a] make up the hedge, and stand in the gap before me for the land, that I should not destroy it, but I found none. Therefore have I poured out mine indignation upon them, and consumed them with the fire of my wrath: their own ways have I rendered upon their heads, saith the Lord God.

Ezekiel 22:30 Footnotes

[a] Which would show himself zealous in my cause by resisting vice, Isa. 59:16 and 63:5, and also pray unto me to withhold my plagues, Ps. 106:23.

Isaiah 59:16 And when he saw that there was no man, he wondered that none would offer himself. [a] Therefore his arm did [b] save it, and his righteousness itself did sustain it.

Isaiah 59:16 Footnotes

[a] Meaning, to do justice, and to remedy the things that were so far out of order.

[b] That is, his Church or his arm did help itself, and did not seek aid of any other.

Isaiah 63:5 And I looked, and there was none to help, and I wondered that there was none to uphold: therefore mine own [a] arm helped me, and my wrath itself sustained me.

Isaiah 63:5 Footnotes

[a] God showeth that he hath no need of man's help for the deliverance of his, and though men refuse to do their duty through negligence and ingratitude, yet he himself will deliver his Church,

and punish the enemies, read Isa. 59:16.

Psalm 106:23 Therefore he minded to destroy them, had [a] not Moses his chosen stood in the breach before him to turn away his wrath, lest he should destroy them.

Psalm 106:23 Footnotes

[a] If Moses by his intercession had not obtained God's favor against their rebellions.

The peasants of tyranny enjoy their festivities of ill-intentioned pseudo-philosophies though the each of them dive head first unto Satanism and contradict every intention of God's purpose wherein man most joyously sets His purpose forth in the actions which illustrate the cause of liberty in both deed and word. The american dream stands as the continuity of that realization of God aiding us in manifesting our heavenly visions unto reality to the degree in which results in the construction of a court system designed for the preservation of the rights which constitute our liberation of mind and continued peace in prosperity thereby increasing the self-evident impotency of those idle dimwits boring ideas of theft and fraud as the illusion of human consciousness. And would those individuals that would desire to call their self american not as well desire to live amongst one another in a peaceful and prosperous state unlike those fallen nations in which people intentionally flee in order that they most assuredly pursue their own happiness elsewhere when awakened to the idea of liberty and private property? Must we conclude the exceedingly wealthy minority of individuals in every nation exercise their property ownership as the means for lobbing government to absolve happiness and oppress free trade? In realizing nations assemble for the breaking of bread self-evidences why an uneducated population would so easily obsesses over that appetite which they see and then keep an apathy toward the knowing of things which they do not see; and, therefore the hidden remains invisible only unto them though it move and swallow them as though they were a predictable harvest to those few individuals controlling the mind of the worldlings.

***Romans 8:2** [a] For the [b] Law of the Spirit of [c] life <u>which is</u> in [d] Christ Jesus, hath [e] freed me from the Law of sin and of death.*

Roman 8:2 Footnotes

[a] A preventing of an objection: seeing that the virtue of the spirit which is in us, is so weak, how may we gather thereby, that there is no condemnation to them that have that virtue? Because saith he, that virtue of the quickening spirit which is so weak in us, is most perfect and most mighty in Christ, and being imputed unto us which believe, causeth us to be so accounted of, as though there were no relics of corruption, and death in us. Therefore hitherto Paul disputed of remission of sins, and imputation of fulfilling the Law, and also of sanctification which is begun in us: but now he speaketh of the perfect imputation of Christ's manhood, which part was necessarily required to the full appeasing of our consciences: for our sins are defaced by the

blood of Christ, and the guiltiness of our corruption is covered with the imputation of Christ's obedience: and the corruption itself (which the Apostle calleth sinful sin) is healed in us by little and little, by the gift of sanctification, but yet it lacketh besides that another remedy, to wit, the perfect sanctification of Christ's own flesh, which also is to us imputed.

[b] The power and authority of the spirit, against which is set the tyranny of sin.

[c] Which mortifieth the old man, and quickeneth the new man.

[d] To wit, absolutely and perfectly.

[e] For Christ's sanctification being imputed unto us, perfecteth our sanctification which is begun in us.

Spiritual imbalance persists in the human race insofar as the purveyors of destruction keep the world in an order which follows their travels through time thus keeping the origin of their wicked new world order alive; as well as all of it's governing decree and degrees of shape-shifting authority in order to keep it's world order disguised as kosher or new or otherwise fed by the energy of it's unaware hosts: foolish people without the knowledge of both good and evil systems of governance. Consider the landowner preventing water access to the neighboring lands thus threatening the survival of a great and many sum of people whom depend on the natural delivery of this water resource – does this example not equally represent a property violation via aggression through dumping pollution into the stream which their neighbors use? In what direction do we then identify as the path toward manifesting a society with conscious awareness of the heavenly things of liberty which await us all? The obvious answer then rests in obtaining that knowledge of God. In exercising liberty we shed the confines of that world of theft and fraud and expose the reality of that world not of this world; and, of which the tyrannical worldlings would wish to hide from public perception: liberty. So then will the nation anew aim for the securing of liberty; and, not for a minority which oppresses the many; rather, for a multitude of self-realized individuals; and, of whom know to refuse every form of tyrannical oppression. Perhaps and only then will that agrarian society not require the false specialties which hurriedly aid that governing of tyranny in direct opposition to the steadfastness of the men of God.

Colossians 2:13 [d],[a] And you which were dead in sins, [b] and in the uncircumcision of your flesh, hath he quickened together with him, forgiving you all your trespasses,

Colossians 2:13 Footnotes

[a] Another end of Baptism is, that we which were dead in sin, might obtain free remission of sins and eternal life through faith in Christ who died for us.

[b] A new argument which lieth in these few words, and it is thus: Uncircumcision was no hindrance to you, why you being justified in Christ should not obtain life therefore you need not circumcision to the argument of salvation.

Colossians 2:13 Endnotes

[d] Eph. 2:1

Ephesians 2:1 And [a],[b] you <u>hath he quickened</u>, that were [c] dead in [d] trespasses and sins,

Ephesians 2:1 Footnotes

[b] He declareth again the greatness of God's good will, by comparing that miserable state wherein we are born, with that dignity whereunto we are advanced by God the Father in Christ. So he describeth that condition in such sort, that he saith, that touching spiritual motions we are not only born half dead, but wholly and altogether dead.

[c] See Rom. 6:2. So then he calleth them dead, which are not regenerate: for as the immortality of them which are damned, is no life, so this knitting together of body and soul is properly no life, but death in them which are not ruled by the Spirit of God.

[d] He showeth the cause of death, to wit, sins.

Ephesians 2:1 Endnotes

[a] Col. 2:13

Romans 6:2 [a] How shall we, that are [b] dead to sin, live yet therein?

Romans 6:2 Footnotes

[a] The benefits of Justification and Sanctification, are always joined together inseparably, and both of them proceed from Christ, by the grace of God: Now sanctification is the abolishing of sin, that is, of our natural corruption, into whose place succeedeth the cleanness and pureness of nature reformed.

[b] They are said of Paul to be dead to sin, which are in such sort

made partakers of the virtue of Christ, that that natural corruption is dead in them, that is, the force of it is put out, and it bringeth not forth his bitter fruits: and on the other side, they are said to live to sin, which are in the flesh, that is, whom the spirit of God hath not delivered from the slavery of the corruption of nature.

We as men must plan and act to reveal the hidden and make self-evident for all men those ills of tyranny.

Children and women remain under the care of good men or within the danger of wicked tyrants. Many of these wicked tyrants today pretend to live the life of the good man and then provide their family a consistent diet of poisonous chemicals hidden within every item of food; toxins well-known to activate soft-kill mechanisms in the victim upon ingesting the substance: substances which foreign mercenaries intentionally inject into our society as means of engaging in quiet biological warfare. Ignorance serves as no excuse for not defending liberty since this type of acquiescence can only savor tyranny.

1 Corinthians 11:29 For he that eateth and drinketh unworthily, eateth and drinketh his own damnation, because he [a] discerneth not the Lord's body.

1 Corinthians 11:29 Footnotes
[a] He is said to discern the Lord's body, that hath consideration of the worthiness of it, and therefore cometh to eat of this meat with great reverence.

Men will always own property at a proportion completely outweighing that of the women and the children. The brotherly priesthood of cannibal overlords hypnotizing the earth would deeply prefer the majority of the population destitute both in liberty and property since the lack of the two forge the means for a tyrannical subversion of society which exalts them with superfluous riches and social status. People in general will own various items either for necessity or novelty – few will ever question the strongholds of the earth and the great game in which we endeavor to render destitute the tyranny which forces men, women, and children into the slavery of the beast system.

Men as the majority property owners remain the chief authority of good versus evil on the earth; though the men of the knowledge of God remain under direct guidance from God for the defense of every individual's life, liberty, and private property though even only a minority of men own land; and two, both the men and women without possession of land will receive some degree of enslavement from individual landowners through their occupying government authority for the construction of a stronghold prohibiting liberty and rewarding the vicious (though it illustriously speak inversions of language with words such as freer or fairer and simply not free or fair); an illusion due to the self-evident reason an aware and free people would not hesitate in overthrowing this faction of treason within the time of one morning. How easy then does the tyrant withholding all land rule the people since that people would wittingly acquiesce their right to the resources of their own land in which they could so easily and privately own through declaring liberty to those captives; and, in this movement amass a repossession of that immeasurable power in overthrowing the tyrants?

Psalm 36:9 For with thee is the well of life, and in thy light shall we see light.

And what can we expect of the tyrants but their choosing political self-immolation through the worship of a religion offering spiritually dead idols as a burnt offering in hope of receiving a whispering in their ear of false wisdoms preaching the suffocation of civilization as the gait toward temporal gain? Do the tyrants not wage war with that image of man whom God designed (for surely they will lose and face perfunctory destruction of their own life)?

What has history shown, time and again, when the great majority of men will not realize their worth in waging war against rulers of kingdoms for the welcoming of the issuance of their own death warrant from that fallen world working desperately to justify it's wickedness as law enforcement? America was once patrolled by peace officers for the defense of civil liberties; in the name of law enforcement does america now destroy civil liberties and refuse the notion of peace officer altogether: a self-evident transformation in that image of church-like uniforms that call onto their posse during a time of emergency and instead now froth at the mouth and stutter in pretended excitement over their paramilitary squadron of black armor and tanks reading

"POLICE STATE;"

and, all of this backed by even chemical weapons, low-altitude armed missile aircraft flying autonomously over every city across the nation all night and every day, grenades, snipers, and fire-bombs and all designed for use against the american people (as proof of what President James Madison Jr. had so forewarned the american people of) – this same tyrannical squadron even used against mango farmers at local Californian farmer's markets, Christian churches for refusing to pay the state, and residents of the city of New Orleans to disarm their homes during a hurricane; verily american-funded terrorism against our own people and all given full-writ to do so with half-retarded government employees that stare at television programming or scroll on their social media "feed" all day. As we today enter the month of January 2020 we learn of the New York United Nations office hiring soldiers with experience in disarmament affairs, political analysis, or in national military or paramilitary service for disarmament and reintegration of american citizens into mass detainment camps; first by disarmament, second by demobilization, third by reinsertion, and fourth by reintegration; and, all of this happening at the same time the feltching Chinese Communists advertise on their national media that america is a lawless nation and must be disarmed beginning with it's stronghold in Texas; oh, but we are supposed to pretend the left is helping us, the damaged divergents, from harming our self by pretending we do not have a legacy of one thousand thousand generations fighting an alien tyranny therefore we will learn to glorify their plastic aura of moral authority by surrendering our human rights to their Satanic overlords.

Exodus 3:11-12 ¶ But Moses said unto God, Who am [a] I, that I should go unto Pharaoh, and that I should bring the children of Israel out of Egypt? And he answered, [b] Certainly I will be with thee: and this shall be a token unto thee, that I have sent thee, After that thou hast brought the people out of Egypt, ye shall serve God upon this mountain

Exodus 3:11-12 Footnotes

[a] He doth not fully disobey God, but acknowledgeth his own weakness.

[b] Neither fear thine own weakness, nor Pharaoh's tyranny.

Whom will the tyrant use to complete His works of death and desolation when the majority of men no longer capitulate to His spell and the few that stand by His side hold nothing but wealth to pretend it shield their flesh? Do these individuals not seek the foreign alien to complete their works of death and desolation? Does history not show us that any society that would forgo the exercise of their liberty thus a loss in property ownership always suffer a foreign occupation of tyrants rendering them destitute unto the whole capturing of their mind; and, first with the capturing of the mind of the women in order to lead the children into battle against their fathers whom instituted the nation in the first place? What historical usurpation necessarily could greater be lectured upon than the introduction of sports (bread and circus) since sports most openly infiltrate the nation while capturing the minds of the women through sporting or showing love for the women of the nation intended for subversion or capture.

1 Samuel 8:11 And he said, This shall be the [a] manner of the king that shall reign over you: he will take your sons, and appoint them to his chariots, and to be his horsemen, and some shall run before his chariot.

1 Samuel 8:11 Footnotes

[a] Not that kings have this authority by their office, but that such as reign in God's wrath should usurp this over their brethren, contrary to the law, Deut. 17:20.

Deuteronomy 17:20 That his heart be not lifted up above his [a] brethren, and that he turn not from the commandment, to the right hand or to the left, but that he may prolong his days in his kingdom, he and his sons in the midst of Israel.

Deuteronomy 17:20 Footnotes

[a] Whereby is meant, that Kings ought so to love their subjects as nature bindeth one brother to love another.

Not all children will turn into dung hunting their own blood for the tyrant though some will succeed this agenda and the least of them, or most vicious, will receive the greatest reward from the tyrant in the compromising of their spirit for a future which can only condemn the true human spirit. Had the people not originally assembled for the purpose of organizing into a nation which identifies with one philosophy above another – what then could the remnant of the population look back to in order to serve as a reminder to those members of society whom have lost their way and think in their ignorance of not individually and publicly standing and speaking out against the system, as the means of forming some type of common sense which parries the tyranny, will not then exhibit the shortcomings of a backbiter reasoning to identify with their own oppressors as spiritually faithful friends in a realm which they now call home? What resonance could so greatly affect a people as that frequency which calls from the promise land unto the majority of each individual's soul therefore a calling which the majority receive and only few respond for the uniting of that common purpose which so well served our fathers above those carnal afflictions rendering lesser men idle unto a pernicious stammering of the mouth as though gravel fill their cheek, muck weigh their boot, and coldness seize their love?

Considering not even one nation today remains wholly competent for an awareness of liberty or true private property (since they so slothfully and unthinkingly love the enslavements of those thefts of taxation) and then realizing this affliction plagues all of the nations of the earth and all of the nations in the books of history we then realize the philosophy of liberty advances to the depths at which consciousness extends it's reach unto it's own preservation from the assault of that consciousness which would assail it's person for none reason other than freely expressing consciousness as itself and not the person which an other consciousness would so quickly and wrongly define as the physical and final reality in which we base law and spirituality upon. Until all of a people can discern the continuity of power within their own consciousness then the majority will not seek representatives to preserve the consciousness which self-evidence reasons as truly set within the outer perception of a lesser consciousness egoically manifesting lukewarm decay in allying similarly weak minds as opposed to uniting with that strength of God's faith delivering an independent mind in pursuit of conscious felicity in the only pathos which binds all things as one movement contrary to that unharmonious perception of false authority infringing on the rights of the individual. The rainbow exhibits God's promise that no tyranny can compel that liberty which lives in similitude with God thus the nature of tyranny first compels it's forces to destroy the natural world through dwelling within the mind of the ignorant whom construct their pathos upon superstition. Self-evidence proves the individual a representative majority; and, this awareness upon further inquiry illustrates an image constructing a more divine pattern and when acting according to true intention of being-at-work will replicate it's consciousness as a base subconscious spreading to other individuals, insofar as that baseness serves as a reminder of our joy in liberty, thus virally permeates it's truth as a center or origin reminding mankind of their spirit emanating from within their own knowingness and outwardly vibrating as a consciousness seeking inward remedy through resisting that tyrannical frequency which would dissolve those perfections of art seizing the moment

for manifesting a clear interpretation of that life of Jesus Christ –
the eternal name guarding the highest spiritual realm by the full
backing of the almighty and living creator of this universe.

Revelation 9:14 *Saying to the sixth Angel, which had the trumpet,
[a] Loose the four Angels, which are bound in the great river
Euphrates.*

Revelation 9:14 Footnotes

*[a] As if he should have said, These hitherto have been so bound
by the power of God, that they could not freely run upon all men
as themselves lusted, but were stayed and restrained at that great
flood of Euphrates, that is, in their spiritual Babylon (for this is a
Paraphrase of the spiritual Babylon by the limits of the spiritual
Babylon long since overthrown) that they might not commit those
horrible slaughters which they long breathed after. Now go to: let
loose those four Angels, that is, administers of the wrath of God,
in that number that is convenient to the slaughtering of the four
quarters of the world: stir them up and give them the bridle, that
rushing of that Babylon of theirs, which is the seat of the wicked
ones, they may fly upon all the world, therein to rage, and most
licentiously to exercise their tyranny, as God hath ordained. This
was done when Gregory the ninth by public authority established
for law his own Decretals, by which he might freely lay trains for
the life of simple men. For who is it that seeth not that the laws
Decretal most of them are as snares to catch souls withal? Since
that time (O good God!) how great slaughters have there been?
How great massacres? All histories are full of them: and this our*

age aboundeth with most horrible and monstrous examples of the same.

Individuals when assembling amongst one another will always select a representative to oversee or translate the communications which they feel must share with a majority either within their nation or interrelated to their nation, or so to say many representatives equally representing the voice of the nation to an agreeable state; therefore, the power which moves from the many representatives will by nature afford the ability for one individual to oversee them all either by power or force.

Hierarchies naturally occur as does the sediment of a river or the things which passion conceives as a thing to observe or act upon though what we must keep close to our heart exists in the knowing of those tightly woven relationships which bound the people together in the first place and keep their desires set at pursuing liberty and not the company of an alien. What then compels one people to ask of their representative for the use of force and another of righteous spiritual power? Presuming the individual seeks to represent the people then some comprehension of liberty must remain present insofar as to govern spirituality requires to seek an office that can not exemplify a worldly office since the appearance which those in liberty seek exists in the inward and perfected image of God and not the outward appearance which can only deliver tyrannical forces extraneous to the human spirit (insofar as that spirit which humans utilize when enacting evil does not represent any human quality whatsoever and exists rather as a virus of spiritual origin hijacking the mind and body of it's host).

Luke 12:54 ¶ [m],[a] Then said he to the people, When ye see a cloud [b] rise out of the West, straightway ye say, A shower cometh: and so it is.

Luke 12:54 Footnotes

[a] Men which are very quick of sight in earthly things, are blind in those things which pertain to the heavenly life, and that through their own malice.

[b] Which appeareth, and gathereth itself together in that part of the air.

Luke 12:54 Endnotes

[m] Matt. 16:2

Matthew 16:2 *But he answered, and said unto them, When it is evening, ye say, Fair weather, for the sky is red.*

Revelation 12:3 And there appeared another wonder in heaven: [a] for behold, a great red dragon having [b] seven heads, and ten [c] horns, and seven crowns upon his heads:

Revelation 12:3 Footnotes

[a] That is the devil or Satan (as is declared verse 9,) mighty, angry, and full of wrath.

[b] Thereby to withstand those seven Churches spoken of, that is the Catholic Church, and that with kingly furniture and tyrannical magnificence: signified by the crowns set upon his heads, and if the same without controversy belonged unto him by proper right:

as also he boasted unto Christ, Matt. 4:9. See after, upon Rev. 13:1.

[c] More than are the horns of the Lamb, or than the Churches are: so well furnished doth the tyrant brag himself to be, unto all manner of mischief.

Revelation 13:1 *And I [a] saw a beast rise [b] out of the sea, having seven heads, and [c] ten horns, and upon his horns were ten crowns, and [d] upon his head [e] the name of blasphemy.*

Revelation 13:1 Footnotes

[a] The Apostle having declared the springing up of the Christian Church and the state of the Church from which ours taketh her beginning, doth now pass unto the story of the progress thereof, as I showed in the entrance of the former Chapter. And this history of the progress of the Church, and the battles thereof, is set down in this Chapter, but distinctly in two parts, one is of the civil Roman Empire, unto the tenth verse. Another of the body Ecclesiastical or prophetical, thence unto the end of the chapter. In the former part are showed these things: First the state of that Empire, in four verses: then the acts thereof in three verses: after the effect, which is exceeding great glory, verse 8. And last of all is commended the use: and the instruction of the godly against the evils that shall come from the same, verses 9, 10. The history of the state containeth a most ample description of the beast, first entire, verses 1, 2, and then restored after hurt, verses 3, 4.

[b] On the sand whereof stood the devil practicing new tempests against the Church, in the verse next beforegoing: what time the

Empire of Rome was endangered by domestical dissensions, and was mightily tossed, having ever and anon new heads, and new Emperors. See in the seventeenth chapter and the eighth verse.

[c] Having the same instruments of power, providence, and most expert government which the Dragon is said to have had in Rev. 12:3.

[d] We read in chapter 12 and third verse, that the Dragon had seven crowns set upon seven heads: because the thief announceth himself to be proper Lord and Prince of the world: but this beast is said to have ten crowns set upon several, not heads, but horns: because the beast is beholden for all unto the Dragon, verse 2, and doth not otherwise reign them by law of subjection given by him, namely that he employ his horns against the Church of God. The speech is taken from the ancient custom and form of dealing in such case: by which they that were absolute kings did wear the diadem upon their heads: but their vassals and such as reigned by grace from them, wore the same upon their hoods: for so they might commodiously lay down their diadems when they came into the presence of their Sovereigns: as also their Elders are said, when they adored God which sat upon the throne, to have cast down their crowns before him, chap. 4, verse 10.

[e] Contrary to that which God of old commanded should be written in the head piece of the high Priest, that is, _Sanctitas Jehova_, Holiness unto the Lord. The name of blasphemy imposed by the Dragon, is (as I think) that which S. Paul saith in chapter 2 of his 2 Epistle to the Thessalonians, verse 4. _He sitteth as God, and boasteth himself to be God._ For this name of blasphemy both

the Roman Emperors did then challenge unto themselves, as Suetonius and Dion do report of Caligula and Domitian: and after them the Popes of Rome did with full mouth profess the same of themselves, when they challenged unto themselves sovereignty in holy things: of which kind of sayings the sixth book of the Decretals, the Clementines, and the Extravagants, are very full. For these men were not content with that which Anglicus wrote in his <u>Poetria</u> (the beginning whereof is, Papa stupor mundi. The Pope is the wonder of the world. <u>Nec Deus es, nec homo, sed neuter es inter utrunque</u>. Thou art not God, nay art thou man, but neuter mixed of both: as the gloss witnesseth upon the sixth book: but they were bold to take unto themselves the very name of God, and to accept it given of other: according as almost an hundred and twenty years since, there was made for Sixtus the fourth, when he should first enter into Rome in his dignity Papal, a Pageant of triumph, and cunningly fixed upon the gate of the city he should enter at, having written upon it this blasphemous verse:

<u>Oraclo vocis mundi moderaris habenas,</u>

<u>Et merito in terris crederis esse deus.</u>

<u>By oracle of thine own voice the world thou governest all, And worthily a God on earth, men think, and do thee call.</u>

These and six hundred the like who can impute unto that modesty whereby good men of old would have themselves called the servants of the servants of God, verily either this is a name of blasphemy, or there is none at all.

Revelation 13:1 Endnotes

The beast with many heads is described

Do the people not entrust some measurable portion of their fate into the hands of whom they elect especially in the event they shed their power for the dwelling under an absolute tyranny which dictates to them their social status in society? What man in society could trust the latter individual with His own fate since that individual would so readily supply a tyrant with the power to steal the means for His liberty?

Obviously individuals must choose one of the two paths available to them: self-governance or enslavement. Self-governance of individuals does not represent majority rule rather this represents minority rule since the individual remains chief among all authority on the earth; and, this topic ought to keep center-stage for our intellectual conductivity energizing free society and serving as a reminder for those things which dishonor the individual and only conclude with a world of disingenuous individuals; and, of whom obsess in the formation of a classist faction treading upon civil liberty in a great game of racing toward the least amount of self-awareness; hence: serfdom. Rule by majority vote then means mob rule within a democracy while individual rule means the democracies of the world at war with our keeping individual liberty within our republic. Today mob rule reigns supreme across the globe illustrating it's most perfect form of that calm of despotism which inspires good men to do nothing as they acquiesce to the theft by taxation from their government and for pretended necessity or security; tyrannical hypocrisy! These presumptuous numptys lack the self-awareness of God creating man to exist as an individual with sovereignty to His liberty and even represent a government of plurality in that God perfectly designed man with equal and unalienable rights preexisting and exceeding the power of any multitude of strongholds writing rules or statutes to presumptuously claim jurisdiction or preexistence over those unalienable rights which exceedingly outnumber the labels which the alien government would mark upon man; and, rights which inherently own the various political systems which remain targets for capture by wicked men in government lusting to usurp such political systems in order to control the mind of many men; therefore, any man proclaiming no government for the individual and by the individual ought to exist do then proclaim destruction to their soul and allegiance to Satan.

Isaiah 52:1 *Arise, arise: put on thy strength, O Zion: put on the garments of thy beauty, O Jerusalem, the holy City: for henceforth there shall no [a] more come into thee the uncircumcised and the unclean.*

Isaiah 52:1 Footnotes

[a] No wicked tyrant, which shall subvert God's true religion, and oppress the conscience.

Matthew 10:25 *It is enough for the disciple to be as his master is, and the servant as his Lord. [n] If they have called the master of the house [a] Beelzebub, how much more them of his household?*

Matthew 10:25 Footnotes

[a] It was the idol of the Acronites, which we call the god of flies.

Matthew 10:25 Endnotes

[n] Matt. 12:24

Matthew 12:24 But when the Pharisees heard it, they said, [j] This man casteth the devils no otherwise out but through Beelzebub the prince of devils.

Matthew 12:24 Endnotes

[j] Matt. 9:34, Mark 3:22, Luke 11:15

Matthew 9:34 But the Pharisees said, [h] He casteth out devils, through the prince of devils.

Matthew 9:34 Endnotes

[n] Matt. 12:24, Mark 3:22, Luke 11:15

Mark 3:22 ¶ [c] And the Scribes which came down from Jerusalem, said, He hath Beelzebub, and through the prince of the devils he casteth out devils.

Mark 3:22 Endnotes

[c] Matt. 9:34, Matt. 12:24, Luke 11:15

Luke 11:15 [a] But some of them said, [f] He casteth out devils through Beelzebub the chief of the devils.

Luke 11:15 Footnotes

[a] An example of horrible blindness, and such as cannot be healed, when as upon an evil conscience, and pretended malice, the power of God is blasphemed.

Luke 11:15 Endnotes

[f] Matt. 9:34, Matt. 12:24, Mark 3:22

In our proclamation of liberty governing our sovereignty we adhere to God's commandments and enlighten to the pursuit of happiness for God's eternal government which the tyrant would destroy by erring from the faith or idolatry of the faithless. Thus we can know the cruel and unusual ghouls would punish the individual in order to usurp their power, prohibit, and then transfer their rights as a funnel transmuting natural energy into a weapon fit into the palm of a greater usurper whom can only form a line in spiritual sand and wage war against the mind defending the philosophy of liberty; therefore, these infidels against human liberty live as a mirage of tone-deaf voices determining their greatest life ambition as reenacting the idol in which they worship most; even the most idle idol; therefore, the tyrant in claiming occupation over an ignorant people builds the momentum of their superstitions into a stronghold of ignorant authoritarians; and, of whom purchase a soirée of circus entertainers (à la the tired archetypes which further the idolization of the state) to act as the people whom individually channel the energy of a state into a religious expedition for the empirical driving of civilization into the fiery hell of a one world governance destitute of any knowledge of liberty or awareness of an individual whose consciousness liberty contains.

The individuals whom will not align their conscience to a majority political faction save their voice from the vortices of a culling which disintegrates their life's ambition (insofar as God gave man ambitious purpose to preserve life, liberty, and property) from fulfilling the womb of destiny; though, when society shall divide itself into the faction of liberty and tyranny – only then would that confused individual without knowledge of God join the faction of liberty and imbue their spirit with the gift of life. The spiritual gap which separates the free man and the tyrant may purely exist in the ability for the free man exercising His faith in liberty to reach His own conclusions by way of discerning the knowledge of God; for in discernment we know our logic gives reason to purpose; thus, honesty provisions our solution with fuel to preserve life and deliver rapid justice to the wicked. Perhaps our rights then exist purely in thought, though real, and this voice which precedes us even unto the alpha of God's own realization creates that omega of our reality in which houses the realms of discovery we choose to live even unto the pursuit of bringing steadfast justice to all of the wicked in this realm and manifestly in this lifetime so that we fiercely and indivisibly oppose the needless suffering from these tyrants. Who might successfully own property when a tyrant commands both thought and trade when a majority gladly endorse the usurping of rights upon every member of society? What type of corruption flirts with that duly elected representative?

Do the corruptions of theft and fraud not offer their seals for the oppression of the majority and appeasing of that minority whom only meditate toward that plunder of an unthinking public? What then compels both the minority and majority to seek union with one another but that realization we must individually take vigorous action in order to seek liberty's preservation shall we earnestly wish for God's vision of mankind to manifestly fulfill; and, for the fulfilling of the perfect law of liberty in that the multitude witness total destruction for those individuals whom wish nightmare upon all? That citizenry whom abandons their civil liberties (this here even meaning to abandon God's way of life) for the worshiping of a tyrant will not always possess the thinking faculty for defining property or that tyrant which they wish to so fervently enjoy as a shadow for the apathy of their heart as He in the same instant forms their obtuse energy into a house of worship which creates a target for the sentient and sovereign individual to destroy shall they earnestly endeavor the blessings of liberty beyond the scope of what the tyrants define as the limits of the individual's capacity or expression under their tyrannical governance. Considering the minority with property and the majority without property – both instances when formed into political factions do represent a majority at odds with that sovereign individual whom would not side with either faction thus stands as His own faction and majority alone; therefore, in this individual's act of being the least of all minorities would in the same instant create the greatest of majorities since God above words measures the potential of man's intention; and, these sovereign powers in man stand ready for the captives to proclaim as their own property; and, in the same instant that they would claim ownership of their life would withdraw their energy from the tyrant's control. All things the tyrant then perceivably owns can only remain under His ownership so long as the people continue their ownership of the idea that a tyrant holds power over them.

What departure from equality can exist greater than the inequality produced from reinterpreting the sovereignty of one's own mind, body, and spirit into a body enslaved to the reinterpretation of life, liberty, and property? Self-awareness knows it's indivisible and unalienable right to life, liberty, and the pursuit of happiness pursues the virtues of honest trade which our efforts bear and our arms aid for the preservation thereof; for what else keeps the majority from usurping the rights of the minority? The rogue legislator so often inspires His unthinking supporters to commit acts of violent insurrection while espousing slogans of anti-fascism or anti-imperialism though these usurpers hypocritically assail the peaceful and sovereign individuals standing for equal rights in the face of those whom tout inequality or infringement of rights as a necessity due to some illusion their commandments act as a proof for their tyrannical acts in order to correct the course of mankind though only liberty can do that. Tyranny as a state of mind truly represents the lack of a human state of mind insofar as though the human act out the tyranny – the state-of-being itself exists as foreign to man in that only a specie designed to consume the flesh of man would so innately desire to harm mankind; therefore, some type of perceived unworthiness toward God's love superstitiously infects the soul of He that would even forgo pursuing happiness to prove His own hatred toward God and mankind in this life time. Any person that would usurp even their own rights and especially those of an other have abandoned all pursuit of happiness; and, in like manner of a volcano after an explosion – this people will form a caldera as it were a pit of unhappiness which can only reject liberty and submit to unwarranted tyranny.

In the same manner that empowered individual in liberty can act as a brushfire or vector with the potential to ignite a majority how then will tyranny expand since it's predecessors can not feel happy or loving at all even unto the extent these individuals seek legislators that would prove their indisputable hatred for their self and fellow countrymen all of their days; therefore, in their co-opting government for the forceful control of the people – do seek a way of life which potentially will make the public feel the same intolerance and weakness as the tyrant thus completing the systems of action or energy-output necessary for a tyrant to obtain the means for fulfilling the highest potential in His seizure of the mind of the women for the take-down of society.

Amos 1:13 ¶ *Thus saith the Lord, For three transgressions of the children of Ammon, and for four, I will not turn to it, because they [a] have ripped up the women with child of Gilead, that they might enlarge their border.*

Amos 1:13 Footnotes

[a] He noteth the great cruelty of the Ammonites, that spared not the women, but most tyrannously tormented them, and yet the Ammonites came of Lot, who was of the household of Abraham.

Ezekiel 32:2 Son of man, take up a lamentation for Pharaoh king of Egypt, and say unto him, Thou art like a [a] lion of the nations, and art as a [b] dragon in the sea: thou castedst out thy rivers [c] and troubledst the waters with thy feet, and stampedst in their rivers.

Ezekiel 32:2 Footnotes

[a] Thus the scriptures compare tyrants to cruel and huge beasts which devour all that be weaker than they, and such as they may overcome.

[b] Or, whale.

[c] Thou preparest great armies.

What outcome does the honest legislator face when the majority which He represents even changes their intention from liberty to immediately demanding He usurp the rights of their perceived political opposition? Would this legislator not suddenly find Himself in the position requiring His most clear articulation of the duty and responsibility for all men to equally defend and protect the rights of all individuals and to fight the ignorance which demands the theft of rightful ownership and fraud of the intelligent truth in which otherwise defends them from that society of plunder and models itself around the anti-art of theft and fraud? This ship of fools using petty theft to extrapolate their global warfare from well-intentioned welfare do hide their international fraud with a knitting of wicked knowledge which in turn culls civilization from it's sovereignty and even unto the ends of despotism though it disguise itself as a pseudonym known as democracy – as though it's tyrants regard liberty as sacred or their sorcery as anything remotely resembling a republic. Central banks as the authority of the standing armies form a chain of command wherein haughty and spineless imaginations endeavor to drunken their minds into hastily accusing and libeling the world in order to justify it's forward progression of occultic anti-knowledge which anagrams against logic and reason for the succession of it's coercions and violence (or simply theft and fraud) which can only vector into an equal and opposite magnitude of force for the reduction of peace and prosperity. Democracy can only promise a government the freedom to eliminate liberty and assassinate human consciousness: yeah, no way to protect the minority from the tyranny of the majority in democracy.

The ignorant whom claim the legislators must complete the will of the majority no matter their slated cause demand not only the usurping of rights in the least but in the usurping of their own conscience and destiny in the most and this can extend outward even unto the destiny of mankind insofar as each individual holds certain immutable keys for unlocking the potential which houses those blessings of liberty. How can this majority claim civility when their intent results in the restriction of unalienable rights for all individuals which directly increases the tyrannical ability of the state and it's harebrained followers? How can this decision to not make any conscious decision at all result in anything except civil ruin unto the forced inscription of worshiping every form of tyranny in the mind of *the man*?

Ecclesiastes 4:1 So [a] I turned and considered all the oppressions that are wrought under the sun, and behold, the tears of the oppressed, and none comforteth them, and lo, the strength is of the hand of them that oppress them, and none comforteth them.

Ecclesiastes 4:1 Footnotes

[a] He maketh here another discourse with himself concerning the tyranny of them that oppressed the poor.

Consider the situation wherein ten million assembled to oppose an hundred million – do the same principles of liberty not apply insofar as those individuals of liberty demand preservation of life and property while this caldera of hopeless fire demands their sacrificing of logic and reason for a life with none? Those tyrants whom would even label all of the flesh of the earth as their own property, or so to say the flesh not their own, must first surrender to the empire which their mind grants acquiescence for none reason but electing their self as a false god; though, in such a scenario this individual can not use any power of God for God reserves His power to destroy such an individual at the appointed time.

Self-governance then means a term in which must keep hidden or defined as a name which no man can speak lest He desire His body chained to the walls of the catacombs within the great dungeon of the tyrants. Property of one's life seems the most self-evident right though even individuals whom profess a desire to preserve their life would as a majority, as history shows, even sacrifice their own life or society for the illusions of taxation and all of it's inherently vicious and psychopathic agencies which parasitically feed off of the public while proclaiming it do so for superlatively anomalous diction and no philosophy could ever or has endeavored to prove their system as immoral or plainly wicked (though this beast system purchase itself time through the slithering tongue of talking-heads and overpaid pseudo philosophers in scantily clad or even slave-tailored clothing; and, the whole of this system described exists as one and in the same with this closed loop system of state-sponsored theft or even thought of as resultant effects which receive false protections of the ego from a system that punishes the Godly and will abstain or prohibit punishment of the wicked which does create a market for wickedness and confusions of tongue chiefly planting taxation as it's king flag on their hill of deception and enslaving mankind into eons upon generations of Babylon's new world order); and, how could such a people view this waste of resourceful energy as means of self-preservation when this promise of self-preservation comes from the men stealing from society which flaunts it's oppressions directly in the face of God and His commandment to not steal. Sovereignty so redundantly makes apparent that life which God designed with unalienable rights including and especially that right to speak freely even unto it's abundantly bold and sharp defense without let. Does this creator God not possess the same liberty for which He grants unto His own image in the form of man from His very inception? Free-will then surely represents that spectrum which enables man to produce liberty or tyranny though abundance favors liberty and herein we pursue this victory unto the light of it's success. One can then think of liberty and tyranny as a separate property or gait for which the human spirit enters – though liberty be the eternal light; and, tyranny be the darkness and the illusion of freedom – since He in tyranny would argue His wilt sufficiently endows Him to commit those tyrannical acts though He remain sinful within the physical realm and pretend as though He lives spiritually enlightened when He had not even neared that spiritual gait in the least; and, the members of society presently seek justice upon Him by way of following God (for His self-evident injustices will God destroy).

Liberty ought to then mean that narrow gait; and, juxtaposed against it: that wide gait of tyranny which the majority of the public so agreeably follow for the sake of vanity or fear of living a hot or cold life or so to say fear of authenticity in a comfortable numbness through apathy whereby living their lukewarm existence appears indifferent to the state of the common fool whom adopt the dull mind of the universal idiot for the false impression of happiness while their inner spirit decay unto the moths of tyranny. Liberty being the philosophy of everything means a certain frequency of individual minds will pursue the equal and opposite form of this philosophy and that philosophy being tyranny therefore we know each of these philosophies point toward the presence of a third philosophy that would contradict liberty, and, yet, sow seeds unto tyranny therefore illustrate one of the colors of tyranny; hence, two paths exist – one of light and one of a darkness which will lead to a deepness so dark that it's web ensnare light thus causing it to glow as though it appeared as knowledge for the taking though it be the evil contradiction blindly propelling those dimwits without care of the knowledge of God or otherwise under the hypnosis of the knowledge of evil since a lukewarm existence only can dizzy the individual into defending evil logic and reason. Perhaps this lukewarm path which can not represent a true path at all then showcases that ghoulish life meandering as a tributary with water in one season and without water in another – simply moving in and out of existence or into the light and and out of the light and into the darkness of that restless tyranny which fuels the desire for money, power, and fame and most effectually works on the economically and spiritually challenged since their desire for money coincides with chasing the illusion that jeer at the animating contest of liberty as though God would regard His men as the outcasts without purpose and not ostracize or exile these jeering enemies; and, especially for such a time as the state of a world ruled by wicked tyrants and not a world defended and preserved by righteous and free men. Perhaps awakening then means a perpetual bending toward that light of truth even as a flowering branch would in producing a new universe as it's fruit; and, even pointing it's potential energy as a light which enters the universe for the full creation of the unborn universe in a delivery from the unseen into the manifestly self-evident form in order to ensure the bending of life in the light of our consciousness breaks with that bondage of tyranny. In either case of choosing liberty or tyranny the individual possesses that power which can mean a property, origin, source, or well-spring of power in which gives rise to majestic or despicably mysterious manners since certain events unfold from pursuing curse or blessings.

The satisfaction of the living rests in their discernment giving vision for knowing the righteousness of God as opposed to that face of outward expression which lies in wait for the innocent and passes opportunity for the evils of a world whose property feigns purity and hates the sublime architecture freely given by God. The spiritual evils of this present realm would create illusions to trap individuals from witnessing and experiencing the higher realms of satisfaction that live without tyranny and in accordance only to the bread of the word of God.

2 Timothy 3:16 [c],[a] For the whole Scripture is given by inspiration of God, and is profitable to teach, to convince, to correct, and to instruct in righteousness,

2 Timothy 3:16 Footnotes

[a] The eighth admonition, which is most precious: A Pastor must be wise by the word of God only: wherein we have perfectly delivered unto us, whatsoever pertaineth either to discern, know and establish true opinions, and to confute false, and furthermore, to correct evil manners, and to frame good.

2 Timothy 3:16 Endnotes

[c] 2 Pet. 1:20

Do the charitable not possess the outcome of the charity as though it were a type of property worth purchasing? And do all individuals present and future face a threat from individuals whom owe their allegiance to a group that would desire famine upon a people as though it were a type of property worth purchasing? In comparing these two examples we must know the true property in opposition to the false property; and, that true property would exist as verily as does liberty; and, so truly had God designed mankind with liberty had God designed mankind with a right to His property in order to exercise that liberty without infringing on any man's civil liberty and this holds especially true for that man whom holds public office and would desire to abuse His own authority for the stealing of property via any pseudonym or statute and especially the immoral and unlawful act of taxation. What society could possibly condemn charity but america today in it's current form as witnessed throughout the nation?

Philippians 1:9 [a] And this I pray that your love may abound yet more and more in knowledge, and in all judgment,
Philippians 1:9 Footnotes
[a] He showeth what thing we ought chiefly desire, to wit, first of all, that we may increase in the true knowledge of God (so that we may be able to discern things that differ one from another) and also in charity, that even to the end we may give ourselves to good works indeed, to the glory of God by Jesus Christ.

America has long fallen from the land of the free into enriching transnationalists by way of adopting the old British system of mercantilism thus leaving the american people stricken with that ignorant and superstitious kind of fear and paranoia even causing them to cheer the flying of a foreign flag (as I have witnessed all throughout Austin, Texas, a city of two million peoples living near twenty-five million more people, for example, in the flying of the United Nations flag atop permanent and public installations) and beg for the enshrinement of a foreign law as their own so that they would make plain their desire for a moniker of their flaming false social justice since we can self-evidently frame the preservation of our liberty; and, as such – these superficial and shallow usurper-entities distort, tax, and regulate as a single crimson tide of tyranny living for the occasion as if they were an alien named "It" harvesting our substance to control mankind into killing itself; one of these most egregious and formal examples of the United Nations usurpation american law exists never so prevalent as the U.N. strong cities initiatives, Agenda 21, and Agenda 2030 – programs which are eugenics systems of total control.

Do we then need any slogan for liberty or could any command, phrase, or utterance represent a slogan in time of need; for example, the people apt for liberty would as well keep apt in the use of the word: "No." Surely certain slogans do fully possess that whole fractal of holographic energy which first accompanied the idea of america and even preceded it's revolution for human liberty – so to say a remnant or literal composite material possessing the part and the whole of that purpose and intent which can only want to pursue and master righteousness so that these lands would dispossess the foundation of that wicked nature and adopt instead that free-will devoid of desire to sin or submission to tyranny and all other programmings of self-fulfilling prophesies manipulating world-view into the elitist houndings of collectivism. Liberty will always remain that path to human enlightenment dispossessed from the energy which brings the ruin of sin and tyranny though those of sin and tyranny will invent all sorts of pseudo philosophies to trick and misguide the cross-eyed and broken-hearted.

What individual can stand before a multitude and proclaim property as no right to man except that tyrant apt to hoard a population as His own property for trade though He claim to provision the people equal unto Himself or their neighbor – as though the civil liberty of property unalienably afforded to every individual by God and not the government of man did not equally harmonize compassion and opportunity in the first place? All throughout human history there have existed this slothful individual whom through their ancestry of disorder join an assembly amongst a multitude of additional slothful individuals; and, of whom all proclaim property as no right to any man; therefore, they compel the state to steal whatever property they can obtain by the use of force (though they spread advertisements requesting the people to voluntarily surrender their goods, thus slitting their spiritual wrists, and upon public refusal do commit acts of death and desolation to steal those goods from the public); and, how can such a thing of stealing goods not as well result in the fraud of the people against their services which the property compels and God gives them advance authority in provisioning even with arms equal to or greater than any state?

What evil possesses a man that He would smirk in one's face as He spit His pseudo philosophy of thieving property from the people as a form of real or necessary enlightenment, and, even perform this stunt without awareness He face perfunctory exile, imprisonment, or reprisal from those men of God whom do represent the righteous intelligence class (class herein meaning the measure of a zeal when weighed contrary to another for the sake of logic and reason to divide the difference of liberty against tyranny)? What psychological mechanism enables an individual to dispossess from their energetic soul and then view society as a purpose which demands the prohibition of individuals and preservation of groups; and, what would disable these groups of individuals from thieving from one another since they all compete to maintain the same countenance or pathos which debases true philosophy in order to receive the immediate gratification of carnal lusts and primarily of the gut-inspired variety; or, even the self-congratulatory nature of their underlings whom constantly self-identify as one group and then another group, and another group, and another group with this slogan, and that slogan, and that slogan since they worship this baseless power as a demigod with powers to deliver the great equalizer of mankind's unearthed potential through that communism of debasing, demoralizing, stealing, and redistribution of wealth to the common man (according to the tyrant the common man can not have equal rights with all men since under such philosophy there exists no creator of the universe endowing men with certain unalienable rights and among them life, liberty, and property as the most base and common sense rights)? Of course only the lemming would harbor a character which measures their character's ability based on the limits for which the government will thieve from them (though this government state this thieving exists for their best interest and represents the base and only form for which the definition of government can operate; yet, every such instantiation can only bring tyrannical war to the free people) such that at some point in time this individual agrees with the present physical decay of society since this would serve as the measure of the property for which He imagined as His chosen spiritual realm and not the one God designed for His people preceding any of the vain and worldly teachings. Certain indelibly stupid and wicked individuals will inquire:

"What authority possesses you to prove or disprove anything since we know language means nothing therefore no thing matters and we all have the freedom to do anything we want without consequence; thusly, not even a government ought to exist for society's preservation and the fact you do not follow my rules means I and my comrades will libelously define and even cause harm to you for whatever reason our logic surmises since our philosophic green-horned-ness does so incredulously paint you as the black, red, and yellow target for our chosen fair and balanced archetype that we shall sacrifice to our stateless-anti-state-anarchist-state."

This folly regurgitated by an uneducated plague of civilization has supported every tyrant in history for the simple exchange of a free gallon of wine to shut them up and compel them to not think past that loaf of bread or weekend circus; and, never so well exemplified as in america today in more than two hundred million psychopathic idiots spending hours per day staring at the psychologically reprogramming warfare device known as the television; or even the self-submitted spy tool known as "Social Media" wherein all mindless and shallow things devour and sway public perception though it's consumers contemptuously excuse and most scornfully lie about the insolence of it's use, for example:

"I am keeping up with friends; I have nothing to hide; I trust my government when they tell me I do not need my fourth amendment anymore; I am too stupid to see how removing my privacy will result in me losing all of my rights and even my life; god damnit, stop warning me or I will call the Federal "my feelings are hurt" hot-line on you."

and, such things must see discussion since these psychopathic idiots openly demand and allow government to exercise these spy tools as the means to suspend the Bill of Rights and outright abandon the fourth amendment so they most wickedly cling to the lie of "keeping up with friends," so they can worship Satanism, pay for unlawful foreign occupation and genocide in The Middle

East, and abandon the ancient and sacred fight for liberty; leave america and move to communist Russia you inhuman, psychopathic, and usurping idiots! Government for these individuals means a thing that only a tyrant could know therefore if the tyrant loses then the people simultaneously lose and win since the conquering of their original tyrant was followed with the oppression from the new and reigning tyrant; though if the tyrant fall amongst a God-fearing people then the people shall rejoice.

2 Chronicles 23:21 Then all the people of the land rejoiced, and the city was quiet [a] after that they had slain Athaliah with the sword.

2 Chronicles 23:21 Footnotes

[a] For where a tyrant and an idolater reigneth, there can be no quietness for the plagues of God are ever among such people.

Acts 5:28 [a] Saying, Did we not straightly command you, that ye should not teach in this name? and behold, ye have filled Jerusalem with your doctrine, and ye would [b] bring this man's blood upon us.

Acts 5:28 Footnotes

[a] It is the property of tyrants to set out their own commandments as right and reason, be they never so wicked.
[b] Make us guilty of murdering, that man whom yet they will not vouchsafe to name.

Habit then forms that self-evident charge of either engaging or removing one's self from possessing that fight for the animating contest of liberty such that entire generations either engage or shrivel in the face of tyranny. How often in civilization does the occurrence of a principled people manifest so as to shed the fear of man in order to enter that society which was promised to their fathers by the almighty God of this universe – a sure promise which no man could ever fulfill without God's express support. However rich or poor – the industrious whom communicate and defend the idea of liberty will prevail over the usurpers insofar as the most industrious will not limit their self in duty or knowledge and therefore will fight against any and all sorts of planned collapse over civilization; and, this can mean imperfectly teaching the poor and idle of the duty and knowledge which can then rest at their hand so that their life and the future of mankind would activate into a society free from the pretenders and religious zealots manipulating the entire economy for the manufacture of poverty for their own gain or seizing of public office for the dissolution of governance and resurrection of tyranny. People of all professions will argue that humans have rose to the heights of civilization before though the truth more closely aligns with only a few individuals having witnessed those heights in liberty which means a property or place not even fathomable among the masses as they choose out their day according to the occasion of vices calming their inexcusably irrational senses which self-reflect their form of ignorance as a derivative of their pretend tranquility though this be such a contemptuous and most passively-aggressive thing since this inaction against tyranny only begets the tyranny they claim to resolve through avoidance of not expressly teaching the public of the self-evident tyranny.

"My weakness strengthens you and your affairs,"

argues the pseudo philosopher. What then could restrain such an assembly of people from pursuing the destruction of their society except those blessings which God gifts to the men of liberty not only for their own life but for even a cure for all of the world? Can we as well reason that the property owners possess the means of creating more industrious action than those without property insofar as those individuals of higher means contain either more elaborate knowledge or abundant resources than those individuals adept at those base tasks of labor which range from skilled to unskilled or otherwise stated as a craftsman and His helpers employed by a statesmen?

What then equalizes rights but that realization that God created all men equal in the ownership of their life, liberty, and property which indivisibly and unalienably reserves them the duty to assemble and overthrow those falsely virtuous individuals threatening their happiness through the theft and fraud of their life and property?

Acts 5:25 *Then went the captain with the officers, and brought them without violence (for they feared the people, lest they should have been stoned.)*
Acts 5:26 Footnotes

[a] Tyrants which fear not God, are constrained to fear his servants.

The fruits of one's labor and innovation of one's character constructs the free market which can only build toward excellence and aspire toward the constant changing of trends which assemble men for the innovation which deprecates the old and makes way for an ever more industrious mankind – industrious since we must eat the food which God would most nourish our body with and consume the word which God would most gladly use for the elation of our soul. One type of pseudo philosophy states men enter society for dignity or pride; for example, the false society of untruth which forms around monarchy or oligarchy (as though one's bloodline delivered authority to enslave men); thus, common sense spells out the abundance which free men trading in a free market will produce since diplomacy and honesty, and not transnationalist trade deals sanctioned by government, will most efficiently innovate industry for the preservation of our liberty. The essence of honor means for a man to publicly declare liberty to the captives as the first means of assembling against a tyrant since the true men will champion the renown of that spirit of the Lord for which we aim to measure and justify our fight for a world of liberty again wherein men wittingly receive their subordination from God and not from any tyrant that would mask that haven of liberty we shall manifest as Heaven on the earth. What then would prevent the assembly of people from destroying those property owners whom arguably enslave the people to enrich the property owners and impoverish the public? Suppose the liquidity of the market would suppress this assembly for a time either due to the people remaining busy in their church or family or by some supposed moral platitude though when famine surely strike some action surely must follow by the men of society so that liberty and justice prevail.

Government will continue even in the absence of mankind since these laws preexisting us govern the interposition and motion of all things. In the imagining of any thing at all does man first govern His mind and in this way do all things including society govern since this same man will govern action from the creation of His ideas; or, said in another way: what man eats in bread and word draws the boundaries of His garden; or, said in another way: truth, like a garden, must be cultivated. How then can a man on the one hand perform a job and then on another hand complain about the work He completes or the pay in which He first agreed to receive lest His complaint rest in those missed opportunities which His most fervent effort would have learnedly afforded Him into a more decisive happiness? Does habit not compel those property owners to oppress He whom does not resist their economic automations and would religion not alter that spirit which embodies both the destitute and the tyrant into one spirit inspired to create a society with decisions designed around acquiring that property of liberty? All throughout this world today individuals complain of capitalism and argue man's desire to trade stems from His worship of money or power when in all of reality all men must eat and to work for one another's mutual defense and preservation in society means to build the efficiency at which men can more readily pursue their happiness without the oppressions of sin and it's guild. True capitalism means to voluntarily trade property for that liberty which compels or persuades men to peace and prosperity or so to say dislodge the mind of man from every form of tyranny. Naturally the *isms* of this world stand to profit off of those controlled individuals whom will agree to expand the scope of any term's original meaning so long as this means they obtain additional unjust power for their tyrant and His shareholders aiding the reign of terror disguised as good intention. How perfect can one individual act insofar as a job, glossing anatomy, vehicle, or home mean nothing in relation to living well since only a moral society with just laws honoring life, liberty, and, property; and, especially by way of men speaking openly and publicly of those self-evident affairs illustrating man's true purpose in fulfilling human felicity will fulfill the life of man and the law; therefore, we must take into consideration how one must view that individual whom obsesses over achieving carnal things above spiritual things in that we must forewarn them of their self-evident spiritual death and absence of spiritual life since they would aim to abolish the means of imagination which they feel threaten their raging ego whereas the men of liberty will aim and achieve the abolishing of those carnal systems which abase abundance thereby burying the tyranny and resurrecting a society of honesty with an imagination for intentionally pursuing truth in the light of God.

Imagine an assembly as a form of conversational warfare to

square off the divisions which separate the right to liberty and wrongfulness of tyranny. Suppose the property owners had enslaved the multitude – do the people not reserve the right to capture the oppressors and free their society? Education of the word alone will not facilitate change without action to prove the just weight of deeds more worthy than the measure of lofty words. What happens in the event the minority of property owners live as free men and that majority without property move as vagabonds from one land to another thereby fostering economic uncertainty for the observer and participant of this type of transient economy – do these innocent and victimized men not reserve the right to defend their property even unto the declaration of war and drawing of blood to keep their life, liberty, and property? So often do the oppressors use government to shield their self from the oppressed and if anything to purchase a little time to encourage the oppressed to forget what ails them hence the use of bondslaves and usury to demoralize, entrap, and placate an envious, greedy, ignorant, servile, soft, spiteful, superstitious, unclean, unwary, and unworthy public and their fellow countrymen.

Revelation 13:16 [a] And he made all, both small and great, rich and poor, free and bond, to receive [b] a [c] mark in their right hand or in their foreheads.

Revelation 13:16 Footnotes

[a] The third place, is a most wicked and most insolent tyranny as was said before, usurped over the persons of men in this verse: and over their goods and actions, in the next verse. For he is said,

both to bring upon all persons a tyrannous servitude, that as bondslaves they might serve the beast: and also to exercise over all their goods and actions, a peddler-like abuse of indulgences and dispensations (as they term them) amongst their friends, and against others to use most violent interdictions, and to shoot out cursings, even in natural and civil, private and public contracts, wherein all good faith ought to have place.

[b] That is, their Chrism, by which in the Sacrament (as they call it) of Confirmation, they make servile unto themselves, the persons and doings of men, signing them in their forehead and hands: and as for the sign left by Christ (of which Rev. 7:3) and the holy Sacrament of Baptism they make as void. For whom Christ hath joined unto himself by Baptism, this beast maketh challenge unto them by her greasy Chrism, which he doubteth not to prefer over Baptism, both in authority and efficacy.

[c] The mark of the name of the beast.

The right to assemble must as well remain a key element of the right to property since without property there can exist no liberty therefore to know liberty means to keep an awareness of that property we own in the virtues of God and His world of real estate; hence, for us exercising our right to assemble means for us the right to overthrow and abolish the men and their institutions which openly plunder liberty and property.

In considering the latter either-or scenario of two factions let us again consider the one scenario of the majority without property seeking to usurp those with property as a majority of uneducated tyrants whose only path in life would seek legislation to redistribute or steal property without any consideration of a response from the people – a gross exaggeration of morality since immorality can not beget morality in the same way a tyrant will not produce liberty and the free man will not submit to a tyrant – lastly, let us not confuse the idle man with the free man since only free men live their lives in the arena and do not imagine their self free in hiding in their church and not making early and often tactical and public declarations of the state of the union. Herein juxtaposes two ideologies fundamental to the view of liberty and tyranny since each philosophy possesses it's own intent and with intent brings action; thus, in naming each action we can name the action of those individuals in liberty as industrious and those conspirators of tyranny as enterprising insofar as the energy in which the tyrants stir will only stir upon the pretext of a false courage to invade the mind and steal property which can only succeed through the use of violence (of which can never represent sharing or courageous since it's use involves theft of the fruit of one's earnest labor). The spirit of the Lord would not wait long for liberty to amass an energy against those seeking to absolve creation and invent an ever growing enforcement of decree or judgment mandating this majority act as one paramilitary unit separate from the citizenry in the same manner as a foreign military presuming itself as law enforcement over the land in which they occupy without any consideration of sovereignty or their own immorality in fighting for the prevailing of tyranny. This type of collectivism can only represent the most base form of tyranny; in that the uneducated or inexcusably tyrannical and most abominable people would invent government enforced pretexts to seize control of the entire economy as if they all arose one day as a vampire from it's coffin even with the countenance of a blood-sucking sadomasochist in forcing an honest people to submit or face war to prove their righteousness against self-evident tyranny. The degrees of tyranny do in fact start with an alien spirit and when entered into human society do appear as collectivism (since collectivism can not include the individual) which innately excludes the idea of peaceful and prosperous spirituality (since under the pseudo philosophies the illusion of abundance can only come from the collective effort and not the individual effort whose production of real estate proves the individual unique and the collective an illusion therefore the collective trusts not in the reality of God whom designed individuals to distrust collectives in order that God's degrees of unique pretexts would remain supreme above those burnt offerings projecting their idol in the place of the living God of this universe); and, a higher degree of order in that collectivism can mean more sharp definitions of their intention insofar as the various *isms* can afford the tyrant additional time to plunder since His true conscience knows His tyranny will fall as do all others; for example: democracy, socialism, communism, fascism, totalitarianism, theocracy, autocracy, caste, oligarchy, monarchy, oligopoly, technocracy and all of these tracts of theft operating under their false flag of taxation or otherwise more rightly known as involuntary taxation or god-dared oppression since the tyrant would dare God although God only bless the free people in mutual defense for their life, liberty, and property. How else could property illegally transfer without an involuntary mandate of subtracting one's fruit of their labor in exchange for the pretending of national security? Theft and fraud remain the chief principals of tyranny. That individual that would wittingly commit theft would in the same instant defraud others of reality and displace the natural motions of the free world. How could any individual fraudulently furnish a good or service without first stealing the mind of their target? The laborer worthy of His wages and the shopkeeper His trade do deliver a good or service. And how did the shopkeeper obtain items to sell unless He crafted them Himself or sold the product of a craftsman; and, does the merchant in trading with the craftsman not equally depend on the continual production of items while He trade with the patrons of His shop with whatsoever currency they shall wish to trade with; be it good fortune, cut or uncut gems, armaments, cloth, fruit and vegetable, herbs, jewelry, lumber, medicine, metals, ore, pelts, services, tobacco, or any other physical or intellectual property which the liberty of man compels them to trade and according to the authority God endues them with; and, without any sanction which false government would decree in delimiting the exercise of their liberty thereof; though, in modern america today a rogue government does suffer the oppressions of violence or enslavement demanding state-approved forms of trade or currency and even demanding the forfeiture of a portion of each trade therefore exhibiting a nation wholly devoid of human liberty and subsisting in a state of pretended liberty though the partiality of such only represent the whole destruction thereof. Industry generates an efficiency in the economy that no man alone could ever facilitate though the tyrant claims in His seizing control of individual liberty thereby seizing control of property and the economy that His decrees even unto the escalations of absolute control will facilitate solidarity or trade when this type of logic only reasons to deharmonize peace and prosperity though such individual arguments boldly spit in one's face with the claim that a tyrant controlling the economy, or "taking from the rich and giving to the poor keeps us safe from our self," when only morality can rightly transfer the energy of love; and, when that morality would go unrestricted – does in fact restrict the immorality of the least and most degrees in society though the immoral gladly seize control of government in order to criminalize morality and legalize immorality as though God would not reward such wickedness with His merry appointment. Morality through honest, free, and open trade naturally divides property unto it's rightful owner while the immoral seek government to initiate violence to steal property and in so doing keep their operation moving as a colonizing army set out for nothing more than to shadow consciousness, sacrificially slaughter the innocent, and at it's true end – achieve absolute extinction of mankind.

Collectivism then really represents a type of assistance initiated by violence though who would want violent assistance unless it was for the mutual defense of preserving one another's liberty and property and not the opposite occurrence of having one's liberty and property stolen while at the same time having to sit idle by threat of violence. These hypocrisies of the tyrant know no end – the only true assistance of the tyrant rests in utilizing such historical precedent to save mankind through ending those calls demanding violence against free humanity. The free market always demands something therefore to assist the free market even in the wake of a tyrannical government does perform the action in which God Himself would demand in order to break that yoke of bondage and diverge His blessings into a harmonious system of divergings infinitely accelerating the direction and expansion of the magnitude and volume of human consciousness and felicity. The ruling elite would desire to portray their idea of a society as a thing in which we must assist or face ostracizing or worse; therefore, in the name of a common good we must concede such a society as nothing more than the survival of the most wicked ruling elite insofar as they assist one another as the untouchables compositing that inner ring of doom. No lasting advancement of society will occur without instruction and understanding of the philosophy of liberty and it's enemy: yeah, that standing army of ideological tyranny.

If any ultimate history of tyranny could present itself as true above other truths then that imbalance of rights we experience as a society and world started small and grew into thousands of years of oppressions which even altered human language to preserve itself and ward off that liberty which would so effortlessly dissolve it's phonetic boundaries. And to what degree does that imbalance favor rumors above truth even unto the idea that hereditary authority came to exist as a rumor which divided the world under the oppressions of thirteen families whom have in the long-past and present worked from the shadows of society to divide and conquer mankind? We can then separate what we mean when we say: 'of the people, by the people, and for the people,' and, juxtapose this against: 'of the mind, by the mind, and for the mind,' insofar as tyranny aims to disconnect man from His mind and spirit, and, in so doing reduce the power and safety of the people until the people then beg for the ideology of the tyrant to further invert reality and intentionally hide the knowledge which would otherwise reveal that one mind which God designed as our vision for liberty. What legitimate proof of ownership could these wicked families possess other than some phony papers or so-called *patents of nobility* when in fact God designed every man as a learned noble in His kingdom and not separate from God into some carnal caste system teaching the intentional saddening of the heart and crushing of the spirit; a carnal system which views theft as righteous and fraud as the honorable trade for the one with the wilt to succeed such a sin? Obviously if mankind allows a few oligarchs to destroy the will of civil disobedience then who of the living does mankind particularly wait upon to rise and then stand against such an evil force when He who dwells within the each of us stands ready, willing, and able to individually use us as that vessel forming into many hands making light work to then open the heavens and flood the world with the knowledge of God such that we astound the tyrants unto a perpetual marveling in that we fulfill God's commandments in the realization that we embody the proof of His animating spirit dwelling within; and, conversely: to not act in treading down the greatly wicked, especially those things which consensus would ignore as lesser or trivial usurpations, means to die without ever having lived.

Perhaps then the illusion of equal property distribution disguises the truth of who oppresses our equal rights since these monarchs have such fattened and willing peasants defending their tyrants as a type of idiotic tradition of worshiping false authority though they have never questioned such a thing in the least for men have gone before them and not only discovered speaking in opposition to such a false power can cause such tyrants to issue a death warrant against them though this can as well also lead to the creation of a new and free nation such as america or Switzerland. No man holds the right to another man's property though this new-age fantasy-philosophy projects we exist as fabric of the universe and while this points toward relative truth – they further bind this notion with the falsehood that anyone can rightly claim ownership of my property and even my life at-will. Even the universe so self-evidently draws borders for how else can a thing contain another thing, the socket contain the eye, the stable it's cattle, the ocean it's water, the heavens it's stars, or the royals their chattel peasants? Does the rock not sit; and, the bird not fly?

Jeremiah 8:7 Even the stork in the air knoweth her appointed times, and the turtle, and the crane and the swallow observe the time of their coming, but my people knoweth not the [a] judgment of the Lord.

Jeremiah 8:7 Footnotes

[a] He accuseth them in that that they are more ignorant of God's judgments, than these birds are of their appointed seasons to discern the cold and heat, as Isa. 1:3.

Isaiah 1:3 The [a] ox knoweth his owner, and the ass his master's crib: but Israel hath not known: my people hath not understood.

Isaiah 1:3 Footnotes

[a] The most dull and brute beasts do more acknowledge their duty toward their masters, than my people do toward me, of whom they have received benefits without comparison.

The new-age philosopher (a truly wicked tyrant) will argue nothing can exist as true since all perception remains indifferent when self-evidence such as violence or coercion can not exist independent of it's cause and the actor can not exist independent of God's mystery; therefore, this pseudo philosopher argues even the consequences do not matter; and, such a thing requires attention since today this type of philosophy acts as even a stronghold in america and throughout the globe with tens of millions of droopy eyes lapping up it's false teaching; for example, pick any *ism*, as though these philosophic conflagrations worship the living creator of this universe when their own texts demand a caste society (among other wicked novelties worth recording); and, for those whom argue these *isms* speak nothing of the sort then to hell with their barbaric tyrants they worship whom do represent false and dead gods: "deities" of unnatural and vampiric energy siphoning that energy which the living God of this universe most purely receives in the worshiping from the whole of a person's being unto Him and not lesser powers; meaning lesser powers do exist and man so often worships these powers and not God though these powers can not surpass the form of an idol or mechanical political system in which God originally designed for the worship of the most high and not the worship of His lesser powers as though these powers were the whole power of God and not simply signs and wonders of His creation.

Kings 1:3 *Then the Angel of the Lord said to Elijah the Tishbite, Arise, and go up to meet the messengers of the king of Samaria, and say unto them, [a] Is it not because there is no God in Israel, that ye go to inquire of Baal-Zebub the god of Ekron?*
Kings 1:3 Footnotes
[a] He showeth that idolaters have not the true God, for else they would seek to none but to him alone.

Truly these false religions entrust in their dead gods to conspire against liberty. True human action exists as unalienable rights unto every man from His creator – that living creator-being-God of the everlasting universe; while false human action means sin disguising itself as lawful or done with protectionism. How could these false gods represent anything except human statutes designed to limit human liberty and enforce some type of caste system empowering tyrants to rule through the taxation of their central banks and absolute oppression via their standing armies?

Would the laws governing Physics not articulate into that Bill of Rights which was previously proven as a self-evident sublimation of the heavens outpouring onto earth? We must then recognize the nature of mankind as those self-evident politics which either embrace good or evil; thusly, to argue good and evil as non-existent and the incredulous quantity of false gods and caste systems as necessary for human existence means to abandon the fertile soil in which God planted us in and forfeit the knowledge which men before us prove worthy unto every man's liberty and happiness.

Consider the assembly as a thing which occurred long after the establishment of a nation and was the result of a long train of abuses by a government against it's people: this as well occurred long after men settled the debate of what necessarily represents life and property and what can not represent that liberty. The american assembly was in fact a revolution in perpetuity with the most alpha and omega of intellectual pursuits on the planet (insofar as true intellectualism ascends into the entering of the animating contest of liberty for the defense of the knowledge of God: yeah, the highest planetary debate) whom refuse the relinquishing of their soul unto those wicked men working to enslave the public? Many times throughout our young american history americans and much of the globe have convinced their self that the revolution for human liberty was lost and the american dream was stopped (since the instigators or tyrants leading the stopping of the liberty movement would proclaim liberty or america as a war-crime which only the brutish royal family must punish through our death by state-funded murder or kindly surrendering to their state). No true man would ever enter society to preserve wicked men and certainly not through the lie of tax schemes promising to preserve their property. We will as free men teach the innocent and the youth of why we fight for the idea of liberty and how this idea exists as the only and most moral approach and intent against every form of tyranny over the mind of man; thus, we live as the civil, strong, and mighty men of renown in the highest sense; and, in our abolishing and overthrowing of wicked men we establish true peace and prosperity and not the submissive type of peace that tyrants require to grant them temporal authority over men and even unto perceptively inconsequential, gratuitous, and unmitigated violence or coercions. The collectivists instigate men of liberty to assemble and reconstitute the preservation of our way of life and property since we would so commonly sense the dangers in allowing men of subhuman character to increase the degrees of government authority unto our own enslavement or genocide. Even under the circumstance of a majority working together to usurp the minority there will always exist individuals of higher intellect within either faction whom abhor the ideology of both factions and defend the philosophy of liberty (which stands counter to all faction) though risk their own life in openly and publicly opposing both factions which can only speak of the philosophy of tyranny; therefore, in His standing as a majority of one – God then looks down from the heavens and gives blessing and favor to this pointed man to further His means into this type of harm's way so that God would bless His deeds with abundance for the world.

Luke 9:7 ¶ *[e],[a] Now Herod the Tetrarch heard of all that was done by him: and he [b] doubted, because that it was said of some, that John was risen again from the dead:*

Luke 9:7 Footnotes

[a] So soon as the world heareth tidings of the Gospel, it is divided into divers opinions, and the tyrants especially are afraid.

[b] He stuck as it were fast in the mire.

Luke 9:7 Endnotes

The common people's opinion of Christ. [e] Matt. 14:1, Mark 6:14

Matthew 14:1 At [a],[b] that time Herod the Tetrarch heard of the fame of Jesus,

Matthew 14:1 Footnotes

[b] Here is in John an example of an invincible courage, which all faithful Ministers of God's word ought to follow: in Herod, an example of tyrannous vanity, pride and cruelty, and to be short, of a courtly conscience, and of their insufferable slavery, which have once given themselves over to pleasures: in Herodias and her daughter, an example of whore-like wantonness, and womanlike cruelty.

Matthew 14:1 Endnotes

[a] Herod's judgment of Christ. Mark 6:14, Luke 9:7

Mark 6:14 ¶ *[i],[a] Then King Herod heard of <u>him</u> (for his Name* *was made manifest) and said, John Baptist is risen again from the dead, and therefore great [b] works are wrought by him.*

Mark 6:14 Footnotes

[a] The Gospel confirmeth the godly, and vexeth the wicked.

[b] This word signifieth Powers, whereby is meant the power of working miracles.

Mark 6:14 Endnotes

Herod's opinion of Christ. [i] Matt. 14:1, Luke 9:7

Would the men of this type of free thought not describe that image of God in which represents the only original intent of man's creation insofar as these men live free of the bondage which lesser men accept as their occasion or occupation; and further, can we not point to america's founding fathers as that very excellent image of the free man; and, whom in history other than Christ can we point toward in properly identifying the perfect action of liberty risen as the individual life and self against tyranny and so widely received as self-evident truth; and, nary do I mean the sinful prophets which only later turned toward God? The true man arises from the light of our universe again, and again, and again, and again, and again to fight this wicked power attempting to overlord the realm in which we live.

Malachi 3:18 Then shall you return, and discern between the righteous and wicked, between him that serveth God, and him that serveth him not.

Property ownership has got nothing at all to do with enslaving one another and has everything to do with freeing mankind since only a free mankind would own property in peace and prosperity with one another in the first place; and, only a wicked mankind would submit to any man and especially that one that would rule the world and raise men as cattle for the propagation of His wicked bishops. A majority of harebrained toads claim america started as an experiment into slavery and not liberty; of course, every notion of such lends itself toward the proclamation of war with honest men since the words written and declared in those days had all to do with freeing mankind from the tyranny of the world though the multitude in those days justified the honesty of other men as an excuse to enslave innocent men; and, only the enslaver of men ought to receive the blame; and, one must particularly implore what exactly represents enslavement since even the free man remains a slave to His own habits thus even the man whom agrees to perform a job remains a slave to whom He aims to please; and, namely enslaved to His own habits which expand or limit His moral obligations.

Although shadow-governments run roughshod over the american public today we still exist as a people that does not openly submit to some type of royal overlord class modulating society into a dumbed-down peasantry of accepting an ever increasing apathy or hostility toward our own existence; or to the exorcism of the knowledge which freed our ancestors from such rule in the first place. Elected representatives with appointed serving times, self-governance, individual-rule, and the american republic remain chief ideas over any form of governance that man would devise outside of the study of the kingdom of God. The slide into tyranny from the liberty of a republic first starts with the enslavements of democracy which smell least of tyranny though with proper foreknowledge will educate the discerner of truth into understanding democracy as one of the many illicit forms of collectivism and despotism since it's invitation into mob-rule will so readily dissuade it's supporters into learning of individual equal rights; yes, rights which by default silence any argument for tyranny as the means for national security. Tyranny's undercurrent will always enslave their self through debt. One can think of debt as a thing which can only injure the mass and velocity of individual economy (micro) thereby accelerating the inefficiency of commerce (macro).

The foundation of civilization depends on trade continuing in a way which supplies individuals with energy to continue their education and discernment without a ruling class enacting usury to tug at the economy and manipulate public policies to the detriment of the people. The absolute tyrant, depicted in stories all throughout time, has so often commanded His enemy, ironically everyone not Himself, to kneel unto Him and He will forgive all debts. The tyrant does not have to think of where money will come from when the entire population supplies Him with the energy which He uses for political favor as though He stood as the central bank and entire standing army oppressing the world. The public after having their naivety used against them in succumbing to the usury or acquiescing to the state's mandate would even grovel at the feet of the tyrant in hope of abolishing their debt; perhaps this action of the peasant could mean they project their natural kindness onto their tyrant and the tyrant reflects back this perception of kindness onto His subjects in order that He erase the thought of He, the central bank, or the standing army existing as a tyrannical machine worth treading underfoot. This absolving of debt only satisfies one of three castes for the tyrant since He must appease or silence these strict divisions which comprise those who see, those who can not see, and those who must be shown; the tyrant rewards those who must be shown the doorknob with the absolving of their debt; the tyrant rewards those who can not see with perpetual plunder of their labor; lastly, the tyrant rewards freedom to no taxation and even distribution of society's plunder to those enemies that would kill the tyrant at the slightest hint of their perceiving any weakness in His wickedry; or plainly stated as those wicked ones who clearly see their tactics used against a free people do model their idol, the tyrant, and then clone His persona into minor tyrants spread throughout the land for the absolute control and enforcement of His pecking order.

The original loaning of money only served to create a target on the back of those that purchased such a fraud and once their debts exceeded the ability for their over-regulated markets to correct – in canceling their debt would only serve to further accelerate the inefficiencies which crush the remaining free market thereby suffocating the least of the existing free market and ultimately isolating all members of society unto the serving of a ruling elite whom force a central bank to feed the standing army for the consignment of it's tyranny. What type of blind patriotism other than the obvious false patriotism of nationalist democracy (often referred to as democratic socialism or otherwise simply stated as the epitome of collectivism, hypocrisy, and socialism) would trade the purest of it's fruits: economic sovereignty for a foreign policy of endless debt and war?

Nahum 2:11 Where is the [a] dwelling of the lions, and the pasture of the lion's whelps? where the lion and the lioness waked, and the lion's whelp, and none made them afraid.

Nahum 2:11 Footnotes

[a] Meaning, Nineveh, whose inhabitants were cruel like the Lions, and given to all oppression, and spared no violence or tyranny to provide for their wives and children.

The american revolution, the great american melting pot, and the global revolution for human liberty has a command post on the earth and that base-station for more than two centuries now represents america; and, more specifically: Texas. Though many enemies walk among us that would elect their self to torture the multitudes to death for their own anti-spiritual gain we can reflect on the vast numbers whom hold no voice across the many enslaved nations for a lack of education or ability to speak freely and thus we must find it incumbent as individuals to enter the arena and spiritually fight the global tyranny that one day humanity might hold a worldwide revolution wherein elected representatives head every nation.

Until americans and the world pursue that happiness found in that duty of defending liberty unto it's highest philosophic end then the downfall of society will continue as a self-evident trend which grows in degrees of danger seemingly every day. No society that would plunder it's economy unto debt and then demand from it's government a cancellation of the debt could not as well expect their government to assume the role of the market in price structuring and namely in the redistribution of wealth through this illusion of equally appeasing the common man or those peasants which remain subjects to the ruling elite (royalty) or wealth management class (dynasty). What good does a man stand to perform when He knows His government will simply diminish His effect through delivering to Him the same reward received of the beggared or of the individual whom simply produces an insufficient product which no sane person would demand or sane economy would keep in the presence of a superior innovation which aids our more perfect union in liberty? What good can society expect of a man if the tyrants in government force society to pay Him the fruit of their labor and how could such a society not exist as an entire population of tyrants at war with one another since only a tyrant controlling them would desire such an environment of oppression?

1 King 15:29 And when he was king, he [a] smote all the house of Jeroboam, he left none alive to Jeroboam, until he had destroyed him, according to the [g] word of the Lord which he spake by his servant Ahijah the Shilonite,

1 Kings 15:29 Footnotes

[a] So God stirred up one tyrant to punish the wickedness of another.

1 Kings 15:29 Endnotes

[g] 1 Kings 14:10

1 Kings 14:10 Therefore behold, I will bring evil upon the house of Jeroboam, and will cut off from Jeroboam him that [c],[a] pisseth against the wall, as well him that [b] is shut up, as him that is left in Israel, and will sweep away the remnant of the house of Jeroboam, as a man sweepeth away dung till it be all gone.

1 Kings 14:10 Footnotes

[a] Every male even to the dogs, 1 Sam. 25:22.

[b] As well him that is in the stronghold, as him that is abroad.

1 Kings 14:10 Endnotes

[c] 1 Kings 21:21, 2 Kings 9:8

1 Samuel 25:22 So and more also do God unto the enemies of David: for surely I will not leave of all that he hath by the dawning of the day, any that [a] pisseth against the wall.

1 Samuel 25:22 Footnotes

[a] Meaning by this proverb, that he would destroy both small and great.

1 Kings 21:21 [a] Behold, I will bring evil upon thee, and will take away thy posterity, and will cut off from Ahab him that [b] pisseth against the wall, as well him that is [c] shut up, as him *that is left in Israel,*

1 Kings 21:21 Endnotes

[a] 1 Kings 14:10, 2 Kings 9:8

[b] 1 Sam. 15:22

[c] 1 Kings 14:10

2 Kings 9:8 *For the whole house of Ahab shall be destroyed: and [c] I will cut off from Ahab, him that maketh water against the wall, as well him that is shut up, as him that is left in Israel.*

2 Kings 9:8 Endnotes

[c] 1 Kings 14:10, 1 Kings 21:21

Heaven and hell exist within the perception of one's spiritual realm and manifests it's self-evidence onto the physical plane through a religious belief set (or simply stated: religion means the whole collection and motion of the invisible ideas within one's mind) which acts as the origin of political decisions (political herein meaning the whole collection and motion of one's visible action) governing every individual. Human action above all separates the philosophers of liberty from those philosophers of tyranny and especially those false philosophies preaching peace and rather meaning submission to tyranny. Do we not witness in the calm of despotism a constant state of survival while with the tempestuous sea of Liberty we witness a thriving and moral people? This illustration of opposites: creation versus destruction outline the character of the tyrant whether He adorn the name of authority, bishop, constable, emperor, Governor, journalist, judge,

King, Lord, parliament, pastor, Pope, President, official, oligarch, monarch, or Sheriff.

Daniel 11:36 *And the [a] king shall do what him list: he shall exalt himself, and magnify himself against all, <u>that is</u> God, and shall speak marvelous things against the God of gods, and shall prosper, till the wrath [b] be accomplished: for the determination is made.*

Daniel 11:36 Footnotes

[a] *Because the Angel's purpose is to show the whole course of the persecutions of the Jews unto the coming of Christ, he now speaketh of the Monarchy of the Romans which he noteth by the name of a King, who were without religion and condemned the true God.*

[b] *So long the tyrants shall prevail as God hath appointed to punish his people: but he showeth that it is but for a time.*

Does the tyrant then aim to teach the people that in the division of property the rights of each citizen will render equal; for only self-evidence teaches us in the equality of rights can opportunity for peace and prosperity remain equal? Certainly that flagrant use of hostility only a tyrant could surmise would so demand every man forfeit His property in the name of preserving society. The effort of a man exists as a product of His labor and no tyrant can ever truly and lawfully own a man's effort through some degree of laws or use of force lest that man succumb to the life not lived for liberty.

Mark 4:12 [b] *That they seeing, may see, and not discern: and they hearing, may hear, and not understand, lest at any time they should turn, and their sins should be forgiven them.*

Mark 4:12 Endnotes

[b] *Isa. 6:9, Matt. 13:14, Luke 8:10, John 12:40, Acts 28:26, Rom. 11:8*

Mark 4:14 *The sower soweth the word.*

Mark 4:15 *And these are they that <u>receive the seed</u> by the wayside, in whom the word is sown: but when they have heard it, Satan cometh immediately, and taketh away the word that was sown in their hearts.*

Isaiah 6:9 *And he said, Go, and say unto this people, [a] Ye shall hear indeed, but ye shall not understand: ye shall plainly see, and not perceive.*

Isaiah 6:9 Footnotes

[a] *Whereby is declared that for the malice of man God will not immediately take away his word, but he will cause it to be preached to their condemnation, when as they will not learn thereby to obey his will, and be saved: hereby he exhorteth the ministers to do their duty, and answereth to the wicked murmurers, that through their own malice their heart is hardened, Matt. 13:14; Acts 28:26; Rom. 11:8.*

Isaiah 6:9 Endnotes

He showeth the obstinacy of the people.

Matthew 13:14 So in them is fulfilled the prophecy of Isaiah, which prophecy saith, [c] By hearing ye shall hear, and shall not understand, and seeing ye shall see, and shall not perceive.

Matthew 13:14 Endnotes

[c] Mark 4:14, Luke 8:11

Luke 8:10 And he said, Unto you it is given to know the [a] secrets of the kingdom of God, but to others in parables, that when [c] they see, they should not see, and when they hear, they should not understand.

Luke 8:10 Footnotes

[a] Those things are called secret, which may not be uttered: for the word used here, is as much as we say in our tongue, to hold a man's peace.

Luke 8:10 Endnotes

[c] Isa. 6:9, Matt. 13:14, Mark 4:12, John 12:40, Acts 28:26, Rom. 11:8

Luke 8:11 [d] The parable is this, The seed is the word of God.

Luke 8:11 Endnotes

[d] Matt. 13:8, Mark 4:15

Matthew 13:8 And some again fell in good ground, and brought forth fruit, one <u>corn</u> an hundredfold, some sixtyfold, and another *thirtyfold.*

John 12:40 *[k] He hath blinded their eyes, and hardened their heart, that they should not see with their eyes, nor understand with their heart, and should be converted, and I should heal them.*

John 12:40 Endnotes

[k] Isa. 6:9, Matt. 13:14, Mark 4:12, Luke 8:10, Acts 28:26, Rom. 11:8

Acts 28:26 *[a] Saying, [b] Go unto this people, and say, By hearing ye shall hear, and shall not understand, and seeing ye shall see, and not perceive.*

Acts 28:26 Footnotes

[a] The unbelievers do willingly resist the truth, and yet not by chance.

Acts 28:26 Endnotes

[b] Isa. 6:9, Matt. 13:14, Mark 14:12, Luke 8:10, John 12:40, Rom. 11:8

Romans 11:8 *[a] According as it is written, [c] God hath given them the spirit of [b] slumber: eyes that they [d] should not see, and ears that they should not hear unto this day.*

Romans 11:8 Footnotes

[a] And yet this hardness of heart cometh not but by God's just decree and judgment, and yet without fault, whom as he so punisheth the unthankful by taking from them all sense and perseverance and by doubling their darkness, that the benefits of

God which are offered unto them, do redound to their just destruction.

[b] A very dead sleep which taketh away all sense.

[d] That is, eyes unjust to see.

Romans 11:8 Endnotes

[c] Isa. 6:9, Isa. 29:10, Matt. 13:14, John 12:40, Acts 28:26

Isaiah 29:10 *For the Lord hath covered you with a spirit of slumber, and hath shut up your eyes: the Prophet, and your chief Seers hath he covered.*

What can that tyrant expect when an assembly of individuals steadfastly respond to His transgression thus forming a worldwide expansion of this steadfast motion as though even the winds of God aid the pursuit to overthrow and abolish every form of tyranny even over night? Would the tyrants whom comprise the ignorant majority and demand a division of labor and property not eventually call for a vote on such a matter as means of quelling insurrection though it further inspire insurrection from the honorable men that will defend unto death their right to life, liberty and property since God so well enjoys seeing His children cause the tyrant to fall or otherwise flee like a phantom at dawn? These tyrants would lead men to worship death and desolation as though it guaranteed them equality of outcome and not the oppression of every opportunity of their life. Can we not deduce that only a tyrannical government of fancy hats and grandiose titles could equally impose oppression while only liberty dwelling within the individual can equally express the proper order of the universe and namely in no violence, coercion, theft, or fraud – the ultimate refutation against tyranny since those individuals in liberty would so steadfastly seek justice upon those criminals oppressing society? Civilization must then discern those self-evident gaits which present their self as a rabbit-hole of choice in every point of life and namely in that narrow gait of liberty as opposed to that wide gait of tyranny; therefore, the narrowness of mind produces the wide gait of tyranny while the openness of mind can imagine the whole vision of the beast and the heavens which so easily presents itself as the narrow gait of liberty which can fit all of the world through though the world so often chooses the wide gait's invitation into the eternal lake of fire. These individuals whom would allow the destruction of their life, progeny, and society work for the identity of a spirit with no love at all – rather they prefer the homogeneous feeling of merely existing as chattel to a state which brands them according to their lack of self-awareness and ability to keep up with the latest state-sponsored trends of fashion, music, and even philosophy though this pseudo-philosophy of the state grant them only illusions of reward for not consciously pursuing a public declaration of liberty to the tens of millions of unthinking individuals following one another nose to ass as a herd of disingenuous locusts consuming things with the smell of bread though they question not the reason for consumption since such folly poison their true purpose in life and preserve that tyrant whom would ensure their ruination. The blind belief in those wicked rulers setting society free perpetuates every greatest known cause to the destruction of liberty and man; therefore, one can think of this blind belief as even an auctioning off of one's own mind for the lowest bid; tallest lie; widest snare; or narrow eye. Since one must trade their thinking faculties in order to purchase the illusion of an economy via central planners – this scenario forms the reservation in which houses an enslaved population constructing it's own walls of collective imagination enslaving them to the god of illusion and vanity. The most beautiful gift from God unto mankind exists never so great than our constant ability to awaken from any nightmare and declare one's life a dream born of liberty in order that we shall seize our righteous power for individual liberty to not only inspire the majority today but to preserve mankind that they may too live as one human race growing ever more near that one mind of the living creator of the universe. Humanity will one day overthrow the tyranny on the land and live according to the harmony of liberty in granting no quarter to thieving and fraud on all of the land until every last corner and vestige of civilization roots out these evils; and, those individuals that would hide in such pilfery will see the light of day as society makes self-evident their drunkenness.

Considering the insanity that will occur under times of duress when the people must reconstitute government in order to redress the grievances of the state – the flood of extra-judiciary privilege unlawfully opposing God's law or that perfect law of liberty then forces the eternal one, God almighty, to swiftly judge the tyrant and the wicked on this earth to justify His law separate from those universally treasonous and tyrannical statutes that man would commit against His fellow countrymen; treason which minds not the vicious use of force staining their destiny and stifling the ascension which His fathers fastened for the defense of our worship for our father in Heaven whom supplies us with the intelligent design for our liberation.

Romans 2:18 And knowest his will, and [a],[b] triest the things that dissent from it, in that thou art instructed by the Law:
Romans 2:18 Footnotes
[a] Canst try and discern what things swerve from God's will.
[b] Or allowest the things that are excellent.

One inversion of the wicked states they worship the architect of the world when this object in which they worship can only mould the destruction of the world and can not rightly possess the name of architect since this would imply a force of intelligent creation and not an intentional destruction of life; thus, we know the almighty living creator of this universe architects the universe to give victory to the peacemakers; thus, self-evidence shows us the individual whom speaks of the architect of the universe does not immediately translate to this meaning that He worships Satan though the wicked would wish the world to believe His words damned Him to their perceptions and even unto the ends of not allowing that man the free expression of His own religious belief.

Matthew 5:9 Blessed are the peacemakers: for they shall be called the children of God.

This design of wickedry which separates property and rights from it's unalienable owner can not possess an unintended consequence since those wicked men so intentionally follow through with those most wicked acts of idolatry which directly blaspheme the living creator. None of these men at the time of their transgression can fathom God eviscerating their world-view unto the untangling of that web of lies and deceit which ushers in the manifestation of God demanding His sons enter the arena of the animating contest of liberty and wage spiritual war against these forces of tyranny whom first captured them and demand they destroy their own soul through completing the orders of death and desolation. Comprehending this tyranny as a tool within the mind of man remains a chief discernment critical to obtaining the awareness which can observe and plan a trajectory of success for mankind's cause of liberty. The new-age pseudo philosophers, whom do represent that multitude of anti-Christs, will argue nothing alters the present moment therefore injustices can go ignored and evil can flourish if it pleases since those injustices and evils will not affect this blind individual fantasizing their own cosmic prophylactic which supposedly preserves them in their pseudo philosophy of remaining idle thereby encouraging and even enabling wickedness.

Luke 12:56 Hypocrites, ye can discern the face of the earth, and of the sky: but why discern ye not this time?

In this circular logic of keeping one's person idle in the face of that evil which sacrifices millions of innocent lives for their own pursuit – this new-age philosopher, which can not talk without speaking tyranny does so in order that they would hypnotize their target and act as that spirit-guide meandering the river of Hades as they invent a type of new-speak which proclaims peace as submission to tyranny and evil as a genetic disposition preceding the birth of the individual thus in their inverse logic they reason the cause of evil as a sinful necessity and unalterable human condition which no God can intervene since their philosophy continues even further stating both sin and righteousness do not exist; or said in another way: "To genocide mankind means to free mankind; therefore death to all means life to all." – an absolute inversion of truth into every extravagant perversion of logic and reason; the very paltry food of the tyrant; though, in this state-of-being we can identify the psychology of the tyrant in that they excuse their self from sin by claiming God chose them to sin for the good which comes after the sin though God would unendingly bless His children shall they not sin at all. The tragedy of course in such false stoicism would view the knowledge of God as a thing to not acknowledge therefore this inaction rewards an absence of knowledge with a public license to sin which can only enlarge the violence of the state and as a result control the rate or scope of which people can sin through a series of permissions such that no individual of the knowledge of God and liberty can near this paralyzing inner circle of hell popularizing the idea that hearing an individual debate the idea of truth requires an immediate punishment via the excessive use of tyranny so society can learn to mark this good individual on their list of evil whereby the state censors this individual's speech and even quarantines their physical body so that the people shall not learn of this individual nor their message and if the people do learn of this individual or hear their message then He who joins forces with Him shall similarly have their tongue removed or their life martyred in order to preserve the degeneracy of this tyrannical state.

Being liberty contains the maxims of all human philosophy and thus the extent of what can absolutely, impossibly, or totally manifest – the logic of our reason then moulds the light of our liberty which no thing on the earth can stop thus achieving for mankind the use of the essence and core of our heavens; and, for our salvation which saturates the heart of all of mankind even unto the charging of it's full capacities insofar as even the carbon atoms comprising the fabric or structure of space-time will animate and then kinetically energize according to the will of mankind's spiritual worship meaning there exists a highest of highs which can only demand and receive the pursuits of mankind's happiness insofar as true happiness means liberty from sin; and, the universe sentiently acknowledges our pursuits as even a life-form calling home to man such that all of these atoms will charge with the potential energy and then emit intelligent information as it were a certain and immutable will of liberty to commit acts of good and design a universe no longer blinded by evil thus existing as a true light leavening the darkness from the four corners of the universe and even unto all of it's polar dimensions.

Matthew 16:6 Then Jesus said unto them, Take heed and beware of the leaven of the Pharisees and Sadducees.

Matthew 16:6 Endnotes

The leaven of the Pharisees,

Jonah 4:11 *And should [a] not I spare Nineveh that great city, wherein are sixscore thousand persons, that [b] cannot discern between their right hand and their left hand, and also much cattle?*

Jonah 4:11 Footnotes

[a] Thus God mercifully reproveth him which would pity himself, and this gourd, and yet would restrain God to show his compassion to so many thousand people.

[b] Meaning, that they were children and infants.

Idle individuals keep a confused mind as to whether liberty means good or evil though liberty can not mean tyranny nor can life mean death since each term can only affirm or deny the other therefore no contradiction will exist which unites the two as the same meaning thus each definition keeps true unto itself insofar as each term knows it's own contrary, origin, and plight. We can then know these progenitors of evil either through acquiescence (intent through unconscious self-expression, plausible deniability, hypocrisy) or intentional and conscious decision-making (absolutely criminal) manifest and rather invocate society as it were that debaucherous calm of despotism and not tempestuous sea of liberty; ashes and not animation; walking dead and not awakening; tyranny and not liberty. We all possess certain strength and weakness thus being the chief reason of mankind absolutely needing one another's voluntary association in this universe of inhuman chaos; and, with our talents we either resist the strengthening of things which persists the matter or we fight the weakness so that we render it into a strength for the purpose of righteous action. I fight to strengthen my character for the cause of liberty through my various talents; and, I intentionally challenge myself daily for whatever service calls upon my art: berserker, defender, carpentry, culinary, herbalist, horticulture, oration, reading, teaching, writing, and all of the masteries which I pursue for my happiness so that mine and my fellow countryman's happiness fulfills for the mutual preservation of our life, liberty, and property against tyranny; and, though we can dually note that the serving of our trade or talent alone does not fulfill the whole law since we must equally make our self that public declaration and force at war with the insensible tyranny.

Micah 3:8 Yet notwithstanding I am full [a] of power by the Spirit of the Lord, and of judgment, and of strength to declare unto Jacob his transgression, and to Israel his sin.

Micah 3:8 Footnotes

[a] The Prophet being assured of his vocation by the Spirit of

God, setteth himself alone against all the wicked, showing how God both gave him gifts, ability and knowledge, to discern between good and evil, and also constancy to reprove the sins of the people, and not to flatter them.

Ezekiel 44:23 *And they shall teach my people <u>the difference</u> between the holy and profane, and cause them to discern between the unclean and the clean.*

Those individuals in pursuit of exercising tyranny focus on controlling absolutely every waking soul of our planet through the division or diminishing of the fruits of their labor. Suppose these individuals choose to dwell within the constant plunder of stealing from one class and delivering to another and that class which received the plunder then sell their booty only to later demand their government steal again what the patron purchased from them. How could any moral man not possess righteous indignation toward that dark army of reptilian-brained imbeciles hiding behind a thin veil of false flags demanding He relinquish the fruit of His labor lest they leave instead with His life on their blood-stained knives?

Acts 12:3-5 *[a] And when he saw that it pleased the Jews, he proceeded further, to take Peter also (then were the days of unleavened bread.) [b] And when he had caught him, he put him in prison, and delivered him to four quaternions of soldiers to be kept, intending after the Passover to bring him forth to the people.*

[c] So Peter was kept in prison, but earnest prayer was made of the Church unto God for him.

Acts 12:3 Footnotes

[a] It is an old fashion of tyrants to procure the favor of the wicked, with the blood of the godly.

Acts 12:4 Footnotes

[b] The tyrants and wicked make a gallows for themselves, even then when they do most according to their own will and fantasy.

Acts 12:5 Footnotes

[c] The prayers of the godly overturn the counsel of tyrants, obtain Angels of God, break the prison, unloose chains, put Satan to flight and preserve the Church.

Do the lakes and streams not collect water freely but when man collects the rainfall do we not witness in american society today the courts imprisoning individuals for collecting rainwater on their own property in which God freely provided? Who would these psychopaths in government imagine would receive the authority of centralization and then planning for redistribution of this water in the first place if not the property owner who first needs the resource and received of it in the most efficient and light manner unto their satisfaction thus giving them even the most efficient ability to share with their neighbors since government would waste all of the portion before delivering nothing at all to the original owner of the water? Only a rogue government could imagine they do not exist as a property of the people whom instituted and facilitated their way of life therefore government possesses no natural rights though the citizens working in government do possess natural rights but only within the strict limitation of ensuring the preservation of civil liberties for the authority in which they serve: the citizen. Only a stupid and forgetful people could imagine their purpose in life as not preserving a civilization and instead then allowing the most intrepidly stupid and evil foes among them to become the lords of evil.

The shift from the spiritual and thus the physical realm from liberty to tyranny shifts as easily as the altering of the public perception from a government which was instituted for the preservation of their property into a government in a society which grants their government the absolute control of every individual's life unto the very end of sabotaging civil liberties and rewriting truth, logic, and reason into a doctrine of a social obedience forbidding privacy and demanding submission to a tyrannically psychopathic ruling elite. The people in owning their life and liberty own their property thus they own the government they institute as their property as well; therefore, in first giving up the idea of self-ownership – the people then succumb to wicked men stealing and then sanctioning their ideas as a form of economic control whereby a rogue government illustrates it's vast deplorability by seizing control of every other form of property from the people such that this concept of stealing property so blinds the physical world with a false spiritual world that the captured property renders into a portfolio of tokens used as politically oppressive systems inherently opposed to the true spiritual world of liberty; therefore, property remains chief among the sacred things for us to preserve since our own life would represent that property to first protect; and, in our discernment we plainly see the eternal connection for preserving life, liberty, and property. The false prophets would wish us to believe our spiritual world does not require force or law to guide our efforts though self-evidence presents to us that most obvious state of wicked men manifestly delivering war against our very state of existence; thus, we fight for the preservation of life against tyranny and we receive the spiritual transformation of God which the lords of evil proclaim as a thing their apathy, idleness, or hostility achieves. We of liberty stand in total defense against the anarchs and tyrants whom hate life, detest liberty, and attack happiness; especially in their denial of the holy ghost and the liberty and joy for which this spirit of living waters unendingly delivers. Property then can never exist as some archaic or meaningless thing of man's creation – rather property exists as a law, even a sacred law, which preexists the creation of man and by the order in which God so self-evidently created for the universe do we then understand His natural law and phonetically articulate our logic and reason according to His life preserving qualities which He so abundantly delivered man above His other creatures and celestial inventions. What force could so envelope society in the absence of the knowledge of God and His sacred laws of property except that worldly spirit of tyranny which hates anything resembling the true living spirit and living waters animating our souls; and, in it's great replacement fills the world with it's ever condensing decay of anarchy which only a tyrant could arrogantly praise; though in His doings He would mark Himself for political destruction both by God and the men with the power at-hand to reckon annihilation of the tyrants at war with the world?

The tyrant approaches a thing as any other man would – a semantical hierarchy of assertions though He invert spiritual discernment into immorality, for example: assailing a civilization through the distortion and manipulation of civil liberties or even the intentional genocide of a population such that it dwindles until full erasure of skilled labor and free trade. Our assembly as a mankind of one mind ought to know even our ideas exist as a property which we ought to freely distribute and redistribute and divide and innovate upon since none can steal the expansion of our spirit (which multiplies it's potency under expansion) – perhaps the best clocksmith produces a competitor – best of luck to the competitor even if He shall perform His best to innovate; though, He may never be allowed under any law to steal the physical property of the clocksmith. Let common sense forever forge our path against the wickedness awakened by those lords of evil and let us keep our supreme law of the land in that perfect law of liberty to force those forces opposing our rule of law and even distorting and manipulating it's intent through whimsical albeit wicked legalese to then abide under our law and keep order in the presence of our civilization such that their evils keep as hidden ideas within the depths of their wretched souls never to see the light of action on any day and even to the extent that the ideas which we bear receive the brunt force of injustice thus preserving our lives into an abundance exceeding the imagination of our devisers of that sublime constitutional republic envisioned at america's founding and conceived of as an infant idea narrowly in whole at the time of the Magna Carta as we have fought and built generations of men to recognize and defend those unalienable rights against those wicked men devising ways to render mankind extinct or in the least the enslaved and insane washers of their fat and slimy feet. Men must manifest their righteous ideas into action since those ideas in action do equally represent the perfect law of liberty and tarred mortar for which feathers society into an awareness which keeps fast toward blessing and not despair.

One additional illness of the pseudo philosophers proclaim fear as a thing in which we must never possess though if we fear not God then how can we love God without fearing man since in liberty I trust God with caring for my instinct to fear above any place else and any man that would proclaim He holds fear for nothing at all hates God first and His own life above all. Tyranny in it's pretended securities of fearing nothing at all then design their idea as both a property and law which they can defend by attacking the innocent and especially attacking those individuals exercising their civil liberties which mean abiding in the kingdom of God on the earth; and, this action according to the tyrant only serves as a reminder of that property which they aim to erase off of the face of earth. How can these tyrants not suppose the being in which set the heavens in motion will not discard of them in the same throe? One can desire to call this force anarchy, monarchy, or tyranny though the fact remains any system of governance which would deny the individual their unalienable rights exists as a governance claiming freedom to sin and not a government instituted by men for the preservation of life, liberty, and property. Those tyrants sold their liberty to the impracticality of an injustice which can only invert reality unto it's own inflections that point and drive mankind toward that unnatural titration manifesting total spiritual enslavement. Tyranny dwelling within the mind of man proves this government a manifestation of individuals presuming their self as not an individual at all and rather a collective authority which can assume the role of an office designed for the restriction of civil liberties even unto a global and panopticonic force of indisputably tyrannical political machinations. That spirit of wickedry embodying the tyrant does dwell within that man as a spirit alien to mankind though God designed the universe and did not design the earth separate from the whole of creation therefore even in the Bible we witness God's clarity concerning the wicked in that this trouble comes from God through the free will of His creation and as a sign or wonder calls home to His children to dwell in that formidable state of righteous worship of the creator in obeying His law and therefore refuting the worship of man and subsequent disobeying of His statutes masquerading as law.

2 Kings 24:3 Surely by the [a] commandment of the Lord came this upon Judah, that he might put them out of his sight for the sins of Manasseh, according to all that he did,
2 Kings 24:3 Footnotes

[a] *Though God used these wicked tyrants to execute his just judgments, yet they are not to be excused, because they proceeded of ambition and malice.*

Ezekiel 30:25 *But I will strengthen the arms of the king of Babel, and the arms of Pharaoh shall fall down, and they shall know, that I am the Lord, [a] when I shall put my sword into the hand of the king of Babel, and he shall stretch it out upon the land of Egypt.*

Ezekiel 30:25 Footnotes

[a] *Whereby we see that tyrants have no power of themselves, neither can do anymore harm than God appointeth, and when he will they must cease.*

Once the individual engages in tyranny as their state of action this motion reverberates as a frequency permeating the wider metaphysical consciousness even unto the opening of that planar gait of hell for the welcoming of more misguided souls into it's carnal misgivings. Perhaps ancient civilizations populate the cosmos though do even they not enforce that law of property and the sacred order for which it divines; for how can anyone contest the eternity of God without denying the operations proving His distinctions and namely the preservation of that moral society which does not tax or possess standing armies or central banks and gives honor to peace and prosperity in the only way unalienable rights could endeavor the luxury of it's tranquility in acknowledging and defending mankind's mastery and stronghold of passion; thus, the infancy of mankind can not be definitive reason for implementing theft as a function of the state – rather, this can only be a diversion turned away from talent – even a legion of these individuals claiming passion, mastery, and talent have nothing at all to do with one's job causing them to succumb to the illness of apathy and idleness which they will pass on to the public in order to overcome them and secretly wish for this tyranny to overwhelm them all so that they can share in the burden of living a life worth less than it's potential (myopic and necrotic burdens they don as normal). The slide into the disorder of tyranny occurs in the moment the individual capitulates or procrastinates their own discipline in the action or knowledge which can not strengthen the neural pathways God imbues with His knowledge to create the faculty for laying the foundation of an avenue treading down every form of theft and fraud in the mind of men and especially those injurious frauds proclaiming a military instituted by the militia receive superior authority over the right of the militia whom own the military outright in the first place as their property. The perfect law of liberty made manifest through the order placed into motion through the righteous action of man gives rise to a series of maxims contrary to one another insofar as concerns the acquiring of knowledge for self or spiritual affirmation since man so passionately looks for signs and wonders as means for recognizing that active connection of God's presence which does mean that feeling of true joy and can not mean the evils which enliven the tyrant through acts of death and desolation or fits of rage therefore even joy can exist as the first property of man's spiritual realm since it's true frequency preserves the entire spiritual world and the homeostatic physical world for which it preserves for it's own likeness.

Exodus 1:22 Then Pharaoh charged all his people, saying, Every man-child that is born, [a] cast ye into the river, but reserve every maid-child alive.

Exodus 1:22 Footnotes

[a] When tyrants cannot prevail by craft, they burst forth into open rage.

1 Samuel 19:15 And Saul sent the messengers again to see David, saying, Bring him to me in the [a] bed, that I may slay him.

1 Samuel 19:15 Footnotes

[a] Behold, how the tyrants to accomplish their rage, neither regard oath nor friendship, God nor man.

Trade alone constitutes the whole law and order of property since it's act transfers that energy which liberty aims to preserve through writing into law it's reminder to the public that would deceive this unalienable right and thieve from a free people even for pretended security for society; though, nevertheless as a proof for their willingness to assume the role of a wicked tyrant in their crimes against the perfect law of liberty as though these murderers, murmurers, and thieves held some type of Godly authority or claim in openly abusing the innocent and sovereign people. Tyrants desire that false power which amasses it's own momentum of anarchy: that anarchy which can only extract energy from the public through theft and fraud via their standing armies and central banks since that spiritual inquisition of temporal capitulation can only maintain it's authority through the present observation and hypnotic ability to enforce a lack of participation from those industrious individuals whom would otherwise animate into the spiritual being God designed for the purpose of overthrowing such statutes. The ability of the tyrant limits itself to threatening hostility against those individuals that would question and fight it's self-evident lying and hate for true knowledge since these tyrants so readily supply the public with the idea that their false knowledge remains supreme over good knowledge and the only route from under the bondage of the tyrant claims we must beg or vote our way out when even america's founders understood well we reserve the right to immediately assemble and overthrow these wicked forces by any bloody means necessary so that we can stand upon this realm and declare liberty to the captives in hope the meek which so readily submit to the tyranny would instead repent of their hypocrisy and join the fight for liberty and stop their willing support and constant payments to the system which has so long enslaved mankind through the vehicle of the spiritually dead.

1 Kings 20:8 And all the Elders, and all the people said to him, Hearken [a] not unto him, nor consent.

1 Kings 20:8 Footnotes

[a] They thought it their duties rather to venture their lives, than

*to grant to that thing which was not lawful, only to satisfy the lust
of a tyrant.*

1 Kings 1:15 *And the Angel of the Lord said unto Elijah, Go
down with him, be [a] not afraid of his presence. So he arose, and
went down with him unto the king.*

1 Kings 1:15 Footnotes

*[a] Thus the Lord giveth boldness to his, that they fear not the
threatenings of tyrants, which otherwise of themselves are afraid
to do God's message.*

Once mankind invokes God to empower them with those
unalienable rights which mankind had for so long acknowledged
though spent centuries not acting as one mind to fulfill – the
illusion of spiritual control shatters; and, in that instant a spiritual
echo forms wherein mankind records this great success as
championed history for the illustration of the blessings we receive
when we believe in God's way to free the world from sin and do
those deeds which ought be done. The pursuit of liberty animates
into a contest for liberty since tyranny only can destroy animation
through war though it hobble about toward nothing good and
congratulate itself as the hero of all heroisms for most closely
following the rules in which the evil one set forth for their blind
and dumb following; and, in the case of today's modern world
driven awry by america's central bank: an example never so self-
evident as the american government stealing from it's own people
and psychopathically destroying foreign lands for that Luciferian

religion which compels it's actors to enjoy and carry-out it's tyrannical orders disguised as bravery, courage, cryptologic linguist, geospatial intelligence analyst, honesty, honor, manliness, strength, warrior and other pomp and vain slogans using compartmentalization to control the weak-minded, unbelieving, and wicked individuals.

Luke 12:57 [a] Yea, and why judge ye not of yourselves what is right?

Luke 12:57 Footnotes

[a] Men that are blinded with the love of themselves, and therefore are detestable and stubborn, shall bear the reward of their folly.

Exercising our unalienable rights guarantees God immediate reception of our deed and with this energy He then multiplies it's effect into a blossoming of blessings the world over and even creates a resonance for which brings joy and inspiration for the multitudes to join in the animating contest for liberty in seeking justice for those individuals taxing the public to keep the world a coercively violent dunescape of warfare and welfare. Our hope then rests in mankind never acquiescing unto tyranny as means of provisioning society with a projection of false civility; for to go along with such a system can only encourage the corruption of that individual's imagination unto the enabling of the most vicious corruptions. America's Founders in identifying Economic and Foreign policy as the chief instruments of the Executive

Magistrate unearthed an elastic and momentous knowledge which illustrates that light of free trade and absolves that darkness of war in the manifestation of a constitutional Republic releasing the chains of bondage unto the purification of the church and the state wherein the people entrust in God to preserve their powers through the people enforcing their government to remain the servant of man and a most fearful master shall the public pursue justice through it's institutions thereby resolving the power structure of the world unto the casting of government parasites into the least of all powers in society while the people keep their indivisible and unalienable rights such that no power on the earth will ever overcome their love for God and His preservation of a society blessing deeds above words. The flow of energy in a market free to punish theft and fraud will lift the suffering of the world and cast it's influence into the eternal lake of fire.

Isaiah 5:17 Then shall [a] the lambs feed after their manner, and the strangers shall eat the desolate places of the fat.
Isaiah 5:17 Footnotes
[a] God comforteth the poor lambs of his Church, which had been strangers in other countries, promising that they should dwell in these places again, whereof they had been deprived by the fat and cruel tyrants.

Isaiah 14:7 The whole world is at [a] rest and is quiet: they sing for joy.
Isaiah 14:7 Footnotes

[a] Meaning, that when tyrants reign, there can be no rest nor quietness, and also how detestable a thing tyranny is, seeing the insensible creatures have occasion to rejoice at their destruction.

Theft and fraud fuel the primary institution of central banks through it's ancillary institution of standing armies and this marriage forms the tyranny for which today we refer to as the military-industrial-complex: a false god instantiating the idolization of individuals basing their understanding of knowledge on the necessity of human action demanding an authoritarian or hereditary government of compartmentalization based on envy and greed as the source of human spirit thus begetting all of this coercive notion's subsequent violent virtue.

***Daniel 8:12** And [a] a time shall be given <u>him</u> over the daily <u>sacrifice</u> for the iniquity: and it shall [b] cast down the truth to the ground, and thus shall it do, and prosper.*

Daniel 8:12 Footnotes

[a] He showeth that their sins are the cause of these horrible afflictions: and yet comforteth them, in that he appointeth this tyrant a time, whom he would not suffer utterly to abolish his religion.

[b] This horn shall abolish for a time the true doctrine, and so corrupt God's service.

***Isaiah 14:13** Yet thou saidest in thine heart, I will ascend into heaven, and exalt my throne above beside the stars of God: I will* *sit also upon the mount of the congregation in the sides of the [a] North.*

Isaiah 14:13 Footnotes

[a] Meaning, Jerusalem, whereof the Temple was of the North side, Ps. 48:2, whereby he meaneth that tyrants fight against God, when they persecute his Church, and would set themselves in his place.

How great an irony witnessed in those individuals whom through their envy and greed toward their neighbor for reason no greater than property ownership, even if that property be their liberty, would lobby the state to steal their property and even their life as a form of equal outcome which can only criminalize our unalienable equal opportunity for life and property.

"COVET ME AND MY!"

These plunderers, ghosts, idolaters, magicians, phantoms, sorcerers, and general deceivers would screed their self into the legislation as a graven image to covet; and, the coveting of these entities only enshrines a standing army in the form of banks and corporations as a rising image of law which can only waste civilization. The assembly of factions compositing the larger world faction of tyrannical order claim their disorder of occupying the authority of language through deliberately misinterpreting logic and reason by threat of violence (a theft and fraud against sovereign humanity) instantly place into perspective the existential threat which they invite upon their own livelihood through misconstruing our kindness for weakness or our intelligent knowledge for their reprieve. Only the heart can truly guard an idea since the mind first seeks a faction as basis to what it thinks even unto degradation and impotency of the original meaning insofar as the greatest ideas give life and restrain tyranny; and, the philosophy of liberty once learned will refuse the teachings of tyranny and the advice of it's individuals whom may as well call their self The Fae Cass Society for the lies in which they promulgate for the shadowing of consciousness.

How could any society reach a state of civilization without exercising their liberty for language which then provisions them with their religion therefore to honor language means freedom of religion in the same breadth and from this notion we can know God Himself wrote the law in heaven for man to not covet since to covet would require the worship of a sinful man and not one's spiritual deliverer? God does not confuse when it comes to His spiritual line in the sand as that perfect law of liberty and to violate such a law would invite the tyrant to steal the liberty of the people therefore to keep the envy and greed of the tyrant at bay the people must write into law those laws of heaven since the more reminders the public can keep then the more liberty they can exercise without any tyrant claiming direct authority to politically punish or prohibit the innocent for acting in their sovereign duty to establish society on their merits which the tyrant would prohibit in order to deliver Himself the merit to rewrite society as though He were God above the living creator preexisting even the stardust which God knit for the formation of this existence. God has drawn the line in the sand and He scorches His opposition. One can then think of theft and fraud as a product of society not reaching the pinnacle of civilization since civility would require at least an absolute reduction of the occurrence of the two and thusly a total absence of the two worldwide would mean a world grown past the stage of civilization into the awareness we live in the free realm of liberty and not the yoke of tyranny which so covetously would express otherwise even unto the theft of life, liberty, and property until the most meek will submit to their false authority. Society can not experience peace without justice therefore each individual of society must fortify their self with that knowledge which civilization demands and a civilization preserving the perfect law of liberty commands. The chief thieves committing fraud as representatives of the nameless wicked one will remain that supreme and ancient dark and dead army of aliens arising from the depths of hell to eat the substance of mankind through their empirically occultic royal dynasty of dynasties of democracies of despotisms of tyrants and of wicked people.

Daniel 7:25 And shall speak words against [a] the most High, and shall consume the Saints of the most High, and think that he may [b] change times and laws, and they shall be given into his hand until a [c] time, and times, and the dividing of time.

Daniel 7:25 Footnotes

[a] That is, shall make wicked decrees and proclamations against God's word, and send throughout all their dominion, to destroy

all that did profess it.

[b] These Emperors shall not consider that they have their power of God, but think it is in their own power to change God's laws and man's, and as it were the order of nature, as appeareth by Octavius, Tiberius, Caligula, Nero, Domitian, etc.

[c] God shall suffer them thus to rage against his Saints for a long time, which is meant by the time and times, but at length he will assuage these troubles, and shorten the time for his elect's sake, Matt. 24:22, which is here meant by the dividing of time.

Matthew 24:22 *And except [a] those days should be shortened, there should no [b] flesh be saved: but for the elect's sake those days shall be shortened.*

Matthew 24:22 Footnotes

[a] Those things which befell the people of the Jews, in the 34 years, when as the whole land was wasted, and at length the city of Jerusalem taken, and both it and their Temple destroyed, are mixed with those which shall come to pass before the last coming of our Lord.

[b] The whole nation should utterly be destroyed: and this word Flesh is by a figure taken for man, as the Hebrews used to speak.

1 Corinthians 12:10-11 *And to another the [a] operations of great works: and to another, [b] prophecy: and to another, the [c] discerning of spirits: and to another, diversities of tongues: and to another, the interpretation of tongues. [e] And all these things worketh one and the selfsame Spirit, distributing to every* *man severally [d] as he will.*

1 Corinthians 12:10 Footnotes

[a] By operation he meaneth those great workings of God's mighty power, which pass and excel amongst his miracles, as the delivery of his people Israel by the hand of Moses: that which he did by Elijah against the Priests of Baal, in sending down fire from heaven to consume his sacrifice: and that which he did by Peter in the matter of Ananias and Sapphira.

[b] Foretelling of things to come.

[c] Whereby false prophets are known from true, wherein Peter passed Philip in discovering Simon Magus, Acts 8:20.

1 Corinthians 12:11 Footnotes

[d] He addeth moreover something else, to wit, that although these gifts are unequal, yet they are most wisely divided, because the will of the Spirit of God is the rule of this distribution.

1 Corinthians 12:11 Endnotes

[e] Rom. 12:3, Eph. 4:7

We can know language forms the first barrier in society to allow the formation of factions which issue warfare and welfare as decrees of tyranny since that tower of Babel would confuse the tongue for their own essential economy which God otherwise disallows although the public so readily abandons the living God for the worship of dead and false idols and gods.

We shall continue in the way of Christ and the founding fathers of america holding genuine intent to eradicate tyranny and inspire self-ownership which fights against the tyrannical notion of stealing individual property as lawful or a moral responsibility for gaining access to social or technological progression or security. America's Bill of Rights was the result of the long spiritual battle following the adoption of The Magna Carta which even itself was set into motion through the manner in which true men acted and worshiped according to those laws governing the heavens. When the individual reaches that awareness and love for God which activates their highest conscious state they then conduct their self according to the action which their spirit of the Lord dwelling within them demands; and, those manners at which this individual then commands bless Him with ever more liberty to even exist as that sign and wonder at war with the wicked one using His tyrants against a free people even if they live unconvinced of their liberty and ask and receive of their own enslavement. The destruction of property brought forth by the idle and intemperate look on to the economy which God provisions for mankind and then seeks to control and dominate this active force of logic and reason such that they reflexively raise that deflated army from hell onto the physical plane therefore any man that would deny it's existence or speak as such that He would argue against the need for His involvement to repel it's advances will then in that instant join with the fallen army as an observer and enabler of their wretched torments and most of all He embodies the wicked one excising His ability from the game which promises Him blessings in the effort for liberty therefore His claim to a blessing outside of this fight can receive no blessing from God or His people.

Daniel 4:21-22 This is the interpretation, O king, and it is the decree of the most High, which is come upon my lord the king, That they shall drive thee from men, and thy dwelling shall be with the beasts of the field: they shall make thee to eat grass as the [a] oxen, and they shall wet thee with the dew of heaven: and seven times shall pass over thee, till thou know, that [b] the most High beareth rule over the kingdom of men, and giveth it to whomsoever he will.

Daniel 4:22 Footnotes

[a] Not that his shape or form was changed into a beast, but that he was either stricken mad, and so avoided man's company, or was cast out for his tyranny, and so wandered among the beasts, and ate herbs and grass.

[b] Daniel showeth the cause why God thus punished him.

If it were so that society did not possess preexisting rights then why would such an argument of eternal law wage against human statutes in the first place if both had not always existed as the contrary of one to another therefore one existing as the property of the people and the other existing as the plunder of the tyrant and crime for which the people reserve the right to seek immediate justice for any such transgression lest the false pastors hypnotize the public into turning their head for an additional lashing on the other cheek. What else could restrain these clowns of evil if those precepts which God Himself governs did not pass through the hands of authority delivering justice to that roaming fog of spiritually disemboweled confusion missing their moment of awakening for a lifetime of insanity and hissing avariceness?

Exodus 5:9 [a] Lay more work upon the men, and cause them to do it, and let them not regard [b] vain words.

Exodus 5:9 Footnotes

[a] The more cruelly that tyrants rage, the nearer is God's help.

[b] Of Moses and Aaron

That foundation of allowing no theft or fraud whatsoever in society stands as the precept and foundation unto all others and the institutions which so commonly birth from these sins manifest into a central bank and standing army drawing forth their powers of tyranny. We must challenge ourselves to open our heart into that spiritual awareness that God delivers us the keys for the entering of that kingdom of God; and, it must remain known that this state exists as the most young idea in all of the world since liberty can even mean a world not at all of this world wherein we witness the self-evidence of it having always pursued tyranny; and, young in that only the innocent or repentant can know the path to liberty since the adults so often nurture their self into the apathy of idly worshiping the machine which abhors the eternity of God thereby making them eternal servants of the fallen world though their obsolete time on the earth and wanton memory shall fade. Spiritual malnourishment plagues mankind since the avenues of it's decay fill with violence and coercion for a world sacrificing the innocent and the immortal man from heaven while giving the keys which hold the degrees of death to the most superstitious since only they would hate God and participate in tyranny through the hypnotizing of an ignorant and superstitious public. Men must know the ideas of liberty which preserve property form the market for which preserves all other property and ideas and when the unjust transgress God's laws we witness their folly and guard our society jealously so that we keep our liberty and righteously represent our God lest we wish to live the life of the backbiter and speak of things without action and justify that idleness with dumb declarations claiming righteousness in idleness; even, and, especially, that idleness of hiding in that church that God Himself would disown and identify it's people as that synagogue of Satan.

2 Thessalonians 2:3 Let no man deceive you by any means: [a] for <u>that day shall not come</u>, except there come a departing first, and that [b] that man of sin be disclosed, <u>even</u> the son of perdition.

2 Thessalonians 2:3 Footnotes

[a]The Apostle foretelleth that before the coming of the Lord, there shall be a throne set up clean contrary to Christ's glory, wherein that wicked man shall sit, and transfer all things that appertain to God, to himself, and many shall fall away from God to him.

[b] By speaking of one, he pointed out the body of the tyrannous and persecuting Church.

This tyranny replicated throughout all of time will guard itself against the men of liberty through the imprisonment and assassination of our identity and even our lives therefore our greatest weapon, even admitted by the tyranny today, exists in our action by faith and knowledge which most permanently represents itself in literature and secondarily in the arts wherein the class of study of liberal arts derives it's phrasing though today the liberal arts university professors teach the art of tyranny and spitefully label their teaching as art and liberal.

Tyrants in forcing men to submit to their dictates ought to know full and well they risk the action of free men under God. The brutish royal family sent swarms of thieving agencies, some called tax-collectors, and were promptly soaked in tar, coated in feathers, and paraded around the town by the men of God that understood the transgression of this false authority and as a result this mounting patriotism was received well by God as He delivered abundant blessings and authority for us to assemble, unite, and fight for our society to overthrow these tyrants out from under our lands. What end could these thieves see lest all they see in their imagination exists as a fantasy of the tyrant wherein they envision a world worshiping them as a living God though like all false gods: they shall die the death. No tyrant will ever force the true believer in God to abandon His ideas through any threat and certainly not the compelling to unbelieve that liberty which man can exercise to fight the tyrant as God's face shines upon the man answering His call; thus, any man that would not hate the tyrant unto the absolute refutation of His existence through the example of His own deeds and public declarations will forever dwell within the life of sin which ensures the funding to empower the tyrant and His lemmings whom oppress society and destroy liberty; and as such, this idle and sinful maker of excuses worships the system which the tyrant built for the purchase of His acquiescence thus illustrates His disobedience to the God of this universe since even He would state the living creator were the tyrant tasking Him with living the life of ultimate sin. The free market compels itself to innovate based on the satisfaction of the customer while the tyrant must propagate deadened ideas to deceive and continue His empire until that fateful and glorious day of exhausting all funds whether spiritual or temporal. The stupidity of the tyrant means His oppressing the people enslaves Him to the wicked one. The road to tyranny paved with a road to freedom will dismiss the philosophy of liberty as the ramblings of a raving lunatic; and, though this stance works to deceive the hypocrite and murmurer with their own self-prophecy of spiritual immolation – this narrative bias keeps them under the hypnosis of that bread and circus thereby causing an acceleration of the zeal in the free market from working under a higher resistance for the reception of the blessings of liberty thus maximizing the self-evidence of that river of stupidity so flippantly mixing politics and religion into a one world government wherein the individuals exercising liberty or at least preaching of a government and religion unto it's pure intention have received the painting of a target upon their head from those tyrants collectivizing for the construction of one military road (ONE BELT ONE ROAD) to govern the planet unto their absolute control for sheer madness

alone; therefore, that road to liberty guarantees eternal life while
that road to tyranny guarantees spiritual death.

*Daniel 8:18 And they shall take the [a] kingdom of the Saints of
the [b] most High, and shall possess the kingdom forever, even
forever and ever.*

Daniel 8:18 Footnotes

*[a] Because Abraham was appointed heir of all the world, Rom.
4:13, and in him all the faithful, therefore the kingdom thereof is
theirs by right, which these four beasts or tyrants should invade,
and usurp until the world were restored by Christ: and this was to
confirm them that were in troubles, that their afflictions should
have an end at length.*

*[b] That is, of the most high things, because God hath chosen
them out of this world, that they should look up to the heavens,
whereon all their hope dependeth.*

The tyrant can only place His plans into motion through forcing
the public into the theft of taxation to fund His endeavor; and,
while the meek may allow their superstitions to overwhelm them
thereby covetously begging wicked men to violently steal their
property or coerce a third-party to commit acts of treason on their
behalf – their ignorance will prove unworthy in the stripping of
their society of every last ounce of happiness. The spiritual canard
of Satan providing anything except tyranny feeds a bumbling
massé of idiots waiting for false super-natural powers to cause
them to rise in significance in society and create a false land of

happiness wherein tributaries of blood flow into lakes of fire, the sky glows swirling hot and scorches the earth, people dwell underground and hunt one another for food, and machines storm through the skies to the sound of silence or unending memories shrieking for help.

Matthew 16:3 *[b] And in the morning, ye say, Today shall be a tempest: for the sky is red and lowering. O hypocrites, ye can discern the [a] face of the sky, and can ye not discern the signs of the times?*

Matthew 16:3 Footnotes

[a] The outward show and countenance as it were of all things, is called in the Hebrews' tongue, a face.

Matthew 16:3 Endnotes

[b] Luke 12:54

Luke 12:54 ¶ *[c],[a] Then said he to the people, When ye see a cloud [b] rise out of the West, straightway ye say, A shower cometh: and so it is.*

Luke 12:54 Footnotes

[a] Men which are very quick of sight in earthly things, are blind in those things which pertain to the heavenly life, and that through their own malice.

[b] Which appeareth, and gathereth itself together in that part of the air.

Luke 12:54 Endnotes

[c] Matt. 16:2

Matthew 16:2 *But he answered, and said unto them, When it is evening, ye say, Fair weather, for the sky is red.*

All dreams of tyrannical empire fade. The men of Liberty preserve current and future generations and perform this duty of civil disobedience against these individuals whom would fire a weapon at their feet and demand they dance and cluck like a chicken.

Taxing citizens, using these funds to coerce the public into oppressing their fellow countrymen, defrauding foreign nations through secretly funding dictators to steal their sovereignty, and forcing the world's entire population to fund it's own suicide of worshiping a non-creator (democracy or any other form of collectivism which purchases that secret poison of mob-rule) – all of this stopped with the simple precepts of punishing and not preserving theft and fraud as the enforced and written law of the land in which keeps the order of society moral and the purpose for which God designed us toward exploring in His infinity of creation and eternal quest for exercising our liberty. The tyrant argues He does not sin at all since the public sins for Him though His intention and action excuse Him and His defenders not from their sinful oppression exhibiting the highest form of existential predation.

Revolution, self-evidently dangerous, continues in america and around the world though among the strongholds today the american public remains chief among the few. The human revolution back to liberty beats strong and at the very core of this revolution exist the heart of the revolutionary and not the false revolutionaries which demand government intervention and redistribution of wealth – the true revolutionaries which know the philosophy of liberty, possess familial and historical evidence proving the philosophy true, and will further show the ideas of liberty as superior in peace and prosperity above all of the false philosophies and religions around the world. We the people, wild as the river, tamed by no oppressor, will fight for liberty and prove our God a mighty creator of armed and ready allegiance to defend liberty, crush the central banks and standing armies, encourage other nations to overthrow their tyrannical government, and corner every state-sponsored dynasty and empire into a hole for which mankind will bury their legacy and false power forever. The core understanding of what force rules the world surrounds the central banks hiding behind standing armies and led by it's chief bishops whom tyrannically destroy the precepts of the rule of law in order that they enslave humanity to an absolute control of illusionary freedom which manifestly culls mankind into forgetting human liberty forever.

Revelation 13:12 [a] And he did all that the first beast could do before him, and he caused the earth and them which dwell therein, [b] to worship the first beast whose deadly wound was healed.

Revelation 13:12 Footnotes

[a] The history of the acts of this beast containeth in sum three

things, hypocrisy, the witness of miracles and tyranny: of which the first is noted in this verse, the second in the 3 verses following: the third in the sixteenth and seventeenth verses. His hypocrisy is most full of leasing, whereby he abuseth both the former beast and the whole world: in that albeit he hath by his cunning, as it were by lime made of the former beast a most miserable ... or anatomy, usurped all his authority unto himself and most impudently exerciseth the same in the sight and view of him: yet he carrieth himself so, as if he honored him with most high honor, and did in very truth cause him to be honored of all men.

[b] For unto this beast of Rome, which of civil Empire is made an Ecclesiastical hierarchy, are given divine honors, and divine authority so far as he is believed to be above the Scriptures, which the gloss upon the Decretals declareth by this devilish verse,

Articulos solvit, synodumque facit generalem,

That is,

He changeth the Articles of faith, and giveth authority

to general Counsels.

Which is spoken of the Papal power. So the beast is by birth, foundation, feat, and finally substance, one: only the Pope hath altered the form and manner thereof being himself the head both of that tyrannical Empire, and also of the false Prophets, for the Empire hath he taken unto himself, and thereunto hath added this cunning device. Now these words, whose deadly wound was cured are put here for distinction sake, as also sometimes afterwards:

that even at that time the godly readers of this prophecy might by this sign be brought to see the things as present: as if it were said, that they might adore this very Empire that now is, whose head we have seen in our own memory to have been cut off, and to be cured again.

The individuals acting on behalf of the tyrant do so for their own reptilian-brained tomfoolery incapable of comprehending their social programming with an education gap too wide to fill though abolishing the central banks will encourage love fill that void although their receiving of bread and circus from the stolen public largess in the meantime imbues them with the legacy of generating bloody hatred throughout society. Their false livelihood will end along with it's grand scheme in shadowing consciousness for the instilling of a common state of fear in man and it's subsequent restrictions of the knowledge of God. The men of God will stir the spirit of the Lord in a way to activate our livelihood as a raging brushfire possessing a distinct resonance and of the resonances does create the largest resonance and clarity of truth of them all. Understanding the low-level criminal, both that petty thief and the multitude aiding and abetting the fraud of taxation, moulds the skeleton key into discerning the psychology of the enemy since this standing army overflows society with seemingly infinite clones of their fattened and avaricious tyranny working to shut the doors of perception and unleash the gaits of hell onto our physical plane through our spiritual window of the heart. The tyrants prey upon individuals lacking sufficient knowledge to escape the trap they built for the people thus enslaving one generation after another and never allowing even the true beam of light to infiltrate society let alone every society therefore no true society can exist that would deny the Holy Ghost thereby in this acceptance of tyranny as a god will allow it's founts of illusion to team with persistence. Men must enter the public debate and correct the court systems in order to expose the empire and peaceably exhaust the tyranny and this action will build a momentum which time and space can not stop. I pray to God the wicked tyrants receive their reward of the wicked on this day and the righteous sons of God eternally receive the light of the Holy Ghost.

Isaiah 49:6 And he said, It is a small thing that thou shouldest be my servant to raise up the tribes of Jacob, and to restore the desolations of Israel: I will also give [a] thee for a light of the Gentiles, that thou mayest be my salvation unto the end of the world.

Isaiah 49:6 Footnotes

[a] To declare my Gospel, to the Gentiles, Isa. 42:6; Acts 13:47; Luke 2:32.

Isaiah 49:6 Endnotes

Christ is the salvation of all that believe, and will deliver them from the tyranny of their enemies.

DEATH

Luke 18:8 I tell you he will avenge them quickly: but when the Son of man cometh, shall he find faith on the earth?

One of the chief debates on the earth surrounds whether the force of tyranny originates from collectivism or an entity. Do individuals tyrannically control the planet for their own pleasure? Who would do such a thing and to what end? How could such few individuals influence the political and religious events on the earth? Everyone lives and dies though how do the wicked transfer this power of absolute control in which they manage into the future so that they and their fellow travelers and progeny perennially manifest control over the present realm? Do we witness a war of realms and do these realms simply war over the physical realm or does spiritual influence infiltrate our realm from their realm as though our realm were separate or even a lower spiritual dimension on the battlefield of intergalactic spiritual warfare? How many people observe this war of realms and how many more wittingly participate in order that they influence the outcome of this war? How much greater of knowledge does the participator of God's word acquire than the idle observer whom lacks certain awareness since only the participant and not the observer of God's word remain wholly aware of the knowledge and the receiver of it's bounty which equips His or Her liberty for the combating of spiritual forces that would otherwise sway civilization into the realms of the underworld?

Luke 17:20 ¶ *[a] And when he was demanded of the Pharisees, when the kingdom of God should come, he answered them, and said, The kingdom of God cometh not with [b] observation.*

Luke 17:20 Endnotes

Of the coming of the kingdom of heaven.

Luke 17:20 Footnotes

[a] The kingdom of God is not marked of many, although it be most present before their eyes: because they fondly persuade themselves, that it is joined with outward pomp.

[b] With any outward pomp and show of majesty, to be known by: for there were otherwise many plain and evident tokens, whereby men might have understood, that Christ was the Messiah, whose kingdom was so long looked for: but he speaketh in this place of those signs which the Pharisees dreamed of, which looked for an earthly kingdom of Messiah.

Judges 17:6 [c] In those days there was no [a] King in Israel, but every man did that which was good in his own eyes.

Judges 17:6 Footnotes

[a] *For where there is no Magistrate fearing God, there can be no true religion or order.*

Judges 17:6 Endnotes

[c] *Judg. 21:25*

Judges 21:25 [b] *In those days there was no king in Israel, but every man did that which was good in his eyes.*

Judges 21:25 Endnotes

[b] *Judg. 17:6, Judg. 13:1, Judg. 19:1*

Judges 13:1 *But the children of Israel continued to commit a wickedness in the sight of the Lord, and the Lord delivered them into the hands of the Philistines forty years.*

Judges 13:1 Endnotes

Israel for their wickedness is oppressed of the Philistines.

[a] *Judg. 2:11, Judg. 3:7, Judg. 4:1, Judg. 6:1, Judg. 10:6*

Judges 2:11 ¶ *Then the children of Israel did wickedly in the sight of the Lord, and served [a] Baal,*

Judges 2:11 Endnotes

The Israelites fell to idolatry after Joshua's death.

Judges 2:11 Footnotes

[a] *That is, all manner of idols.*

Judges 3:7 ¶ *So the children of Israel did wickedly in the sight of the Lord, and forgot the Lord their God, and served Baal, and [a] Asherah.*

Judges 3:7 Footnotes

[a] Trees or woods erected for idolatry.

Judges 4:1 *And the children of Israel [a] began again to do wickedly in the sight of the Lord when Ehud was dead.*

Judges 4:1 Endnotes

Israel sin and are given into the hands of Jabin.

Judges 4:1 Footnotes

[a] Hebrew, added, or continued to do evil.

Judges 6:1 *Afterward the children of Israel committed wickedness in the sight of the Lord, and the Lord gave them into the hands of Midian seven years.*

Judges 6:1 Endnotes

Israel is oppressed of the Midianites for their wickedness.

Judges 10:6 ¶ *[a] And the children of Israel wrought wickedness again in the sight of the Lord, and served Baal and [b] Ashtoreth, and the gods of [c] Aram, and the gods of Sidon, and the gods of Moab, and the gods of the children of Ammon, and the gods of the Philistines, and forsook the Lord and served not him.*

Judges 10:6 Endnotes

[a] Judg. 2:11, Judg. 3:7, Judg. 4:1, Judg. 6:1, Judg. 13:1

[b] Judg. 2:13

Judges 10:6 Footnotes

[b] Or, Syrian.

Judges 2:13 *So they forsook the Lord, and served [d] Baal, and [a] Ashtoreth.*

Judges 2:13 Endnotes

[d] Judg. 10:6

Judges 2:13 Footnotes

[a] *These were Idols, which had the form of an ewe or sheep among the Sidonians.*

Judges 19:1 *Also in those days, when there was no king in Israel, a certain Levite dwelt on the side of mount Ephraim, and took to wife a [a] concubine out of Bethlehem Judah,*

Judges 19:1 Endnotes

A Levite's wife being an harlot forsook her husband, and he took her again.

[a] *Judg. 17:6, Judg. 18:1, Gen. 25:6*

Judges 18:1 *In those days there was no [a] king in Israel, and at the same time the tribe of Dan sought them an inheritance to dwell in: for unto that time all their inheritance had not fallen unto them among the tribes of Israel.*

Judges 18:1 Footnotes

[a] *Meaning, no ordinary Magistrate to punish vice according to God's word.*

Genesis 25:6 *But unto the [a] sons of the [b] concubines, which Abraham had, Abraham [c] gave gifts, and sent them away from Isaac his son (while he yet lived) Eastward to the East country.*

Genesis 25:6 Footnotes

[a] For by the virtue of God's word he had not only Isaac, but begat many more.

[b] Read Gen. 22:24.

[c] To avoid the dissention that else might have come because of the heritage.

Genesis 22:24 *And his [a] concubine called Reumah, she bare also Tebah, and Gaham, and Thahash and Maachah.*

Genesis 22:24 Footnotes

[a] Concubine is oftentimes taken in the good part for those women which were inferior to the wives.

Tyranny then can only represent a design of spiritual discernment wherein wicked men manifest the philosophy of death on the earth. America's Founding Fathers all possessed a keen awareness of the death cult plundering mankind with their excuse that our existence were a gift or effigy wherein the death cult's sacrifice of the free world through the destruction of our flesh and spirit made an atonement for their traveling through time as though we were the virus and they the host ensuring generations and centuries of mankind dwell under their false providence of truly wicked spirits that no good or sane individual would ever consider joining lest they spiritually surrender to the spiders whom God eternally damned.

The cult of death must forever concern mankind's imagination shall we endeavor to guard our human liberty from their temporal illusions of despotic tyranny.

2 Samuel 10:12 *Be strong and let us be valiant for [a] our people, and for the cities of our God, and let the Lord do that which is good in his eyes.*

2 Samuel 10:12 Footnotes

[a] Here is declared wherefore war ought to be undertaken: of the defense of true religion and God's people.

These false powers have thus far largely succeeded in chaining down mankind's potential through shadowing the vision and dreams contained within the fractal of liberty. The veil in which this death cult designs creates an image of tyranny with wanton power which most hypnotizes the weakest individuals amongst society thus setting a foundation for the pattern on which their web ensnare more idle souls unwittingly participating as a pawn against our ancient and sacred battle for human liberty which will always represent mankind's true battle worthy of and signifying our original intent by order of the universe's design at the time of the creation of man and woman: let there be peace on the earth. God forms the alpha and omega while the cult of death would anagram itself against His design in order that they deceive and tempt mankind into suffering their oppressions. The action of these spiders makes self-evident their manifestation as a ritualistic feast upon mankind's innocence.

As men in defense of civilization and liberty we support the cause that all ancestors of all tribes in their most true form sought for mankind to preserve so that one day mankind fulfill that sacred responsibility of living up to the standard of that holy ghost dwelling within man which had always captured our imagination and love though perhaps the history of mankind reveal a constant toiling and missed opportunities in succeeding the deeds which God rewards with His promise of world-wide peace and prosperity or otherwise stated as that full articulation of the spiritual realm of heaven onto the physical plane of earth; however, we must discern our responsibility, as it were peril, in addressing and confronting this common enemy waging spiritual war against the liberty of mankind. The driving force under this death cult keeps knowledge buried thus outside of the control of the free people whom would learn of such power in order that we the people rewrite the function of knowledge from it's previous state of oppressing mankind and for our promised destiny in the duty of fulfilling human felicity.

2 Chronicles 14:5 And he took away out of all the cities of Judah the high places, and the images: therefore the Kingdom was [a] quiet before him.

2 Chronicles 14:5 Footnotes
[a] He showeth that the rest and quietness of kingdoms standeth in abolishing idolatry, and advancing true religion.

Luke 11:52 [a] Woe be to you, Lawyers: for ye have [b] taken away the key of knowledge: ye entered not in yourselves, and them that came in, ye forbade.

Luke 11:52 Footnotes

[a] They have of long time chiefly hindered the people, from entering into the knowledge of God, which ought to be the doorkeepers of the Church.

[b] You have hidden and taken away, so that it cannot be found anywhere.

Speech exercises our most common liberty since it's use popularizes the practice of that knowledge man would preach in order that the multitude discern what we ought to tolerate and what intolerant tyranny infringes on the rights of the individual. Let us not confuse the chivalry of bridling one's tongue with the cowardice of restricting one's self from discernibly, immediately, instructively, inwardly, eternally, understandingly, openly, outwardly, sharply, steadfastly, wisely, and wittingly refuting the sins of tyranny.

1 Kings 1:10 But Elijah answered, and said to the captain over the fifty, If that I be a man of God, let fire come down from the heaven, and devour thee and thy fifty. [a] So fire came down from the heaven and devoured him and his fifty.

1 Kings 1:10 Endnotes

The captains over fifty were sent to Elijah, whereof two were burnt with fire from heaven by his prayer.

1 Kings 1:10 Footnotes

[a] He declareth what power God's word hath in the mouth of his servants, when they threaten God's judgments against the wicked.

Acts 4:13 [a] Now when they saw the boldness of Peter and John, and understood that they were unlearned men and without [b] knowledge, they marveled, and knew them, that they had been with Jesus:

Acts 4:13 Footnotes

[a] The good liberty and boldness of the servants of God doeth yet thus much good that such as lay hid under a vizard of zeal, do at length bewray themselves to be indeed wicked men.

[b] The word used here, is Idiot, which being spoken in comparison had to a Magistrate, betokeneth a private man, but when we speak of sciences and studies, it signifieth one that is unlearned: and in accompt of honor and estimation it importeth one of base degree, and no estimation.

Simply going along with and not fighting the death cult nurtures it's culture and delivers precedent to it's oppressions therefore the self-realized individual deliberates and then fights it's compulsions if not for their self then for the defense of the innocents without their own representative defender of liberty even if that representative be the spirit of the Lord dwelling within them that would animate their idleness into that representative defender of liberty for their self and the world shall they uncover His mission and strength in perilous times for the preservation of the peace and prosperity for the world.

Consider america's illegal, undeclared, and unconstitutional wars and the blithering praise so heavily laden on those individuals whom illegally occupied these foreign and sovereign lands that one could almost think the constancy of such compulsive and intercessionary celebration of immorality as a form of performance mockery though it rather perfectly illustrate a plague of Stockholm's Syndrome for the fabrication of defending freedom or security at home though their ignorance and viciousness only did grow the beast in which they claimed to defend against thus inviting God's wrath onto american lands since we as the wicked world empire be both the host of the beast and at the same time the carrier of the torch of liberty being we possess that enlarged population of philosophic defenders of liberty though we be presently outnumbered, but not outwitted, by tyrannical anti-christs. Our hope rests in these blind and warmongering men and women of america turning to God and praying for forgiveness and showing God their earnestness through altering our government to it's original state of not allowing central banks or standing armies to enter and then pervert our society in the knowingness that God in our resurrection of discernment will turn away His wrath and spare this world of the coming judgment. Imagine tyranny as an entity separate from the mind though existing within the mind of man and therefore in this man's imagination will the face of the tyranny express through His own physical image and this uniform which He bears over His mind's eye masks the dictates keeping His aim aligned with the wilt separate from any talent of God.

Ezra 9:14 Should we return to break thy commandments, and join in affinity with the people of such abominations? wouldest not thou be angry toward us till thou hadst consumed us, so that there should be no remnant nor any escaping?

This face of death which pervades society through a multitude of anti-Christs stands ready to articulate it's tyranny through violence and coercion in order that it dissolve constitutionality and borders across the world and reform the nations and people of the world into a one world government wherein the wicked one leading the death cult openly and publicly rules the world and liberty vanishes as a mirage along with all of it's faith and justice. The old adage we remain our greatest enemy holds true insofar as even we restrain this greatest enemy and keep those friends we presume friends though we face the same fear and first danger in becoming enemies of one another or even delusional friends to the enemy of all friends: yeah, do not give time to the enemy.

In pursuing happiness we must keep an awareness for our life and liberty and face the challenges which we as individuals in society encounter and especially those challenges which the tyrants illuminate through their thieving the public and defrauding us of our God-given liberty to expand the peace and prosperity of civilization and not only for our society but as well civilization on the earth. No individual can benefit their self without extending aid to the society around them though what does it necessarily mean to benefit one's self when we must regard the teachings of Christ and the tyranny in which so often, if even indefinitely, oppresses our fellow countrymen. Clearly one's vocation and instruction can not exist independently of the problem or solution thus only He whom would keep a constant illumination upon His oath to preserve life, liberty, and property in society would first lay the foundation of confirmation for the rest of society to wage a successful war against the death cult. Our unalienable rights written into reminders known as our Bill of Rights challenges this multitude of anti-Christs in that without this hedge men would have nothing to look onto in order for them to bring justice to the wicked; and, with the most clear interpretation of justice such that we need not reinvent the wheel nor forget to serve justice to those puppets beholden to their puppet-masters.

Luke 19:8 [a] And Zacchaeus stood forth, and said unto the Lord, Behold, Lord, the half of my goods I give to the poor: and if I have taken from any man by [b] forged cavillation, I restore him fourfold.

Luke 19:8 Footnotes

[a] The example of true repentance, is known by the effect.

[b] By falsely accusing any man: and this agreeth most fitly to the master of the customer's person: for commonly they have this trade among them when they rob and spoil the commonweal, they have nothing in their mouths, but the profit of the commonweal, and under that color they play the thieves, insomuch that if men reprove and go about to redress their robbery, and spoiling, they cry out, the commonwealth is hindered.

When Founding Father Benjamin Franklin wrote about

individuals dying at the age of twenty-five and not buried until age seventy-five He was speaking specifically toward the imagination or that spirit of the individual and their willingness to pursue destiny in a spiritual life of purpose in Christ and fulfill the duty of defending liberty though these ghosts that allow their spirit to die live the rest of their days as clay treaded underfoot. Benjamin Franklin in speaking on the topic of spiritual death sought to animate or stir the inward spirit of the public that they would discover spiritual rebirth; and, verily the entire gospel of faith preaches this rebirth and liberty from sin. The pseudo philosophers will argue the idea of rebirth means reincarnation, as though Steve was always reborn into Steve only to face the responsibility of reconciling the sins of the buried Steve (thus form their basis for that false philosophy of hereditary rule and Satanic worship though even the royals outwardly claim to worship Christ to flatter the fools they oppress: yeah, those fools that do not do what Christ profess), or even freedom to commit sin without consequence (since they so readily argue knowledge and language does not exist and mankind be synonymous with evil) though the Godly rest easy with a sound mind knowing the time of the thief, especially that spiritual thief, receives absolute destruction from God since they wittingly live as His enemy; and, He reward indivisible goodness and favor to His people whom answer His call.

1 Corinthians 1:26 [a] For brethren, you see your [b] calling, how that not many wise men [c] after the flesh, not many mighty, not many noble are called.

1 Corinthians 1:26 Footnotes

[a] *A confirmation taken of those things which came to pass at Corinth, where the Church especially consisted of the basest and common people, insomuch that the philosophers of Greece were driven to shame, when they saw that they could do nothing with their wisdom and eloquence, in comparison of the Apostles, whom notwithstanding they called idiots and unlearned. And herewithall doth he beat down their pride, for God did not prefer them before those noble and wise men because they should be proud, but that they might be constrained even whether they would or not, to rejoice in the Lord, by whose mercy, although they were, the most abject of all, they had obtained in Christ, both this wisdom, and all things necessary to salvation.*

[b] *What way the Lord hath taken in calling you.*

[c] *After that kind of wisdom which men make account of, as though there were none else: who because they are carnal, know not spiritual wisdom.*

The emergency we face exists as a spiritual one wherein the cult of death would restrict our abundance unto famine and gird itself (though this cult only will curse their self unto total destruction) in hopes of keeping the free man from awakening into that spiritual quest of perpetual rebirth wherein the hope of Christ light the eye with that blue hue and our spiritual dreams see realizing; and, though we would wish our spiritual and physical death to occur at one time and not years apart let us not allow our flesh to grow weary or even separate from the holy spirit as witnessed in abundance throughout civilization wherein multitudes live in total fear of putting on that power of God designed for them in resisting the faintings of the flesh and deprogramming the massive automation shift being imposed upon us from the machinations of the death cult.

1 Corinthians 1:18 For that [a] preaching of the cross is to them that perish, foolishness: but unto us, which are saved, it is the [j], [b] power of God.

1 Corinthians 1:18 Endnotes

[j] Rom. 1:16

1 Corinthians 1:18 Footnotes

[a] The preaching of Christ crucified, or the kinds of speech which we use.

[b] It is that wherein he declareth his marvelous power in saving his elect, which would not so evidently appear, if it hanged upon any help of man: for so man might attribute that to himself, which is proper only to the cross of Christ.

Romans 1:16 For I am not ashamed of the Gospel of Christ: [a] for it is the [b] power of God unto salvation to everyone that believeth, to the Jew first, and also to the [c] Grecian.

Romans 1:16 Footnotes

[a] The second part of the Epistle unto the beginning of Chap. 9. Now the whole end and purpose of the disputation is this: that is to say: to show that there is but one way to attain unto salvation

(which is set forth unto us of God in the Gospel, without any difference of nations) and that is Jesus Christ apprehended by faith.

[b] God's mighty and effectual instrument to save men by.

[c] When this word Grecian, is set against this word Jew, then doth it signify a Gentile.

Rebirth delivers that spiritual rejuvenation which outpours the spirit of the Lord onto the physical plane such that we illuminate the life of Christ and bring to awareness the dangers of the death cult whom must be brought to justice. The death cult wilt not believe in the occurrence of any good event since their life revolve around rotting good things according to their self-fulfilled prophecy.

The force of good and evil in their representation of life and death both showcase their own architecture of vertical and horizontal dimensions which span time from their own beginning to their own conclusion as we know each action represents an equal and opposite reaction thus Godly intent wards off the absoluteness of evil and not without the action of the Godly whom tend to their good works in the light of day while the evil work from the shadows and under the cloak of darkness.

***Jude 1:9** [a] Yet Michael the Archangel, when he strove against the devil, and disputed about the body of Moses, durst not blame him with cursed speaking, but said, The Lord rebuke thee.*

Jude 1:9 Footnotes

[a] An argument of comparison, Michael one of the chiefest Angels, was content to deliver Satan, although as most cursed enemy, to the judgment of God to be punished: and these perverse men are not ashamed to speak evil of the powers which are ordained of God.

Evil works like static to blend into the atmosphere and expand it's creep as even a fungus colonizing the decay in order that it consume innocent souls until it burst forth with masochistic princes manifesting their dark theater of multi-dimensional hell onto our sovereign physical plane. The Godly will not hide the foundation of their faith nor their logic and reason constructing the architecture of their society as self-evidenced through america's Declaration of Independence. God gave us knowledge that we would establish a history, even that Kingdom of God on the earth, in order that we provision mankind with the resources necessary to learn from our past and preserve the present and future with an architecture of His design and in this way do we witness the self-evidence of that cult of death exercising theft as it's religion and fraud as it's politics in order that this death cult keep it's tyranny in season.

1 John 3:20 For [a] if our hearts condemn us, God is greater than our heart, and knoweth all things.

1 John 3:20 Footnotes
[a] If an evil conscience convinceth us, much more ought the judgments of God contemn us, who knoweth our hearts better

than we ourselves do.

Maintaining vigilance against theft and fraud means the individual must keep a countenance or constitution indifferent and even politically and religiously at war with the religion of theft and politics of fraud. The cult of death remains so pervasive today that it's growth succeeds in triplicate as it's forces sacrifice the innocent and unborn by the tens of millions in the name of women's rights thus removing the spiritual shield which would otherwise deflect every other evil born out of this most wicked blood ritual sacrifice; and, especially that evil plague of war disguised as foreign occupation for ally or national security purposes. This power vacuum of the death cult grants spiritual passage to their retarded followers whom know not that this vacuum descends into a bonfire of God's design wherein all whom enter shall not flee the wrath. The spiritual realm of liberty wherein righteousness treads down theft and fraud grants men talents with a weight which only the partakers of it's fruit can know. The members of society ascending their progeny into the hands of the courts of God even as it were the Kingdom of God with Jesus Christ as the King of Kings does set forth the principles in the rule of law as a hedge against these inhuman statutes existing as burnt offerings unto God wherein such false pursuits can not receive the blessing of God thus our assurance rests in His word sharpening our ways out of imperfection and eliminating the dimensions which harbor the actors and philosophic juggernauts and sentinels of the death cult. Though the vacuous cult of death manifesting as it's various occultic strongholds have succeeded the manifestation of their wickedness for a season – their robbing, killing, and stealing will end along with every other usurpation they seize for the harming of our family's life, liberty, and property; yea, we whom refuse to worship their ways and instead worship the living creator of the universe whom makes self-evident His abundance and steadfastness for the overthrow of this cult of death in the pouring out of His spirit to preserve us and tread down the enemy; yea, victory reserved for we who understand this death cult desires us to destroy our self and not the death cult – for shall we raise our sword against them then they shall flee as the phantoms they are at the coming of our dawn. Though this wicked force would wish their self to be that event horizon capturing mankind we know the constant physical arrival and constant spiritual presence of Jesus Christ terrifies the death cult and delivers us the awareness of revival, revelation, and revolution for that event horizon of peace on the earth.

1 John 2:10 He that loveth his brother, abideth in that light, and there is no occasion of evil in him.

Mankind sits at a cross-roads of mind, body, and spirit – the philosophy of death or the philosophy of liberty. God designed the true purpose of life for the individual to tread down this death cult and it's tyrannical forces enslaving mankind to it's false mind, body, and spirit. Faith then illuminates our path since faith begets action, or participation, and not the idleness of observation thus our righteousness illuminates the juxtaposition of wickedness threatening capture of our liberty.

1 Thessalonians 1:3 Without ceasing, remembering your effectual faith, and diligent love, and the patience of your hope in our Lord Jesus Christ, in the sight of God, even our Father,

Living with faith means to live with hope only for our Lord Jesus Christ and the knowledge He gave to us in order that God deliver us the free-will at-hand to escape the dangers of the death cult's realm though we can not escape the ever-present emergency confronting mankind with it's threatening beasts standing idle as one army at the four corners of earth and awaiting the idolatry which animate them into a fiery dragon.

Proverbs 19:21 Many devices are in a man's heart: but the counsel of the Lord shall stand.

The cult of death desires men to not stand and to remain in the sitting position in the dirt for all of time so that mankind will never see the light of grace and joy again. This cult maintains a steady aperture toward the erecting of it's devices against humanity and intellectually challenges all men to confront it's automation and declare self-evident those novelties which encompass it's sphere of influence. The death cult has created the world in their like image – a great game controlling all human activity and endeavoring to sacrifice mankind on it's graven altar.

2 Peter 2:2 [a] And many shall follow their destructions, by whom the way of truth shall be evil spoken of.

2 Peter 2:2 Footnotes

[a] There shall not only be heresies, but also many followers of them.

Consider that society which would seek it's own purification and the things in which plague this society chiefly consisting of those two parts composing the whole operation of the death cult: theft and fraud. What would it take for society to recognize the immorality of theft and fraud and then act to seek justice for these transgressions instead of masking it's effects through claiming their embargo as necessity or tradition? The coercive and violent centralization of power achieves temporal control over society through the conversion of the people from independent thinkers into worshipers of the red carpet of blood in which their idols walk upon during ritual holiday. This death cult leaves a trail of blood so great that one would have to ignore the markings which trace it's origins directly to the wicked one manifesting an architecture antithetical to the architecture in which God prescribes in The Bible; yea, that very architecture in which america's Founding Fathers wrote into law and unto it's written perfection at the time of america's founding; though, this does not mean a government of men perfected the control of people nor does it mean the sins of men mean the architecture fail as so many pseudo philosophers would lay as their claim in deceiving and funneling more misguided people into their Satanic system of caste society wherein civil liberty dies and their blind followers amass until the appointed time of that great massé which kills them all; yea, this means we relinquish the control of government to God's discipline in whom we trust and by His orders do we conduct the offices of governance for the providence in which He promises.

Psalm 33:10 *The Lord breaketh the counsel of the heathen, and bringeth to nought the devices of the people.*

Jude 1:6 *[a] The [c] Angels also which kept not their first estate, but left their own habitation, he hath reserved in everlasting chains under darkness unto the judgment of the great day.*

Jude 1:6 Endnotes

[c] 2 Pet. 2:4

Jude 1:6 Footnotes

[a] The fall of the Angels was most sincerely punished, how much more then will the Lord punish wicked and faithless men?

2 Peter 2:4 *For if God spared not the [a] Angels that had sinned, but cast them down into [b] hell, and delivered them into [c] chains of darkness, to be kept unto damnation:*

2 Peter 2:4 Endnotes

[a] Job 4:18, Jude 6

2 Peter 2:4 Footnotes

[b] So the Greeks called the deep dungeon under the earth, which

should be appointed to torment the souls of the wicked in.

[c] Bound them with darkness as it were with chains: and by darkness, he meaneth that most miserable state of life, that is full of horror.

Job 4:18 *Behold, he found no steadfastness in his servants, and laid folly upon his [a] Angels.*

Job 4:18 Footnotes

[a] If God find imperfection in his Angels, when they are not maintained by his power, how much more shall he lay folly to man's charge when he would justify himself against God?

This scripture directly showcases the two threats facing mankind which men must vigilantly confront with eternal hostility: the heathen, or that wicked death cult, and it's devices. The cult of death targets the civil liberty of our political speech and religious worship knowing these powers as our foundation for human felicity to seize control upon and enforce their state-sponsored politics and religion. This death cult desires to hold counsel among the righteous through seizing control of government office thereby delivering their wickedness immunity to act both as a channel to receive energy and gait to sacrifice energy and increase the scope of their secrecy in society. The key position in our republic concerning freedom of speech denotes the press and the key position in our republic concerning freedom of religion denotes The President since the press be the head and the President the tail – the cult of death would render the press red and the President the dragon which would empower all other central positions of governance to abort their powers of decentralization which would otherwise preserve property and instead we would see a supplantation of these key power slots with contradictory figurines designed to foment national peril through the confusion of the tongue.

Deuteronomy 32:31-33 For their god is not as our God, even our enemies being judges. For their vine is of the vine of Sodom, and of the vines of Gomorrah: their grapes are grapes of gall, their clusters be bitter. Their [a] wine is the poison of dragons, and the cruel gall of asps.

Deuteronomy 32:33 Footnotes

[a] The fruits of the wicked are as poison, detestable to God, and dangerous for man.

What role does the press and the President fulfill if not the preservation of life and property for the liberty of the people whom instituted that constitution for the illumination of their representative-offices? All members of a society exist as citizens and only a free society will recognize even the government workers, employees, representatives, and the like also as citizens with no powers which no other citizen does not equally possess thereby proving no man be above or below the perfect law of liberty. Any entity whom would shill for a purpose separate from the preservation of liberty, for example a thief believing their false title of tax collector, as though this were lawful and not inviting their doom from the men of God, would remain the enemies of humanity and always in collusion with the central banks in order to subsidize the corporations and elect their influence to propagandize the people into a state of inaction and derision of unthinking reaction in order that they self-restrict their civil liberty and even convince their self into believing tyranny as an impossibility and any teacher of such ideas must receive immediate condemnation from the commune through labels such as reactionary or conspiracy theorist; and, even to the point of exile or even state-sponsored murder if the free people shall not surrender their right to speech which means that right to life since speech be a thing of the mind and through the window of the spirit makes manifest a frequency and vibration of mind, body, and spirit as though this animation shone the life-force and tree of liberty bearing the fruit of the knowledge of God – therefore speech delivers all other liberty since an assembly of people – from their sovereign citizens acting as the press (alpha) to their sovereign citizen elected as Sheriff, Governor, or President (omega) form the entire republican contract and reality in which mankind must live and not beholden to any oppression of liberty both for our self and our friends of the world. We can then think of that restriction of civil liberty of the press and enlargement of the abuse of powers of the President as the demand which begs for the people to increase the frequency and awareness of public information as the false authorities gain ever more secrecy in the occupation and enslavement of society thus we witness righteousness and life on the right and destruction and death on the left; and, with a lukewarm majority in the center – swaying as grass or confused sheep sinning that they may keep the beast in operation and their President aiding the silencing of the people either through intent or acquiescence though even acquiescence be the spiritual intent of spiritual death. The rottenness of that philosophy of death tastes so sweet to the bitter souls professing it's flatteries as goodness. Both the press and the President must maintain and publicly declare often the presence of the cult of death and how we as men of God must fulfill His commandments and purge this national emergency through immediately pursuing the wicked unto justice and keeping an open line of communication with one another to discuss the tactics of that static structure using it's wicked minions for it's dynamic induction of culling mankind as it's occultic sacrifice to their Luciferian god.

Psalm 44:19 Albeit thou hast smitten us down into the place of [a] dragons, and covered us with the shadow of death.
Psalm 44:19 Footnotes
[a] Or, whales: meaning, the bottomless seas of tentations: here we see the power of faith, which can be overcome by no perils.

Societies under the command of God exhibit the free society of privacy while the society under the command of the cult of death exhibit the tyrannical society of secrecy. Liberty means privacy, for example: locking one's home, while tyranny explicitly authorizes government secrecy as means of abolishing individual privacy and weaponizing itself to destroy every other form of liberty and property. Free societies should do all within their bloody power to prevent their government from exercising the canard of secrecy against them. Does the individual committing a crime in secret fulfill the requisite of a crime? Likewise does the society treading down the wicked unto it's very ends fulfill the perfect law of liberty? I suppose the difference in individual privacy and government secrecy imply a system of oppressive governance or even a death-inspired cult abusing the birthright of the people as means to achieving it's ends. What happens to that society which would punish all forms of theft including and especially that theft of taxation which psychopaths in government deem lawful according to their finger-pointing at signatures, statutes, votes, or laws written by wicked men whom have tricked the public into trusting and then knitting their life into it's wicked composition devoid of human liberty?

Isaiah 27:1 In that [a] day the Lord with his sore and great and mighty [b] sword shall visit Leviathan, that piercing serpent, even Leviathan, that crooked serpent, and he shall slay the dragon that is in the sea.

Isaiah 27:1 Endnotes

A prophecy against the kingdom of Satan.

Isaiah 27:1 Footnotes

[a] At the time appointed.

[b] That is, by his mighty power, and by his word. He prophesieth here of the destruction of Satan and his kingdom under the name

of Leviathan, Assyria, and Egypt.

Will the majority of things not eventually fall unto the dependence of a god at war against our liberties and independence when the people overlook the least of these things which we know to design the whole fashion of governance thereof? What society could stand in the midst of perpetual favor toward a government that would use secrecy to war against logic and reason until absolute seizure of all of their land? What type of individual does God look for when He weigh earth against His measure and ask of His people to reconstitute His economy and disrupt no more their liberties and independence which will otherwise disappear unto slavery forever? What compels the individual to think even the name of The american Republic to mean our nation forms a democracy when the title of our nation itself declares us a republic and therefore not a democracy lest this individual think the two as one in the same since He view Himself not an individual at all and rather a collective of that *ism* which conquered His imagination and soul thus He sequester His own sovereignty to the pomp vanity of shallow knowledge sent down from the offices of secrecy or even secret armies and not the orderly duty of preserving life and property under God? Any society that would surrender their privacy for government secrecy would in that same instant surrender every other civil liberty thus no longer exhibit the pursuit of happiness; these deserters of truth would rather adopt the uniform of that proud hypocrite merely existing as chattel to a wicked ruling class. Secrecy punishes the innocent, usurps the law for blanketed martial law, assassinates the self-aware whom speak freely of injustices while claiming their wickedness justify self-preservation or national security, and will forever represent the cult of death and their exercise of eugenics as means of keeping their manifestation that apparition determining whether to keep or discard the society it falsely claims to defend.

2 Chronicles 19:9-11 And he charged them, saying, Thus shall ye do in the fear of the Lord faithfully and with a perfect heart. And in every cause that shall come to you of your brethren that dwell in your cities, between [a] blood and blood, between law and precept, statutes and judgments, ye shall judge them and admonish them that they trespass not against the Lord, that [b] wrath come not upon you and upon your brethren. This shall ye do and trespass not. And behold, Amariah the Priest shall be the chief over you in all matters of the Lord, and Zebadiah the son of Ishmael, a ruler of the house of Judah, shall be for all the [c] King's affairs, and the Levites shall be officers [d] before you. Be of courage, and do it, and the Lord shall be with the [e] good.

2 Chronicles 19:9 Endnotes

and exhorteth them to fear God.

2 Chronicles 19:10-11 Footnotes

[a] That is, to try whether the murder was done at unawares, or else on set purpose, Num. 35:11; Deut. 4:41.

[b] Meaning, that God would punish them most sharply, if they would not execute justice aright.

[c] Shall be chief overseer of the public's affairs of the Realm.
[d] They shall have the handling of inferior causes.
[e] God will assist them that do justice.

Numbers 35:11 *Ye shall appoint you cities, to be cities of refuge for you, that the slayer, which slayeth any person unawares, may flee thither.*

Deuteronomy 4:41 ¶ *Then Moses separated three cities on this side of Jordan toward the sun rising:*

Even in modern america today the least educated of individuals maintain some type of knowledge regarding the wickedness of our pseudo intelligence agencies operating in total secrecy though they lack the education as to why they must not tolerate this design quartering hostile enemies on our soil or why we must pursue the absolute absolving of these agencies whom execute individuals at-will and answer only to the wicked one confusing the tongue of the nation into accepting such self-evident immorality. Most americans today maintain some type of knowledge regarding C.I.A.(Central Intelligence Agency) kinetic action in the assassination of President John Fitzgerald Kennedy; and, to this day, many government documents remain sealed under "official secrecy" citing "national security" as justification for not allowing the american people their indivisible, God-given, and unalienable right to read what the foreign-terrorist-occupied and rogue government wrongly keeps from we the people of whom do acquiesce our authority from otherwise treading down this rogue and hostile design of lunatics at war against our liberty. All of this disgusting secrecy premises upon the falsehood that our rule of law can not discern current events therefore a shadow carbon-copy of government must exist to override the things which the rule of law can not do which means doing things totally illegal and enlisting an ignorant public to superstitiously believe the suspension of the rule of law preserves their rule of law.

The individual contains within their epigenetics the eternal inscriptions which form the pillars of light vehemently opposed to the hopeless secret societies subverting the minds of men unto tragedy around the world. We the free people discern that knowledge which sets the precedent for our historical war against that cult of death whom herald their self as earth's guild of factions choosing out which cartels receive the status of royalty and which nations receive the enslavement of another in a great game of realms warring over absolute control since mankind's first corruption. These circles of cults would save nothing in the world except their oath to secrecy in order that their subterfuge proceed into utterly incomprehensible degrees of world oppression even a million million years of earth without the light of God to spark the imagination of mankind into a spectral fire of torches driving out the thieves and murderers. Our ancients had always gone to war against this wicked cult of secrecy even unto the illumination of every form of violent overthrow in order that we succeed our opposition against the planning of the death rituals desolating civilization since we the free people well understand

God designed man and civilization to live in harmony and will with our eternal vigilance forbade that death cult which teach theft and fraud for the alteration of society from it's dynamic state into that of a stateless or static apparition forming the signpost of hell on the earth.

Deuteronomy 4:40 *Thou shalt keep therefore his ordinances, and his commandments which I command thee this day, that it may [a] go well with thee, and with thy children after thee, and that thou mayest prolong thy days upon the earth, which the Lord thy God giveth thee forever.*

Deuteronomy 4:40 Footnotes

[a] God promiseth reward not for our merits, but to encourage us, and to assure us that our labor shall not be lost.

We as the Godly naturally pursue means of peacefully absolving this yoke of bondage which binds itself to that oath of Satanic vibrations. Virtually no individual, except for the wicked, would desire to remain a slave – and this point further recognizes that the cult of death live as slaves one to another that they may bind their self into an oath with the wicked one and push His agenda as one force against those heavens which promise destruction and great leavening upon the wicked. Even in today's modern world when an individual flees america the probability of our rogue government recapturing this individual remains extremely high; and, especially when that person flee for tax purpose; although, the very notion of theft under the pseudonym of taxation embodies a wicked government of secret operations since it conceal this crime as though it were lawful and not a crime or immorality at all; even further, even when the people vote for this theft – God's law still applies and His reconciliation will effectively weigh the matter though this realization does not grant man reprieve to remain idle and not wage spiritual war against this governance of secrecy.

Deuteronomy 5:7 Thou shalt have none [a] other gods before my face.

Deuteronomy 5:7 Footnotes

[a] God bindeth us to serve him only, without superstition and idolatry.

The cult of death divides and conquers the world through using borders to create economic sanctioning in order that it use some nations for war and others for play. All throughout earth tyrannical nations pose as indifferent from one another although they all fly the same philosophic flag in being under the rule of dynasty and royalty or some other form of collectivism wherein tyrants oppress the people and cull civilization as though free people were a crucible, herd, gift, or object sent from their Luciferian god as a reward for their wickedness. Dozens of nations remain under the rule of the brutish royal family today with some estimates suggesting as high as one sixth of earth directly and openly subsist under the authority of their secretive and wicked rule; secretive in that it and not the public knows the intent of it's own origins or final destination and public in that anyone can see the public information showing them their head of state: yeah, their slave master. The royal family grips the neck of their peasants with such soft cantor they champion the frigidity of it's placid distractions as it were an eternal holiday; a landrace of apathetic, avaricious, boring, confused, envious, and unfulfilled individuals knit thousands of generations ago into the matrices of that royal caste lair. The progeny of these ancestors whom have chosen to live under royal rule for so many centuries have developed a type of learned preconditioning to accept the tyrannical programming of the death cult first in it's physical layer of power made manifest through it's standing army of fattened royals and second in it's perceived intellectual power via it's central bank which uses the idea of free as a bargaining chip to placate the public into the various *isms* which make them to feel the type of intellectualism they perceive in the high seats ruling them. We of Texas and america by and large represent that potent population on the earth with a lineage of individuals violently opposed to tyranny and well-aware of it's origins in the cult of death hence our battle-cry of "Liberty or Death," and "Victory or Death."

Philippians 1:11-14 *Filled with the [a] fruits of righteousness, which are by Jesus Christ unto the glory and praise of God. ¶ [b] I would ye understood, brethren, that the things which have come unto me, are turned rather to the furthering of the Gospel, So that my bands [c] in Christ are famous throughout all the [d]* *judgment hall, and in all other places. Insomuch that many of the brethren in the Lord are boldened through my bands, and dare more frankly speak the [e] Word.*

Philippians 1:12 Endnotes

he entreateth of himself and his bands:

Philippians 1:11-14 Footnotes

[a] If righteousness be the tree, and good works the fruits, then must the papists needs be deceived, when they say that works are the cause of righteousness.

[b] He preventeth the offense that might come by his persecution, whereby divers took occasion to disgrace his Apostleship. To whom he answereth, that God hath blesseth his imprisonment in such wise, that he is by that means become more famous, and the dignity of the Gospel by this occasion is greatly enlarged, although not with like affection in all men, yet indeed.

[c] For Christ's sake.

[d] In the Emperor's court.

[e] The Gospel is called the Word, to set forth the excellence of it.

America, though stumbling as we always had in fighting to succeed our revolution for human liberty, marches according to those core principles of defending life, liberty, and property; and, with our efforts we shine as the tip of the spear on the earth in spiritually combating these wicked forces thus ripping the veil of this spiritual tyranny wide open – knowing our hope in Christ be answered and mankind see the light from that narrow gait we preach from for the uniting as one spirit of the Lord in mankind for our mutual defense and preservation of life, liberty, and property on the earth.

Many thousands of years ago our great ancestors determined this death cult uniforms itself in secrecy for the culling of civilization; and, we as a people must bring to light the significance of combating this danger with the organization of our civic, historical, and technological knowledge in order that we may exercise our liberty and depart from sin and the fallen ones. These wicked troglodytes pursue their agenda unto every excess without any regard for the abuses which they attempt to justify through their reasoning and logistical consensus insofar as their swarms of agencies form an operation or continuity of governmental logistics which cites it's intelligence as the reason which countermeasure all others even if the chaos their secrecy foments multiply the chaos which they claim to quell. Our ancestors understood well the dangers of closed communication and state-sponsored concealment of information or speech as opposed to open communication and free speech: those things which God's authority equally distributes to man though the ignorance of man would wish to criminalize such liberty for temporal gain. The power we commit into society in delivering to each individual (since removing the yoke of bondage delivers liberty to the multitude) their right to bear speech and arms forms the basis for morality to level any intolerance which would distribute it's knowledge amongst a council of despots whom would then aim to stop men from entering the tempestuous sea of liberty that in this stopping they might further their cause in reducing heightened awareness amongst the public which dulls the public and separate their conscience unto dependency of that illusion which criminalizes individual and thus national sovereignty or distorts and manipulates the expression and meaning of sovereignty unto absolute perdition. The people will forever keep their favor from God if they shall equally trust the citizens with the facts more than the presumption of wicked ne'er-do-wells in secretive factions perpetuating the lie of keeping the people safe. In the event true peace emerges and crime diminishes – secretive groups will even invent dangers through their own hands in order that they continue the charade of demoralizing the intellect and spirit of joy in the people in hope the death cult maintain some type of false heroic status in society; or, even further, keeping occultic groups practicing the art of death against a free people for their own Satanic rituals whom would otherwise discover the power to overthrow their oppressors. Logic and reason will forever govern society. As long as the death cult can hypnotize the public into accepting it's facts as truth then the public will never discover their own liberty nor a civilization with liberty; and, how this civilization without liberty can call itself civilized at all alludes my own self-evident reasoning. Even under the circumstance of america's Founding Fathers possessing the highest potency of knowledge amongst civilization during their time on the earth this only allowed them to draw a border for a small fraction of earth with other individuals whom understood the idea of liberty as self-evident logic for man to reason His entering into that Godly society; and, even further, defending unto death the declaration and continued independence of this nation; whereas the majority of earth today still succumb to the various forms of peasantry via any false authority of dynasty or royalty. When Australians, Canadians, Jamaicans, Bahamian, or United Kingdom subjects argue "The Queen does not rule over us. Her Majesty tis' tradition and stands independent of our state sovereignty!" self-evidence then witnesses these individuals as ignorant and superstitious to the highest order thus the lowest order of what we self-evidence as trustworthy individuals or definable as an individual with awareness of their sovereignty since any self-realized individual would not relinquish their self-awareness to the illusion of hiding within an enslavement of orthodoxy perpetuating oppression under the veil of freedom since their monarch allow them to toil unto shameless shame under the various types of poverty of the mind so long as they steer their imagination away from individual sovereignty and the philosophy of liberty.

Luke 2:1-2 And [a] it came to pass in those days, that there came a decree from Augustus Caesar, that all the [b] world should be [c] taxed. (This first taxing was made when Quirinius was governor of Syria.)

Luke 2:1 Endnotes

Augustus Caesar taxeth all the world.

Luke 2:1 Footnotes

[a] Christ the son of God, taking upon him the form of a servant, and making himself of no reputation, is poorly born in a stable: and by the means of Augustus the mightiest prince in the world

(thinking nothing less) hath his cradle prepared in Bethlehem, as the Prophets forewarned.

[b] So far as the Empire of the Romans did stretch.

[c] That is, the inhabitants of every city should have their names taken, and their goods rated at a certain value, that the Emperor might understand, how rich every country, city, family, and house was.

Even though thousands of years ago our ancestors sorted these things out the weight of evil permeating from the death cults and secret societies of this planet looms precariously though our spirit be a beast unlike any of theirs shall they stir our awareness up against them. In that regard one can view liberty as the only tool for chipping away the foundation of the royal order and bringing down it's tower of babel unto destruction and erasure of it's hierarchy such that all individuals recognize the possession of our equal rights under God's perfect law of liberty thus making way for humanity's ascension into the version of a type-one civilization wherein liberty prevails with the chaining down of that tyranny unto those sublime commandments in which God inspired men to write and daily fulfill. Mankind must abandon contentious arguments surrounding skin color since we know hereditary power fuels this civil unrest and with the overthrow of such powers we as a people will in the least give rise to that eternal education which accelerates the liberty movement and keeps civilization from sliding into the dark ages of man existing as an ant colony under the worship of that superficial idea of civil democracy pretending to resemble the same image or likeness of civil liberty though that civil democracy represent the tyrannical collectivisms and not the civil liberty which defends the individual from all collective mob rule which minds not to bludgeon the philosophic defender of individual liberty and equal rights unto death or desolation.

Daniel 7:11 *Then I beheld, [a] because of the voice of the presumptuous words which the horn spake: I beheld, even till the beast was slain, and his body destroyed, and given to the burning fire.*

Daniel 7:11 Footnotes

[a] *Meaning, that he was astonied when he saw these Emperors in such dignity and pride, and so suddenly destroyed at the coming of Christ, when this fourth Monarchy was subject to men of other nations.*

Those monarchs masquerading as civil society do so for none reason other than to serve the purpose of the state which enslaves them to their own ignorance of the state of their nation. This governance whose architecture only can arbitrarily restrict civil liberty forms their society around a closed state wherein all types of prohibition against civil liberty criminalize the individual that would open their heart thus open society to the dangers of love wherein the state would oppose their way of life unto hostility due to their nature in exposing their closed society to the dangers of the desire of money and fear of God. While the majority of Earth enjoys their apathetic life devoid of adversity, replete with comfort, tranquility, and the illusion of wealth – those brave defenders of liberty preserve their right to the duty of an open society wherein such personalities that invent imaginations of oppression over them do then face the man of a certain moral code that particularly and perfectly hate the immoral men portraying their self as immortals and certainly a congregation of them that would subject centuries, or even one instance, of people to their false religion of barbarous politics. Open societies rarely exist and the few whom openly wield their liberty face a colonization of imitators that would justify the infringement of civil liberty as an excuse to criminalize the exercise or mention of civil liberty. The only true manner in which we must conduct our self in order that we sharply oppose these imitators whom would close our society (in the same manner we witness them in their exercise of closing their own imagination) exists in continuing to exercise our civil liberty and fight even unto death to keep our liberty from these vile aliens and creatures of the night whose mouth foams with the creep of a long and forgotten distant horror which seeks to bridge the gap of our space-time continuum and then divide and conquer nation-states until they resurrect what our good father in heaven did dead and bury so long ago. When that cult of death shall raise it's sword against ours we shall not flee nor shall we cower or submit; nay, we shall fight with such steadfastness the wicked will cower, submit, or flee from our berserking guard and jealous advances. These imitators would argue we must oppose the threat of the foreign nations by exercising their same laws while at the same time professing this treason does not represent an infringement of civil liberty or infringement at all and anyone whom shall posit such an idea –

"Why, he, He be the treasonous idolater we must burn at the stake!"

As in all war, the threat presents the greatest danger of all, thus we must arm our purpose with that vigorous action which unites many people in a phalanx against tyranny. The cult of death threatening the world constantly supplies itself with greater than the threat it proposes and that supply being the blood of the innocent by way of ritual sacrifice and sanctioned war; though, many argue these things exist as one and the same. American society right now has invariably stripped itself of every civil liberty in the name of opposing the danger of a foreign nation threatening to steal our civil liberty (though such a system exist as a concerted effort of the tyrants through their cult of death). This reign of terror continues today and threatens the entire world with it's once free army now turned into a religious ceremony wherein it's chief tenant today self-evidences a reduction of civil liberties for domestic and foreign individuals (though they hypocritically take an oath to the american constitution; and, perhaps we should abandon this document altogether and only take an oath to our Declaration of Independence since we can deduce all logic and reason for the governance of true human liberty therein). This death cult, or lesser power feigning greater authority and power, obscures it's presence as though it were an unknown entity or unknowable enemy perpetually forcing civilization unto civil war though we shall know our enemy far greater in magnitude than they shall ever pretend to know us thus we recognize their authority as that of the dung beetle using it's forearms for walking and hind-legs for backward rolling an ever larger ball of dung as it were it's tyranny accumulating more death in their attempt to form a path of world domination though they mark their self for utter destruction by the righteous authority on the earth which concentrates into the hands of the living such that our knowledge of God deliver that power of God unto us to bear the fruit of liberty as that reward for treading down the wicked by way of being righteous and that righteousness bearing the sweet fruit. While the charlatans of society may express their disdain for the often slow effects of the rule of law – no rule can exist of greater value in society than opposing the rule of the death cult through the enforcement of our perfect law of liberty.

Deuteronomy 5:22 ¶ *These words the Lord spake unto all your multitude in the mount of the midst of the fire, the cloud and the darkness, with a great voice, and [a] added no more thereto: and wrote them upon two tables of stone, and delivered them unto me.*

Deuteronomy 5:22 Footnotes

[a] Teaching us by his example to be content with his word, and add nothing thereto.

When the individual gains awareness of this death cult on the

earth and the persistence of it's presence since the dawn of man —
the individual then experiences a metaphysical alteration of their
mind, body, and spirit, which God Himself instructs through the
armoring of that individual's mind, body, and spirit to dutifully
respond with the pursuit of knowledge ensuring their thriving
contribute to that great mending which preserve the liberty of
mankind. What comes of the nation that would champion the
survival of it's government over the survival of it's liberty but
spoil? What world will we awaken to one glorious morning when
the ember of liberty sparks into a fire and enflames the soul of
every individual? Which traditions will reemerge on the earth
when the theft and fraud cursing mankind unto our own absolute
enslavement to this death cult abolishes under the justice of our
direct pursuits? Perhaps the only value to ascertain in preserving
the survival of a nation without a tradition of liberty would mean
that certain hope in the soul of that nation which minds not the
martyrdom of their body so that the body of the church prevails
separate from any spiritually carnivorous state of wicken
influence. The tradition of independence in the americas has faded
in direct proportion to the loss of our civil liberty. The state may
survive; america may survive; our flag may survive; even our
constitution may survive; however, if the people will not enforce
the constitution and the defense of liberty then the survival of the
defenders of liberty will go extinct in the midst of a multitude of
anti-christs inheriting the world to perfect it's destruction. Who
can speak highly of a nation when it's traditions preserve the state
thus ensuring the capture and elimination of the defenders of

liberty insofar as to even teach of liberty means to fight for liberty aright and to assemble men for the overthrow of the tyrants and continuity of our liberty means to rightly declare liberty to the captives of tyranny in this moment of now wherein exists all blessings, hope, materials, people, and substance for true liberty? The brutish royal family may head a nation though they prohibit liberty and distort and manipulate civilization thus they value the tradition of oppressing liberty as the chief governance over earth (though their ignorant peasants superstitiously claim their calm of despotism not an oppression at all). How can any tradition survive without it's defenders therefore even to do nothing at all defends that tradition of oppression thus tradition alone can never mean liberty? How can this death cult persist without murdering the unborn whom inherit liberty in the very womb of God's design? The object in which the cult of death seeks to eliminate exists in the individual's imagination of their self first existing as an individual and second as an empowered individual with the full power of God to set into motion the chain of events which render idle men into the participants of their own liberation.

Thessalonians 1:11 [a] Wherefore, we also pray always for you, that our God may make you worthy of [b] this calling, and fulfill [c] all the good pleasure of his goodness, and the [d] work of faith with power.

Thessalonians 1:11 Footnotes

[a] Seeing that we have the mark set before us, it remaineth that we go unto it. And we go to it, by certain degrees of causes: first

by the free love and good pleasure of God, by virtue whereof all other inferior causes work: from thence proceedeth the free calling to Christ, and from calling, faith, whereupon followeth both the glorifying of Christ in us, and us in Christ.

[b] By (calling) he meaneth not the very act of calling, but that selfsame thing whereunto we are called, which is the glory of that heavenly kingdom.

[c] Which he determined long since, only upon his gracious and merciful goodness toward you.

[d] So then, faith is an excellent work of God in us: and we see here plainly that the Apostle leaveth nothing to free will, to make it checkmate with God's working therein, as the Papists dream.

The dipoles which consist of good and evil hold their own veils of architecture and hierarchy to attract the counsel of each for warfare in the heavens. The good with their fear of God and the wicked with their fear of man act as those key motivators in which the wicked use to design that veil of secrecy around them in order that they hide the spiritual warfare from that public whom threaten their extinction. The sons of God fear God for they worship God and not man while the sons of Death fear man for they worship man and not God; and, these truths of the ungodly do we know as self-evident through their Satanic and Luciferian religion which speak philosophic things of spiritual death as their justification for physically harming their self and the innocent for their graven altar of sacrifice.

2 Chronicles 32:16 And his servants spake yet more against the Lord God, and against his [a] servant Hezekiah.

2 Chronicles 32:16 Footnotes

[a] Herein we see that when the wicked speak evil of the servants of God, they care not to blaspheme God himself: for if they feared God, they would love his servants.

The gravest danger we face as free men exists in this death cult being permitted access to our legislation which will entrench them into society for even eons and allow them to popularize their wicked culture and grow their new succession of ages for the culling of civilization. Time and again this happens when this death cult uses their problem-reaction-solution paradigm to divide and conquer the population through the promise of securing the threat whether artificial or real, however, through the avenue of restricting one or many civil liberties in the name of alleviating the threat.

1 Kings 13:33 Howbeit after this Jeroboam [a] converted not from his wicked way, but turned again, and made of the lowest of the people priests of the high places. Who would, might [b] consecrate himself and be of the priests of the high places.

1 Kings 13:33 Endnotes

The obstinacy of Jeroboam.

1 Kings 13:33 Footnotes

[a] So the wicked profit not by God's threatenings, but go backward, and become worse and worse, 2 Tim. 3:13.

[b] Hebrew, fill his hand.

2 Timothy 3:13 *But the evil men and deceivers shall wax [a] worse and worse, deceiving, and being deceived.*

2 Timothy 3:13 Footnotes

[a] Their wickedness shall daily increase.

This supposed ability to increase security through secrecy of the state or censorship of the public only serves to mortally wound the state of our union and can only succeed through the taxation of the people (often named subsidy), otherwise known as theft, since without these stolen public funds there would exist no energy to fuel these idle people in government for their immoral cause of pretending theft aids society when these career thieves only can form a cult of apathetic ingrates reeducating society into a state of suggestive thinking wherein the nation worships the vampires as heroes and views the heroes as apparitions robbing the cult from their shifting society into the shape of a civilization without any liberty at all. The death cult looks upon society as a dwarven bonsai tree receiving the edifices of their torture. We as individuals must not permit the progression of the death cult, take control of our sense of urgency, and stop these demons from usurping our language and subverting our articulated values.

This type of knowledge appertaining the treading down of the death cult, and this cult's enslaving of mankind since the beginning of time, contains the world-view that our first order of business require us to remove these wicked men from public office and then bring the awareness of this cult to the public in order that we enlarge the scope of our efforts against them and disassemble their tyrannical network unto total overthrow. A people whom have assembled as a nation for the purpose of maintaining awareness of and defense against this death cult do so for the preservation of their liberty and know full and well they must continually teach the youth in perpetuity with the expansion and maintenance of their republic and for their individual sovereignty.

Exodus 15:1 Then [a] sang Moses and the children of Israel this song unto the Lord, and said in this manner, I will sing unto the Lord: for he hath triumphed gloriously: the horse and him that rode upon him hath he overthrown in the Sea.

Exodus 15:1 Endnotes

Moses with the men and women sing praises unto God for their deliverance.

Exodus 15:1 Footnotes

[a] Praising God for the overthrow of his enemies, and their deliverance.

The potential to activate certain awareness in the multitude of individuals around the world persists since only a lack of awareness dissolve the foundation for everlasting systems of education and governance; yea, systems which preserve the rights of the individual and the futurity of their civilization. I overheard a novice Indian Chess player ask a Chess Grandmaster, "Does my caste determine my Chess ability?" My heart sank for a moment as I captured a glimpse of the suffering tyranny has inflicted upon this man and generations of His family and community and the centuries of efforts throughout our world until my heart lifted and I realized He perhaps may be the first man in His lineage to break the curse and question such a thing with all boldness of faith. True discernment unlocks that potential energy which multiplies abundance for the realm of civilization; and, also reverses the false social constructs and caste mentality used as tools of the death cult. These tyrants ranging from the free citizen to the highest ranking government representatives walk in the halls of every place of society waiting to hear of some type of threat or crisis as an excuse to assemble government and it's military for the unconstitutional disassembly of the rule of law through the criminalization of the individual's civil liberty. The free press must continue to expand so that the exposure of reality illuminates the imagination of society in order that secrecy absolves, dissent to tyranny increase unto total proclivity, and justice be delivered to the wicked. When the death cult can not succeed with censoring the truth – they then will use the stolen public funds obtained from their crime organization of tax-collectors to create their own press corps of propagandists in the aim of flooding the perceptions of the public with their own narrative-bias such that the truth be stifled by the vicious defenders of the fake news whom have received their programming from the death cult to coercively or violently respond to truth-tellers in order that they act as the outer-shell of defense to the cult which expands the inner shells or scope of their intent or meaning.

2 Chronicles 32:12 Hath not the same Hezekiah taken away his high places, and his [a] altars, and commanded Judah, and Jerusalem, saying, Ye shall worship before one altar, and burn incense upon it?

2 Chronicles 32:12 Footnotes

[a] *Thus the wicked put no difference between true religion and false, God and idols: for Hezekiah only destroyed idolatry, and placed true religion. Thus the Papists slander the servants of God: for when they destroy idolatry, they say that they abolish religion.*

Passion ultimately burns through the facade of this death cult whom wishes to extinguish the flame of liberty by any means necessary. No obedient peasant would want to possess that property of liberty which the tyrant abhors. Ideas as property and freedom as an expression of any idea even the philosophy of liberty or the philosophy of death manifests an order of the universe from the metaphysical to the physical thus the two juxtapose one another in spiritual warfare.

The american dream continues as a rebirth of an awareness which identifies both our peril and kingdom of God at-hand. The forces of good and evil were from the beginning of mankind at war with one another in the theater of man's relationship with God and woman. When imagining those individuals of liberty against those tyrants – what standard can differentiate one individual opposed to the other but the awareness within that individual which delivers full defiance to that death cult. We the defenders of liberty receive that glory that the tyrants pretend to claim through their vacuous slogans and harebrained financial schemes of world-war proportion. The revolution for liberty interdimensionally and intradimensionally forged against the cult of death revolves in a victory which the ignorant and superstitious must come to know at the time of their rebirth into that Godhead of true consciousness. God glorifies our deeds through the great alignment of men adorning an unquestioning faith in their action of righteous defense of liberty as their source for happiness and cure for life on the earth. Faith without action terminates faith unto vanity. The pen being mightier than the sword means the people maintain the duty toward that responsibility of being the press armed with that knowledge of liberty against the forces of tyranny whom understand their role in assailing our free press whom act as that forcefield, hedge, and shield against all wickedness since public knowledge be that light assuaging the darkness. This wall which the press forms can even mean the first and final authority in determining the reality of a separation in church and state thereby allowing the liberty of man to fully exercise His freedom from sin and not make Him complicit in sin in forcing theft as the human statute superseding the rule of law thus the action of the free man demonstrate to the youth the exemplary religious and economic sovereignty which chains down the death cult from their possessing the minds of society for their own empirical and tyrannical cause.

Leviticus 20:6 ¶ *If any turn after such as work with spirits, and after soothsayers to go a [a] whoring after them, then will I set my face against that person, and will cut him off from among his people.*

Leviticus 20:6 Endnotes

They that have recourse to sorcerers.

Leviticus 20:6 Footnotes

[a] To esteem sorcerers or conjurers is spiritual whoredom, or idolatry.

Recognizing mankind's natural enemy as the death cult serves as the primary baby step toward acquiring that fear and knowledge of God and why we defend our garden of eden and every herb on the earth which God designed for the preservation of our liberty against those tyrants that would criminalize any part of the garden as their excuse for the corruptions of our church and state and the varying societies of earth's wider civilization. God provides a great covering to preserve life and property when the deeds which He commands fulfill. Each of these deeds move like feathers on an eagle flying mankind on the wings of God's word. Imagine a world with freedom of the press and the central theme of this press focused on economic and foreign sovereignty in order to govern mankind into that political and religious purity which beget every form of peace and prosperity thereby turning away every form of theft and fraud; thus, removing any excuse from the powerless tyrants to steal from the public via the arbitraries of taxation and it's subsequent malfeasance of economic and foreign policy which beget every form of warfare and welfare for the dissolution and destruction of peace and prosperity. No force on the earth could arise to stop such an impenetrable defense though the dark armies of death lean on their cause in their chosen life-path of a separation devoid of the spirit of the Lord in the doings of their master's demand for reasons unknown to the master or the slave since both adore their enslavement to an off-world, alien, anti-intelligence which govern the possession of their wickedness into circles of ancient death cults. The slaves of this cult of death must let go of this hand of death misguiding their destiny, open their eyes, and awaken onto the living creator of the universe whom does possess a name of perfect Godliness.

No matter what example of war presented throughout history any sovereign government seizes control of the press in order to preserve it's dynamic tactics and static structures thus we witness in american society the death cult having turned our government rogue in the executive declaration of a constant state of emergency and foreign adventure in order to fascistically seize control of the right to free speech and continue their empire of subterfuge upon america and the world. The death cult will always and ceremoniously form into one cohesive unit whose efforts of self-discipline seek that reward of destruction of their perceived enemy whom righteously demand the disclosure of certain facts for additional self-evidence of that war waged against our intelligence from that morally wicked counter-intelligence exacting it's perversions over a free people whom when acquiescing to such oppression do then confirm their lack of discipline, intelligence, material resources, or public awareness in preserving their own sovereign governance. This cohesive unit that forms to defeat a common enemy will withhold information from the individuals even going so far as to remove their label of citizen and redefine them as civilian in order to excuse their systematic or claimant accidental killing of free and innocent people.

Jeremiah 7:6 And oppress not the stranger, the fatherless, and the widow, and shed no innocent blood in this place, neither walk after other gods to your destruction,

The uniting of government and press during a true war of self-defense occurs naturally though when the people without any vote at all have their government go to war or enact sanctions on domestic or foreign people then this illustrative self-evidence of treason hearkens to the work of that death cult looking to cull the earth of free men. Pretended security, arbitrary sanctioning of individual liberty, prohibition of speech and religion, an unlimited expansion of government authority: all designs for the instantaneous capture and seizing control of a people and their nation thereby empowering the enemy nation from within to issue it's effects of damaging the economy and sense of tranquility in the nation and in effect enslaving the citizens to the very military in which the militia, or even stated as free men, instituted and swore an oath to tame. This proxy army receives it's instruction and reward from the death cult and their instinct to viciousness can only be outmatched by their ignorance in acting as that hostile force against their own nation as though the public were the rival force in the way of their mission since this rogue government does so very well forget their archetype of intent first came into being as the servants of the masters whom instituted them. If the american people ever find out what really happens within their government then in as little as six hours time the sheer multitude of individuals whom rise with the power of God will stand ready to fight and die for the cause of liberty and declare victory to the captives of tyranny.

Jeremiah 7:11 *Is this House become [a] a den of thieves, where-upon my Name is called before your eyes? Behold, even I see it, saith the Lord.*

Jeremiah 7:11 Footnotes

[a] As thieves hid in holes and dens think themselves safe, so when you are in my Temple, you think to be covered with the holiness thereof, and that I cannot see your wickedness, Matt. 21:13.

Matthew 21:13 *And said to them, It is written, [e] My house shall be called the house of prayer: but [f] ye have made it a den of thieves.*

Matthew 21:13 Endnotes

The house of prayer.

[e] Isa. 56:6-7

[f] Jer. 7:11, Mark 11:17, Luke 19:46

Isaiah 56:6-7 *Also the strangers that cleave unto the Lord, to serve him, and to love the Name of the Lord, and to be his servants; everyone that keepeth the Sabbath, and polluteth it not, and embraceth my covenant, Them will I bring also to mine holy mountain, and make them joyful in mine House of prayer; their burnt [a] offerings and their sacrifices shall be accepted upon mine altar: for mine house shall be called an house of prayer for [b] all people.*

Isaiah 56:7 Footnotes

[a] Hereby he meaneth the spiritual service of God, to whom the faithful offer continual thanksgiving, yea themselves and all that they have, as a lively and acceptable sacrifice.

[b] Not only for the Jews, but for all others, Matt. 21:13.

Mark 11:17 *And say, We have piped unto you, and ye have not danced, we have mourned unto you, and ye have not lamented.*

Luke 19:46 *Saying unto them, It is written, [h] Mine house is the house of prayer, [i] but ye have made it a den of thieves.*

Luke 19:46 Endnotes

[h] Mark 11:17

[I] Isa. 56:7, Jer. 7:11

The fashion then of a house of people of one mind and body unitedly fighting for the cause of liberty aim for that fashion which unite the people of their nation with that spirit of the press in order to divide and conquer the minds within their own government and keep their civil servants as that entity instituted by the church whom instituted our nation and house of the Lord whereby our people, militia, and press form as one union together, alongside our king of kings and Lord in heaven, which further illustrate that holy spirit of decentralized power and flattened hierarchy wherein the civil liberty and knowledge of the individual creates the exercise of free trade which morally regulates economic and foreign policy, ensures government enforce prohibition of infringements upon the individual's civil liberty, God witnesses a free people enforce the criminalization of taxation, and these free people elect representatives whom watch their appointed lemmings succeed their promise in the enforcement of the perfect law of liberty in order that we stand united on that one rock of salvation wherein no sandcastles of infringement stand to shadow the consciousness of mankind from honoring God's eternal authority. The people reserve the right to keep and choose the hirelings whom comprise their institution of government. These hirelings will always (perhaps this be a lesser understood aspect of natural law) aim to expand and abuse the scope of their power and especially when the theft of taxation offers them the hidden knowledge of occultic realms with real evil powers though the sum-total of this false power can not outmatch or outcompete that heightened level of awareness, peace, productivity, and prosperity of the individual's liberty and not even with their illusion of fancy devices obscuring peace since we stand ready to defend as spirits of readiness prepared for invasionary war from that wicked counter-intelligence which God designed to fail against the shield of those deeds which God Himself instructs us to hear and then do.

This death cult inspires the people to beg of their government to redefine society into three permanent parts: the government, the public, and the citizen, insofar as each of these groups receive their own permissions for rights. The rogue government would define the individual declaring liberty as the clear and present danger facing the nation as witnessed even in today's america with elected representatives claiming supporters of the constitution as domestic terrorists. This peril facing mankind and our society rewrites logic and reason to activate the devices which slide society into tyranny and continue to suffer ever more sorrowfully under the ever-tightening control of the death cult that professes itself the preservationist of earth and public society. The oddity of this death cult's logic in separating the individual from the public exists as that clear and present danger they wish to cover through the refocusing of the public, or the unthinking individuals, into the agenda of stripping the individual of their rights with the illusion of handing a superior power or right to the public through giving government the secrecy of quietly criminalizing free speech and all other types of individual liberty and privacy in order that they seize control of human and material resources.

"MOVE OUT OF OUR WAY."

The demand of the death cult never hesitates to mount it's agenda on the back of the people. This pretended cause of social salvation when unrestrained will always expand until what previously represents the public now advertises a society of incompetent individuals incapable of knowing up or down, right or left, heaven or hell, liberty or tyranny, life or death; thus suffering the inability to reverse the damage which they originally begged of for the false resolution of their happiness which only liberty can mitigate against. The departure from reality exists as the only form of power which the state can advertise and then use to capture souls for the pursuit of additional systems of subversion weaponized against the minds of men even unto distorting and manipulating the minds of all of the earth into the subterfuge and rewriting of the world economy and geopolitical landscape into the vision and like-image of the death cult. The establishment of a certain flow of power grants this death cult the ability to modulate state governments in order to aid their own religious ceremonies of sacrificial slaughter or purposes unknown though for the permanence of their Satanic machinations which establish Satanists as the masters of the world even under the illusion of calmness with the state perceivably under the watch of a dynasty or royalty though these killer klowns only form a permeable layer of obscurity with the stench of that death cult puppeteering world events through the systemic culling of civilization.

Isaiah 56:10 Their [a] watchmen are all blind: they have no knowledge: they are all dumb dogs: they cannot bark: they lie and sleep, and delight in sleeping.

Isaiah 56:10 Endnotes

Against shepherds that devour their flock.

Isaiah 56:10 Footnotes

[a] He showeth that this affliction shall come through the fault of the governors, prophets, and pastors, whose ignorance, negligence, avarice and obstinacy provoked God's wrath against them.

There do exist many layers of this death cult though in general terms the captured society appears as a caste system from beginning to end: the standing army of peasants and tyrants, the central bank of corporate and royal overlords, and finally the death cult of Satan.

"GET BEHIND ME SATAN."

The demand of free men remains the same yesterday, today, and forever. The maker of excuses waits on the Lord while the free man knows that power of the Lord dwells within and presently at-hand; thus, idleness means to worship Satan outright with the only payment He would ask of His true deceivers.

Genesis 3:4 *Then the [a] serpent said to the woman, Ye shall not [b],[c] die at all,*

Genesis 3:4 Endnotes

[a] 2 Cor. 11:3

Genesis 3:4 Footnotes

[b] This is Satan's chiefest subtlety, to cause us not to fear God's threatenings.

[c] Hebrew, <u>die the death</u>.

2 Corinthians 11:3 But I fear lest as the [a] serpent beguiled Eve through his subtlety, so your minds should be [b] corrupt from the simplicity that is in [c] Christ:

2 Corinthians 11:3 Endnotes

[a] Gen. 3:4

2 Corinthians 11:3 Footnotes

[b] This place is to be marked against them which loathe that plain and pure simplicity of the Scriptures, in comparison of the colors and paintings of man's eloquence.

[c] Which is meet for them that are in Christ.

Whether considering ten thousand years ago or the infinity of time ahead of us – the reason for this war against mankind presents itself as a clear personification of intelligent communication exhibiting the desire to defend the guilty through creating a system of checks without balance since such a congregation or cult wilt only worship the illusion of authority and war against the true religion of God's innocent authority.

Isaiah 51:9 Rise up, Rise up, and put on strength, O arm of the Lord: rise up as [a] in the old time in the generations of the world. Art not thou the same, that hath cut [b] Rahab, and *wounded the [c] dragon?*

Isaiah 51:9 Footnotes

[a] *He putteth them in remembrance of his great benefit for their deliverance out of Egypt, that thereby they might learn to trust in him constantly.*

[b] *Meaning, Egypt, Ps. 87:4.*

[c] *To wit, Pharaoh, Ezek. 29:3.*

Psalm 87:4 *I will make mention of [a] Rahab and Babel among them that know me: behold Palestine and Tyre with Ethiopia, [b] There is he born.*

Psalm 87:4 Endnotes

So that there should be nothing more comfortable, than to be numbered among the members thereof.

Psalm 87:4 Footnotes

[a] *That is, Egypt and these other countries shall come to the knowledge of God.*

[b] *It shall be said of him that is regenerate and come to the Church, that he is as one that was born in the Church.*

Ezekiel 29:3 *Speak, and say, Thus saith the Lord God, Behold, I come against thee, Pharaoh king of Egypt, the great [a] dragon, that lieth in the midst of his rivers, which hath said, The river is mine, and I have made it for myself.*

Ezekiel 29:3 Footnotes

[a] *He compareth Pharaoh to a dragon which hideth himself in the river Nile, as Isa. 51:9.*

This illusion of serving a common good which excludes the rights of the individual can only serve a public that serves as it's own standing army prohibiting their own exercise of civil liberty. How must free men act for the immediate dissolution of this blasphemous deceit overshadowing society? How must men assemble and fight such a tyrannical force without immediately assembling for the manifestation of serving immediate justice to the death cult and without any fear of these wicked men and only with a fear for what God designs for us shall we not endeavor to succeed the instruction of His eternal promise? How must men conduct their own character when their own court systems illustrate that clear and present danger ready to imprison their self and their fellow countrymen for simply working to reconstitute the intent of a Godly court system? The laws given by the death cult that the men within the court systems would defend continue in direct contradiction to the rule of law and succeed only through a standing army of disingenuous and deceitful swarms of ignorant and superstitious *law enforcement* pretending that the following of any rule they receive in their job as that of an incontrovertible and of unquestioningly greater authority than their oath to the constitution which they so readily desecrate through the blind enforcement of unconstitutional orders even if the courts state the unconstitutionality as constitutional though we witness the courts so often exclude the vote of the citizens and operate government as it were rogue from the free men whom first instituted their public affair and way of life. Their wicked desire to eat out the substance of the free man blinds them from seeking truth and governs them into the enslavements of a death cult redesigning their mind to accept spoken word as a crime and thought as a weapon which must see elimination to prevent the spread of it's hypnotisms.

The true intention of the liberty movement means to break that yoke of bondage with the death cult therefore we must manifest a revolution against this force with every generation throughout eternity. Traditional war involves public declaration, battle-lines, and constant public awareness; however this war we fight maintains the most fierce conflict men could ever surmise. The sons of God for liberty juxtaposed against the death cult show the only two real philosophies on the earth at war with one another since God divide every other philosophy unto only one; and, we the sons of God do not live to threaten the life of others, rather we live to preserve life; while the death cult act for the purpose of ending our way of life. The threatening of our way of life demands a response from us; and, these pseudo philosophers whom argue that standing idle and meditating on positive vibes or good things in order to absolve this threat do illustrate their intellectual incontinence positioning them as an additional pawn in which the standing army uses for the expedition of tactics culling mankind. Around the world we do not witness a cluster of nations orderly defending liberty rather we witness only america and perhaps Switzerland openly declaring liberty to the captives of the world (though each of our governments openly and continually conspire against, and declare an end to, our sovereignty; also I in no manner discount or dismiss the efforts of those individuals presently at war defending their sovereignty; perhaps then this orderly defense then means that assembly of people which had succeeded the war for liberty and now presently illustrate that robust economy surrounding the preservation of civil liberty even when times appear rocky). Nations such as India profess their self a free society though what caste system of fiat currency could profess itself free while not even mentioning the philosophy of liberty as their aim or justification? This type of false free society advances it's suffering into a higher order of complexity which can even mean it aids the fostering of that growing enemy around the world forged against the individual fighting for liberty. This tyranny possesses the mind of individuals thereby requiring no appearance of formal war since it's metaphysical usurpation dissolves the bonds which otherwise affectionately unite us. Our struggle against this death cult unites the fierce and scorned patriots in the shared duty against this death threat that we will together survive as friends putting a stop to the standing armies and central banks funding the destruction of the free world. This war demands the sharpness of our spiritual sight to first gain discernment of it's threat and then use our information as a weapon to dissolve it's influence. Our aim then pursues a world of friends forged against the forces of theft and fraud and living their life with property and happiness under the trust of God and not under the subterfuge of secrecy and other canards of dynasty, officialdom, or royalty sold as the fiefdoms of balkanization, order, project, security, or taxation.

Bread and circus; media and entertainment: the things which steal self-discipline from the people and even allow them to serve this facade as inventious reason to ignore, fight, or deny the existence of the threat which presently, uniformly, and viciously impose it's philosophy of death upon mankind. The people and their press must act now to expose and bring immediate justice to this death cult which through it's self-evidenced act of treason does show it's hostile design combating every man, woman, and child on the earth such that it maintains a constant state of war against the independence and liberty of the living; therefore, to understand it's inquisition and then discern the action to take ought to move into center stage in society and luckily men have gone before us and we now know this fight as the animating contest of liberty. The general public and the press included act as if some type of war declaration must be made on the television or with some supposed official government release of papers outlining the problem and war preparations. Our own conscience would demand we repel this death cult threatening our way of life and not await any declaration from any man or press outlet since the self-evidence of this death cult's crisis upon us speaks so clearly that those without the inclination to recognize or discern such a threat do live the spiteful life of hypnotic derision. Can we not witness the most simple form of national peril through the abuse of our courts and dangers on our streets? What force then do the ignorant and superstitious suppose could empower such insurrection but that death cult which lulls the public to the lullaby of spiritual suicide? We must as well recognize the significance of our ancestors in achieving for us the existence of a nation which on the surface defends individual liberty to challenge the death cult and the various tyranny they embed into the mind of their subjects (though criminal elements of government presently showcase illegal and unconstitutional exceptions to our own rule of law). The public and the press when maintaining their own state of dysfunction in regard to confronting this war beseeching us forms a gap which the death cult in the unification of their mercenaries and press do seize upon through secret and public declarations of war. For shall we form our front with the discipline which God prepared for us – only then shall we remain prepared for war at all times thus retaining that eternal readiness to thwart the tyrannical advances of the death cult. Each individual acquiring the awareness of this death cult does by order of the universe then lower the shields of it's defense through the exposing of their devices of deception which torment the masses. The role of man must act as a light to paint the vision into the eyes of society from the youth to the old, rich to the poor, educated to the uneducated, such that we free civilization from the net and rather haul souls into tempestuous safety exceedingly away from these polluted waters.

What do we as a people consider literature or even history or what means truth or falsehood and how do we progress and what defines a loss of progression or remaining the same? How could civilization progress when each individual defines this notion without congruency? How can we define liberty without illustrating the action which break with it's constraint? The idleness of the individual begets that disease which renders civilization into a state of imminent danger and exacerbate all other crisis which righteous action would otherwise annul. The idle await orders of sacrifice from their death cult so that they satisfy the hunger of their god feeding on civil scorn as a blight upon this bright realm. The public so proudly stand idle for the announcement of a danger which encourage them to recognize a crisis and then feel an integral purpose in their life since such a false announcement would as well ask of them some type of action for said crisis as witnessed with the destruction of New York's twin towers and subsequent unconstitutional genocide and slaughter of millions of innocent citizens in the Middle East by way of the United States military, and co-conspirators, along with their providing weapons to terrorist organizations to fuel the vane and wicked effort of the hypocritical, shallow, and unthinking american people; though, the public was so easily trapped by the powers whose endangerment preexists all recorded history for a purpose which can only cull weak minds and misconstrue world events in order to raise standing armies for the preservation of the death cult. Self-evidence proves such a scope of clarity into the existence and present danger of this death cult that these individuals whom would deny this present peril for the hope of some illusion of official announcement granting them authority to feel endangered only illustrates the mire which compounds the mind of the fallen as they ignorantly hide behind their superstitions; and, out of this countenance of stupor do grant the death cult the currency to feverishly rampage mankind. Many individuals throughout the world today possesses the seasoning of that intelligent effort which marches closer than ever in ripping the veil completely off of this death cult and their various crusading military orders and secret occultic death societies enacting battle plans to torture individuals and enslave mankind for the temporal wicked power of accessing even greater wicked dimensions which further establish a firmament of absolute control over their grid and network of career satanists beckoning for additional immoral teachings to entrench their reign.

Proverbs 28:2 *For the transgression of the land [a]* <u>*there are*</u> *many princes thereof: but by a man of understanding and knowledge* <u>*a realm*</u> *likewise endureth long.*

Proverbs 28:2 Footnotes

[a] The state of the commonweal is oftentimes changed.

Many of these secret societies mask as open public societies and often certain individuals that expose these secret societies through the breaking of their secret oath risk being politically targeted or assassinated for exposing the evil to the light of day. These groups will always manifest their self as long as mankind turn a blind eye to the secret societies and secret oaths which elect their self the one-eyed king over the spiritually blind.

The philosophy of liberty and the philosophy of death existing polar opposite of one another simultaneously form an architecture and world-view antithetical to one another; and, both equally possess the potential to manifest, through participation or observation, a world in their like-image. Throughout the world the public have received the programmings of a specific world-view which rapines itself down the narrative of channeling wicked spirits for the normalcy bias of social conformity in their keeping up with pomp and vain media and entertainment. Adhering to the narrative-bias rewards it's closest allies with the officialdom of celebrating the erosion of the foundational principles of life, liberty, and property. The order of this death cult employs specific tactics for their own dynamic structure for the division and conquering of mankind. These individuals whom openly spiritually excise their self from the spirit of the Lord do not view their self as a human being apart of our great struggle for liberty.

Isaiah 29:24 Then they that erred in spirit, [a] shall have understanding, and they that murmured, shall learn doctrine.

Isaiah 29:24 Footnotes

[a] Signifying, that except God give understanding, and knowledge, man cannot but still err and murmur against him.

The individual in defense of liberty against the death cult must know we secure the victory through the stalwart tactics for which our steadfast purpose in Christ grants for our authority in the valiant alteration of the outcome of any plans of this most sinister death cult. As a people we must commit our self to the discernment which teaches the youth of such a thing so that not only do we rear a nation with such knowledge but that we rear a government which bear the fruit of this excellent pursuit of happiness. The public and their press must form as one business of men in the free trade of their own ideas and property in a war waged against those individuals that demand their taxation in order that they engage in cold or hot war against them. Free trade leads to peace while theft under the pseudonym of taxation leads to war. America's founding fathers well understood this present danger facing mankind and acted accordingly through the awareness and discernment that any other purpose the people surmise in life were a pomp and vain thing built on a foundation of ignorance and superstition which does attract a market of crooked mules ready to reform said market as a modular assembly within the death cult for the gaming of the economy against free trade since the foundation of such trade be in the spirit of our Lord with His love given freely to all. These forces of tyranny unified as a cult of death shape their self through the various secret societies and manifest either hidden in plain view in the case of royalty or not even murmured and only shared in secret in the case of the occult and it's various financial and intelligence institutions usually comprised of hereditary selection though primarily focused on those individuals that can most strictly implement the philosophy of death on the world and that does mean that philosophy which most strictly adheres to destroying liberty on the earth through providing an exhaustively thorough illusion of freedom which does mean a population of individuals incapable of articulating liberty or forming their own self-evidence for what constitutes liberty and tyranny or freedom from sin. This death cult would desire we do not learn of their tactics for if we learn of the gestations of their alien mission against mankind then the people upon learning such a thing would demand justice and even call for the death warrant of this cult as the world orders into a moral society which enjoys to hunt down this wicked death cult in order that they live in a free society of individuals whom individually and not governmentally determine their own trade of property and money since that moral government guard the privacy of civil liberty and not the secrecy of official security.

This cult of death at war with the human race cares not of what culture, nation, origin, race, religion, tongue, or tribe acting as the blockade and hedge dividing their path. The monocratic order of satanically wicked and devil-worshiping tyrants command the world in opposition against us through the demand we worship their ranks with a false faith in their planned obsolescence. This conspiracy born of evil enhances it's powers only upon the influence which infiltrate the minds whom give charge over their foreign and economic policy to these wicked controllers. Covert subterfuge forms the primary order and indefinite means for which binds the order of secret oaths. This emotionless and vicious circle of spineless demons stare coldly upon our desire for a free world as a border for which they aim to dissolve into the false idea that words and ideas hold no meaning thereby leading the blind into a quiet war with one another as these individuals comprehend not the invasion of drunken power into their psyche as they sign over their lives to a spiritual vacuum which dance in crimson robes around a fire of bones signifying their allegiance to the hypnotizing order of that death cult appointing wicked acts of power over men and not with an intelligent design but rather as a structure of feeders consuming the material world in the same manner a deranged man may attempt to jump into a sea of lava in hopes of passing through it's golden essence into poppy fields of communist utopia. Even as a child I understood the third world was without fair elections and subject to the oppressions of proxy armies and their dictators empowered through corrupt factions in the first world. How did this multi-generational replacement of elections with subterfuge occur except through the infiltration of culture with a cult of death generating it's own gladness on the screams of the innocent? Elections form the hallmark of any free and open society; and, in fact, free society ought to deport individuals whom refuse to vote in order that they exile the self-proclaimed tyrant upending justice and peace. Even in the awareness of free society and achieving of elections the people must still base their determinate course of destiny in opposition to the subterfuge awaiting to capitalize on their ignorance and superstition; though, history shows the occurrence thereof to form within the children of those individuals whom instituted free society since liberty like a dream fades into decadence and parades in nightmare. When the people replace their unconditional love in the knowledge of God with a pride for their self or country they then beget every intention and institution with a fear of man such that they cede their power unto the structure which moulds wicked men into the transceiver of twisted fates which embolden the wicked since society then defends wickedness and not liberty or true love as their god. The influence of free trade and diplomacy expunges the influence of violence and coercion whether this means muting the frequency of occurrence or eliminating the state-sponsored variety. God creates man equally in that we innately know our free choice and equally discern the tactics of fear which wicked men use to gain absolute control over our lives whether this means to steal my property in this moment or steal the destiny of mankind through that theft and fraud disguised as federalism, nationalism, or any *ism*, taxation, or national security. These inversions of reality flip the above into the below and the below into the above and perish mankind through it's psychological torture imprinting individuals with the spiritual desire to seek mental harm unto the physical harm of their own body and by extension the mind and body of the church though the spirit for which they aim to harm be the invincible one thus they injure only by unawareness all else whom aim to follow His path.

Deuteronomy 18:15 ¶ *[f] The Lord thy God will raise up unto thee a [a] Prophet like unto me, from among you, even of thy brethren: unto him ye shall hearken.*

Deuteronomy 18:15 Endnotes

God will not leave them without a true Prophet.

[f] Acts 7:37

Deuteronomy 18:15 Footnotes

[a] Meaning, a continual succession of Prophets, till Christ the end of all Prophets come.

Acts 7:37 *[a] This is that Moses, which said unto the children of Israel, [u] A Prophet shall the Lord your God raise up unto you, <u>even</u> of your brethren, like unto me: him shall ye hear.*

Acts 7:37 Endnotes

[u] Deut. 18:15, Acts 3:22

Acts 7:37 Footnotes

[a] He acknowledgeth Moses for the lawgiver, but so that he proveth by his own witness, that the Law had respect to a more perfect thing, that is to say, to the prophetic office which tended to Christ, the head of all Prophets.

Acts 3:22 *[b] For Moses said unto the Fathers, The Lord your God shall raise up unto you [a] a Prophet, <u>even</u> of your brethren, like unto me: ye shall hear him in all things whatsoever he shall say unto you.*

Acts 3:22 Endnotes

[b] Deut. 18:15, Acts 7:37

Acts 3:22 Footnotes

[a] This promise was of an excellent and singular Prophet.

This death cult expresses the literal exhibition of an alien guerrilla army sent to ravage earth as though it were a village of sleeping and vulnerable minds using the night to beckon for the selling of their soul to the devil of their cause. The death cult had realized long ago that marching an army onto our lands leads to our victory thus this death cult moves in the public through the shadows of their mind and enforces their reign with all sorts of signs and symbols to intimidate the weak-minded into surrendering their liberty or free expression through the corruptions of their thought and action. We the people must burn this monolithic death cult into dust. Various global enterprises, for example the materials or petroleum and weapons industry, fund these dark armies as they hide their symbols of rapacious arrogance in the open; for example: the Shell company illustrating the hair upon the head of the inbred and self-entitled queen; or the McDonalds logo representing the thirteen royal families; and *this* occultic list never ends. The hereditary death cult of interbreeding family imagine they hold the keys of wickedness which lock mankind away from our potential though those keys dwell from within the power of the Lord. Thousands of years of accumulated stolen wealth will never silence that weapon of speech which crush this sphere of influence shuttering the minds of men. They would rather encapsulate the strong, awake, and youthful, into vials of blood and tonic for their own spiritual games of control to shadow humanity and engrave their initials on our tree of liberty or as expressed through the movie *The Matrix* whose intent was to make the public aware of the stated mission of this death cult: enslave mankind as individual battery cells which electrically power a technocratic control grid for the suffocation of all life on the earth lest it's wicked influence expand such that it shutter the existence of all known life in the cosmos hence the dangers witnessed in the war of good and evil in the movie series *Star Wars.*

Many will argue over the name of this death cult whether (and I ascribe this death cult or doomsday cult to none subdivision and only attribute it's presence to that higher semantic which when spoken in present language transliterates into evil) archons, chabad, demiurge, marxist, zionism, or any other presumptuous and self-congratulatory definition even if a multitude agree their perceptions prove the collective-name they identify (since these collective-names so often represent even multiple competing factions within the named faction; for example: the Kurds, a nomadic tent-dwelling and mercantilistic people referred to as the Kedar in The Bible; and, this example of the Kurds does not represent an example of a group which overactive imaginations claim to be the controllers of the world though it does represent a group which wicked factions use as pawns for balkanization; i.e. carving out eastern Syria for a U.N. member state; empires making cracks, building statelets, perpetuating war, and repeat) as those individuals placing the physical world into a motion which composes a singular machine; however, names and identity mean everything when justice treat the each of them as the same death cult, rather than some type of corporate shield bearing one of the many *ism* names, thus achieving our ends in individual and national sovereignty. One must look no further for the proof of this death cult than those individuals expressly engaged in the political realm throughout all nations and why would they engage in such a thing if not to seize control of the nation's military and as a political-military class then exercise authority over the education of the public through controlling the money supply and which educational institutions receive funding or sanctioning based on their ability to teach the things which politically or militarily enhance, harm, or support the machine. All of this acts as one layer unto itself thus the system renders it's highest university institutions into political science programs in order that they create the scientific class as a form of royalty that weaponizes the political and military class to a degree that separates them from the public as though they were an alien race milking the general public and foreign world even as though all of the world were foreign unto them; thus, therein lies the philosophy of death which feed on everything innocence creates. Whether we traverse the scope of this death cult's institutions, names, and titles, bares little difference to the effect which we aim to achieve in having the public discern the end-game of this death cult in remaining bound to their secret oath combining their machinations into a device, matrix, or new world order of that philosophy of death.

Rumors have suggested The Internet was created in order to draw weakness into the lower ranks of the death cult in order that they most efficiently locate their most weak tension points and inject reinforcement into these weaknesses so that they more tightly weave their agenda into a strength whose ability instantaneously sends energy or information to enact action of any scale across any distance or even destroy an entire civilization with or without a missile launch or even fire particle-beams from satellites to instantly torch entire nations; weaponized laser technology have rendered nuclear warheads into today's common grenade. One can not discuss this death cult without the mention of their chief religion being the false science of eugenics and their chief politics being subversion or the false countersubversion of subterfuge. Their central banking diplomats march alongside their fellow standing army of economic and political scientists to the false flags of divide and conquer. The constructors of this tyranny, that death cult, comprise those individuals wittingly flying the false flag of socially-just superiority as though their posture of tradition were that origin and specie of true power and not the remnant of a fallen idol whose outward appearance emboldens fallen people to paint it's epithets upon every public avenue when their farcical countenance exists as the absolute furthest example from the abstraction in which they fail to even remotely portray through their compository wicked devices.

Psalm 74:4 *Thine adversaries roar in the midst of thy congregation, and [a] set up their banners for signs.*
Psalm 74:4 Footnotes
[a] They have destroyed thy true religion, and spread their banners in sign of defiance.

Imagine an individual upon donning a certain fancy outfit finds reason within their person to then demand whomsoever receive the pointing of their finger must now involuntarily conscript into their army. The royal family and their wider death cult possess none difference. The simple peasant will answer,

"Well these people doth be royal and as a commoner I shall

honor what they call they self through being they subjects and if you too kain't do the good work of keeping yo head down then we gon' hurt ya's or turn yas' over to dem royals fer redgecation."

Further questioning of the empty-minded and hollow spirited peasant yields little results though exemplifies ample proof of a confused slave slumbering in the matrix for a social credit which they shall never find. The disciples of the royal death cult live horrified of the fact they continually choose to spiritually disembody their self and regurgitate the lies of what God would use to expedite the end of their time on the earth; and, may their time come ever more swiftly.

The death cult do not shy away from their agenda as one can so easily witness the self-evidence of their tenants throughout the various writings, public white papers, books, manuals, and even legislation outlining their desire to subvert mankind. Though many of their writings, especially those deemed national security, remain in secret the public almost always witness the declassification of such documents though only fifty years later. If a leak of such a document or plan occurs then the control of this death cult orders through it's secret channels (even if this order be previously understood as a doing-business-as or like-being-like or not a direct call-to-action) for the erasure of this information such that the public receives no knowledge of the situation or those that do learn of the leak then receive counter-intelligence propaganda to unlearn what they had learned or in the least cause a division of opinion which succeed in conquering the imagination of them all.

Whether the thing of secret were an individual or information weapons systems the cult of death acts to hide it's reveal and convincingly lull the public into the perception that the system make no mistakes warranting suspicion of their cause or intent. When a member of the press attempts to unearth certain truths the death cult having previously inserted their spys amongst the various media outlets as editors and other top executives then ensure the agenda of the occult does not infiltrate the awareness of the public and if it does they then coordinate as a standing army from within the corrupted government and press to alter the public perception and delimit the expansion of human consciousness. The occult most effectually extends it's reach through manifesting hidden control over the members of society (i.e. stuff thy face with false food and stuff thy ear with false knowledge in order that thy peasant exhibit proper unthinking and ant-colony behavior). This example serves to highlight how even those individuals unaware of the greater evil act as tools for the greater evil in attempting to silence the free flow of thought and ideas which communicate that higher knowledge and true intelligence sufficient for the rendering of the tyrant into the inanimate footstool of society. These silencers hold many tools in their repertoire of deception of nail-biting and ankle-biting over every last word and detail as they seek self-affirmation in their own destitution to draw others near their misery in hope of roasting another soul on their altar of blasphemed destiny. Those worthy fighters in the Kingdom of God instead of receiving praise from this inverse world all receive the threat of a force which would silence their minds. This is the method of the dark army fighting for the philosophy of death: their cold war moves in stealth in order that they deter mankind away from liberty and raise the cult of death into the heads of state thereby giving them unlimited resources to materialize their spiritless tyrants into a spiritually dark lord devoid of joy and overpowered with every hue of wickedness. The fiery discipline of this apparatchik ought to terrify any discerning man into total soberness and turn the stomach of that society which would abhor it's demands and enrage and engage the republic which gain awareness of the wicked and their active devices even if they be disguised as apples, pastors, or toaster-ovens.

One must ponder the happenstance of two enemies uniting as friends against an evil more greatly threatening them than any power previously perceived as necessary for their defense against one another. The men of God discern the disturbance in the force and recognize their duty and purpose in seeking to illuminate other men in this fight against wickedness which has plagued mankind with ushering in their own destructive wisdoms throughout all of the ages. Men fight over religion and politics through debate and war though mankind spends eons without fighting the powers which compel them unto their own divide and conquer in the first place either for a lack of awareness of these certain powers or whom shall control these powers; and, though the clear answer remain in equal rights, or powers, which God Himself ordains, the death cult shadows the mind of the public from this knowledge in order that this public remain under their slave-state. The death cult has no interest whatsoever in a discerning people operating in a free society with awareness of the equal distribution and rule of this eternal and infinite flame of liberty hence the constant assault and subversion upon america and the ideas of liberty. Does this occult aim to keep as few people as possible under their control or does self-evidence not teach of the subservient individuals within this secret oath all competing for the chair of the most evil one while aiding one another as co-conspirators for a power they subconsciously know they will never obtain though they openly race toward it's gathering as it were a momentum of inanimate rock made temporarily animate from the mountain dislodging it's incompatible form?

Ephesians 4:26-27 [a] Be [b] angry, but sin not: let not the sun go down [c] upon your wrath, Neither give place to the devil.

Ephesians 4:26 Footnotes

[a] He teacheth us to bridle our anger in such sort, that although it be not, yet that it break not out, and that it be straightway quenched before we sleep, lest Satan taking occasion to give us evil counsel through the wicked counselor, destroy us.

[b] If it so fall out, that you be angry, yet sin not: that is, bridle your anger, and do not wickedly put that in execution, which you have wickedly conceived.

[c] Let not the night come upon you in your anger, that is, make atonement quickly for all matters.

The great disturbance in the force separating good and evil acts as a frequency of energy aligning individuals to it's magnetic pulse in order that the wicked assemble for the dismemberment of the innocent and the good assemble for the shrinking of the wicked. The wicked wear the image of a wave-form intentionally manifesting actions to suffer the life-force of individuals into a sacrificial energy for their illusory god-form in which they worship therefore forever removing the tyrant from the power of God unless that tyrant repent and earnestly and totally give their self over to that prince of peace. The defender of liberty possesses both the knowledge of God and the knowledge of evil and with this knowledge then lives according to the knowledge of God in that like-image and wave-form of God in which He designed for us to complete His works both in deed and spirit and to the best of our faith and knowledge.

PRESENT

STATE OF

AFFAIRS IN

AMERICA

The division amongst americans today stands as tumultuous perhaps as the months leading up to our american revolution on 4 July 1776; and, however real or manufactured the perception or factual state of our peril – and concerning whatever stream of consciousness or reason self-evidencing a demand for men of God to deliberate and act – there exists an avarice upon these lands grating the soul with visions of blood and light. The central banks have impoverished america's middle-class and God looks on to see who among the american people will rise to fight for His world suffering the force of the undead in their manufacture of the elimination of mankind or civil liberty in the least; and, on the streets the innumerable wicked conduct their self with all manner of violent threats believing that none shall object to the illusion of their false and incompetent authority seizing political control over american society and the world and engaging in an unmitigated persecution of Christians domestically and abroad even with U.S. tax dollars and military force; and, even using government to ban public prayer, criminalize free speech, ban american flag t-shirts, and burn our Bible and Bill of Rights and Declaration of Independence; and, all under the guise that we must as a people promote ignorance in order to deprecate the superstition of questioning government, secret societies, secret oaths, and secret proceedings; this force of insatiable wickedness reasons we the people must adhere to their devilish perceptions and remain silent when physically or spiritually assaulted by the enemy from within our own borders; but, what they can not see appears as ultra light beams from God giving His full authority and power to the individuals on this land to destroy these grand dragons and bird-brained ostriches summoning the most undead of demons to kill us after having finished their intentional and manufactured collapse and genocide of civilization as though the enemy could successfully breakaway into an untouchable civilization of immortals or evade the judgment from the pursuits of our systems of justice whose proving of cause and effect in a civil society reproves the perfect law of liberty and the intentions of our God and fellow countrymen.

The world-view of many americans fails to align with reality or discern the false consensus of strangers seeing the world through eyes of deception and only now deftly marvel the dark arts coercing them into turning away from God and liberty; and, the sepulcher of sand for which they previously stood and worshiped upon now washes away with their tide of false narratives attempting to bend our reality unto their submission which does serve as notice for us to to strengthen the formation of our defenses and reveal of their repeating lunatics these contrived narratives as though their lies were their cosmic prophylactic and not a standing army uniformed in barn-red with white cross-hairs painted on their middle and with the intention of oppressing free people in america and the world which only works on human-beings without the education of their history and love of the beauty in a mind, body, and spirit to expose the generally excessive imposition of tyrannical inquisition justifying it's wickedness with their prideful and hypocritical oath to martial law; a double-mind; which, as an agency of continuity of governance does separate them from their oath to the rule of law and command of them to cause the genocide of all life on the earth and even in the name of favoring or saving plants over people as though genociding mankind for a world of plants without people could benefit the consciousness for which only man, and not animals or plants, will know.

A type of new-speak in america has emerged wherein tens of millions of individuals now claim extra-judiciary rights for their newfound political correctness or religious class moonlighting as trend-inspired mental illnesses; for example: feminism, trans-gender, ableist, trans-specie and a whole soiree of "trans" labels all related to how one prefers to operate their own sexual organs or even cut off their own limbs in order that government ensure them protectionisms or in the least use these false genders and pronouns as political leverage for the criminalization of free speech and mass imprisonment of individuals for "misgendering" this new god-class which lends itself into a more subtle type of this trans-feminist-gender-confusion subterfuge agenda wherein corporate press works tirelessly to replace male leaders with females even going so far as to replace drill sergeants with women so the officers have access to a harem of comfort-girls in these never-ending wars, including the unconstitutional and corporate "war on terror" the boors so gleefully cheer on (a drone-strike kills a caveman four thousand miles away and hypocritical and foolish americans cheer while the Clintons and Soros walk free – surely american hackers do not launch foreign missiles to aid the military-industrial-complex while the corporate press prints one-liners "Der leadership of dis enemy cheer americas pain;" surely not), wherein the name of democracy and political correctness elects these female drill sergeants to literally outfit male soldiers in red high-heels and march them down public streets as a show of this tyrannical force of demonic transvestites (crotch-rot trannies: america's new authority figure, truth filter, and death bringer) occupying the americas by the threat of violence and to accentuate a falsehood of friendliness and relatability – a mask to mute the seriousness of a military and divert attention away from the true role of that same military now being constructed into an attack formation for the crushing silence of free speech and defenders of human liberty whom american government now officially defines as home-grown american extremists (the true ramp-up of which began under President Ubama though the Bush-Clinton crime syndicate laid the foundation); for example, Seattle government paying transvestites hundreds of thousands of tax dollars to strip-tease for them as local media video-tapes for their nightly news programming; or the County and school systems across america under the funding of the state enter our public institutions and sexually groom schoolchildren with transvestite convicted-pedophile men so that there be none question that the state fully endorses the unveiling of a demonic army by way of offering them a platform to promote their pedophilia in public libraries and public schools for teaching particularly the youngest school children to literally masturbate, hump, and physically insert dollar bills into the G-string being worn by these mentally retarded or Satanically possessed transvestites as though a spaceship of demonic killer klowns from outer-space landed for an all-out assault on the good conscience of mankind with witnesses reporting a label on the trap-door of this ship reading 'LGBTQP' apparently painted on with the blood of sacrificed straight men; and, first by attacking the individuals that do not officially address these boglodites properly while yelling:

"WE ARE YOUR FRIENDS. IT'S MA'AM; NOT SIR. WE COME IN PEACE. THE RAINBOW FLAG IS OURS NOW YOU DIRTY CHRISTIANS;"

and all the while claiming this demonic activity as the necessary upgrade for the seizing control of the intelligencia seats of our nation and this does mean the attempted bloody-coup of every Executive, Legislative, and Judicial seat for the burning of america and handing of our bodies and land over to international cartelmen which all must be accommodated by our government to enforce a prohibition of criticisms against this new god-class or standing army faltering our society from within the defensed watchtowers; or, how about the unofficial psychological intelligence operation known as 'black lives matter;' and, or, other shallow efforts and repeating people bumbling about as a globular slug driveling their trail of false narratives for the scalping of the political landscape and oozing of it's creep until it violently overthrow common sense, disappear every challenger to these counter-intelligence narratives, and enforce myopic social conformity as though we were North Korea and not mankind's greatest assembly of people to ever set foot on the earth with the intention of promoting one nation and one world order of, for, and by the defense of human liberty; and, not a world of phony people planting illegal military bases within every nation across the planet while paying covert proxy armies to piss off the world then waiting around for these unconstitutional bases to be targeted by militiamen so the corporate presstitutes can grandstand on national television as the thought-leaders of the world now that they seemingly have justified their arrogant criminalization of every amendment in our Bill of Rights for the low-low-low cost of a debt that ten trillion years of american civilization could never pay as well as the cost of the militarism suffocating america and the world while claiming it's illegal bases as sovereign soil though it violently violate the sovereignty of every nation in the world and the american people whom would never have voted for their public largess to be stolen for such a stupendously incompetent foreign policy though this incompetence only can reflect the ignorance and superstitions of the people encouraging the immolation of true american culture and human liberty: yeah, commerce with all and alliance with none; yeah, as though america is the global arranger of that marriage or summer fling called war.

The self-described thought-police bullying every american they can identify have now organized into a coalition force of paramilitary units designed to sabotage all individuals voicing their disagreement to the prohibition of free speech and this veritable announcement of forced authoritarianism erecting idioms against us such as 'hate-speech' (while they deny the implementation of their online and physical covert action begetting future events) disrupt the dissemination of information exposing their activity, degrade the individuals disseminating the information, and deceive the individuals without leadership and looking for the path to true information with one of their more wicked cloaks of stupidity being: "None shall doubt the credentials of mine and these fine institutions," or "Full stop," when their real motive lie somewhere in the landscape of exuding their cringe-worthiness even by repeating one another's words pretending they finish each other's sentences as though any of this information ops of suggestive influence or technical disruption would not in the same instance give us the power to uncover their true identity or signature intent to hunt and sacrifice the imagination of the believer with the full backing of a legislature openly defining and criminalizing free speech as outright physical violence and not simply a formless and victimless expression of physical waves of sound from a holographic realm of spiritual creation and meekened unity; though, their fantasies only reverberate racial division with ignoring and importing tyrannical and malignant Islam (though many Islamic peoples state this show of force be not Islam at all but in fact a state-sponsored false-flag from places of global influence which works well enough even to compel Islamic religious leaders and scholars to call for the death of white men and rape of white women while the wealthy white liberals in america will not denounce this and in similitude applaud these barbaric notions as scholarly and austere humanitarianism; yes, the rich white liberals have all taken on the role of a psych warden for the criminally insane and their danger is so existentially crazy and real) even patronizing the public with calling tyrannical Islam the religion of peace (never-mind the numerous videos of Islamic husbands close-hand slapping the face of their wife in the middle of their marriage ceremony, Islamic preachers throwing homosexuals from atop buildings to their death, bathing and drinking from a cow's spraying golden shower of urine in public, the bombings and canings and stabbings and stonings and beheadings and cannibalism and public necrophilia and boy-wives) after one of the crazed lunatics runs in circles killing people repeatedly screaming *Allahu Akbar!*; how can this not be the weaponization of a society and their government in a war against loving thy neighbor as thyself including demonizing and promoting disgust and hate of the family unit and the perseverance of true men and the ornate beauty and intelligence of women and the love of all loves: Jesus Christ; even while proposing the genocide of Christians with one hollywood movie after another depicting killing white men or men of European descent (as if all men do not share a common ancestor; or technological illustration of genetic diversity proves to anyone a division of race justifies the means to keep mankind divided and does not simply showcase familial decisions from an even more common common-ancestor over time; which, ironically enough these divisions of confusing the male and female gender work hand-in-hand with inspiring racial division since all sorts of labels accompany these official race narratives; i.e.: *orange* man bad); and, even castration or execution of male children as regularly and publicly suggested by the Sharia law loving feminists (who can name a greater oxymoron when we know Sharia law exhibits the opposite of equal rights? And can there be a bottom to their feints of shifting their political narratives; for example: trans-exclusionary-radical-feminists or cis-gender-non-binary-genderqueer-third-gender: seriously, batman? Get fucked by the non-binary camel or elephant you rode in on and give me a fucking break you Sharia law and tyrant-loving beasts and phantoms of the night. We are a free people not to be brain-washed or tread on.) and deluded college professors; or Hollywood's portrayal of the alpha male as the secret bad guy taken down by a secret operation claiming to justify the suspension of constitutional rights while cold-sweating, disgusting, fidgety, greasy, panting, mildly retarded, stuttering, and testosterone-deprived beta males storm the home of a patriotic american citizen for "dangerous speech" while damn near one hundred literal military combat vehicles line up outside with a foot-soldier army to match the heated seats of it's interior and exterior cabs as one dozen helicopters and unmanned drones armed with smart bombs "secure the airspace" to ensure an atmosphere of totally fascist and unconstitutional martial law as some sort of open exhibition of the successful takeover of america in the case of the political targeting of libertarian activist, Marine, patriot, Congressional and Presidential candidate Adam Kokesh for simply displaying a video of Himself with a shotgun during the same season of a President Barry Hussein Ubama politically charging american society with His signing of foreign legislation at the United Nations to seize all firearms nationwide (and do what with the "counter-revolution" pray-tell: of course Ubama & Co. plan was to genocide the free people of this nation while His ignorant supporters (mostly rich white liberals acting as the handlers for collectives of non-white non-governmental organizations and voters) think it was some type of necessary eradication of "white people" or "white supremacists" as some sort of means to pomp up an illusion that the only americans left that understand liberty have white skin (and they want to use their liberty to enslave you? Fat chance.) and every non-white demands a fascist takeover (while the media ignores "non-white" americans publicly advertising and voicing support for liberty)); and, in any case sample of the litany of tyrannical causes flooding our lands we witness what proves to be a displacement of american society with a beast system issuing a public and unpunished license of killing and especially in the case of it's Department of Homeland Security with it's main tenant being to eradicate the fourth amendment and primarily by hiring the utter dregs and pedophiles of society to publicly molest children at airports and other places of public transit and secondarily by warrantless spying and facial-recognition scans everywhere in public and even in the privacy of one's own home and all for a world I.D. and Chinese communist social credit score system (A.I.: advanced arithmetic disguised as sentient physics) while claiming it would be a crime to drop the hammer on this self-evident insurgency of lawlessness; a chilling effect quickly causing american society to devolve into a narco-pharma state indifferent to today's state of Mexican affairs and we even narrowly face the point of no return wherein americans will be extradited and tried as Chinese citizens in Chinese courts or imprisoned in Chinese labor camps before having our organs harvested for offending the impotent, stupid, and felching Chinese communists and George Soros' of the world kissing babies and eating ice cream cones in public while in private eating babies and kissing crystal balls to summon a weaponized scrying over the world; a situation of which more immediately remedied by the act of civil liberty (bring on this civil war against us and our liberty if you must) and even the annexation or purchase of (1) Canada, (2) the Caribbean, Bahamas, Bermuda, British V.I., (3) Australia and Oceania, (4) Liberia, (5) Greenland, (6) Iceland, (7) Scandinavia,

(8) Portugal, (9) Ukraine, (10) Crimea, (11) North and South Korea, (12) Antarctica, (13) Honk Kong, (14) Taiwan, (15) Vietnam, (16) Laos, (17) Cambodia, and (18) the north half of Mexico including walling off this narrowed corridor (an idea exceedingly more futuristic and sane than allowing the overwhelming majority of these territories to remain the direct or indentured servants by-proxy of the British Crown); and, all of these peoples recognized as independent and sovereign colonies within nation-states for the assembly and preservation of their unalienable right to their life, liberty, and property; and, each colony with their own Bill of Rights, Declaration of Independence, and Sheriff, each nation-state with it's own electoral college and President; and, each citizen with the authority to freely exercise their speech for the enforcement of the most near-perfect representation of that framework and republican governance enshrined into the constitution as a defensible reminder against the tyranny in the minds of men and a serious expansion of the cause of liberty and not by force but by the ideas and philosophy of liberty (despite the populists' claim that country or dignity and not liberty and tenacity unites people).

The labels these disingenuous sycophants repeat and swath at their political opponents involve a slew of ridiculous canards; for example: racist, homophobic, misogynist, patriarchal nazi, cis-gender-privilege-white-skin-blue-eye-devil, and all sorts of other divisive, spiteful, and envious garbage designed to psychologically crush the accused, enlarge the church of Satan by way of replacing truth with falsehood, and accuse the absolutely unaccusable of the most gawkish accusations hence their pet-project of demonizing the original preacher of liberty and perfect image and son of God: Jesus Christ; and, for great reason, after-all: for what must a person do when confronted with a deharmonization of reality from hoards of gibbering buffoons flying from every crack, crevice, street corner, alleyway, causeway, subway, thoroughfare, and walkway in order that they enter through the backdoor of logic and reason and programmatically accost with hostility He whom the social engineers distorted the archetype thereof in order to manipulate the perceptions of superstitious fools being spoon-fed semantical propaganda in order that they best prepare their self to correctly perform the dance of exhaustive hyperventilation unto blind rage at even the memory, mention, sight, or sound of the good man as though we the people would not in the least refuse submission to Satanic war lords since it be they and not us rooted as the subservience to a neural-network of mind-control triggering idiots to think they with officiality can when encountering their most rare and primordial existential threat strip that person of their papers, houses, or effects and without any provocation while claiming to portray peaceful resistance to the violence of speech by being violent to those who first forgo violence for speech: yeah, leftists shaking violently with anger everywhere. The left has even stated that to even question their self-evident conspiracy to persecute an innocent men without fact or witness is itself a conspiracy which does imply their intent and showcase their reactionary conduct of denial, disruption, degradation, and deception when free men pursue true justice; truly the days of brazen Satanism set before us and in fullness of their inversions even teaching schoolchildren in official curriculum to believe all women, erect Satanic churches and statues everywhere, tear down america's Christian churches and historical american statues, open witchcraft general stores everywhere, ban anti-women comedians, jokes, and words, or that men can have babies and women can donate sperm, or men can compete as women in female sports; and, in this new world order heterosexual relationships end and human-beings come from genderless global hatcheries though this be a small step before these hatcheries reform into a vehicle for converting the human race into a permanent comatose state of performing the role of a thermal and psychic energy source for the algorithmic time-dilation, cosmic fuel, and historical vector for the positional functioning of the dynamic matrix wherein the mind of every human being is inserted into a holographic and multiverse projection where the imagined world operates as real as one without the people being plugged into this matrix; and, as well, many intelligent people with weak nerves claim this be our present reality today though the fact we possess the singularity of having the man Jesus Christ to defend means quite the contrary and luckily we as a human race stand at a time to keep us within God's heavens and not without His favor in being trapped or transformed into a memory within a computational program controlled by a breakaway civilization whom their self keep willingly attached to the spirit of Satan with the blindness that whispers in their ear that no alpha God plans the omega of their fiasco.

Every kind of american today still holds a high regard for the original precepts of liberty and with whole admiration supports our statesmen standing in defense for human liberty and especially those statesmen of our present-day including the stalwart and former Congressman from Texas: Ron Paul whom early and often preaches of equal rights and liberty for all individuals on the earth and a restoration of our republic to it's constitutional boundary. The times be such a way in america that the latter statement would even and immediately elicit from the general public a profoundly hostile assault against us even with abrasive screaming often described as autistic screeching or a toddler-like temper tantrum (thrashing on the ground while screeching) which has occurred at such a high frequency that journalists have extensively documented this phenomena and most notably occurring at rate conducive to a critical mass in the immediate aftermath of President Donald John Trump's successful election with all sorts of these deranged individuals hollering unto madness, maiming their perceived political enemies by using steel bike locks as an assault rod, or roasting their political enemies alive in hot tents for a spirit cooking event (this ritual described in greater detail in the book of Leviticus) that does as well involve consumption of certain flesh and blood and burning of the unspent remains into dust and all before cheaply discarding the old dust into the yard (this event perfectly depicting a portion or too near of a resemblance to be anything not this ritual in question in the first Guardians of the Galaxy film when the character Groot dies and dancing light emerges to float through the air in a mystical manner and not that this be a vision but rather a true occurrence lighting the faces and some of the draping wall around the pit of scorching rocks in the black of night and is not an illusion and is another example of Hollywood revealing the method of their more inner secret and Satanic rituals (though being popularized and spread like fire) of deception and sacrifice as a form of normalcy bias and I know this to be true because I was one that escaped this edge of the sword with seconds to spare: evidently this light energy that emerges is our life-force or innocence which is absorbed as black magic by the surrounding practitioners (their self guarded by thick blankets as their ancient chants open the portals and Lord give me protection for exposing their chants which their threats aim for none to ever expose without being totally hunted down)), and arresting the good samaritan and setting free the criminal and all of this madness officially excused as *political correctness:* self-evident imprisonment of those individuals all along the watchtower and high office for the protected coup, secret arrest, torture, and burial of body and event of innocent citizens with these ghouls formed against us and even their minions pursue us in public to bite us, force their self upon us, pinch us, rob us, slap the back side of our head, spat on us, and trip us; celebrity athletes farting on us; the act of foes in their folly of being this and that standing army waged against our spiritual duty to be the hand with the sword of knowledge for the conquering of their imaginations whom so readily invent (1) devices against Christ, (2) infringements, (3) usurpations, and all other sorts, types, and stinking generaldoms of subterfuge while even stating: "Jesus Christ deserves what He got because He would not shut His fucking trap." in a manner self-evident with desiring to deprecate known truths. The ignorant be so tangential to the tyranny we face and whose ignorance can not be respectably measured without first recognizing they believe such childish things as democracy and socialism before going on and on and on and on and on and on and on and on and on and on to argue liberty means legalizing slavery, socialism means "guaranteeing a basic level of dignity" (whatever in the fuck-all this means but the challenged and deluded people do use this phrase as an anthem for infringing on civil liberty and claiming to enjoy their calms of despotism) and will refuse to comprehend [logic and reason] making every form of theft and fraud illegal and especially that theft of persons which be that entourage of slavery and underworld without love for God, neighbor, or self.

How must we address those individuals whom desire to destroy equal rights and compose stupendous examples of horrific individuals or groups of stupefyingly horrendous individuals for the parading around of self-proclaimed extra-judiciary rights which does mean the exercise of those oppressions antithesis to the powers of justice and of man's granting of powers for the institutionalization and resolution of our just and orderly powers whose state of liberality provisions us with the dissolution and abolition of those prohibitions suppressing liberty by way of storming the castle of God and man: yeah, oppressions witnessed in american society with the descending upon american citizens on Texas soil with flamethrowers and tanks in the case of the Waco, Texas massacre or militarily seizing a home without a warrant in Odessa, Texas for having multiple plastic Christmas trees visible through the front window and from the road (hostile warrantless examples number in the thousands or even millions when including the unconstitutional T.S.A searches). Do we then identify them as anarcho-marxists, clockwork elves, communists, demons, fascists, interdimensional fae, little green men, Satanists, twerps, yellow-bellys; or simply recognize them through the like-image which their intent reveals: conquerors, colonizers, deceivers, destroyers of life and property, manipulators of self-evident truth, or interdimensional cro-magnon and mad monsters engaged in a hostile takeover of reality – owned as pawns by their occultic masters to bring desolation, destruction, and famine to the free world. Logic and reason translate no sense to the colonizers and when any one defy logic and reason they then ask of their master to use them for treason for they go on in their reasoning that the american revolution was intentionally and originally a genocidal colonization effort in itself when it was in fact the free spirited luminaries and visionaries of the free world uniting in spiritual war, which we took unto victory, against every faction of dynasty, mafia, and royalty upon the face of this earth (of which was pre-formed as one world government of absolute genocide) thus throwing into the lake of fire a mass of babylon whose most powerful empires rumble about earth as a land-locked storm stalking the horizon of the visionary dreamers and of whom unite real powers by way of their civil liberty and spiritual path in following Christ to naturally and triumphantly assemble for the empathic overthrow of that alien colonization force working to deprecate free thought and replace the word of God with the absence of thought.

Today when an individual uses these words: *equal rights* the pretend conqueror (though they intend to use a foreign military to conquer americans into a one world government; maybe these goons are infected with zombie-parasites mind-controlling it's host :shrug:) immediately, libelously, and publicly label that individual a racist which has caused many americans to be the victim of having their homes raided and arms seized by a rogue federal government and for some far-fetched and secret ruling (and rumored to first be determined by fixed computer algorithm which does effectively, if wholly true, prove the usurpation of our governance by way of an unelected technocracy being the funnel through which technology increasingly and autonomously determines and controls the functions of governance, and primarily with the duty of officially censoring individuals and information even with surreptitiously libeling individuals as "anti-semitic," or an "anti-semitic-trope," a "homophobe," "racist," a "bigot;" and, never-mind the fact *semitic* translates to *Arab* therefore to announce a need for increased security by way of demanding the world conform to or obey the false definition of words (for example redefining semitic from Arab into Jewish in order to libel their political enemies as anti-Jewish for criticizing Israel's state government and not the Jewish people) be wholly wrong on it's face, immoral, and illegal; and, especially considering secret courts criminalize free speech for the reconstitution of caste conformity.

Many Satanists within the Christian church exercise sorcery to herd the meek Christians within the church with an odyssey of authoritatively analgesic claims; for example:

"Satan promotes equal rights."

or that

"Liberty is a political fantasy not a political reality."

and then go on to reason this by claiming equal rights is defined by judgment or power equal with God therefore any individual whom proclaims equal rights must mean they follow Satan with the intention or likeness of bringing down the people of God. This fake Christian inverts every intention of Jesus Christ's teachings in that we exercise our liberty in a revolutionary war for equal rights under the trust of God and between all men to set free the captives of tyranny. Student University manuals today even claim the statement "I am not racist" or "It's okay to be white" proves the speaker of such a statement as in fact a secret racist whom must be publicly exiled even by death warrant; statements which our Federal government now literally investigates as domestic terrorism and militarily interrogates american citizens found to express such a speech in this new world order (but everything is completely normal in america; just turn on your television and dine in hell you filthy and stupid americans). The sordid blasphemy against free speech and independent thought crests today with such force that our fellow countrymen sheepishly hide in their delivery and warehouse jobs while trembling at the thought of being the change or that public figure of renown for our nation thus compelling them to live the life of a lie that can do no deed for their family greater than devoting their weakening intelligence to the gibbering away of their intellectual powers and resources toward inconsequential things and not the strengthening of ideas and preservation of mankind's futurity since God does design men to align their intent with their action and resolve the mystery of Satan's self-evident attack on our society's individual liberty. The philosophy of liberty stands in the way of the tyrants seizing total control of earth thus the tyrants work tirelessly through their international bodies to render america a slave state of their corporations whom presently erect swarms of banks and officers for the preparation of martial law around the world; and, we know this to be the case with their bold and public proclamations of: "America is separating families at the border. Open the borders now. No border; no wall; no U.S.A. at all." or "America was never great and will never be great." or "Defending a nation's border is a *border publicity stunt*." and all of this for the flooding of our borders with disease and human traffickers while the left promotes billion-dollar ebola vaccine contracts (remedied with Vitamin A and Vitamin C and not injecting your self with the live ebola virus – the federal government is even making such a statement of free speech illegal), unvetted access for a literal army of narco-cartelmen, and dissolution of the rule of law, america, and our Bill of Rights. The government of america exhibits it's own evil deeds through their pursuits into illegal and unconstitutional wars; however, under no circumstance would this mean every single individual in america, from the youth to old, hold responsibility for these actions and absolutely not that individual whom receives the pointing of a finger from the ignorant and superstitious proclamations of the general public, "A witch!" Though the real canary in the coalmine be the fascist foreign military going by the name of ANTIFA terrorizing american citizens primarily in the northeast states since the public down south would justly and promptly kill these jellyfish in self-defense for the things ANTIFA does to the public up north; and, let us not forget ANTIFA fights alongside the head-chopping, Christian murdering, terror group ISIS and Al-CIA-DUH in the Middle East while flying the exact same flags in america and the stupid assholes of this nation have the audacity to existentially continue this threat of our people with the claim that this fascist group wearing the same uniforms, flying the same flags, and performing the same dynamo tactics in america as overseas be stunning and brave and not at all the same group overseas. This lunacy witnessed all throughout america has devolved into veritable civil war in an increasing number of municipalities with Virginian men actively forming militias to meet a United Nations disarmament invasion (individuals even murder one another over hot and spicy chicken sandwiches worth one thousandth a troy ounce of Gold each) while we even witness an exceeding of the murder rate per capita qualifying an area as one in an active state of civil war in the case of Chicago which much of the world today refers to as Chiraq to parallel the fact that more people get killed every month in Chicago than within the borders of the illegal U.S. military occupation of Afghanistan and Iraq combined though the source of such murder in Chicago be that self-evident unconstitutional war on drugs which force the uneducated and the youth into the armies and proxies of the american politician's drug cartels which has created an environment of human trafficking and white van kill-teams disappearing citizens for human experiment and other Satanic ritual sacrifice in what the Satanists term "using up" when referencing the type of attack they enjoy most on their "expendable subjects;" and, how could we not trace the source of this evil back to the unconstitutionality of taxation since government legalizes these wicked illegalities for their self which inspires a monkey-see-monkey-do attitude and even a market to contribute to the personalities turning disgusting evils into a growing market and trade even – with a tourism sector with private Hollywood and other hush-hush elitist parties wherein certain celebrities have openly discussed elite parties wherein expensive tickets purchase entry into watching individuals get murdered; and, an example of this demonic elite party of a few hundred individuals being popularized to the door-knob public is illustrated with video channels on the dark web charging thousands of individuals for entry into a raffle with the winners determining how the *antinomians, associates, Balobians, Black Order, Gnostics, kollective, The Finders, The Seekers, ONA/O9A, nexions, Numinous Way, Rounwytha, or White Star Acception* (or whatever in the hell these targets of spiritual damnation want to call their self) murder an individual and with as many as one dozen individuals per night and per channel being tortured and murdered in secret and on live video feed and in the most unimaginably grotesque, horrifying, and deeply shocking format that would make any sane individual potentially lose their mind though many argue that the people being murdered chose to willfully agree to the matter and though she or he in their agreeance may be joking when they show up to the party though the party is not [joking]: Satanic terrorism is on the rise and it amplifies it's ambiguity and subversion by way of sinister dialectics with playing anti-Christian *insight roles* throughout various groups in society be it Frankism, Hinduism, radical Islam, neo-nazism, national socialism, and even Buddhism (praying on the dupes and less-than-intelligent or "human dross;" is it really any wonder so many socialists despise Christians and then have Buddhist idols all over their home while social media so readily supplies the Internet with the celebratory worship of this false religion) with the aim of destroying western civilization even if that means playing the bad actor in american or european socialist parties, competitor intelligence, terrorist jihad groups, or killing business figures, journalists, and political activists (all encouraged by the group claiming to not be a group) whom pose a threat to the continuance of their illegal acts and operations.

A Colorado Sheriff advised me highway shootings remain a daily occurrence and of course the media will not report such findings since these events contradict the state-news' official narrative of demanding americans open their border without vetting anyone which will cause untold numbers of illegal aliens to overwhelm states like Arizona, California, Colorado, New Mexico, and Texas or even major cities like Chicago so that the interim authority of these regions be unconstitutionally governed by foreign and international bodies inventing ceremonial law, rules, or human statutes which command americans to subvert our own way of life by redefining some and eventually all territory as official ghettos under their pseudonyms such as *sanctuary area* wherein illegal aliens gain free reign and even tax-fueled credit cards by the government for what purpose but to endanger the public (as we had witnessed in the federal government repeatedly bailing out illegal aliens from jail, absolving them of their crime, and setting them free again within the U.S. – literally a god-like class of people or antinomians living outside the rule of law by being protected by antinomians in government whom were voted for by a scourge of antinomians in society whom were raised by antinomians although they fancy their self Liberals or Marxists or Progressives or Socialists which is why none of them will ever associate with Classical Liberalism which is true conservatism) and wreak all sorts of havoc though some illegal aliens (another phrase causing people to be fired from their job and threatened with imprisonment) admittedly do intend to serve God well for the house of the Lord there does exist a literal flood of extortionists and Satanists crashing over america's southern border with no intent but to kill, steal, and destroy; and, the fact that our government has created this catastrophe specifically with the war on drugs can not ever go understated and it is incumbent upon

1. Grace Shao, Christine Wang, Evelyn Cheng, Vivian Kam. "China accuses US of 'sinister intentions' after Trump signs bills supporting Hong Kong protesters." *China Politics*, CNBC, 27 November 2019, https://www.cnbc.com/2019/11/28/china-condemns-us-bills-supporting-hong-kong-protesters.html. Accessed 4 January 2020

americans to end the drug war which really is a war on the american people and has allowed a new world order to emerge from within these series of events, which would not have otherwise occurred without these events, wherein our own government may as well be at Defcon 5 against the american people; China's Foreign Ministry even stated, "It will only make the Chinese people more united and make the American plot doomed to fail," when speaking on the topic of americans resisting their tyrannical subversion of american society thus proving which foreign enemy particularly has successfully occupied our government from within whereby innumerable agencies receive unconstitutional authority to cut our constitution into little pieces and use america as the world empire to keep the entire world in poverty or war and all allowed by the unconstitutionality and Satanic schism of taxation thus the american people must learn the requisite that a people of liberty eliminate every form of taxation by principle and not by books since we of liberty well understand this taxation to be immoral by fact that theft and taxation are synonymous with one another and theft is immoral and this immorality of hiring force to involuntarily steal money from people shall not ever be the progression of society since only the calm of despotism do to their company what no free people would do to their enemy: yeah, the culture that steals for applause; yeah, the rebelling against mom and dad culture by way of extreme insanity and outrage; yeah, the culture that would not even throw a bone to a dog.

America's rocky mountains have long been known to be filled with practicing Satanists, and what a joy for the child and human sex trafficking Satanists to receive seemingly endless amounts of human dross and sacrificial lambs from these undocumented human flesh offerings courtesy of the incompetent assholes hijacking american government so they spend billions of dollars for a marketing campaign in america and the third world to openly invite one point five billion people into the barren and rural lands of america and the heavily populated regions with promises of free stuff; and, in Europe their government literally seize businesses and homes, forcefully kick and punch the citizens in the throat until they leave the premises, change the locks, hire an on-call plumber to respond to toilet-plunger maintenance calls all day, and then move in these government migrants and future voters; and, most of these Satanists coming and going within these mountains hail from Hollywood and other skull and bones, blood and oil, ore and plunder, gold and booty, Ivy-league and elitist-oriented, royal strongholds and institutions, lesser and greater black magic and demonic induction, invitation, invocation, offering, and worship to the frequency and resonance of an artificially intelligent and mechanized system of dungeon-masters, crypt-keepers, chanting gait openers, and puppets offering human blood ritual sacrifice of the children and innocents to feed the system who feeds them the attention of false power; which, an accumulation of articles of fact appear as power but can not be power thus what they source they shamelessly steal from innocence even the occasional lone traveler or political activist whom these Satanists befriend before trapping through deception and slaughtering them as a lamb-offering before a large party of these self-proclaimed Satanists, body-snatchers, sorcerers, spirit killers, vampires, and witches whom revel in their wickedness, worship that dark and dead lord and spirit of Satan, and fill our government offices and medical institutions with their facsimile of people.

Locals of the San Luis Valley speak of Mount Blanca as the center, crown, or central intelligence vortex of ley lines on the earth which the unbelievers and Satanists view as their source of demonic power on the earth while the believers in Christ of this region argue that this mountain be the original and fabled Mount Zion of earth thus the source of controversy in those oppositional spiritual powers of good and evil on the earth and who could compose a more refined argument for the powers of this world than this when considering the course of known historical events and present state of affairs across the world today and the trajectory at which liberty ought to travel when freeing the world from the bondage of sin and slavery: of course that would be the single most defensed mountain range on planet earth; of course; and, who could ignore the american government's innumerable public and secret bases and tunnels implanted within these mountain ranges; all one has to do is drive through the area and enter into certain mountain passes with the radio turned on to receive covert transmissions of secret intelligence classes, for example, a class teaching students about helicopters released to the public in 2000 that were flying surveillance missions as top secret aircraft during The Vietnam War; or stay overnight and witness unexplainable lights (indifferent to the Marfa lights though presumably hyper-advanced technologies acting as aircraft; i.e.: advanced ceramics with a solid state motor made out of exotic magnets which were excavated as a complete craft or machine from earth and not made by men on the earth as far as we know though some argue the monsters beyond the edge of the map come from an inner earth whose entrance is located along Antarctica's sixty to two hundred thousand mile coastline (discounting the potential coastline breaching it's potential perimeter as a bay, harbor, or inward bound sea and it's tributaries and lakes and rivers for example); or even flown today from ancient and deep oceanic bases of indeterminate origin insofar as how one may measure the agencies of a government and find no source of such an agency to possess any such bases or such craft or even such knowledge of such craft which cautions many to seek a source of the intelligence of the use of this craft; and, people then question or turn toward either human beings or another self-imposed super race of human beings or higher beings from within the earth and jettisoning from the depths of the ocean and into our skys and beyond into intergalactic space, or maybe all they do is interdimensional or metaphysical, and even further magnitudes of energetic order or rather what the Bible describes as the fashion and patterns thereof or famous physicists spoke of when referencing the enfolding and unfolding orders of the universe and this infiniteness of the expanse of our universe compels us to logically reason the idea of our individual liberty and the infinite source and evidence of truth under God that we with our liberty do oppose a self-imposed royalty even if or whether they come from a castle or the royals are truly shape-shifting reptilian squid whose eggs were barnacled upon the rocks of certain asteroid and meteor showers and whose falling and burning like stars into our ocean did heat and awaken the hatchlings in order that the alien race occupy the depths of hell on this planet in sub-ocean super-bases with trillions of beings and for millions of years at a time shall they reign unless in a moment's notice the public shall enlighten to the philosophy of liberty and only when such a world endeavor to attain this feat will they then have so interwoven composure with form that the very functions of society from travel to trade will reflect the liberty which is that select treatment of the individual which stands in total contradiction of that which we see through political factions at war with one another since they possess the word of freedom but not the idea of liberty and what Jesus Christ much more greatly did for this world above all of the others; magnitudes beyond the prophets so infinite that His magnitude be the alpha and omega of infinity). These fallen fiefs arise again with the name of thief so that their demand of taxation be of the same oppression and origin as their tyrannical ancestor's of monarchy; and even, herein, the state of the world be such that tyrannical monarchy be the most blinding illumination of phrasing a redundancy thus we know the people must be early and often reminded of why we rise and fight; and, why they live.

The civil war happening in slow motion today in america manifests in many other ways, though, unlike america's first civil war of uniforms and battle-lines; rather, we witness a clash of philosophy causing untold tens of millions of job loss, assault, and violence wherein the overwhelming majority of this violence stem from these wicked spirits seeking to abolish america and our bill of rights and even the free-minded individual when they so encounter the individual who with ease identifies and witnesses their true identity beyond that spiritual veil of physical, mental, and spiritual pomp and vanity: yeah, The Federal Reserve has perched our economy into that most precarious trap of facing total economic collapse, verily any day now lest the awakening accelerate and drive us into liberty, and God knows what horrors shall unfold then. These wicked devils live their lives as The Bible describes they will do and that means progressively following the forward trail of blood toward their own destruction in an attempt to take the free world with them. This civil war appear as a gradual slide into tyranny and as a landslide does accelerate the image of alarm witnessed by the believers to sharpen their steadfastness and evade the famine. Homelessness, illness, suicide (many farmers), family suicide, group suicide, ritual sacrifice-suicide – events exponentially increasing their frequency with the decay and degeneracy of american society with such force that no statistic accurately portray the truth of our present great depression without this aid of literature whose hope be in Christ Jesus to shed light into the world and convey His love to those individuals imprisoned in the realm (whose entry require the turning away from Him) with such power that He shock the heart of the dead unto that awakened discernment whose only inclination be to build on the last standing rock: yeah, for the defense of human liberty.

Traveling around america from the years 2015 to 2019 I had witnessed individuals and entire families by the masses living in their automobiles along river-ways and washing their clothes in buckets before hanging their clothes to dry in nearby trees; and, even living in Wal-Mart parking lots by the hundreds within one's own field-of-view and by the dozens of lots and tens of thousands of people per som aught capita; and, even parked by the thousands along the neighborhood roadways near town; and, what about the people living in entire tent cities springing up in every public space imaginable; and, even homeless shelters so full that it's outdoor sidewalk refrain from abandoning the drunk, broken, sad, sleepy, and wandering people and zombies; even the sidewalks and parking lots across the street from the homeless shelters remain lined with a caterpillar-like tent-city snaking through the downtown sector with contaminated dog, cat, rat, and human feces mixed about filth and diseased intravenous needles strewn about every pathway even as though it's creep flow about the ground as a red-carpet welcoming even more vehicles lining up as a form of emergency housing; and even people sleeping under park shrubs or in an office-lot tree; sleeping bags and tents of illegal aliens springing up along our Texas creeks; every underpass and overpass clamoring with cold and hungry souls and many of them even having some type of work though the monthly rent across the nation rise at a rate that no good answer come about when figuring how do people keep paying five or ten times the rate of rent from a mere ten years ago and how does homelessness and job loss increase at the same rate these apartments fill and how does the rent equal seven or even ten times the average income today and what brazen idiot can not track all of this economic terrorism to the unconstitutional Federal Reserve system, it's fiat currency, and our duty to abolish it so that we return the economic sovereignty into the hands of the righteous people for which it belongs; an uncertainty of which has narrowly instituted unstable work environments even with employers enjoying their newfound ability to hire and fire a completely new staff several times per quarter, corporations borrowing debt to create the illusion of profitability, and all of the while being proud of their self for losing money by the hour as they witness their own way of life engulfed in the all-consuming fire of political correctness ("We refuse to hire millennials!" Most boomers believe all millennials have no skills whatsoever and show up to public venues everywhere with headphones and gadgets attached to every part of their body like Inspector

Gadget.) even as it were they publicly stood about the street and asked of the public to light the flame for the petrol dumped about their body. As if the homelessness crisis were not bad enough it is now being recorded in Austin, Texas and Florida that the United Nations is now micro-chipping homeless individuals (mark of the beast) as a gateway into the cashless society wherein this chip allows them so-call free access to food, shelter, travel and supplies; couple this with the super-hotels being built in the Middle-East with ten thousand rooms, seventy restaurants, and presumably only a handful of entry and exit points and it is easy to paint a picture of a future wherein the people are kept as chattel by a world-elite while they slowly merge with the machine in which gradually replaces their physical body – actually the list is for an effective checklist system and this is all a conspiracy theory and everyone should turn their television on and shut up.

One morning I even witnessed a man and woman with six young children climbing out of the sleeper cabin of a new pickup truck. Only a fool would travel unarmed in these day's of impoverished desperation, as we witness the corporate mercenaries send in their death squads to shoot our public places, schools, churches, and businesses, or place their entire family in such dire straits that any discerning man knows that family stands a high risk of robbery or killing by mafia for kicks or loot or other vagrant lunatics and outside of america of course we see this mafia and wandering vagrant lunatics quite literally driving the nations of the world into the ground; and, as such we must remind our fellow americans of the origin of our gun rights being rooted in self-preservation from the mafia and every other form of tyranny since we follow Jesus Christ and not their dead idols; of course; of course; of course. Peace officers all across this nation randomly and indiscriminately discharge their weapons in the general direction of the public at-will; for example, a man in Austin, Texas stepped out of His vehicle upon request and with His highly-visible brown leather wallet casually in-hand (and this must be noted to underscore the political gerrymandering of words as the tyrants use any excuse to claim law enforcement safety be their reason for the termination of our Bill of Rights and even the termination of our life which has created such a displacement of civility that the federal government may as well had already codified into law the necessity for the citizen to perform some type of ritualistic jitterbug dance to disarm the aggression of their government robot designed to charge every crime as guilty until proven innocent which has resulted in many people spending more than one decade in prison without ever having been convicted or seen before a jury of their peers, asking questions later and never now, and scooping the citizens into and through the unconstitutional justice matrix so the unthinkers get paid, the citizen become extinct, and america fade as a distant memory with the story of this realm spiritually turned over to the submission of gas-lighting and placating of the self with every type of fantasy except when it appertain the open exercise of wickedness as legalized governance which they will never go to the length of offending Satan by not perfecting His ways as they genuflect and giggle at the opportunity to deliver their overlords commanding them to dishonor God and country in being the boots on the ground for the new world order while simultaneously cackling or onerously smirking at the believers with the eyes whom toll: "Question me not or die now. Believe the lies or die. Speak truth before me and I will show you the darkness of demons I cultivate. Show me not the light lest you be mobbed.)" at His side and the peace officer immediately quick-drew His firearm and fired at the man one or multiple shots; and, although the two men stood ten feet apart this incompetent public servant shot clear over the still man's head – something which no clear-minded, discerning, and healthy man could ever achieve without Himself first being fired upon. And – speaking of scoops: northwestern territories in america have planned to compost human bodies and no longer bury or burn them which does create a business out of using humans as plant fertilizer thus inspiring a demand or market-share for an increase in production of human flesh; and, please: spare the attempt of convincing me Satan did not directly summon this inverted care for the dead or that this does not threaten the biological health or moral parallels of society or does not reflect some type of black magic ritual of reversing thousands of generations of best practices whose practices were discovered through the abominable failure of this pseudo-intellectual movement to upend the most base elements of common sense; and, in fact even government-subsidized military manufacturers have invented entire fleets of autonomous body scooping vehicles (presumably with on-board processing for complete disposal or final kill mechanisms) for the battlefield truly showing the ominous direction of technology in our world which was depicted in the 1973 film Soylent Green wherein the government uses up the public, or human dross, as a source of food; and, this technology does not even spell-out the horror which the technocrats wish to employ in order to take humanity down with them: technology is currently being pursued wherein an autonomous and gelatinous blob moves about absorbing, consuming, and digesting organic matter and converting this energy into more gelatin causing it to grow without stopping in size and presumably even causing it to consume ever larger materials like people, entire forests, cities, states, planets, solar systems, and galaxies. Focus, attention-span, empathic, peaceful, and a sympathetic nature: all of these qualities of a free society flee america causing a dark winter to infringe on every good conscience.

Millions of individuals all across this nation currently and have already packed up and moved to another country or state in what appears as a mass exodus out of communism. The interstate highway systems designed by President Eisenhower have suffocated what little economy remains in the rural parts of america as the highway exits continue to be literally removed from accessing small towns and private industry or moved far enough away from the town that it inconveniences or confuses anyone whom would wish to seek it's township for business or trade before continuing in their travels thus illuminating an effective implementation of sanctioning private economy and foreign attrition for the starvation of what little private economy remains in this whored-out and utterly decimated american republic; and, none can argue that the multitude of small towns, which be the overwhelming look of america, appear as bombed-out villages rotting to pieces with only one or two military-industrial-complex-owned fuel stations per borough, commonweal, commonwealth, county, parish, state, or territory with the remaining work in the area being related to and subsidized by the materials sector of this military-industrial-complex (e.g., gas and oil). This economic malfeasance forces individuals into the global corporate funnel as individuals skip over the towns and spend their money in the larger cities and specifically at the international corporate places of business which vacuum money out of the local economy and into the hands of the foreign nations which accelerate the deflation of american economy thereby encouraging the rogue central bank to inflate the currency and continue the deflation of the gross value of the american dollar; and, all the while more and more youth enter the work-force year after year only to experience a market which was designed to punish and even prohibit creativity in order to destroy the american dollar and society and never so apparent as the more than one hundred percent drop in value of the american dollar since the creation of The Federal Reserve system in 1913. Austrian economist Peter Schiff even spoke on the topic of the american dollar dropping a measurable eight percent in value during the twelve months from 2017 to 2018 – an additional eight percent on top of it's ninety-eight percent drop in value since the 1913 Federal Reserve Act which gave rise to the immoral and unlawful fractional reserve banking system – a fancy name for an institution designed to steal, kill, and destroy we the people; for how else could Gold move from eighteen dollars per ounce to eighteen hundred dollars per ounce unless by theft of international proportion.

Hyper-inflation remains the new normal and the public keeps largely unaware of the origin of the business-cycle and how the printing of fiat money violates their contract and trust with their government – a government of whom have through the exercise of this theft they call fractional reserve banking or quantitative easing: abandoned their oath to the constitution, foregone their trust in God, and gambled their hedgings on the television programming elucidating their darkened fog of translucent silvery nightshades for the fancying of a nightmare which eliminate free people (whom stead fast to the work which invest the interests of God and the mystery of His energy working in the lives of men); thus, the enemy wanting to conquer the spirit of the Lord withdraw their self-awareness for bending, kissing, and submitting to wicked men. The individuals enslaved within this beast system of wretched spiritual torment will never admit they lack the discernment to reorder their lives since that act would demand of them to accept Jesus Christ into their heart and expose the system which design hostilities against our liberties and primarily with the sabotage of imagination wherever it arise which does mean the summoning of sorcery against the flame of human liberty and continuity of their war of worlds for a perpetual new world order wherein the people come to worship their captivity for bread, circus, false heroisms, and every calm of despotism causing the eyes of the people to dim and droop.

Mainstream media, entertainment, psychiatrists, psychologists, Senators, Congressmen, Legislators, Judges, students, teachers, professors, journalists, reporters – every stratum of society now openly declares (with the veiled threat of government persecution to support their claim) the belief in God as a mental illness; thus, we [according to the unbelievers] must assume the position and forcefully submit to the reasoning embarking on the formation of government concentration or detainment or reeducation camps for the imprisonment of free-thinking individuals lest they accept the new way of thinking in this new world order (and never-mind the empty and emergency federal government facilities discovered with hundreds of thousands of war-time caskets and fleets of United Nations combat vehicles nor the one half million foreign troops training on U.S. soil at any given time nor the daily atmospheric, oceanic, and underground nuclear detonation testing nor the chemical spraying which blots out the sun and discolors our horizons). The revolving door so historically prevalent in it's quarantining individuals for the act of speech or thought has infringed upon the civil liberty of mankind throughout all of our written history but as well there have stood men fighting to assemble, engage, and forge society against these tyrannical forces whose intent openly contradict happiness and liberty (i.e. "No; we will not have any liberty; but, what we will have for you [sharpening snivels of cacklingness] ... "). These people that would enslave society to no freedom of speech or religion assume citizenship means correcting to the edict of the higher authority in the palace and any objection to their insolent demands require the security of a military to protect their egoic insecurity thus opining the illusion of hardened enforcement of the self-evident act wrestling my liberty as though it intends on submitting my will for the wearing of a mind without the sanity of individuality or questioning of oppositional forces and their nature of barren defiance toward the power of God's wisdom and history of Jesus Christ even going so far as to commit the acts of burning books with military authorization for a targeted erasure and subterfuge of the circles of influence surrounding the primary and secondary layer of influencers dispersing or adhering to the like or opposing circles of influence in order to blockade the modulation of information whether sanctioning or erasing individuals (shadow-banning or even assassination) or their accessing information within the entire mind that we call Internet and with the use of it's tyrannical Google operating system coupled with it's eastern and western hemispheric directives of Facebook and Twitter acting as the primary and secondary layers of online covert action for gathering or sanctioning information in order to discard or keep individual learning within or without a likeness or opposition to the conformity or narrative bias of censorship or promotion of ideas or individuals or information in real-time as the algorithm identifies, redefines, or discovers an emerging test case or likeness of a predefined archetype for the granting of certain access or permissions request for some type of Internet access or views (e.g., manipulating the population of public listings and hiding true measures of popularity to control or steer or stifle narratives while even applying this model to predicting or preventing world events) which does create an atmosphere of official censorship and control of the minds within society for none reason more rightly defined as propagandizing the american people unto the criminalization of their civil liberty; or, rather, the murder of mankind's truth in destiny. This intellectual segregation of government involuntarily enforcing the funding of information forces the technocracy to group society into towers of control in the same like manner that one could separately classify a blue, green, red, or yellow window for the creation of a target by which the algorithms war-game against and whose powers be promoted for the cause of robbing, killing, and stealing all of the hopes and dreams from the people of the world; the ability to with greater ease drive a coup without blood, create chaos where there be none, and accelerate the interdimensional rip which opens the declarative gaits of primal hell.

The manufacture of this ugly and disdainful world-view has produced in america a nation of adolescent-like adults legalizing child sacrifice wherein the state of Virginia executes children after birth, even a week or month later (and with discussions of up to age three which segways into death committees ordering the killing of senior citizens and eventually all citizens for whatever reason the wicked men in government decide), under the guise of abortion (doctors literally tossing and mangling living and crying babies into painter's buckets like automotive parts or "keep'n'um'comf'fa'ble," said with the hostility of a Frenchman from Louisiana occupying Virginia governorship while most other states even rip them from the wound and then violently stab them with steel weapons through their skull while the infant literally punches and fights (video of this even from the womb) for what amounts to intentional chumming of their brains and maiming of the innocent child's life unto physical torture and then death before then chopping their body parts into prepared pieces and throwing them on a bed of ice for legal human trafficking markets and overwhelmingly these practices be advertised as a solution for "Empowering women..." on print or media with the force of an interdimensional insurgency though this is particularly marketed toward the African american community since Margaret Sanger is the dear leader of the very racist abortion proponents of whom are mostly rich white liberal women with a lesbian girlfriend or feminist boyfriend (Who can continue to believe what these tattooed alligators speak? Feminism and eugenics have verily merged as one. Sub-cultures within feminism have even emerged wherein people popularize the sharing of diseases so along with wife-swapping there is bug-swapping.) and alongside advertisements with photos of women smiling as they watch soft puppies roll in the cool grass of a hot afternoon as their ninety-pound effeminate white husband in the background sports His new beard-implant while drinking craft beer and holding His eyes and mouth wide-open (soy face [excess of estrogen hormones from soy consumption (Starbucks lattes; illuminati logo; symbology; occultic power structure)]) for a photo with His protandric hermaphroditical monastic gender lesbian tri-christian-curious-evangelist friend Desmond Sparkles who recently turned right of left to left to right to be more climate-change active by like and such and such with the plane flying to the third-world country and the such as and the like-like but my district is litter and poverty and the such as with the mud-hut in the foreign country and the twitter photo such-as; which, in turn has produced the unintended consequence of a mafia-controlled market of child sex trafficking and mass organ harvesting which does include the Satanic Chinese Communists and their state-sponsored mobile kill-vans and organ-harvesting prison-camps into this carnivorous feast – a network of spiritually rotten dynasties feeding on the public as their bread-offering from their false God; also, speaking of Virginia – this state has recently proposed a bill to declare firearms and martial arts training as an act of terrorism which of course will be considered an add-on to the unconstitutional Patriot Act so that any american citizen in the eyes of Virginia (and growing national support?) must be disappeared into one of america's many unconstitutional concentration camps including the death camps at Guantanamo Bay. So-call climate-change activists literally reference transgenderism as a solution to earth's changing climate (which means mentally-retarded people using the authority of government to reclassify their gender by personal choice) which they claim as man-made and therein lies their open secret: "Haioouowl*daaahhewyhhooeyyoaue* [man];" the evil upon the earth which must be eradicated by a government army in the name of saving the climate; and, while all of this sounds ludicrous the so-call climate change activists literally have called for reeducating the public into the idea that heterosexuality (human procreation) must be eradicated to repair earth's climate; and they take this idea even further calling heterosexuality "delusions of heterosexism" or "heteronormativity" as the cause for society wrongly viewing every other form of sex as deviant (sex with earthworms is absolutely deviant) and all other sorts of invented names and psychological warfare tactics of obscuring the intent of their purpose in being the demoralization and genocide squad formed against mankind; and, what this has to do with climate change self-evidences nothing at all lest of course we follow through with their insidiously false logic that their occultic reasoning mandates the stopping of human reproduction world-wide and of course this will result in the end of mankind therefore the saving of this so-call climate catastrophe when looking from the soap box of those eyes bent on the centralization of power via converting by color of law the deviancy of society into a maximum of false principles whereby false flags, hoaxes, or superstitions govern the perception of reality; for example, *Smolletting* wherein a fake hate-crime is used to steer public opinion or personally gain; also, much of this being backed up by their own claims that not only does this squad teach society to hate men but that being a man exhibits toxic masculinity therefore universities must be paid by government to force-feed stupid teachings to the most bright individuals of society for their eradication and therein lies the entry into the debate of genociding men and cloning human-beings as mechanized and weaponized test-tube subjects stowed away or in a state of preparation awaiting these military orders demanding cyborg-robots defend this babylon dungeon of legislative matrix, machine, or grid of neural-network systems with the mask of fake A.I. given legislative-powers to algorithmically automate the governance of society while superimposing the totally false idea that this control is not infinitely enfolded and unfolded upon itself but rather this notion realizes in the same instant a society with the total removal of self-governance therefore the total illusion of self-governance and within the bondage of tyrannical forces dehumanizing and mechanizing logic and reason; and, what do they mean necessarily about toxic masculinity but the ability to discern, exhibit, and succeed the goodness of God and to perfectly hate the sinking ship of Lucifer and Her damned fools. On the one hand the american government encourages the murder of american children and on the other hand a mass of individuals whom claim they support pro-life do send their youth off to take up arms and fight in illegal wars overseas; wars so terrible that moderate figures estimate three to seven million innocents were killed by this so-call act of democracy from american government while naming the loss of the life "collateral damage" (an idea as moderate as the incorrect and so-call idea of *moderate rebels* fighting in The Middle East; a phrasing which we do ridiculously hear so often stupidly mentioned by the [mainstream media] press or government puppets; ignorantly repeated to keep hidden the fact these moderate rebels invented savagery and american [allies] government funded this terroristic military operation in conjunction with foreign powers hijacking the american government to usurp our liberty and produce endless, global, and overseas war and all of this hinged on the fact the american people love to lie and sleep and delight in the sleep that worships the world without understanding the philosophy of liberty and do their eyes and face not say it all when any one of them shall realize peace and prosperity is the only way and not an artifact of heresy) and the hypocritical fake conservatives claim the number of dead innocents was only one half of one million – the psychology of the fake conservative: "Thou shall not kill my youth until age of eighteen and only then can they die without cause after they fly overseas to fight illegal, unconstitutional, and undeclared wars to murder the youth of foreign lands for reasons which no sane individual could ever honestly believe;" thus, this scenario exhibit the blow-back and kinetic action caused by blind emotion and unthinking Stockholm Syndrome; and, all of this – for what: to stifle domestic and foreign economy, sanction information domestically, and extract foreign resources to enrich the wicked rulers thus enslaving the civilized world to the spiritually deaf and dumb world-view of accepting life as a thing devoid of the philosophy of liberty; therefore, the innocent and strong must give way to this playground for wicked men experimenting on mankind as we were laboratory rats and not spiritual fountains of infinite creation.

If subservient and slave-like be what the new world order wants out of us – then not in america or any society rightly discerning liberty shall they enter into without the fire eyes of the holy reading the eyes that lie. Those individuals whom name their self a political party form this holy crap of democratism which trades in the market of warfare and welfare and stands as that force of democratic parliamentary Monarchy in total opposition against america and human liberty. All logic of the lie reasons that mankind's total spiritual enslavement under a collectivist mob exhibits the true spiritual expression of humanitarianism and if any articulation shall be spoken for the devising of a society without this commital act of state-sponsored violence or coercion then this source of interventionism must be met with state prosecution. The true expression of our true God does bare the reality of a prohibition of involuntary taxation and today's macabre argument against sovereignty does not unconfirm our duty and right to assemble and declare null and void this infringement upon individual liberty; only when true discernment permeates society will that society experience the true liberty of truly prosperous and truly peaceful association. The rulers have deprecated even the most foundational aspects of our rule of law by blaming the second amendment for the wickedness of men thus pitting against americans hoards of drooling boors flocking like the locust to consume the substance of our economy and overthrow the sustenance of our reality so clearly outlined in the Bill of Rights while at the same time literally awarding their most idiotic cult members attempting to erase the second amendment with Bill of Rights awards at civil liberty award ceremonies (pure laughing-stock blasphemy) from the rogue so-call civil liberty unions whose devotion to liberty be as honest as the devil claiming to discover truth in the teachings of Satan. This is a simple program of the left: (1) take away our second amendment,

(2) fill our streets up with police in an attempt to compensate for law and order, (3) make the people worship the police-state, (4) and, finally purge the divergents. We even witness illegal aliens and paid provocateurs senselessly murdering people, even being freed of the crime, while our politicians use these isolated incidents as cannon fodder to rail their own constituents with famine-level taxation. These cowardly and deranged lunatics even claim that the defense of the second amendment exists as a conspiracy theory promoted by Russia when no further stretch of the imagination or impossibility could ever unfold since the Russians lust for an even greater disappearance of their soul into the abyss of Communism; and, all of the while the american people verily enjoy to keep their liberty and keep those literal bastard Communists from infringing their shoddy ideas into our liberty thereby making it self-evident those individuals whom champion the dissolution of our civil liberty be the Communists and enemy that Christ and our forefathers spoke of and the enemy be not us whom manifestly in this life proclaim liberty to the captives of tyranny in God's eternal quest for us to tread down that intemperate and vicious facsimile of justice and truth. How do these people review history and not realize democide as the number one cause of death throughout all of recorded civilization except to ignore history, hate knowledge, and persecute the champions of history, knowledge, and our God?

An epidemic of individuals today work to actively usurp america without the mildest depth of historical or practical knowledge otherwise known as common sense since this army of usurpers dismisses history in order to fit their context of usurpations for the honoring of their overlords promising them stylish rewards for plundering the society of liberty: yeah, even fake voices of authoritative condescension purchasing an ability to know less and persecute ever more. Spiritual illness manifests itself as physical war and unfortunately this blight does plague our world. I can not help but think time and again america was based on equal rights and this battle for human liberty has waged since the dawn of man. The questions appertaining humanity's origin certainly frighten much of the population into conforming into ignorant and superstitious worldlings and this does especially include the practice of religious impurity or simply tyranny which distinctly separate itself from the religious purity of liberty thus the dishonest evade the reality of such an idea in order that they further separate their self from confronting the genesis of feelings associated with darkness, nothingness, void, and the time separating our life from death and that existence without earthen awareness; and, sadly enough, they miss the opportunity to overcome the darkness and witness the light and experience in the glory and joy of Jesus Christ and His love for we the people: yeah, that force in which men enforce God's commandments and introduce the world to true authority and power appearing before them as free men engaging in their duty to appeal to God before men and to do the things which ought must be done against the spite of the face without reflection and whose tyrannical soothsaying fashions mystic armies against our worship of the divine God; and, today contributes to what can only best be described as a nation treading heavily in deep waters as it were even an eclipsing of the foreshadowings of exodus and witnessing of destruction upon the multitude: yeah, many, many revelations with all roads being traced to central banks funding endless and unconstitutional war (not "all roads being, um, traced to, um, Saudi Arabia and, um, China, um, therefore, um, we, um, must, um, logic into *teh*, um, World War III, um, Iran, um, *teh*, war on terror, um, and the like such as and the such like, um."), lobbying of spys to infiltrate and occupy the seats of america's representative government, and ensnare political society with every type of highway robbing, secret killing, sabotage, and all for the aiming to keep a superstitious public within the confines of a fear-laden flood of fabricated emotions demanding dead statues rise above the living creator and destroy western civilization by way of shutting down Christianity through the state-sponsored preservation and promotions of Buddhusim, Hinduism, Neo-Nazism, and Islam in order to hide the obvious force at war against Jesus Christ: Satanism. The articulation of the vision of liberty would according to the wicked mafia be the sole motivation for their culling of mankind into a watery grave; contrarily that articulation act as the fuel for He whom contains within His vested interest the duty to exercise His powers for the revolution of the spirit of the Lord. The idea in america today or for anywhere in the world for that matter that we must conform to the hostility of vicious intemperance and surrender our liberty for a life without images and words ought to compel any sentient individual to rise up and pursue that happiness which God

[678]

delivered us authority in completing. One can not remove the rights of the individual without restricting that individual's life from having access to their liberty; and, under the authority of God's almighty vision for our individual life which does remain inseparable from that gift of life in which God imparted to us at conception and with His full authority to combine life and liberty to be His property and not subjects to some parliamentary democracy pretending to war against Monarchy while at the same time raising a standing army within a republic under God for the criminalization of the individual's liberty.

We witness today the hell of that realm in which the alien occupiers of our liberty do build in self-evident matters; for example: the selling of our rights and divesting of our foundational strength via the immorality of taxation, or the sending of lethal weapons to foreign nations when the american citizen would have purchased spiritual weapons otherwise and of which would be ten thousand times more powerful than any theft of public funds which does enable immoral decisions of government rats behind closed doors for the animation of fleets of mechanized Valkyrie-squid determining who lives and dies ... while the moral approach would be the people and not the government choosing and purchasing supplies for a foreign nation; and, especially when our own nation be in such peril that our countrymen require every bit of our mutual assistance for how else could we be of the spirit if we allow our government to steal our funds and ship away our energy while claiming our problems be our own to solve and not their corruptions as though we stood incapable of thinking of where the enemy sit within society as He enlist government violence to thieve mankind's destiny; though these hobgoblins pretend to challenge the intellect – they can only steal one's time and alter the course of the destiny whose time they stole therefore the path of the hero is that path of paying for the sins of the people. These psychopathic thieves claiming their uniform protects them from america's rule of law or that my liberty be a hostile alien does encourage our God to move against their attempted seizure of the alpha and omega powers of society – powers which I and my God reserve the duty to preserve in order that we reprove liberty in a republic as the keepers of life and property and wager of spiritual war against their theft and fraud causing impure government and religion to be involuntarily imposed on the people. A market well-regulated by the citizens will naturally well-regulate their militia to keep their government from the disorder of underhanded dealings inherently opposed to peaceful and prosperous human action.

The description and the discernment of the citizen and the individual requires the individual to keep steadfast to seeing crime as a self-evident form of theft or fraud and knowing markets as a sovereignty of the individual and phenomenal mystery of this realm; we the people decide what currency we wish to use and government shall not have any say in currency thus the hand and role of economic and foreign fate, policy, and power ought to be and rest in the care of God's people. The ruling elite obtain foreign interest to divide and conquer mankind with militarily enforced injustice as we witness with the rising police state across america wherein our federal government intentionally and wittingly designs hostilities over our liberties, including not protecting and serving citizens, and, instead standing down to violent mobs curb-stomping young women, government standing down during school shootings, and burning businesses and homes in the case of the intelligence agencies' psychological operation: "the black lives matter movement," (which was absolutely promoted by the technocracy to inspire copy-cats and inflate the occurrence of a thing which was not at present-time a thing which then contributes to the new world order's wider false narrative of there being a national crisis where there was not one before; and, no, not at all was there a long-standing global crisis which our forefathers knew and warned of with the hope and prayers that we the people of this earth would assemble and defend against the tyrannical assault on our liberty in order that we proclaim liberty to the nations of the earth and witness them cover their people with all glory and power of God). The central banks and standing armies even today work desperately to collectivize mankind into governments of theft and plunder rather than we self-declare sovereignty under God (sovereign unto God's government and not the inventions of hostility shame-dumping an entire nation to wage war against ten million free thinkers whom would rather not have five hundred million more undocumented illegal aliens show up for a godhood-ticket combined with voting rights so none shall miss out on the opportunity to illegally vote for more free stuff and have sixty-six children per woman at a spa-like government hatchery, "I make you more baby. Please; sir, I can no has some more cola...;" of these wicked men set about their day to shatter dreams and seek the misery for which their father in hell promises for being good little boys in spitting venom at the men of God) to do His will even justifying our position of illumination winning the war against those individuals collectivizing in order that they impose war over us while attempting to shame us into their choosing of death and not liberty thus we fight their tyrannical advances which they will always fail to disguise as anything not a totalitarian push with their literal raising of their voice to match the increasing frequency at which they proudly and shamelessly invent lies with the delusion that they placate, end the imagination, or deaden the nerves of their victim or satisfy or patch up the thing which pulls them up thereby preventing them from never amounting to anything truly honest: a double-minded cult with a lie in one hand and a body-bag in another as the wicked all idly lie in wait for the orders from their idol demanding they skewer the men comprising this civil republic so that none more shall stand to correct their wicked ways, and, yea, we stand fully aware of the purpose for which God delivered us into fulfilling with full self-awareness of that knowledge concerning God's ancient, eternal, and historical opposition to that very cult of death living on today as a gestating and cultish association of dumb, confused, and disempowered worldlings worshiping the light of God through the colored darkly of idolatry therefore entirely missing the discernment for which delivers them salvation and not their present intentions of worshiping the carnal spiritual structure, which does compel them to constantly display a carnal mating strategy designed to breed and grow the kingdom of Satan to even more lazily sacrifice a diminishing God-fearing people, endeavor to learn even greater the arts of deception within their corporate religions of atheism, naturalism, or part-time-Christianism which all creates the coldness of a power vacuum only a wicked ruler could know to operate for the continuance of His oligarch and their divide and conquer tactics inflicted upon civilization as their subjects line up to stand in a three-way brawl of determining whose superstition be the champion of the Sunday matinee – and all on the day that Christ ought to be fully celebrated and revered by the breaking of bread of His church with all glory given to His victory so self-evidently manifest in our lives. The winner of the oligarch's imaginary war delivers precedent to one group over another thus templating the hierarchy of secret authority and it's issuing of black magic keys in the form of one group of individuals being granted authority to do what the other groups can never do thus this unequal rights be the governance of systems for which so many americans today claim to defend as an american system though narrowly all of them have no idea the word liberty even exists and this inflection of reason can not go understated or without fiery exclamation.

The individuals presently consuming the substance of america believe society be a pie which so-call authorities in government must split into chambers of easily controllable and even consumable class systems for the scaffolding of their authoritarian rule. The realm in which God designs remains unperturbed by the evils of this universe therefore only our fear of man and not God alters the perception of the present realm into the disorder of a civilization forging ahead without the love of God. The neo-classical philosophers of today whom truly represent the synagogue of Satan argue one must only imagine without any action to enter the realms in which they choose or imagine possible as though we lived in a world of scrying and not intention; for example: the peaceful world without the threat of violence, coercion, theft, or fraud; and, this act of pledging allegiance to that faction of projectionists (and most notably within the democrat party today and also contained within the operatives planted in the libertarian and republican political parties) and though this opposition to reality exist across the spectrum of political ideology it does grow with the force of corporate, covert, and public funding in the case of government delivering billions of dollars to universities in order that psychological warfare operatives disguised as college professors experiment with designer drugs on expendable subjects at unconstitutional and secret bases domestically and abroad or public universities and even all across the occupied republic of Texas; and, while all of this pseudo philosophy of accepting idleness be the governance of systems which collectivists mandate for the burial of the perfect law of liberty and sanctioning of God's commandments and coercing a free people to fight or die for the deeds which God Himself demands be done to deliver the innocent from this state of bondage. The highest irony of this notion rests in the fact the progenitors of this philosophy root their self into a fallen and destitute place of vibration similar to those nations which they claim to supersede and should they visit these more fallen nations they shall not discover the philosophers of liberty in hiding in hope of building a swell from within the nation which overwhelm the hearts of their people and lower the weapons against the framers of free thought; nay, the philosophers of liberty wield their weapon of speech in public and that speech be the declarative proclamation of liberty to the captives of tyranny. No matter their falsities of naturalism which openly deny God – their proof will eternally remain that of a series of individuals spiritually enslaved to babylon. Men of high character and liberty will assemble and stand as an army in the streets speaking truth for necessity of audible vibration which the crisis of today warrants as a call to action for any discerning people whom see the weakness of the tyrant and understand the excellence of exercising God's disciplines through the open rebuking of wicked men and their strongholds formed against us as self-evident revelations show us that they intend to displace us and destroy or silence us and even quiet the spirit of the Lord upon the land; truly, exercising one's God-given rights is out-smarting the state. The outright fearfulness, paranoia, and blatant brainwashing of the people today all remain literally convinced the world will end in five to twelve years due to their religion which so often changes names as we had already witnessed with 'global warming' and then 'man-made climate change' and then 'climate change' and now 'heteronormativity-made climate change;' and, although this fascist mass of mask-wearing black-and-red-flag-bearing-think-green-police politically shield their self with mentally incapacitated children as their political hawks being forced to read purely partisanal messages (which so readily attach to the pleasure stimuli of stupid people) from a teleprompter and for the announcement of a one world government without freedom of religion or speech: we the people continue the work of exposing their charade of hostility against logic and reason. This force of tyrants presently work to sacrifice the people or convict us for defending our self from their original and intentional aggression of infringing on our persons, houses, papers, and effects with even politically targeting us economically through the fraud of libeling our character and enlisting an army of blood-drunk dragons and carnivorous ostriches to sabotage the commutativity of we the believers thus we to a certain degree remain spiritually invisible to these tone-deaf unbelievers as they run about in their mob of killers pursuing the death of innocent people as though human beings were their test subjects to expend thus proving their minds were programmed from an off-world entity constituting them with a monarchical force which only knows no other design but the implementation of hostility against civil liberty and ignorance of our strength in assembly: yeah, blasphemy so stupendous that one's witness even thunders in defiance against the self-evident inversion applied to common sense as a coercive justification for their injustices upon our civil society.

I once phoned into a local emergency phone-line, this event also occurred while Ubama was in office and this declarative can not go understated since it's diction governed a strong atmosphere of silent obedience and paranoid avarice and fearful intemperance, only to be hung up on not once but seven times in a row with seven different dispatchers before the eighth department responded to my call to action; the timid dispatchers whom hung up on me said my voice was too serious and they did not like my audibly urgent inflection (articulate and passionate inflection is now a crime: dotingly whisper like all of the other dotards or die is this beast's only and final warning; these enemies are very advanced NPC's – like lobsters marching toward the ceremonial sea shelf suicide while carrying any divergents with them) or rather this scenario all frightened them too much and made it apparent to them that I was somehow forcing them into the vagueness of an intellectual fetal position or compelling them to reveal their true nature as a simpering baby incapable of acting like a human adult:

"What's the matter? You do not understand why being serious was criminalized under the new-think laws and how literal nazi hate-speech and scared and triggered your seriousness causes us simpering babies to simper like babies while our simpers wail through the night because your violence of hate-speech persists and we know what you do to be total affirmation of hate-speech because your mouth opens and my ear hears the tone of speech without the sound of words?"

– who in the hell hires for or works within an emergency capacity only to then with ease mentally crumble as I had witnessed in their child-like voice and general stupidness devoid of all discernment, resourcefulness, and seriousness of an adult; that type of naked idiot would even search for the question mark after a rhetorical statement in order to further justify their own stupidity in the stupid conversations they conduct with their self as some sort of justification for their proclivity to escape self-awareness and as though their Buddha idol gave them some formidable or omniscient enlightenment to grace the world with their abominably pathetic and submissive inaction during global crisis (this slug even arrogantly claim giving recognition to emergency is an invention of the mind and not a reality: truly wicked muppets – the very opposite of a Saint or servant of God) so that the parliamentary democracy their limp-wrists intentionally feed fly away like sparrows with their morning light and even as this scenario were a spiritual declaration of a mental submission damning them to a hell wherein they exercise not their magnanimous and God-given ability and strength to deliver practical ideas from heavenly visions: yeah, spiritual contention; and, this spiritually challenged people so well enjoy their slavery of dwelling under an ever greater calm of despotism that they build their lifeless existence around the expectation of numbing their humanity though they even profusely mutter they do so little for the sake of humanitarianism; and, this notion can even hardly scratch the surface concerning the peril mankind face when believing that america's two hundred and forty year young experiment grants any man reprieve from entering this world and not fighting the antiquated tyranny of dynasty and monarchs shuttering the men of self-governance whenever in the world these men show their face to God before men. We of liberty in the condoning of peace must keep a keen awareness of the wicked walking down their carpet of blood while tempting every generation to live a life without the bloody revolution preserving individual liberty. The urgent transmission which President George Washington heeded and made no excuses for not following created for him a dynamic of strategies to choose out with His God so that He would run astray not Himself nor His people into the periphery of masking the white stone in which the happiness of God's people pursue when a man makes Himself open to surrendering His life to Christ for the cause of liberty on an earth full of increasingly hostile designs against free expression and moral objection. The call in question was for an out-of-control big-rig literally running men and women off of the road – and this scenario remains commonplace throughout this great country and of such a frequency that the words of the deniers of these events (e.g., "These events do not exist; you are just paranoid and too unsuccessful to have a millionaire mindset for getting everything you want in life and ruling the world with whatever it takes. Pahhssshaaww. Mic drop. I love Obama and I do not care if He signed illegal international treaties banning guns in America.") would even lie about the contents of their own sandwich if it meant purchasing the gavel of government to force upon a society a cult of genderless freaks rewriting creeds, oaths, tongues, and tribes for a new dark age or informational singularity wherein information ceases to exist. One other time I phoned into the emergency phone line to report a credible threat against my life while being stuck in the sand on a rural road and after some thirty minutes a Sheriff's Deputy arrives and within one or two minutes of His arrival an [presumably] F-18 scorched our heads some two hundred feet above and with such acceleration and sound-breaking speed we had not known of Him until the upward thrust of the jet lay it's all-encompassing thunderous sound upon the land directly over our head causing the Deputy to fall backward to the ground as He simultaneously look up in befuddlement and terror. The jet flew straight up until disappearing before making a couple more passes at roughly six hundred feet and two thousand feet. Two or three days after having been vacant from this valley I drove west to reenter the valley only to be greeted on my northern flank by two F-18s at approximately 6,000 feet overhead before lowering into an acceleration at some 3,000 feet due west. There is grave danger and great safety in the lines of communication open today as the eyes of liberty diminish in number and the evil awaken all around. Some two weeks later I tracked the individual whom threatened me and had a deputy arrest Him. "Officer safety" or "national security" comes to mind when thinking of the excuses our government uses to suspend our constitution and Bill of Rights: a hypnotic trance of extremely programmable behavior wherein anyone with a pulse can witness literal mind-control victims robotically compelled to engage knowledgeable good samaritans with hostility while at the same time any voice of authority can switch off their programming since they remain so susceptible to suggestive thinking even causing them when told to lurch and grab a hot potato with their bare hand (smh); and, although common sense vacate america with a terrible sucking sound a Godly authority does fill the room causing men to be reminded of critical thinking and their mental wherewithal which was hypnotically switched off though they still commonly fall into a literal narcoleptic deep sleep when a true voice of liberty commandeers their delusions to affix the reality being intentionally usurped by their dead gods. A majority of the american people have apparently undergone a spiritual excision from the spirit of the Lord and that labyrinth of common sense and self-awareness and thus we witness a remanifestation of the enemy on these lands and in this life to perform their automatic and unthinking ritualistic nature of seizing control of individual liberty and torturing the innocent and righteous whom perform their duty to keep and bear the illumination and liberty of God.

Our speech and armaments provision us on this sea of liberty with the power to set our God before us so that He living through us submit the forces and powers of the alien coercing governments and institutions into oppressing free people with violence. Violations of civil liberty have been normalized as a social expectation and an official and highly-paid and even worshiped profession of the state whom receive official department training teaching them that home grown extremism or home grown terrorism engage in the articulation or act of defending one's civil liberties (because surely *home grown* has nothing at all to do with home grown weed or classical home grown liberty or the liberty garden or the liberty of which Christ taught to proclaim to the captives) as an official national security risk and imminent domestic terror threat which the federal government receives full authority under Congress to declare an endless state of public and national emergency to indefinitely suspend the constitution, indefinitely imprison and even torture american citizens without due process, notice, warrant, or acknowledgment or admission of incarceration or whereabouts; and, even to the degree that President Hussein Ubama publicly executed a seventeen year-old american citizen via drone-strike; imagine: bombing free people ("Derrr; he's a god dern terrrist ain't got no rights derr'mmk." No more due process in this soviet america.) whom belong to a nation which was never intended on spiritually starving to death by official assassination, spying, torture, and genocide of it's own citizens; faux military-might or faux philosophy of strength through might: an abomination and a turning away from peace and prosperity.

Never in my life had I ever imagined america would arrive at such a time as today that even as I write these words I pray to God almighty His message move as that brushfire of liberty around the world and convert the course of events into a single trajectory of liberty so that we witness the reignition of that flame of character whose igneous form bore the rock of our salvation so that none ("I am no one." - a common chant or utterance of the wicked of america today for which the Godly reply with "I am a child of God given a destiny, name, and purpose by Him to live with joy, steadfastness, and truth.") question the reason why men jealously guard against that spiritual death usurping nations with their international crime syndicates whose only agenda be to alchemize the blood of the innocent into a fuel for the central banks and standing armies so that they then shadow the imagination of society from remembering that free system of health and liberty which even lengthen the human life-span well beyond a dozen centuries once the light of God fill all men and then move as water toward the winds of injustice.

The spirit of the Lord possesses no inclination to construct what wicked men construct in devices and other machinery for the waging of war against the pursuit of our happiness. This idea of equal rights lives on as a forbidden fruit in today's america and even as it were the border which forbade our entrance or perhaps even outline our imprisonment rather than living on as the result of sovereign minds institutionalizing republican self-governance as a design to preserve the life and property of all tongue and tribe; and, by the way, would in time elevate and expand common sense in direct proportion to the expansion of our liberty and deprecation of tyranny which does mean all people achieving the authority in which God designed for people to remain in a state of being whose cause of self-ownership reveal the layers of a constitutional republic as the sustenance for which all tongue and tribe had envisioned and spoke of in so many spiritual and visionary ways. The highest state of awareness for any republic recognizes their individual liberty as their source of self-evidence for the preservation of a society prohibiting wicked governance.

The threat of global warfare remains more probable now than

any other time in recorded history, especially in light of President Trump assassinating top Iranian military commanders during a time He claims He can not arrest the traitors within our own government and our representatives do little to nothing about the siege of millions of illegal aliens crossing our southern border (and while I do empathize with the fact this Iranian leader was a protected man riding the deep-state gravy-train via the endless Middle Eastern wars and america in some way has to end the militarism in which our own government in fact started so Trump did cut the deep-state's plan off at the pass since this ends what would have otherwise led to magnitudes of greater war; thus Trump's actions do put on notice all deep-state operatives not excluding Ubama or Soros as well as encourage the anti-corruption people to continue the fight for liberty in their own nation; and, yes, philosophically america needs to just come home and stop all of the militarism and foreign occupations; it still must historically noted – the mindset of today's geopolitical landscape in order that america learn and not doom itself to repeat the incredulous militarisms of today), as not one single nation on the earth can forgo exhibiting some type of civil unrest and mass poverty as the parties who demand more fruit of the labor of the people do accelerate into the purview of that one world beast system of nightmarish governance. Old adages reference a rare type of individual, insofar as by rare we can mean throughout all of known history as "of the dirt" or "salt of the earth" or otherwise pure in their intention and wholly designed by God to overcome the sorcery of necromancers thus the fulfillment of God's truth as an individual breathed into life from the dust of clay and water and into the express intent for which God order's all things of the universe in an eternal reminiscence of the power which love and order flows and not the illusion whose only expectation plans for the outcome of wicked men culling mankind into a lake of fire; and, not that this person be perfect but rather the imperfectness in stumbling and then following God. The power then with which we work to achieve as individuals and free people must reflect the perfectness of God's intentionally abundant design − a design for which the challenged and hostile people seek to tear down and displace the free people from their home and force them into the conformity of a hostile design of alien intent and whose decay of colonizing nations (america was bought) perform the social colonoscopy which be best left to God and not tyrants. For any society to impose it's rule upon us as opposed to that rule of law grounded on that foundation which be the gospel in Christ Jesus ought to understand we well intend on remaining free men and not subjects flying flags of surrender lest they be our own banderillas to entice and destroy the enemy. This purpose driven against us serves us no good now or ever for the future or history of any republic seeking to defend that perfect law of liberty; and, any assembly that would reveal itself engaged in the overthrow of a free people shall be rewarded with the full attention and responsive duty of that people shielding their lands with the justice of the Lord and with no regret or remorse for showing the world the look of the land of the free.

We openly witness infringements upon mankind's first and

second amendment; legislation forbidding the individual their unalienable God-given right to a third and fourth amendment; indefinite suspension of the court's acknowledgment of a fifth and sixth amendment; government death squads disappearing and torturing citizens in absolute secrecy for which their own legislation outlines without the american people having been considered for a vote though not even a vote by wicked people could unrender God's law from eternally defining such a thing as an act of wickedness; and, we especially witness the sound of crickets when searching for the seventh, eighth, ninth, and tenth amendment unless the state require any amendment to shield itself from the intellectual revolution of the individual making light of the state's tyrannical renditioning of the spirits of the land and their preservation of the spirit of the Lord; for example, the unlawful persecution of journalist Julian Assange and innumerable other political activists and even to the point now that simply expressing a political opinion in public as innocuous as "It's okay to be white." warrants a terroristic secret interrogation (incontrovertibly alien and hostile persecution and act of terror upon the sovereignty of the individual's free speech) from the federal government's FBI Joint Terrorism Task Force – a rogue agency of book-burners, brain-wash victims, domestic terrorists, deluded pre-crime stoppers, thought-police, and television-obsessed ignoramuses which every God-fearing american and Christian should work toward the congressional abolition of such an agency and all like-agencies and replace them with absolutely nothing except for the unmitigated constitutional authority in a republican system of voluntary taxation begetting every abundance of involuntary peace and prosperity. A secret continuity of governance quietly fuses total secrecy into one mining expedition for the procurement of human intelligence designed for a more perfect global governance. We witness the exaggeration of every amendment beyond the ten in order that they usurp our Bill of Rights and replace americans with a force which will shoot our dogs and wives and even replace our flag in order to never encounter again the knowledge of true historical machination living each day and season to tell of our King of Kings: Jesus Christ. This occult cast against us has determined our idea for the defense of individual sovereignty stem from some unspeakable mental hazard which exists in the realm of vanity rather than the only perceivable outcome of attempting to enslave a people whom aim in keeping free. The great many of spirits of the past always enslaving man to false idols was always perhaps this grand and false delusion of government or state security by way of stealing from the people under the pseudonym of taxation; and, where did all of the true defenders of mankind go anyhow and how did the children of a free people learn to become so enslaved to so few and weak agents of evil whom openly exercise fear, intimidation, and human slaughter as a replacement for morality; yea, the deliverance of abundance from the unseen to the satisfaction of every man's spiritually worthy hunger upon the face of this earth. The globalist occupiers of america and the world exercise their religion of climate change through paying for our world's systematic depletion of resources and atmospheric shielding and once the earth receive our sun's unfiltered energy, even excessive UV-B radiation, this will cause earth to accelerate toward a collision with a celestial body not excluding that potential collision with our sun or the rendering of our atmosphere stricken by hellfire from waves of unmitigated solar flare, meteorites, and radiation – an event which presently intensify it's threat in combination with potential strikes from every kind of celestial object: yeah, the globalists want to suck us into the sun; and, though we face endangerment from the natural world we as well experience the endangerment being threatened against us by our own government by way of artificially increasing spatial threats; for example: government programs fly large white military aircraft day and night while spraying all of the public and across the face of this earth with gaseous and cross-hatch patterns containing billions of tons of aerosoled aluminum and barium salts and presumably accompanied by a cocktail of all sorts of other immunosuppressants, lead, selective seratonin reuptake inhibitors, pathogenic pneumonia, excitotoxins, cognition disruptors, and God knows what else and all the while scientists world-wide officially record a twenty-percent dimming of the sky and stopping of our access to the homogeneous state of solar energy which does in the least totally disrupt critical rhythms of earth's auxiliary resources as well as provide for us an illustration of the chaos the psychopaths in government will sink down into in order to justify their authoritarian and political psychosis of seeking to embargo every naturally occurring synchronicity of the earth – the technical disruption of a harmony for which we find to more perfectly or with more clarity deliver that abundance which we all innately seek in the worship of Jesus Christ and not in the worship of government or it's diarrhea of unfounded advice which government now so regularly offers up with intimidation and violence.

The globalists even predictively program the general public with their higher tiered plan of jettisoning off of this earth with a few chosen slaves (since their Satanic countenance require them daily to spiritually torment innocent subjects) to board their craft (which will surely self-destruct when reaching intergalactic waters) for the restarting of civilization under the eternal bondage of existing in an intergalactic ship characterized and chartered by psychopaths claiming to seek refuge anywhere but earth whether this means on an uninhabited, habitable, or terraformable planet with a single or binary star system of one or multiple viable venues like our neighbor Alpha Centauri, although mankind in general retains such little access to the true nature of knowledge for which mankind already codified in long-past that there may be habitable moons within our solar system potentially colonized by an ancient race of humans controlling earth like a prison planet or rather they humbly keep to their self with the belief that earth pose them no threat whatsoever by way of their ancestors ensuring such continuity of intergalacian relations; and, this type of system which philosophers have articulated for centuries continues into the expanse of intergalactic space and time with higher orders of human's and of ever greater advancement of knowledge and technology and for the defense of our most ancient truths as though we all be lost in some spectrum of mental craze which God invented as a stumbling block to inspire us to overcome and forever search for the gravity of His liberty. "Saving earth" to the new world order means Satanically and scientifically engineering earth and man in order to intentionally collide us physically or spiritually with the lake of fire upon the sun and even in a year's time shall this false intelligencia diverge unto absolute secrecy and expansion (though many would irately object to the notion there exists no absence of absolute secrecy and then go on to claim the shadow government be in all practicality an alien race controlling us with a futurity of space and time perhaps ten thousand centuries in length thus we subsist under their tutelage as a human would in the taming of a dog; perhaps government facilities with human clones exist and a master-race of telekinetic mongrels is being leaked into the public by shadow governments; perhaps liberty produces exceedingly greater humans and governments work double-time to prevent or steer away the discovery of the self; perhaps the government preventing or steering away such an ascension is a government of magnitude or a men in black with ways of meeting our disruption or opposition to their systems); and, at the least we know the wicked admit the name of their religion as Science as though it and not God were the boundless armor and shield deflecting every bad idea and chiefly it's admitted sworn enemy of religion since religion of purity prevent best it's desire to use government enforcement to facilitate their experimentation with sovereign individual's, their mind, and body so that all of mankind become their mechanized androids robotically constructing an intergalactic empire even if that meant the using up of every individual on the face of this earth within a human hatchery megastructure confining every human body into a coffinesque chamber while keeping them in a state of sedative suspension in order that the systems of their flesh act as the source of psychological and thermodynamic power governing an algorithmic matrix of machines as though every individual of mankind were conceived as a micro unit involuntarily merging with this vast machine and whose wider articulation performs one autonomous protein recital in the following of desires of that one architect existing as the only sovereign human being outside of this crystalline matrix; and, herein we find the primary architectural structure of philosophy of this Satanic cult of death and it's intelligence agencies anagraming logic and reason with official censorship and secrecy as some sort of validation for the override of common sense and morality.

Whatever this international force we witness within the shadows of civilization and it's secretive collectivization of the four winds of the earth into one beast governance mixing up the earth – they succeed none of this without the refueling of their coffers with armaments and human trafficking. Our local authority having now been absolutely seized by the hands of the highest bidders or gamblers throughout the various international and foreign or alien oligarchs abuse the free world as it were their power to be brokered in a for-your-eyes-only market which can only exercise violence or coerce mankind and keep us within the acceptance of what can best be described as the medieval times in terms of what our liberty would otherwise produce in comparison to this alien occupation of having our public funds stolen via taxation to then only be used against us in the most twisted ways. America's economy, now under total seizure of international authority, have produced a closed loop system of agricultural, pharmaceutical, and medical control by being fed poisonous foods then being prescribed toxic drugs and finally being wrongfully executed by the failed medical system who regularly witnesses it's own doctors and nurses intentionally killing patients presumably for the sake of wickedness since so many of them even admit they had no idea why they committed such egregious acts.

American courts today remain riddled with unfair elections and blatant abuse of the right to a fair and speedy trial and especially in the case of our great state of Texas wherein a young father faces jail-time for not allowing the non-biological mother of His son to medically mutilate the young child in the name of this neo-sodom-and-gomorrah culture plaguing the nation wherein multitudes of doltish babblers assemble strongholds within government in order that Satan reward their exercising of the color of law for the national implementation of forced mutilation of the public's genitalia or for the simple chemical castration of them through aerosol spraying the sky, or injecting substances into the cosmetics, food, and water supply even including cockroach poison, embalming fluid, and highly experimental and exotic psychedelic drugs and all of this being given the green light by our federal government; even our vaccination industry remains afflicted with the mass-production of hormone-blocking or hormone-inducing chemicals though the label for all these products claim "safe and effective" and the insert of the product boldly states "sudden death" or suicide as a potential side effect; only the ignorant would either not read the product's information or certainly not possess the wherewithal to know the difference between a toxin and a shoe and given these parameters of the general public being afflicted and the government endorsing the transaction – this whole shenanigan appears as a self-evident scheme to toxify an ignorant american public with enough force to lobotomize what little gray matter they utilize and then use this cavity of vague stupidity as the mothership to induct them into the monopolistic insurance and medical tyrannies and never-mind the circumstantial evidence that government often produces and experiments with weaponized enzymes, super-bugs, nano-technology, and pico-technology even rumored to be designed for race-specific bio-engineering reason (start and stop life or start and stop race-specific viruses uploaded through their intranet or black-web or otherwise preprogrammed with an intentional seek and destroy mechanism; and, why race-specific other than the fact these Satanists at their very core practice eugenics and population control to maintain their multi-generational occultic monopoly) while even aerosoling this weaponization of technology into the sky in the form of microscopic smart dust and specifically this technology is rumored to be researched and developed for use in these pico particles and whose actions can occur without recognizing it's distinctions though the effects of lobotomizing the

R.N.A. (Ribonucleic acid) be self-evident as a soft or slow-kill weapon being implemented globally with every metric denoting the rising cancer and suicide rates or the falling birth, intelligence, fertility, and population rates; and, so much so that even entire continents like Africa be the global spiritual guinea pig for this chaos of releasing biological weapons onto a population and in their case in the form of AIDS, Ebola, and Malaria which when considering the sheer amount being dumped into Africa, in combination with the Chinese building mega-cities on the African continent, does reflect an autonomous standing army of super-bugs surrounding a people; and, perhaps the new world order's super-bugs will always remain their tip of the spear for the ushering in of a new world order as was witnessed with the Bubonic plague, or in the case of america today – the creation and mass release of flu-like virus (killing millions in america since mystery virus' including immortal cells accompany this pseudonym of *flu* and in the least is known to exist and be impossible to remove from every surgical instrument or steel item at every hospital and including of the hospital's basins which could suggest evidence as to how two to three hundred thousand people die on accident at an american hospital every year and why the very wealthy order brand new instrumentation for their own surgeries) with easily-triggered mutational adaptations formed by a cocktail of other pathogenic horrors like exotic and immature pneumonia-inducing fungoids either by forced intravenous injection or even aerosol spraying by the ton via these large military drone aircraft blanketing valleys and skys which do kill crops, eliminate human fertility, and spike cancer rates; and, all for the quieting of the american public and the third world (which would otherwise attain enough resources to flee to america and evade the death chamber of their own nation or simply crawl out of poverty and enrich their own nation) by way of plague or injustice. This scale at which the royals operate in their injecting societies with killer bugs or hoards of migrants work as a calendar to reset the strongholds of civilization and ease the tension forming against the royals as they cruise into their next millennia of total control.

In as little as ten years in america the age eight to forty-eight demographic has undergone a successful psychological assault of their imagination with a majority having fully committed their life purpose over to rewriting textbooks or in general sabotaging knowledge by claiming america must submit to the eastern and Islamic world; for example, we even witnessed an alteration of the melting point for steel in official textbooks after the professional implosion of the World Trade Center towers (more than three thousand Architects and Engineers bring attention to this matter today since everyone knows now that this criminal demolition has a mountain of scientific evidence to support the claims countering any official narrative including the discovery of an incredibly advanced compound of nano-thermite scouring the site post-implosion among many other glaring novelties) when Bush, brutish royalty, C.I.A., the Chinese, the Clinton crime syndicate, perhaps even the KGB since self-evidence would portend the facts align with all intelligence agencies being a spoke of the CIA hub and itself being a spoke to the more ancient and hidden hub or spoke of hubs etc ..., MI5, MI6, Mossad, Ubama, Saudi intelligence, and the Soros-partnered endeavor to claim authority over america's Bill of Rights and first by creating a problem and then providing the solution through the elimination of our fourth amendment; and, even with one human statute disgustingly named *The Patriot Act*. Merging government with the falsely contrived necessity of identifying and protecting made-up classes of people such as the state-sponsored abolition of biological genders and creation of infinite genders excluding male and female does fabricate class warfare through baptizing or simply hypnotizing the public into worshiping protectionisms for the mentality of warfarism and welfarism since both of these ideologies be one of two eyes upon the same dragon with it's third-eye belonging to the abyss toward which it's deceived truly look onto; and, as far as the case of the father's boy being potentially subjected to frankensteinian mutilation – during the course of this writing this particular case had [thank God] garnered such national attention that the Governor of Texas and friends intervened to the best of their ability resulting in the boy now attending school and living life as a biological boy (His own choosing) and not the life of that prepackaged and force-fed hogwash from the greater demon occupying His non-biological mother whom was programmed by the technocratic social engineers through their network of universities and entertainment-driven worship of money and it's subsequent false power attempting to convince Him to deny His reality and declare He must now live as a biological female though the unconstitutional issue still persist that the psychotic and Satanic Judge with the fully-vested [unconstitutional] powers of the state government demand neither the mother or father be permitted to discuss the case until the boy reach the age of eighteen years; which as well violates the right of the free press to obtain knowledge of the case from the mother or father which proves the Satanic government coercing or sanctioning individuals and our economy into surrendering their God-given right to forcefully defend their liberty to assemble or in the least greatly reduce our ability to increase the frequency of our liberty as means of soft-killing the liberty movement. Judges across the spectrum from Federal, State, and Local courts remain ripe with corruption – supposedly as they always had performed which was a major cause for delivering inspirations of justice for our american patriots during the american revolution that led to the founding of our nation – an american revolution which does continue today; and, even today this remains more clear than ever as america has finally elected a President demanding to end the endless unconstitutional and illegal wars fomented by corrupt factions in the military-industrial-complex within america and factions of whom work endlessly to impeach and imprison President Donald John Trump for literal made-up reasons and self-evident hyperbole; in fact, on 4 December 2019, post 5PM CST, after the initial impeachment hearings vehicles were peeling out everywhere in rage and even into the following early morning hours. These same losers whom tried and failed to muster up an energy and presence like that of President Trump had in times past and prior to His Presidency elatedly posed with Donald John Trump in photographs with the more than apparent reflection in their own eyes of a self-proclamation of their arrival in the world in having obtained money, power, and fame (in either case – irrelevant to the matters of God insofar as He look not for sin but for deeds glorifying Him) only highlighting their hypocrisy and desire to hold the attention of the public even when malfeasance be their obviously dull tool and as they now treat His excellent diplomacy as their own existential threat.

The states narrowly face civil war once again and over the same common sense issues of the right to bear arms and freedom of speech wherein those individuals whom ruthlessly desire to restrict the individual's right to bear arms and their right to freedom of speech be that same colonizing force for which arrogantly and wittingly supported and worshiped Hitler unto genocide and today this same unthinking cut-out of a human being assembles in such great number that they continue the stinking legacy of doing business as an unelected international oligarchy of tyrants for the seizing control of american land through declaring portions of american property *international territory* in the case of an increasing number of United Nations occupations on our soil coyly termed "indefinite temporary stay" within america in the name of global security thus raising the bar from the lawlessness of national security into babylon worldwide with no restriction of it's global jurisdiction even though we possess absolute and certain duty to honor our right in denying the quartering of a foreign occupation on our soil as ought to be expected of any civilization for what else defines civility but sovereignty and defiance to tyranny. Most american states have in one way or another managed to decriminalize Cannabis (also known as 420, Afghan, Afghani, Afghanica, america's founding crop, bhang, bhangi, bread, brick, brick weed, bubblegum, bud, Buddha, cabbage, cheese, chronic, the crust, dagga, dank, ditch weed, dro, fire, flower, ganja, gas, God's chief herb, grass, hash, hashish, haze, hemp, herb, hindu kush, hydro, the herb used in Jesus Christ's holy anointing oil, kind, kind bud, kush, landrace, the liberty tree, loud, lye, ma, marijuana, mary jane, medicine, merihuana, mexican brick, nug, Pakistani, panama red, pot, purple haze, ragweed, reefer, schwag, sensimilla, spliff, sticky icky, strawberry cough, Thai stick, trees, weed, wild tobacco, and wizzle) though the lawlessness of government continue with it's endless regulations of restricting liberty and opening the door to the legalizing of criminality since mankind long ago defined the boundary of criminality as theft and fraud and by these things can we discern every crime thus our ancestors early and often publicly declared and philosophically rejustified the proper weight and measure of criminality and today we continue the efforts of our ancestors and our Declaration of Independence from the founding of this nation thus these regulations first and foremost illegally regulate our Bill of Rights and by this fact will then serve the low-hanging fruit meaning those tyrants leading indoctrination campaigns with easy-bake celebrities in order to give a disguise to the things which the banks and corporations would want to say in order that they manipulate society for the disposal of their secrets through hypnotizing the public into the submission of this false authority funding and promoting demonic activity. The criminalization of our private property under the guise of decriminalization of a set list of property be so constricting that one with the mildest education be hard-pressed to claim this decriminalization as a form of legalization since the government has shown itself to recriminalize Cannabis and terrorize americans at-will with using this false crime to instill a chilling effect of expecting a tyrannical government to suspend the fourth amendment at-will which does mean forwardly marching toward the opposite direction of liberty and wholly toward tyranny by way of exercising paramilitary operations for a citizen's violation of unconstitutionally legislated civil infractions. The more avenues of american society one peers down when viewing from the lens of that individual exodus for liberty the greater the despotism witnessed and even at the most casual of events as righteousness be met with snake-eyed infinitisms.

The State of Texas, arguably the last stand or final safe haven for liberty within america and on the earth; (Switzerland only has sum eight million citizens, literally the population of today's Houston, Texas, unlike america with some three hundred and twenty million or Texas with sum thirty million (government numbers and statistics today must be as high as fifty to eighty percent lower than the true metrics in most accounts and certainly due to their delivering unmitigated access to illegal aliens over our border; and, these people must be vetted despite the objections of the left-tards; and, concerning the risk of plague from destroying our population though the wicked today only smirk when presented with such an idea for they know the intention of their own dark heart therefore they ignore the ebola deaths of illegal aliens happening in Texas today and by extension ignore the reality of flirting with a pandemic)) exhibiting revolutionary statehood and of which contains within it far greater zeal and numerous account and witnesses appertaining the defense of liberty and the spiritual tests which God has apportioned to the individual than any living nations on earth combined (exceeding zeal concerning the nature of the world empire declaring war against us either in open in the case of the brutish monarch or in secret today in the case of the United Nations though they be accompanied by all of the usual players; e.g., Bilderberg, Council on Foreign Relations (CFR), CIA, Mossad, MI5, International Monetary Fund, The Sabbatean Frankists, The Vatican, etc...), though we witness the slave-state now occupying Texas does complete the works of death and desolation upon our own citizens and lands whether that be our person, houses, papers, or effects, – truly everything from criminalizing america's founding crop of Cannabis to prosecuting individuals on the basis of false witness or unfounded gossip acting as prosecutable facts or other delusional exaggerations of an interdimensional-kundalini-serpentine-succubus-super-state ruling the earth from within a DMT dimension (((<([filetype:]|||[=)dm[...-..-]T.$^_-$]);>))). The ignorant and superstitious citizens numbering near three hundred million today view citizenship and paying taxes as synonymous with morality or national sovereignty thus fund their own slavery to stupid ideas and wicked men using their nation's military to ethnically cleanse virtually every area of the world via virtual battlefields manned by soldiers in america flying armed drones among other things and by way of causing every individual in every nation whom genuinely believes individual and national sovereignty and not foreign military occupation to assemble for their own defense and to only then be killed by foreign mercenaries for defending their own land thus culling the world of culture and free-thinkers while being left with a civilization reanimating tyranny world-wide.

All over the world the appearance of tyranny manifests as a dark and howling, bloody, and frigid enforcement of tyrannical law, unmarked black uniforms, invisible military robotics with body armor and algorithms designed to hunt and quit the life of human beings (imagine unmanned facilities autonomously slaughtering the world), and even manned and unmanned war drones and tanks equipped with biological, chemical, computational, kinetic, laser, nuclear, psychological, radiation, sound, thermal, and any other weapon which wilt aid their Satanic orders of death inflicted upon a free people (and even state-sponsored slavery in the case of the unconstitutional thirteenth amendment legalizing slavery; and, the fact all amendments past the initial ten be unconstitutional; or, said in another way: diversions from the totality of truth appertaining the contents and constraints of each original amendment for the preservation of our civil liberties (yet the pseudo philosophers argue that the very word amendment means 'up to interpretation' therefore they reason government shall infringe (though they shall not) and we shall be the ones to defend that which the government shall not ever be permitted to do and especially not unto totality (that totality of the erasure of liberty)) for we shall strike them down as the ceremonial swatting of the flies before the decorative feast; this whole notion that "we the people decide how much of your rights to regulate," yeaaa; no; the ten amendments are not hedges for trimming; no, the trimmings are the fungus rotting the brittle and starving tree of liberty; or, another colossally stupid argument: we can not have a constitutional republic because we must slowly walk back the tyranny in stages and must not have a revolution doing what Christ demands of us; is it really any wonder the people with this type of stupid logic is God's clear example of the stupidest creatures among men. Because americans pass the law does not mean the law is american or constitutional and all laws passed after the constitution shall be subject to review with only one law per review per ten years before approving or rejecting and then moving onto the next inquiry which threaten to infringe upon our civil liberty and assuredly deserves our unwavering dismissal.

America as 3.5% of earth's total population today imprisons more individuals than all of the world's prisoners combined and those prisoners are our own citizens – an absolute criminal abomination since as high as two out of three of these prisoners remain imprisoned for a victimless crime (a logical impossibility and self-evident constitutional crisis). The sheer insanity of labeling the present state of affairs in america as the land of the free and home of the brave today resonates with only the most idle and stupid men whom revel in their wiltingness to turn a blind eye to the total infirmitism rotting the core of their soul unto the merging of it with an atrocity whose befalling can only be saved by heeding the foreshadowings of their nation's demise while earnestly working to warn or revive the strength of their God's liberty for their own sake and in the name of God in order that we preserve the destiny of mankind and right now at-hand defend the innumerable domestic and foreign innocents by way of learning of the philosophy of liberty and doing that which must be done to defend it's cause from the practitioners of death and desolation. Only those most few and noble men continue in the way of the Lord to expose the intentional dumbing down of america by way of absolute secrecy of public information. The greatest triumph, and ignored topic of the press, concerning President Donald John Trump to date was to ban foreign lobbyists for life and domestic lobbyists for five years to stop the brute force of the tyranny from within our government and for which He and the Presidents to come along in the future will hopefully follow suit in the reinstatement of these bans. We must as free men endeavor to avoid the great marveling which can take place when witnessing hundreds of millions of individuals championing the selling-off of their life and property for a trade which forbade their liberty and deliver them the equivalent of a barrel of wine every four years as the means of shutting up their high frequency intellect and drive from otherwise witnessing justice against the wicked.

Certainly we must focus on these central bankers destroying our currency for pretended security and unconstitutional foreign wars abroad though americans as well possess an inherent duty in preventing individuals from seizing such powers of office; however, we must not do as so many do-nothings profess today in the placing of sole blame on the citizens since they be not the ones ordering the military to commit the acts of death and desolation upon domestic and foreign lands as the Bible so clearly outlines since the tyrant be the doer of tyrannical acts and indoctrinator of the youth in His raising an army of tyranny for the razing of civilization in the name of saving civilization though He clearly mean saving those individuals wicked enough to chant, "Nein; nein; nein;" at Satan's feet. Government is responsible for as many as five hundred million murders this last century and the american government is responsible for as high as two percent of these murders and upon innocent non-combatants.

The left openly dismiss facts or become selectively outraged at the revelation of facts that can not fit their false narrative and in fact dismantles their falsehoods thus we witness what appears as a foreign alien occupation inventing a type of new language wherein the alien inverts the knowledge of God while simultaneously claiming to be the progenitors or final discerners of fine knowledge therefore in the instant they make their godhood known to the plebs then all law-abiding citizens must recognize their criminality in not worshiping lies and inversions and submit to the cringiness of the delusion while contributing to the swift overthrow of their own civilization. The use of the idea of sovereignty as the supreme law of the land was always sanctioned by Monarchs and the tyrant to keep mankind away from that all-powerful and unpredictable timing which man finds in the awareness of individual sovereignty by following God according to His intention and not according to the state's inscriptions or prescribed blasphemy. Perhaps this uncontrollable power in it's absoluteness be the most terrifying thing for a civilization to consider as the great wonderment of our purpose looms upon the wary soul of every man whom keeps well aware of the clock ticking toward certain eternity. Imagine God laughing at the end of a wicked life and crying at the beginning of a new life. Forever can not be a place or a time so did man come from space or did time engineer man to create space within this heaven of liberty which does reign over those forces of wickedness worshiping their gods or colloquial "clockwork elves" so that they siphon ancient and wicked knowledge from a realm of devices and ultimately for their institutionalization of mankind's neural association in strengthening the public's worship of forever being the hearer and doer of the death cult's antidote to the anodyne and stimulant of liberty.

One must wonder the nature of the watch and how the elites came to realize that the quartz crystal pulsates with an acceleration in exact congruence to certain known celestial bodies and why one would desire a population of people to attach such a device to one's own body if not to maintain wireless control of that individual and their world-view thus monopolizing the imagination of individuals when this idea of imbuing our body with a crystal or gem would advance into the prowess of knowing which gem potentiate the energetics of the individual, even if that one remains unknown today, and as a result acting as a natural resource of free energy or defragmentation of the world's deprecated energy. Enslaving mankind to the false weights and measure of time and not seasons creates a ledger for wicked men to trade as a portfolio of slaves under the illusion that He control His and their time. Slavery can never be of the same accuracy or harmony as the timing of God's work and perpetually requires man to rejustify His device against God's appointments lest God's expediency accelerate His season.

Today's tax system operates like all theft: pay the mafia's tax or die; thus, creating the illusion that paying the mafia be the salutations and path to liberty. I envision this false modern world as a small marble-set with which Monarchs trade territories within by way of military force and paid-for by taxation; and, these Monarchs are as balloons lifting and then displacing the idea of civilization's foundation as a result of their using theft to succeed the crown of control over society; and, the people hold the scissors to cut all ties with this cancer though they be taught from youth they will shatter as an egg and be unrecoverable if they cut the balloons away that have supposedly kept all things afloat since the beginning of time. We must cut the balloons of tyranny away and land on our feet as the sons of God. How the balloons attach to civilization demands a more refined inquiry into how easily each individual carries the entire weight of their own string – a string of false, or ignorant and superstitious, world-views that individuals do not self-govern or possess unalienable rights given freely by the living Creator of the universe: yeah, that alpha and omega giver of life and trouble of death, the beginning and the end, our source, origin, and original originator of origin's infinite dilation of space-time.

Americans have abandoned the honest money of Gold and Silver as their moral approach to trade and now place all of their faith (as it were their programming to gamble their family against the nature of God) on fiat currency and other pump and dump schemes, for example: the E-Mail from a "Nigerian prince" offering untold wealth after one shall be so inclined to deliver this prince an offering of one lump payment (whose addition grows and grows until the idiot learns to stop believing lies) for the reception of untold wealth; or, other various scam-artists via dating, medical, political, or wellness scams which require the merger of a veritable fool and a con-artist and all of which occurs by the tens of millions of occurrences throughout the world making it an additional attribute of the international mafia-driven enterprise since it can expand the scope of the scam from the theft of property to the theft of persons, papers, houses, and effects or states and continents which self-evidences wickedness and none Godliness thus birds of a feather do flock together as discernment would have it; and, especially when we look at the obscurity of fiat currency produced in secret meetings with secretive computational code (coincidentally enough as well these systems and types of systems of control will merge with the immoral and rogue voting system (secret code?) or in the case today wherein the federal government says North Korea can not have digital currency but our own government can take away digital currency from it's own people and then serve up a big-tech sponsored state version with the dmt.slavery upload) on computers via sorcery or wizardry code delivering the appearance of currency though it be a temporary commodity of novelty which inflate unto unfathomable worth only to it's original investors and only before the faith and the value disappears from their own wallet; the people ought to make their own decisions on currency but one fiat tied to another solves nothing good. The policies which the american government is imposing on North Korea appear to seek control and not amends with North Korea since america is demanding North Korea do this, or do that, and all of this demanding other nations do anything for america is more of this Satanic militarism portending to be the policemen or tyrants of the world hypocritically opposed to the philosophy of liberty. Our once civil society remains as volatile today as that fiat currency in which enslaves americans to warfare and welfare. Sadly millions of these cryptographic fiat currency weevils argue Gold holds no purpose in a civil society when no greater denouncement of one's own intellectual prowess and honesty could unfold since the dishonest invariably hate honest money though they conflate their hatred for honest money by claiming dishonest men using honest money means the problem be with the honest money and not the wicked men making trades for the delivery of war against the honest men honestly seeking to bring the wicked to justice. Americans today use Gold in many of our most important electronics equipment which ironically enough makes certain this fiat digital currency can not function without the sovereignty of Gold's function; how is it the perfect money is both prehistorical and predeterminately governing the course of invincible revolution. Gold's value could be outlined in entire volumes of encyclopedia; the same can be said for Cannabis; God; agriculture; The Bill of Rights; George Washington; James Madison; The Bible; Jesus Christ; Townes Van Zandt; Martin Luther King Jr.; Alex Jones; Doctor Joel Wallach; O'Sensei Morihei Ueshiba; Ron Paul; and Maram Susli.

The libertarians today seem the most rare breed of them all in america. Why on the earth was Morocco the first people to recognize america as a nation other than we the people of america? What had Morocco so similarly empathized or sympathized with us americans in our war against the brutish crown – that neck of the death cult's face? And who better to fight and defeat this global empire of tyranny but the spirit of the Lord which be most prevalent in that wild american spirit today – that great american melting pot of every political and religious stripe united for the cause of liberty? Today there exist those of us in america investing into human liberty and a majority, even near ninety percent of the nation, subverting human liberty. Our founders warned us of the alien and foreign people (alien and foreign to God) afraid of government and not God since it be their misplaced trust which enlist the dark armies of Satan against us and our God: yeah, our founders, like Christ, were weaponized for success – footsteps I want to follow; footsteps the enemy calls the victim mentality in order to ignore true victory. The tongue of the friends of government constantly repeat their overlord's murmurings; for example, with the voice of nails screeching on a chalk-board: "But; but, ..., but, ...Scandinavian socialism ..." Of course none of their false platitudes stand the test of truth and we can know their jihad against logic and reason will crusade onto future assassinations of believers well into the centuries beyond this book as the terran defenders of peace and prosperity be blessed with the duty in arming free people with the word and the knowledge of God delivering us unto the whole restoration from the zerg of these froward archons, tempests and valkyrie.

I once wondered how, pray tell, the plague of the medieval times took place and now I know this as one self-evident truth which a free people must consider and receive as an utmost serious condition entered into the catalogue of God's knowledge as to how the alien royals wage war against free men when they be so fed up with our excellence that they pull the hammer and call on their Lucifer to destroy us; and, namely I speak of biological warfare since it's devices will remain for some time far in advancement, efficacy, and totality beyond that which wicked men presently attempt to devise through their telescopic technology of world annihilation (telescopic in it's multi-faceted ability for peering or seeing beyond or into recognizable points or unknown pictorials for whichever bract of knowledge men so choose to implore; be it their ability in narrowing the field of view for hidden elementals or for the extraction of a visual component targeted by utilizing bioluminescence at such an unfathomable scale that it's use inspire the technocrats to apply it's function to viewing in real-time the architecture of economy and sciences such that this uncovering or revelation of digitally displaying consciousness will shift mankind's focus from the light of the television to studying the light of this geometric super-lattice in order that we ascend into, through, and beyond our primary and secondary epochs of civilization following the times from which we stand within today; and, moving in such concentricity to the circuitry which God delivered in the first place that we as a human race will self-reflect as one mind and recognize the sovereignty of our church and spirit in liberty acting as God's upward mobility for the manifestation of God's bread). Obviously what I speak of being the importation, without any vote from the people, or even if it were a vote by way of kangaroo-court usurping foundational law as some supposed new-think upon which the falsehoods of modernity base their divisional conquering upon, of multitudes of foreign peoples entering sovereign lands under the guise of refugee status (a true migrant invasion which the left label a migrant crisis to hide the inherent national suicide of literally surrendering the sovereignty of one's own nation to one hundred nations of people living in the squalor of mental, physical, and spiritual poverty and while forcing the population to pay every one of them a salary potentially even higher than their own) thus bringing upon the people of the city and lands every disease which the immunity of the waiting citizen contains no inherent rebuff save the rifling through of that knowledge of God which tells us to eliminate the consumption of artificial or deprecating foods like gluten and unnatural ingredients and then replace what we eat with the living waters of greens, fruits, roots, flowers, nuts, soft-cooked eggs, bone broth soup, naturally occurring pink salt from the state of Utah or the Himalayan mountains, colloidal silver, nascent iodine, olive leaf extract, oil of oregano, apple cider vinegar, black elderberry, echinacea, ginger, ginseng, ginkgo biloba, the many herbs of the monarda family, mincing a clove of fresh garlic then waiting ten minutes before consuming raw (not more than three at once), and, all of the various healthy sea kelp, sea vegetable, chlorella, turmeric, and ninety essential nutrients of sixteen vitamins, twelve amino acids, sixty minerals, and three essential fatty acids that can with discipline imbue the body with it's own inherent immortal and supernatural immunity and healing capacity. This example we witness being played out in america with the american federal government importing illegal aliens from the tropical jungles of Africa and South America, the deserts of the Middle East and China, and all sorts of shithole countries, and then directly importing them into the downtown square of San Antonio, Texas: the middle of a city with some three to seven million people with direct access to other neighboring major cities totaling some twenty-five to forty million people – pure insanity; a ticking time-bomb awaiting an outbreak of plague; an intentional flirtation with introducing famine and plague to civil society.

Europe remains heavily under this type of assault and the poor example of diplomacy being exercised therein now suffers the evil and stupidity of american authoritarians demanding all of the americas suffer the same fate in the name of false platitudes such as cultural appropriation or diversity or inclusivity (discrimination begets inclusion) or political correctness or tribal beings (tribalism: a synonym for antinomianism, barbarism, carnalism, frankism, gnosticism, or Satanism) or rational thinking beings (this expression of the left-hand path went from rational beings to rational thinking beings from 2017-2019; "We're just living life to the fullest! We so woke. Our words got so many syllables. So take your vaccines and hand your guns in to the United Nations so we can take more selfies in front of the Bali green-screen." Real life is death to these people. If you had never cried out to God then you had never lived.) though they only wilt conscientiously, consistently, and hypocritically persecute that which they do not agree with or understand thereby being the animation of whoreishly wicken contradiction. In either case of america or Europe we witness the same experience of interspiritual warfare being waged against earth for the usurpation of the individual's liberty; and, the death of liberty will result in the destruction of sentient life on the earth so what sense does it make for the profoundly arrogant to support a foreign occupation of sovereign lands. The mirage of this death cult echo as a voice anchored in the reptilian ego of a globally personic vice which cancerously consume culture in a bid to erect an unelected aristocracy of a European Union, African Union, Asian Union, North American Union, and South American Union first by conforming americans into the *little princess philosophy*: [with a bug-eyed and slack-jawed mouse-like inflection and in addition whose pronunciation of anything with the letter 'S' then inflects an ultrasonic and whistling hiss],

"Little princess: like everyone gets a trophy and we hate men because men are bad because inclusivity, mansplaining, and the such as, manspreading, testicular bill of rights, such as and the, toxic male privilege such as, toxic masculinity, oh em gee and the such as like, muh patriarchy, and the such as, and we love our Somalis – oh, they're so good; oh, they're so sweet; I kill my kids; Babies are a virus in the womb and the such as and the like such as; and there is no such thing as the soul I just love it when Islamic men beat me and tell me how worthless I am and the like such as;"

and, second by forming one monolithic super-state of publicly declared or self-described assholes, feminists, or fuck-boys (the act which be the currency and non-disclosure agreement (NDA) of their cult) in open defiance against God in their deconstruction of civilization into an image of a one world government which strike down individual liberty in the name of their Luciferian religion which does mean a population demonically equalizing the obsession of their self hate with the hate of their neighbor and God. The obsession of americans with entertainment and media, or bread and circus, has created multiple generations of individuals knit into a quilt of brainwashed repeaters taught by their social engineers into dolling around on the couch all day as if they were the conservative repeaters of irony by stupidly worshiping false gods named Q and even endlessly staring at fictional plays on their wireless devices or tractor-sized television-sets for as many as nine hours per day, or seventy-eight thousand hours in their diseased lifetime, as they burn away their destiny and life by the hour and all the while the Satanic pentagon admittedly funds at a minimum of two billion dollars, or forty-eight metric tons of our citizenry's Gold (though in reality this Gold be stolen from the banks of foreign nations since america no longer owns this wealth and our entire economy remain afloat on the illusion of value thus our rogue government goes to the open market to purchase Gold with fiat money in a bid to appear sustainable which does cause many nations to travail in pain and ask of the central banks for their Gold back as the self-evidence of a ponzi scheme arise with the spread of that knowledge concerning the illegality of central banking being more broadly understood as the source of contempt and attracting of obstructionists to thwart diplomacy for an intentional subterfuge of peace and prosperity), per year on state propaganda and specifically designed for the organization of an endless campaign of distorting and manipulating the mind's of american citizens and free people and all in order to further program unthinking adults into the slavery of infantile minds worshiping their apathetic, complacent, and subservient ego in order to preserve the fattened and artificially mentally retarded ego of the government whose defenses first design a social government around the slave in order that these slaves act as walruses herded by shark to a homeward-bound island except with cross-eyed law enforcement sadomasochistically enjoying their hostility against americans in the suspension of our Bill of Rights at-will, and even immorally mass-incarcerating the youth and trying them in court as adults for even thinking or speaking a world-view separate from their dumbed-down and programmatically filthy government bullshit laden with green and red dollops of Frank's deceit and topped with all sorts of yellow sprinkles and snow-white powder of Jekyll island greed shifting public debate into hallways of cubed mirrors reflecting society's grassy knoll as it were the state's beer-goggles role-playing another Titanic Benghazi.

The crisis we face today combined with the fervency of those individuals whom seek to deliver justice to this tyranny and correct the course of mankind's destiny for liberty has resulted in an avalanche of knowledge pouring into this present realm at such an unprecedented rate that it exponentially flood the nations though the wickedness on these lands consistently and presently appear to equally and oppositely match our expansion of awareness as we overwhelm and cut them off at the passage of time. The fiat currency has shook every market of free men to the brink of extinction as it with constant trajectory further shift the geopolitical dynamics into a quake of uncertainty portending tyranny and not the elated uncertainty of knowing the abundance of demand and supply meeting every horizon thus propelling all discerning men to stand guard at the narrow gait and go into the burning fire and save as many souls as possible; and, we must contest the argument that this be the nature of the world forevermore since God would prefer not the presence of a tyrannical government on the earth and would rather all of His children obey His mighty commandments and thrive in that kingdom of God on the earth as in heaven thus what we face today be a crisis unlike any other due to the nature of this technocracy which threaten the very existence of mankind in an instant and though all things be spiritual something great has happened which mankind may not fully comprehend for an indefinite period of time in that the ability for any tyrant to erase civilization in a moment's notice with atmospheric, biological, nuclear, or particle-beam capability be unlike any power our publicly available historical records match or reveal.

America's proxy armies constantly assault The Middle East and render it's economic potential essentially dysfunctional in a concerted effort by criminal elements of the military-industrial-complex to destabilize then balkanize the nations into regions which reform into member states of the united nations and eventually the European and African Union or whatever world government imposes it's wicked reign until it achieve one world governance of absolute tyranny. This false idea of policing the world in the name of parliamentary democracy while feigning opposition against Monarchy does so at it's own peril since democracy be the thing for which america does not and hopefully refrains from ever collapsing into since we keep in the hearts of many the american republic which swear eternal hostility against every form of tyranny and it's democratic tactics (a thing inherently devoid of and opposed to honest diplomacy) in the minds of men. This false diplomacy which constantly repeat democracy or dignity as some type of ticket validating their sanity has perpetuated itself unto millions taking to the public streets with corporate banners and slogans so terrible and immoral no sane nation would desire the witnessing of such an emergency scenario: yeah, corporate campaigns advertising corporate slavery as individual freedom; for example, the common, disgusting, ignorant, and wicked murmuring: "I kill my kids." in reference to the supporters of a feminist movement popularizing the sacrificial murder of america's children under the guise of government-subsidized medical offices empowering women with "choice," though this exclude the sovereign choice of the life of the defenseless child being murdered; or "Kill those brown people. Kill them sand-niggers. Turn that there god-dern desert into a glass parking lot herrrrmmk." (Who could ever wonder how a people morally opposite of the so-call south's saintly men would as well receive the deep-south political slurs and these slurs would be used to demonize any political opposition by familial or geographic association?) in reference to the tens of millions of literal Satanic vampires disguising their self as good Christians in america as they prop up Satan with their undeclared and unconstitutional invasion of The Middle East and the entire world for that matter with our global empire presently occupying the entire face of this earth as any tyrannical empire openly would do during the course of it's irreparable fall; and, sadly – this ignorance persists today and will for generations as this ill knowledge passes from one empty mind and corrupt heart and into another.

From the iron-hand of government-enforced education or the tearing apart of family for owning the private property of God's chief herb or not sinning by performing man's requisite duty on the earth in refusing the immorality of taxation and the subsequent folly self-evidenced by it's metathesis patterns classifying the american people as property of the land which government manages and not the property of God for which the liberty of the people manage thus we openly refute the famine first offered up as democracy but even herein we find the victimization of the american citizen across these lands whose innocence God declares but this participant of tyranny does grow their army against us and consciously commit every conscious act of evil.

Many today argue america was always a war society and will always remain a war society; and, this superimposed affirmation from the politically correct and totally wrong american does necessarily bolster itself as confident or even complementary but more rather as a tone of marked arrogance condescendingly addressing us that we shall never overcome the lusts of war (which be the thing plaguing the world and the thing which we of liberty recognize as the plague to overcome and not perpetuate; nor not ever should we be forced to perpetuate the religion of war under pseudonyms like, "War on Terror," which can even fabricate and overcome it's own pseudonyms of "This Terror Group" or "That Terror Group" calling for peace or strength through war) and war be what saves us when because we look not onto government or ourselves and only look onto Christ to live through us since He won every spiritual war and what we aim to do now as a nation and world-wide movement is to keep our individual liberty and that does mean restore our nation's government and society to the highest end of liberty until there be no more plague of war though the wicked argue liberty be evil in a failed attempt to escape their stupidity in a witting effort to ignore the cause of liberty and pretend all people want to live under varying miseries of authoritarian or collectivized statism therefore they ignore free trade and drone on about capitalism while equating capitalism with violence and preachers of free trade as creators of violence through a teaching of some hidden meaning which only the sorcery of capitalism would do. No words be capable of accurately reflecting this demonic vibration emanating from the warmongering worshipers of america's illegal wars; so much so that they even refer to the war as a constant sacrifice thus proving their religion of sacrificial slaughter of their progeny to ignorant and superstitious cause as the thing pretending to hide the torments of Satanism.

The shadow government usurping america operates under many names including black ops, OCA, The Central Intelligence Agency, The National Security Agency, No Such Agency, Men In Black, NASA (widely contended as the ancient and shadow-government transcending the history of mankind's languages and times; a continuity of governance; or central intelligence agency predating and outlasting or also reigning over all nation-states and perhaps a government under the command of non-human entities even if this term is synonymous with individuals whose own self-image and spiritual worship is a constancy of being-at-work from within a non-human entity; and, to what degree do these entities or individuals embody liberty or tyranny: a topic of which can branch off into the exploration of secret agencies hiring psychonauts in their psychonautics division to document the novelty and topic of DMT and attempt to map out the dimensions of that realm for the retrieval of it's occultic information and implementation of that information for the absolute oppression of mankind), and many other acronyms representing some bullshit agency of the rogue usurpation of our individual liberty.

Estimates have suggested as high as seven out of ten american's personal savings equal to no higher in value than the equivalent of forty ounces of Silver. How have the american people been taught to not know Gold as the value which orders human economic affairs; and any citizen that would accept otherwise has traded the value of his money for the value of bathroom paper? The overwhelming majority of americans today live with that enslavement of debt to their home, vehicles, credit cards, etc ... [now more increasingly with common expenses like food or car repair]; and, government has colluded with debt and loan companies to rig the contracts and the markets to double or triple the debt of the people; and, at-will in what appears as a self-evident and intentional act of economic sabotage in the knowingness that in the eyes of this operation the controllers view the customer as one of their debt slaves inducted into their system as early as eighteen years old and Lord knows america's enslavement to debt and famine of knowledge ought to teach them how to distinguish the honest money in Austrian Economics from Keynesian economist's eternal contention toward individual sovereignty.

Avarice and debt explode while entertainment-media drown the public with images of the walking dead, zombies, vampires, and other necrotic themes; even to the degree that the time they devote toward this theme does equal that time or greater than any other individual's church worship; parents even regularly dress their children as diseased, disgusting, and gruesome images of wicked killings; who would want to celebrate their children by parading them around as death but an associate of the death cult; and, let us not forget either the ignorance surrounding that Satanic holiday or the lust for an artificially intelligent (admittedly devoid of intelligence and replete with programmatic automation) transhumanism singularity wherein the wicked constantly propose a world of machines to merge with flesh for the manufacture of a world wherein sincerity reigns over truth; a veritable mark of the beast robot military which will look indifferent and even far worse (assuming such worsening could even be graded once the implementation of certain horrors and silencing of men ensues) than the vision which the movie *The Matrix* provisioned the public with. Couple this with the movement to legalize euthanasia world-wide wherein sullen individuals declare Amsterdam the 'motherland of euthanasia' and wish to deliver this *gift* to america for "the greater good;" the insanity of this route of ideas produces with it even more insane ideas like the legalization of 3d-printed machines called *suicide machines* though they be literal death-chambers outfitted with nitrogen-gas canisters and presumably with a built-in button-pad or joystick-with-attached-button so one can play Politically Correct Jeopardy on their way to hell except they escape to nothing they imagined and this life or space God removes is immediately replaced with a space crawled into with the force of ten thousand trucks slamming against every organ as one is hammer and sickled into a hypnagogic state preventing them from escaping the flood of an all-consuming terror and without any potential for a reversal as their life-force explodes from within their brain, chest, guts, heart, and eyes; their mind accelerates and suspends into a state of transcendent light making time itself warp and smear clarity wherein after having made amends for their sadness or screaming out to God to ask of Him to return to them the life He stole – He shows them the time they stole as enemies of Him and the life shown the gait to the eternity of hell for which they were so forewarned of so many times before as they scoffed at the love lending a drink to them. The transhumanism sells itself in the same manner with the claim that people will achieve Godhood though the people whom will *try on* such a device will literally die even if the cyberkinetics or cybernetics insert for the procedure state: "U dai nao n00b. Your impulse copy to cloud-drive. Jeffrey Epstein is alive. -1337;" and, given the numinous way of the public today this insert will easily fool the foolish into thinking their friend who was "transloaded" to his phone-list survived the digital transformation during the death-chamber procedure therefore they too will survive the transformation upload; and, as terrible as this sounds this scenario is where technology is presently headed and is being popularized and used today and will create a growing vacuum of subjects willing to devote their divinity not to destiny but rather to the absorbing of mankind into a great culling machine designed by the wicked one architect in the pits of hell. Government manifests itself in a similar manner with citizens in a constant state of fear as all positions of government including military, police, and representatives increasingly reflect the image of the public by way of intentionally hiring emotionally deaf, dumb, fragile, soft, and volatile individuals with a hostile insecurity toward the reveal of true knowledge (and true individuals: Julian Assange, Roger Stone, Andrew Breitbart, Michael Hastings, Aaron Swartz, Ahed Tamimi, Dinesh D'Souza, Ron Paul, Maram Susli). The Federal government now makes every excuse to enlarge the standing army presiding as a foreign occupation over america and recruit as many anti-american individuals as possible and without ever having them sworn in as officers to perform the officer duty in question thus accelerating, by sabotage of laws and norms (deprecating county and state laws and funneling or overwriting all laws into the Federal Government for example), the economic collapse with their hiring of individuals by the millions to occupy the innumerable non-government organizations (NGO) and government check-points accompanied by their kill-squads comprised of out-of-work, paranoid, trigger-happy, and unimaginative people or even illegal aliens hired into this global government's eugenics operation disguised as tax-collectors and while dressed in uniforms so advanced they retain the option of invisibility cloaking or a black so dark that it's top secret material absorb all light causing it to hypnotize any onlookers while they prance about like killer demonic ballerina barbies happily murdering citizens left and right as their stupid prisoners mop up every last trace of american blood; and multitudes of these police even newly hail from the third-world nations, like Somalia, with little to no assimilation to the tribes, stripes, and stars of the american culture of married-in cultures thus leaving them with the world-view of doing in america what was first seen in their nation which has resulted in numerous unfounded killings by these incompetent public servants (and it feels dirty to even call them a servant since they be moreso a secret demon than a public servant).

The delusion of there being a different result than corruption from a faction or political party has resulted in the criminalization of individual liberty. One can only imagine for a moment the fright that would ensue if in the name of freedom our american military will with foreign aliens fly a flag reading *coalition forces* to commit acts of death and desolation on american lands and in the name of being a good person or defending freedom, "just doing my job and following orders," or "just paying the bills," and whose orders were from assholes and coke-heads inside the american government ordering them to "correct" the ideology of the people (even if that ideology is the philosophy of liberty) with the spread of their loving nature at a rate of thirteen hundred feet per second. Consider the delusion of our general public for a moment: the tyrannical cartel occupying america now regularly carts off to jail through kangaroo courts considerable amounts of our representatives and even go so far now to reason that "It's okay if they imprison Alex Jones for false crimes because Trump has got a plan." These people have no idea of our peril and remain totally disconnected from reality and wiltingly cut off from God. One thing remains certain today and in the foreseeable future as we know america has and presumably always will be under the threat of some type of philosophic civil war imposed by a wickedness breeding bad ideas into tens of millions of people for fear of the republication of the ideas of liberty; and, that thing that remains certain is that this civil war to keep our liberty rages with such fury today even the professional sports teams in america stand tall for the song 'God Save The Queen' and do immediately follow-up this blaspheme with avoiding eye contact with other men while in slow-motion kneeling in disrespect to the american flag as some sort of failed effort to appear strong as soon as the stadium announcer declares *"Please stand for our [america's] national anthem."* In no way do I condone a nation being a cult by way of the public repeating morning diatribes rooted in the sale of our nation's flag by a hungry salesman but the intent of these people be to not even prove their psychosis that america was a mistake but rather to do such acts as a declaration of their foreign government's occupation of our nation ("You're wrong america! We the social justice warriors say you European invaders took america from the indigenous people, and raped and pillage, and brought diseases, and desecrated culture, and made the grossest example of genocide in recent history, this is hard to not think about. I can't even. Sorry-not-sorry. Fuck off homophobe-racist-sexist-bigot-literally-hitler."), especially when that foreign government be Satan's fallen army making another stab at defeating free men and making plans at dividing and conquering the nation-states of the world into a tyrannical one world government before killing everyone remaining and leaving earth to the cockroaches; a complete and total reversal of a people whom once discerned spiritually and not that victim mentality found in wickedness. We have even seen video evidence of adult supporters of these celebrity tyrants totally incapable of opening a tin can of food for reason of not having the knowledge of using a large-handled and modernized manual can opener with rubber grips and 3d-printed plastic blade-turner; a literal infantilization of the american public to the very exploratory extant of one's imagination on the subject (americans are not having a healthy amount of children anymore and a population collapse is on our horizon and not only here in america but this occurs world-wide even causing Poland and Hungary to pay families to reproduce); the adult infants even believe that President Trump's sons illegally hunted the extinct triceratops dinosaur causing them to protest this obvious sign of patriarchal racist hedonism by marching by the ten thousand while wearing hats in the shape of literal vaginas called *pussy hats;* and, this standing army of vaginal-hat wearers is but a continuation of the branch of the feminist cat-hoarding society wherein disgusting and fugly women smelling of been gay, hominee, and moth-balls hoard cats at home while they drive to national parks and hide from the public while the sun is out as they post photos of their self with their comrades and radical lesbian islam-feminists (islamofist, islamosister, islamoscissor, islamopascifisters) all day as they post "Fuck Trump" photos on social media proving they hide in national parks all day hoping no one draws a conclusion between their culture and the Missing 411; Mark Dice in His man-on-the-street interviews video-taped these total idiots in California failing to know what the 4 July 1776 represents, and a laundry list of other unbelievably real examples of their frightening stupidity including lining up at big-box stores for days (occurring all across the country and for items that can be ordered online for a fraction of the price) before entering the store and trampling one another to death or fist-fighting one another over ten cent socks, proving these total idiots have no common sense whatsoever and they occur in such high numbers it appears true american citizens are outnumbered by these total idiots; and, even as video often emerges of them being bitten by a rattlesnake or literally tossed into the air by buffalo for attempting to place their face next to the wild animal for a photo; or pissed on by cows in India; or eaten by monkeys in Africa; or disgusting and fat old men being adopted by someone their own age and treated like a six-year-old while suing tanning parlors for not waxing their balls and glory hole: an infantilization of such mental-midget proportion that it's literal stink would act as the legislative shield to overthrow reality and the men of this nation standing in defense of human liberty and in open defiance against their tyranny ("It's ma'am! Now wax my balls and ass or I will scream racist and the United Nations will be here with their migrant army wearing their walrus-sized underpants to impeach your President and disarm and kill you Christians and even if my balls and ass get waxed we are killing you Christians anyway! No Racist; No KKK; USA Go away. No

Russian Collusion please Hillary come my way."). These monarch-loving fiends live the life of a perpetual hissing first to honor their cockroach overlords, second to seek the growth of their den of vipers, and third to murder every philosopher of liberty and especially that image of Jesus Christ dwelling within all men; and that does mean their target goal to be the genocide of all demographics across mankind.

1. Peter Schiff. "Peter Schiff Debates Abolishing Minimum Wage at Yale Political Union." *Peter Schiff YouTube Channel*, Peter Schiff, 10 Oct 2017, https://youtu.be/v1m9qz1DSE4. Accessed 4 January 2020

Famous Austrian Economist Peter Schiff debated 'Abolishing Minimum Wage' at Yale Political Union in New Haven, Connecticut on 3 October 2017 and the students literally abused His time with their driveling snot on their shirts while hissing like reptiles at Mr. Schiff in an attempt to drone out His audibility and convey to their peers that none shall question their Satanic countenance systemizing the resurgence of babylon's demands and for the securing of their authority to keep the knowledge of honest money hidden from the world. For ten thousand thousand centuries this alien force of ungodly hissers have slithered about the night retaliating against God's shining light and they appear everywhere in america today as a sight and stench so foul. Though the vice of wickedness clench it's fangs upon the neck of america there be Godly leaders among the ash rising from the young to the old. Perhaps mankind for far too long have lived without measuring the consequence of unthinkingness and this apathy toward truth drives the persecution of the thinker free from thinking sin and into the realm of liberty. Perhaps this liberty movement restore those leaders instituting that certain and immutable semantics which strata the animating contest of liberty into focal points of regenerative information and substance which concentrate into a potency whose awareness expand the remnant and revive the market for a correction of law and order and deprecation of tyranny such that we pass this inscription of discerning knowledge and language from our blood onto the blood of our progeny that they may safely shepherd the sheep of earth from the jaws of death. Congressman from Texas Ron Paul shattered a certain fragility in this day and age of the nation and in so doing delivered a clear message to the standing army oppressing us and as a result greatly spread the brushfire of liberty even to the strengthening of our morale for this clear test which God prepares for the each of us in the american-revolution continuum; the liberty revolution be real and that liberty revolution on the earth be american today and primarily commanded in central Texas whose true forces guard west, west-central, and the gulf region of Texas with the knowledge of God and the armaments to tactically flush out any opposition.

The wicked continue with their idea that our Bill of Rights be outdated and must be replaced by intentional authoritarian governance devoid of individual liberty. Americans in possession of the mental illness which accuses our latest twenty sixteen election of Russian collusion (never-mind Hillary Clinton's selling of Uranium to the Russians for nuclear armaments to be used against american gun-owners: yeah, nuclear armaments which Representative Eric Swalwell (representative of a foreign enemy) did threaten to use against us americans when publicly contesting journalist, patriot, and Sergeant Joe Biggs via social-media; or butch-dyke Hillary Clinton's and creepy Joe Biden's quid pro quo of several billion U.S. taxpayer dollars delivered to Asian, African, and European oligarchs) possess the highest mental incapacitation and retardation narrowly fitting the exactness of such a bewilderingly intentional nature that it inflict many millions of americans with open madness though upon further reflection self-evidences these same americans as the very hissing families whom condemned President George Washington and fled to the brutish-monarch-occupied *Ô Canada* (oh; yes: marvelous is that nation of people whose ancestry fled liberty to worship tyranny); Ô Canada's anthem: French; america's anthem: american. Representative Swallwell truly is a bellweather of the New World Order; Texas and many other states had a military operation called Jade Helm imposed upon us and there was no withdraw as far as we know and much evidence supports the fact that all people are militarily watched at a level of Defcon 5 with unmarked black helicopters dropping altitude in the dead of night to intimidate or rendition patriots or the staging of military events with falsely discharged nuclear warheads accompanied with announcements that Hawaii face impact; and under the cover of this Jade Helm or other unconstitutional programs and false flags and other hoaxes implemented to inspire national emergency, mass riots, terror attacks, and the joining of the forces of evil to destroy the intelligencia of our american revolution. All of this national emergency jargon has led to programs as treasonous as Ubama's Civilian army (obviously a copying of Adolf Hitler's subversion tactics), federal programs delivering surplus military equipment to local law enforcement (militarization of police in preparation for martial law), CIA delivering weapons to terrorists, the corruption of Hollywood with the government creating police shows wherein the police openly defy the constitution and the show's primary objective (they receive transcripts directly from the Department of Defense [once called the Department of War]) appears to popularize the torture of the citizen and their rights (and whose viewership mainly consist of government employees), weed being labeled contraband when contraband can only exist in prison and not in a free society, fat-ass and half-retarded cops violently tackling to the ground docile and unarmed, quadriplegic, autistic young children while strapped to their wheelchair while claiming, "People used to show more respect to the police." (Sorry, jackass, the child is obviously mentally and physically incapacitated.) Patriot journalist of God and political prisoner: Julian Assange recently suggested the brutish monarch as the force behind the attempted sabotage of america's twenty sixteen election but one must look no further than any election in america to discover the americans that confronted and overcame the crown have always faced sabotage from the royals that would seek to possess the people as chattel peasants. Governor Jesse Ventura was interrogated by the CIA for winning governorship via the independent party ticket in order that the CIA mitigate against this never happening again (obviously illegal and rogue institution usurping our sovereignty and must be politically laid to rest; repugnant behavior in a free and open society).

Along with attempts to destroy america's Bill of Rights and Declaration of Independence, one additional target for sabotage remains america's electoral college which prevents mob rule from dissolving that perfect law of liberty. All efforts of the forces of tyranny today, in the past, and certainly in the future, debase logic and target the most reptilian reason of the human psyche by forcing a tribalistic group-think into the uneducated agents of evil in order that they commit programmable acts from the orders of the intelligence agencies in high places. The fear of robotics culling civilization remains a high fear and permissible probability today insofar as government pays whipping-boys like Elon Musk to waste their money and deceive the public and especially with government's additional manufactured billionaires or billionaire-manufactured-governments or what about the rumors of hundreds of trillionaires endorsing the culling of civilization even up to ninety-nine percent genocide (oh; right: that was Bill Gates); and, one must look no further than the Georgia Guidestones to fully comprehend the wicked ruler's tactical scheme bearing all sorts of wicked combinant strategem. Bill Gates even had entire plane-loads of Polio disease-ridden "vaccination" needles delivered to the third-world for what reason other than competition with His fellow house of Satan members in their most dangerous game. Vaccination remains a hot topic today and for good reason with the innumerable questionable substances wittingly or spiritually coinciding with compounds perfectly fit for corruption of one's cognition, mobility, and even sudden death syndrome as diseases like Autism sky-rocket in occurrence from one in many-ten-thousand to one in thirty-three. The government's answer: target the non-autistic Amish people and force their children to receive the autism transformation or steal their children and sell them to the human and sex traffickers thirsty for more O Negative. Children went from no vaccinations during the youth of my great-grandparents (while their parents and grandparents lived well over one hundred years of age and with a high functioning life of sharp mental clarity) and then within a matter of decades – only a few decades ago – a half dozen vaccinations increased to sum seven dozen shots per youth today, and now the benchmark moves to seven shots per injection with forty-nine shots within seven injections (admittedly seven per injection ...), in what appears no less than a concerted effort to: (1) engage in boondoggle; (2) intentionally soft-kill the public while claiming unintentional consequences of their most noble act of public safety or national security though no market in our world be free to choose or explore it's own route of vaccination without secretly going against the grain of government statute; also: how coincidental can this all be when this seemingly rogue Centers of Disease Control (CDC), in the name of eradication, do store uncontrollable diseases and we know this by these diseases, such as black plague, frequently finding their way into squirrels (primarily in the federal government's illegally owned national parks; resources which belong to the people under private ownership and not the government and their destruction of resources; national parks have literally turned into an international scheme to steal private property in america, keep us exposed to tyranny, and prevent us from going to the stars even in one decade's time) and people although the government constructs security recursions for itself in attributing such occurrences to squirrels consuming rotten rodents for example.

Our people in america have remained a hot topic for two and one half centuries now for no reason but Godly people living here and questioning or verifying the provocative – the things which the unbelievers can not personally confront since their spiritual relationship be so bound to Satan that as they aged out of childhood and left the security of their blankey they then grew into and within the four walls of Satan's veil while learning to build a life of expectation around this vice squeezing them today and giving their face and beliefs that appearance of a sour apple pucker. We do as americans possess certain discernment in knowing the things of God as opposed to those things inherently designed to destroy or tear down the image of God thus delivering us unto salvation through the joy of knowing the matters we reason compel us to escape the edge of the sword so in considering this why then have we as a people now determined the course of events better left to the surrendering of our sovereignty over to foreign nations such as Israel regardless of people's interpretation of the Bible since america shares no such history in being created for the reason of enslaving our people as indentured servants to foreign nations but rather we live as the firewall for sovereign people that would seek refuge in our lands although we can know the Bible does not explicitly state the nation of Israel can not ever be the same thing as what God would speak of in the Bible when referencing the people of Israel since He does explicitly state the people of Israel be scattered throughout the lands which does reason that a nation that would fly a flag of Israel would almost inherently be the false flag of Israel since these people lie if they say they keep the traditions of what they claim to defend; and, besides our american revolution has all to do with proclaiming liberty and rendering every thought captive to the obedience of Christ and not anything at all to do with involuntarily stealing from our own citizens to then deliver weapons of war to multiple factions opposed to one another in foreign war while claiming we righteously defense or manage the outfitting of foreign men with supplies or factions from the forces against them while at the same time pretending to not know how the opposing faction be so militarily hardened or intelligently elusive or self-replicating when we can know through countless examples of the military-industrial-complex caring for america's rogue generals to provide a scapegoat from otherwise earmarking uniformed americans from the crime and responsibility of having illegally received secretive contributions and orders to control and fund the praxis of each and every proxy's faction for the intentional subterfuge of americans under the false flag of continuity of governance, national security, or intelligence community's necessity (intelligence "community:" *"Thank you for surrendering your sovereignty. We love you."*). What do the american people get today then but constant propaganda literally shouting official state propaganda into every home via their device: "Stand with Israel now and forevermore." or "Stand with Israel." and by stand this means surrender our property and the american dream for a foreign policy of welfareism and to the tune of two hundred dollars per Israeli citizen per month at a cost of one hundred dollars per american per year and all of this ruckus so our american government can stand in open defiance against us and the exercise of our liberty.

Revelation 2:9 I know thy works and tribulation, and poverty (but thou art rich) and I know the blasphemy of them, which say they are Jews, and are not, but are the Synagogue of Satan.

Revelation 3:9 Behold, I will make them of the Synagogue of Satan, which call themselves Jews, and are not, but do lie: behold, I say, I will make them that they shall come and worship before thy feet, and shall know that I have loved thee.

Criminal elements within the military-industrial-complex have hijacked american governance for the enlisting of american youth into illegal wars and even for the pretended cause of "defending Israel," (why would a military not be for the purpose of defending one's own nation and if one wanted to defend Israel then why not live there as an Israeli citizen and within the Israeli military defending the Israeli lands? America is not Biblical and Israel is Biblical therefore the entire world must live their life to militarily defend the Israeli government even if that means genociding all of the Israeli people in order to preserve the Israeli government according to this failed argument.) which does mean invade Iraq and Syria and steal their land and resources while shielding their self from criticism in the name of saving the Iranian tent-dwelling nomadic gypsy-vagrants going by the name of Kurdish people whom have zero historical proof of land ownership or a nation whatsoever and quite the contrary in that the Bible confirms their nomadic lifestyle in it's constant reference to the Kurdish people as the Kedar; and, never-mind the Bible teaching about the Israelites and Palestinians constantly engaged in sin against one another in an endless tribal war of self-prophesying religious extortion and political defibrillation – obviously this has no bearing on the situation. All of earth and not a small stretch of beach in the Middle East be that holy and sacred ground God would love to see for mankind to defend against the alien forces of tyranny. Journalist Abby Martin interviewed Israeli citizens in Israel and one citizen after another glowed as they spoke of their dream for an absolute genocide of neighboring Arabic people and their nation-states (the very definition of anti-semitic and the incongruency of imagination and reality) and their God of Israel even provisions them with authority to govern the God of the Christians as they mockingly spit at Jesus Christ and geo-conquest for a God of whom none shall know but the state and certainly this knowledge will evade the people of Israel for a season. This line of thought contending america must surrender it's sovereignty for the greater good always reverts to the wicken idea that if every individual simply minds their own business then government will ignore and not oppress the people which does expressly convey the lie that true happiness lies in obeying government by ignoring the reality of government and as a result deludes the challenged people with ignoring the reality of God calling to His people to proclaim liberty to the captives of a disobedient and tyrannical government.

Daily dangers today involve mass murders by way of greedy governments and envious individuals. The environmental agency, again funded by theft thereby sworn to that intention, poisons wild game populations including coyote, deer, hog, rabbit, frog, bird, turtle, wolf, the myriad of other varmints and large game roaming our lands, and even the soil and living waters and wild forage suffer; and, if that were not enough they indiscriminately slaughter every wild donkey and horse on our flowing amber waves of american grain while staking their justification on the security of public health via plague prevention (one or even four dozen horses roaming som aught million acres: give me a damn break – who can honestly believe this without calling bullshit and demanding a restoration of our fallen republic); or, what about the federal government under President Barry Soetoro Barack Hussein Ubama threatening to imprison americans for having unpaved roads on their land with the claim that dirt tossed into the air from the wind be a literal potentially fatal toxin requiring or even granting approval of suspension of our constitution and federal seizure of our land for what amounts to that self-evidence of a communist takeover wherein devils occupy government and forcefully seize all property until shutting down every last means of production with the end-game being famine; or, we even witness this same federal government incompetently or intentionally dumping ["spills"] millions of gallons of wastes, estimates ranging from five hundred to even one thousand gallons per minute, composed of heavy metals (cadmium, chromium, cobalt, mercury, nickel, plutonium, lead, radiation?), other contaminants (phosphorous or biologicals?), and mostly highly toxic and brightly-colored orange arsenic-bearing sludge into Colorado and New Mexico rivers and the respective ground water systems entering the lands of private citizens, Arizona, Texas, Mexico, and the Gulf of Mexico; or how about the american government covertly and forcefully renditioning and infecting African americans with diseases under officially secret programs; or even the covert diffusions of *Lysergic Acid Diethylamide* (LSD) into the water supply of European towns and potentially or probabilistically american and Texan air, food, medicine, or water supply for that matter since our own CIA has so well documented the experimentation of LSD and other exotic drugs inside of what they reference as their expendable subjects when they request experimental test cases at the foreign bases illegally procuring individuals so there be no question why Agent Eli Lilly be the source of their intention when they wire a New York City hotel room with recording equipment to research the expendable subjects that their drug dealers they hire sinisterly lure into the hotelroom outfitted for officially covert analysis and experimentation; imagine the horror and lessons we face today in knowing that american citizens minding their own business face the threat of our government not only leading the genocide of our people but the sinister act of sneaking around our neighborhoods as though they were Slender Man: the CIA secretly renditioning our own brothers, sisters, mothers, daughters, fathers, husbands, wives, children, pastors, farmers, salesman, teachers, and whomever else these filthy leprechauns deceive; and, speaking of rendition – numerous journalists had even recorded on video our own [most presumably] government in black vans and armored vehicles "practicing" the renditioning of people outside of the illegal, treasonous, and unconstitutional globalist world government meetings in Philadelphia – perhaps these renditions were real and the staging of such scenarios were not for the obvious tactic of further inspiring a normalcy bias into the american culture: to make casual what ought to strike furor or terror into the heart of any discerning citizen which would thus inspire an immediate manifest refutation of the capture and murder of our own people by our own government in open daylight under the auspices of official or total secrecy being the reason for sanctioning free speech!?). All of this faux benevolence openly champions: (1) the end of our literature; (2) the end of mankind since we can with discernible ease know our story flows from the cornerstone of liberty.

This same agency sent Federal agents from faraway states including the U.S.-Mexican border at Arizona to attempt to seize county and private property and public and private roads in Nevada at Bundy Ranch, and also North Texas near and on the

Red River bordering Oklahoma and Texas, and lastly in the state of Oregon; all the while claiming the use or ownership of the property was invalid due to some tyrant in government declaring (though this particularly was a tremendous tyrannical coalition of forces against the american people as though we lack the religious will to sink our political teeth into the neck of the ignorant tyrants superstitiously believing they owe their life to their god of the state; truly a historical anomaly and official announcement of the beginnings of unwarranted and nationwide martial law kicking it's hell through the door of civil liberty; every thing was at stake or on massive alert as the future of america hinged on the critical time period of our own government monitoring all communications and making arrests based on the words spoken thereof even with their pansy and patsy operatives maneuvering through every public meeting and organization to gather intelligence toward the mounting of the wider tyranny begging for more insight into how to further prevent the public from our accessing of our constitutional provisions in order that they seize one state, two states, and even fifty elections under this umbrella of one bloody coup) that their lands were a sacred turtle sanctuary and other erroneous, farcical, and nefarious reason capable of turning the blood hot of any sane and God-fearing man and especially that straight-shooting man engaged in the experiment of our american revolution for human liberty. This same government even erected literal free speech ghettos in the barren desert near Bundy Ranch wherein signs pointing toward square outlines of brightly-colored tape on the ground declare speech outside of that fifty square foot zone as illegal; and, all of this blasphemy manifesting on the lands of free and sovereign people while a literal growing physical standing army composed of their own federal government fight to merge local, state, and federal governments into one seemless martial law takeover and all for their Satanic new world order wherein wicked men become and believe the lies. Naturally the american spirit was stirred and the abomination of a free-speech zone, though a side-issue, did paint the morning sky red, and was torn down as the cowardly, dipshit, incontinent, incompetent, ineffective, impotent, myopic, piss-ant, pussy, spineless, useless feeder, Satanist, and weak tyrants were chased off with their electrocution-torture devices by the mighty american men – a true allegory of things to come; even far exceeding the dangers and more nearing the end-game of what we face today in this head-fake of the left and the right wanting to disarm americans, seize our lands, impeach our sovereign elected President, and rendition the history of a nation and the uniting of our native and non-native peoples though our spirit be ancient and sacred; and, let us not forget the feds are even keeping elected representatives from entering secret impeachment hearings: the true form of soviet-style authoritarianism (Sheriffs, the only authority higher than President, must seize authority and arrest these treasonous usurpers to restore our republic). Luckily the spirit of the Lord dwells within many and armed free men repelled the advances of the tyrannical government in The Last Stand of Bundy Ranch on 12 April 2014 as many dreams and cattle were rescued from the illegal theft by way of a rogue federal government indiscriminately incarcerating men and illegally stealing (yeah we must remind the people stealing is illegal) their property to then hand the land over to Senator Harry Reid's son for use as a Chinese solar farm (though most cattle were indiscriminately rustled and shot to death on Bundy land from Satanists flying in american government helicopters before camouflaging hundreds of the murdered livestock with a dusting of dirt – and a putrid majority of the nation even mocked the victims (the Bundy's and the american people) as though the reason we defend our land were insignificant and worthy in itself of the subterfuge imposed by such international lawlessness; and as we the people did at The Last Stand of the Alamo in 1836 – we must and will persist in our duty to keep prepared for the assembly of our liberty's preservation wherever our God and His republican kingdom of heaven on the earth shall stand.

Men must wait on no official announcements of war and act always since liberty goes not unchallenged. The Last Stand at Bundy Ranch was rigorously documented by patriot journalist of God: David Knight in His reporting for Alex Jones' Infowars news outfit. Satanists within our government did later hunt down and murder on live-television some of our public figures engaged in the american revolution for liberty like LaVoy Finicum on 26 January 2016 after His engaging of the federal government's tyranny in Oregon. The Bundy's truly stood as the hedge in stopping a great unraveling which was forming as a mudslide to take the nation with it in as little as six months time with other skirmishes forming in Oregon, Washington state, Utah, and Texas while a general background noise of civil unrest rustled throughout these great states bordered against the total failed continent of nation-states in south America – issues causing millions to steam across our southern border and mostly as a result of the unconstitutional U.S. fiat currency and war on drugs officially enlisting corruption and starvation on their lands. So many of these evils seemingly slip through the cracks and then surface as a system of issues hours or decades later even before it's victims were even counted that this force of tyranny become self-evident as each new generation bear the ensnarement of banking institutions wielding a corporatocracy of tyranny.

Within the higher architecture of governance in america the central banks and standing armies persist in a way that could potentially strike america's Founders with a dumbfounded marveling. The lower architecture of government, so to say the daily life interactions of the general public, displays a veritable battle of good versus evil as the lukewarm public competes to satisfy two masters thus providing enough babel for the wicked to foment unrest against the efforts of the good. The Bible speaks of the evil riding their horses in a manner specifically to endanger the righteous and even with modern day transportation today we witness this same truth. Sadly the population of individuals whom pursue the successions of tyranny runs through the very depths of american society. President Benjamin Franklin's own son murdered americans for the brutish crown just as today's rogue federal government undeservedly murders the very most patriotic and Godly men of this nation and the men going about their own nations abroad. Our civil war has shown us that elite social engineers do brainwash people into joining their announcement of a new world order which does force the hastening of the public into assembling with a wartime discipline; a discipline for which should not during any time ever abandon the will of the people or lessen to the degree that it's most rudimentary practices face extinction.

American families today keep at political war with one another unlike anytime in american history since the last Presidency did not go in favor of the warmonger Hillary Clinton (true wicken scribe and whore of Satan's army; one man even murdered His own family while blaming Trump's winning the Presidency over Clinton as His reason; main-stream media even prepared and mass printed "Madam President" magazines and shipped them out for arrival on the day of Trump winning the Presidency since the system was so convinced it properly rigged another american election – so what did the system do but call for Trump's impeachment six hours after His inauguration before waiting six months to come up with a false reason for why they sought impeachment) and Her unabashedly weathered and whorish jezebels with their stable of dull, effeminate, feeble, and stupid boys and yes-men; though, the military-industrial-complex worked very hard to steal the election, and even continues to reverse the results of the election today som three years later, by way of brainwashing an ignorant public into believing the famished communists of Russia could influence a patriotic and wealthy man like Donald John Trump to win the Presidency and kill every american for a prize from the Russians – truly a fantasy and farce of the chemically-lobotomized, infantile, and underdeveloped minds under the hypnosis of the most advanced military-intelligence-propaganda known to man – advanced in that only someone so stupid could think it's solution as their unicorn ride to rainbow safety. Press articles each year have even advertised tactics to upset one's family in order to protest against President Donald John Trump and particularly at family events like Thanksgiving or Christmas (holidays which the Satanist news outlets openly rename like friends-giving or X-mas) and the articles go on to talk about how Thanksgiving must be forgotten as a day where white devils oppressed peaceful injuns and squaws therefore this can not be a day long-remembered even if it can easily be proven to represent a symbol of unified effort from every culture of the world living within the americas for the overthrow of the world empire and establishment of a clear home base to pursue the happiness found in mankind's liberty and as a nation of one mind and one people with peoples going by the name of america. This political division, which does represent the very definition of civil war (since the first ninety percent of a war be psychological), extends into every local municipality, state docket, and federal inquiry inverting the justice system into a device of absolute injustice rendering fraud as fact and spiritual wickedness as the flag to replace our stars and stripes. Unbelievers masquerade as moral majorities and fascists masquerade as classical liberals; leftists masquerade as liberal and conservatives masquerade as independents; men masquerade as women; women masquerade as men; some men masquerade as women being men; some women masquerade as men being women; some men and women masquerade as children or furry animals; judges masquerade as God; police and military masquerade as dumb animals; churches masquerade as Christian; Satanists masquerade as morally upright; witches masquerade as enlightened; the swamp masquerades as healing waters.

Rumors of Presidential assassination fill the air even by the hundreds of thousands of mentions on the Internet's public forums which journeys through the minds of one billion moronic, morose, and myopic fooks and twits. The defenders of liberty demand declaration of a constitutional crisis in order to arrest the usurpers in Congress and the Senate while the Democrat Party lobbies for a foreign military to disarm or kill american citizens in the name of their Satanic version of america. Former Congressman from Texas: Ron Paul advised unalloyed patriot journalist of God: Alex Jones that Alex was buying into the neo-conservative (neo-con) perspectus and Alex Jones in His cognitive dissonance rushed Ron Paul off of His radio show although some twelve months later Alex has moreso come around to Ron Paul's point-of-view in light of President Trump's certain dereliction of duty in defending free speech. Judges are even ruling that scandalous and noxious speech is illegal and by that definition this book is surely illegal according to that incompetent tyrant wearing His glory-hole robe. Free speech means freedom of impugning. Free speech means freedom of speech calculated to lessen the authority and dignity of the court, mortally wound the integrity of the judiciary, and expose the improper administration of justice. A vicious politic wants to silence religiously protected speech: yeah, with hostility and force convince us to not voice our opinions or thoughts. No statesmen has stood as near the like-image of america's Founding Fathers, in deed and word, as Ron Paul; and, even Alex Jones joins them by the virtue of the people in the heights of renown thus further underscoring the peril of our fog of war. The fact of the matter remains that the President's sole job be dedicated to the preservation of our life and property by way of the Economic and Foreign Policy and that duty and responsibility to accurately implement, without any required vote from the people, and keep what america's Founding Fathers created – only then when any sitting President pretend He be not capable of abolishing unconstitutional agency and especially that pink elephant of our unconstitutional and toxic central bank – we then when residing within that enslavement of thieves given absolute power of the state to destroy life and sanction property – do possess that President in obvious dereliction of duty to no longer perpetrate lies and instead immediately use executive privilege to abolish every agency whose creation was only possible through the consumption of taxation and this does come with the intention of ensuring a great restoration of the principles of liberty and our republic and a flushing out of tyrannical babel demanding permanence over the sovereignty of our lives. Even with President Trump erecting tariffs over foreign nations – all of this tinkering with collectivism will force americans to pay more money for the same goods thus this game of convincing other nations to see our side by the force of taxation show itself to be but a game – the truth shall set us free so let there be liberty and criminalize taxation in all of it's forms again. Other strong statesmen outside of Ron Paul can include His own son, Medical Doctor, and Kentucky Senator Rand Paul and none more excellently impress upon me as truly honest men than He though Florida Congressman Matt Gaetz does emerge from obscurity to join the ranks (though we await His revelation of ending The Federal Reserve); and, although Rand Paul even gerrymander and waver His form in attempting to appease the faction which would enslave us to a world of factions thus consensus would reveal Him as generally lukewarm and not a first-class pick of classical republicans (underscoring the peril of our times and His timidness earning Him the appeal of a third-rate libertarian although even this phenomena remains magnitudes of higher excellency than any of these fake neo-conservatives pushing for endless and unconstitutional warfare which inherently enables the slavery of welfarism and subsequently the violence of warfarism with both boondoggles occurring domestically and abroad) pursuing the restoration of the american republic with the vision President George Washington or Ron Paul envision thus instilling a feeling of a nation stranded without a life-boat of representatives carrying our flag of victory across icy waters and if a certain word could glance the elucidation of this particular citation of philosophic indignation then regular prolonged absence of form or intentional vagueness while under the artillery of direct assault fits the bill. Ron Paul and Alex Jones remain the highest stake contestants in the animating contest of liberty since they lead the people with the philosophy of liberty and bear the brunt force of it's opposition which was the cause delivering that pedestal of Presidency to President Donald John Trump and His subsequent opposition to so many of the inversions from this anglo-saxon death cult though the talking-heads of corporate press constantly work to keep the light focused on their self in order to not lose their Satanic lifestyle which does mean not releasing hold of the example they impress upon in living the life diluted with envy and greed. Though we can say President Trump and men like Him be in general good and not wicked men – their express lukewarm philosophy measured in action and not word darken the world and immunize the wicked strongholds which would otherwise fall by the abolition of our central bank thus disengaging the scaffolding of the world's standing army and freeing of our focused intelligence into an ultra light beam intelligently designed for the diminishing of all other resources of this rogue state. Sadly these maxims remain mostly hidden from the public in america even today though we do make great headway in infiltrating the public debate. The constant assault on the censorship of the free speech of individuals ought to remain the single tool that inspires this debate once again as censorship today be so widespread that the state currently demands official censorship of our President while even arresting and convicting His friends on totally fabricated charges in the case of patriot Roger Stone in an attempt to prove their political vendetta of our offending Satan as their cause for spiritual warfare. And they even threaten patriot Alex Jones with arrest and the fake and challenged people still say Trump waits to do the big things. I suppose the sheep will repeat the same nonsense when the foreign boots on the ground unconstitutionally jail Trump too:

"I tell you what Mr. George He's then there planning that dern great escape by golly gee He sure is ... sure as the sun sets on the Sangre De Cristo mountains!"

FUTURE

ABILITY OF

AMERICA

American Economic and Foreign Policy controlled by the President and voted for by the american people will remain as the only power of authority guaranteeing a legitimate american republic standing for the defense of life, liberty, and property. The american people and the people of the world must recognize the falsehoods of democracy (that fascist idea only pronounced by children) and become educated on the diplomacy of a self-evident republic standing for the defense of the philosophy of liberty and by this virtue will mankind pursue happiness in earnest. Democracy presupposing itself as indifferent to diplomacy does ignore and mock the idea of a true and realized republic since the natural deference of democracy be to jealously guard the groups governing the cementing of a democratic mob-rule in opposition against that self-aware idea of a republic for which God himself designed for the preservation of individual liberty. Never before in our known human history have the free people of this earth established a nation holding the philosophy of liberty as the highest law of the land through the enlightenment that it be the eternal and perfect law of liberty to establish on the earth what God spoke of as being-in-heaven. The disposition for which our ancestors achieved focuses americans into a free assembly of people living together in one nation and at length (consider this notion against the communist Russians and the length of their moronic despotism in what they claim is the last safe-haven on the earth given it's perceived permanence) for the formation of one mind in Christ through men securing the architectural formalities of being the individual representative government whose laws order the foreign world to cease and desist their infringements of individual liberty. When america's Founding Fathers stated, "Trade with all. Alliance with none." this statement enlightened the people into the higher patterns which form the more perfect union of Economic and Foreign Policy (of which directly controls the powers of peace and prosperity over a nation) and allows the people, or the market, to discern which adaptation best meet the criteria of liberty and which governance restricts our liberty by promising their regulations will regulate for us what only our liberty can regulate thus they intend to steal liberty in order to exceed the role of their seat in society and claim their idea of a market be superior to the promiseland wherein people witness the spirit of our Lord squash those infringements from those aliens of strange lands who we self-evidently know to contain an estrangement of the unbelievers from the knowledge of God and the slide into man's ignorant logic with all sorts of superstitious reason to place their natural fear in man and not in God. To trade with all implies to trade without the accompanying of theft by any individual including those pretending their human statute passed in legislation guarantees them the right to thieve through taxation though this be no right at all but a formality of pretended measure usurping and subverting the blessings of liberty or even a hell which no free society will stave off for long without war or a total loss of their civilization. Thus when the Economic Policy of our nation again imbues with the blessings of liberty through no taxation unto all individuals of the earth then innovation will exponentially multiply and alleviate the suffering which the plague of war stirs throughout the globe from simply controlling the absolute means of economic sovereignty from channels within the overwhelming majority of governments on the earth; and, those channels of entrainment can even be international finance, spiritual, oligarchy, dynasty, though in general the shape-shifting of consciousness into the mottled perception of a communista world that must continue to be at war for the necessity of an oppression disguised as a progressive preservation of some perceived greater good. The communist look of disappointment is their nationally approved and standardized outward facial expression: "Not a problem." The difference in americans possessing that security of a global power through the decentralization of power means we enlist the anonymous citizen and individual, whether known or unknown, as the origin, owner, and focal point of rights and power thus recognizing no loss or transfer of energy unto fancy titles or hereditary lineage through acquiescing to their oppressions or concentrating immoral and undo power unto these tyrants thereby shackling the tyrants of the world to the decisions of the multitude of individuals whom govern human destiny aright. So long as at least even one government on the earth guarantees such preservation of property which concretely establish the excellence of that very life dwelling within man we then preserve the fruits of our labor such that the governance of people influence in accordance with the spirit of our Lord and that influence fracture and dissolve the tyranny which can even mean the assembly of an intelligence network forming a stronghold of churches across the nation preaching God's greatness and not a people (as the big churches do today) censor the perilous injustices of the land and the call to action to both pray and do the deeds which ought be done lest we fall without recourse. America has still not achieved such a thing nor has any government on the earth though we can know in our heart the greatest potential for such an occurrence across the whole face of the earth be present thus within the hand of the american citizen holds the key to doors which open toward proclaiming this birth-right to those captives of tyranny in order that we manifestly in this life grow God's kingdom even unto unimaginable scale from where one presently stand as was always the case for believers in freeing the world from abject tyranny since the beginning of time and will remain the case for every revolution as we head so clearly into the waters of witnesses as these individuals whom witness had so clearly witnessed when witnessing The Magna Carta, The american Republic, The

Republic of Texas, and our continued victory for liberty; these events form like morning dew and bring with it a sea of plenty whereby none assembly of the unbelievers shall overcome us. In truth the defender of liberty be not even a classical liberal but rather a classical republican and this division of original intent create the market demand to corrupt minds into factions willing to forget the honesty of a Republican's Republic in order that the forgetful have their seat reserved for them at the roundtable of fictional fairy-tale. The greatest brilliance of america's Founders was to show the way for the world to achieve mankind's potential narrowly overnight. The american President holds the power to abolish the unconstitutional bureaucracies including the Internal Revenue Service, all spy agencies, the central bank, the hundreds of paramilitary "SWAT" teams (a foreign occupation of U.S. soil with the illusion of friendly in wearing our flag and being our ignorant neighbors that would prefer to abandon the liberty of a militia for the very economic slavery from which we fought against in a war unto victory for the establishment of a republic and in defense of our liberty and by the name of america and nature of liberty; and, one can even name or slander the great I am for preaching the philosophy of liberty to the captive world and this open slander be permissable by me insofar as one shall not infringe on mine or my countryman's liberty to speak or think; no, not even if one deceives Himself into government office and declare Himself King over the King of Kings Jesus Christ and our perfect law of liberty which need not any illusions from these wicked rulers whom be so heavy-handed and quick to distort what man discerned so long ago and will continue to rightly discern in knowing Jesus Christ as the invincible and perfect image standing in eternal hostility and vigilance against these wicked rulers; we still hold the sword of Christ's victory to bring low the strongholds in three day's time), abolish the jobs of the eighteen million government employees (will americans be so stupid to allow this number to grow to one hundred and eighty million or even one quadrillion?) and every one of the unconstitutional institutions acting as that standing army weaponized against the church and usurping our God given rights, and even withdrawing the illegal military occupations – all things illegally stealing funds from the public under the guise of taxation and national security. Theft, otherwise known to the demonically-possessed Satanists and thieves as taxation, does not guarantee liberty; in fact taxation will only guarantee the expansion of tyranny, expedition of widespread death be it the philosophy thereof or the arising of that foe army which inflict such egregious acts upon the innocent, and constriction or even erasure of liberty. We must not abuse the ideas of liberty by pretending they be a balancing act rather we must fully immerse our education and actions into the full expression thereof and only when americans pursue such matters of the heart will their government then begin to reflect a government in defense of individual liberty and hold full accountability unto it's legislators in the gaining of that awareness which can only know to mean liberty by doing liberty and by the fact of this matter will tyranny be brought low even unto our treading of it underfoot shall the wicked force us to mix their blood into our mortar for the towering of impenetrable walls surrounding every egress and pass upon our lands.

One glorious day entire libraries will devote their resources to housing volumes of literature dedicated to dispelling the immorality of taxation and though this concept be understood simply and completely to the clear-minded there still exist a multitude of individuals enslaved to the articles of theft which arrest society to it's own ignorance and superstitions thus self-evidence illustrates the overwhelming majority of civilization still worship immorality since theft be the shell of the fraudulent core which divide the world upon factions and whose wrestling to obtain the power to use the stolen public largess does further man's separation from the rock of salvation; therefore, in recognizing such an affair will america then establish a future which includes liberty and deprecates theft from it's current psychological state of governmental enforcement which teaches that in order for an individual to receive equal rights or common sense they must first be forced by the threat of violence from a state to surrender their money or be executed and since the whole world does not have liberty or preach liberty then we too must do this thing that the commoners, or idiots, see as good, natural, or necessary.

Theft and fraud go hand-in-hand as both a lever and fulcrum one to the other though they be one thing and not separate from another as even be the case with the Economic and Foreign Policy of a nation which elevate the discourse from a lesser stature of shuttering one's own intelligence and instead focuses on leavening the infringement of civil liberty as the only true means of serving social justice; and, as a warrior ought to do when confronted with multiple rungs upon countless tiers of theft before our very eyes in our Economic and Foreign Policy which will ultimately excise the Satanic philosophers occupying government thus reducing government to the standard of civility and not brazen and dumb hostility since we can know at this point that our markets will restore a certain respect for life, liberty, and happiness and cause an expansion of awareness that no repeater demanding state violence could silver-spoon around and rather any [expectant] mumbling utterance of theirs would expose their lack of character to the public as that of a pathology of degeneracy wherein all that they demand requires government violence to impugn market behavior; therefore, what we achieve in a liberty first priority be the purification of religion in order to deserve a purity of governance which preserves the purity of markets and the more pure the freedom of religion then the more aright will the state preserve civil liberty and the religions adopt trade and abandon every sanctioning facet of war.

Any civilization engaging in the allying with other nations forms the basis for fraud and corruption whose flow produce an order of war-time discipline to the people whereby honoring God and not obeying the order of wicked men preserves for them the status of a representative citizen, militiamen, and final constitutional authority of the nation; and, by virtue of principle corrupts the faction of allies forming the basis of the death cult against God and man. Trading lives for money and stealing property to acquire allies results in a Satanic empire razing the world as though it were the stomach of a wild beast feasting without lamentation. Allying with no nations and trading with all nations must keep as our only and most true governance for lasting peace and prosperity and for our domestic tranquility in the americas and the prosperity of the love we share for the foreign world. All other routes of taxation via tinkering with this or that will only beget illusion and multiply the repeaters of democracy expressing their perfect hatred for God and the defenders of the republic. Trading with all nations and allying with no nations guarantees we keep an open invitation to friends with all people, even with the hope they duplicate our success in absolving their own tyrannical governments, which will confound the enemy upon earth, and open the door of love to fallen nations and people that we may unite without the despotic rule of monarchs, oligarchs, aristocracies, theocracies, and especially not enslaved as subjects to the militarily hardened stronghold of authoritarians picking our people from their teeth. God makes all of these things possible when we keep out the unbelievers from injecting their Satanic sarcasm of taxation as the cause of our court systems and morally prohibit that unthinkingness causing us to fight and defend foreign nations from a thing which we learned well to defend against and need not impoverish our own nation for the fixation upon another nation which can only result in the damnation of our own. America has already proved such a model as that highest achievement for mankind through this sharp rise into awakening that we be better off resolving our matters without aristocracy or oligopoly and instead exercise our civil liberty to combat the subversion which cause our liberty to show the whole fashion of the spirit of the Lord for which the unbelievers go to war against proves that the cost with which we spend will exhaust the funds and the spirit of tyranny. The call for liberty in america at the least guarantees us time to a more lighted present reality that we may alleviate the pressures which compel individuals to martyrdom and rather cover society with that knowledge of God which compel us all to dynamically explore the infinite and static structures of liberty and that we may also chain down the undead greater demons for all of eternity. Education in liberty will preserve our churches which separate the state from our private property concerning our life, liberty, and happiness, and work to the continuance of teaching the youth of the knowledge of fearing God and not man that they may always preserve their defenses for the whole fashion of their life and property thereof from the grasp of the tyrants that seek government office to inflict physical, mental, and spiritual wickedness upon the public. America must move from it's current state of one-eyed pastors into a public with all eyes open as a flock of one mind which does not keep itself blinded by flesh and instead keeps active in healing everywhere their eye shall aim to save in a great deepening of what God purges for us through the act of our hands in order that we through Him lift out of wicked times and adventure into the lives of spiritual frequency which vibrate songs of love and not without the preparedness for war to preserve the property and the life of true happiness which resonates perfectly with what God is − the eternal and reigning champion of spiritual warfare. Through our spiritual warfare for God and liberty we shall witness God almighty abolish the manufacture and sale of physical warfare and shall the undead arise against us we shall tread down thee whom dare us even. Americans possess this ability to elect a President to secure a proper Foreign and Economic Policy even immediately as not even an election must be required or waited upon since the people reserve the right to assemble, redress their grievances, and reform government for the implementation of the proper role and function of a constitutional republic. Proper representatives whom do not conclude they be the official oppressors of the people but rather the servants of the believers of God for the cause of liberty secure the courts of God in the land of america for all people of the world to seek refuge from the hell of tyranny flooding the earth thus raising the significance of america into that of a visibly lighted mountain surrounded by a darkness covering the world without the people Jesus Christ spoke of coming into being for a new world – the first step being their mind accepting the possibility of a lasting happiness in a new life and then comes the discernment of the potential which God provisions man through the abundance rooted in His word. The brushfire of liberty will spark a single interest of the individual and from there grow into a spectral fire of winds which sway the grass and ignite the soul for an eternity of mankind losing not the translation of God's love. The people must decide here and now do they choose to pursue Heaven or Hell; Liberty or Death? A heavenly Foreign Policy does not ally with any one and a heavenly Economic Policy does not sanction trade domestically or abroad. The future of america and logic of mankind depends on such Godly reasoning. The people must not submit to the acceptance of individuals within government to exercise powers which can not be rightful powers of a government at all; no, not for any individual; not even within government; none allowed unequal rights whatsoever and especially not that damned ability to thieve or defraud or grant permission to thieve or defraud or be coerced without our reconciling unto justice from this deception of being thieved or defrauded; thus, we must jealously guard the market as we do our liberty so that we too shall do as our fathers and exercise our liberty in the marketplace of ideas which shall not entertain or host the tyrant or their flattery. In our Economic and Foreign policies do we find the heavenly places where the corruptible and the corrupted aim to deluge insofar as banks and corporations so often be the open declaration of war against the people by way of maintaining status as state-sanctioned demons publicly committing mass-scale theft and fraud through false moral platitudes.

In today's format of ignoring what our founders intended and what God promises america keeps the thieving and fraudulent banks and corporations in a trajectory of expansionary growth through illegal wars and the welfarism which follows thus keeping the righteousness of God from growing the new world born out of liberty from it's potential growth rate; and, this waning of some liberty here and not there; then and not now; faints the awareness of liberty from taking root as that formidable and foremost philosophic harmony of self-evident metaphysical architecture and this does mean an intelligent structure of individual action creating a distribution of waves in accordance to the frequency and vibration of true love. The tyranny over this earth has held a monopoly on banks and corporations, which does mean the monopolization of central banks and standing armies, insofar as their means of securitization be the free reign of exercising theft and fraud disguised as fanciful terms such as subsidization, infiltration, subversion, and subterfuge which does mean the usurpation of the rule of law which ought to be regarded as synonymous with the perfect law of liberty, and through this monopoly the youth to the old have their destiny's shifted into combating the false paradigm imposing it's classist rule of every oppression which silence speech and punish thought in what amounts to a politically charged religious order of wicked demons constructing lies as they were strongholds and threats as a varying order of compartmentalization controlling the potency at which ensnares would-be saints and places them at war against those saints of whom experience in their endeavors a sharpening of the equipment granting them access to ascend the lines upon the tower of babel in order that the red dragon be seized and separated from it's head.

Americans must continue to freely grow their founding crop of Cannabis knowing they keep absolute sovereignty in this act and no state government oversight ought to weigh the prosperity of the market since the government governing best would be the citizen accepting or denying the trade of the good or services produced so long as those goods or services do not infringe on the civil liberty of any individual at any time whatsoever and for all private trade and public matters which does mean keeping the government within the boundaries of preserving civil liberty therefore delivering justice only to theft and fraud and keeping these civil servants within their public duty of minding their own damned business concerning both the domestic and foreign aspects of diplomacy and trade; the sustenance of mankind's futurity depends entirely on a free people discerning God's word that this plant be kept as the crop and household treasure of the people and for their economy of God's kingdom; yes: Cannabis be the medicine which heal the nation but as well Cannabis does fulfill over fifty thousand known industrial uses for the provisioning of the people with the very "green" solution that the confused masses push though they wrongly lobby for the criminalization of economic liberty through their tired argument that liberty be the cause of tyranny and reason for which they demand an authoritarian one world government wherein a caste system departs from history in the same manner igneous and sedimentary rock depart from one another before mineralizing dinosaur bones or in the like-manner of magma and it's effortless ability to reanimate earth's crust and remove it's tepid tale. One particularly wicked juxtaposition which the tyrant haughtily imposes and for all sorts of various reason as though they dropped a magic ball containing an explosion of light which shot forth projections of a swirling vortex of violins with ten thousand miniature ringing bells looped around each wound string like a lighted path of dancing and sentient candlesticks and all with golden arms adorned with white gloves dripping with strings of fire and reflecting envious keys of perdition yet all they produce sounds of underwater drums and the screams of dying rabbits as they prove their separation from the grounds of humanity which they so much despise and hate: "Well then; name those fifty thousand uses right here on this street corner at this here bagel stand or the people ought not have Cannabis at all! You prove my point! Your silence is deafening."

The monopolies over this earth have held onto facsimiles of industry by unconstitutionally hiding behind the shield of government and for the acquiring of subterranean resources as an excuse to prevent the people from enlisting the free energy of the sun and other magnetic or superimposed energies; and namely, that energy resource and most abundant crop of all mankind: Cannabis. All of earth can thrive with Cannabis whether we need it to articulate into plastics, oils, gas, insulation, concrete, metal composites, clothing, carpet, glass, medicine, food, shelter, and virtually any other industrial material presently sourced through the global military-industrial-complex' dangerous game of enslaving the individual. The banks fund their endeavor while the standing armies protect their investment and keep the perception of the public molded to the world-view widely held by the public as it were their very religion and boundary of matter-of-factness. America need not look onto tyranny to balance the innumerable tangents born out of liberty but look only onto more liberty to have it's abundance wash away the effects of tyranny disguising itself as though it were the synonym with the power to replace liberty and of which the unbelievers so clearly articulate as contained within and not without the word of freedom; or, in the least: the progenitors and defenders of tyranny blame our liberty for the tempestuous economy which only individual liberty will continually solve with free trade.

The economic power of cannabis available to americans alone possesses an exponential potential since it satisfy so many demands of the market – well more than would ever be required to absolutely eliminate poverty and nullify the desire for war and unto complete removal off the face of this earth; though, mankind risk the slide from liberty to tyranny; perhaps God rewards certain tests that mankind often wrongly views as an obstacle which does mean the potential for mankind to do away with tyranny for we know an eternity of salvation exists and persists – such goes the mystery and happiness we pursue. Honoring market behavior as opposed to submitting to the unconstitutionality of government regulation will allow those market behaviors to guarantee the highest quality and deprecate those ideas antithetical to innovation, form, and function. Medicinally Cannabis does hold certain qualities that be often capable of rendering the mentally incapacitated slave into a defender of liberty with eyes to see and ears to hear though this medical or spiritual phenom ought to particularly be primarily within the abilities of the Cannabis Sativa (full of cannibinoids activating the CB1 receptors) and not the Cannabis Indica (full of cannibinoids activating the CB2 receptors). One of the most notable colloquialisms of today be that effect on first-time experiences with Cannabis Sativa when watching the main-stream television media and entertainment in what some describe as, "A breaking of the spell." insofar as the discernibly tone-deaf voice fractalizes from it's scrying tyranny and into a potency for which it never knew and of which it's hypnosis had so deceptively forbade hearing or seeing to a degree those individuals previously falling under such spells be suddenly broken loose as an avalanche of consciousness entering the heart of the newly discerning and awakened eye witnessing the nightmare which has enveloped their present state of affairs and greater reality as it impose it's will of death and desolation upon the reality of their progeny and all of mankind such that this governance of wicked men reign with such brute force that to witness the firmament of it's symbols and passive language from the control of one's person add color and sound to the realm previously understood as gray and now being in that place outside of that matrix of babylon (an alien and miserable place of worshiping the matrix and denying the maker to keep cut off from the God dwelling within the individual and dissuade the heart from conducting frequencies of love universally larger than this plague of war). The rebirth of the spirit happens out of the sheer joy at receiving the one Jesus Christ who receives truth through God and makes this truth self-evident on the earth for man so that He be the defender and testament of God's word in order that we the people preserve life and property forevermore.

A constitutional Economic and Foreign Policy will reanimate the intention of not only the founding of this republic but as well the intention of God for mankind and if no life be breathed back into these Federal policies and the local governments do not cut off the infringement of the State and Federal governments then all other policy at the federal, state, and local levels will keep subordinate to these two rogue control arms occupied by a foreign intelligence operation chartering the nation and our liberty into hostile waters for which there be no recompensing of such intentionally blasphemous sin. We as americans must exercise liberty to resolve this issue of the oligarchy distorting and manipulating the flow of mankind with all of their ill logic and it's duplicitous tactics; and, one way for certain we will achieve this be through the advertising and teaching to other nations to engage and overthrow their tyrannical governments and resurrect and restore the liberty of mankind which was stolen by subterfuge and to do so either by peace when their government submit or force when they fight; and, when any nation shall overcome the tyrants on their land will they then deserve the implementation and use of that sublime and lightweight framework of the Bill of Rights and not only for our design but for all of mankind's defense, preservation, and settlement of individual liberty and national sovereignty. No longer will the earth tolerate these tyrants and their program of controlling the means of production which self-evidence teaches us their suffocations spiritually force industry to point toward homogenization of our culture or a scarcity of our harmony or an abundance of theft and fraud upon us such that it's stressors ruin us and raise wicked spirits as state authorities which make the path of least resistance against them a counter-intelligence operation of controlling the minds of individuals into exercising least their highest potential and instead culling society into the formation of a wave going against state troopers whom live in complete contradiction and ignorance to the sublime nature of a learned and skilled mankind which would otherwise overflow the boundaries of imagination and lift the second, third, fourth, fifth, sixth, seventh, eighth, ninth, tenth, eleventh, and twelfth dimensions, times, and worlds out of their fallen status and reunited again into the rebirth of a new spiritual body and church which be like the peace and prosperity of the original world (not the false first world of taxation today which does mean the thing more properly defined as a second world) by way of tempestuous free trade and not calm despotisms; and, this can only happen when we increasingly spread the awareness with each future generation to dislodge the tyrannical power structure and chief burr under mankind's saddle; and, we know this power structure be wholly insignificant compared to the power of God dwelling from within the each of us which can only produce excellent works and perfectly hate evil works to the degree that discernment will one day compel all men to tread down wickedness and expose the lukewarm enablers of wickedness whom in their feigning enlightenment can not enter the animating contest of liberty and will remain frozen in time as elemental proof of the eternal glory of Jesus Christ treading down tyranny so that none stumbling block keep down that man of prayerful deliverance and action.

The question ought then rest in the heart of every man and

woman: what do you know about God designing your purpose and destiny in fulfilling the role of a defender of human liberty? Are you one with working to think at something? Anything? How will you defend the thing which God wishes us to declare and proclaim? We must lift one another up and aid one another in mind, body, and spirit for the defense of the cause of liberty and resistance against all forms of tyranny wherein individuals seek to suppress what we know as mankind's truthful destiny in Jesus Christ and then use that energy of tyranny which forms against our efforts as additional means for the boldness which only knows to sharpen itself unto the acquiring of additional responsibilities of glory and power and for the continuance of instruction and practice for the securing of the knowledge of God in order that we more greatly harden our spiritual stronghold of society and keep steadfast to our discernment of the song of our Lord's trumpet while not looking and looking and looking and looking and looking for any sign of the time as do the googly-eyed worldlings. Americans must adorn their heart with the suffering of our ancients and wear upon our neck the spiritual warrior mentality again and with the aid of the knowledge of God and that does include the teaching of the evils of history and the triumphant victory of those overcomers acting on the righteousness of God as that purpose at which fuels revolution and so that our song we sing be:

Glory,
Glory,

Glory

thy name

Jesus Christ

unto the expanse

of the heavens

and fullness

of our heart

forevermore.

The best solar energy collectors are plants and so we begin with Cannabis as one of the foremost free energy resources since it alone can supply the world's clothing, food for members of society and their livestock, every type of air and land and sea and space fuel, medicine, plastics, oil, and individual and macro economic trade, and all materials for terraforming new frontiers, potentially even advanced ceramics and other exotic spatial materials for spacecraft or for the type of travel at which the public presently deems impossible; perhaps even delivering us the economic plan to pursue happiness all of the way down the path to the mapping out of the known universe spanning the alpha and omega of dimensions, space, and time – perhaps the Bible achieves the full articulation of the knowledge that God would demand from men and our struggle lie in us overwhelmingly defeating our self and avoiding the hands of God's eternal profoundness so clearly outlined in His book of life. The Founders taught of liberty in it's proper context and not what the heathen describe as escapism or extremism. Liberty only makes sense common again when the individual holds the highest authority in government in a hierarchy which then flows to the County and then the State and finally the Federal government as a display of the weakest and most subordinate agency of government at the federal level and into the high office of the citizen or individual (not civilian; stop saying civilian you idiot; we are a nation and not a combat zone) thus americans must fully comprehend the Bill of Rights as a hedge for the free individual and a hedge upon the face of the earth and not simply a cultural document delineating one tribe over another but rather a declaration of the individual's independence against the superstitious ignoramuses of the world and they must be spoken of with such utter contempt and detestation for their inhumane welfarisms and grotesque violence – all of which they disguise as morally superior and beyond reproach lest one speak above their breath causing the perverseness of these wicked tools to believe they receive an open invitation to deliver violence to the light-bearer. We must expose these deniers of liberty whom early and often pretend they defend constitutionality while exercising double-speak to support their cause in limiting the exercise of rights. When americans again find their self in the scenario of liberty facing extinction our spirit must seek and establish routes of liberty with friends of liberty who continue that economy within God's promise in Christ. The courts and the people ought to forever reject unconstitutionality no matter how great the perception of advancement in technology claims to have thunk a thing beyond the sublime realization of equal rights (which was never fully realized) and only God knows when we must secure liberty within the year or have centuries or even thousands of centuries to go before establishing liberty on the earth.

We must keep President Thomas Jefferson's vision alive; a vision which I firmly believe be that vision which Christ preached of at length appertaining that world-wide agrarian society standing in defense of life, liberty, and property (insofar as the heathen so often view the combinations of words which teach about a thing as their justification for the setting of a standard which grant them authority to cease thinking and assail the teacher of a thing since the heathen reserve not the ability for critical thinking which be the reason they dehumanize their self unto the status of heathen in the eyes of God and not a human in a state of being [human], as though they reserve the right to distort reality and declare speech a physical assault of their ego therefore the self-evidence of criminal assault and deservedness of the entire justice book being repeatedly flogged and thrown at this being of self-awareness, their witnesses, and the very foundation of society from which the teaching be taught and for the purpose of deluding and not sharpening their reality thus such combinations of word which exceed the scope of merely speaking for the purpose of sacrificing time for fool's flattery must not be performed within their abominable presence). Language and not technology will guide our peace and prosperity. Human action will either speak good or evil for itself though the good must discern as a judge of the good against the evil. Americans must resolve domestic and foreign disputes with the perfect law of liberty and not bombs or bribes.

Americans whom oppose war be those defenders of liberty and the defenders of tyranny will continue to call the non-interventionist: an isolationist; which, does mean an inversion of self-evident reality. Benjamin Franklin stated wherever He shall find liberty shall be His nation therefore we must as our ancestors had performed so well at doing in keeping steadfast to overcome the sting of Satan and keep encouraged in the nomadic transformation of our liberty as we gladly walk home to the promiseland with Jesus Christ and not thinking Him some where over there and not here (as the Satanic Bibles and general deceivers of reality's easily deceivable things state) but face-to-face and within the individual's at-hand power to faithfully commit acts of liberty under the care, supervision, and trust of God and not be one of the soothsayers whom fill our churches with haunted souls that pray in the darkened place which promise them faith without action is the command of the hour: yeah, God damn stupid's vagueness and surely God damn their idleness to hell.

In the discovery of new lands or space will we learn and study God's trajectory for us; and, in our obeying of God's defensible things will He design for each of us the word for our mind to procure the water of the body and from thenceforth will all like-defenses flow unto purity and unto eternity when the children receive the teachings of their parents. When the human statutes be removed and our society can reapply our knowledge to the economy we will render barren wastelands into brooks and meadows, farms and churches, peace and prosperity, charity and not taxation, imagination and not automation, design and not destruction. Many individuals abiding under the Synagogue of Satan disguised as american Christian churches wrongfully advise that Romans 13 proves all individuals must do the things which any government one lives under does command of the individual ("God made that government! Obey it!" Really? God made the government that said kill Christians? Not Satan? Explain that, stupid; ...(see: Pastor Chuck Baldwin)) which first be a sovereign right of God and not government (though this entirely contradict our oath to the constitution since in all reality our Bill of Rights overlays as a long-form oath to God's ten commandments (the true governance of earth)) and this be God's will and if the government decides that being a Christian be unfit then we must allow the government to kill us and our families however treacherous and treasonous the affair; nay, we shall not succumb to such stupid weakness. Within america's government exists numerous checks and balances to ensure corruption does not take foothold from within our government; however, let self-evidence be the cause for proof that such defenses remain only as good as the people whom institutionalize the representative authority over that function of market behavior which the members of society receive by the gladness of ordaining a nation asunder the trust of God. Americans can and will enforce the idea that the individual be the highest authority since liberty belong only to the individual thus no agency, entity, or governance shall arise and claim authority over the individual without in similitude waging war against liberty and the individual. The Federal government will stop their seizure of private property under the guise of public lands or natural preservation since pristinity and every type of property belong to private ownership and not this delusional citizen sitting in government while claiming false authority to indefinitely control property under the authority of the state (blah blah blah ... false in that He grant Himself rights which other men do not have therefore they be not rights at all and the glaring proof of a criminal usurpation of the rule of law). Americans must take into the highest account that consideration of punishing those individuals usurping our rule of law and not allowing them to continue their access to public affairs in order that we not only incarcerate these individuals but as well incarcerate the force of tyranny which attempt to compel us into destroying our liberty and society for some weaselly excuse like necessity, security, or tradition.

Public execution best fits the punishment for high treason since there be no question of the precedent and proof of justice (and our government today so readily lies to the american people repeatedly claiming they bury our same enemies out to sea again and again even hours after the repeated capture and second or third or fourth burial of the same bogey-man), in the moment of their high treason do they exit and transfer their energy from our realm and society and enter into the dead army rising from the grave to war against free men. The daft will argue no evil shall be met with evil in a dishonest attempt to allow the wicked to evade righteous prosecution; or, even: no one has a right to shoot anyone when arguing for their desire to ban arms and claim no individual has the right to self-defense. Due to the nature of social media and it's powerful ability to transcend the trade of culture and transfer of information – this transference of individual free speech, along with the individual's privacy, must be defended at all cost if americans wish to keep free; thus, we must endeavor to continue the pursuit of open-source technology regarding cloudware, hardware, and software since the tyrants seek to use algorithms to engineer our untimely fate by way of corrupting every character of information traveling through space and time. The minerals and raw material to create such devices be as well apart of this world game of war with americans occupying the nation of Afghanistan for the last two decades while guarding their poppy fields and lithium mines for the benefit of Chinese communistas for what amounts to nothing more than the banks determining how the standing armies protect their own investment for their fellow banks to then administer a false perception onto the globe by guiding the otherwise free attainment and dissemination of wealth, from the land owner to the end user and into a total mass deception from censoring voices to censoring free men in the market of ideas who trade to keep their substance separate from treason.

How will the world ever advance if even america struggles with advancing the cause of liberty? How will we ever succeed our cause if the majority of americans forsake their duty in pursuing justice for the wicked? We must keep our voting authority by forever voting with paper ballots since the threat of the technocrats would render all votes onto the digitization of computers in order that they with ease manipulate the vote and subvert the american republic. The only true path forward for americans even into the multi-billion-by-trillion-by-quintillion year infinitum of the continuance of time-space we must cast hand-written ballots as to ultimately and intelligently defer the extension of property (save me from the false platitude of claiming mankind's enlightenment or evolution will overcome disagreement or voting since such a system could only consist of that calm of despotism) cast from one person's possession into the possession of the ballot counters to guarantee a true outcome without forgery. Obviously we as human beings today can perceive a technological perfection of wireless informational transmissions though this perfection of perfectness be so many centuries from today we can know at least for half a dozen more centuries the technology for such use will be corrupt and wholly untrustworthy for a free society (the dishonest men today refuse to entertain the debate of medical harm (5G millimeter waves) since so many of their overlords control the corporations which inflict medical harm upon the public and then research uncovers an articulated relationship with secret oligarchy and world banks). Regardless of whatever device americans possess for the transference of information our communications have always held as tight as they will always hold but this shifting of public perception alone does not always tightly bind us to the cause of liberty and we know since the beginning of time, that among tyrants, and among the defenders of liberty, we constantly succeed through the changing of season and times to keep the perception and reality of liberty alive in order that we do not allow the wicked to witness the blood they wish to shed for none other purpose than blood-ritual-sacrifice. Had the american revolution never succeeded then today the people would exclaim,

"The computerized devices we share information upon will certainly attain peace and prosperity when the state aggregates and curates our information."

America in solving these issues of liberty most efficiently solves our own issues which will overflow in the resolution of foreign matters as the citizens of these foreign lands see that what we do and what we believe works as the means to the ends which all people seek. When an american wants to help another nation with war then that american must pack their bag and assemble with those forces at war for foreign logic and reason and under no circumstance ought a government of liberty find excuse in war for taxation of the public since the best fighters feed their own family first and no free society surrender's it's liberty for the lie of temporary security which is a deep sleep from atop the watchtower. America's future destiny does not depend on the technology which we see; rather our future depends on the living who witness liberty and know better than tyranny. The Bill of Rights guarantees man the ability to exercise peace to create an innovation without restraint of His civil liberty and to keep free from sin. Innovation creates a higher efficacy of the economy and does not eliminate our necessities by creating a vacuum of the economy; rather the higher intellectual means attain a new perspective for the economy for which the economy was seeking to achieve for efficiency's sake in expanding the peace and prosperity of civilization from our bedrock of manufacturing to our men pointing the way. America must return it's manufacturing to our lands since any nation which would not manufacture it's own goods would in no way be within the realm of their own sovereignty. In retaining our manufacturing domestically we prevent the worst of tyrants from infiltrating our government and institutionalizing economic destruction. Perhaps this effect of americans recapturing their own nation be the course for cause for our perpetual human revolution for liberty that must continually cleanse and purge the bowels of society with that pure water of affection which founts from the bosom of civilization and pours it's soul over the lands of eternity and awaits mankind's rediscovery of how easy the decision be to restore the matters of the heart into a garden of eden and pursuant to the happiness which keep liberty's vigilance in honor of the origin and means of eternity's manna.

The free-minded in worshiping God particularly concern their illustrative pursuits of knowledge with the knowledge of God thereby concerning their self least with the ideas of carnal affliction insofar as they learn of carnality but do not become it's causality as do the heathen in order that they more perfectly keep a union with the teachings of the left-hand path and whose governance by pomp and vain measure does draw borders around earth to suspend the necessary confrontation of one's self with the loving of thy neighbor as thyself which does mean we live in a world as it transparently were a prison-planet and sporadic war-zone. America's greatest friends in liberty could very well be the Middle-East though the oligarchs create and then corrupt factions in order to keep the Middle-East decimated in war for reason of keeping their people at the same state of cultural barbarism, or inherent void of civilization, from which the west recorded them as narrowly one millennia ago. The philosophy of liberty founting from america as it's present bedrock will teach the people to keep and bear their arms while simultaneously learning to adopt the precepts of human liberty and exercise their rights without succumbing to individual theft or fraud even if that theft or fraud be under the guise of state-sponsorship claiming it's veil of secrecy and extra-judiciary authority as exceptional necessity when it be the very entity of Satan spiritually at war against us. This does mean that when in the event of being in a state of our republic that our state choose out it's day to officially claim the philosophers of liberty as tyrants then let their speech be free; for what they aim to do in rendering our civil liberty a distant memory be the very thing a true tyrant would do while we be a child of God and a man prepared for the glorious defense of our liberty; a place from which He freely gave to us knowing that we would respond to the call of that responsibility of defending against all enemies foreign and domestic. Since we can know the truth of this slide of liberty and tyranny swaying and moving in waves we can also know that all people of the earth, especially americans today since these are the lands that have so thoroughly advanced the philosophy and cause of liberty, surrender all Satanic ideas appertaining the false duty in remaining the policeman of the world by way of militarism or state-sponsored occupation, whether that false pursuit present itself in the air, ground, sea, space, or the telecommunications of the domestic and foreign world and this pursuit of policing market behaviors will never result in the prospering of people and will only result in the systematic genocide of the natural inhabitants of the land thus the elimination of liberty forever. A free america will discern the significance of deserving their current government. How then will a score of socialist governments war with one another while claiming to fight over the roots of civilization when liberty alone be the blemish-free and robust roots of civilization and the tree thereof and the isms of the world be nothing more than the opposition of liberty and oppression which surreptitiously force society to use it's body to water the tree of liberty? Does self-evidence then teach that the borders of a nation be the spiritual boundaries of our spiral realm and not the physical boundaries which shallow and vain people would claim as symbols of oppression for how could the oppressor oppress without He assailing the body politic of another therefore that which He assail be not the symbol of oppression for they receive the blunt force of oppression therefore causing them to be victimized and rise to defend against oppression; thus, we must come to resist the Satanic pseudo-intellectual's argument that "there are no victims; only volunteers" since good, evil, and the word be the things which govern the politics and religion of mankind and the antimatter and matter, or darkness and light, of the universe; though these wicked arguments and phrases can be catalogued for use in locating and freeing innocent people trapped by the Satanic scourge.

America ought remain "The Great American Melting Pot" insofar as I do not perceive any illusory perception instructed into this meaning but rather an enlightened awakening of melting the facade of tyranny and an enjoying of the potential humanity has to offer when race, color, creed, and national origin do not foretell a cause for concern of war but rather effect the increase of frequency for celebration of our fellow countrymen and mankind as people awaken to the liberty within all of the people and again americans will witness nationwide block-partys as the people again unite as true neighbors in a land of free people in their keeping watch over their liberty from the advancement of tyranny disguising itself as stupidity or exposing itself as violence. The parabola of issues which concern americans do not coincide with those base concerns which entrap entire nations since our chief philosophy be the liberty to wholly submit to the God of this universe and not the submission to a government of men. Americans and the world must forbid the creation of central banks and standing armies knowing full and well that technology does not alter the human condition of being faced with good versus evil and these factions of central banks and standing armies tilt the destiny of mankind unto evil and not good by way of theft of the public largess which defraud the individual of their liberty and property. The idea and notion of these institutions must be shunned by all discerning people. They will work to erode each of our liberties beginning with speech and then arms in order that we can not freely (by unlawful human statute which is of tyrannical decree) possess our greatest spiritual weapons during the time we experience when faced with every form of spiritual chaos which exhibit best the state of war as our opposition early and often imprisons our countrymen as though they disparage us at the same frequency of a nation gorged with enemy occupiers in their capturing of thousands of brigades.

America in the nineteen fifties possessed the ability to feed all of earth many times over and today struggles to feed it's own diminishing middle-class, and even it's own family in many cases, and this surplus of abundance in the nineteen fifties was but a minute fraction of the potential that america will uncover when the people again wholly discern far beyond what we have witnessed in the upright mobilization of the philosophy of liberty. The wealth of the people was stolen from central bankers through the allowance of the people and now central banks erect standing armies to steal what can not be spiritually stolen from the people in order that they turn the land over to the brutish crown – the entity of which modern-day Israelites claim america stole the land from in the first place and must be held militarily accountable via royal interdiction which does mean killed in war (Come and take it then you god-damned pussies; Pray y'all can withstand a tenth revolutionary ass whooping and remind all your fellow cracker-jacks and royal ass-lickers to wear their bright red uniforms with a large white X over their middle and also not to forget their giant furry black hat draped with silver bells; oh, and march in a single file line into an open field while announcing your presence with the singing of God Save The Queen you soft and stupid twerps). American media today regularly pushes to normalize the idea that americans must abandon our fight for liberty and lust to live under the tyranny of the monarch again. Americans must stop their defense of foreign lands, by way of the theft of taxation, if they ever wish to see true liberty, peace, and prosperity on this earth since such acts of false platitudes only deteriorate international relations, expedite genocide, encourage poverty, stir civil unrest, and blight civilization with war and we know war always stifles the development of economy for a generation or more. America descends into the dark-ages by pursuing allies across the world and a Foreign Policy enlisting america's standing army to occupy every nation upon the face of the earth and supposedly as an ultimatum for the provisioning of americans against foreign threat; provisions which we know as the creed of deception from the deceivers pretending to act as the moral obligation whose constant shifting of public appearance disguise it's camouflage of broken logic, insolent hypocrisy, and unfounded reason lest a keen awareness expose these warmongers whom in their lostness of searching for love at the bottom of a bottle do desire a world of warcraft for their false religion of ketamine freedom which usurp and make hidden to them every form of liberty. Whatever the case if you know someone who is lost, and there are lost people, then we have got to find them. We must not quarrel over which region be the fount of civilization (probably Syria; absolutely not China or Russia) though we must necessarily assemble to settle all quarrels for the remediation of liberty and as such we then will supply our society with the ideas founting all moral civilization in rightly defining morality and wickedness since any honest man knows the wicked provocatively deliver, without appointment or invite, quarrels to the righteous since our love for God and His wisdoms judiciously prove the disobedience of the wicked and the wicked perversely believe power only comes from the fear of men thus the wicked find reason in promoting fear of them thus in their perverseness do the fallen manufacture war for an order of false valor. How then do we disassociate from the argument of what God would not align us with since those things which God would not align us with so self-evidently be lost-in-translation throughout our space and time on the earth thus shifting the identity of the believers into the muddied realm of the unbelievers as the unbelievers through their tyrannical nature cause mankind to merge as one beast system? This knowledge of God acts as the energy-well which propels mankind, fuels economy, delivers individual happiness, and cures the individual whom finds not joy in their life though they so often arrogantly and deceivingly claim to find joy without God or the acceptance of Jesus Christ into their heart; and, self-evidence teaches us that that individual without the love of Christ remains cut off from love and in a pomp state of worshiping illusion and all things vain; and, for whatever reason: compels them to defend a Satanic state ...

The cult of death stand in the way of mankind even as it were we hung about a thread of rope which even itself dangle upon a fractured branch bearing heavy fruit and tossing about the wind in the portending of an inevitable peril as birds land and go, storms, tectonic plates, fires, and cosmic radiation contribute to this atmospheric instability and all of those things of systems which God made to govern and even the governing of things for the regeneration of this generation's universe rattling and reverberating against the equal and infinite force of the butterfly's winds. We must march the direction of resistance and forge paths narrow enough to know it's visionary and wide enough to justify inviting the sheep to our reality self-evidently forged against the soothsayers buying their iron-clad factions to then hang upon their silk web. Whatever america's potential – one reality for mankind will persist in that one spirit of the Lord equally dwelling within man and provisioning us with that realist nature embodying the love of God and guarding against the envy which steal life and hate property. The american Dream entails we set our hearts upon those virtues and standardize the acceptance and manifestation of visionary dreams and choose out the manifestation of our liberty which exist entirely outside of the scope offered by the tyrants whom command of us our obedient silence so that we take on the responsibility of forgetting, impeding, and muting the spirit of the Lord. We shall not succumb to waiting centuries for the candle to be invented or be ordered by law to wield our torch for the treading down and sacrificing of the chandlers. A free society, and this be what america aims to keep, regards the idea of tyranny with the utmost seriousness in order that we keep aware of those dangers which erode historical, governmental, and moral architecture. The youth when shown the way will pass on this knowledge to where it must stick as mortar for the true keeper of time: liberty in the heart and at the hand of man, His children and wife, His fellow members of society, and especially His countrymen. One day this knowledge will expand the individual lifespan into unfathomable numerals of centuries which will exponentially increase the potency of our liberty and trajectory toward potential preservation and beyond. Knowledge will compound and it's effect will expand the sphere of influence such that the things of mystery today be revealed and those weak worldlings who wrongfully guarded it's knowledge for the rendering of it's capacity into wicked use shall vanish. Americans must remain torch-bearers for truth and resist every form of tyranny in every mind and every system acting with hostility toward the mind whithersoever we go keeping always attentive and willing to identify and hear and see and learn of those things of God and never succumb to that apathetic complacency garnering excitement over believing lies rather than asking of God to deliver us adversity in order that we sharpen and well-temper our fortification and then leaven and even banish tyranny from this realm. Idleness be the enemy of liberty, unbeliever of love, and constancy of superstitious lore. Knowledge resists tyranny and education indoctrinates the tyrants. Only the individual can exercise liberty in self-governance thus most strictly regulating the markets which a multitude of self-aware individuals institutionalize through the free assembly of men forming government to process the designation of life, liberty, and property's preservation and not for the surrender of our wit to the control of a force seizing absolute control of the means of production in society; and, from this inequality of rights produces kingdoms infringing upon kingdoms. Today's greatest inventions and ideas be not in the hands of society since unconstitutional laws have governed the formless idea into the realm of physical property (so long as one be so corrupt and wealthy to pay the courts to unconstitutionally sanction an idea) which no person can reproduce when certain powers have spent the proper money and bent the bendable channels of influence to keep the public one with their torch and separate from the candles which would lift the veil from the eye of society. Free energy and ancient systems of liberty versus blood money; individual sovereignty versus ancient dynasty; the perfect law of liberty versus human statutes; proselytization versus revelation; love versus retaliation; perception versus self-evidence; righteous indignation versus indignity; self-awareness versus mob-rule; laws versus human statutes; men versus aliens; ideas versus edict. What must we innovate upon but the knowledge of liberty in order that we achieve that agrarian society which free man onto His own private property and free men into their own society of liberty though this reality be so totally self-evident when learning of the stewardship of the republican and eternal preservation of liberty and a moving away from the falsehood of democratic freedom and all of it's blasphemous forms such as monarchical parliamentary democracy.

Super-soil; bio-char; compost tea; gravity aquifers; cisterns;

aflaj; qanat; geodesic earthen homes and villages; hand-held solar or gravity-powered device that spits out gallons of pure water per minute; passive subterranean or even passive air-cooling towers or passive rain producing or water capturing towers; keeping the earth covered with one meter of wood-chips or organic matter for medicinal and substantive food production or for terraforming hungry or barren wastelands, water storage, or climatic regulation or restoration; constructed wetland systems; Nikola Tesla's infinite energy; the Searl Effect Generator (SEG); hippocratic oath versus the hypocrite; Isaac Newton's occult studies; not allowing even the immorality of taxation to enter society; a world with communicative abundance under the assault of the heathen's sticks and stones and all of this totally avoided when men work of one mind in Christ to worship God and perfect the ease of His noble obedience in what the world may see as a performance of interdimensional arithmetic in the unleashing of exponent resources for a happiness which they can choose to fight against or thrive with as liberty shuts out tyranny for eternity. Do these same practices which set us free not anagram against those hereditary oppressors whom enslave mankind through seizing control of those things which God delivered us autonomy and authority to privately possess? Self-evidence inclines one to discern our ideas and practices of law and order to reflect our beliefs against our actions, our expectations against our outcome – for if we believe the land devoid of water then the land be without water since our imagination be without the revelation of the source of water and so forth in like manner concerning the infinite of proportion and scale. The cult of death depends on bending our will to the torments of an imagination whose vision worships false images and uses these false images as a template to constrict and not expand consciousness thus constricting resources and expanding the intemperance and viciousness of the public which form the state of a mind economizing poverty and outsourcing war since the domestic corruptions always involve operating government outside of law. The cult of death presently knows americans to be the primary force standing as the hedge against their plans of ushering in a new dark age and what we reveal will in time result in an overflow of freeing our nation and at least one additional nation so the highest nations on the earth will no longer be a standalone front of america and Switzerland but perhaps ten dozen more angelic nations and all working as one hive-mind to keep the forces of tyranny on the sewered streets of a diminishing third-world (since the nature of the third-world will diminish in direct proportion to the spread of the joy of the Lord since His arrival always delivers His people), and, of whom, as well work to purge the tyrant's multiverse and join the defense for liberty. With our literature as our guiding primary weapon we will free all markets of medicine, industry, agriculture, food, arts (since the cult of death presently control even the arts by slaughtering the chief artists and musicians whom threaten most their mafia underworld) and every seat of representative governance in order that we remind, reprove, and reteach the ways of liberty to all of the youth forever and ever and ever: Amen. Consider the philosophy of liberty the highest linguistic fractal or symbol which leaven the infinity within the enfolds of eternity's unfolding. The program projects an infinite number of ways in which mankind can travel though the free route which God provisions us with and so that we have the power to create a narrow and straight path to unveil the whole mystery even at the appointed hour shall His people light their eyes upon His majestic mystery and speak and do the things which He instruct. No longer will mankind give authority to individuals whom claim God ordained them to perform evil and no thing on the earth matters and words be a thing which they can use to harm men and not a thing for us to set men free from the harm of the wicked. Japanese philosophers speak of heaven being where we stand thus train at-hand we must. Perhaps Heaven be what man when holding the chains of the constitution then lowers onto earth and the heights of heaven be the continuance of the youth in future generations perpetually separating mankind from hell and into the angelic Christendoms of higher awareness and conscious vibrations whose capturing of ideas unto the obedience of Christ manifests every provision for our lives and property acting as the proving grounds for mankind's lost temple such that we train as men to pass the tests which God with Godly proof of works and reason and not ungodly men would have us do in order that He discern His duty in accepting the responsibility of doing the deeds which cause men to receive the blessings of liberty on the earth and manifestly in this lifetime. One could hope the tyrants of the world will repent and join the people of the world as individuals worshiping Christ although history shows tyrants be so turned over to wickedness that their spirit must come to know the fullness of it's hell unto that grave which fit all of time's obsolescence. No individual be capable of escaping the belief of their own mind or the actions of their own body nor will any nation escape the belief of their own foreign relations or the actions of it's economy. Releasing grip on the tyranny be the sure method to falling in love with liberty and witnessing the vision of our creator God whom built it all to then destroy the wicked and resurrect the spirit from within us all.

The Bible, 1599 Geneva Bible, Tolle Lege Press, 2006.

Made in the USA
Middletown, DE
21 April 2021